Opera and Ideology in Prague

Eastman Studies in Music

Ralph P. Locke, Senior Editor
Eastman School of Music

Additional Titles on European Music and Musical Life since 1900

A complete list of titles in the Eastman Studies in Music Series, in order of publication, may be found at the end of this book.

Opera and Ideology in Prague

in Prague

BRIAN S. LOCKE

UNIVERSITY OF ROCHESTER PRESS

First published 2006

University of Rochester Press
668 Mt. Hope Avenue, Rochester, NY 14620, USA
www.urpress.com
and Boydell & Brewer Limited
PO Box 9, Woodbridge, Suffolk IP12 3DF, UK
www.boydellandbrewer.com

ISBN: 1–58046–233–2

Library of Congress Cataloging-in-Publication Data

Locke, Brian S., 1972–
  Opera and ideology in Prague : polemics and practice at the National
Theater, 1900-1938 / Brian S. Locke.
    p. cm. – (Eastman studies in music, ISSN 1071-9989 ; v. 39)
  Includes bibliographical references (p.   ) and index.
  ISBN 1–58046–228–6 (hardcover : alk. paper)   1. Opera–Czech
Republic–Prague–20th century.   2. Music–Political aspects–Czech
Republic–20th century. I. Title.
  ML1724.8.P7L63 2006
  782.1094371′209041–dc22
                          2006020813

A catalogue record for this title is available from the British Library.

This publication is printed on acid-free paper.
Printed in the United States of America.

To Donna

Contents

Illustrations

Musical Examples

Tables and Figures

Preface

Positive criticism, from both professionals and laypersons, could accomplish much here; unfortunately, its state today shows that, on the basis of our isolation, and having grown up among the "young postwar fighters," it has churned out more or less personally pointed, comfortably convincing, and attractive slogans about the decadence of foreign art and the elevation of our art above that of all nations of the world, thus fostering a "healthy" conservatism and petty-bourgeois indolence, simultaneously with an inability to healthily express the [critic's] personal relationship to the real values of artistic works. From whence come all these tiring and shaming arguments, not touching the core of the issue and expressing themselves only through the assembly of mutually antagonistic theories, within which Smetana's name appears like a *deus ex machina*, invoked to help in the most convoluted circumstances.[1]

This quotation, from an essay by a young composer, Josef Stanislav, in 1924, expresses in two sentences what this entire book attempts to solve: the problem of why the incredibly rich musical sphere of Prague in the early twentieth century has remained all but unknown to Western ears for three-quarters of a century. And yet the circumstances, while certainly convoluted, were not always as dire as Stanislav would have us believe, and there are a great many artistic creations and critical ideas that inform the greater understanding of European modernist culture in its day. Thus, the second goal of this book: to bring the individuals, ideologies, and operas of the Prague community into English-language musicological discourse, and so to provide a local context, not only for household names such as Janáček and Martinů, but also for the modernist "mainstream" of Europe in the fin-de-siècle and interwar periods.

The present text began as a Ph.D. dissertation at the State University of New York, Stony Brook, *Music and Ideology in Prague, 1900–1938*, completed in 2002; it was then transformed through substantial revisions to its present state, with almost every chapter split into historical and analytical "halves." Several new sections were added, notably the nineteenth-century prequel, the post-1938 epilogue, the Mánes Group, and most of the discussion of Zich's *Vina*, while almost all others were augmented with new research or ideas. Many of the smaller topics became the subjects of conference papers in the intervening years, including ones on the "Dvořák Affair" and the "*Wozzeck* Affair," Jeremiáš's *Bratři Karamazovi*, Ostrčil's *Legenda z Erinu*, Czech interwar jazz, Czech Zeitopern, and the aesthetics of Hostinský, Nejedlý, and Očadlík. These papers in turn prompted the publication of two articles: "'The Periphery Is Singing Hit Songs':

The Globalization of American Jazz and the Interwar Czech Avantgarde," *Journal of the American Music Research Center* 12 (2002): 25–55; and "Decadence, Heroism and Czechness: The Reception of Ostrčil's *Legenda z Erinu*," in *Socialist Realism and Music*, Musicological Colloquium at the Brno International Music Festival, vol. 36 (2001), ed. Mikuláš Bek, Geoffrey Chew, and Petr Macek (Prague: Koniasch Latin Press, 2004), 71–82. I would like to thank both Thomas Riis of the American Music Research Center and Mikuláš Bek of Masarykova Univerzita for their permission to reuse portions of my work in this book.

A great number of individuals assisted in the creation of this book in its many forms. Certainly the project would never have achieved the scope it did without the formative input of Joseph Auner and Jane Sugarman, my dissertation advisors at Stony Brook. Their guidance informed my methodology and style, but also allowed the full exploration of my musicological imagination. From the beginning, Michael Beckerman also assisted in the development of ideas from the perspective of Czech music studies; his moral support also proved inspirational and essential through this process.

For help in funding my initial research, I acknowledge the generous Doctoral Dissertation Award of the Social Sciences and Humanities Research Council of Canada, which gave me the chance to undertake my first research trip in 1999. Special thanks also go to various institutions in Prague: the Hudební archiv Národního divadla, for making available so many Czech operatic scores and libretti; Český rozhlas, whose archive provided unreleased recordings of several of these works; the České muzeum hudby, which allowed me to view letters and manuscripts by the composers in my project; the Městská knihovna, the music department of the Národní knihovna, and the periodicals department of the Národní muzeum, all of whose staffs were kind, courteous, helpful, and above all patient, despite language barriers and cultural expectations.

Other individuals in the Czech Republic who assisted in this endeavor are the very encouraging and helpful PhDr. Jarmila Gabrielová, director of musicology at Univerzita Karlova; PhDr. Mikuláš Bek of Masarykova Univerzita, whose invitation to present a conference paper in Brno developed into a research trip in October 2001 and a publication; PhDr. Markéta Kabelková of the České muzeum hudby, Mgr. Zuzana Petrášková of the Národní knihovna, and Mgr. Aleš Březina of the Nadace Bohuslava Martinů, all of whom helped me achieve my research goals in Prague. Particular thanks go to Helena Čapková and Jana Pavelková of the Hudební archiv Národního divadla for their warm-hearted generosity and helpfulness during my protracted sojourns in their midst, to PhDr. Vlasta Reittererová for welcoming me as a colleague in the field of Czech modernism, and to my friend and colleague Mgr. Aleš Opekar for his assistance at Český rozhlas. PhDr. Marie Dohalská-Zichová, granddaughter of the composer Otakar Zich, was also very helpful to me in my search for *Vina*. My wonderful conversations with all these scholars gave me some much-needed insight on the cultural climate of the historical period I chose to study. Special thanks also to Barbara Eger of Universal Edition A.G., Vienna, who helped me in locating the unpublished bilingual edition of *Strašidlo v zámku.*

Later, certain individual scholars helped me to shape my project as it transformed from dissertation into book. Foremost among these is Geoffrey Chew, whose insight, encouragement, and support continue to be invaluable at every turn; it has been an honor to glean his expertise in the field of Czech fin-de-siècle modernism. PhDr. Bohumil Fořt, my friend, colleague, and former Czech teacher, has been a tremendous source of strength during this process, providing me with continuous language instruction, assistance with translations, and tireless reassurance. My editor, Ralph Locke, has also inspired me to continue this research despite all obstacles, and his energy and excitement have guided me toward the best possible expression of my ideas. During the copyediting process, Louise Goldberg and Martin Nedbal also contributed greatly to the final format of the book.

With regard to my musical examples, I acknowledge the following:

Novák KARLŠTEJN © Used with kind permission of European American Music Distributors LLC, U.S. and Canadian agent for Universal Edition A.G., Vienna.

Křička SPUK IM SCHLOSS, ODER BÖSE ZEITEN FÜR GESPENSTER © Used with kind permission of European American Music Distributors LLC, U.S. and Canadian agent for Universal Edition A.G., Vienna.

I acknowledge also Jan Andreska, heir of Alois Hába, for his permission to use excerpts from *Matka*, and Mgr. Jana Budíková, niece of Otakar Jeremiáš, for her permission to use excerpts from *Bratři Karamazovi*. All other excerpts by composers contained in this book—Otakar Ostrčil, Josef Suk, and Otakar Zich—are in the public domain according to the Czech Copyright Act.

Other friends and colleagues deserve mention for helping me along the way: Derek Katz, Judith Mabary, Alma Santosuosso, Susan Cook, Richard Taruskin, Jennifer Bain, Marcia Swanston, Aileen Laurin, and Andrew Sarty all contributed to my ability to create and complete this project, along with the faculty, staff, and students at the universities where I have taught. Special thanks go to my parents, Phil and Jean Locke, not only for their generosity but also for their faith in me as an individual; my father also helped as a proofreader at various stages of this research. I would like to acknowledge the members of both my family and my wife's family, the Jeffersons, whose encouragement enabled me to keep going. First among all these, however, I would like to thank my wife, Donna, for her unflagging love and belief in me throughout the entire project, as well as for her assistance during my research trips. None of this would have been possible without her, and it is to her that I dedicate this book.

Notes to the Reader

Because this is a book full of names, terms, and historical data unfamiliar to most native English speakers, I present the following guides to the reader. In addition, there is a Personalia in appendix 1 (p. 339) and a chart of operatic premieres in appendix 2 (p. 349). While none of these purports to be exhaustive, it is hoped that they bridge the linguistic gap that might otherwise hinder an understanding of this rich history and repertoire.

1. Pronunciation of Key Names and Titles

Czech words are stressed, for the most part, on the first syllable. They also have certain elongated vowels (indicated by the acute accent, **á, é, í, ó, ú, ý,** as well as **ů** and **ou**) that can fall on either stressed or unstressed syllables; unaccented vowels are simply short in length. Beyond the issue of vowel length, most Czech vowels correspond to those of Italian, with the exception of the diphthong **ou** [oh-oo].

The Czech alphabet contains certain accented consonants: **š** [sh], **č** [ch], **ž** [zh], **ř** [rzh], **ť** [tyuh], **ď** [dyuh], **ň** [nyuh], each of which serves to soften the consonant in question. In addition, the symbol **ě** [yeh] softens the consonant immediately preceding it. Czech has one digraph, **ch**, pronounced as in the Scottish *loch*. All consonants are pronounced, no matter how clustered they appear. Most are roughly equivalent to Germanic norms, including the pronunciation of **j** as [y] and **c** as [ts]. **S** is never [z], and is never [š] before hard consonants, unless written as such. **Z** is never [tz].

The following list gives approximate pronunciations, according to North American English:

Bratři Karamazovi	[BRAT-rzhee KA-ra-ma-zo-vi]
Legenda z Erinu	[LE-ghen-da ZEH-ri-noo]
Karlštejn	[KA-rl-shtayn]
Matka	[MAT-ka]
Poupě	[POPE-yeh]

Preciézky	[PRETS-yehs-kee]
Strašidlo v zámku	[STRA-shid-lo FZAHM-ku]
Vina	[VIH-na]
Vojcek	[VOY-tsek]
Zrání	[ZRAH-nyee]

Hostinský, Otakar	[HOS-tyin-skee, OT-a-kar]
Jeremiáš, Otakar	[YEH-re-mee-ahsh, OT-a-kar]
Ježek, Jaroslav	[YEH-zhek, YAR-o-slav]
Kovařovic, Karel	[KO-var-zho-vits, KA-rel]
Krejčí, Iša	[KRAY-chee, EE-sha]
Křička, Jaroslav	[KRZHICH-ka, YAR-o-slav]
Nejedlý, Zdeněk	[NAY-ed-lee, ZDEN-yek]
Novák, Vítězslav	[NO-vahk, VEE-tyes-slav]
Očadlík, Mirko	[OH-chad-leek, MEER-ko]
Ostrčil, Otakar	[OS-tr-chill, OT-a-kar]
Vomáčka, Boleslav	[VO-mah-chka, BO-le-slav]
Vycpálek, Ladislav	[VITS-pah-lek, LAD-yi-slav]

2. Glossary of Institutional Names and Other Important Words

The two most important Czech nouns that recur in this book are **hudba** (music) and **divadlo** (theater); four adjectives, **český** (Czech), **hudební** (musical), **moderní** (modern), and **národní** (national) also appear throughout. Note that each of these may also be displayed with varied endings, such as **českých**, **hudebního**, **divadla**.

Journals are often called **listy** (pages) or **revue** [REH-vee].

Administrative bodies are often called **spolek**, **společnost**, or **družstvo**.

České filharmonické družstvo—Czech Philharmonic Association
Devětsil—"Nine Strengths," an avant-garde literary group, also called Poetists
Družstvo Národního divadla—National Theater Association
Hudební klub—Musical Club
Osvobozené divadlo—Liberated Theater
Podskalská filharmonie—Podskalí Philharmonic
Přítomnost—The Present (a new music society)
Spolek pro moderní hudbu—Society for New Music [Spolek]
Společnost Národního divadla—National Theater Company
Stavovské divadlo—Estates Theater/Deutsches Landestheater
Umělecká beseda—Artists' Union [UB]

Two words that I use throughout my analysis are **důslednost** (consequentiality) and **náladovost** (no precise translation: mood-orientation), derived from the aesthetics of Hostinský.

3. A Word About Musical Examples and Translations

In the captions for the musical examples, I indicate page and measure numbers (in most cases, from the published piano-vocal scores). Novák, *Karlštejn* (8/1–4) thus refers to mm. 1–4 on p. 8 of the Universal-Edition piano-vocal score of that opera, listed in the Bibliography. Exceptions are Suk's *Zrání*, which requires measure numbers only, and Zich's *Vina*, which is unpublished. *Vina*'s numbering scheme thus refers to (volume: p./mm.) of the manuscript vocal score listed in the Bibliography. Finally, the text accompanying Křička's *Strašidlo v zámku* appears in Czech, despite the fact that its vocal score was published in German (see discussion in chapter 10, n. 28); my source for the Czech text is an unpublished bilingual vocal score in the archives of Universal-Edition A.G. Wien (see Bibliography) and reflects the 1933 Estates Theater production discussed in this book. All English translations in this book are my own.

Abbreviations

The following abbreviations are used throughout all endnotes and bibliographic citations in the book. For the most part, they reflect those commonly used in Czech-language bibliographies and dictionaries, with the exceptions of those I have altered for greater specificity (e.g., *HR-S*, *S-HL*, and *S-HL (II)*). Note also that some of the journals changed names during the course of their publication; I have included these subsequent titles under the same abbreviation for the sake of simplicity and because these journals are always kept under the same call number in Prague libraries and elsewhere.

Publishers and Organizations

ČRo—Český rozhlas, Praha (Czech Radio Prague)
HA-ND—Hudební archiv Národního divadla (Music Archive, National Theater)
HMUB—Hudební matice Umělecké besedy (Music Publishers of the Artists' Union)
ISCM—International Society for Contemporary Music
MŠANO—Ministerstvo školství a národní osvěty (Ministry of Education and National Culture)
SNKLHU—Státní Nakladatelství Krásné Literatury, Hudby a Umění
Svaz DDOČ—The Workers' Union of Theater Amateurs of Czechoslovakia
UB—Umělecká beseda (Artists' Union)

Journals and Newspapers

A—*Der Auftakt*, 1920–38
ČH—*Česká hudba*, 1895–1939
ČK—*Česká kultura*, 1912–14
ČR—*Československá republika*, 1918–32
ČS—*České slovo*, 1909–43
D—*Dalibor*, 1879–1913, 1919–27

HR—Hudební revue, 1908–20
HRo—Hudební rozhledy (Brno), 1924–28
HRy—Hudební rozhledy (Postwar), 1948–
HR-S—Hudební revue-Smetana, 1906–7
HVk—Hudební věstník, 1908–27, 1934–41
    Věstník československých hudebníků, 1928–33
    Věstník československých hudebníků z povolání, 1934
K—Klíč, 1930–34
LL—Lidové listy, 1922–45
LN—Lidové noviny, 1893–2000
LUK—Listy pro umění a kritiku, 1933–37
MdS—Musikblätter der Sudetendeutschen, 1936–38
ND—Národní a Stavovské divadlo, 1923–30
    Národní divadlo, 1930–43, 1946–62
NL—Národní listy, 1861–1941
NO—Národní osvobození, 1924–39, 1946–48
NP—Národní politika, 1883–1945
NSv—Nová svoboda, 1924–38
P—Přítomnost, 1924–43
PP—Prager Presse, 1921–38
PL—Právo lidu, 1892–1999
R—Rytmus, 1935–48
RA—Rozpravy Aventina, 1925–30
RP—Rudé právo, 1920–38
S-HL—Smetana-Hudební list, 1910–27
S-HL (II)—Smetana-Hudební list, 1936–38
T-LHM—Listy Hudební matice, 1921–27
    Tempo-Listy Hudební matice, 1927–35
    Tempo-List pro hudební kulturu, 1935–38
TT—"Tam-Tam" Hudební leták—Gazette Musicale, 1925–26
V—Venkov, 1906–45
VPR—Vest Pocket Revue, 1929–30
ZSVN—Zprávy Společnosti Vítězslava Nováka, 1980–95

Timeline of Modern Czech History

1620–1918	Provinces of Bohemia, Moravia, Silesia within Austro-Hungarian Empire
1918–38	First Czechoslovak Republic (with Slovakia and Subcarpathian Ruthenia)
1938–39	Second Czechoslovak Republic (Czecho-Slovakia, minus Sudetenland)
1939–45	Nazi occupation (Reichsprotektorat Böhmen und Mähren, minus Slovakia)
1945–48	Third Czechslovak Republic (plus Sudetenland, minus Ruthenia)
1948–89	Czechoslovak Socialist Republic (postwar communism)
1989–93	Fourth Czechoslovak Republic (after "Velvet Revolution")
1993–present	Czech Republic (minus Slovakia, after "Velvet Divorce")

Chapter One

Introduction

Nationalism, Modernism, and the Social Responsibility of Art in Prague

Throughout the early twentieth century, the musical community of Prague was the site of intense artistic creativity and aesthetic debates that both reflected and helped shape the cultural life of Czechoslovakia at the time. As Europe entered the twentieth century, profound social changes affected the course of its history, in the realms of politics, culture, and both collective and personal identity. These changes were greatly influenced by ideologies, some held over from the nineteenth century, others transformed by the new era. In the artistic sphere, the new possibilities of cultural interaction forced a confrontation between traditional aesthetic views and the threat of cosmopolitanism. In the years between the turn of the century and the collapse of the First Czechoslovak Republic in 1938, the predominant issues that affected the discourse of music in Prague were nationalism, modernism, and the social responsibility of art.

After 298 years of somewhat parochial existence under the Austro-Hungarian Empire, citizens of the five provinces[1] that became an independent Czechoslovakia on October 28, 1918, experienced twenty years of the most idealistic and Western-oriented democracy in interwar Central Europe. Although not without serious internal problems, this oasis of free thought and cultural endeavor came to an end on September 30, 1938, with the Munich Accord, in which the powers of Europe signed over the country's border regions in order to appease Nazi Germany. Just five and a half months later, the Czechoslovak Republic ceased to exist when Hitler's armies occupied Bohemia and Moravia, leaving Slovakia as a puppet state. Like many national groups throughout Central and Eastern Europe, the Czech, German, and Jewish populations of these provinces experienced far-reaching political shifts in the early twentieth century that affected their view of themselves as individuals, as members of an ethnic group, and as participants in a larger European community. These shifts were reflected in an extraordinary flowering of artistic production in Prague and other centers, but nowhere more than in the musical community of the capital, which played a key role in the ongoing reformulation of Czech cultural identity. While Prague began the twentieth century as merely a provincial city within Austria-Hungary, after 1918 it was suddenly transformed into the capital of one of the most democratic states in Europe, where the interaction of its three resident ethnic groups placed it among the most cosmopolitan cities of its day.

Scope of This Study

This book will present an overview of music history in Prague, with a particular concentration on composition and criticism in the years 1900–1938, and on the aesthetic and ideological debates that shaped these activities. The repertoire presented here, in order to demonstrate the importance of these debates in compositional practice, is either opera or other musical genres in which text plays a prominent role, since the theater and literature were also integral to the formation of Czech identity at this time. The following chapters alternate between a narrative history of the Prague musical community and a series of eight analyses that explore major representative operas, as well as one important programmatic orchestral work, Josef Suk's *Zrání*. The analyses are tied into the main narrative by means of the critical reception of each work, where the ideological theories were put most concretely into practice.

Although fundamentally interconnected with music making and culture in Central Europe in the early twentieth century, particularly with the Austro-German sphere, the generations of the Prague community examined in this study have nevertheless not received due scholarly attention until now. Indeed, the dearth of knowledge outside the Czech Lands regarding all but a few composers—Smetana, Dvořák, Janáček, and Martinů—hinders an understanding of the Czech circle as a whole, and scholars have ignored the German-Bohemian contingent entirely.[2] An exploration of the activities of Prague musicians and their reactions to more general artistic developments sheds light on the larger picture of European modernism, as seen through the lens of the local. Heretofore the narrative of early twentieth-century music has prioritized solely those individuals whose music has retained wide exposure to the present day, thereby producing a highly selective and teleological view of this period. Since even "famous" composers lived and worked in an environment of their lesser-known peers, whose daily involvements had an impact on their own, traditional historical narratives render an inaccurate and dissatisfying recreation of European musical culture in the modernist era. In this way, the present text seeks to contribute to the retelling of music history in the early twentieth century, already under way since the mid-1990s through other detailed studies and reinterpretations, and in the large-scale rediscovery of a vast amount of repertoire.

What applies to the traditional narrative of European modernism also res-onates within the microcosm of music history in the Czech Lands, where the highly idiosyncratic styles of Janáček and Martinů have received the lion's share of scholarly attention, particularly since 1989. While this phenomenon has pro-duced excellent scholarship and has served to introduce some extraordinary repertoire to the musical world, there has been no English-language study of the Prague musical community to date. Since the Prague sphere was, for the Czechs in the early twentieth century, the dominant cultural milieu, against which fig-ures like Janáček and Martinů consciously reacted (often voicing their positions in print), a study such as the present one can surely contribute to a greater understanding of these two figures. In light of the aforementioned scholarship, however, I have chosen not to concentrate heavily on either Janáček or Martinů, in part also because neither composer spent any significant portion of his cre-ative career in Prague, preferring instead to avoid the maelstrom of professional and aesthetic intrigue continuously raging in its musical community. While Janáček and Martinů do make occasional appearances in the present narrative, I have limited these to points where their music or ideas had a specific impact on the debates in the city.

In terms of repertoire, this study concentrates primarily on the operas of early twentieth-century Prague composers, for the reason that the National Theater was the most hotly contested cultural space in the city, and that, through opera, Czech composers were expected to represent the larger collective identity. The eight operas I have chosen for musico-dramatic analysis were selected not only because of their compositional strengths, but also for their relative significance in the community, reflected particularly in the criticism of the time. Such is also the case with the ninth composition, Suk's tone poem Zrání, which is based on a significant work of literature and which found itself at the center of a fierce controversy in the early days of independence. As I attempt to show in the sub-sequent analyses, each of these eight compositions also presents a synthesis of the ideological debates of the time, thereby participating in the discourses of nationalism, modernism, and the social responsibility of art.

Alongside the creative efforts of Prague musicians lies the extraordinary growth of music criticism in the early twentieth century, both in terms of the city's specialized journals and the daily press. The highly charged debates among composers, critics, performers, and audiences regarding the conflicts between traditional and modernist aesthetics, and between national and cos-mopolitan worldviews, offer a new window into our understanding of similar processes going on at the same time throughout European music centers. A sig-nificant portion of the following study involves the exploration of a series of important ideological polemics that helped shape the Prague music community, changing the way its members dealt with each other as Czechs and Germans in the city, as well as with the outside world. These "Affairs"—the "Dvořák Affair," the "Suk Affair," the "Wozzeck Affair," just to name a few—involved a great amount of published writing of a frequently caustic nature, producing an environment that served to stifle creative activity as often as to encourage it. These crucial debates affected the musical contributions in a continuous manner, and even more tangibly, the cultural policies of institutions such as the Conservatory and National Theater. Music and culture in general were held in such high esteem in early twentieth-century Prague that not only did these debates spill over into the daily newspapers on a regular basis, involving nonmusicians in protests of various kinds, but in the most extreme cases they also became the subject of controversy in the Czechoslovak legislature. That these debates were taken up with such vehemence throughout these years and with such palpable impact on the compositions themselves reflects several important and unique characteristics of Czech social and cultural life. In this respect, as the narrative will show, music in Prague was possibly far more influential toward the construction of communal identity at this time than was the case in other European centers, including Paris and Berlin.

Three Ideologies

As I shall trace over the following chapters, nationalism was one of the most contentious ideologies to influence the path of music making in Prague. Nationalist feelings were constantly shaped by the single-most divisive cultural issue of the region: the cohabitation of Czechs and German-Bohemians. The interaction between the two linguistic groups, while surprisingly minimal despite their close proximity, nevertheless shaped their attitudes toward themselves and each other, both in the waning years of the Habsburg Empire and during the First Republic. Czech nationalism, for instance, was defined precisely in relation to the German presence all around them, and quite often, modernity was perceived as a longed-for goal, the path to which was blocked by what many Czechs considered the repressive force of German art and culture. The Czechs' and Germans' willful ignorance of each other's musical activities, while offering an interesting statement in itself, inhibits the researcher's attempt to reconstruct the total picture of musical life in the city. Prague's ratio of population at this time—some 93 percent Czechs with a 7 percent German-speaking minority[3]—produced a situation where Czech musical activity virtually dwarfed the efforts of the German-Bohemians, whose legacy is all but inaccessible in the post-1945 archives. Although the majority of the Jewish community of Prague associated itself, particularly in the early years of the century, with the German cultural sphere instead of the Czechs, after 1918 (and especially after 1933) the tendency shifted dramatically, provoking many Jewish composers to form significant allegiances with their Czech colleagues.[4] Thus, in the present study I have chosen to concentrate mainly, but not exclusively, on discourses and compositions in the Czech community.

The second ideology, modernism, is crucial to an understanding of nationalism, in that modernist aesthetics of art were often seen as a key component of national identity, on the part of both Czechs and German-Bohemians. Although still strongly influenced by Herderian romantic nationalism, members of the Czech community also relished the opportunity to form cultural ties with countries other than Austria, thereby provoking a long-term struggle between nationalist and cosmopolitan/ modernist aesthetics and values. Most artists and thinkers involved in the musical community saw artistic (and in particular musical) modernism as an integral part of Czech national tradition, within the context of which each new contribution had to be evaluated. Thus, even nineteenth-century figures such as Smetana were held by many Czech critics and composers to be "modern" long past the currency of their style in the rest of Europe. Somewhat paradoxically, many of the same individuals also saw modernism as a necessary phenomenon to be acquired in order to catch up with the rest of Europe, particularly after 1918; modernism, allegedly integral to Czech tradition, had to be maintained and/or regained, even by means of outside influences. For those opposed to radical change, modernism was viewed as an imported product having little to do with Czech national culture, and conversely, as proof of the moral superiority of Czech conservative values by comparison. The German-Bohemian community, on the other hand, had no such psychological dilemma as a group with regard to cultural interaction in Europe. As representatives of the ruling majority before 1918 they enjoyed fruitful exchanges with the rest of the German world, a situation that continued after Czechoslovak independence despite their sudden loss of power and privilege as a minority in the new state. With the political shift of 1918, the perception of Czech–German relations was reversed, as several Czech institutions perpetrated acts of vengeance on their German counterparts in the effort to reduce the size and importance of German cultural hegemony from the Austro-Hungarian era. Thereafter, the German-Bohemians were forced to find their own artistic voice in the face of Czech domination, and their increased participation in modernist musical activity eventually regained the respect of the Czech avant-garde in the 1930s.

A third ideology, the social responsibility of art, arose as a consequence of the two conflicting ideologies of nationalism and modernism. The debate over the promulgation of high art to a wider public had already been in motion since the late nineteenth century; moreover, for many commentators, it was the national and moral responsibility of modern music to encapsulate the entire Czech collective. On all sides of the ideological spectrum this rhetoric seemed to encapsulate the urgency of doing what was morally correct for Czech society, whether in terms of the preservation of tradition or specific artistic legacies, the assimilation of "non-Czech" influences as a source of cultural rejuvenation, or as in many cases, both of these arguments simultaneously. These ideas had a strong historical precedent. Not only had musicians been considered an integral part of the Cultural Revival in the late nineteenth century (specifically Smetana), but the aesthetic principles of the revivalists were often held to be modern in a way that transcended temporal boundaries, often on the level of a moral creed.[5] In this manner, it was relatively common for new compositions to be considered "truly Czech" and "truly modern" at the same time, through the righteous adherence to a tradition whose modernity would never fade. The ongoing implementation of a "modern tradition" was thus a social necessity, bearing the responsibility of carrying the moral imperative of the Cultural Revival to future generations. As the twentieth century progressed, the ideology of social responsibility became increasingly attached to left-wing politics, reaching a peak with the largely social-ist Prague avant-garde of the 1930s, whose politicization of art occasionally rivaled that of Weimar-era Berlin, albeit with strong nationalist overtones.

The interconnectedness of these general tendencies, however, does not indi-cate the degree to which the musical community of Prague was fraught with ten-sion, caused by the debates discussed in the following chapters. While in theory the general goals of Czech nationalism, modernism, and the social responsibility of art may have been similar for most individuals, they often saw the specific roots of Czech tradition in differing places. As such, composers and critics located the main model for Czech composition variously in the music of Smetana, Dvořák, Fibich, the aesthetics of Hostinský, or even in universalized notions of what Beethoven or Wagner represented. These "legacies" prompted a variety of opin-ions as to which composers had the right and/or responsibility to represent mod-ern Czech music to a national or even an international audience. Since these individual musicians were often affiliated with major cultural institutions in Prague, such as the Prague Conservatory, the National Theater, the Czech Philharmonic, and Prague University, these collectives came to represent factional voices in a very powerful way. Czech contemporary music making, be it composition, perform-ance, or criticism, was therefore almost constantly under attack from one or more sides of the factional divide, since new music usually met with the charge of "nečeskost" (literally, "un-Czechness") for representing a supposedly fraudulent vision of modern Czech music. That such a charge was not only artistically but also *morally* reprehensible demonstrates the degree to which art was thought to bear a responsibility toward Czech society. In no respect, then, could a composer hope to have a work critically accepted without being subjected to a thorough exami-nation of its connection to a musical legacy, its situation within the complex of contemporary debates, and its merit with regard to representing the nation in a responsible way. Indeed, the constant contestation of culture and its symbols in the musical community was so much in the public sphere that it can be said to have formed a crucial part of Czech identity during these years.

Czech Musical Identity and Its Parallels to Russia

Michael Beckerman has helped to define Czech musical identity as a porous concept, socially constructed and constantly being redefined in the context of politics and social change.[6] While certain formal or even gestural similarities can be found across the range of music written by Czech composers, these instances can be explained by a system wherein artists consciously modeled their music on each other's work as a referential canon, a phenomenon also epitomized by the quotation of "nationalist" tunes and folk songs.[7] Particularly with regard to the history of Smetana reception, Beckerman found that all other ideological "messages" that claimed to be integral to Czech music and essentialized the music as an expression of the collective national spirit were imposed on the repertoire from without, either by the composers themselves or by subsequent writers on music. Such a formulation describes succinctly many of the aesthetic and ideological debates that shaped ideas of Czech musical identity, both in its crucial, formative stages and throughout the early twentieth century.

Many similarities exist between the history of music in the Czech Lands in the era of nation-building and that of other linguistic or ethnic groups in Central and Eastern Europe. There are, however, just as many crucial differences, encompassing social, cultural, and political factors that distinguish the community from Russia or Germany, to pick the neighboring nations to which Czechoslovakia has often been compared. Richard Taruskin's insightful study of the discourse of Russian musical nationalism in *Defining Russia Musically* is extraordinarily helpful in understanding the Czech context, revealing both similarities and differences.[8] The present study and Taruskin's are both based, in part, on contemporary scholarly views of nationalism as a social construct, generated by a middle-class intelligentsia that sought to represent a collective of its own selection and definition, reflecting the demands of a specific time and place. Taruskin describes the "mythos of authenticity and exclusion" surrounding the imaginary realm of Russian "national" music, created partly to assert an assumed moral authority, and partly to distract from any cultural shortcomings Russian musicians may have felt in comparison with Western Europe.[9] The same can be said for the musical ideologues of Prague, who were, as in Moscow and St. Petersburg, supported by a battery of like-minded journalists whose rhetoric helped to define and strengthen the terms of the discourse surrounding the concept of a modern "Czech" music. As was the case with Glinka, Smetana's followers very quickly converted the musical elements of the composer's style that were, by and large, a personal variation on current Central European models into an ahistorical symbol of ethnicity. The following chapters show that Smetana's compositions, particularly the operas, were frequently used as a yardstick by which "Czechness" could be measured. Although rival factions openly disputed the validity of this claim until the end of the nineteenth century, a discursive shift around 1900 is revealed by the growing use of Smetana's music as almost the sole norm or authority in judging both Czechness (i.e., similarity to Smetana) and difference.

Taruskin places a high value on the "myth of otherness" in the formation of the Russian nationalist ideology in music in the nineteenth century.[10] His phrase embodies the self-imposed romanticism and exoticism that for Russian artists and thinkers was bound up with the formation of national identity in the modern era. A similar myth of cultural difference existed among the critics of Prague in the ongoing exclusion of foreign composers (and those Czechs who were overly influenced by them) from their own, morally superior category. In contrast to the Easternness exploited by the Russian national school, however, the "otherness" of the Czechs never contained any sense of exoticism. Belonging as it did to a Western European monarchy for the first eighteen years of the century, and then representing an interwar democracy, Prague lay wholly within the cultural sphere of Central Europe, particularly because of the well-connected German-speaking segment of the city's population. As a result, any post-1900 attempts to exploit a Czech folk character among Prague composers were half-hearted (in comparison to Russian counterparts), in that most composers actively took part in German- and French-influenced musical discourses for the majority of their careers.[11] Such a situation forced the journalistic rhetoric of Prague critics away from exoticist otherness, and led instead to a form of self-righteous conservatism, just at the moment when Czechoslovakia became an independent state in 1918. It seems that, precisely when Czech culture found itself on an equal political footing with its neighbors, certain of its representatives became somewhat embarrassed about their stylistic proximity to Western practices—in other words, that cultural differences were no longer as pronounced as they ought to have been.

As it was described in the critical rhetoric of the time, the sense of identity demonstrated by Czech composers leaned much more toward the collective than the individual, such that the purported goal of every artist was to speak for the community (or the nation) rather than just him/herself. The heavy importance placed on "collective" expression meant that virtually everyone was in danger of not meeting a set of ill-defined criteria, mostly based on the personal style of Smetana. Various Czech commentators' exclusion of individual Czech composers from the definition of a national identity affected almost every artist mentioned in this study, including Dvořák, Fibich, Novák, Suk, Zich, Hába, Weinberger, Janáček, and Martinů, as well as a host of other personalities from every generation, including Smetana himself. Such a situation sought to negate the reality of a cluster of individuals linked by language, common heritage, or geography, each contributing according to his/her own personal experience and ability; instead, the prevailing system of aesthetic judgments favored an imagined collective identity, which, ironically, was often used to exclude just as many individuals as it included. With the possible exceptions of the 1890s and the early years of the 1930s avant-garde, subjectivism was seen as a distasteful aesthetic stance, morally opposed to the socially minded achievements of the Cultural Revival. For a composer to express him/herself just for the sheer joy of the musical content (art for its own sake or *l'art pour l'artismus*) was to ignore the Czech people and therefore to betray them, for if an artist were not linked with a sense of immediacy to "the people," he/she would be more likely to be susceptible to dangerous outside influences, and therefore prone to lead the nation astray. Similarly, a composer could not simply choose to follow a musical style from abroad without public repercussions. Behind the oft-stated charge of cosmopolitanism lay the fear that Czech musical culture was essentially no different from that of other European nations, springing as it did from predominantly Wagnerian, Lisztian, or Brahmsian sources, and only as far back as the mid-nineteenth century. Thus, it was often a matter of pointing a finger at one's neighbors lest they point first, since everyone's style was derived from somewhere else in recent memory—Czechness only ran so deep.

As with the Russians, various parameters were put forth as a means to exclude individuals from authentic Czechness in music, including economic success (Dvořák), formal training (all those at the Conservatory, most prominently Suk and Novák), lack of formal training (Zich), or concentration on more popular genres (Nedbal, Kovařovic). Perhaps the exclusionary tactics with the most serious ramifications were those based on religion, wherein the Jewishness of a composer such as Weinberger or Schulhoff might be perceived as Germanness (or simply non-Czechness); or class, such that a composer practicing outside of Prague, like Janáček, Zich, or Jeremiáš, might be considered second-rate, whereas in a socialist context those artists with pronounced urban or cosmopolitan characteristics could be criticized for their distance from "the people."[12] Obsessed with the idea of collective, national musical identity, Czech commentators, rather paradoxically, constantly sought ways to divide the collective into those who belonged and those who did not.

This discussion is not to say that Czech composers never acted as individuals in such an environment. On the contrary, most creative artists, by and large, made stylistic choices independent of the critical discourse that raged in the music press. In many cases, too, certain composers' works could influence contemporary thought about larger aesthetic issues, such as expressionism, neoclassicism, or popular culture. Most often, however, individual compositions contributed to the ongoing debate in such a way that the changes they introduced were so incremental as to be almost unnoticeable. While this tendency produced a smooth course of transition for the local music history, it also served to prolong the discussion of aesthetic issues that were long out of date, a factor that in turn slowed the progress of compositional change.

One further noteworthy similarity between Czech musical culture and Taruskin's reading of Russian nationalist ideology is the debate over the predominance of either absolute or program musics; Czech post-Wagnerian critics (figures comparable to Stasov and the Russian nationalist composers) sided with the latter.[13] This debate shaped the history of music in Prague in fundamental ways in the nineteenth century, in that all other arguments, regarding national expression, larger aesthetic issues, or simply personal politics, had as their musical core this binary opposition. This musical struggle was manifested in the arguments over the interpretation of Wagner during the Cultural Revival and subsequently over the constant reconfiguration of Smetana's oeuvre in the Czech musical community, both of which related directly to the larger attitude toward national identity and cultural interaction.

Intercultural Relations and Music
Inside and Outside the Czech Lands

Another key component in the formation of cultural identity in the Prague context was the problematic interaction between its linguistic groups, which gave the city an inherently multicultural character in the early twentieth century. The attitudes of Czechs and Germans toward each other influenced their perceptions of the outside musical world, including European modernism. As the domestic situation changed, therefore, so did the relation to the international one, fluctuating constantly between acceptance and rejection across the entire era.

Although much of the music making in the city was carried on with an attitude of willful ignorance on the part of Czechs and Germans toward each other's endeavors, with actual interaction kept to a minimum, their cohabitation influenced the sense of identity on both sides. Every event caused a reaction in the opposite quarter, provoking a reidentification of self, and of both domestic and foreign "others." Prior to 1914, during a period when the Austro-Hungarian regime rigorously maintained a system of societal norms, there existed a greater sense of cultural openness between the Czechs and Germans in Prague, particularly in the institutions where the linguistic factions were forced by necessity to cooperate (albeit on German terms). This situation, however, played out somewhat contrary to expectation in the general attitude toward the rest of Europe and in the interaction with foreign musicians and styles. In the Habsburg era, the Czech community was relatively open-minded toward fin-de-siècle European modernism in order to stave off the threat of enforced cultural isolation (efforts that can be read as an extension of political self-determination). Ironically, this interest in contemporary music outside of Bohemia most often focused on Austro-German composers such as Mahler or Strauss. Conversely, the German-Bohemian musical community, as a satellite of Vienna, never had to exert itself beyond the merely provincial status it enjoyed prior to Czechoslovak independence. This attitude resulted in a dearth of interest in new music (especially before the advent of Zemlinsky in 1911) and a prevailing conservatism that was only slowly overturned in the interwar era. Thus, the stylistic gulf, as well as the extreme nationalist tensions between the two linguistic camps, resulted in strong animosities during the war years, the outcome of which was felt throughout the years of the First Republic.

After 1918, the situation took an extreme about-face, particularly in terms of which camp was considered the bearer of cultural authority. For the first time in their existence, the German-Bohemians began to worry about their survival amid relative isolation under the thumb of a Czech government. Their eagerness to make up for lost time in forging connections outside of Bohemia was demonstrated by the efforts of Erich Steinhard at *Der Auftakt*, a journal that became a lifeline to the rest of the Austro-German musical world after independence. For almost the first time, the Germans of Prague pursued an active interest in contemporary composition, perhaps as the fruit of activities long sustained by Zemlinsky. The self-determination of the Czechs, meanwhile, had an extremely negative effect on their German neighbors, and the ensuing process of purgation served to sever all ties in cultural life for a period of years: the fates of the German Conservatory professors and the Estates Theater administration (outlined in chapter 5) are testament to this almost violent urge for separation in Czech society. That the careers of prominent Czech musicians, too, particularly Suk, Nedbal, Šak, and Kàan z Albestů, were subjected to suspicions and false "charges," shows the virulence of the anti-German feeling in the early years of the First Republic. Quickly, the two communities began to define themselves as morally victorious, unfairly punished, modern, true bearers of tradition, and the like.

After approximately two years of belligerent interaction, the Czech and German musical communities of Prague just as quickly began to ignore each other again, this time with a greater sense of purpose dictated by the politics of the time. No longer concerned with mere cultural survival, Czech musicians saw the lack of involvement in German-Bohemian musical life as a socially conscious duty, particularly as the latter had taken such a pronounced interest in the potentially dangerous modernist forces now coming into the country from abroad. The Germans, under Steinhard, Zemlinsky, and subsequently Finke, fought to maintain their position alongside the Czechs in the international cultural forum, such that, by the inauguration of the International Society for Contemporary Music (ISCM) in 1923, they demanded equal representation in the form of a German section of the Czechoslovak committee. Interestingly, it was these efforts, as well as Steinhard's open policy of contribution at *Der Auftakt*, that gradually brought the two linguistic factions back into a sort of minimal contact in the late 1920s.

True interaction, however, would come only with the ascendancy of the younger interwar generation under the leadership of Hába (who had already begun to publish in *Der Auftakt* with greater acceptance than among the conservative Czech establishment). It was in the Hába circle that figures such as Schulhoff, Reiner, Ullmann, Ježek, Burian, and Krejčí could interact as equals, each contributing to the cause of avant-garde art. The situation was not to last, however, as both domestic and international politics forced a further bifurcation of Czech/German cultural life after 1933; the new music community, with its relative absence of "Aryan" Germans (excepting perhaps Finke), remained outwardly unaffected by this split before the end of the First Republic. All of their cooperative efforts, however, could not prevent the decimation of their numbers after 1938. Nevertheless, the rapprochement between linguistic camps under the aegis of the avant-garde was not a chance happening, as the sense of cultural interaction both within and outside the national borders was strongly tied to the acceptance and/or rejection of European modernism and its perceived effect on the moral fiber of Czech society.

The interaction of the dominant Czech musical community with compositional circles from outside their borders in this period reveals a somewhat elusive relationship, but one that nevertheless helps to shape our understanding of the achievements described in this narrative, with all their relative strengths and weaknesses. Indeed, it is important to consider first and foremost that, despite the perceived cultural isolation of the Czechs—a phenomenon created largely by the political divisions of the mid- to late twentieth century, as well as the language barrier—the music of the fin-de-siècle and interwar periods in Prague was not written in isolation, but rather in full consciousness of the various trajectories of the early modernist era. Despite the efforts of critics to dissociate their notions of Czech musical identity from the rest of Europe, it is undeniable that composers in Prague actively contributed to a larger discourse of European compositional thought. It has already been stated that the late nineteenth-century standards of Czech "modern" music, established by the careers of Smetana, Dvořák, and Fibich, were built upon the largely Wagnerian, Lisztian, and Brahmsian stylistic vocabularies inherited from Central and Western Europe. While many Czech composers of the early twentieth century were affected directly by Smetana's brand of Wagnerianism, the cosmopolitan aesthetic of the 1890s also served to introduce waves of influence from abroad, whose effects could be felt all the way to the 1930s. It was the generation of Novák, Suk, and Ostrčil—and no less the mature career of Janáček, also blossoming at this time— that introduced various elements of impressionism, expressionism, polytonality, and verismo opera to Prague audiences, often (although not always) through the admixture of folk elements. Even this reworking of folk musics in a high-art modernist framework seems to have more in common with contemporary efforts by Bartók and Szymanowski than the idealized, iconic folk references found in Smetana, for example, and the surrounding musical material presents an interesting reception of Strauss's and Mahler's fin-de-siècle scores. After 1918, with the pronounced shift away from Germanic influences of all kinds, the Czech community chose to emulate French culture throughout the arts; while poets imitated Apollinaire, composers also rushed to acquaint themselves with the latest developments from Paris. One such endeavor was the well-known occasion of the Czech Philharmonic's presentation of Albert Roussel's music, which intrigued the young Martinů and led him to study with Roussel and ultimately emigrate to the West. The Parisian connection also helped solidify interests in jazz, populism, and neoclassicisms of various kinds, while a strong connection to Busoni's Berlin masterclass reinforced the trends of *Junge Klassizität* and microtonality. Thus, even when, in a fit of exasperated conservatism, the composer Emil Axman issued the call to "Leave aside foreign tongues, speak your own!" and turn back to the traditions of Smetana, he did so in the effort to sift through the multitude of European modernist influences making their mark on the Prague of his day.[14]

* * *

This book seeks to present an intricate web of individuals, ideologies, and works hitherto unknown outside of the Czech Lands. The result is a large-scale examination of the nature of Czech musical identity in this era, contributing to a broader understanding of modernism in the early twentieth century and its relationship to nationalism.

Chapter Two

Smetana, Hostinský, and the Aesthetic Debates of the Nineteenth Century

In order to gain a full understanding of music in Prague after 1900, it is necessary first to explore the aesthetics of music during the nineteenth-century Cultural Revival, and the roles of Smetana and Hostinský in it. In many surveys of music history, it is often assumed that music in the Czech Lands began with Smetana, the so-called "Founder/Father of Czech music," or more specifically with his return to Prague in 1862 after several years abroad.[1] While this rhetoric certainly plays into nationalist narratives that have held sway since the late nineteenth century, it is impossible to deny the rapid development in Prague's musical activity after 1860, a situation owing in part to Smetana's participation. Smetana, of course, had been the product of several different precursors, including the influence of the New German School and an extended apprenticeship in Sweden as well as the substantial music education he received prior to his departure from Prague in 1856. Indeed, the dates of Smetana's absence are more than a mere biographical detail: they fall during the years of the repressive Alexander Bach era that held sway throughout the Austrian Empire until 1860 (see discussion below). As such, Smetana's years of exile, return, and subsequent accomplishments on native soil say as much about the artist as about his political and cultural milieu, since his mature career could have happened only after the post-Bach easing of restrictions. Significant in this regard are the new performing venues and cultural institutions—most prominently the Provisional Theater—that gave a sense of permanence to Czech musical endeavors. Most important for the present discussion, the so-called Cultural (or National) Revival, already in its third generation by 1860, could finally be expressed in open, rhetorical terms, amid a growing Czech-speaking and Czech-educated public. All of these components were necessary for the participation of composers and critics in the movement, since public performances, particularly

of dramatic music with Czech texts, demanded institutional support and provoked waves of commentary, especially at this early stage. Thus, while music had
already had a substantial history in Prague prior to Smetana's return, the community quickly became an ideological hotbed, spawning polemic debates over
the definition of "Czech music" within a few short years.

Granted, Smetana did bring a higher level of compositional professionalism
to a city whose creative energies had dwindled well before the 1848 revolution,
and Smetana's presence within the post-1860 debates contributed greatly to
their prolongation. Nevertheless, these developments are also reflective of a
growing trend throughout Europe: the politicization of art, particularly concerning those trends labeled "progressive." Smetana's music and that of all subsequent composers in late nineteenth- and early twentieth-century Prague, as
with most communities in Europe, arose in an atmosphere where greater and
greater social implications were attached to the pieces themselves. Indeed, the
narrative of music in Prague after Smetana can be read broadly as representative of the position of music in the late romantic era, a period when increasing
numbers of artists were compelled to come to terms with modernism and its ideological bases. In order to gain a sense of the scope of change in this era, however, we must turn back to the years prior to 1860.

Music in Prague before Smetana

While the political and cultural history of the Czech Lands is readily available to
English readers in recent texts such as Derek Sayer's *The Coasts of Bohemia*, it is
worthwhile to give a thumbnail sketch of the period after 1620 as it pertains to
music history.[2] Prior to this date, the Czechs had enjoyed political independence
under a Habsburg monarch, with an indigenous aristocracy and a sizable population of Czech Brethren, the local Protestant sect. Early in the Thirty Years' War
(1618–48), however, at the battle of White Mountain, the Czechs lost their independence and became subsumed into Austria: many of the Czech Brethren,
scholars and aristocrats, either converted to Catholicism or emigrated, some as
far away as America. The aristocrats that remained were quickly Germanized,
many settling permanently in Vienna. With the patronage system almost completely disabled, therefore, Czech musicians were suddenly at a loss at a time
when increasing numbers were set to attain professional status.

Despite these hardships, the Czechs began to develop a thoroughly organized
music education system, possibly as a remnant of the celebrated court of Holy
Roman Emperor Rudolf II, who had chosen Prague as his seat in the late
Renaissance. By the mid-seventeenth century, as their language was gradually
being forced out of schools and daily life, even the smallest Bohemian and
Moravian towns began to produce performers and composers of the highest
professional caliber. While aristocratic families such as the Rožmberks in

Southern Bohemia did much to foster the arts on a local scale, the sheer volume of musicians forced many to emigrate by the early eighteenth century. Indeed, it will be remembered that a large number of composer-performers of the so-called Mannheim School were first- or second-generation Czech émigrés, and that Gluck and other German-Bohemians had received their first music education in Bohemia: Burney's famous description of the province as the "Conservatory of Europe" was not without basis.[3] Such rhetoric was gladly appropriated by subsequent generations of romantic nationalists, including some who made the excessive claim that the Czech émigrés were solely responsible for the late-eighteenth century Classical Style. Still, it is undeniable that the contributions of Bohemian-trained musicians influenced certain soon-standard genres, particularly "reform" opera (Gluck), the woodwind concerto (Stamic family), the melodrama (Benda family), and somewhat later, the lyrical piano piece (Voříšek and Tomášek).

As tempting as it is to think of these émigrés as long-suffering artist-patriots, forced away from their homes and native language by the machinations of the Habsburg counterreformation, it must be remembered that the concept of collective or national identity was intrinsically different prior to the 1780s. Bohemia and Moravia had been provinces in a network of states within the Holy Roman Empire for several centuries, and the émigrés, tremendously successful in "foreign" courts, were merely working their way up the existing hierarchy of culture in Europe. Perhaps by virtue of availability, all Czech composers of the eighteenth century set German, Italian, or Latin texts exclusively, using themes from mythology and history in the stylization of authors such as Metastasio. Furthermore, the proud acceptance of such high-profile German composers in their midst as Mozart, Beethoven, and Weber points to a more porous sense of identity than the romantic nationalists would care to admit.[4]

With a German administration and aristocracy, it is natural that the rise of municipal theaters in Prague and Brno at the end of the eighteenth century should be a German-language phenomenon.[5] While the permanence of these cultural institutions can be read as a step toward the increased Germanization of Czech culture, it also provided a limited venue for Czech productions: initially in the form of spoken drama and Czech translations of German operatic repertoire, they came to fruition in the first original Czech opera, František Škroup's *Dráteník* (The Tinker) of 1826. John Tyrrell describes how these first modest productions, amounting to a mere two hours per week, sparked the aspirations for more substantial works and greater public representation.[6] Established in 1783, the so-called Estates Theater, along with the foundation of the Prague Conservatory in 1811, marked the beginnings of municipal music making in a sustained and organized capacity, although the latter institution merely granted official status to the music education system described above. Parallel to these artistic developments, the growth of a Czech-speaking middle class in the early nineteenth century ensured not only an audience for music at these institutions, but just as important, a recurring crop of students and artists identifying them-selves—and their music—as Czech.

The growth of a self-consciously Czech high-art culture after approximately 1800 was one of the results of the Cultural Revival. This oft-discussed phenom-enon was a multigenerational nationalist project started by a few individual scholars and amounted to rediscovery (and reinvention) of the Czech language, followed by the creation of a system of arts and media around it, based on the romantic nationalism of J. G. von Herder. Herder's philosophy stressed the reawakening of a people (particularly the people of Central and Eastern Europe) through, among other things, the collection of folk poetry and music. These materials would assist in recreating the linguistic basis of a culture by means of its closest link to the soil—the peasants, a social echelon that had sup-posedly preserved the oldest cultural forms.[7] Such a project was particularly appropriate for the Czech cultural situation, since most educated citizens of Bohemia and Moravia before 1830 spoke German exclusively, regardless of their ethnic heritage, with Czech spoken only in small villages by peasants. Using Herder's model, Czech scholars such as Dobrovský, Jungmann, Havlíček-Borovský, and Palacký ushered in a cultural renaissance, inspiring generations of young authors and artists to write in their "mother tongue" (which most, including Smetana, had to learn as a foreign language).[8] As Czech-language schools gradually gained precedence in Bohemia and Moravia (a by-product of the Cultural Revival), increasingly larger social groups began to think of them-selves as ethnically Czech, a phenomenon that can be seen in the official Austrian census, as well as in the rash of name changes in the latter half of the century.[9] The social stratum most affected by these changes was the Czech bour-geoisie (a class virtually created by the Revival), whose ascent was aided by a flowering of the arts, including literature, scholarship, journalism, painting, and, from the 1860s, musical composition.

One of the immediate aspirations for the revivalists was a form of cultural self-determination expressed in the permanence of institutions such as the Czech National Museum (founded 1818), the aforementioned Conservatory, and increasing demand for representation on the theatrical stage. This permanence was also reflected in the middle-class musical community, more of whose mem-bers were remaining in Prague; most prominently among them were the Estates Theater conductor Škroup and the chamber music composer Václav Tomášek, whose salon in the Hradčany district provided an important meeting place for Czechs and non-Czechs, including prominent visiting artists from abroad.[10] Nevertheless, these crucial, if modest, activities did not immediately flower into a large-scale production of Czech-language works: several of Škroup's later operas, as well as those of his successors, had German texts, as did the songs of Tomášek.[11] Indeed, one gets the sense that the fledgling community had gone as far as it reasonably could within Metternich-era Austria, with any further growth hindered by the aftermath of the failed 1848 revolution.

All branches of the Cultural Revival experienced a setback for the period 1848–60, the so-called Bach era, named for Franz Josef's repressive minister of the interior who instituted one of the most intolerant regimes in Austria's history. Designed to suppress nationalist aspirations among the Slavic and Hungarian provinces of the Empire, Alexander Bach's plan called for increased Germanization in cultural life, along with severe restrictions imposed by censors. For the musical community of Prague, struggling to achieve any sense of continuity, this period was disastrous: it put off plans for a Czech-language theater in the city and precipitated yet another wave of artistic emigration. While several budding composers for the theater were among those who departed (including František Skuherský and the by now elderly Škroup, who died in Holland), the most prominent among them was Bedřich Smetana, who left in 1856 for Göteborg, Sweden, after several unsuccessful years of running a piano school in Prague. Prior to his departure, Smetana was a modest composer of small piano pieces and had only attempted two works for large ensemble: it was in Sweden that he truly began his career as a composer and conductor of note, largely as a result of his assimilation of the Lisztian tone poem, and gradually, the Wagnerian music drama. It is the coincidence of art and politics, therefore, that enabled Smetana to return to Prague in 1862 with his modern compositional techniques, freshly bolstered by his increasing success in Göteborg, right at the point of the collapse of Bach's autocracy. Franz Josef's dismissal of Bach in the wake of the 1859 military defeats against Napoleon III at Magenta and Solferino ushered in a new era of cultural openness for nationalists throughout Austria, and it is precisely these events that enabled the Czech musical community finally to contribute to the Cultural Revival.

The decisive cultural shift in the musical community was twofold: the Emperor finally granted permission for long held plans to build a Czech theater; and in anticipation of the event, in February 1861, the Bohemian nobleman Count Harrach announced a competition for the composition of a new Czech national opera. Smetana's response to both projects, embodied by his return to Prague in 1862, has often been hailed as the birth of modern Czech music. While it is certainly true that a musician of his artistry and cosmopolitan experience could only benefit a musical community just now achieving permanent performance institutions, it should not be assumed that Smetana found himself before a blank slate. Indeed, as the composer's subsequent difficulties with that community attest, the Czechs had had plenty of time to formulate deep-seated opinions about music and collective representation, even in the absence of overt expressions of nationalism during the Bach era.

Music in the Cultural Revival and the Role of Smetana

As with other branches of the arts and society, the Cultural Revival marks the main division point between Czechs and German-Bohemians in music history.

The Czech community used it as a tool with which to distance itself culturally from the perceived oppression of the Austrian regime, whose representatives they saw in their German-speaking colleagues around them. Such cultural separation was extremely difficult in a city filled with bilingual (or German-only) institutions such as the Estates Theater, the Conservatory, and Prague University. Each of these would split into parallel administrations by 1920, a development instigated by the opening of the Provisional Theater in 1862. German-Bohemian musicians, meanwhile, also found themselves in a new position: whereas, prior to 1860, they had enjoyed a fair amount of status in the multicultural Prague sphere, acting as a bridge between visiting foreigners such as Liszt, Schumann, and Berlioz and their less connected Czech colleagues, no longer were their endeavors appreciated. Indeed, in the late nineteenth century Prague became a decreasingly important center of German culture, a state reflected in the provincial level of musical activity there. Eventually, in the waning years of the Habsburg regime, this increased pressure on the social structure of the Czech Lands forced its German-speaking inhabitants to take a more active interest in music as an expression of local identity. Indeed, any interest in new local compositions was at a virtual standstill until Heinrich Teweles took over the directorship of the Deutsches Landestheater (previously called the Estates Theater) in 1910, at which point he hired Alexander Zemlinsky to help revive the musical atmosphere among Germans in the city.[12] Thus, in the late nineteenth century, the Czech musical community met with almost no local resistance with regard to the expansion and promulgation of their cultural endeavors.

The opening of the Provisional Theater and Count Harrach's contiguous opera competition suddenly provided both venue and repertoire for a Czech-language genre that had so far not achieved any works of prominence. Such a decisive shift also guaranteed primacy for opera in Prague for both critics of the day and subsequent historians. The importance of the new genre was so great that performances were heralded as national events and the directorship of opera at the theater was expected to provide, if not secure, the future direction of Czech music. Small wonder that every Czech opera director until the Second World War was faulted for choices in repertoire (including their own compositions) by some portion of the fractured critical spectrum. Despite the nationalist illusion that Smetana's arrival, the opening of the theater, and the "birth" of modern Czech opera were essentially coextensive, such an opinionated, Wagnerian composer as Smetana could never have suited the tentative, parochial atmosphere in Prague during the first post-Bach years, at least not without substantial problems. And indeed, Smetana was refused the first opera director's position in 1862, and his turbulent eight years in that role (1866–74) set a pattern of belligerence between compositional leaders and critics in the city for several generations.

Nevertheless, Smetana's first two operas at the Provisional Theater, *Braniboři v Čechách* (The Brandenburgers in Bohemia, 1865) and *Prodaná nevěsta* (The

Bartered Bride, 1866) were extraordinarily successful, largely because their patriotism was obvious and their Wagnerian traits less so. These two works, along with the orchestral cycle *Má vlast* (My Country, 1874–79), solidified Smetana's reputation in the musical community of Prague. The common description of *Braniboři v Čechách* as the first modern Czech opera is true only if one associates it with the composer's Wagnerian operatic paradigm, fully adopted only with his third opera, *Dalibor*, a few years later. In fact, there were already several composers writing for the stage in Prague at the time, in various subgenres (including opera, operetta, Singspiel, and incidental music), though not always in Czech or based on "national" themes. It was Smetana's synthesis of compositional skill, large forms, subject matter from Czech history or folklore, and the latest German stylistic models that placed him in the best position to "create a national music": to this was added the rhetoric of self-promotion, where his own efforts became inseparable from the moral achievements of the Cultural Revival.[13] His main departure from the approach of his contemporaries was to avoid the direct quotation of folk sources in favor of an idealized recreation of them, a technique that could more easily blend with his prevailing Wagnerian compositional language. As such, the rejection of the naive, rudimentary "ethnography" found in the stage works of the time corresponded closely to Smetana's demand that a truly "national" music be up to date in its expressive means.

Although the sheer quality and popularity of *Braniboři v Čechách* and *Prodaná nevěsta* gained Smetana many admirers and supporters, his Wagnerian aesthetic stance and uncompromising attitude toward his peers' inadequacies became the basis of opposition against him. By the mid-1870s, because his stature in Czech cultural life far exceeded that of any other musician, the bitter controversy that shaped his late career deeply affected the entire Czech musical community. The main question became whether Wagnerian-influenced and/or program music could belong within Czech national music and whether Smetana could stand as its representative, both inside the (as yet imagined) nation and abroad. Fueled in equal part by the deep-seated conservatism of the Prague bourgeois stratum (which comprised the majority of the Czech artistic realm), this particular ideological conflict remained largely unresolved until more modern issues supplanted it with independence in 1918. Indeed, the success or failure of all Czech artists and their compositions during these generations can be understood as tangentially related to the Prague reception of Smetana in the 1870s.

The political life of Smetana's Prague reflected the sharp divisions in artistic circles; indeed, much of the factionalization was underscored by the bifurcation of the so-called Old Czech and Young Czech parties in 1874.[14] The Old Czechs, whose political policy was one of passive resistance to the Austrian regime in the form of a thirteen-year boycott of the Imperial Assembly, had a stranglehold on the cultural institutions of the city, the most important of which was the Provisional Theater. In this respect, Smetana's difficulties in maintaining his position as opera director at the theater were a result of the administration's politics, and the ideological opposition to the stylistic choices in his compositions reiterated the conservative stance of the Old Czechs. His contemporary Wagnerian aesthetics found resonance in the liberal Young Czech party, as well as in the Umělecká beseda or Artists' Union (hereafter UB), founded in 1863 by a circle of open-minded intellectuals of all artistic disciplines. Initially an informal gathering place for creative artists to discuss aesthetic issues in the absence of politics and institutional administrations, the UB quickly formed three parallel divisions, for music, literature, and the plastic arts. Each division had its own president and secretary responsible for the maintenance of membership and the organization of events; in the music division these events included various concert and lecture series, and after 1871, a publishing house (Hudební matice Umělecká besedy or HMUB) with various affiliated journals. Despite its idealistic beginnings, the UB gradually came under Old Czech domination by the 1880s, which changed the group into an official bastion of the artistic establishment.[15]

Thus, when the young Antonín Dvořák began his ascent to international success in the mid-1870s, it was not simply as another composer alongside Smetana within the Prague musical community, succeeding solely on the merits of his own music. This latter aspect may be true beyond the Czech borders, but in the Prague context he was seen increasingly as an individual embraced by the politically conservative Old Czechs, likely chosen consciously as a rival to the senior composer. Furthermore, it was frequently implied that Brahms's support of Dvořák not only pertained to matters of musical style, but also Old Czech conservatism through their connections to Vienna. From this viewpoint, Dvořák's early career was based in a complex of cultural/political nuances that reveal the Old Czechs' relationship with Austrian cultural policy: while boycotting the Assembly, the party worked alongside German authorities at so-called utraquist institutions, a stance that the more openly confrontational Young Czechs (including Smetana) opposed.[16] Many commentators, including those in his own day, measured Dvořák's success alongside the solidification of Old Czech power in Prague cultural life. Conversely, the younger Zdeněk Fibich, who studied abroad and whose Wagnerian tendencies and affiliation with Smetana were evident from the beginning of his compositional career, faced a lifetime of ostracism from the musical establishment: the political connotations of such artistic choices often prevented his music even from being heard.

By the 1880s the complex political network within Prague music community included yet another significant factor: in 1881, after two decades of planning and public fundraising, the National Theater (Národní divadlo) was opened, an achievement that marks the zenith of the efforts of the Cultural Revival in music and drama.[17] Although the inaugural performance was reserved for Smetana's opera *Libuše* (which had been composed over a decade before and whose premiere had awaited this ceremonial occasion), the theater administration, controlled by the Družstvo Národního divadla (National Theater Association), was Old Czech in orientation. As a result, the National Theater became a site for the contestation of differing representations of Czechness on the stage, including the "ownership" of Smetana in the decades after his death in 1884. While almost all of the composer's eight operas were accepted into the repertoire (albeit in severely altered versions by V. J. Novotný), his radical Wagnerian ideology was not tolerated by the theater administration, which resulted in a toned-down body of work, normalized to coincide with the ideals of the establishment. On the other hand, this shift also corresponds to a gradual rapprochement with Wagner's style (in however a conservative and diluted manner), as evidenced by the late operas of Dvořák and their popularity among the conservative elite. As we shall see, this confused state of affairs continued to exclude the more ardent followers of Smetana and Wagner, most prominently the aesthetician Hostinský, who was increasingly ostracized from the establishment, and Fibich, whose attempts at success at the National Theater were thwarted time and again. This ideological conflict would also form the basis of the debates of the coming century regarding nationalism and modernism in music, as well as the initial stages of the discourse around the social responsibility of art.

Hostinský, Pivoda, and the Aesthetic Polemics of the Late Nineteenth Century

One of the most interesting figures of the so-called National Theater generation, Otakar Hostinský (1847–1910) also played a role that was perhaps the most difficult to define. His system of aesthetic paradigms, however, would pervade almost all of the ideological debates of the early twentieth century, whether or not subsequent artists and thinkers could trace their intellectual heritage directly to Hostinský himself. A fervent supporter of Smetana from the late 1860s, he had absorbed the doctrine of Wagner's music dramas from the time of his studies in Munich.[18] Intimately associated with the UB in its early days, his work as a music critic represented some of the most informed contributions to the field at that time in Prague. Later in his career, his lectures on aesthetics and music history at Prague University formed an alternative to the officially recognized Conservatory curriculum, attracting a small group of dedicated students who went on to promulgate his theories in the succeeding decades. Hostinský's career reflected the ideological shifts in the musical community after the opening of the National Theater, in that, despite being one of its greatest proponents, he was increasingly shut out of the establishment, even while his idol, Smetana, became its cultural property. By the time of the early years of the twentieth century and its first polemics, Hostinský had withdrawn from cultural life, his crucial involvement reduced to a series of shadowy references. Nevertheless, his philosophical discussions of the role of art in Czech society and his contribution to the aesthetic polemics of his day left an indelible mark on its future debates.

As Miloš Jůzl relates, the musical life of Prague was already divided into opposing camps by 1869, for and against Smetana, who by this point had been director of opera at the Provisional Theater for three years.[19] The opposing camp, firmly situated in the sphere of Old Czech politics, was led by the influential voice teacher and critic František Pivoda (1824–93), although its ideological policy was dictated in many respects by the politician František Rieger. Pivoda, one of the founders of the UB and a contributor to many contemporary Prague journals including the Old-Czech *Pokrok* (Progress), initially supported Smetana's bid for the conductorship of the Provisional Theater, and fervently advocated *The Bartered Bride* as a model for Czech national opera. Had the composer continued in the folkloric style of his second opera, Pivoda would have been content, since he was formulating a theory regarding the essential Slavonic character of Czech music, an ideology based in the then-popular pan-Slavic movement (manifested politically in Rieger's concept of Austroslavism, largely ineffectual for the Czechs). For Pivoda, pan-Slavism in music was best embodied through operas that were essentially strings of folkloric quotations in a Singspiel setting, such as could be found in the handful of Czech operas attempted since Škroup. Smetana, meanwhile, rejected this model, theorizing instead that the role of national opera should be to idealize folksong through high art, rather than to quote them directly. Such idealism would free the composer to follow the most progressive musical trends in Europe without being stifled by local, parochial traditions. As a direct result of this aesthetic schism, Smetana and Pivoda publicly parted company in 1868 with the premiere of *Dalibor*, an opera that firmly tied the composer to Wagner's operatic aesthetics.

Pivoda's reaction in *Pokrok* was to charge the composer with attempting to Germanify Czech music, thereby threatening its moral ascendancy and endangering its very existence.[20] It was doubly insulting to the critic that such a Wagnerian musical language should be used to depict a heroic character from Czech legend who was renowned for his musical ability; Pivoda later suggested that Smetana's main character be renamed "Dalibor Wagner." In a review from 1870 he accused the composer of exercising a monopoly over Czech composition:

> Against this [monopoly], the general opinion must be heard more distinctly; otherwise, we will not cultivate our own forms for long, and our opera will not surpass the stage of being hostess to a foreign entity, which might suddenly take over the role of landlord, even here, if it has not already happened thus.[21]

It is interesting to note that even at this early stage, the German influences of one composition could be felt to threaten the entirety of what constituted "Czech music." Pivoda also claimed that Czech singers were unable to master the roles, a situation that shut them out of the monopoly and simultaneously opened the door for foreign artists. Smetana responded nine days later in *Národní listy* (National News), the Young Czech daily paper, claiming that the director of a vocal school where the only repertoire taught was "*Il Trovatore, Rigoletto*, and similar works" had little right to make such pronouncements. In a similar article he denounced Pivoda's tactics, saying, "You babble something about *Wagnerianism* without knowing what it is."[22] Clearly, the core of the debate had as much to do with the reception of Wagner in Prague as with any grand statements about the national identity of Smetana's music; the latter, however, would outweigh the former in the eyes of posterity.

It was within this volatile environment that Hostinský made his first forays into music criticism, writing for the journal *Hudební listy* (Music Pages), which he edited with fellow Smetana supporter Ludevít Procházka beginning in 1869. Some of Hostinský's main contributions to the Czech aesthetic discourse were written at this early stage of his career, and therefore had an impact decades before the turn of the century. Three essays, "Art and Nationality" (1869), "Wagnerianism and Czech National Opera" (1870), and "On Program Music" (1873, written for the subsequent journal *Dalibor*), provide a cross-section of their author's position in the debates, as well as of his methodology and allegiances in the musical world. In each of these essays, Hostinský began with a binarism, where the two opposing forces of aesthetics and art history formed a dialectic relationship whose outcome was a truly modern, national music. In "Art and Nationality" he used this paradigm to probe the dichotomy between the universal application of artistic statements (in the aesthetic realm) and the tendential quality of an art too attached to a specific time and place (as fostered by art history).[23] For Hostinský, the basic question became one of whether or not art could be national, and if so, whether it was a necessary component of all art: simply put, whether the "national" and "universal" in art were coextensive. Since beauty, for Hostinský, was conditioned by the local cultural environment, multiple variations of "national" beauty could coexist without negating each other. He reasoned that each nation had a collective taste that was differentiated from private, subjective fancy; national taste was based on the psychological character of a society, reflected not only in art but in every other aspect of life as well. Unlike subjective fancy, it did not force judgments about beauty, but rather presupposed a complete aesthetic system: in this regard, beauty and nation were independent concepts, and any nationalism that forced judgments on art was intolerable.

In a series of statements that would shape the discourse all the way to the postwar socialist era, Hostinský declared that art and society must have a mutual relationship, creating an organic link wherein artists educated and ennobled society. To make this link complete, artists must base their creative work in the psychological makeup of their society, in "national soil," but without being dependent upon it (as, one supposes, Pivoda's contingent was). Ever conscious of the divisions in Czech musical society, Hostinský drew a distinction between "national" and "patriotic" aesthetics, where the former embraced the entire interior life of the people, while the latter was merely for external show. Similarly, while patriotic art might shun all foreign influences, national art could allow a moderate amount—enough to eliminate isolationism without creating too much competition with the local tradition. Certainly the most "national" element for Hostinský was language, which was manifested in music by the vocal repertoire, most prominently by opera. Here the melodic and rhythmic components of vocal writing could mirror the natural flow of the language, and by extension, the internal psychological basis of the nation. In a remark that reflects his deep immersion in the doctrine of Wagnerian opera, Hostinský concluded that the evocation of the nation through operatic vocal writing lay at the center of a composer's artistic statement, such that its psychological core could be taken to the proper musical and logical conclusion. Such an expression was not simply abstract, mannerist, or formalist, as was the tendency with more external, "patriotic" nationalisms.

The crux of the debate was the binarism of *důslednost* or "consequentiality," wherein a composer or work displayed the appropriate responsibility to see an artistic statement to its necessary end, versus *náladovost* or "mood-orientation," in which artistic statements were dependent merely on subjective states. This binarism, while never theorized explicitly by Hostinský, pervades his criticism and that of his followers as an implicit system of aesthetic judgment, appearing frequently in reviews as late as 1938. *Důslednost* was always a positive characteristic, signifying not only the logical development of a musical idea or textual theme, but also due attention to the moral consequences of the artist's aesthetic choices and their impact on society. *Náladovost*, conversely, referred to a general superficiality on the part of both composer and composition, as though such music was written for the composer alone and all aesthetic choices were made in a state of total obliviousness to their effect on an audience. In accordance with one of the main tenets of post-Revival thought, *důslednost* showed an altruistic objectivity that was lacking in *náladovost*, a condition that often stood as the embodiment of negatively charged subjectivism. As is made plain in the subsequent narrative, the interior/exterior relationship of *důslednost* and *náladovost* could be made to fit any number of debates regarding composers, works, and ideas of all kinds. Indeed, as with most of Hostinský's binarisms, this paradigm was not exclusive to Czech music alone, but was free to be used in the assessment of various musics, as seen in the critic's own remarks regarding Italian bel canto opera, Gluck, and German romanticism in general.

Miloš Jůzl, one of the foremost Czech historians of philosophy and aesthetics in the late communist period, summarized the system of binary oppositions in Hostinský's criticism and theoretical writings in the following manner:

Progress	Conservatism
Nationalism	Cosmopolitanism
Music Drama	Opera
Dramatic perspective	Purely musical perspective

Dramatic flow	Closed musical numbers
[Dramatic] realism	Formalism
Content	Virtuosity, formality
[Unity of] Style	Eclecticism
[Musical] Stylization	Naturalism
Natural Expression	Unnatural expression[24]

While this list provides an excellent delineation of both general aesthetic and music-related binarisms, it also assists in the definition of *důslednost* (left-hand column) and *náladovost* (right), connecting them to broader debates over content versus form, stylistic unity, and Wagnerian operatic reform. In fact, much of the above can be considered an extension of Wagner's own writings from a quarter-century before, specifically in his polemics against French and Italian opera. It is important to note here that Jůzl's use of the term "cosmopolitanism" does not refer to the worldly view of Czech national culture that Hostinský himself advocated, but rather to the promotion of non-Czech composers and works at the expense of Czech ones, simply on the basis of popularity. As the above discussion shows, nationalism was also pitted against patriotism with perhaps greater aesthetic consequences, since such a dichotomy sought to define the portrayal of Czech culture itself as either Wagnerian or folkloric, respectively. Already in the polemic between Smetana and Pivoda this division had been manifested in the question of whether folksong influences should be stylized or left in their natural state as quotations. By the time post-Wagnerian aesthetics were in full swing amid turn-of-the-century modernism, both in Prague and across Europe, Hostinský's binarisms would have a strong resonance—small wonder they formed the basis of subsequent debate in the city.

Hostinský's "Wagnerianism" article further explored the nationalist implications of progressive music, such that his defense of the neoromantic German school of composition turned into an advocacy for its use as the basis of modern Czech opera.[25] As with the preceding article, Hostinský's thesis rests on the subtext of a social division between conservative/patriotic and progressive/national factions. The aesthetician sought to defend not just the specific musical traits of Wagner's oeuvre, but also the principles behind them. Although the surface of the music could be refuted by some as intrinsically German, it was the modernity of Wagner's ideas that Hostinský considered to be the only viable starting point for a Czech national music. Citing Gluck's operatic reforms as the origin of Wagner's and Smetana's modern outlook, he described their use of "real" characters, the clear declamation of the text, and the process of merging set forms into dramatic wholes as crucial to satisfying the demands for a national music, both in Germany and for the Czechs. For Hostinský, each of these three items revealed the internal life and thought of the people, whether through role models on the stage, the foregrounding of language, or the presentation of a modern dramatic scheme that "conquers eclecticism," respectively. To prove his point, Hostinský proposed the reverse argument—that simple, unadulterated folksong serve as the model for national opera. With the assumption that such an opera would be modern (i.e., through-composed) in its formal layout, he demonstrated how the placement of a naive, essentially lyric set piece would make the overall dramatic structure unsound, thereby destroying the modern, unified concept of opera. Wagner's model, on the other hand, with its stylistic unity and declamatory style of singing, would reveal the dependability and liveliness of the Czech national character when used by a composer such as Smetana.

In 1872, when the three-year-old journal *Hudební listy* went over to an Old Czech publisher, Hostinský resigned and Pivoda came on as his replacement; within the year, Procházka and Hostinský established a new music journal, significantly entitled *Dalibor*, from which they could defend their position against Pivoda's circle. The debate became quickly polarized between two personalities, with Hostinský providing a rebuttal to every significant Pivoda article.[26] Hostinský's use of binarisms in print, therefore, whether between progressiveness and conservatism, nationalism and patriotism, Wagnerian music drama and number opera, were not only manifestations of an aesthetic creed, but also represented direct attacks on a rival ideological faction.

The third major essay of his early years, "On Program Music," was perhaps the most important, in that the author combined his approach to the debate on Wagner with his philosophical standpoint of aesthetic formalism.[27] For Hostinský, the polarity between aesthetics and art history presented a tension between the preservation of the beauty and stylistic purity of each art form on the one hand, and the historical tendency toward the merging of artistic disciplines on the other. In his view, despite the critics' frequent denunciation of program music as the "embodiment of the musical anti-Christ," this compositional approach represented a welcome solution to the dichotomy between aesthetics and art history.[28] If the arts must merge, the highest attention must be paid to their interrelationships in the whole, a task that only the *Gesamtkunstwerk* was able to do. Constructed as an elaborate response to Eduard Hanslick's polemic with the New German School, Hostinský's essay began by supporting Hanslick's standpoint of aesthetic formalism, seeking not to overturn it completely, but rather to demonstrate that such a methodology could be applied to program music without compromise.[29] Hostinský asserted that in the aesthetic system, musical notes were just notes, and any idea-content they supposedly conveyed, including beauty, was imagined externally by the audience. Differentiating between forms of idea-content in music as "spoken" or poetic, and "unspoken" or musical, he posited that music was able to stimulate the audience to arbitrary subjective reactions, but that these should not be confused with objective beauty, which came from known musical relationships. Related to Hanslick's discussion of "sounding architecture," Hostinský's argument held that musical content was either the abstract temporal movement of spatial forms, which was proper, or the mimicry of extramusical phenomena by musical means (i.e., naturalist tone-painting), which he deemed old-fashioned and absurd. If the form of a larger artistic work consisted of the concatenation of the mutual relationships of the individual parts on multiple levels, multiple artistic disciplines could then be juxtaposed without harming the doctrine of aesthetic formalism. Thus, a poetic program could serve as a stimulus for musical composition, without the necessity of existing as the musical subject itself, as was the case with tone-painting. It could also express what the music could not: namely, an idea content other than a purely musical one. The composer's method of conveying the program to the audience would then be through stylization rather than mimicry, forming an analogue to the Wagnerian technique of stylized declamation advocated earlier, and a reflection of the Smetana/Pivoda debate mentioned above. The synthesis of stylistic purity and merged artistic disciplines had a larger significance that was twofold: it could potentially teach composers how to discover new, purely musical forms; and as such, would produce a progressive relationship between the arts, creating a modernism that transcended temporal boundaries, as Haydn, Mozart, and Beethoven had accomplished. The implication in Hostinský's prose is that modern composers who followed the New German School ideology—particularly Smetana, in the local context—would remain modern beyond their time: this view would shape not only the reception of this composer's music but also the many polemics surrounding his legacy in the twentieth century.

After *The Two Widows*: Smetana, Dvořák, and Fibich

In March 1874, Hostinský began a three-year sojourn outside of Prague as a tutor to an aristocratic family; in his absence, Pivoda, along with a circle that included younger contemporaries such as Karel Knittl, Jindřich Böhm, and Max Konopásek, virtually held court in Prague's musical life at *Hudební listy*. Hostinský's departure also signaled the weakening of the Smetana faction. The composer himself, after the problematic premiere of *Dalibor*, did not have another opera produced at the Provisional Theater until *Dvě vdovy* (The Two Widows) in 1874, insofar as the superbly nationalistic *Libuše* of 1872 was destined to wait until the opening of the National Theater in 1881. *The Two Widows*, a parlor comedy based on a French play by Félicien Mallefille transplanted to the Bohemian countryside, was perhaps the greatest disaster of the composer's career, provoking as it did the ire and ridicule of *Hudební listy*, and therefore the disrespect of the Old Czech cultural establishment. These events proved extraordinarily ill-timed, falling amid the reversion to an Old-Czech administration at the Provisional Theater, the onset of Smetana's deafness, and his resignation from the post of opera director, all within the same *annus horribilis*. Taken together, they form the final pivotal moment in the composer's career and thus contribute to the definition of his legacy among romantic nationalists throughout the twentieth century.

The atmosphere of cultural politics in Prague was in a state of near paranoia at the time of *The Two Widows'* premiere. Events such as Pivoda's publication of Schubert's *Die schöne Müllerin* with a bilingual text, or the performance of Beethoven's Ninth Symphony by the Philharmonic Society in 1873 provoked critics of both sides to volleys of rhetoric and nationalist posturing.[30] Smetana's comedy, with a text of foreign origin and based on Auber's model of dialogue-based number operas, was easily seen as a weak link in the pro-Wagner faction. A review of the opera, signed only with the cryptic "-tt.," denounced the work as Wagnerian, composed "for orchestra with voice accompaniment" by a "certain emerging mole-hill" (i.e., in comparison with the "mountainous" Wagner).[31] The unknown author considered the lack of closed forms and inclusion of prose sung dialogues in *The Two Widows*, both elements of late nineteenth-century operatic reform, to be merely "frivolousness." The tone of the article indicates the degree to which it was important for the conservative faction to attack Smetana, not through the reasoned analysis of any flaws the work might have, but through outright rejection to the point of belittling the composer as a person. The reaction among Smetana's supporters was utter astonishment that such tactics could be used with regard to an artist of national importance.

The almost cultic aura surrounding Smetana that persists to this day in Czech society can be said to have started precisely at this point. For Hostinský, Procházka, and others, it was inconceivable that any work by their musical hero could meet with a negative reception on any level, an attitude echoed even more so in the polemics of the early twentieth century. Although *The Two Widows* has never been considered Smetana's greatest work, to disagree with its place in the growing canon of Czech composition in 1874 was, for some, to commit an act so morally reprehensible that its effects would be felt by the nation for generations. Indeed, this very issue would reappear in 1907 as part of a vehement debate, and the work itself was still viable as a model for modern opera as late as 1911. The myth of the untouchable status of Smetana, situated alone above the collective of Czech culture as the sole possible model for its music making, was already firmly in place by his death and continued, ever stronger, until its institutionalization with the Smetana Exhibition of 1917. After the apotheosis of one such individual, then, no others could possibly be afforded such a luxury. For Hostinský's followers, one was either an undeservedly unsuccessful composer, martyred to Smetana's cause (as were Fibich, Foerster, Ostrčil, and Zich), or an undeservedly successful one, whose fame was bought at the price of Smetana's glory, and whose music could, therefore, never represent the Czech collective.

The composer whose reception in Prague best fits the latter description was Antonín Dvořák, whose successful career outside the Czech Lands was disproportionate to his slender fame at home. Indeed, it is surprising that a composer whose position in the late nineteenth-century orchestral repertoire is now largely uncontested should have been the object of such contention in his home environment. As we shall see in following chapters, this phenomenon was a direct result of his international fame, particularly in the realm of absolute music. Although Dvořák composed in many genres, including dramatic ones, the participants in the ongoing aesthetic polemic quickly typecast him as Smetana's "instrumental" counterpart; conversely, his operatic endeavors became objects of ridicule for Hostinský and his supporters. This reading of Dvořák's music and its role in Czech culture forms yet another link between the absolute/program music debate and contemporary issues of nationalism.

As indicated previously, Dvořák's success in Prague depended to a certain extent on the good favor of the Old Czech party, and on Rieger in particular in the 1880s. In the minds of Smetana's supporters, there was a direct connection between Old Czech influence (which was considered to be utraquist), Dvořák's Austrian state stipend, Brahms, Hanslick, anti-Wagnerianism, and international fame. The coincidence that Dvořák achieved his initial breakthrough in Vienna at the same time as Smetana's disaster with *The Two Widows*, deafness, and resignation from the conductorship of the Provisional Theater was not lost on the Czech Wagnerians, who equated Dvořák's ascendancy with a betrayal of the older composer. (Similarly, Dvořák's success beyond the Austro-German lands, in England and the United States, was often juxtaposed with Smetana's death, as though it were immoral for another Czech artist to have any sort of ambition when the only possible musical model had been martyred to the cause.) Almost as revenge for the mistreatment of *Dalibor* and *The Two Widows* at the hands of Dvořák's supporters, the pro-Smetana critical faction of Prague attacked Dvořák's 1882 opera *Dimitrij* for the political and aesthetic ideals it was held to represent. Set in pre-Petrine Russia with a story that forms a sequel to *Boris Godunov*, Dvořák's work was at once an attempt at grand opera and an evocation of the pan-Slavist ideals promulgated by Pivoda and others in the Old Czech artistic circle. The latter connection was solidified in the minds of many by the fact that the librettist, Marie Červinková-Riegrová (who also wrote the text for *The Jacobin*), was the daughter of Old Czech leader František Rieger, whose conservative politics included a favorable position on pan-Slavism.

In late 1874, toward the end of the debate on *The Two Widows* (and, significantly, prior to the composition of *Dimitrij*), the Pivoda supporter Max Konopásek published the article "An Analysis of the Slavonic Music Question," in *Hudební listy*. Konopásek asserted that, since each nation's music was dependent on the people's speech, and because the Czech language had been unduly corrupted by German, Czech folksongs and music based on them were worthless as contributions to pan-Slavic music making.[32] The only option, therefore, was to explore the historic roots of other Slavic cultures (from which he chose the example of the Ruthenians, whose largely pastoral society was said to have preserved the oldest speech and song patterns), and to ignore the developments of modern music in the West. Nevertheless, *Dimitrij*, as a conscious effort to rejuvenate the grand opera style of Meyerbeer, cannot be read as a rejection of Western music. It was, however, labeled by Hostinský and his followers as a reactionary work—the very antipode of Smetana's efforts—that consequently reified the connection between conservative aesthetics and antinationalism (even though *The Two Widows* had used Auber as a model). Many of these formulations were not stated so directly in the criticism of the era. Nonetheless, from the time of the *Dimitrij* premiere onward, Hostinský was singled out as Dvořák's main opponent. For this reason, the aesthetician was gradually ostracized from Czech cultural life as the Old Czechs solidified their control over musical institutions in the city.

The third composer of stature in Prague in the waning years of the nineteenth century was Zdeněk Fibich, whose vocal support of Wagner and Smetana also excluded him from the Czech cultural establishment from the beginning of his career. His only two significant involvements in musical institutions were three years as an assistant conductor to Smetana's replacement, Maýr, at the Provisional Theater (where he was relegated to conducting operetta, 1875–78) and a single year as dramaturge of the National Theater before his death in 1900. Between these commitments he was dependent upon work as a freelance composer and as a teacher of piano, theory, and composition in a private studio. Although the latter activity may not have been extraordinarily lucrative, its contribution to Prague's musical life had an importance that stretched well into the twentieth century. Despite his failure to gain a post at Prague Conservatory (where the director, Bennewitz, was unable to persuade the administration to hire him), Fibich taught an impressive list of musicians, including the critic and composer Emmanuel Chvála, composer and future National Theater conductor Karel Kovařovic (1862–1920), the composer Otakar Ostrčil (1879–1935), and the critic Zdeněk Nejedlý (1878–1962). Fibich was also active alongside Hostinský (who had served as librettist for the opera *Nevěsta messinská* [The Bride of Messina]) in the aesthetician's ongoing struggle with the Pivoda faction after Smetana's death. Their participation in the polemic was particularly significant at the point when the conservative establishment sought to bring Smetana into the pantheon of national Czech artists on their own terms. Perhaps most important, Fibich would join Hostinský in shaping a new generation of thinkers, thereby consciously attempting to preserve Czech neoromantic ideology and create a legacy for their role-model, Smetana.

The 1890s and the Rise of a New Generation

After the solidification of cultural power among the National Theater generation and their appropriation of Smetana as a norm within the bounds of conservative-nationalist taste, there occurred two important developments in the final decade of the century. First, the appearance of a new generation of Czech students, the first to enjoy a system of firmly established cultural institutions, changed the landscape of Prague's musical life, such that new personalities began to dominate the concert and operatic stage. As a direct result of this development and the attendant shift in musical styles, many in the Old Czech establishment began to soften their attitudes toward the debates of the past, to the point of hiding or rewriting their own involvements in the confrontations of the 1870s. In general, the 1890s were a decade of cultural and political liberalism in the Czech Lands, when artists of all persuasions experimented with more cosmopolitan influences. Two specific examples of this are the poet/novelist Julius Zeyer and the painter Alfons Mucha, both of whom spent time in Paris and other West European capitals, assimilating many of the cultural forms they encountered there. The generation that began its compositional and scholarly careers at the very end of the decade would be the driving force behind the debates on nationalism, modernism, and the social responsibility of art in the new century, shaping the path of music and cultural identity in Prague for several decades.

Second, the decade also saw a resurgence of dramatic music by Czech composers, occasioned by the emergence of Foerster and especially Kovařovic as popular composers of opera, the melodramas and late operas of Fibich, and not least by the return of Dvořák from America in 1895 and his subsequent operatic production. The popular taste of the new Czech bourgeois audience inclined toward lighter genres and less complex musical expression, thereby accounting for the abundance of comic operas, operettas, ballets, and pantomimes, all represented by Kovařovic in the early part of the decade, but also reflected in the work of Jindřich Kàan z Albestů, Josef Richard Rozkošný, the young Oskar Nedbal, and even in Dvořák's *Čert a Káča* (The Devil and Kate, 1899).

With the ascendancy of the Czech bourgeoisie came the institution of salon music making, somewhat belated by several decades in comparison to similar developments in Paris and Vienna. As such, salons became a very approachable venue for young emergent composers in Prague, including Vítězslav Novák and Josef Suk, who composed much of their early piano, vocal, and chamber music for performance in this environment.[33] Much of this bourgeois musical activity, itself quite open to contemporary influences from abroad, became an object of disdain for those left in the Hostinský faction, as evidenced by even the very earliest writings of his student Nejedlý. Ironically, the so-called "progressive," Wagnerian faction now stood in opposition to young composers who were fast attaining the label of "modernist" throughout the music community of Prague, and whom the Wagnerians considered too cosmopolitan to be truly "national" artists in the mold of Smetana. Thus, an unusual situation developed, where the modernists were nurtured by the salons of Prague, while the proponents of a "modern, national" culture gradually slipped into conservatism, since their efforts to find a viable, new representative of Smetana's ideals had come to naught, especially with Fibich's exclusion from mainstream musical life.

In the mid-1890s, amid the decline of Old Czech conservatism and the appropriation of Smetana's music by the cultural establishment, members of the faction that had originally supported Smetana twenty years before renewed their struggle against their original opponents. Alongside Hostinský and Fibich emerged Josef Srb-Debrnov and Antonín Čížek, who sought to expose once and for all the identity of the author of the *Two Widows* review from *Hudební listy*.[34] This incident reveals not only the lasting importance of the issues of nationalism and social responsibility from the time of the Cultural Revival, but also the desperation of the Pivoda faction as they felt the tide of public opinion turn against them—a phenomenon occasioned by their own assimilation of Smetana. Srb-Debrnov and Čížek succeeded, if not in proving the authorship of the article beyond doubt, then at least in tarnishing the reputations of Pivoda, Knittl, and other contributors to *Hudební listy* in the early 1870s through the implication that their attack on Smetana was in essence an attack on the moral achievements of the Cultural Revival. Simply put, Pivoda and Knittl behaved as though they had something to hide, refusing to divulge the authorship of a dissenting opinion from twenty years before.

Part of this deliberate obfuscation stems from the direction that the debate over the influence of Wagner on Czech music had taken in the intervening years. Knittl (along with his Conservatory colleague, the theorist Karel Stecker) had come out against Hostinský and Fibich in a series of attacks that labeled the aesthetician as having misunderstood Smetana, thereby damaging the composer's reputation and chance at success during his lifetime. What Hostinský's student Nejedlý later called "the younger Pivoda generation" read Smetana as a defender of the rights of absolute music *in opera* against the threat of Wagnerian influence. Hostinský, therefore, in his prior defense of Smetana as having created a modern Czech music "alongside" Wagner, had misread his idol, having made him out as nothing more than an epigone of his German contemporary, and therefore as an "antinational" composer.[35] The seemingly inexhaustible polemic and the unaccountability of Hostinský's opponents finally forced him out of the debate in the late 1890s, after which point he advised his main successor, Nejedlý, to refrain from such belligerent tactics. In this respect, the Pivoda faction retained its place in the musical establishment, having warded off their main sources of threat of the past quarter-century.

Hostinský, meanwhile, continued to develop his aesthetic theory of music, publishing a major treatise, *Nauka o hudebních zněnách* (The Theory of Musical Sounds) in 1878, and creating an influential lecture series on the history of music at Prague University. Shortly after the turn of the century, three years before his death in 1910, he published the lengthy essay *Umění a společnost* (Art and Society), which summarized his efforts on the topic throughout his career.[36] This work, which forms a parallel to similar discussions at this time in Western Europe regarding the social (and/or socialist) role of art in the modern world, also served as a major milestone in Czech musical aesthetics, touching on many issues that would reappear throughout the early twentieth century in different contexts. In essence, the essay can be regarded as the main link between the endeavors of the nineteenth-century Revivalists and the musical modernists of the early twentieth century. Cast as an argument for the very existence of art in a bourgeois, materialist society, Hostinský's argument proceeded from the use of art as entertainment to its necessity in terms of human education, citing the need for the internal (i.e., intellectual and spiritual) development of "the people" of a nation. Although he was never explicitly socialist in his writings, he recognized the cultural needs of levels of society broader than merely the regular concert-going public. So, too, was art to be made accessible to the masses in the effort to educate them, thereby forging a unity between art and a national audience that would benefit both agents.[37] Through a discussion of the dialectic of utility versus monumentality in art, Hostinský proposed a synthesis, wherein society would be not simply entertained, but rather uplifted by progressive art, which reflected the people's highest, idealized emotions on an atemporal and universal plane.[38] The conformity of art to this social task would render it beautiful because it would both reflect and idealize the inner, emotional state of "the people," thereby elevating the taste of the entire nation: "in itself it becomes the driving motive and goal of artistic creation and simultaneously the yardstick of its value."[39] The true artist would therefore struggle against the forces of blasé mediocrity to create progressive art as a social duty. Despite popular opinion to the contrary, Hostinský stressed that such art should not be simplified or in any way tailored to the masses, since such measures would fall short of the aforementioned goal.

Hostinský's efforts would not be in vain: by the time *Art and Society* was published, Prague was in the midst of a nationalist and modernist upheaval that would last until Czechoslovak independence in 1918. While the seeds of this unrest can be found in a multitude of sources, including national and international politics, developments throughout the social structure of Europe, and the rise of modernism in all the arts, the catalysts for change in the Czech musical environment were relatively few in number and specific in impact. Although the main iconoclast after 1900 was undoubtedly Zdeněk Nejedlý—about whom much more will be said in the coming chapters—before the turn of the century one voice, Ludvík Lošťák, strongly advocated a modernist revolution in Czech musical culture. His manifesto, "An Open Letter to the Young Musical Generation of Bohemia and Moravia," published in 1896 in *Dalibor*, promised such a revolution:

> If a cadaverous immobility and fearfulness dominates in any branch of Czech art, then doubtlessly, first and foremost, it is the case in music. Already for years [Czech music] has been wholly and exclusively in the hands of a few older lords who have merely their own interests and successes in mind, while not caring about the interests, hopes, and ideals of the younger generation in the least. . . . We all feel the results of their tactics, and very cruelly and bitterly at that. . . . There is a whole group of us in Bohemia and Moravia, a group of young men whose young souls are kindled by a true love for artistic ideals, even though the realization of our ideals is impossible, since we are not

admitted to the arena of public activity and influence! And so it is our sole lot that we be dwarfed, stifled, and finally extinguished in the darkness that pervades in a fog of selfishness and jealousy!![40]

Lošťák's views on how this revolution should take place musically, however, were somewhat commonplace and conservatively nationalistic. Moreover, his reaction to his surroundings, while mostly based in generational animosity (as seen in the above quotation), was likely aimed toward the perceived cosmopolitanism of his teachers and the attendant relinquishing of nationalism as a priority throughout much of the 1890s. Although his manifesto attracted the attention of several other students, his lack of organization and inability to translate his fiery words into leadership in the compositional sphere reduced his impact severely. As we shall see in the coming chapters, it would be others—the composers Novák, Suk, and Ostrčil, and the musicologist Nejedlý—who would serve as the main voices of modernism in the first two decades of the new century.

Chapter Three

Legacies, Ideologies, and Responsibilities

The Polemics of the Pre-Independence Years (1900–1918)

The date 1900 is not widely held to be a significant point of division in the musical history of Prague. The previous decade had witnessed a spectacular flowering of compositional activity, including Dvořák's "American" period, Fibich's late operas, and the first publications and performances of the new generation of Novák, Nedbal, and Suk. Between 1890 and 1910, much of the musical life of the city had continued on course since the opening of the National Theater in 1883, with the addition of a new German opera house in 1886, chamber concerts at the Conservatory, orchestral concerts with the Czech Philharmonic after 1901, and ongoing lectures in music history at the University. Various journals that had existed for decades continued a modest existence, while others came and went without much impact. Amid these outwardly serene activities, one seemingly insignificant event proved enough to trigger a series of artistic and aesthetic debates, as well as to initiate one man's long career in the field of musical and social criticism. When Zdeněk Fibich died at the age of fifty in 1900, his twenty-two-year-old theory student Zdeněk Nejedlý resolved to settle old scores—to put all his energies into shifting the balance of power in musical Prague—and so to alter the course of music history in that city.[1]

From the early years of the century, the most important ideology surrounding music making in Prague was nationalism, a factor that affected all the arts, and more directly, politics. By the turn of the century, the work of the Cultural Revival was complete, and the generation that first appeared in the 1890s was now beginning to achieve professional status; Czech society was no longer quite so focused on the foundation of representative institutions, but rather on the exploration of different modes of thinking about themselves and their place in Europe. The Czech population of the city (as throughout the provinces of Bohemia and Moravia) was divided into a variety of camps that favored differing strategies regarding the future of the nation, from total autonomy via revolution to passive assimilation with the German-Austrian majority. These divisions were matched in the musical community, where shades of national feeling intersected not only with similar policies at cultural institutions but also with aesthetic attitudes toward the music itself, be it conservative, modernist, aggressively nationalist, or openly cosmopolitan. As a result, while proclamations regarding the musical identity of the Czech collective issued from all sides, no consensus was possible; furthermore, the voice of the individual creative artist was often explicitly ignored, in that his/her subjectivity somehow detracted from collective achievements. While more will be said in chapter 4 regarding Czech fin-de-siècle modernism, suffice it to say that contemporary composition was granted increasing nationalist importance by 1914. Ironically, this ideology often burdened modernist composers unduly, in that their every creative act was upheld to an almost impossible moral yardstick. Thus, while it is true that nationalism ran rampant throughout Europe in the years before the First World War, rarely did the critical divide serve to inhibit modernist expression so directly as in the Prague environment.

Another result of these factional divisions, both musical and political, was a series of localized polemic "affairs," carried out generally in the music press, but often spilling over into the daily news. In all cases, the polemics involved either Nejedlý directly or one of his university students, who by 1911 were ready and willing to pen vituperative articles for their mentor. While on the surface the debate raged over the legacy of Smetana, Dvořák, and the alleged duties of their contemporary representatives, these polemics served ultimately to bring the Czech musical community into a confrontation with the modern era, where the responsibility of the individual artist lay wholly toward the collective. Although the often pugilistic stance of Nejedlý was seen by his contemporaries as merely vengeful, anti-establishmentarian hate-mongering, it can also be said that the content of his attacks (amid the "Knittl Affair," the struggles over the National Theater, and the "Dvořák Affair") displayed a desire to rectify various "wrongs" he perceived in Czech music making. Interestingly, Nejedlý's efforts were directed more toward social, moral, or general aesthetic evils rather than toward specific musical attributes. While this bias has often been cited as proof of the critic's musical shortcomings, more revealing are the possible connections in his prose to contemporaneous discourses on immanent analysis (à la Adorno), idealism versus realism, and most important, the long-term legacy of Wagner as figured in the debate between absolute music and programmaticism. By the First World War, particularly with the rise of widespread patriotism as evidenced by the Smetana Exhibition of 1917, Nejedlý's paradigm of a national, modern, socially responsible Czech music had gained ground, to the point where many of its tenets were accepted by individuals across the entire critical spectrum.

Nejedlý's Early Career

The debates around nationalism, modernism, and the social responsibility of art that came to the fore after 1900 were not new to the Prague cultural sphere.[2] The arrival of Nejedlý on the scene brought the discussions (which had been dormant for about five years) to a more acute level, turning aesthetic differences of opinion into virulent and often personal assaults. He began by attacking the musical establishment in order to correct certain injustices he perceived toward his vision of Czech music, or in some cases, simply toward his friends. One of Nejedlý's best-known efforts was the synthesis of his concept of the Czech musical past—in which the positive legacy of Smetana ran alongside the negative influence of Dvořák—with contemporary composition. This scheme pitted the "Smetanian" composers Foerster and Ostrčil against Dvořák's former students Novák and Suk. Such a development not only increased the relevance of the outdated arguments but also forced his contemporaries to choose between individual visions of modernism, a stance that effectively excluded possible alternatives.

Nejedlý's anachronistic obsession with Smetana was linked directly to the debate between program and absolute music; in its local context, the argument acquired nationalist overtones, much as it had in the previous generation with Hostinský. As the century progressed, Nejedlý introduced increasing amounts of modernist rhetoric into the debate, asserting that a modern, "Czech" music could only spring from the operatic and programmatic models of Wagner and Smetana. Although his opponents in the musical establishment initially believed that such a dependence on "foreign" models served only to negate the "national" element in Czech music, which should be derived from folk sources alone (an ideology reminiscent of Balakirev and others in the Russian Five), younger composers began to incorporate newer styles from abroad, such as impressionism around 1900. Nejedlý rejected all of these notions, countering that a truly national music was based in objective idealism, not realism, naturalism, or passing subjective trends. These latter approaches, he felt, belittled their national subject matter through mundane quotation, mimicry, or insufficient deference to Smetana. In other words, truly modern, national art must edify the audience through higher artistic aims, and Czech music must strive to be both modern and national in order to fulfill its social mission. Much of this rhetoric was evident even in the critic's early career.

Zdeněk Nejedlý was born in 1878 into a musical family in Litomyšl, Bohemia, the same town where Smetana had been born fifty-four years earlier. His interest in the formative periods of Bohemian history (the Hussite period and the nineteenth-century Cultural Revival in particular) led him to study history and aesthetics at the University in Prague. His passion for the music of Smetana, however, led him to study music theory briefly with Fibich, and to have Hostinský as his university adviser. From both teachers, Nejedlý received an unshakable reverence for Smetana as the founding force and supreme model of modern

Czech music; he also inherited their positive stance toward Wagnerian music dramas, which Smetana and Fibich had introduced into Prague musical life. Hostinský in particular had promulgated these and other "modern" developments in opera, which he felt showed a greater responsibility toward the needs of the burgeoning Czech society than did the more provincial musical models used by other nineteenth-century composers. By 1900, as a result of these opinions and the ongoing struggle against Smetana's opponents, the arrival of an energetic young ally was a welcome development for Hostinský and Fibich. Indeed, the musical writings of Nejedlý's early career imply that the young man was groomed as an ideological successor to his teachers. Although Nejedlý had sought instruction in the positivist school of Jaroslav Goll, whose doctrine was to avoid sociological and ideological analysis in favor of causal, fact-based history, the impact of his musical and aesthetic instruction steered him precisely into the social issues of nationalism, modernism, culture, and eventually socialism.[3] Furthermore, it was his strong personal relationships with Hostinský and Fibich that made the deepest impression on the young student, who by the age of twenty-two was ready to take up their cause in the midst of formidable adversaries.

When Fibich died in 1900, Nejedlý was just beginning his career as a historian, having already published a positivist monograph on the Hussite theologian Jan z Rokycan in the previous year. Within a few months of Fibich's death, Nejedlý inaugurated his career as a music critic with a scathing attack on Dvořák's *Rusalka*, in an article that appeared in the journal *Rozhledy* in May 1901, less than two months after the opera's premiere. Already in this short review we see many of the basic criteria that Nejedlý would use throughout his critical oeuvre. "Dvořák's *Rusalka*" began with the assertion that "music drama is the sole possible form for modern opera," implying that Dvořák's latest work must be judged by Wagnerian standards.[4] Nejedlý went on to declare that the music should submit to the text; that the opera's large-scale form should be dramatic, not musical; that closed musical scenes are "absolutely inadmissible"; and that leitmotivic material should, "through its form, placement, and changes, make psychological moments as clear as possible."[5] In each of these criteria we can see the legacy of Hostinský's Wagnerian teachings, now directed more specifically at an individual composer. Perhaps most confrontational was Nejedlý's contention that *Rusalka* was antinational and un-Czech on two fronts: its declamation was faulty in both melodic contour and rhythmic placement ("What *less* can we demand from a national composer, than that he respect our language?"); and Dvořák's inclusion of folksong melodies was trivial, undramatic, and in direct opposition to the ideals of Smetana. This line of argumentation not only continued Hostinský's thirty-year-old construct of declamation as a marker of national identity, but also connected it to the discourse on idealism versus "realism" in music. After quoting Smetana's thoughts on this topic, Nejedlý reminded his readers of the suffering that both Smetana and Fibich endured on this account.

The implication is that *Rusalka* continued the domination of the conservative pseudonationalists who had tried to suppress Smetana's and Fibich's music in the preceding decades (i.e., Rieger, Pivoda and Knittl), although Nejedlý was careful not to make this connection directly. While he conceded that the orchestration of *Rusalka* was excellent, he took this opportunity to reinforce the idea that Dvořák's true musical home was the realm of absolute (particularly chamber) music, and not dramatic music in any form whatsoever. As if this were not enough, the critic asserted that Dvořák's music was unoriginal, the composer having lifted musical material from Smetana's *Dalibor* and *Libuše*, Wagner's *Ring Cycle*, and Kovařovic's *Psohlavci* (The Dogheads).[6] As a final touch to this litany of defamation, Nejedlý issued a challenge to the critical community at large, asking whether they had failed to realize that dramatic quality is a necessary trait of modern opera; whether they had recognized its absence in *Rusalka*; and whether they refused to acknowledge the value of speaking the truth about Dvořák to the listening public.

To the musical community of Prague in 1901, Nejedlý's attack on *Rusalka* would not have come as much of a surprise, given that he was the product of two creative, yet contentious, minds—Hostinský and Fibich. What was surprising was the directness of Nejedlý's belligerent tone and his virtual battery of arguments: he seems to have presented not just a review of a single contemporary work, but an all-encompassing worldview including music, drama, nationalism, progress, and ethics, both artistic and journalistic. His emphasis on the "modern" instead of merely the "progressive," while somewhat novel for Czech criticism, reflected the new era in which he was living, since by 1901, modernist aesthetics and above all rhetoric had become a permanent fixture throughout the artistic spheres of Europe.

Belief in the absolute authority of Smetana, in both written word and musical model, was perhaps Nejedlý's most obvious trademark. Indeed, he evoked Smetana in almost every musical tract of his career, always as the messianic "Founder of Modern Czech Music," a towering figure whose extensive shadow was a continuous reminder of the tremendous moral achievement of the Cultural Revival. Very often he used Smetana's music as a means to strike down "lesser" musicians in a seemingly incontrovertible comparison; sometimes Smetana might also appear in a historical context as a martyr who suffered at the hands of his dishonorable adversaries. Each of these paradigms was also available for use with regard to any of the composers that Nejedlý considered to have "inherited" Smetana's legacy, most prominently Fibich, Foerster, and Ostrčil. Such a system of judgment was contingent upon an ahistorical concept of modernity, wherein the spirit of Smetana was treated as a model for new compositions, particularly in terms of opera, more than a quarter-century after his death. Further trademarks of Nejedlý's critical style appear in the binarisms of the dramatic versus the trivial, the psychological versus the sentimental, originality versus eclecticism, Czech versus foreign (particularly "Viennese" as an embodiment of bourgeois triviality), and—although mostly implicit at this stage—modern versus conservative, in both compositional style and cultural/political outlook. While Nejedlý in 1901 applied each of these paradigms to the *music* of Dvořák's *Rusalka*, he refrained from making explicit connections between Dvořák's character or career and Smetana's adversaries of the 1870s.[7] The outward appearance of "Dvořák's *Rusalka*," then, is of a feuilleton on how (not) to write a modern opera, rather than a polemic on the nature of Czech musical culture, past and present, despite the concatenation of wider concepts and allusions. The overall effect is one of redrawing Czech musical identity, wherein only one individual, Smetana, and a handful of like-minded artists were allowed to represent the collective, from which all others were excluded, be it for stylistic, ideological, or moral reasons. In the coming decades, Nejedlý had ample opportunity to make these arguments explicit, even exhaustive; interestingly, his approach to this realm of total cultural warfare led at first not through Dvořák, but through Fibich.

As a challenge to the musical community that had ignored Fibich during his lifetime, Nejedlý resolved to devote a long-term project to bringing his teacher's music to the public consciousness. This plan had deeper roots than merely to make up for the dearth of biographical or analytical publications regarding Fibich and his music at the turn of the century. Intimately associated with this gap in Czech music literature were the other results of the unresolved tension that had persisted since the 1870s: the general ambivalence toward Smetana's music (i.e., not including the severely altered Novotný editions), the exclusion of Hostinský from musical life, and the dim future for the young composers most closely associated with Fibich (specifically Foerster and Ostrčil). As with the *Rusalka* review, Nejedlý was able to weave these sometimes disparate threads into a complex series of arguments about the past, present, and future of Czech music, creating a historiography that would influence generations of musicians in Prague.

Nejedlý's first few monographs fulfilled these plans amply. In *Zdeněk Fibich, Founder of the Scenic Melodrama* from 1901, he not only published the first full-length study of his teacher's music, but also sought to elevate what he felt to be Fibich's flagship genre, the melodrama.[8] For Nejedlý, the high artistic quality of these melodramas and their subsequent dismissal by the cultural institutions of Prague were not only emblematic of Fibich's undue neglect in the public sphere, but also indicative of a large-scale misunderstanding of Smetana's heritage and of Czech culture in general.

With growing boldness, the young critic set out to declare his overall historiographical conception in his 1903 *History of Czech Music*, a slim volume that nevertheless encompassed material from the pre-Hussite years all the way to reports of the prior season's theatrical performances. Some of the most interesting writing comes from the latter half of the book, divided into two large chapters: "The Era of Smetana," which delineates Czech music history up to 1884; and "The Era of Fibich," which provides details for the following two decades, a time

Nejedlý had witnessed firsthand. The volume, one of the most comprehensive of its kind to appear in Prague at this time, provoked the ire of the musical establishment through the implication that only Smetana and his followers were truly Czech and modern.

Already with these chapter designations we see the author's inescapable bias, having named the entire era after two composers at the expense of all other musical activity, while simultaneously constructing a compositional "lineage." Indeed, by 1903, Nejedlý was already beginning to promulgate the system of lineages that he would use to define both the history and present-day state of music in the Czech Lands throughout most of his career. Despite some rather dubious factual statements and stylistic connections, Nejedlý maintained that those figures in Czech music who held a positive attitude toward Smetana and his music were somehow spiritually descended from him. In this manner, Fibich, who had actually studied abroad, was treated as Smetana's heir apparent, and while Ostrčil had certainly studied with Fibich, Foerster was also interpolated into the lineage in their midst, without regard for historical accuracy or stylistic continuity.[9] In opposition to Smetana's "lineage," Nejedlý constructed a parallel one fostered by the Conservatory: with Dvořák as the nominal head, and virtually any other late-nineteenth-century Prague composer lumped into the bargain,[10] this "lineage" was responsible for the miseducation of the new generation of Novák, Suk, Nedbal, and Karel. Nejedlý's chief analytical tool was to label Smetana's lineage aesthetically and continuously "modern" (a designation that grew increasingly ahistorical), while, in his view, that of Dvořák became inescapably and unequivocally "conservative," both in musical style and political outlook. The atemporal modernism of Smetana's lineage could also tap into any other significant composer or trend from abroad, beyond the direct connection to Wagnerian style: at times, Nejedlý and his followers would attempt to demonstrate spiritual kinship with Mahler, Liszt, Berlioz, Beethoven, and even Gluck, all of whom were suitable models for modern Czech culture and society. Conversely, Dvořák's lineage could be connected with anything overly popular, transitory, or personally distasteful to Nejedlý, such as opéra lyrique, verismo, impressionism, and occasionally Richard Strauss. This system of lineages, couched in the terminology of modernism, and to some extent, the artist's social responsibility in the sphere of culture, was primarily directed toward defining the identity of a Czech national music, partially through the exclusion of a substantial portion of Czech participants. It is important to note that, while Nejedlý described the musical characteristics of individuals such as Foerster, Ostrčil, Novák, and Suk, he evaluated them predominantly in terms of their contributions to a collective, virtually ignoring the impact of subjectivist aesthetics—a concept encoded in his discourse as weak and potentially damaging to Czech identity as a whole.

In many respects, Nejedlý's attitude concerning the representation of musical Czechness tended toward a rigidity that belied his allegedly progressive, proto-socialist politics: Czech modernism, while aesthetically atemporal, was limited to a single model in Smetana. Indeed, within a short space of time, his modernist standpoint grew increasingly outdated and conservative as a result of his resistance to change. In this way Nejedlý's position is reminiscent of the Brahms-Wagner debate, wherein the more "progressive" Wagner became associated with right-wing politics, while the musically conservative Brahms (like Novák and many others) had connections to liberalism.[11] It also foreshadows somewhat the Soviets' adoption of a repressive nineteenth-century canon in the name of revolutionary politics in the 1930s.

The History of Czech Music also related Nejedlý's highly incriminating saga of Smetana's opponents from the 1870s, particularly Pivoda and Knittl; both were described as having promulgated Old Czech political and cultural conservatism against Smetana, eventually roping Dvořák into their faction. Despite many bitter implications, the latter composer was still not openly attacked in Nejedlý's *History*: rather, he was portrayed as a misinformed and indecisive artist of talent whose career as a Czech National Composer was marred by a susceptibility to Viennese fame and power. Novák and Suk, too, were benignly categorized as "young conservatives," a designation that both demonstrated their cultural inheritance from Dvořák and ignored their burgeoning status as the leaders of the young modernist generation in Prague. In their place, Nejedlý heralded Foerster and especially Ostrčil as the brightest hopes for Czech music; in the case of the latter, this was indicative of an alliance of growing importance between the author and composer. With the *History of Czech Music*, Nejedlý clearly delineated a faction of adversaries, against whom he would proceed to struggle for most of the next quarter-century.

Prague Conservatory and the "Knittl Affair"

With or without Nejedlý, the years between 1900 and the First World War were ones of precarious transition for the Conservatory, which had so far retained its status as a bastion of Old-Czech political values as well as its links to the like-minded Artists' Union (UB). The unflagging support of Dvořák and his music among the faculty stemmed from his role as Conservatory director, from the time of his return from America in 1895 until his death in 1904. During this time, professors Karel Knittl and Karel Stecker reinforced the composer's advanced masterclass with instruction in theory and introductory composition. The Conservatory system produced a host of well-trained young composers throughout the 1890s, with Vítězslav Novák, Josef Suk, Oskar Nedbal, and Rudolf Karel at the forefront of the group. The experience of the first three composers in particular was shaped by the three-year hiatus (1892–95) caused by the departure of Dvořák for America: during these years, the bulk of the instruction was given by Knittl and Stecker, who prepared the students for the advanced class, which resumed upon Dvořák's return.[12] With the latter teacher, however, Novák, Suk, and Nedbal made the transition from satisfactory students to widely appreciated professionals; by the last years of the nineteenth century, Novák had achieved success in Prague society with a number of published songs and piano pieces, and both Nedbal and Suk had begun touring Europe as members of the Czech Quartet. Despite Nejedlý's charges of conservatism, by all accounts these students' education was relatively cosmopolitan for the time, since Novák's and Suk's compositions from the early years of the century already reveal a comfortable openness to fin-de-siècle Viennese modernism and impressionism.

When Dvořák died in 1904, Stecker and Knittl remained on the faculty. According to Stanislava Zacharová, both professors not only gave their students a thorough musical education, but also attempted to influence them with a positive view toward Smetana's former opponents, particularly Pivoda.[13] They and the rest of the musical establishment (the Conservatory, the UB, and the journal *Dalibor*) viewed the entrance of Nejedlý on the musical scene, and particularly his growing influence at the University, with considerable misgivings, as evidenced by their various attempts to limit Nejedlý's voice in print. As Nejedlý argued in his *History of Czech Music*, the continued success of the Conservatory implied the victory of conservative forces in Czech culture, to the particular detriment of Smetana's and Fibich's music, amounting to outright rejection in the case of the latter. That anyone should gain cultural superiority over the moral and artistic achievement of Smetana was an obvious sore point for Nejedlý; even worse was the fact that one of Smetana's original opponents was still in a position of cultural power, forty years later—Karel Knittl, now director of the Conservatory.[14] Knittl, however, had not responded to the overt criticism in Nejedlý's *History*, forcing the situation into a stalemate that none of Nejedlý's badgering could alter.

In late 1906 a catalyst arrived in the form of music educator Josef Theurer, who was a strong believer in Smetana's music, and therefore ideologically sympathetic to Nejedlý's cause. In November of that year, Theurer gave a lecture in Prague in which he claimed that the appreciation of Smetana's music was at an abysmally low point, and completely incommensurate with the respect due a National Composer. Theurer's efforts became the start of a year-long conflict known as the "Knittl Affair," in which Nejedlý's mandate of a modern, socially responsible Czech music was to play a decisive role, ushering in a new era where Czech musical identity was defined more by exclusion than by acceptance. The lecture ended with an open rebuke of contemporary Czech musical society, which over time had accepted not only Smetana's opponents from the 1870s, but their fraudulent judgments as well—"proof of the pathology of our situation."[15] Furthermore, the obvious public silence on the matter was for Theurer a direct result of the opponents' continued status in positions of cultural authority:

> These personages could well have destroyed Smetana, undermining his health and life—but to *speak* about it, to *name* these people after almost forty years—that would

already be an offense! On the one hand, to beat to death the first Czech genius—on the other, the anxiety, lest any shadow fall on the names of those who didn't think twice in *acting* thus![16]

In the absence of any specific names, the lecture received positive feedback; nevertheless, when pressed to come forward with this vital information, the author quickly ceded the honor to Nejedlý, who immediately published a review of Theurer's lecture, in which he stated:

> The public was enthusiastic and even applauded Dr. Theurer after these words. Did they know the importance of this? I doubt it. . . . Whoever sees Smetana's enemies only in Pivoda and Maýr knows that era very poorly. . . . Behind [them], however, stood other people. . . . Among the living personages the main musical opponent of Smetana, who despite all precaution has not changed his views even today, is *Karel Knittl*, director of the Conservatory of Music in our Smetanian nation. In 1873 Knittl stood up against Smetana with all possible means. And today? He is the true evil spirit of our young generation, which he has completely constricted in the nets of the old anti-Smetanian reactionism. . . . The saddest phenomenon is that our progressive papers have lent themselves to this sickening comedy, and who in the *ignorance of things* pursue the resurrection of anti-Smetanism, indeed not suspecting from whence it comes. . . . The society that applauds Theurer with moral indignation today will similarly applaud Knittl's helpers tomorrow, and will ostentatiously acclaim the principles that Smetana struggled against, with the sacrifice of his life![17]

While Nejedlý's attack clearly focused on Knittl, the implications of his denunciation reached the younger generation, whose individual members he too refrained from naming. Again, several Nejedlian traits come to the fore, particularly that of Smetana's martyrdom. More veiled is the meaning behind the description of Knittl's undeserved status "in our Smetanian nation": since for Nejedlý the true Czech nation was one infused with Smetana's values, Knittl's success represented the victory of un-Czech elements. The reference to the younger generation, already described in the *History of Czech Music* three years earlier, was not so much an attack on Knittl's students as an allusion to the moral obligation toward the future of Czech art. Nejedlý, here and elsewhere, bemoaned the fact that most of the composers and performers in Prague were receiving a fraudulent education (from the "un-Czech" Knittl), the basic tenets of which went against his belief in Smetana as the only true model of modern, progressive, and creative thought. Hence, Nejedlý refrained from reproaching the students, at least until they had attained positions of cultural authority themselves. As he would do in even more explicit terms later with the "Suk Affair" of 1919,[18] the critic was attempting to purge an individual he felt to be harmful to his concept of modern, socially responsible Czech music, excluding him, however belatedly, from the communal identity of the nation.

At first, Nejedlý's review met with total silence. This tactic, as Zachařová relates, was most likely reached by consensus of Knittl and his Conservatory/UB supporters.[19] Clearly, such a personal attack as Nejedlý's could go no further without some form of public rebuttal; hence, none was forthcoming. But as fate would have it, Karel Knittl passed away a mere four months later, on March 17, 1907, at which time almost every newspaper in Prague carried an obituary of the Conservatory director, written by former Conservatory students.

Perhaps the most detailed obituary came from Conservatory historian Jan Branberger, whose extensive account in the UB organ *Hudební Revue-Smetana* (Musical Revue-Smetana) amounted to a total rehabilitation of Knittl, albeit through the obvious omission of the deceased's critical career and his possible participation in Pivoda's campaign. One of the most interesting aspects of Branberger's obituary is the almost point-by-point countering of Nejedlý's claims from the previous November's article. For example, he stated that, "Knittl's attitude to [music] theory best demonstrates his modernism, the basic trait of his character, for the wider, uninitiated public," and that the late professor was much abused for his progressiveness, which was often in advance of even the German theorists.[20] In a strange paragraph full of oblique references, Branberger elaborated on Knittl's modernism in its historical context:

> A rare soul—under whose influence everything was always harmonious with the truth— he could bridge the chasm of different convictions and opinions, just so that an idea— progress—could be applied and flourish. Knittl was a *progressive* of pronounced character. He always researched and sought out the new, he set out to convince and to win in the name of the newest achievements—he never remained standing by things which perhaps 30 or 40 years ago were modern (pseudo-progressive)—he always adhered to what was the best and most correct in all trends, even if [the matter] came out one way or another.[21]

To those readers well versed in the ongoing debate—as those of *Hudební Revue-Smetana* undoubtedly were—Branberger's insinuations would have been quite clear. The seemingly arbitrary "perhaps 30 or 40 years ago" obviously refers to the Smetana controversies, and the opposition of a "pseudo-progressive" who stands by outmoded theories can only be Hostinský, with whom Knittl had quarreled in the previous decade. Branberger's veiled references, coupled with the insistence that the Conservatory director had worked selflessly for future generations of musicians by trying to raise the level of their education, were a direct provocation of Nejedlý, indeed a long-awaited rebuttal using his opponent's very same rhetoric of modernism and social responsibility through education.

The polemic developed quickly at this point. In his articles for the daily newspaper *Den* (The Day), Nejedlý rejected Branberger's obituary, particularly in that it ignored the most "incriminating" aspect of Knittl's career: his involvement with Pivoda in the attacks on Smetana in the 1870s. By 1907 the issue had a greater, more emotional impact than historical accuracy could account for, especially since the creation and promulgation of Nejedlý's lineages; that his ideology had already gained widespread attention is evident in the vehemence of the UB's defense of Knittl. It was Nejedlý who finally mentioned Knittl's probable contribution to Pivoda's journal *Hudební listy,* citing the most crucial editorial—the denunciation of Smetana's *The Two Widows* in mid-1874, signed by the mysterious "-tt."[22] From this point on, the crux of the debate rested on Knittl's authorship of this article, a point refuted energetically by Stecker and another Conservatory historian, Boleslav Kalenský. For Nejedlý, the mere fact that Knittl had contributed at all to Pivoda's *Hudební listy* during the years in question was incriminating evidence enough. Given the vociferously anti-Smetanian content of all the "-tt." editorials, Nejedlý was at a loss to understand why Knittl had never owned up to it, especially after having openly used the same signature in his polemics with Fibich and Hostinský twenty years later. With mounting ethical outrage, Nejedlý refused to pardon such an unconscionable act.[23]

The "Knittl Affair" died down after only a few months, since Stecker and Kalenský refused to discuss the cultural implications of either the *Two Widows* article or the reasons for its hidden authorship. The last straw came when Kalenský, writing in *Národní listy* on July 31, 1907, put forward the unsubstantiated claim that the article had been written by a relative of Nejedlý's, who could now count himself among "the family of Smetana's enemies."[24] For Nejedlý, the taste of his own medicine was too much: he dropped the polemic entirely, disgusted with the unethical tactics of the Conservatory clique.[25] In a letter to his supporter Artuš Rektorys, he wrote: "The entire thing in *Národní listy* is so inexpressibly shameful that I can only keep silent about it. I hope, however, that others will be found who will expose the unfathomable amorality of the behavior of *Národní listy.* Just a little example: *against* me is now the authority of he who allegedly wrote so shamefully against Smetana."[26] Nevertheless, Nejedlý had struck a serious blow to the credibility of Prague's musical establishment, raising doubts as to its members' ethical behavior, both past and present. With regard to institutional politics, Nejedlý's criticism questioned the rights of the UB and Conservatory to represent the Czech nation in music, claiming that they had not displayed the appropriate degree of responsibility toward the cultural education of society. Perhaps most crucially, the rhetoric on both sides implied the exclusion of a large segment of the musical community from the collective Czech identity, mostly on the basis of forty-year-old grudges, but also with reference to the perceived modernness of each other's aesthetics, and the attendant ramifications for Czech society.

The most bizarre aspect of this debate is that a single negative review—already thirty-three years old, older than Nejedlý himself—could hold such emotional and political weight for both sides in 1907. The vehement defense of Knittl by his supporters implies an unspeakable shame over his alleged denunciation of *The Two Widows,* a modest opera that contributed comparatively little to the nationalist cause in the first place. It is equally hard to imagine that such a debate could be taken seriously elsewhere in Europe, with the possible exceptions of Budapest and Warsaw, where Bartók and Szymanowski were in the midst of prolonged controversies with their respective cultural establishments. But Nejedlý's interest in reforming culture was not that of Bartók or Szymanowski; rather, he used Knittl's imperfect history as a means to test the mettle of his opposition and to make his views on modernism and social responsibility known to the general public. Having provoked his first full-fledged polemic, Nejedlý could place himself with satisfaction among his fellow martyrs Smetana, Fibich, and Hostinský. Perhaps it is not surprising that he himself would subsequently "expose the unfathomable amorality" of his opponents.

Nejedlý and the National Theater: The Polemics, 1907–11

After the "Knittl Affair" had died down and Nejedlý had vowed to back away from any confrontation with Stecker and Kalenský on the topic, the musical community of Prague saw relative peace for a few years, particularly at the Conservatory. Nejedlý, too, seemed content, in that he acquired a post as music columnist at the influential nonmusic daily *Den* in 1907, and in the following year was named professor of musicology at the University. *Den*, which lay within the Young Czech political sphere,[27] enabled Nejedlý's ideas and opinions about art, culture, and society to be disseminated to a much larger readership than ever before, lending him a significant degree of prestige. It was from this vantage point that, as a newly appointed member of the Czech Council of Arts and Sciences with a growing number of followers among his students at the University, he attempted to make inroads on changing the cultural policies of the National Theater. While some of the ideological debates had touched upon the University and the National Theater in the past, the years before the First World War would witness a change in perspective, wherein these institutions formed the main vantage points in a controversy heretofore focused on the UB and the Conservatory. The issues at stake were ones of direct relevance to both the musical establishment and Nejedlý, since, among all the cultural institutions of Prague, the National Theater was perhaps the most contentious, representing as it did the culmination of the nineteenth-century Cultural Revival and thus a normative model for Czech musical identity. The struggle, largely fostered by Nejedlý, would solidify both factions, and in turn influence the course of compositional history in Prague, shaping the attitudes of critics and composers on all sides.

At this point, the National Theater in Prague was barely a quarter-century old, and had as its musical director the composer and conductor Karel Kovařovic. Like Ostrčil and Nejedlý, Kovařovic was a former student of Fibich's; his operas and operettas had been quite popular in the 1880s and 1890s, particularly the historical tragedy *Psohlavci* (1897). When the Young Czech party made its bid to wrest the National Theater from Old Czech domination in 1900, Kovařovic made his directorial debut, continuing in that position until his death in 1920. During these two decades, while virtually ceasing his activity as a composer, Kovařovic became the constant focus of cultural struggles among Prague's musical community. Initially out of favor with the powerful publishing firm of Mojmír Urbánek, who had supported the pre-1900 regime, both Kovařovic and the National Theater administration consistently received bad reviews from that company's journal, *Dalibor*.[28] As a consolation, the opera director sought refuge among the luminaries of the UB, even though their relationship was somewhat nebulous and many dramatic productions still received bad reviews in their journal, *Hudební revue* (Musical Revue).[29]

Equally tenuous was Kovařovic's relationship with Nejedlý, who was suddenly a voice to be heeded at *Den*, a paper that counted many influential National Theater subscribers among its readers. Alongside his usual resistance to institutional authority, Nejedlý's particular mantra throughout his years at *Den* was the urgent call for change in the National Theater's policy toward Smetana's operas, particularly with regard to the constant use of V. J. Novotný's substantially altered editions in place of the composer's original versions. The critic's barrage of complaints against the frequent performances of the Novotný versions was always accompanied by a host of moral implications regarding the duty of the supposedly *National* Theater toward the legacy of Czech music, which he defined as the operas of Smetana, Fibich, and Foerster.[30] Despite his frequent dissatisfaction, Nejedlý treated both conductor and theater with a positive outlook, since he felt that, despite its drawbacks, it represented the most likely venue for the future production of modern Czech operatic works.[31] In this respect, he endeavored to use his growing cultural clout at *Den* to educate the National Theater administration as to what he considered the true direction of Czech culture. Nejedlý's tactic was somewhat successful, in that Kovařovic gradually allowed communicative links to be formed with his most vociferous critic. The happy result was the reinstatement of the original Smetana cycle in May 1909, under Nejedlý's advisorship. For the latter, this was a moral victory that gave him considerable hope, not to mention self-assurance: the promise of influence through *Den* had paid off. Indeed, through good times and bad, Nejedlý would refer to the 1909 Smetana cycle as a benchmark to which all future cultural events should aspire. Undoubtedly, this seemed to be the start of a new era for Prague's musical community, wherein Smetana, Fibich, Foerster, Ostrčil, Hostinský, and Nejedlý himself could be enshrined.[32]

This small victory, coming after a series of uphill battles since 1900, would actually be the precursor to the most turbulent half-decade in Prague's musical history, both for Nejedlý and the musical establishment. By 1909, the National Theater administration, with Kovařovic in tow, had constructed a large-scale scheme to consolidate their cultural power, while at the same time excluding and isolating those who might threaten their regime, particularly Nejedlý. The first blow came on September 1, 1909, when Nejedlý was dismissed from his job at *Den*; the editor, Ladislav Klumpar, cited a general disagreement between Nejedlý's critical outlook and the future direction of the newspaper.[33] Indeed, after Nejedlý's departure, *Den* became a staunch supporter of Kovařovic and his work as director of opera, and the critic was left without a regular venue for disseminating his views on Czech culture in print.[34]

While for a time Rektorys was able to publish occasional studies by Nejedlý of a musicological nature in the *Dalibor* journal, which he edited for Urbánek, such a practice was not tolerated by the publisher as a rule. By January 1910, however, the publishing situation in Prague had changed somewhat with the Young Czechs' acquisition of the most important daily newspaper, *Národní listy* (National Pages), and the new editor invited Nejedlý aboard as music critic. It was a position potentially even more significant than his work for *Den*; nevertheless, Nejedlý would not enjoy his new status for long. After only three editorials, Nejedlý was dismissed on February 16, 1910.

It was the first of Nejedlý's editorials, a discussion of the political motivations behind the dismissal of dramatic soprano Růžena Maturová from the National Theater cast, that prompted a drastic reorganization at *Národní listy*. This particular editorial was only one of many throughout Prague's journals that month on the same topic, and it could be that the theater administration was trying to make an example out of Nejedlý, its most notorious heckler. Nejedlý reasoned, as could be expected, that the loss of Maturová from the company meant that no one at the National Theater was qualified to sing Smetana's and Fibich's roles with the dramatic and psychological impact that operatic integrity demanded.[35] To dismiss Maturová would therefore signal a tremendous failing of the Theater toward the cultural education of the nation. Since the shuffling of the operatic cast was a move planned as far back as 1908, that is, before Nejedlý's Smetana cycle of 1909, it was Nejedlý's ill fortune to have sent Kovařovic a copy of his new monograph, *J. B. Foerster*, the day after the Maturová feuilleton, in the hopes of repeating his success with a Foerster operatic cycle. His encroachment on the fronts of both Maturová and Foerster was reason enough for the National Theater to strike back.

However much Kovařovic himself was or was not an agent in the above proceedings, the opera director had not been idle in the preceding months. Having endured a decade of tense relations with Urbánek's *Dalibor* journal and the UB's *Hudební revue*, the winter of 1909–10 witnessed a remarkable reconciliation on all sides. Kovařovic had been invited by the UB in 1908 to create a performance edition of Smetana's last composition, *Pražský karneval* (Prague Carnival), which was a smash hit in the following season. When Nejedlý, inevitably, began to question the motivation behind a revision of Smetana, the UB closed ranks and refused access to the edited score, thereby protecting Kovařovic and halting the discussion. Meanwhile, Kovařovic's ballet *Na záletech* (Going Courting, 1909) attracted the favorable attention of *Dalibor* despite Rektorys's open disapproval. Gradually Urbánek and Kovařovic forged a seemingly indissoluble bond between *Dalibor, Hudební revue,* and the National Theater. To seal this pact, the UB elected Kovařovic an honorary member, in the very same week that Nejedlý received his dismissal from *Národní listy.* It is perhaps no coincidence that Antonín Šilhan, the critic who inaugurated Kovařovic into the UB, and who had been a student and vociferous supporter of Karel Knittl, replaced Nejedlý as music critic of *Národní listy.*[36]

As a consequence of these transactions involving the three leading cultural institutions of Prague, both *Dalibor* and *Hudební revue* also began to weed out contributors who may not have desired such a union of Young Czech-based cultural power. Prior to Nejedlý's Maturová feuilleton, Rektorys had ensured his participation and also that of his student Vladimír Helfert in *Dalibor,* while other Nejedlý supporters such as J. B. Foerster, Otakar Zich, and Hubert Doležil had written for *Hudební revue.* With the exception of Foerster (who was more respected and resided abroad), all the other authors were ejected from their positions by the end of 1910, leaving them virtually no venue for publication.[37] To top it off, Rektorys was dismissed as editor of *Dalibor* in October 1910, to be replaced by Kovařovic's assistant, the conductor and composer Rudolf Zamrzla (who had cowritten *Na záletech*). For the National Theater, the UB, the Conservatory, and the publishing house of Urbánek, the circle was complete, both in their cultural power and in their exclusion of Nejedlý. If only temporarily, the establishment had been forced to redraw the accepted lines of the Czech musical community more sharply than had been necessary since the time of Pivoda. Their removal of opposition was merely an illusion, however, and one that inevitably weakened their hold on cultural power in Prague.

The Nejedlý Circle: *Smetana-Hudební list* and Hudební klub

With the disruptive events of 1910, Nejedlý's career and public image were at an all-time low, with virtually all doors closed to him in Prague except at the University, where he had been lecturing for the past two academic years. These isolating circumstances were not without their benefits, however, since they forced him to consolidate his forces; as a fully independent agent he would no longer have to vie with the powers of the musical community for access to a broader public. Nejedlý's lectureship not only gave him ample opportunity to express his views on the history of Czech music, its composers, historiography, and aesthetics, but also enabled him to build up a contingent of followers as a counterpart to the Conservatory/UB clique. As with his own experience under Fibich, Nejedlý's new generation of students would be molded in his own image, approaching Czech music history with the same anti-establishmentarian attitude and fervor. A brief description of the group is necessary for a complete understanding of the years before Czech independence and the events in which they would take a leading role.

Nejedlý's group of young musicologists came from a variety of backgrounds and experiences. Several among them had already begun careers, either in music criticism (Artuš Rektorys), music theory (Josef Theurer), or composition (Otakar Zich, who also lectured on aesthetics at the University). Among the younger generation, the most important figures at this time were Josef Bartoš, who had left the Conservatory to study under Hostinský and Nejedlý as well as at the Sorbonne, and who earned a living teaching French; Vladimír Helfert, who studied with Kretzschmar and Hostinský, and whose time in Prague preceded a noteworthy academic career in Brno; and Hubert Doležil, who began his career in Moravia and worked as a critic in Prague after independence. By the time of Nejedlý's dismissal from *Den*, *Národní listy*, and *Dalibor*, all of these young men had become so linked to their mentor's path that their exclusion from Prague's musical life was inevitable. In an act of responsibility toward his students and followers, Nejedlý established, in the last few months of 1910, an independent music journal and a forum for public lectures and presentations. As the sole organized entity outside the circle of the establishment, Nejedlý's group could provide alternative readings to the normative views of Czech musical identity and its role in the nation and society. In so doing, they were in fact able to effect changes that transformed Prague musical life in the years prior to independence in 1918.

Named after their spiritual predecessor, *Smetana-Hudební list* (Smetana: A Musical Journal) commenced on November 4, 1910, with a sixteen-page issue that can easily be read as a collective statement of the Nejedlý circle's musical and cultural beliefs. After an unsigned introduction that served to foreground some lengthy Hostinský quotes, Zich's analysis of Smetana's *Hubička* (The Kiss) appeared as the journal's first article, followed by Helfert's description of the importance of the University's musicology program within Prague's musical community. The third article was Nejedlý's attack on Kovařovic and the National Theater in "*Psohlavci* and Its Smetanism," which outlined precisely how and why Kovařovic had misread the heritage of Smetana's music dramas, producing an opera whose continued success was proof of the fraudulence of current musical conditions.[38] The issue was rounded out by reviews of recent compositions by Foerster and Ostrčil, a section entitled "Dokumenty—Fibichiana," and a multipage overview of theaters, concerts, and "Musical Life." Within its few pages, Nejedlý, Helfert, Zich, and Rektorys demonstrated their allegiance to the compositional lineage of Smetana–Fibich–Foerster–Ostrčil, as well as their self-sufficiency at the University.

The December 16, 1910, issue ran Helfert's article "Musicology at Our University," which contained the brief notice that:

At the beginning of 1911 the Hudební klub [Musical Club] will come into existence; started by Nejedlý's students, it will be firmly tied to the University, and its goal will be to organize lectures, debates, evening concerts, and to maintain continuity between the attendees of University musicology lectures and the supporters of the Hudební klub.[39]

Along with the aforementioned followers and students of Nejedlý, several others took active roles at the organizational level: Ferdinand Pujman, an engineering student and failed tenor who would become scenic director at the National Theater; and the young composers Karel Boleslav Jirák and Emil Axman, both of whom had started at the Conservatory under Novák and were subsequently attracted by Nejedlý's theories. Beyond this central group, there were attendees numbering in the hundreds (including a substantial number of female University students), almost all of whom were in their early twenties; Rektorys was among the oldest participants at the age of thirty-four.[40]

With its combination of lectures and concerts, the Hudební klub attempted to challenge the authority of the Conservatory, the National Theater, and in particular, the UB (which also sponsored concerts and lectures in support of its favored composers), merely by breaking their respective monopolies on music making and criticism. Petr Čornej aptly remarks that "the importance of Nejedlý's activities was expressed in the most varied manner and we can say that with Nejedlý, the Hudební klub rose and fell."[41] Of the 125 events sponsored by the organization over a sixteen-year period, 86 were lectures by Nejedlý.[42] As we have seen with the content of *Smetana-Hudební list*, the programming of the Hudební klub was centered around the composers supported by Nejedlý: Smetana, Fibich, Foerster (who lectured on his own compositions), Ostrčil (an analysis of whose recently premiered opera *Poupě* was presented by Helfert at the second lecture in 1911), and in later years, Jirák and Otakar Jeremiáš. Outside of this well-worn lineage, we see the Nejedlý circle's attempt to stake out a territory of musicological expertise: Nejedlý and Helfert lectured on the Czech composers of the eighteenth century; Nejedlý also led analyses and lecture-recitals on *Tristan und Isolde, Der Rosenkavalier, Ariadne auf Naxos*, and Beethoven's quartets. Most significantly, six evenings in January 1912 were devoted to the symphonies of Gustav Mahler, at which Ostrčil and Bedřich Čapek performed the musical examples for Nejedlý's analyses.[43] The choices of these composers, particularly the modernist ones, were in conscious opposition to those championed by the musical establishment; as with Nejedlý's opinion of Strauss, these allegiances were constantly being redefined. One seemingly anomalous event of the earlier years was Hubert Doležil's analysis of Novák's cantata *Bouře* (The Storm) in February 1912, which lauded the work as "epochal" the day before its Prague premiere.[44] Such a move was likely an attempt by Nejedlý's circle at attracting the allegiance of Novák himself, whose Conservatory masterclass was fast becoming the most important in the city. It is interesting to note the near total lack of discussion about Nejedlý's other opponents, specifically Kovařovic, Knittl, and later adversaries such as Suk or Janáček. Dvořák was represented solely by Josef Bartoš's two-part lecture on the composer's chamber music, subsequently published in *Smetana-Hudební list* and decried as an abomination by the entire body of Conservatory and UB associates. It was through the dismantling of such a revered icon that Nejedlý and his circle would exert the most profound changes on the Prague musical community and the way they viewed themselves in the modern age.

A Crisis of Identity: The "Dvořák Affair," 1911–14

Bartoš's lectures in March 1912 were a further elaboration on views he expressed in an earlier article that appeared the preceding October in the independent journal *Hlídka Času* (The Times Viewpoint). Bartoš's "Antonín Dvořák" was disguised as a scholarly reflection on the late composer's seventieth birthday, after the passage of "proper distance from the artistic work." As the succeeding months would show, however, the article was more likely the premeditated catalyst for a full-scale attack on the musical establishment by the Nejedlý circle than an attempt at serious musicological analysis. With *Smetana-Hudební list* as their main mouthpiece, Nejedlý, Bartoš, Helfert, Zich, and Doležil sought to remove the mantle of glory under which Dvořák and his music had existed since the latter's return from America in 1895. Their efforts, which would touch upon issues of nationalism and politics, cultural conservatism and modernism, compositional integrity, as well as all genres of music (most notably operas, symphonic poems, and chamber music), caused such a violent and prolonged uproar in the Czech musical community that the phenomenon is still known as the "Dvořák Affair."

Despite the acknowledged risk of being charged with "heresy" at the hands of the musical establishment, Bartoš immediately exposed many myths he perceived to veil the true stature of Dvořák the composer: "that Dvořák, in spite of all his charisma, was not among the chosen ones by whose names we signify musical epochs; that he was no poet, that he was only a poor dramatist."[45] In a direct comparison with the creative methods of Smetana (the "great legislator"), Bartoš felt that Dvořák relied solely on instinct, and that his compositional development was too sudden for him to retain any continuity as an artist. In a passage that combines imagery of high art and left-wing politics, the critic stated:

> If [Smetana's] personal and artistic development were considered a complete dramatic poem with a tragic fifth act, by contrast Dvořák's life looks toward the future a hundred times over in order to compensate for the dire straits of his beginnings. The living drama of the musical proletarian makes a transition in its second and third acts to an everyday stage-play, not without a touch of certain bourgeois character.[46]

The final reference above to the influence of the bourgeoisie on Dvořák's work hints at one of Bartoš's main arguments: that Dvořák failed to have any thoroughly conceived system of artistic values, being susceptible to outside influences instead: whether the vagaries of bourgeois taste, fame in foreign countries, conservative forces like Brahms, or simply "mood"—a formulation derived from Hostinský's binarism of *důslednost* and *náladovost*.[47] The result was a "système d'incohérence," which dissipated any self-criticism the composer ever had. For Bartoš, Dvořák's lack of control over his own artistic production allowed Brahms and Hanslick to turn him into a reactionary; subsequently, when he tried to assimilate Wagnerian trends into the late tone poems, the result was disastrous. "I know no more tragic moment in Dvořák's work than this. *Dvořák bought this idea of progress with his own artistic ruin.*"[48] In a gesture that recalls Nejedlý's *Rusalka* review from ten years before, Bartoš concluded with a salvo at the Czech musical community, whose "uncritical glorification of [Dvořák's] *entire* oeuvre seeks to mask the paucity of work on the Dvořák question itself. . . . Lazy convenience must step aside in favor of genuine work."[49] In no uncertain terms, Bartoš was suggesting that the accepted historians of the UB and Conservatory make way for the Nejedlý circle and their new retelling of Czech music history. This new history proposed nothing less than the reformulation of Czech musical identity, excluding in the process Dvořák, and by implication, the entire musical establishment of fin-de-siècle Prague.

Almost simultaneously with the appearance of Bartoš's "Antonín Dvořák," Nejedlý published the monograph *Česká moderní zpěvohra po Smetanovi* (Czech Modern Opera Since Smetana), which boldly redefined the history of Czech operas from Fibich onward.[50] Of its six chapters, the first three were dedicated to the stages of Fibich's operatic development, with the remainder divided between his three most prominent "students": Foerster, Ostrčil, and surprisingly, Kovařovic. Although the chapter that analyzes the last composer's work is extraordinarily negative to the point of slander, the most problematic aspect of the monograph is its obvious exclusion of Dvořák's nine operas from the history.[51] Judging from the title alone, the implication was that for Nejedlý, Dvořák's operas were neither Czech nor modern—their exclusion was a passive aggression perfectly aligned with Bartoš's article, which had repeated the hackneyed maxim that Dvořák's strengths lay only in the realm of absolute music. Alongside his well-worn arguments about the necessity for progressiveness in music, Nejedlý amplified the importance of Czech nationalist sentiment in this history, and more significantly, introduced in print his concept of the social responsibility of the truly national artist. It is important to note that nationalist sentiment for Nejedlý (as for Hostinský) did not refer to overt patriotic display, but rather to an intricate web of psychological characteristics that the composer imparted to his work. This layer of the music is what attached "truly Czech" composers to their *lidový* (i.e., folk, or at least nonbourgeois) audiences, turning the act of composition into a moment of popular cultural education. As usual, all roads led to (and from) Smetana:

Art, too, has a national duty; it must be more than just art. Although artistic merit is indeed a prerequisite of true, national art, it is not the only goal of art for a nation longing for its own revival. Art must therefore have a task outside itself: any "l'art pour l'artismus" is a luxury for the nation at such a time. Smetana therefore creates revivalist music, in the way that Palacký created revivalist history. It is a music for the entire nation, for the strengthening of national life. Since the nation was made up of primarily folk strata, the basis of the new national art is "of the people" [*lidovost*]. . . . To a certain extent, [Smetana's] poetry is a surrogate for folk life and can be the source of new music, but only inasmuch as the real life of the people is expressed in it.[52]

Dvořák's operas, therefore, by their exclusion, were examples of "l'art pour l'artismus," irrelevant to the true goals of the nation, and inexpressive of "the real life of the people."

The immediate reaction of the UB-centered community to Bartoš's and Nejedlý's publications seems to have been to share the rebuttals among a variety of different critics. Jan Löwenbach, a critic and historian with strong ties to the Conservatory, responded to the *Hlídka Času* article in a subsequent issue of the same paper.[53] Löwenbach began with some general statements about the sorry state of Czech music criticism, which had allowed such outdated arguments to be prolonged. In a tone that bespeaks a sense of maturity and reason (in comparison to his younger opponents), Löwenbach judged the Nejedlý circle as having failed to analyze their subject "empirically using multi-sided concrete musical material . . . [instead relying on] a viewpoint of Wagnerian music drama retained as an *a priori* formula." The result for Löwenbach was an aesthetic simplification, the main "sacrifice" of which had been Dvořák's operas.[54] Finally, Löwenbach unpacked the "Hegelian" formulation of progressive versus conservative, stating that both labels should be used only in relative terms. Throughout his essay, Löwenbach showed himself to be not a great defender of Dvořák, but rather a critic fighting to preserve the integrity of his field against what he saw as unscholarly, baseless attacks.

One of Löwenbach's colleagues, and among the most important of Novák's composition students from these years, was Ladislav Vycpálek, whose concert reviews appeared regularly in *Hudební revue*.[55] It was Vycpálek's task to review *Česká moderní zpěvohra po Smetanovi* for that journal, concentrating on its most contentious points. In the exclusion of Dvořák, Vycpálek felt that Nejedlý had presented the history of Czech opera merely "how he might really wish it to be," and that most of the rejection of Kovařovic was childish and tactless in its approach. One of Vycpálek's more general points was that "Prof. Nejedlý is unable to view [operatic] development without bias and can only express himself in superlatives of affirmation or negation," which adversely affected his reading not only of his foes' music, but of his protégés' as well.[56] In a final thrust, Vycpálek judged the book to be a mistake, premature in its conclusions: future historians would realize that "up to 1911 we had no modern music dramas since Smetana," and that Novák's and Suk's (nonoperatic) music would be valued above the works of Fibich, Foerster, and Ostrčil.[57]

Beyond these opening salvos by members of the musical establishment, most of the polemic was carried out throughout 1912 by Boleslav Kalenský in six articles for *Dalibor*, which he published under the rubric "Dvořákiana." Kalenský, who had been vocal in the Knittl Affair five years earlier, concentrated his efforts on saving the reputation of Dvořák as an artist of national standing, basing most of his arguments on biographical details. In the effort to overturn Nejedlý's martyrization of Smetana due to Dvořák's unjust fame, Kalenský strove to show the opposite, citing Dvořák's "moral worth as a person," and his suffering at the hands of Smetana, Hostinský, Nejedlý, and Bartoš. Unfortunately for Kalenský, his highly impassioned, subjective tone made him an easy target for Nejedlý's clique. The latter group openly mocked Kalenský's sentimental glorification of Dvořák in *Smetana-Hudební list* and another new independent journal, *Česká kultura* (Czech Culture), edited by Nejedlý and his colleague, the literary figure F. X. Šalda. With few changes the skirmishes went on through most of 1912 in a similar fashion.

In November of that year, however, the "Dvořák Affair" entered its next stage with the publication of Helfert's ironically entitled article "Více Dvořáka!" (More Dvořák!) in the November 18 issue of *Česká kultura*.[58] Helfert continued the overtly belligerent tone of Bartoš, introducing the argument that Dvořák's character and upbringing prevented him from being a truly Czech artist, allowing him only to achieve the level of a humble "muzikant" or village musician. Helfert described this compositional type as dating from the counterreformation (a concept that allied Dvořák with the hated Austrian regime), which automatically negated any chance of originality, artistic reflection, or possible contributions to "musical culture" on the part of the composer. For Helfert, the internal inconsistencies of Dvořák's music revealed the overall chance outcome of his creative process. Although he conceded a certain amount of talent to the composer in terms of orchestrational ability, Helfert felt that operas such as *Dimitrij* were an anticultural anachronism that served as a "document of the times"; ultimately, this outdated component of Czech musical society was weeded out by "the great work of Smetana." This *muzikantský* element was for Helfert inherently Czech and therefore all the more dangerous: as part of the reactionary half of Czech music making, Dvořák's music represented an obstacle for "modern culture," the importance of which was paramount with regard to popular education. Dvořák's marked rhythms and "trivial, easily perceived, but contentless melodies," admittedly attractive to the audience, were dangerous in that they would give foreign audiences a poor impression of Czech music. Of greater worry for Helfert was the fact that such music did not encourage the domestic audience to strive for anything better (including, rather significantly, Novák's music among the list of desired representatives). In a final word of optimism, Helfert noted that the Czech public was not responding to the celebrations put on by "the artificial cult of Dvořák" with their attendance at concerts.[59]

The immediate reaction of Prague's musical establishment to Helfert's article was a forceful rejection of its tenets and those of preceding statements by the Nejedlý circle. On December 15, 1912, there appeared in almost all of the city's daily papers a protest signed by thirty-one of the most prominent composers, conductors, music educators, and critics. The list of signatories included many significant names, such as Stecker, Kovařovic, Zamrzla, Conservatory director Jindřich Kàan z Albestů (who had succeeded Knittl), Czech Philharmonic conductor Vilém Zemánek, all four members of the Czech Quartet including Suk and Nedbal, and the Conservatory-based composers Rudolf Karel, Jaroslav Křička, and Vítězslav Novák. The protest decried the "tactless and insulting expressions" by Bartoš and Helfert, which the signatories "could not calmly overlook." Only near the end did the text mention Nejedlý as orchestrator of the struggle against Dvořák enacted through *Smetana-Hudební list* and *Česká kultura*, though without further commentary as to the critic's aesthetic program. The final line read as follows:

> It is our duty to object publicly to these expressions of fanatic prejudice, and we protest against their crude and base tone, in which immature and uneducated people presume to speak about a master of world renown.[60]

Nejedlý was quick to counterattack, and his first strategic move would serve as a model for the rest of the Dvořák Affair. Indeed, the article "The Struggle over Dvořák: Personnel," which appeared in the January 3, 1913, issue of *Smetana-Hudební list*, marked the point at which Nejedlý himself overtly acknowledged the leadership of his faction. The article enumerated the thirty-one signatories according to their institutional affiliations in order to analyze their relative weakness as individuals, or any fraudulent culturopolitical power they might profess to have. He was attempting nothing less than the elimination of his enemies from the Czech collective by means of removing them from the context of their official organizations, since, as individual subjective voices, they had a slim chance of representing society. At the end of this long charade of finger-pointing, Nejedlý included the name of Vítězslav Novák, "who also signed the protest, although his opinions on Dvořák's work are well known. Let's think, however, that he did so out of a student's piety toward a teacher. Surprises are not excluded here, however."[61] To round out his article, Nejedlý went on to discuss two prominent figures who refused to sign—Ostrčil and Foerster, the latter still in residence abroad—despite the alleged pressure to participate in a mass rejection of anti-Dvořák criticism. Nejedlý's "Personnel" article is significant not only in the thoroughness of its response to the protest; it also marks the turn of the Dvořák Affair away from issues strictly pertaining to that composer's music, and toward the critical persecution of the thirty-one signatories on the part of Nejedlý and his followers instead. Perhaps the most important development introduced by "Personnel" was the shift in the discourse from historical symbols to modern music and its living representatives—Novák particularly. It is here that we see the direct influence of the ongoing debates on the identity of the musical community of Prague, which, according to Nejedlý, now more than ever felt the need for a national, modern, socially responsible music.

The End of Musical Naturalism: The "Novák Affair," 1912–16

Besides the Nejedlý circle's continued harassment of Kovařovic, which had been under way for quite some time, the surge of critical judgment against the music of Vítězslav Novák was the most important outcome of the 1912 protest. Over the next five years, each successive premiere of a Novák composition met with a barrage of bad reviews in *Smetana-Hudební list* and elsewhere; nevertheless, the composer had the strong support of the entire staff of *Hudební revue*, including his former teacher Stecker and his student Vycpálek. The change in focus of the polemic was by no means instantaneous after the protest, however, and only gradually were the issues distilled into the opposition of Nejedlý and Novák as polar personalities within Prague's musical culture.

Looking back at Nejedlý's earlier attitude toward the slightly older composer, it is difficult to determine exactly how the critic envisioned their future relationship. Although Novák, as we have seen in the *Dějiny české hudby* of 1903, was immediately suspect as a result of his Conservatory training, Nejedlý seems to have considered him a possible candidate for initiation into the Hudební klub circle—indeed, a conquest through which he could encroach upon the domain of the UB. While it is clear that no sort of lasting friendship was ever established, Nejedlý enacted a series of overtures toward Novák around 1910, before the critic had met with his rejection from the Young Czech newspapers and when the composer was enjoying the most successful period of his career. Perhaps most significant was the monograph that Nejedlý started at this time, the task of which was to present an analysis of the psychological depth of Novák the artist, whom he considered to be among the most modern representatives of Czech music.[62] Started during the period when Nejedlý's friendship with Ostrčil had temporarily cooled, the monograph charts the transferral of aesthetic paradigms—formerly reserved for the inheritors of Smetana's legacy alone—to the newest member of the Conservatory staff. Indeed, Nejedlý's prose in the Novák study was startlingly laudatory, to the point where Novák was treated as a "revolutionary" who gradually and methodically rose above his restrictive Conservatory upbringing; Dvořák and any influence on his student were mentioned only in passing. Also appearing at this time were a handful of reviews by Nejedlý that praised the symphonic cantata *Bouře* and *Pan*, the five-movement tone poem for piano solo, both from 1910. It is this state of affairs, then, that can explain why Hubert Doležil dedicated a full evening's lecture to *Bouře* after the Dvořák Affair had already begun, and why Nejedlý expressed his surprise in "Personnel" over Novák's participation in the 1912 protest. Such a move by Novák would have been perceived as a rejection of so much accumulated critical goodwill, a commodity very difficult to come by in prewar Prague.

Novák's decision to sign a brief protest against the Nejedlý clique, amid thirty other musicians who had many more grievances than he, was most likely an entirely passive gesture: by his own admission, he signed only under the emphatic suggestion of his friends Zemánek and Křička.[63] Nevertheless, it would prove to be a decisive moment in his career, unleashing a critical backlash that prompted a personal depression, which in turn cut short the most creative and successful period of his compositional life. The initial results came quickly: in January 1913 Novák premiered the orchestrated version of *Pan* (which had been enormously successful in the original piano version) with the Czech Philharmonic under Zemánek, and the work promptly received a disparaging and vindictive review from Josef Bartoš in *Smetana-Hudební list*. Bartoš, whose article appeared in the next issue after Nejedlý's "Personnel," recounted his gleeful anticipation of the upcoming Novák premiere, especially in light of the original *Pan*—a piece of idiomatic piano writing he had considered "brilliant," "nobly intimate," and "modern."[64] The orchestrated *Pan*, however, was too much like *Bouře*, which Bartoš maintained had a completely different musical character and faulty orchestration to begin with. Using descriptions such as "dull," "inept," and "contrived," Bartoš judged that Novák had lost much more than he had gained in orchestrating *Pan*, a decision that revealed the composer's overall weakness.

Soon after, Nejedlý and his other associates joined the fray: throughout 1913 Nejedlý resumed his monograph on Novák, which he had put aside in 1910 in a time of more favorable relations. The second part of the Novák study (published serially in *Smetana-Hudební list*) was highly charged with the insinuation that the composer, for all his revolutionary promise at the start of his career, was ultimately a disappointing cultural representative, whose brand of modernism was only a mask for deep-seated subjective and reactionary tendencies. For Nejedlý, the influences of Strauss and impressionism and the incorporation of Moravian and Slovak folk sources in Novák's music[65] all pointed to the dreaded *naturalismus*. This aesthetic, with which a composer could allegedly only imitate or describe the surface features of his composition's subject, had been decried as fraudulent by Hostinský decades earlier. A term the critic would also use against Janáček's *Jenůfa* in 1916, *naturalismus* was anathema to Nejedlý's concept of truly modern, dramatic Czech music, which was inherently psychological in its approach, scope, and impact, and which positioned artistic and ideological content far above mere compositional form. Anything not related to the idealist philosophy he had inherited from Hostinský was, in his eyes, anticultural. In to this category he also placed French impressionism and Italian verismo for the same basic reason—that the composers of such music (including Novák) could never attain the ideal state of representing the inner psychology of the people. "Naturalist" composers were hence extremely subjective in their approach, an aesthetic Nejedlý held to be immoral and irresponsible toward society.

Novák's negative experiences with the Nejedlý circle worsened with the composer's growing interest in theatrical music. With the exception of Suk's two melodramas from the turn of the century, none of Dvořák's acknowledged successors had produced anything for the stage, let alone a full-length operatic work, allowing Nejedlý to claim that the National Theater belonged exclusively to Smetana's lineage. When Novák began to make serious plans for an opera after 1910, the critic's optimism quickly turned to horror: while the cantata *Bouře* had been destined for the concert stage and was (for Nejedlý) constructed upon symphonic, not dramatic principles, the cantata *Svatební košile* (The Wedding Shirt, premiered 1914) was too obviously an operatic study to pass unchallenged. Conceived by Novák as a more dramatically focused alternative to the better-known Dvořák setting, the work was trounced by both Nejedlý and Helfert as having failed precisely in this dramatic component. For Helfert the cantata signaled the "End of Musical Naturalism," in that it described only the external characteristics of the drama (the setting and general mood, captured in the orchestral music), and inevitably missed the necessary psychological aspect.[66] For Nejedlý, evoking Hostinský's binarism of *důslednost* versus *náladovost* (i.e., music based on artistic consequences versus music based on mood), the music of *Svatební košile* was more dependent on the composer's subjective fancy than on the logical or moral consequences of musical thought.

Novák's first opera, the one-act *Zvíkovský rarášek* (The Zvíkov Imp, premiered 1915) fared just as badly in a five-page review with which Nejedlý opened the sixth year of *Smetana-Hudební list.*[67] Perfectly in line with the change in rhetoric since the protest, Nejedlý judged Novák's first opera to be suspect by virtue of the composer's prolonged experience with lyric instrumental music: Novák's dramatic inability was made explicit by his rigid attachment to each word of the libretto and lack of a larger psychological understanding. In Nejedlý's opinion, the music of *Zvíkovský rarášek* concentrated exclusively on external aspects of the comedy (such as mimicking the raising and lowering of wine goblets) instead of emulating Smetana's model of heart-warming comic emotion that opens a window to the human condition—in a nutshell, the argument of idealism versus naturalism. On the whole, he deemed Novák's relation to dramatic composition unhealthy, "both for Novák and for our dramatic music, for it is too external, not internal."[68] Regrettably, for Nejedlý, even Dvořák's contributions were more suitable in light of his paradigm of modern Czech opera, since they at least demonstrated an attempt at dramatic understanding. Without such a goal, *Zvíkovský rarášek* had no reason to exist, and any critical support (which in this case came only from Václav Štěpán) would merely serve to (mis-)lead Novák down a similar path for future operatic projects.

Shortly after the completion of *Zvíkovský rarášek* in the summer of 1914, Europe was engulfed by the First World War, and its effects had been felt in Prague for an entire year by the time of the opera's premiere in October of the following year. Czech national feeling was running high in all aspects of society, including the depleted musical community, many of whose younger members had to fight amid the despised Austrian army. Certain political and cultural figures, inside and outside the Czech Lands, began to make serious plans for an independent Czech state with the decline of Austria-Hungary's military fortunes: most famously, Tomáš Masaryk and Eduard Beneš petitioned Western powers in the hope of creating a pro-Western democracy. Various composers incorporated this surge of nationalism in their works, including the young Conservatory graduates Ladislav Vycpálek and Boleslav Vomáčka, whose compositions reflect both the crushing anxiety and the thrilling prospects of the times. Vycpálek's song cycles *Vojna* (The War, 1915) and *V boží dlani* (In God's Palm, 1916) and Vomáčka's *Výkřiky* (Outcries, choral, 1918) and *1914* (song cycle, published 1923) all use a more uninhibited modernist palette, occasioned by the extremes of emotion in contemporary society. Neither was their teacher, Vítězslav Novák, silent at this time. Shortly after the completion of his first opera in the early days of the war, he started work on a second, this time a comedy with a nationalist message: *Karlštejn*, a work whose pivotal reception by Nejedlý and the public will be discussed along with the musical analysis in chapter 4. The war years would also see the culmination of Nejedlý's efforts to enshrine Smetana, as well as the beginning of a new era with Janáček's operatic debut in Prague.

Nejedlý, Janáček, and the Smetana Exhibition

One of the most significant events in Prague musical life during the First World War was the premiere of Janáček's *Jenůfa* (or *Její pastorkyňa* as it is known in the Czech Lands) on May 26, 1916, at the end of the season prior to Novák's *Karlštejn*. While the circumstances surrounding the composer's struggle with the National Theater and Kovařovic are well documented, a short discussion of Nejedlý's reaction to *Jenůfa* will reveal how the reception of Janáček's compositional style merged with contemporary issues in Prague. In comparison to the power Nejedlý exerted over the reception of Novák's work just months later, the critic's rejection of *Jenůfa* did not hinder its success in the least, as it is still the most widely known Czech opera of the twentieth century.

In his article "Leoš Janáček's *Její pastorkyňa*," published in *Smetana-Hudební list* in August 1916, Nejedlý began with two rhetorical statements, in which he expressed his wonder that the opera could be so successful after the long disagreements between the composer and Kovařovic; and that the leader of what he termed "conservative Moravia" could turn around to become the "official representative of Czech musical modernism."[69] As it turns out, Nejedlý's main cause for the musical and moral rejection of Janáček lay in the latter's alleged sympathy for Pivoda at the very beginning of his career: according to the critic, Janáček's short-lived journal *Hudební listy* (published in Brno, 1884–88) welcomed contributions by the younger members of Pivoda's anti-Smetana, antimodern faction. From this point of departure, Nejedlý was able to connect Pivoda's aesthetic aims to every aspect of Janáček's music, most prominently in terms of the supposed pan-Slavonic underpinning of the composer's speech melodies, the roots of which could be found in the pseudo-ethnographic approach to folk-like art music.[70] In an extension of the binarism of naturalism versus idealism, the critic linked

Janáček to virtually all possible musical "offenders" of the day, including Strauss and the verismo composers (and by implication, Novák and the impressionists, argued elsewhere). In this respect, the speech melodies had nothing to do with either a scientific reproduction of folk speech or even correct operatic declamation (i.e., idealized, as Hostinský had legislated it): it was instead the work of a dilettante who had cast long outdated (i.e., Pivoda-esque) principles in false colors of modernism. After comparing *Jenůfa* unfavorably to Foerster's *Eva* and Smetana's *Hubička* (two works that, for Nejedlý, embodied the ideal of modern folk opera), he concluded that neither the story nor the music of Janáček's opera portrayed the moral value necessary in a "national opera." With a plot and score too regionalized to stand for the whole of Czech society, the opera had also forged connections to compositional streams (pan-Slavist, verismo) too international to be representative. Amid all of his blatant misreadings, Nejedlý's aim seems to have been to discredit Janáček—a major artistic force just on the eve of his rapprochement with the Prague musical establishment—by any means possible, including a highly tendential link to Pivoda and to issues long outdated, but kept alive by the rhetoric of Nejedlý himself.[71]

Simultaneous with the premieres of both *Jenůfa* and *Karlštejn* were the preparations for an event that would finally galvanize the Czech community in a unified statement of national musical identity: in 1916, specific plans were made to create an exhibition honoring the life and works of Smetana. On May 6, 1917, at the Ethnographic Museum in Prague's Kinský Gardens, the Smetana Exhibition opened, displaying manuscripts, letters, photographs, and other documents, curated by Nejedlý and a group of individuals from throughout the Prague community.[72] The project was specifically designed to appeal to the nationalist sentiments of the wartime Czech public and was, predictably, overwhelmingly popular, tallying over ten thousand visitors by June of that year.[73] Although clearly the work of the Nejedlý circle, who saw it as a victory of their vision of Czechness in music, the exhibition also gained a large number of supporters among the Conservatory/UB contingent as well. As such, the growing unity of opinion surrounding Smetana as a symbol of Czech musical identity can be regarded as a major step in the normalizing of culture in wartime to traditionalist standards, "ironing out" dissenting or factional voices for the good of the collective. That Smetana, a figure from the Cultural Revival, was now reinterpreted as the only model for a modern musical culture in Prague (signaling the partial acceptance of Nejedlý's platform) also meant that the city's compositional circle took a large step toward conservatism, even antimodernism. To this end, some of the most experimental Czech composers of the prewar and wartime period (for example, Vomáčka) now abandoned their modernist aesthetic in favor of models that were almost a half-century old. Indeed, this event and its aesthetic ramifications would shape the future of Czech music making for quite some time, renewing a tension between national and cosmopolitan ideals that would not abate until the rise of a new generation in the late 1920s.

The rhetoric surrounding the Smetana Exhibition reflects these trends. Helfert's brief description of the various exhibits referred to the whole project as a "pious" act, the "consequences" of which were directed toward creating a "sanctuary" worthy of a National Composer.[74] He stressed the "pure, objective" nature of the curators' efforts, not designed to be popular in the manner of most patriotic displays; such a focus conformed to Hostinský's binarism of true nationalism versus superficial patriotism in the previous generation. Most significantly, Helfert's rhetoric sought to encapsulate a sense of national completeness brought about by the exhibition (which reflected that of Smetana's art itself):

> The exhibition, through its organization and objectivity, completes with certainty a significant national-cultural project, for if the knowledge of and a deep and unconditional respect for Smetana's work penetrate our society in such a lively manner, so will it also open an understanding of our own, purest Czech music and the fullest expression of our national character.[75]

Not even Nejedlý's antagonists at *Hudební revue* felt the need to counter any of these claims, even though much of the discussion served to affirm the normalization of the critic's reading of his idol, a point of great contention in the past.

In a time of extraordinary nationalist feeling, Smetana and his achievements reached an apotheosis that elevated them above the factionalization of contemporary Prague, bringing the debate surrounding his legacy to a (provisional) close. As such, focus returned to the issues of modernism and the promulgation of art in society—discourses greatly affected, positively and negatively, by the Smetana Exhibition as well. With the imminent collapse of Austria-Hungary and the achievement of Czech political sovereignty, the lives of the individual agents in the debate over Czech music and culture would be different, and their priorities would change irrevocably from the years before the war. It is snow time to gain closer acquaintance with the composers of fin-de-siècle Prague and the music that had proved so worthy of debate.

Chapter Four

"Archetypes Who Live, Rejoice, and Suffer"

Czech Opera in the Fin de Siècle

Introduction: Musical Life in Prague

The ideological debates discussed in chapter 3 reveal much of the vibrancy of the Prague musical community in the pre-independence era, and a discussion of the actual musical production of the day—concert life, musical styles, and the composers themselves—completes the picture. It is certainly true that the polemics of Nejedlý, Stecker, and others occasionally departed from contemporary experience, concentrating more on minutiae from decades past. As with the "Novák Affair," however, these issues continuously had a direct effect on contemporary composition, helping to shape, for better or worse, the direction of Czech modernism and its relation to the rest of Europe. Public tastes, too, were affected by these print wars, since the programming of institutional concerts directly reflected the ideological and stylistic leanings of those in power.

If taken as a whole, concert life in turn-of-the-century Prague offered an astonishing array of choices. The possibilities were severely limited, however, if one's attendance followed national or linguistic lines, and concert and opera reviews published at the time seem to imply a strictly segregated audience, particularly with the approach of the First World War. Prague's German community, while increasingly in the minority (with the rise of Czech middle and lower classes in the suburbs), was still within the political majority of Austria-Hungary, and its programming choices reflected a desire to preserve its cultural status. Since opening its doors in 1783 the so-called Estates Theater (also known as Deutsches Landestheater, or Stavovské divadlo in Czech) had been under German administration, which allowed only a modicum of time for Czech performances prior to the founding of the Czechs' Provisional Theater in 1862. After this point its repertoire was exclusively German, with productions in both theaters on a similar scale, which is to say, increasingly insufficient for opera in the late nineteenth century. Not surprisingly, shortly after the completion of the much larger Czech National Theater, the Germans responded in 1888 with their own Neues Deutsches Theater, a larger building that was equipped to mount productions of Wagner and other late romantic composers.[1] Despite their expansion, however, opera at the theater under Angelo Neumann (director 1888–1910) remained quite conservative, reflecting the pillars of German tradition, up to and including Wagner, as copyright restrictions were increasingly lifted over the era. The programming aesthetic eventually changed, first with the Prague premiere of *Salome* in 1906, and then with the acquisition of Alexander Zemlinsky, modernist composer and Schoenberg's representative in Prague, as opera director in 1911. As with Kovařovic at the National Theater, Zemlinsky had to contend with conservative tastes for operetta and a general lack of interest in modernism—a situation that prevented the performance of any new works by German-Bohemian composers until Finke's *Die Jakobsfahrt* in 1936.

With two German stages to one Czech stage (the Provisional Theater had been physically incorporated into the National), increasing demand for Czech-language theater was met by the opening of the Vinohrady Theater in 1907. Started as an incentive from conservative Old Czechs, whose private company, Družstvo Národního divadla (National Theater Association), had lost control of the National Theater in 1900, the Vinohrady Theater was run as a business from first to last, with little pretension toward artistic intellectualism. Set in a wealthy inner suburb and directed by Kovařovic's predecessor František Šubert, the theater catered to popular tastes for operetta and light operas from abroad, as well as a large selection of spoken drama. The modest opera department, headed at first by Ludvík Čelanský (1907–9, 1913–14), attempted nothing more demanding than d'Albert's *Tiefland* (1909) with the bulk of performances devoted to Offenbach, Johann Strauss, Lehár, and the Czech Karel Weis. When Ostrčil took over the reins in 1914, his attempts to impose a more "serious" repertoire in the form of recent works by Foerster and Zich was met with only a lukewarm response (accolades from the Nejedlý camp notwithstanding). The situation at the Vinohrady Theater continued in this way until 1919, when its opera department was permanently disbanded (in favor of spoken drama) and absorbed into Prague's other companies.

Despite the many criticisms against it, the National Theater was able to provide audiences with the widest selection of repertoire in Prague, including a vast number of full-length Czech operas. In light of Nejedlý's many reproaches against Kovařovic's twenty-year regime as opera director (1900–1920), it is perhaps surprising to discover that Smetana's eight operas received the lion's share of performances (1,103 total), with *The Bartered Bride* far ahead of all others (396). *Dalibor* (169) and *Hubička* (142) also received respectable numbers, to which only Dvořák's *Rusalka* (133) and Kovařovic's *Psohlavci* (126) could compare.

With some notable exceptions, such as Dvořák's pantomime opera *The Devil and Kate* (83), most other Czech operas saw performances well below these figures, including works by Fibich (115 total), Foerster (51, 27 of them after 1918), Novák (33), and Ostrčil (23). Nevertheless, all but the most insignificant of Prague's opera composers could count on at least a half-dozen performances of their work under Kovařovic: Janáček, residing outside the city, was made to wait (60 performances of *Jenůfa* and *Mr. Brouček*, all of them after 1916).

Kovařovic also had to bend to his upper-middle-class subscribers' demands for operetta and ballet, which were fully supported by the administration as guaranteed revenue. Since 1900 the Young Czech party, whose liberal politics grew increasingly conservative by the end of the Habsburg era, had operated the theater via the private company Společnost Národního divadla (National Theater Company). Although Kovařovic had a personal interest in both light opera and ballet (having composed several of each, often published under the French "translation" of his name, Charles Forgeron), his relationship with the administration and their negative attitude toward modern Czech music became ever more fraught with tension. Nationalist feelings certainly played a role in this respect, as did Kovařovic's warm encouragement toward younger composers, most prominently Ostrčil, whose early works were always premiered shortly after their completion.

Operas by foreign composers occupied an interesting position in the National Theater repertoire, since they neither received top billing nor were totally ignored. On the contrary, Kovařovic introduced and maintained a wide variety of European operas, usually performed in Czech translation. The most favored of these were *Evgeny Onegin* (126), *Carmen* (109), *Mignon* (79), *Les Contes d'Hoffmann* (70), and *Aida* (68), all to the chagrin of the Nejedlý contingent. Wagner was better represented than most, with respectable figures for *Lohengrin* (63), *Tannhäuser* (61), and *Der fliegende Holländer* (54): other composers were usually overrepresented by a single opera, with only sporadic performances of others. As such, virulent nationalist critics of the theater complained unfairly that foreign operas were preventing the promulgation of Czech high art—in fact, it was precisely this attitude that blocked the production of any modern European operas in Prague for quite some time.

The Czech Philharmonic, although a much newer institution, also proved to be a hotbed of ideological debate prior to (and after) independence. Initiated in 1895 as a revenue-building enterprise for members of the National Theater orchestra (led by Dvořák), it was soon forced to become independent after a performers' strike. The ensemble was reconstituted in 1901 under the aegis of the České filharmonické družstvo (Czech Philharmonic Association), with the somewhat maverick Ludvík Čelanský as its first director. Čelanský, who was championed by Nejedlý for his brilliant Smetana interpretations, found himself at the head of the single professional instrumental ensemble in a city that overwhelmingly favored opera. The great demand placed on the orchestra, from Prague all the way down to the tiny hamlets where they frequently played, produced a huge variety of repertoire but weakened its quality substantially.[2] When Čelanský moved to the Vinohrady Theater in 1907 (as noted earlier) he was replaced by Vilém Zemánek, whose work with the orchestra brought its output to a more consistent level, albeit at the cost of a more adventurous repertoire. Zemánek faced internal conflicts between the administration (whom he was perceived as supporting) and the orchestra members; the situation came to a head on the eve of independence with the performers' expulsion of their conductor on both political and artistic grounds (see further discussion in chapter 5).

Much of this instrumental activity was sustained by the graduates of Prague Conservatory, which also offered symphonic and chamber concerts as well as public lectures in support of its students. The Artists' Union (UB) also held similar events for the public, with a concert series that stretched back to the institution's inception in 1863. Although the series, which achieved a systematic regularity in the period 1886–1903 under the title *Populární koncerty*, was purported to expose its members to the most up-to-date music from the rest of Europe, in reality its offerings were slim and conservative. The concerts continued with less frequency until 1911, but with a greater representation of local contemporary composers, particularly Novák and Suk, who each received full concerts dedicated to their works. The final concert on February 8, 1911, entitled "Young Vienna," contained compositions by Schreker, Schoenberg, Korngold, and Bruno Walter, a program that likely served more as a curiosity (or even a boundary for acceptable taste), rather than an open-minded exploration of artistic possibility.[3] Although heavily laden with its own ideology, the Nejedlý circle's Hudební klub provided exposure to a more challenging repertoire in an interactive, student-based atmosphere (see chapter 3).

Another significant society of this type was the so-called Podskalská filharmonie (Podskalí Philharmonic, named facetiously for a suburb in South Central Prague), a private organization of musical figures all closely connected to Vítězslav Novák. Novák was at the height of his creative powers and cultural influence in the period of its operation (1901–17), and the group's activities closely conformed to his artistic evolution. The "Philharmonic" itself was, in actual fact, a discussion group whose biweekly evenings were enhanced by live musical examples of recent compositions from all over the continent, including works by Reger, Debussy, Scriabin, and Schoenberg, well before their respective concert premieres in Prague.[4] Much like Schoenberg's Verein für musikalische Privataufführungen (itself soon to be replicated by Zemlinsky in Vienna), these compositions were performed in reduction for piano or small ensemble. The group also served as a private venue for previewing its members' (primarily Novák's) compositions before an audience of like-minded peers, occasionally culminating in modest collaborative projects reminiscent of the Belyayev circle in St. Petersburg. Although not a formal institution per se, the Podskalská filharmonie had a closely monitored membership (excluding women until their leader, Novák, married in 1912) that conformed primarily to those of the UB and Conservatory, not to mention the infamous anti-Nejedlý "Protest" of December 15, 1912.[5] Most important, while such a closed group could not influence the direction of larger public musical tastes in the city, it helped to determine the aesthetic attitudes of its very well-placed members, who in turn were crucial in shaping the collective style of Czech modernism. In fact, through the progression of its programming choices (initially an exploration of lesser-known Baroque and Classical compositions, gradually adopting a more modern repertoire until the eventual exclusion of all else), the Podskalská filharmonie traces its various composers' exposure to—and acceptance of—modernism as a larger cultural movement.

Composers and Musical Styles in Prague

The early years of the twentieth century present the first full glimpse of the tremendous creative renaissance that would encapsulate the Prague musical community for the next four decades. The student generation of the 1890s, described at the end of chapter 2, attained professional status after the turn of the century and influenced their younger contemporaries in a much more immediate fashion than at any other time in the community's history: the Podskalská filharmonie is a prime example. It was a time of young leaders, particularly since none of the older generation presented a strong artistic voice that could fill the gap left by the deaths of Fibich and Dvořák. The two most likely candidates, Foerster and Kovařovic (both around forty at the turn of the century), were variously absent from the creative community, living abroad or occupied with conducting duties, respectively, and it is unlikely that their predominantly conservative styles would have provided models for prospective modernists. As a result, Novák, Suk, and Ostrčil, all younger than thirty in 1900, are upheld in the standard histories as the main purveyors of Czech modernism, with Rudolf Karel and Otakar Zich in supporting roles. This cluster of individuals, from which radiated an ever-increasing array of students, disciples, and enthusiasts, produced a body of work that surprises the listener with its freshness, high quality, and uniqueness of compositional voice. It is, however, a repertoire that sits uncomfortably under a monolithic definition of modernism, since it conforms neither to retrospective (i.e., "reactionary") postromantic tendencies, nor to a clearly defined avant-garde. It is a product of its fin-de-siècle generation in Europe, with whose trends it was intimately connected at the time of its inception in the late Habsburg era.

In the wake of Dvořák's and Fibich's deaths, it would seem that opera had finally relinquished its position as the dominant genre of the Czech musical community. The tremendous burst of activity in the final years of the nineteenth century, which saw the creation of *Šárka*, *Eva*, *Psohlavci*, and *Rusalka*, produced a subsequent lull in quality: it was several years before any one work created a lasting impact. There were also various new directions to explore, with modern chamber music bolstered by the Czech Quartet and a rash of song cycles prompted by the wave of Czech decadent literature of the 1890s. Nevertheless, amid the growing variety of new compositions and stylistic directions in Prague, it was still opera that most encapsulated the identity of the musical community, particularly in the ongoing search for a modern expression in the genre. When those in the younger generation finally attained operatic success, their work was considered to be a direct reflection of the critical debates in which the composers found themselves; with such public attention cast upon them, these works could not help influencing the debates in turn. Although its composer's viewpoint was anything but unequivocal in these turbulent times, Ostrčil's 1911 opera *Poupě* (The Bud) was often upheld as a fulfillment of Nejedlý's aesthetic paradigm. Conversely, Novák's *Karlštejn* of 1916, by virtue of its reception, became the most important opera from the ranks of the so-called musical establishment. Ironically, both of these composers, as well as their close colleague Josef Suk, came from a similar stylistic background, despite what their contemporary critics may have argued.

Shades of Modernism: Suk, Novák, and Ostrčil

While the next generation of music critics was already continuing the factional divide in Prague's musical life, the composers Novák, Suk, and Ostrčil were, for the most part, staying clear of the gathering storm. Both Novák and Suk had already had some success in publishing and performance, and by 1900 their names were on the lips of Prague's bourgeois elite as the most likely to lead the modern generation of composers into a new era. Although the generation of Novák, Suk, and Ostrčil is referred to as "modernist" in the Czech musicological literature, their modernism must be understood in relative terms, especially since the state of composition in Prague has often been criticized as conservative and provincial, particularly in comparison to developments in Vienna and Paris at the turn of the century. While it is true that several of the newer musical styles, such as impressionism, extended tonality, and bitonality came to the Czech musical community quite late, and the direct influence of Mahler and early Schoenberg was felt only briefly by a few individuals,[6] it cannot be said that composers like Suk, Novák, and Ostrčil lacked a vital spirit of musical exploration. As can be expected, a certain tendency toward expressions of nationalism appeared in the oeuvre of many of the fin-de-siècle Czech composers, usually manifested in some sort of connection to folk music or poetry. Nevertheless, the "Czech modernists" did not use folk (or folk-like) music in a way comparable to Smetana and Dvořák, but rather incorporated contemporary harmonic and stylistic features throughout, particularly in the accompaniments to their many folk-song arrangements. The result is a curious blend of "traditional" (i.e., self-conscious) simplicity and a cosmopolitan elegance often reminiscent of Debussy or Strauss. It is important to note, however, that a large portion of chamber and orchestral compositions at this time (as well as the entire output of certain composers) had little or nothing to do with direct expressions of patriotic nationalism, through the use of either folk song or historical/folkloric subject matter. Many times, if a folkloric connection exists, it is textual rather than musical; or if it appears in the score at all, it lies buried in a single melodic or rhythmic motive, with little else to identify it as "national" to the non-Czech listener. Despite all of these exceptions to the traditional conception of nationally representative music, each work can be read as an attempt to define the modern Czech collective in music.

Novák and Suk, both coming from the ranks of the Prague musical establishment, have been treated as parallel personalities since their graduation from Dvořák's masterclass in 1897. Although Suk, as a composer, initially received less attention than Novák, having most of his time occupied by his participation in the Czech Quartet (alongside Hoffmann, Nedbal, and Wihan), his name was the one most closely associated with Dvořák's, not only as a result of his marriage to the composer's daughter Otilie, but also as an indication of their stylistic proximity. This latter factor, which had mostly to do with Suk's preference for instrumental genres, was linked to the widespread consensus that Dvořák's true calling lay in the realm of so-called absolute music, a generalization that would overshadow Suk's career as well. In Nejedlý's opinion, Suk's stylistic allegiance to Dvořák carried a stigma that reflected badly on both the younger composer and his generation, so much so that the critic never penned a positive review of Suk's music throughout his entire career.[7] The compositional connection between Dvořák and his student was further strengthened by the dual tragedy of Dvořák's and Otilie Suková-Dvořáková's deaths within the same twelve-month period in 1904–5. Suk, already in the process of creating an extended symphony in mourning for the loss of his father-in-law, composed the final two movements in memory of his wife. This anecdote was well known throughout Prague's artistic circles, and the premiere of the *Asrael Symphony*, op. 27, in 1906 became permanently associated with its composer's public act of grieving. *Asrael* also became a stylistic turning point in Suk's career, since almost all of the composer's subsequent large-scale works involved some degree of autobiographical reflection; it also represents his first true exploration of a modernist musical language, with an intensity of expression and a density of motives and orchestral part writing that had no parallel in Czech musical experience. Although the post-Wagnerian legacy is still quite apparent, as with his older contemporaries Reger and Scriabin, Suk's polythematic technique and fluidity of phrasing mark out an individual territory, which is so crucial in the modernist context. In many respects, *Asrael* became the earliest model for a modernist Czech orchestral style that would reappear in symphonic and operatic works of Novák, Ostrčil, and others for a half-century.

The artistic pairing of Novák and Suk was preserved by the two composers' lifelong mutual admiration and respect. Perhaps more important for the perception of Prague's concertgoers, Novák and Suk were held to be at similar artistic stages, with many "newer" stylistic characteristics in common, a phenomenon that served to identify them as a group rather than as individuals. Nevertheless, Suk's post-Conservatory years were altogether different from those of Novák, who formed crucial ties with musicians in Moravia and Slovakia and built up a widely respected private composition studio in the Vinohrady suburb of Prague. By the time he commenced his duties as professor of composition at the Conservatory in 1909, Novák had already taught a considerable number of important students, including Ladislav Vycpálek, Boleslav Vomáčka, and Erich Steinhard, each of whom would contribute greatly to Prague's musical and critical activity over the next several decades.

Novák's compositional career was also significantly different from Suk's; his passionate interest in Moravian and Slovak folk music strongly influenced his compositions from the turn of the century onward. The *Sonata eroica* for piano (1900), the symphonic poem *V Tatrách* (In the Tatra Mountains, 1902), and the orchestral *Slovácká suita* (Suite from the Slovácko Region, 1903) each popularized the composer's reputation as a new, modern voice in Czech music, while also solidifying his connection to regions east of Bohemia. Of more scholarly interest were the many volumes of *Slovenské spevy* (Slovak folk songs, 1900–1930), to which Novák provided piano accompaniments in his own characteristic idiom. The musical language that Novák employed at this time, monothematic as opposed to Suk's polythematicism, also tended toward what came to be called musical impressionism: the tone poems *V Tatrách, O věčné touze* (Of the Eternal Longing, 1903) and *Toman a lesní panna* (Toman and the Wood Nymph, 1906), and the song cycles *Melancholie* (1901), *Údolí nového království* (The Valley of the New Kingdom, 1903), and *Melancholické písně o lásce* (Melancholy Songs of Love, 1906) demonstrate Novák's growing interest in coloristic orchestration, parallel chords, diatonic ninths, thirteenths, and whole-tone clusters. While many commentators have described a vital connection to Debussy's music, Novák had strong feelings on the subject in later years: "Often people have written about my impressionism as if it were taken over from Debussy. This is not correct at all. I already felt things in an impressionistic way with *Melancholie*, thus at a time when Debussy was just getting started and moreover quite unknown in Prague."[8] Vladimír Lébl asserted that Novák's brand of modernism took shape through his contact, on the one hand, with Moravian and Slovak folk music, which he abstracted both melodically and harmonically, and on the other, with the symbolist poet Antonín Sova and the painter Joža Uprka, the three of whom shared ideas regarding modernism and expression in art. Such a compositional trend represented at once an allegiance to accepted, folklore-based nationalist expressions and a method by which the composer could bring "national" music into a more modern, cosmopolitan musical realm.

This stylistic change, which amounted to a departure from the Conservatory model of composition, proved harmful for the most important artistic connection in Novák's early career: from the time of the first performance of the *Sonata eroica*, the composer's relations with Dvořák cooled substantially.[9] It was for this reason that Nejedlý sought out Novák's allegiance during this period and began a series of studies that reflected positively on the young composer's development, in the hopes that a "Dvořákian" would convert to the opposing faction.[10] Novák's turn toward modernism, through symbolist poetry, impressionist harmonic language, and timbre-based scoring techniques, led to yet another great stylistic affinity: as elsewhere in Europe, the Prague premiere of Richard Strauss's *Salome* in May 1906 created a sensation among the younger members of the musical community that was lasting in its effect. Indeed, Novák was at the perfect point in his career to benefit from such an influence, having already written several lengthy tone poems with a variety of programmatic bases. The first traces of Strauss in Novák's artistic consciousness appeared in *Toman a lesní panna*, based on a poem by Čelakovský that had earlier inspired a tone poem by Fibich. The response to this work, including a surprisingly generous review by Nejedlý in the nonmusic daily *Den*, was overwhelmingly positive.

The exposure to Strauss also reinforced Novák's latent desire to embark on an operatic project. Novák had always written vocal music, including some challenging work in his latest, "modernist" style (particularly *Údolí nového království*); he had even attempted various operatic projects over the decade since his student days.[11] Nevertheless, as Lébl pointed out, opera was not such a straightforward task for Prague's new modernist generation, given the dual legacies of Smetana and Dvořák, not to mention the less exalted work produced since then by Rozkošný, Kàan, Nedbal, and others, which lay in the direction of pantomime.[12] Opera, the productions of which often required a public space of nationalist importance (as was the case in Prague, given the history of the National Theater), was by far the most contested genre in these years dominated by rumblings of national self-determination. Furthermore, opera was automatically assumed to represent some form of collective identity—despite the audience's increasing discomfort with the modernist musical language—rather than the subjectivity of the individual artist. As Janáček's subsequent tribulations with *Jenůfa* would clearly show,[13] modern Czech opera and its reception among the musical elite of Prague was at a crisis point in the years before the First World War.

Nine years younger than Novák and five younger than Suk, Otakar Ostrčil was widely considered to be the most junior member of the newly emerging modernist generation, but yet the one most active in the realm of operatic composition. The youngest son of a bourgeois Prague family, his musical interests came second to his parents' wish that he pursue academia; his musical studies consequently proceeded part-time in Fibich's private studio, rather than at the Conservatory. It was through these private composition lessons that the teenaged Ostrčil formed the two most important relationships of his career. The first was with Fibich himself, who seems to have groomed Ostrčil to be his compositional successor in Prague's musical community.[14] The second was a lifelong friendship with Nejedlý, who was only one year his senior and a fellow student of Fibich at this time. While the devotion to his teacher would be felt as a strong compositional influence long after Fibich's death in 1900, Ostrčil's relationship with Nejedlý would define his career much more substantially. Indeed, for their more than thirty-five-year acquaintance, Nejedlý would pen the lion's share of prose on Ostrčil and his music, so much so that the critic's work has overshadowed all other scholarship ever since.[15]

Ever since the 1903 *History of Czech Music*, Nejedlý had described Ostrčil as the most modern of his generation: not only was he the most youthful (which, for the author, meant the most progressive), but he was also virtually the only "direct descendant" of Smetana's and Fibich's creative genius. In actual fact, Ostrčil's compositional style was not that far removed from that of his contemporaries, mainly Novák and Suk, in that the bulk of his orchestral and operatic music employs a post-Wagnerian harmonic language (influenced at times by Mahler and Strauss), often with a densely contrapuntal web of motives. According to Nejedlý, however, it was Ostrčil's compositional inheritance from Smetana and Fibich that gave him a distinct and indisputable advantage over Novák and Suk (with whom Nejedlý almost never compared Ostrčil directly), since only he had received the "artistic laws" of truth and progressiveness.[16] By virtue of having pursued his musical education away from the Conservatory, it was commonly assumed that Ostrčil, like Nejedlý, stood in an antagonistic position to all forms of the musical establishment. When the young composer's career continued in this direction (after university he took a job as a German teacher), Nejedlý could proudly state that "not by chance did all those who adhered to the program of the young [generation] seek and find their livelihood outside of our musical institutions of the age."[17] With the possible exception of Foerster (who lived abroad until 1918, and whose main links to Prague's musical community were through the two younger men), Nejedlý considered Ostrčil the only imaginable candidate to lead Czech musical culture into the modern era. Such a distinction not only prevented the young composer from having an artistic voice - completely separate from his lineage (and from the collective of anti-establishmentarians), but also made him into a messianic figure whose responsibility for the future course of Czech music making he could not possibly hope to fulfill, especially amid the debates raging during the fin de siècle. Thus, in Nejedlý's eyes, Ostrčil was at once an individual, by virtue of his inheritance, and a representative of the collective identity, much as Smetana had been understood to be.

In his biography published shortly after Ostrčil's death, Nejedlý described how their friendship was based on common artistic and ideological convictions: following the premiere of Foerster's *Eva* in 1899, the two young men professed their devotion to modern Czech music right outside the National Theater.[18] Nejedlý also felt that Ostrčil had a stronger personal affinity to the "folk-based" heritage of Smetana and Fibich than to bourgeois Prague society, even as a young man; the critic reasoned that Ostrčil had steered away from the "reactionary" Conservatory sphere in choosing Fibich as his mentor.[19] In this respect, it helped that Ostrčil's compositional focus, like that of his teacher, tended toward opera and dramatic music in general. To solidify the concept of an artistic inheritance from Smetana and Fibich, Nejedlý strove to make specific connections between Ostrčil's early operatic efforts and the flagship works of his predecessors. The most significant example of this occurred, rather symbolically, at Fibich's death, when Ostrčil was working on *Vlasty skon* (Vlasta's Passing), an opera whose plot provides a sequel to both Smetana's *Libuše* and Fibich's *Šárka*, and whose libretto had previously been considered by both composers.[20]

An interesting window into the early careers of the two young friends is provided by their attitudes toward musical developments outside the Czech Lands. In his Ostrčil biography, Nejedlý described how they were both initially excited by modern trends in the music of Strauss and Mahler, without, it seems at first, having heard any of their music. They eagerly attended the Prague premieres of Strauss's *Feuersnot* and *Till Eulenspiegel*, but after a while became convinced that Strauss was not the ideal leader of musical modernism; it is probably not a coincidence that "this [opinion] was confirmed for us when the conservative faction, at home and elsewhere, expressly received Strauss with enthusiasm."[21] At this point, Ostrčil and Nejedlý turned to Mahler's music with great anticipation, knowing almost nothing about him until the Prague premiere of *Lieder eines fahrenden Gesellen* in 1901, an event that confirmed their hopes. Ostrčil confessed shortly thereafter that "now I would follow Mahler into a fire."[22] The composer's early fascination with Mahler's music led to Nejedlý's pronouncement that Ostrčil was the Czech embodiment of Mahler's aesthetic of modernist musical expression, which formed yet another dictum that would last his entire career.

The success of the Fibich-inspired opera *Vlasty skon* at the National Theater under Kovařovic in 1904 led to further projects in music for the stage: most important, the Straussian opera *Kunálovy oči* (Kunála's Eyes, 1907, set to a play by the decadent Czech writer Julius Zeyer).[23] In his glowing reviews of each of these works, Nejedlý reinforced his views that Ostrčil was the only young composer in Prague worthy of the epithet "modern," both compositionally and in terms of his character; indeed, as he later asserted, in a true artist these two facets of life were inseparable.[24] This pattern of approval continued unabated, despite the temporary cooling of the two musicians' friendship in the years 1906–11, apparently as the result of Nejedlý's disapproval of Ostrčil's amorous interest in Gabriela Horvátová, a soloist at the National Theater. It is also very likely that Ostrčil sought to distance himself from Nejedlý's unfettered extremism during this turbulent time (the beginning of which coincided with the "Knittl Affair"). As a result, when Ostrčil commenced a new operatic project in 1909, it was, for the first time, wholly in the absence of his main ideologue and self-appointed publicist.

Ostrčil's *Poupě* and the Legacy of *The Two Widows*

Recognized as one of the most striking contributions to Czech-language opera in the prewar period, Ostrčil's one-act opera *Poupě* (The Bud, 1909–11) has all but disappeared from the National Theater stage since the early days of communism.[25] Premiered in 1911, it held a unique position among the Czech operas of its day, being the only relatively successful work of its kind from the prewar period; a modern comedy based on informal dialogue, it was often upheld as a model for younger composers during the First Republic. One of the most problematic aspects of the opera is its relationship to both tradition and modernism, situated as it is between Smetana's comedies (particularly *The Two Widows*, which likely served as a conscious model) and modern compositional techniques, verging at times on an expressionist vocal style of the type heard in *Salome* and *Elektra*. The conflict between past and present musical styles intersects with a second conflict—between national and cosmopolitan aesthetics—that together create a tension that is particularly fortuitous for opera in general. For a comedy such as *Poupě*, however, such tension remains ill-defined, making it difficult to place Ostrčil's work comfortably in the larger repertoire. Indeed, as subsequent analyses in this book will show, Czech comic operas retained their position as a locus of modernist operatic expression much longer than was the case in most compositional circles in Europe at this time, where comedies tended to have less demanding scores. The phenomenon of the Czech modernist comedy produced a certain hybridity in the works themselves, which, in a larger sense, is indicative of the problematic position of Czech composers in the context of European modernism, and is not unlike the problem of situating the comic *Der Rosenkavalier* comfortably within a "mainstream" of modernist expression. Finally, while Ostrčil's music was always assumed to be in accordance with Nejedlý's paradigms, the composer's relative silence about his own work allows us to question whether or not *Poupě* was in fact truly representative of any one faction in Prague's musical community.

Coming as it did after wave upon wave of folkloric comedies and historical tragedies by Czech composers, *Poupě* would have been refreshing for the audience at the National Theater in 1911. Ostrčil's musical language, too, had changed dramatically from *Vlasty skon* and *Kunálovy oči*, which were still firmly in the vein of Fibich's expressive, Wagnerian model. In his newest opera, the thirty-two-year-old composer explored a harmonic and gestural territory that few of Prague's prewar concertgoers would have been exposed to, especially from the pen of a homegrown artist. *Poupě*'s score is an expertly condensed web of relatively few motives, which "easily become etched in the memory, such that we follow their psychological changes, even to the most subtle gradations."[26] The harmonic language, while still not thoroughly expressionist in the manner of Ostrčil's postwar compositions, has much in common with the gestural language of Strauss's tone poems, or of Schoenberg in *Gurrelieder* or *Verklärte Nacht*. One of the most immediately audible "modern" characteristics of Ostrčil's work is the vocal style that, although it had rarely been seen among Czech composers, quickly became a hallmark of a specifically "Prague modernism" that is differentiated even from Janáček's idiosyncratic sound. What makes this vocal style so distinctive is a marked disconnection between singers and accompaniment, in that the solo lines are almost never doubled by instruments; moreover, the vocal melodies (which are mostly declamatory in nature) are quite unrelated, thematically and most times even harmonically, to their surroundings. Indeed, Ostrčil's singers almost consistently present nondiatonic tones in an otherwise tonal context, the resolution of which is only implied—briefly—amid a series of astonishingly frequent changes of harmonic direction. The result is a strange feeling of discomfort amid familiar (i.e., tonal) musical surroundings, at once modernist and conventionally operatic. Although declamatory singing was nothing new by 1911, its specific usage by Ostrčil and subsequently by Novák, Zich, Jeremiáš, Burian, and others, represents a local, collective attempt to come to terms with modernism and thereby to demarcate (albeit in moderation) a specifically Czech territory within it, without recourse to the folklorisms of the nineteenth century. *Poupě*, as the first work of this type to gain recognition in Czech musical circles, can as such be considered a model for many other subsequent operas written in Prague in the early twentieth century (see further discussion of Ostrčil's vocal style below, pp. 82–85).

In the effort to create a modern operatic comedy where text and especially dialogue could be foregrounded, Ostrčil carefully researched the field of contemporary Czech plays to find a suitable libretto. In F. X. Svoboda's *Poupě*, which had premiered in 1903 and received a new production in 1908, the composer discovered a bittersweet conversation piece, whose dialogues offered a substantial amount of space for musico-dramatic development.

Characters:		
	Klán, a widower and country landowner	bass
	Anežka, his daughter	lyric soprano
	Ladislav, a medical student, his nephew	lyric tenor
	Kučina, owner of the neighboring farm	baritone

The plot is exceedingly simple, set in a single, unbroken scene on a winter's evening at Klán's farmhouse in the countryside outside of Prague. Anežka, an adolescent girl on the cusp of adulthood ("The Bud" of the title), has attracted the attentions of two young men: one, her cousin Ladislav, an impetuous medical student visiting from Prague; the other, Kučina, who has loved her from afar for quite some time. At the beginning of the action, the household is awaiting Kučina's arrival, each individual anticipating the possibility that the neighbor will reveal his love for Anežka this very night. Trying to divert his cousin's attention, Ladislav pours out his heart to Anežka, offering the girl her first kiss in the midst of a charmingly naive dialogue. When Kučina arrives, Anežka has planned to

(*continued*)

speak with him privately, so that she can ask him not to love her, since it annoys her; if she were to ask him this as part of their general merrymaking, she reasons, he would not take it harshly and everything would come out right. As she begins to implement her plan, however, she hesitates and the strategy backfires: Kučina, terribly hurt, pensively informs Anežka that he must depart, never to return to their house. Gradually, Anežka realizes the seriousness of her words, and shaken by the potential loss of her childhood friend, she begins to reminisce with Kučina about the wonderful moments they have shared. The scene grows more passionate as Anežka discovers that it is a lifetime of love for Kučina that will sustain her into adulthood, rather than a transitory infatuation for Ladislav. The opera closes with a merry scene, wherein the happy couple informs the surprised Klán and Ladislav of the evening's outcome.

Already within the context of this bourgeois parlor comedy, it is easy to see that the crux of Svoboda's play lies in the exploration of interpersonal relationships, conflicting perceptions of human nature, and the emotional maturation of the individual. In an effort to preserve these dramatic nuances, to get away from traditional operatic conventions, and to keep abreast with modern developments in opera abroad (as with *Salome* and *Pelléas et Mélisande*), Ostrčil set Svoboda's text directly, providing a score of arresting beauty, wit, and grace. Dramatically speaking, *Poupě*'s libretto is one of mundane conversations rather than grand theatrical scenes in the traditional sense, and the reader of Svoboda's original without Ostrčil's contribution might conclude that the climax dénouement (Anežka's change of heart) is reached almost without anything happening on stage whatsoever. Yet, Ostrčil clearly demarcated his scenes to allow for shifts in dialogic content as well as dramatic impact. As Nejedlý strove to demonstrate in his 1911 monograph *Czech Modern Opera since Smetana*, it was Ostrčil's music that added a layer of considerable emotional and even moral depth to Svoboda's parlor comedy. Hearkening back to the aesthetic formulation of Hostinský, it was precisely this psychological interiority that, for Nejedlý, best spoke to and represented the Czech collective, paradoxical as it may seem.

It seems that, for Nejedlý in 1911, not only was Ostrčil's *Poupě* everything one could hope for in a modern Czech opera, but it was also inseparable, both stylistically and ideologically, from the tradition of Smetana, Fibich, and Foerster. Much in line with his commentary from previous years, Nejedlý stated that "these attempts at Czech opera from contemporary life all have one precursor: Smetana's *The Two Widows*, a work doubly rare in that it was found to be quite new in an era already so long ago."[27] Immediately we get the sense that Nejedlý's comment is more than just a stylistic comparison: after the "Knittl Affair," no reference to Smetana's comedy could be taken simply at face value. By placing *The Two Widows* and *Poupě* at either end of a long and honorable tradition of

Czech-language comic operas (described at length in his 350-page *Czech Modern Opera*), Nejedlý was attempting to confer a heightened, *modern* status on both works, to spite his increasingly hostile adversaries.

In his analysis of *Poupě*, the critic's reasons for the comparison are numerous. Both operas were, for Nejedlý, quintessentially modern portrayals of Czech society in their respective eras. This point is somewhat hard to concede, given the multiple similarities in plot that make both operas more representative of 1874 than of 1911: both stories take place at the country estates of upper-middle-class landowners, and revolve around similar themes of love, flirtation, and the choice of a spouse. Indeed, there is little to attach *Poupě*'s dramatic action to the modern world, given that it takes place indoors in a romantic, wintry setting, complete with horse-drawn troikas and sleigh bells, and in the total absence of any reference to modern social, cultural, or technological developments. Nejedlý's identification of *Poupě*'s modernness had less to do with a tangible dramatic action or setting than it did with the psychological underpinning of the characters' interaction.

The most significant argument in favor of *The Two Widows*' influence is that its main characters are also named Anežka and Ladislav, and that the plot revolves around the interactions of four individuals, including Anežka's cousin Karolina and their farm manager Mumlal. This last character, like Klán, comments on the young lovers from an ironic (albeit disapproving) distance. Smetana's Anežka, like Ostrčil's, must decide whether or not she loves Ladislav (her only suitor in this case), even though she still mourns her recently deceased husband. After Karolina makes her jealous through childish flirtation with Ladislav, Anežka decides (also in a soliloquy) to cease her mourning and accept Ladislav. The tone of the opera is more frivolous than psychological, in keeping with the style of comic opera at the time it was written. While the similarities of the characters of *The Two Widows* may have influenced Ostrčil's decision to choose Svoboda's play, even as a sign of allegiance to the pro-Smetana cause, Nejedlý makes no mention of such details in any of his many discussions of the opera.

The strong dialogic component of both Smetana's *Two Widows* libretto and Svoboda's play was a second important link that enabled Nejedlý to introduce another of his (and Hostinský's) well-rehearsed maxims—that a truly modern opera would observe rules of "correct" Czech text-setting. The stronger the treatment of dialogues in an opera, the greater occasion there was for the composer's artistry (and implicitly, Czechness) to be revealed. In this respect, Ostrčil's choice of a preexistent Czech play did him much credit in Nejedlý's eyes, since it also revealed a link to Fibich's work in the genre of melodrama, and compensated for any nationalist fervor it might lack as a nonfolkloric parlor comedy. The analysis in *Czech Modern Opera* also contains a description of how Ostrčil turned to a stage play in order to escape from the formal conventions of nineteenth-century opera; the increased reliance on dialogue in *Poupě* was a sure sign of this intention, for which *The Two Widows* (rather paradoxically) was again a model.[28]

A less tangible trait of *Poupě* for Nejedlý was its "positiveness of life": "it emphasizes life in its liveliest aspects especially *as a whole*"; "it warms us and . . . makes us smile at the truth"; "it is a *musical comedy* in the new sense of the word"; "it is a Smetanian comic opera."[29] This warmth apparently came from the "seriousness" of the humor, a trait both of Ostrčil's personality and one inherited from Smetana's model of comic operas. As a reflection of modern Czech society, serious, "living" humor was at once *lidský*, or "human," and *lidový*, or "of the people," in a proto-socialist sense. The latter attribute Nejedlý reserved for the most special cases, where an artist had not simply copied the surface characteristics of the folk, their lifestyle, and music, but had internalized a psychological element of the Czech (read: nonbourgeois) people in a manner that escaped verbal definition. The more human or universal an artwork, the more it could be said to represent the Czech people, since both concepts implied the absence of subjectivism and its alleged immorality. That Ostrčil's opera contained no reference whatsoever to the folk, either dramatically or musically, was apparently irrelevant to Nejedlý's greater point.

In Nejedlý's argument we also find a hint of the aesthetic of "healthy art," so common among politically motivated European commentators on culture at this time: *Poupě* is credited as springing "from simple, contemporary life . . . where drama must be expressed in the most untouched purity."[30] Throughout the ensuing analysis, Nejedlý also described the young lovers Anežka and Ladislav as belonging to the same simple and innocent realm. More relevant to the drama, perhaps, was the aforementioned psychological layer that Nejedlý credited to Svoboda's text and particularly to Ostrčil's music. The drama of *Poupě* took place more in the psyches of the characters (most important, Anežka) than visually on stage or even in the words themselves. In this respect, Ostrčil's music assisted on a supradramatic level, in that it was able to provide the necessary psychological preparation for the climax.[31] Perhaps most important for Nejedlý, this internalized drama of emotions represented the perfect merging of high art and popular humanity, a unity that only a truly Czech artist could attain, with Smetana (and latterly, Foerster) as a model.

In much of his analysis, Nejedlý was quite perceptive, especially about the interrelationships of music and drama. I contend, however, that while there are many "modern" aspects to *Poupě*, they often operate contrary to Smetana's operatic model, and in spite of the many superficial similarities to *The Two Widows*. It therefore becomes a question of whether Ostrčil was attempting to modernize Smetana's model for comic Czech operas or to break free from it; from either perspective, *Poupě* represents a radical alteration of Czech musical identity as the first opera whose music sits firmly in the twentieth century. Aside from the aforementioned vocal style, the most obvious sign of musical modernism is Ostrčil's harmonic and gestural language, which goes beyond virtually every other Czech-language opera written up to this point, with the exceptions of Janáček's *Jenůfa* and *Osud*. From the outset the harmony implies a polytonal undercurrent, as first occasioned by the orchestral accompaniment to the discussion of sleigh riding in the opening scene (4).[32] The staccato chords and oscillating bass patterns tend to move by common-tone motion, but without any sense of progression or home key. Many of the climactic passages within scenes also employ a rapidly shifting tonal orientation, such that it is difficult to predict the chord of resolution (37–38), while other tonal centers are undermined by the extreme use of nonharmonic neighbor chords (58). In a similar manner, Ostrčil made considerable use of ostinato figures to shape extended passages, a device that allows the gradual increase of chromaticism in the upper voices (35; also used by Janáček, Bartók, and Szymanowski at this time). Gesturally, the music of *Poupě* is akin to the exploration of registral extremes and radically differing types of phrasing, used in combination or in quick succession, found in music of his contemporaries particularly reminiscent of Schoenberg's fluid use of voice leading around the turn of the century (14). The result is an astonishing complexity of voicing that, owing to the brightness and levity of Ostrčil's scoring for this comedy, does not make the overall musical texture unduly dense.

The melodic motives that Ostrčil used throughout *Poupě*, appearing predominantly in the orchestra without the participation of voices, are flexible and versatile in a wide range of dramatic situations. These motives, unlike most of their nineteenth-century precedents, do not appear initially in any sort of harmonically or texturally simplified presentation, but rather in their full chromatic complexity (ex. 4.1a, Ladislav's motive, 8; 4.1b, Anežka's motive, 18). As an extension of this technique, *Poupě*'s motives easily contribute to the textural thickening of a passage, revealing the composer's skill at motivic overlapping and combination (ex. 4.2, the combination of all four characters' motives, 143).

Ostrčil's orchestral music helps greatly to characterize the four personalities that interact throughout *Poupě*. Indeed, reading Svoboda's original text apart from the music, the crucial differences between the two suitors, Ladislav and Kučina, remain rather nebulous, such that Anežka's ultimate choice of Kučina comes as somewhat of a surprise. Ostrčil, however, amplified Ladislav's nervous energy, giving his prolonged love scene with Anežka an underlying feeling of strained frivolity. This effect is expressed musically by the overwhelming paucity of melodic and harmonic resting points, very few slow, sustained passages (the exception introduced by Anežka at the words "That's enough now!" 38), and the almost total lack of silence. While Kučina's subsequent love scene with Anežka begins in a similar mood (in keeping with Anežka's plan to ask him, in a joking fashion, not to love her), his shocked reaction to Anežka's question provokes a long passage of introspection, captured musically by extended, Straussian, overlapping chromatic phrases, and the abandonment of the prevailing *scherzando* tone. Thus, each suitor receives a musical character that helps Anežka make her choice, as it were; more important, it enables her to grasp the importance of maturation through an adult relationship, as opposed to childish infatuation.

Example 4.1a. Ostrčil, *Poupě*, Ladislav's motive (8/1–2).

Example 4.1b. Ostrčil, *Poupě*, Anežka's motive (18/1–2).

Each of these aspects of atmospheric and dramatic differentiation also characterizes Anežka herself, since the musical world of *Poupě* represents her whole psychological being and its development over the course of the opera. In this respect, the gradual and subtle changes in mood affect her interactions with each of the other characters, creating a large-scale developmental scheme for the entire work. Like many of the one-act operas of the fin-de-siècle period (e.g., *Salome, Elektra, Erwartung,* and *Bluebeard's Castle*), *Poupě* consists of a series of smaller, subsidiary scene divisions that link together, often alternating between sections of high dramatic import and moments of relative repose. Ostrčil deftly changed multiple parameters of the music at these structural points, including tempo, rhythmic motive, tonal centering, and general mood, in order to capture the relative dramatic urgency of the moment. Striking in this regard are Anežka's two brief scenes on stage alone (43–49; 72–76), which pass through a surprising number of abrupt changes, each building to its own localized climax.

The first of these scenes, "Blázne jeden!" (He's a crazy one!), offers an excellent example of Ostrčil's method of detaching the vocal line from its

Example 4.2. Ostrčil, *Poupě*, final measures of the opera with all four motives (143/9–13).

surroundings, thereby helping to establish a Czech modernist operatic school centered in Prague. As Anežka wavers between thoughts of Ladislav and Kučina, her orchestral accompaniment moves through a series of stable, repeating patterns, above which she supplies a relatively innocuous—but not melodic—declamation of the text. At the moment, however, when she abandons the pressures imposed by these two men and turns inward to examine her own desires, the relationship between voice and orchestra changes perceptibly with a presentation of her motive, marked *con elevazione*. Anežka begins a lengthy passage of arioso, complete with melismas and other examples of text painting suggesting the forest birds she wishes she could become (ex. 4.3a, 47). The sense of flight that she mimics is reflected in her utter detachment from the complex orchestral accompaniment: singing in short, one- to two-measure gestures, her phrasing does not match up with any of the instruments, nor does the contour of her

[And to soar over the flowers]

Example 4.3a. Ostrčil, *Poupě*, avian melismas in Anežka's soliloquy (47/5–6).

[And not to know about anything, except my own happiness!]

Example 4.3b. Ostrčil, *Poupě*, unprepared modulation (48/6–8).

line resemble any of those surrounding her. The orchestra, meanwhile, presents a multitude of gestures that, while conflicting with Anežka, still exist within the late romantic musical vocabulary, including *siciliano* triplets and pulsating syncopations. The complex harmony, chordal but barely functional, offers very little support for the singer, in that she almost never receives common tones to assist in modulation; similarly, her melody offers no assistance in predicting the outcome of these modulations, particularly at the climactic ending of the passage (ex. 4.3b, 48). Nevertheless, despite the concatenation of diverse gestures in close succession, the solo passage does not give the effect of stylistic splintering when taken as a whole. Anežka's quixotic vocal line can be taken as a more expressive extension of her more straightforward declamatory singing at less dramatic moments, exhibiting continuity from scene to scene and a wide spectrum of emotions overall. Ostrčil's technique, while not perhaps immediately identifiable as "modernist," became a signature of other opera composers in Prague for the next quarter-century (even appearing—albeit in a substantially altered guise—in Alois Hába's quarter-tone opera *Matka* of 1931). *Poupě*, though modest in dimension and dramatic impact, would have a musical impact beyond its pages.

The most crucial scene of the entire opera is the "tryst" between Anežka and Kučina, which begins in a frolicsome mood, and is prolonged unbearably by Anežka's hesitation. The music that opens this scene is dominated by Kučina's motive, which repeats through almost every measure, lightly articulated (103). As Anežka begins to implement her ill-advised plan, the weight shifts to her motive, which forms the basis of a rather awkward-sounding ostinato in the bass (105). Another ostinato takes over as her painful hesitation begins; it is a tense, angular pattern, loosely based on the contour of Kučina's motive. As the situation worsens, the parallel chords in the upper voices drift away from the tonal center, such that, when Anežka utters her poorly advised request ("I want to ask you not to love me!"), there seems to be no hope of tonal resolution (ex. 4.4a, 107). The long-awaited A-flat major resolution occurs with the exclamation of Kučina, who repeats her request, as though in shock; the ostinato accelerates, erupting into a frenzy of overlapping motives, and finally disintegrating completely (ex. 4.4b, 107–8). What follows is the most abrupt atmospheric and musical change in the opera. The tempo drops to its slowest rate so far, remaining so for more than twenty pages of vocal score; the harmonic rhythm also decelerates, such that long passages are declaimed over sustained chords in the orchestra. The melody that dominates the orchestral music is a pathetically chromatic, overlapping version of what Bedřich Čapek identified as Kučina's love theme.[33] Prolonged silences and long interludes abound, and the painful awkwardness on stage is reproduced by a seemingly endless chain of dissonances that resolve into each other (ex. 4.4c, 108). After Anežka has awkwardly and unnecessarily described her rationale ("I know well that you love me, but it annoys me"), we finally receive an E-flat minor cadence, which hangs tragically in the air until Kučina speaks. The music that accompanies Kučina's introspective utterance is a marvel of quiet tension and noble simplicity: Ostrčil wrote a D-minor phrase, where the sole melodic line, in the low bass register, interacts subtly with Kučina's apologies for his prolonged silence. It is one of the most starkly revealing, psychological moments of music in the opera (ex. 4.5, 110).

From this moment on, the music of *Poupě*, with few exceptions, tends toward greater and greater simplicity of expression, as Anežka enters the emotional world of adulthood, leaving behind her childish infatuation for Ladislav forever. Luxurious waltz meters and slow tempi predominate, with two poignant moments providing examples of Ostrčil's technique of revealing the psychological

[I want to ask you not to love me!]

Example 4.4a. Ostrčil, *Poupě*, climactic build–up (107/8–12).

[Not to love you!]

Example 4.4b. Ostrčil, *Poupě*, A-flat "resolution" (107/13–15).

depth of his characters: first, as the couple begins to reminisce in earnest (amid a subtle mixture of $\frac{3}{8}$ and $\frac{2}{8}$, 126–27); and second, during Anežka's *lentissimo* declaration of her true feelings, without pretense. The latter passage, the completion of Anežka's happiness, is expressed as a single, eight-measure phrase in A-flat major, wherein the sense of progression is never in doubt, despite the ever-present chromatic coloration (ex. 4.6, 135–36). Ostrčil's music at this moment has the simple elegance we have waited for since the beginning of *Poupě*, and forms a suitable counterpart to the tortured passage in example 4.4a, which had also culminated in A-flat. It is this declaration, and not the final, awkward scene—where the couple reveals their news to Klán and Ladislav—that serves as the resolution of the opera, both dramatically and musically. Indeed, after the intensity—and sincerity—of this moment, the final scene is strikingly unsatisfactory, in that it attempts to return to the comedic frivolity of the opera's earlier scenes, whose insincerity had been transcended by the climax itself. Ladislav's cryptic final comment, "You are amazing, Anežka, amazing! It all turned out well

Example 4.4c. Ostrčil, *Poupě*, Kučina's love motive (108/27–35).

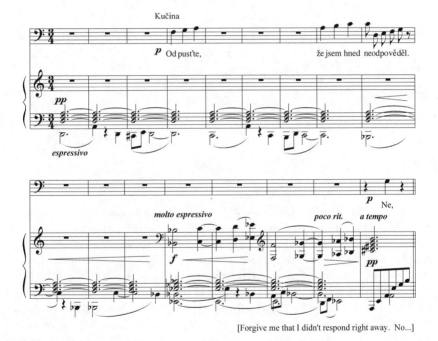

Example 4.5. Ostrčil, *Poupě*, Kučina's response (110/1–17).

for you! You are remarkable, really remarkable!" together with the unity implied in the combination of all four characters' motives (ex. 4.2b), both belie the unexpected upheaval in the lives of the individuals on stage, and the opera ends without any further resolution. This shortcoming, while minor in comparison to the strengths of the opera, is symptomatic of the Janus-like position of comic opera within musical modernism.

[Now I am happy, now I am like a bird, now,
now I am free, now I look forward to everything]

Example 4.6. Ostrčil, *Poupě*, Anežka's happiness (135/21–23; 136/1–6).

The music for *Poupě* reveals a complex negotiation of modernist and traditional operatic styles, complicated by their relationship to the largely introspective drama. While Ostrčil did succeed in portraying musically the psychological depth of his characters, particularly Anežka in her journey to adulthood, thereby fulfilling an aesthetic formulation asserted by Hostinský and Nejedlý, he also achieved a sense of operatic interiority not accounted for by nineteenth-century models. It is this sense of inner journey, enacted through the music, that puts *Poupě* more in line with modernist operas such as *Elektra* than with a parlor comedy such as *The Two Widows*. Nevertheless, the comic directness and accessibility of the opera's expressive style, particularly with its jovial dance meters and relatively light orchestration, put it at some distance from the "mainstream" canon of early modernist operas. Although the vocal writing, with its ongoing separation from the accompaniment, may achieve an operatic style distinct from earlier Czech models, it is less likely to convey a pervasive impression than the lighthearted and largely traditional orchestral writing that marks this work as a comedy in the first place. As with *Der Rosenkavalier*, another serious, "interior" comedy of human emotions, it is difficult to include *Poupě* comfortably in a narrowly defined categorization of modernist opera, yet it is equally impossible to exclude it from a discussion of the modernist musical and dramatic vocabulary in which it operates.

In his 1936 biography of Ostrčil, Nejedlý added further insights to his initial analysis of *Poupě*, written a quarter-century before. While the critic reused much of his analytical prose from *Czech Modern Opera*, he substantially changed his opinions about the relationship between *Poupě* and its supposed model, *The Two Widows*. He still admitted that Ostrčil's comic opera was in essence Smetanian, for all the reasons (e.g., "serious humor") mentioned above. Nejedlý also continued the discussion of the psychological impact of *Poupě*, although with an important difference: while both operas operated in many ways on an internal level, he argued, *Poupě*'s psychology was fundamentally different from its precursor's, particularly with regard to the musical treatment of the heroine, which was all but incomparable. This was perhaps an acknowledgment that Ostrčil's modernism and his heritage from Smetana were strange and uncomfortable bedfellows. Indeed, *Poupě* offers a curious stylistic mixture of nineteenth-century comic opera and fin-de-siècle one-act music drama, between retrospective and modernist aesthetics: as closer scrutiny reveals, it was *not* the modernist side of Ostrčil's work that retained a link to *The Two Widows*. Despite the many superficial connections between the two comic operas, *Poupě*'s music served to overturn many of the possible ways in which *The Two Widows* could have been used as a model: in this respect, it represents a substantial alteration of the image of Czech opera, now turned decisively toward modernism. It was (to quote Nejedlý's rather apt chapter title) the beginning of "a new path," both for the composer and his musical climate in Prague.

Whether or not *Poupě* was as significant a representative of collective artistic expression for the entire Czech nation as Nejedlý hoped, it is certain that its effect on the musical community of Prague was considerable. In an era of impassioned, career-altering polemics based on clear ideological divisions and compositional lineages, Ostrčil's work was surprisingly well accepted by critics and artists on both sides, despite his apparent allegiance to Nejedlý. Indeed, up to the early interwar difficulties with conservative critics like Šilhan, the young composer's work and activities were always respectfully assessed by his contemporaries—as though the product of a nonpartisan individual—and Ostrčil's continued silence amid the prevailing controversies did nothing to alter the situation. With such a well-written opera, he gave Nejedlý all the ammunition he needed to bolster his arguments for his own lineage's righteous domination of the genre, particularly in the absence of any such works from the "Dvořákians." Ironically, *Poupě*'s success is also measured in the number of subsequent operatic works that draw on its fledgling modernist style, vocally, orchestrally, and dramatically, by composers on both sides of the critical divide, most significantly in the case of Novák and his students. As the century pressed on and the Habsburg era drew to a close, the supposed stylistic divisions between the lineages grew ever narrower, and nowhere more demonstrably than in the all-important world of opera.

As we have seen in chapter 3, just after the premiere of *Poupě*, the writings of Nejedlý provoked the entire musical community to anger, with individuals and entire institutions reacting en masse to his iconoclastic criticisms of Dvořák and his "lineage," regarding both compositional style and cultural representation. One of those most at risk was Dvořák's most prominent student, Novák, whose turn toward opera during the First World War provided the impetus for Nejedlý to shift the focus of his polemic from historical to contemporary issues. In so doing, he forced the composers of Prague to take a stand, whether they wished to or not, on the role of modernism in Czech society—and in their own compositions.

Novák's *Karlštejn* and the Modernist "Feminization" of History

As with many other local communities in early twentieth-century Europe, modernist composers in Prague went through a long period of indecision, caught between the desire to express something revolutionary and the reluctance to abandon recently acquired traditions from the late nineteenth century. In the case of Prague these recent traditions were Wagnerian, and complete departures from this vocabulary—itself so radically different from pre-1860 Czech composition—were virtually unthinkable. The result was a series of compromises between Wagnerian tradition and more up-to-date styles, which, in the effort to appease both sides of the equation, often expressed very little to contemporary audiences. The typical problems of alienation associated with modernism were only exacerbated by the countercurrent nationalist urge to represent the collective identity of specific audiences through art. As the most publicly recognized composer in Prague, with the greatest stylistic influence and noteworthy success in most genres, Novák was the most likely candidate to master this delicate balance. But, as we have seen in the preceding chapter, the circumstances surrounding Novák's critical reception had begun to affect the direction of his work after his participation in the Protest of 1912. As such, any decisions regarding large compositional projects—such as operas—were undertaken in the context of public disputes over who could represent the Czech collective, and with what ideology.

Coming after a series of powerfully expressive tone poems and symphonic cantatas that showed him at the height of his career, Novák's first foray into opera, *Zvíkovský rarášek*, was at best ineffectual. A short historical comedy without any substantial plot, it left little impression on most critics save Nejedlý, who used it as welcome ammunition against his latest enemy. Novák's second opera, *Karlštejn*, was designed to create a much more significant statement, in terms of both dramatic content and musical language. *Karlštejn*, composed in 1915, was to be Novák's modern national opera.

Based on a historical Czech subject, Novák's choice of *Karlštejn* demonstrates the public importance of expressions of nationalism in wartime, as well as the fundamental difficulty in meeting these expectations through modernist music. For Novák the extroverted aspect of most patriotic music was aesthetically somewhat foreign, especially given the impressionist, idyllic character of much of the composer's oeuvre to this point. The result is that *Karlštejn*'s nationalism does not follow the typical Herderian model, to which Smetana's operas were more closely allied. In much the same way that Ostrčil's *Poupě* diverged from the model of *The Two Widows*, Novák reinterpreted romantic nationalism through the modernist tendency of his music for *Karlštejn*—itself another "serious comedy." Novák's modernism, with its obvious debt to Richard Strauss, was a challenge to, if not a direct act of provocation toward, Czech wartime audiences, who were experiencing a phase of aesthetic normalization after decades of freer expression in opera (for example, Fibich's *Šárka* and Kovařovic's *Psohlavci* from the 1890s). Thus, musical modernism could have been construed as both anti-traditional and foreign, a dangerous combination in such highly charged patriotic times. Nejedlý in particular read Novák's opera as a feminization of both Czechness and the Smetanian tradition, a view that not only speaks to the feminine bias of the plot, but to Novák's specific brand of Straussian-inflected modernism, which he conceived as "weak," and hence not truly modern at all. Both musically and dramatically, Czech critics and audiences perceived *Karlštejn* as a weak link in the debate over nationalism in music at a time when a show of collective strength was of the utmost importance.

Yet all outward signs imply that Novák's intention was to provide another work for the canon of Czech national operas on historical subjects. Based on Jaroslav Vrchlický's historical comedy from 1883, *Karlštejn* takes place at the castle of the same name, built in the fourteenth century by Karel IV, the Czech-born Holy Roman Emperor and King of Bohemia, to house the imperial jewels. Vrchlický exploited the legend that, because of the political and religious importance of the site, no women were allowed into the castle.

Characters:	Karel (Charles) IV	baritone
	Queen Alžběta (Eliška) Pomořanská	dramatic soprano
	Duke of Bergamo, emissary from Rome	tenor
	Alena, Eliška's handmaiden	lyric soprano
	Pešek, servant at Karlštejn, beloved of Alena	tenor
	Arnošt z Pardubic, archbishop of Prague	bass
	Ješek z Vartenberga, burgrave of Karlštejn	bass
	Castle watchman	baritone

Act 1: Karel's new bride Eliška arrives at Karlštejn with Alena, seeking to gain entrance to the castle in disguise as page boys with the help of archbishop Arnošt. Karel appears with the duke, who has come from Rome to pressure

(*continued*)

the king into moving his seat of government to Italy. Despite the duke's insinuations that the castle is an illicit pleasure palace filled with hidden women, Karel maintains that Karlštejn is instead a sacred retreat where he can find relief from the pressures of public and conjugal life.

Act 2: The duke begins a search of the castle for Karel's hidden concubines. The disguised Eliška succeeds in evading his gaze, and enters the imperial bedchamber as the replacement for her husband's evening attendant, Pešek. Alena reveals her identity to Pešek, and the two are almost discovered by the duke.

Act 3: In the bedchamber, Eliška encounters the duke, whose aggressive interrogation turns into a seduction; legendary for her strength, Eliška breaks his sword in two and sends him away. Karel enters and begins a discussion with Eliška about love, honor, and the virtues of a noble distance from the beloved, during which time he discovers the identity of his page boy as that of his wife. Realizing that her husband truly adores her even in the solitude of Karlštejn, Eliška hastily repents her transgression and vows to leave the castle: in a show of good faith, however, Karel recants his mysogynistic decree and accepts her presence there. The duke departs in shame and the royal couple leaves Karlštejn together, enabling the king to reenter the world, a changed man.[34]

Novák's decision to write an opera on Vrchlický's play was at first purely nationalistic, based on its setting in a beloved Bohemian castle and its portrayal of Karel IV (the ruler of the Czechs' "golden age"), whom the composer intended to introduce on the operatic stage as a historical substitute for "that incapable weakling, [Franz] Josef I."[35] Seriously depressed about both the war and his critical reception as an operatic composer, Novák found in *Karlštejn* an uplifting subject on both fronts. With its heroic portrayal of a beloved monarch, Novák intended to place his work in the canon of Czech historical operas, which included Smetana's *Braniboři v Čechách*, *Dalibor*, and *Libuše*, Fibich's *Šárka*, and Kovařovic's *Psohlavci*. Ironically, it was his musical and dramatic treatment of the subject matter that denied *Karlštejn* its place in that canon, particularly in the eyes of Nejedlý, who regarded it as further proof of its author's inability to represent the Czech nation in music, especially since much of the drama unfolds from the perspective of an "erotic" female character. From the general reaction to *Karlštejn* it is evident that Novák's music for such patriotic subject matter was altogether too challenging for the general public in its harmonic and gestural fluidity. So, too, would the lack of obvious, singable vocal melodies throughout the score—the legacy of Ostrčil's *Poupě*—negatively impact audiences who were more likely to equate patriotism with musical populism and accessibility, especially in wartime. In this respect, Novák's operatic rendition of national history, while dramatically effective in its own right, was too individualistic for the collective imagination.

In both the play and the music, the central theme of individual and national redemption through righteousness is carried out through the portrayals of the three main characters and the way in which they interact.[36] Initially King Karel IV appears much as he did in the popular consciousness: benevolent, highly intelligent, but distant from his subjects. As the personification of Czech sovereignty he is untouched by the emotional conflicts around him. Nevertheless, by the end of the opera, Novák and his librettist provided an increasingly intimate portrait of the monarch, undermining the notion of noble infallibility set up at the beginning. The overall effect is one of correcting history, where the status of a figurehead (and by extension, the nation he represents) can be placed in doubt, then redeemed only by a modern reassessment. Queen Eliška, in opposition to the relatively passive Karel, appears at once as protagonist, antagonist, and catalyst for the drama. As a woman forbidden in the castle, her entrance is an aggressive act that disturbs the status quo, making her solely responsible for the change in her relationship to Karel. As a threat to the sanctity of Karlštejn she represents at the outset a threat to the nation, and in penetrating the castle she reverses the traditional gender roles allotted to active males and passive females—a circumstance that increases her "menace." Of less importance to Novák was the fact that, historically, Eliška Pomořanská (Elisabeth von Pommern) was a German princess; any insinuation during wartime that her Germanness contributed to her intrusiveness would have been likely unacceptable with the Austrian censors. The Italian duke, on the other hand, represents the foreign counterpart to Eliška's feminine threat and provides a considerable obstacle on her path to intimacy with Karel. In the larger context of the opera, the duke is the main antagonist, in that he seeks to inhibit the eventual reconciliation of the royal couple. Whereas Eliška's desire is to be united with her husband in a greater sense of spiritual Czechness, the duke's ultimate hubris is his lack of understanding of what this means. Equally significant for the audience is his political threat, in which he seeks to undermine the position of the Czech Lands in the Holy Roman Empire; such an act implies the negation of the fabled Czech "golden age," and by extension, one of the most important tenets of modern Czech nationhood.

Musically, the opera is constructed using a dense web of motives that represent the various characters, the castle itself, and Prague. Although the opera contains a relatively small number of actual motives, the variety of their presentation, juxtaposition, and combination provides a rich palate of musical material. It is important to note that the vast majority of this activity occurs in the orchestra alone, without the admixture of vocal forces. For patriotic effect Novák also employed two well-known tunes of ancient Czech provenance: *Hospodine pomiluj ny* (a vernacular Agnus Dei setting) and *Saint Wenceslas Chorale*, which appear somewhat gratuitously at the ends of the first and second acts, respectively. As with *Poupě*, Novák's soloists receive mostly nonmelodic, declamatory material that challenges the harmonic basis of the accompaniment through nondiatonic tones. Harmonically, the music of *Karlštejn* explores the region of late-romantic semifunctional tonality, with frequent forays into bitonality, a device that was experiencing a surge in popularity across Europe at this time, as seen variously in works by Szymanowski, Stravinsky, and Bartók. Novák's bitonality is usually a localized phenomenon, relating directly to the juxtaposition of multiple motives, each in its own key. While the weighty leitmotivic texture is ultimately an inheritance from the post-Wagnerian tradition, Novák's opera also betrays the continued influence of Richard Strauss's techniques of melodic and harmonic prolongation, and of compositional devices akin to French impressionism, such as parallel chords, whole-tone scales, and atmospheric orchestration.

In the midst of this rich motivic, polytonal, and largely contrapuntal fabric, it is easy to lose sight of the main thrust of *Karlštejn*: that of a *comic* representation of historical figures. Indeed, in addition to the serious undertones regarding gender and nation that the plot itself suggests, the opera's music stands as a weighty counterpart to *Zvíkovský rarášek*, for which Novák had provided a score of simple textures and easily identifiable melodies, much like what the audience might have expected for a patriotic wartime opera. While *Karlštejn*'s music does include comic scenes, such as the duke's rantings about illicit pleasures (set to pervasive siciliano rhythms) and the extended second-act duet between Alena and Pešek, the opera is predominated by a Wagnerian framework of dense orchestral counterpoint and open-ended scenas. Furthermore, as with *Poupě*, there exists in *Karlštejn* a certain tension between modernist aesthetics and those of comic opera as a genre, complicated here by an overtly nationalist setting: the fact that even Czech audiences, who had much experience with "serious" Smetanian comedies, rejected Novák's opera speaks to the problematic nature of the work.

It is hardly surprising that the motives should be the locus of this musical and dramatic tension, reflecting the characters' interrelationships, as well as imbuing the score with a certain nationalist import. In this respect, the frequent appearance of King Karel's motive (ex. 4.7a, 8)[37] forces many of the other motives into a direct musical opposition: its prominent rising fifths have their complement in the rising fourths in each of the motives of the queen (ex. 4.7b, 14–15), Prague (ex. 4.7c, 36), and Karlštejn itself (ex. 4.7d, 1), with which the opera opens. While the king and his inanimate possessions musically evoke a sense of stately power, with dotted rhythms, narrow, controlled ranges, and a firm sense of meter, the queen alone breaks these boundaries. By adding another rising fourth to her original one, her music takes on a radically different shape (often marked "passionato"): it rises quickly into a higher tessitura, in fluid gestures tied over strong beats. On the whole, Eliška's motive seems to possess greater opportunities for development than Karel's more rigid rhythms will

Example 4.7a. Novák, *Karlštejn*, Karel's motive (8/1–4).

Example 4.7b. Novák, *Karlštejn*, Eliška's motive (14/9–12).

Example 4.7c. Novák, *Karlštejn*, Prague motive (36/6–9).

Example 4.7d. Novák, *Karlštejn*, Karlštejn motive (3/1–3).

allow, and its implied quartal harmony sets it apart from the clear tonic-domi-
nant relationships of the other motives. Given the pervasiveness of these
motives, this system of opposition, both national and gendered, not only helps
characterize the solo roles, but also carries the dramatic action and brings about
the resolution of the opera.

Indeed, the queen's will to enter Karlštejn and be reconciled musically and
dramatically with her husband propels the entire plot. Significantly, the librettist
Fischer placed her entrance at the very beginning of the libretto (rather than
halfway through the first act, as in the original play), so that the audience may
hear her viewpoint much earlier than anyone else's, including the king's. This
viewpoint, however, may have contributed to the opera's lack of success, placing
the entire nationalist statement in a feminine context, which would have been
construed by the wartime Czech public as "weak." Her statements to Alena in the
opening scene provide a moving account of her mental state, in a comparison
between her emotional needs from Karel and the impersonal demands made on
a monarch:

> Just count the days, how long it's been since we've seen each other! How many loving
> words might I have heard since my wedding? . . . The only things that demand care are
> his subjects: today a new city and tomorrow the crown council, now an assembly of elect-
> ors, then a guest from Italy, now taxes, then gifts, then improvements to a bridge, and
> tomorrow, like today and yesterday, the untiring care a thousand times over, now about
> statues and buildings, now about the trim and the painting of Karlštejn castle! [*she ges-
> tures threateningly in the direction of the castle*] (9–12)

In the following arietta, "Ne, Aleno, to nenávist," one of the few relatively
closed segments in the opera and its first moment of climax, the queen expresses
a desire to be reunited with her husband; as the text of the passage indicates, this
anticipated union will happen after her penetration of his secret, private space.[38]
This notion inverts the traditionally gendered binarism of domestic "feminine"
solitude versus the public mobility given to men. The highly sexualized atmosphere of the moment is mirrored in the music, which is the most energetic and
cadentially driven material the queen receives in the opera. Indeed, this excerpt

[How I love you, my Karel, my lord and King!]

Example 4.8. Novák, *Karlštejn*, Eliška's G-major arrival (16/7–10).

witnesses the transformation of her character, from the candid innocence of her motive on the text "only the wistfulness of the young heart," through undulating triplets and a series of surprising key changes, to the moment when she joyfully reveals her intentions once inside the castle. Her G-major arrival on the text, "How I love you, my Karel, my lord and King," is easily an erotic climax, which carries over into a more chromatic afterglow of several measures (ex. 4.8, 16). However, the sheer harmonic brightness of the excerpt, along with the candor of her expression, allays any immediate suspicions of the character as a femme fatale; the arietta thus provides a bias for the audience that they will view the drama from her seemingly sincere vantage point.

The second scene brings the first moment of deception in the opera, when the queen, fearful at the approach of the friendly archbishop Arnošt, hides her identity in the disguise of a monk, provoking an instantly noticeable change of tone in her music. Before Arnošt she seems to lose the composure she held in Alena's presence, facing her first obstacle to entering the castle. The open-ended arioso passage at "Neříkej královno" is prompted by the archbishop's polite refusal of assistance on her behalf. Her response, "Do not say 'Queen,' when my modest wish is not be fulfilled," is accompanied by a Tristanesque rendition of her own motive (ex. 4.9a, 23). Shortly after, the moderate flow of the passage is interrupted by a strikingly static four-measure segment, whose celesta chords give a sense of ironic distance to the words, "A beautiful puppet, dressed as a foreign servant." The dramatic outburst on "Nemožno!" (Impossible!) reveals the intensity of her outrage: it also provides an example of the disunity of the whole scena, which incorporates a shifting density of accompanimental texture and relatively little cadential direction throughout (ex. 4.9b, 24). In comparison with the Straussian brightness of the previous scene's arietta, this arioso has a preponderance of angst-ridden seventh chords that interlock chromatically without much hope of resolution. Interestingly, the cadential closure in D minor/major arrives

[Don't say 'Queen,' when my modest wish is unfulfilled]

Example 4.9a. Novák, *Karlštejn*, Tristanesque rendition of Eliška's motive (23/4–6).

[Impossible! Impossible! I hear that every moment,
for here is a moral barrier and there an inherited custom]

Example 4.9b. Novák, *Karlštejn*, Eliška's dramatic outburst (24/4–9).

only with the offstage horn call announcing the king's approach, and is thus not part of the queen's music per se (26). This scene illuminates an important aspect regarding the queen's relationship to her surroundings: she describes the castle as the only obstacle in her achievement of both a healthy marriage and a sense of native Czechness. This latter point introduces a dimension of foreignness to

[Surround yourself openly with beauty, love, and lovers]

Example 4.10. Novák, *Karlštejn*, The Duke's "tarantella" (152/11–14).

the queen otherwise missing in the text of the libretto: rather, the opera high-lights her quest to become Czech (a welcome sentiment in wartime Prague), thereby diffusing her representation as a threatening foreign woman encroach-ing on native male territory. Thus, her entrance to the castle is on terms that are, for the most part, gender-based instead of national, despite her irreverent jibes at many of the hallowed symbols of Karel's regime (the establishment of Prague's New Town, Charles Bridge, the seat of imperial government, and Karlštejn itself). Musically, however, the tension between the feminine voice and the nation is fur-ther aggravated by the harmonic instability of the passage, which demands reso-lution here more than elsewhere in the opera—and therefore stands a greater chance of alienating the audience.

Dramatically, the main challenge to Czech national sentiment is reserved for the duke, whose character also transgresses along religious and sexual lines in his increasingly personal obsession with hidden women at Karlštejn. If the duke stands for foreignness and blasphemy, the resulting corollary is a rather confus-ing conflation of Czechness and sacredness, a pairing that sits at odds with the largely anticlerical, bourgeois nationalism maintained by the Czechs since the mid-nineteenth century. Furthermore, as a foil for the religious and patriotic Karel, the Italian duke is presented as an irreverent pagan, a strange and some-what ironic attribute in a political representative of the Roman church. It is thus difficult to determine—especially in the context of the wartime Czech audi-ence—precisely which national group provides the opera's focus of xenophobia, or whether foreign vice in general is depicted as a foil for Czech virtue. The duke's motive, described by Poliakova as a tarantella, readily (and rather sim-plistically) identifies him with a foreign quality (ex. 4.10, 152).[39] Indeed, it is the jaunty atmosphere of the duke's music in general that prevents the reading of his character as an extreme threat to either the royal couple or Karlštejn: such flippancy will not start a holy war, despite the implications of his speech. His only moment of musico-dramatic weight is his near-seduction of the queen in Act 3, where the highly charged sexual atmosphere provides the most modernist music in the entire opera (see discussion below).

Compared with the machinations of both the pagan duke and the unhappy queen, King Karel appears as an oasis of calm, serenely content at Karlštejn in his personal, sacred space, away from the pressures of both government and intimacy. Shortly after his arrival on stage in Act 1, Karel delineates the difference in his perceptions of the castle and the outside world:

> I love Prague; but Prague, heart of my Bohemia, belongs to my people, as does the whole of Bohemia. Here [at Karlštejn], however, is the seat of my soul, where everything belongs to me: battlements, chapel, towers, and roofs. Everything you see here is my empire and the work of my spirit, and my heart would not share it with anyone. (36–38)

As a paragon of Czech masculine virtue, Karel has the heavy burden of representing the nation, its people, and the strength of its historical lineage in *Karlštejn*. Like Smetana's Libuše, he must imply his knowledge of the next several hundred years of his people's history. Although not blessed with the gift of prophecy, his words to the duke in the third act carry similar weight:

> And this is my dream, not in one generation and not in one hundred years, but a dream whose completion perhaps my grandchildren's great-grandchildren will have the privilege of seeing: that this land, which you look down upon as if it were an orphans' asylum with deathly cold air, was once a starting point for a new authority of the people's spirit. That my land, from which I want to control nations, was not poverty-stricken and despised, but was like a shining light, like a crowned queen. That this heart, in whose pulsation resounded the beat of the whole continent, hammered with native life and became the artery of the world. (164–67)

Through Karel, the symbol of Czech masculinity becomes one of possession: not only does he rule, but he also owns his surroundings, and his first monologue reads like an itemized list of personal assets at Karlštejn. Without a doubt, Karel's escape to his castle is to a place unambiguously associated with masculinity, as opposed to Bohemia, the "crowned queen," in which he feels somehow less at home. His avoidance of Eliška, a strong woman from the outside world who refuses to be possessed, is an extension of this attitude, in that she threatens to remove his last masculine escape—the castle itself, which can be read as the essence of Czech autonomy.

The music of Karel's first scene does much to further our understanding of Novák's sense of a Czech monarch: the accompaniment, at times contrapuntally dense, revolves around the motives of Prague and Karlštejn, giving the entire passage the flavor of a march. Although the overall shape of this solo segment is similar to that of the queen's arietta, with long crescendos in phrases of rapid tonal juxtapositions, Karel's vocal line, unlike hers, works against the accompaniment

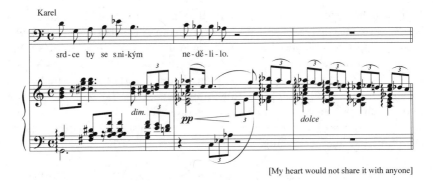

[My heart would not share it with anyone]

Example 4.11. Novák, *Karlštejn*, A-flat major interpolation (38/2–4).

rather than being shaped by it. Where the queen seems fixated on desire, Karel's music only allows for distant fatherly pride, apart from a single moment of child-like tenderness, evoked by a sudden A-flat-major interpolation (ex. 4.11, 38). His joy is therefore rational and cerebral rather than overflowing, directed universally rather than at a specific object of obsession. Within this context, both the queen's illicit presence and the duke's attempted destruction of Karlštejn as a spiritual haven may be seen jointly as a feminization and de-Czechification of the king's national space.

From the outset, the king's refusal to discuss politics with the duke undermines the queen's equation of the castle with the demands of royal duty. Furthermore, Karel's noble, unsulliable character serves to obviate the irony of the duke's assessment of him as the master of a den of iniquity; this mistaken judgment does much to further the dramatic action, in that it turns the queen into living proof of hidden women in the castle. Most of the opera's plot, however, only indirectly involves Karel, whose existence in the first two acts is little more than a "provisional" deus ex machina, signaling the temporary close of action with well-marked, "national" Czech tunes. In keeping with the mode of irony, the climactic scene of the opera falls shortly after the queen discovers Karel's true nature as an adoring (however distant) husband: as such, the characters gradually learn what the audience already knows—that the king is an unimpeachable paragon of Czech virtue, who deals nobly in encounters with both foreigners and women. That this resolution is achieved dramatically through irony, and to the accompaniment of austere, polyphonic music and an angular vocal style, goes against the accepted image of Karel as "Father of the Homeland." Overall, his depiction as a cerebral, distant figurehead makes him significantly less approachable as a symbol of Czech collective identity.

After overhearing a comic dialogue between the servants Alena and Pešek in Act 2, the duke's pursuit of hidden women at Karlštejn gains momentum. It is during his hunt for Alena in the third act that he eventually finds the queen, whom he believes to be the same person; that she is discovered in the king's bed-chamber provides further proof of Karel's fall from grace. This scene, dramatic-ally and musically, is the most sexually charged of the opera, even more so than the subsequent, climactic encounter between the king and queen. Not only is the duke completely convinced of the queen's gender *before* he sees her (in his initial statements offstage), but he fully intends to seduce her as a culmination of his search: his tone is one of mocking, as though belittling her for her failed masculine disguise. The queen, however, simultaneously defends her disguise, her honor, and that of the king:

Duke: It is a beautiful night, full of stars, my golden page. Don't you feel how the summer is scented outside? Don't you hear how the Southern blood resounds through my heart? Wouldn't you like me to carry you away?

Queen: What do you want? What are you asking? What do you dare to do? Traitor!

Duke: Let's stop fighting! A kiss, a hug, and forgiveness! . . .

Queen: (jumps toward him wildly, tearing his sword from its sheath; she breaks it and throws it at his feet) Here is my answer. (141–45)

Precisely in this moment, when the duke's suspicions bubble over into lust, Novák provides a musical setting that is aggressively discordant, where the marked restraint that predominates the rest of the score is swept away in a tor-rent of progressive tonality. The vocal lines are at their most unmelodic in a trad-itional operatic sense, having to accommodate for radical key shifts virtually on every beat. Novák's orchestra momentarily erupts with an intensity equal to the storm scenes in *Bouře*, equating the negative, uncontrollable aspects of human passion with musical modernism (ex. 4.12, 146). Although the duke remains oblivious to the queen's royal status, his attempted seduction provides the seeds

[(My) succulent viper! Irritable, treacherous, brilliant!]

Example 4.12. Novák, *Karlštejn*, The Duke's passionate outburst (146/9–13).

of her eventual recognition. Indeed, the key point of this scene—when Eliška breaks the Duke's sword, itself a bitonal juxtaposition of A-flat major and C minor—not only overturns the power relationship between the two, but necessitates the intervention of the king, and with his entrance the climactic encounter of the opera.

Coming after a scene of intense drama, Karel's appearance restores musical stability to Novák's score, and in a dramatic sense, continues his prevailing repression of emotions that is increasingly in need of change. One of the most interesting and ambiguous aspects about the scene between the king and his disguised wife is the precise moment of recognition, prior to which the audience is presented (for the second time) with a prolonged scene of open flirtation, ostensibly between the king and his page boy. Gradually, it is the latter's resemblance to Eliška, as well as the unexpected strength in an individual of his/her stature, that convinces the king that it is his wife standing before him. The music throughout this scene, far from the stormy intensity of the duke's violent seduction, presents a chain of unresolved phrases with a prolonged Straussian yearning that builds toward this selfsame conclusion. In effect, the climactic moment of recognition, presaged by frequent motivic references, is not the king's, but the queen's, when she realizes he has *already* discovered her identity. As a result, the power of disguise that she had wielded up to this point is stripped away from her, leaving her defenseless and in a position of supplication before her husband. The prolonged demand for harmonic resolution is met only with awkward silence, which does little to alleviate the musical and dramatic tension.

The penultimate scene, arriving as an interruption at such a delicate moment, is perhaps the most complicated of the opera. In a gesture of good faith, Karel facilitates the queen's escape before the reappearance of the duke, who enters presently with the "guilty" Pešek and Alena. For the duke, this revelation represents a victory over the king, proving Karlštejn to be a sacrilegious fraud through his capture of Alena, whom he believes to be the same "page boy" as the Queen, and thus the *only* woman in the castle. Realizing the duke's mistake, Karel has a chance to reassert his own virtue, and arranges his wife's subsequent entrance as a chance encounter: she appears for the first time in royal clothes, apparently having lost her retinue (i.e., Alena) on a hunt that very morning. This gesture, while continuing the subterfuge in place from the beginning of the opera, does so on new terms, with everyone but the duke "in the know": it also subordinates the question of feminine presence beneath that of national and spiritual superiority, redeeming the Czech nation in the face of the duke's accusations. The change of fortunes implants a reversal of power, in that the queen is invited to pronounce judgment on her servant and Pešek. In the spirit of comedy, she orders their banishment from the castle and the royal retinue, provided they *marry* immediately, thereby nullifying the duke's "victory." Curiously, she continues with an evaluative comment toward Alena:

For that which you undertook tonight, you will not escape the retribution you deserve. The strictest punishment awaits every woman who dares to bring to this castle her feminine distrust, her feminine weakness, and her feminine passion. . . . Woman is the only genuinely guilty one. (209–10)

The moralizing tone of this statement is at first shocking, until it is read with an eye toward the irony with which Alena has been "dismissed": obviously, the queen is referring to her own daring, distrust, weakness, and passion, taking the blame for the entire deception toward her husband. Indeed, the queen implicates herself during her pronouncement of guilt, albeit in music alone (ex. 4.13a, 210): alongside her words "Woman is the only genuinely guilty one," the audience hears her motive, beginning in a low register. By "strictest punishment," we may infer that the queen hopes for a result similar to her maid's—to be reconciled with her beloved, and as such to justify her passionate course of action. The remark, however, remains disconcerting, given that Eliška's viewpoint has been foregrounded to such an extent in the opera. Similarly, her tortured scream on the word "passion," accompanied in the full orchestra by a chromatic flourish that forms a recurring motive, aligns her statement with the negative symbolism of modernism as an uncontrolled, dark force (ex 4.13b, 209). Just what is fraudulent pretense and what is sincere confession is unclear at this point, necessitating further resolution before the opera's conclusion.

The final scene of the opera is striking in that it is the only time the royal couple converses openly with each other, with all pretenses lifted. It is a resolution that also offers a denouement, carried out both dramatically and musically. The orchestra captures the effect of rapprochement succinctly, turning from a chromatically harmonized recurrence of the queen's motive, reminiscent of her Tristanesque first-act arioso, to a simultaneous presentation of both Karel's and Eliška's motives in C major (ex. 4.14a, 212). In a low tessitura, the queen repeats her plea for forgiveness, proceeding to relinquish all demands for admission to her husband's castle, as though nothing has been gained from her efforts; that she does this to the fanfares of the Karlštejn theme only serves to underscore her surrender. In fact, the entire passage of music is lifted from Karel's first-act monologue, so that she declares the castle's "rightful" ownership to the accompaniment of her husband's music. The recurrence of the sudden A-flat-major interpolation, however, is now an occasion for the king to gaze back out into the world (ex. 4.14b, 214); he takes over the remainder of his music until the cadence, which is now interrupted by yet another passage of music quoted from earlier in the opera. The text of this second crucial interruption reveals Karel's decision to lift his ban at Karlštejn, and to leave the castle to start a new life with his bride. Most important, he sings these words, "Take me with you," to the accompaniment from *her* first-act arietta, prolonging the cadential motion with the same pent-up desire for resolution (ex. 4.14c, 216). The G-major cadence, where Eliška had earlier predicted the moment of calling her husband back to a

Example 4.13a. Novák, *Karlštejn*, Eliška's pronouncement of guilt (210/11–13).

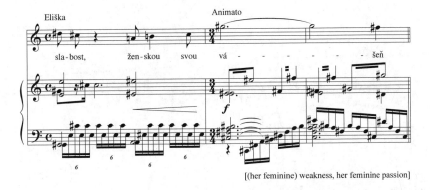

Example 4.13b. Novák, *Karlštejn*, chromatic flourish (209/10–12).

life of youth and love, arrives with Karel's words, "With you I want to go toward a new life," sung to *her motive.* Evidently, his wife's actions have brought him to the realization that a separate, masculine, national space is not worth the price of alienating his beloved. Eliška has exerted a power, not in terms of controlling her husband, but to the effect of changing his opinions about love and human relationships. In the final scene we witness, in both text and music, a mutual implosion of wills: the king's authoritative presence has caused the queen's capitulation, but it is she who has instigated a change in Karel, the "Father of the Homeland," and by extension a change in the audience's perception of him as a stable, historical figure—an alteration that had far broader, if unsettling, implications in wartime Prague.

Karlštejn's Reception and the End of a Modernist Leader

Despite Novák's high hopes for the acceptance of *Karlštejn* into the canon of "national" Czech operas, its critical reception was sealed by the turbulence of the

Example 4.14a. Novák, *Karlštejn*, opening gestures of final scene (212/5–13).

[Look, what a godly morning!]

Example 4.14b. Novák, *Karlštejn*, A-flat major interpolation in final scene (214/7–9).

[With you I want to go towards a new life]

Example 4.14c. Novák, *Karlštejn*, appearance of Eliška's G-major music in final scene (216/4–8).

composer's prolonged dispute with Nejedlý, as well as by its modernist and protofeminist interpretations of Czech history. Premiered at the beginning of the National Theater season on November 18, 1916, Novák's opera was the first work in the history of the theater to replace Smetana's ceremonial opera *Libuše* as the work to inaugurate the season. The nationalistic fervor in Prague during wartime was such that Smetana's music had achieved the cultlike status for which its supporters had so long agitated. Similarly, Nejedlý's Hudební klub found its greatest following during these years, the audience being attracted by the lecturers' calls for a "modern" voice in Czech music that could respond to both the "national" legacy of Smetana and the responsibility of leading "the people" toward the future of culture. Indeed, the nationalist-oriented Smetana Exhibition of 1917 would take place only months later, solidifying these concepts in the public imagination (see chapter 3). It was in this difficult climate, at a theater whose position was increasingly embattled by questions as to its patriotic stance, that Novák attempted to gain popularity with a modern comic opera about historical figures. It did not help *Karlštejn*'s chances that its composer had followed neither of Smetana's "national" models—comic folk tale and historical tragedy—opting instead for an introspective, almost intellectual comedy that cast doubt on commonly held perceptions of Karel IV, Eliška, the nation, and the roles of men and women in it.

At the premiere itself, a crowd of nationalist-minded students began chanting "My chceme Libuši!" (We want *Libuše*) when Kovařovic appeared at the conductor's podium; the opera's performance was able to go forward only after the arrival of the police and restoration of decorum. The next morning the students' leader, the promising young composer (and former Novák student) Jaroslav Jeremiáš, denounced Novák's opera in a feuilleton; his claim was that nothing of *Karlštejn* could be considered Czech, except the name.[40] Within a month after the premiere, two scathing articles by Nejedlý appeared in *Smetana-Hudební list.* Nejedlý concluded that Novák, by not following the "national" paradigms set out by Smetana's operas, had shirked his responsibility of portraying the greatness of Czech historical figures and their innately "popular" spirit. Faulting the librettist Fischer for cramming Vrchlický's original play with incomprehensible "symbols" that confused both the sense of comedy and the clarity of the characters' depiction, Nejedlý also felt that Novák was incapable as a composer of handling such delicate subject matter.[41] Citing *Svatební košile* and *Zvíkovský rarášek* as examples, the critic rehashed his views on what he felt was Novák's sole compositional ability: merely to describe his subject in a naturalistic way, without approaching an understanding of the psychological depth of the drama.[42] Nejedlý summarized the composer's creative method as "absolutely foreign and inaccessible," no doubt referring to the prevailing Straussian tendencies in the score, as well as the nontraditional treatment of the nationalist subject matter. Given a subject with as many serious implications as *Karlštejn*, this textual and musical ambiguity became morally questionable for Nejedlý, in that it did not provide a socially responsible model for the Czech people. The use of the castle as the setting for such a work Nejedlý found "disorienting," depicted in a manner closer to a marketplace than an exalted royal residence. More important, the opera's representation of Karel IV, Father of the Homeland, was not "royal" enough, nor was it even particularly Czech: thus on two counts the king had become alienated from the spirit of the people. Compared to the elevated portrayal of King Vladislav in Smetana's *Dalibor*, Novák's Karel was pretentious and boring, especially in his appearances during the quoted hymns (thereby negating the effect of the overtly patriotic music). Indeed, for Nejedlý, the only facet in which Novák succeeded in part was his portrayal of Queen Eliška, whose feminine eroticism was captured by the largely descriptive, "undramatic" nature of the composer's music. Still, her music "endangers our sympathy for Eliška as a queen," who exhibits the "passionate nature of the hero-ines from the latest French comedies."[43] On the national front, Nejedlý consid-ered it demeaning that the queen should be made to deride such symbols of Czechness as Karel and Karlštejn; throughout his essay, it is clear that the critic failed to see her as any sort of protagonist whatsoever. Nejedlý's implication is that the erotic element of Novák's music was both too foreign and too feminine to play any role in Czech identity; this formulation reflects a paradigm of the "masculine nation" that could be satisfied musically only by Smetana. When Novák applied his musical eroticism to a dramatically ambiguous use of "national" symbols, the result was fraudulent, insulting, and morally reprehensible:

> Novák is a spirit [that is] artistically purely ironic, or as we could just as well say, artistically purely egoistical, which never escapes itself. . . . Therefore no artistically altruistic tone ever echoes in his work, either national or universal, nor has Novák ever felt any continu-ity with the larger development of national art; he only ever applies his artistic tastes with-out regard for any sort of tradition of national art. His cold, yes, negative relation to Smetana's art certainly shows this most objectively.[44]

Although Nejedlý made no direct reference to the "Dvořák Affair" in his review of *Karlštejn*, his method of analysis, his conception of drama and music in opera, and the growing sense of a moral obligation to the Czech people all link this skir-mish to the larger debate. All the more interesting in this context, then, is Vycpálek's review of *Karlštejn* in the literary journal *Lumír*: while the young com-poser and former Novák student initially thanked his teacher for providing a "gift, the like of which our nation does not often receive," Vycpálek went on to say that the orchestral primacy of *Karlštejn*'s music was "incorrect."[45] As a com-poser who had already worked substantially with vocal music, Vycpálek felt that Novák's singers were working "against the orchestra," and that "Novák sooner wants to characterize using the orchestra rather than the voice, and that the bearer of the drama is, for him, first the orchestra and only in second place the people on stage."[46] In this remark we hear the young composer's discomfort with the modernist separation of the vocal line from its intensely contrapuntal surroundings, a particularly Czech technique to which he himself would contribute in later years. Foremost for Vycpálek, his teacher had failed to provide operatic archetypes in his music, in the manner that Gluck, Mozart, Wagner, "and, most convincingly of all, our Smetana" had. These archetypes would not only be the bearers of the dramatic action, but would also provide (in the case of Smetana) a mirror for the Czech people:

> What does the immense importance of Smetana consist of in our musical art, or even in our life as a whole? That once and for all, for eternal time and in a truly perfect manner, Smetana provided in musical speech the archetypes of the Czech man, be it countryman or landowner or noble. It is not the plot material of Smetana's operas that moves us, but the archetypes who live, rejoice, and suffer in the bounds of those plots. For: we are they.[47]

The nationalist flavor of Vycpálek's message, the adherence to Smetana, and above all the abandonment of his earlier unquestioned loyalty to Novák (which had included the defense of the orchestrated *Pan*) all point to a substantial change in both his attitude and the dimensions of the larger debate. Indeed, it is more than likely that the efforts of the Hudební klub were having an effect on the general cultural sphere in wartime Prague, in that their nationalist, pro-Smetana message had been adopted even by one of the UB's staunchest supporters. Such a trend, as we have seen in chapter 3, would bear fruit in the 1917 Smetana Exhibition. Vycpálek's expressed desire for the normalization of archetypes also points to a general resistance toward modern readings of history, a statement that applies as equally to the sexually subversive aspects of the drama as to the modernist tendency of Novák's music. Although *Karlštejn* is, to quote Karel, predominantly a nationalist opera about the "new authority of the people's spirit," its comic irony and all-too-human passions did not sit well with the reinforcement of tradition needed by Czech collective identity in 1916. In the king's abandonment of his castle, the Czechs saw modern art abandoning its people.

The years of the First World War, however, were to be merely a stopgap before the true flood of modernism in all its variegated and cosmopolitan forms. As Europe was fast approaching the dawn of a new era, its musical community began a process of fragmentation into a variety of aesthetic groups: no less so in Prague, where the stranglehold of the UB and Conservatory was breaking down among the newly emerging younger generation, whose aesthetic attitudes did not necessarily conform to those of past leaders. Novák, once hailed as the candidate to bring Czech culture into musical modernity, was beginning to lose his supremacy on the concert and operatic stage, in no small part because of his inability to form an expressive bond with Prague audiences. Such was the fate of early modernists, however, whose music neither conformed to past traditions nor formed a circle of avant-garde enthusiasts. After 1918, the indecision of the age would manifest itself in a host of new problems, where the alienation of the audience left critics and composers to bemoan the future of art.

Chapter Five

The Pathology of the New Society

Debates in the Early Years of the First Republic (1918–24)

On October 28, 1918, a monumental change took place that altered the course of Czech society for the succeeding two decades: an assembly of figures from Czech political life gathered and issued a proclamation of independence, thereby ending 298 years of Austrian political and cultural domination. A new Republic was born that included not only a union of Czechs and Slovaks (for the first time in their history, creating borders that had never before existed), but also new minority populations of German, Hungarian, Polish, and Rusyn citizens, with which the new government and society had to contend. Almost overnight, attitudes changed in Prague's Czech-speaking musical community regarding cultural interaction, from perceived isolation to openness, from marginalization to domination, while for the long-standing German community these changes happened exactly in reverse, occasionally with disturbing and violent consequences. Although for the Czechs the era started with an overwhelming sense of optimism, by the mid-1920s this exuberance had sharply abated, prompted largely by fears of the modern, cosmopolitan world they had rushed to embrace. Conversely, for the German-Bohemians, the initial anguish of dispossession gave way gradually to a new, if limited, cooperative spirit, particularly with other German cultural centers.

Musically the new era paralleled these social developments, in that a new openness to modernism and foreign influences in 1918 was soon replaced by an anxiety over the potential loss of Czech national difference and tradition. Most other issues affecting the arts, such as the desire to reform cultural institutions and the question of individual and collective artistic expression, were connected to the central dichotomy of cosmopolitanism versus isolation. Despite the recurring waves of extreme insularity that swept the community, these debates in fact reveal the proximity of the Prague sphere to other musical centers throughout

Europe, where similar issues were in active discourse at the time. Significantly, critics in Prague often used the term "pathology" to describe the vast changes under way in Czech society, denoting a fear that the excitement induced by sudden freedom would wreak havoc if unchecked by traditional moral values.[1] In this way, the citizens of the new Czechoslovak Republic came to fear the modern world and each other for their participation in it. In the early days of independence, the entire Czech musical community endured a terrifying purge of its "Germanic" elements, including not only the German-Bohemians from cultural institutions but also all those Czechs whose perceived allegiance to the new state was anything but unequivocal. In the 1920s, many also viewed the modernist reorientation of the National Theater as a dangerous threat to national identity. The acceptance or rejection of foreign artistic influences acquired central importance with the 1924 festival of the International Society for Contemporary Music (ISCM), when many of these anxieties came to the fore. And as chapter 6 will show, these tendencies affected the reception of local composition as well: while Suk's tone poem *Zrání* was celebrated for its depiction of the maturing Czech nation, modernist operas such as Zich's *Vina* (Guilt) and Ostrčil's *Legenda z Erinu* (Legend of Erin) fell short of acceptance by a critical community suddenly having to redefine itself.

In comparison with the political and social turmoil in Germany, which met the dawn of the new era with months of revolutionary violence and bloodshed, such occurrences were kept to a minimum in Czechoslovakia. Indeed, until the finalization of the national borders at the Versailles conference in 1919, German-Bohemians and Czechs played a waiting game that concentrated more on the issue of German participation in the new Czech parliament than a belated display of force. Czech society, meanwhile, sought to fulfill the consequences of self-determination and rabid wartime nationalism with a purge of all those who did not meet the ideological standards of the Republic from its social and cultural life. As such, any cultural institutions that had retained vestiges of "utraquist" Czech-German collaboration were quickly divided along linguistic lines, and many prominent individuals, notably Suk and Nedbal, endured intense public scrutiny, being suspected of traitorous activity during the previous regime.[2] This ill feeling in the musical community reached a low point with the aggressive takeover of the Deutsches Landestheater in 1920 by a Czech mob who felt the ownership of Prague's oldest theater (and its subsequent annexation to the National Theater) was their unquestionable national right.

It is one of the greatest paradoxes that such a time of intercultural hatred should occur simultaneously with a sudden desire for all things foreign across the arts in the Czech community. As this chapter traces, for musicians, this sudden rush of cosmopolitan aesthetics was inseparable from a thirst for European modernism, as though only with independence could composers and critics finally catch up to the cosmopolitan world. Given that a certain "progressiveness" was always held to be part of the aesthetic of the Cultural Revival, Czechs initially felt cosmopolitanism to be a fulfillment of their national character. Many key figures embraced French culture with the rhetoric of long-lost brother-hood (in part as an extension of anti-German sentiments); composers looked with interest upon developments in impressionism and early neoclassicism as well. Once the first contact with the new influences had been made, however, the shock of cultural differences proved too much for most, particularly those worried about the maintenance of Czech musical traditions amid the new moder-nism. Because pre-1918 Czech modernism was generally felt to be grounded in equally "modern" traditions, many feared that new musical developments from abroad would threaten the Czechs' musical identity and hard-earned independ-ence—that both tradition and local modernist achievement would be nullified by an outside threat. Those influences at one time felt to be a necessary rejuve-nation of local traditions were now seen as "pathological." As a result, within a few short years, Czech modernists retreated to a conservative aesthetic position with the claim that their traditions held a greater degree of moral authority, and as such, lay closer to the essence of modernism itself. Such an isolationist tactic, however, incurred largely by a generation whose careers had been sidetracked by the war, only served to hinder (if not prevent) the development of a true Czech avant-garde movement until the rise of a new generation in the late 1920s. Within this context, the debates regarding the individual artist's repre-sentation of collective identity still raged, now exacerbated by the problem of musical leadership in the era of modernism.

The New State and Its Cultural Goals

Nine months before Czechoslovak independence, Vladimír Helfert published the essay *Naše hudba a český stát* (Our Music and the Czech State), which took stock of Czech musical life in his generation, concentrating on its status during the war. Instead of lamenting the cultural oppression of the Habsburgs or the depletion of resources during wartime (as many such discussions were quick to do), Helfert criticized Czech cultural institutions for being too German, and therefore "un-Czech":

> The development of our music today aims toward complete autonomy. And our musi-cal life should be conscious of this situation. Unfortunately, so far, it is not. I ask: do our musical conditions even remotely respond to the high state of our musical production? Were they [i.e., musical conditions] conducted so that our music's autonomy could come to full application? In other words: were our musical conditions really Czech musical conditions? The answer is very sad.[3]

Helfert went on to criticize the main institutions of Czech musical life for ignor-ing a substantial portion of current compositional activity, creating an "unintelli-gible and unnatural dualism" within "musical culture."[4] Particularly to blame were the National Theater and the Czech Philharmonic, which had not lived up to the "Smetanian ideal" in which they supposedly had been founded, and the dangerously collaborationist Prague Conservatory. By ignoring the younger generation of Czech composers (as well as the music of Smetana himself) in favor of Wagner, Verdi, Puccini, and Nedbal,[5] the administrations of these institutions demonstrated that they were only interested in the economic success of culture as a capitalistic venture. Citing National Theater director Kovařovic's rejection of three recent Czech operas as a willful neglect of national duty, Helfert called for the overthrow of the present "closed oligarchic society that carries out its business out of public reach," and the subsequent democratization of the National Theater administration.[6] The National Theater could be truly *national* only under state control, administered by a body of artists paid by the state: such a system would restore the necessary relationship to art and thereby destroy the "unnatural dualism" in Czech culture. Helfert called for similar changes to the Czech Philharmonic, at that time directed by Vilém Zemánek (according to Helfert, "a *German* who has no relation to Czech works whatsoever");[7] by replacing Zemánek with L. V. Čelanský on the basis of his excellent performances of *Má vlast*, "we would once again have a really *Czech* Philharmonic—not only in name, but also in artistic direction and in full spirit."[8] Of much greater "national shame and disgrace" was the "utraquist" administration of the Prague Conservatory, led by the Bohemian noble (and salon-music composer) Jindřich Kàan z Albestů. For Helfert, the bureaucratic regime at the Conservatory not only endangered what he considered to be an obligatory educational component of musical culture, but also hindered the necessary drive toward a "living, new, progressive art."[9] Helfert tied this Nejedlian axiom of socially mandated modernism to the language question at the Conservatory:

> Our Conservatory cannot keep step with contemporary art. A second, and for us even more serious, defect is that the Prague Conservatory is an *un-Czech* cultural institution. The linguistic utraquism is an insult to our art in this day and age. Let's just ask ourselves, what share do the Germans have in our musical culture? It is therefore incomprehensible that the sole Conservatory in Bohemia is Czech-German. Or better said, *German-Czech*.[10]

In a curious twist of logic prefiguring many events of the early First Republic, Helfert assumed that the democratization of the Conservatory (again, to be placed under state control) was equivalent to its de-Germanification, implying that Czechoslovak democracy applied to Czechs alone. The general feeling throughout Czech society that Austrian bureaucracy had long hindered their democratization fueled this opinion.

Helfert now turned toward the future of Czech composition, calling for a rejection of the prevailing romantic individualism among composers. "Let go of your egoism [and] realize that you are members of a national cultural whole, whose blossoming must lie in your hearts!" commanded the critic, with the certainty that the "Smetanian" mission of social responsibility, humility, and self-sacrifice would benefit art, culture, and the nation.[11] For Helfert, this trinity of cultural ethics also needed to spread to music criticism, whose partisan antagonism he (with unwitting irony) deemed unhealthy. The antidote to this situation was the messianic "artist-composer," who, in the footsteps of Smetana, would take up the leadership of musical factions and continue the fundamental purity of Czech music: it was the duty of music criticism, then, to "prepare the soil" for this new generation and its leader. Written prior to independence, Helfert's text simply presented a utopian version of the prewar existence to which he had been accustomed. Prefiguring the future course of Czech music criticism in the early 1920s, his imagination excluded the possibility of influences from the world beyond the Czech Lands and any alternative modernisms it might offer, resulting in a vision of cultural (albeit democratic) isolation.

Otakar Nebuška, in his article "Česká hudba a česká samostatnost" (Czech Music and Czech Independence) from the July 1918 issue of *Hudební revue*, sought to counter Helfert's arguments. The Artists' Union (UB)-based critic felt that Helfert's vision of change was hampered by inconsistency, disproportionality, short-term thinking, and a desire for ideological, as opposed to concrete, solutions.[12] Although he agreed with the idea of greater artistic involvement in Prague's cultural institutions, he also emphasized the necessity of being conscious of the outside world and of foreign (i.e., West European) music, "since a poorly understood and executed self-sufficiency would result for us in self-intoxication and finally suicide."[13] Finally, Nebuška wrote openly about Helfert's rather misplaced diatribe against the factionalization of the critics—a situation to which Helfert himself had contributed a significant part over the previous seven years. As a result, Helfert's use of Smetana's name had been to the detriment, rather than the betterment, of Czech musical society. Nebuška concluded: "Let us leave aside [the question of] whether Smetanas live among us today, for the future will decide this. . . . Thus, let the only leader of factions be the *idea* of hard work, honesty, and impartiality—neither for nor against—love of truth in art and life, and the desire for individuation and artistic creative strength."[14]

The differences in opinion between Helfert and Nebuška reveal more than the usual bias toward individual artistic figures such as Smetana or institutions like the National Theater. The expressions of each were based on a use of political language that demonstrates a schism in their respective cultural viewpoints. For Helfert, the leader of a future, "healthy" Czech music (potentially Foerster, as he at one point wistfully imagined) was a composer who denied his individuality, and yet through his personal work performed a lasting, if only conceptual, service to the Czech people. Presumably, this lifework would serve as a model for other Czech composers to follow, evoking a utopian ideal of nonpartisan brotherhood, anonymous in its unanimous acceptance of the leader's view of Czech art and modernity. Nebuška's view, on the other hand, stood radically apart from

Helfert's messianic vision: in no way implying a single cultural leader, his equally utopian future allowed for the contribution of artists as idealized individuals, living up to their fullest potential without submitting to any other artistic rule than "the idea of hard work, honesty . . . and the desire for individuation." While each of these viewpoints would evolve throughout the interwar period, it is possible to trace in them the main elements of anxiety toward individualism in art and the threat of foreign influences in the writings of subsequent critics and composers.

Both critics' demands for the future hinged on large-scale schemes of government intervention in the arts. Over the course of the first few years of the First Republic, many of the aforementioned ideas came to pass, particularly with regard to music institutions, by means of MŠANO, the newly formed Ministry of Education and National Culture. MŠANO's secretary Jan Branberger (previously involved in the Knittl Affair against Nejedlý) proposed a five-point restructuring of government involvement in Czech musical life, including financial support for the Czech Philharmonic, the creation of a Music Chamber to regulate performance standards, the reform and nationalization of the Prague Conservatory, and the development of music education in society at large via the musicology program at Charles University.[15] It is noteworthy that in Branberger's plan, most of Helfert's and Nebuška's suggestions were taken into consideration, with the prominent exception of the National Theater, whose administration was retained by the private Společnost Národního divadla (National Theater Company), a group originally backed by the right-of-center Young Czech party. The Společnost had been in power since ousting the Old-Czech-based Družstvo Národního divadla in 1900, ushering in an era under the general direction of the conservative Gustav Schmoranz and the musical direction of Karel Kovařovic, whose problematic leadership was discussed in chapter 3. In the absence of a governmental takeover, Schmoranz and Kovařovic remained in power as Czech musical life began its transition to democratization.

With regard to all of Prague's musical institutions, however, one significant change took place that reflected the strong influence of Nejedlian criticism: immediately after the dawn of the new era, artistic advisory boards were introduced into several administrations. The most significant body of artistic advisors belonged to MŠANO, itself a concatenation of wildly divergent cultural and political allegiances: in the initial setup, Nejedlý and his student Doležil were pitted against the likes of Janáček and Conservatory/UB associates Šourek, Štěpán, and the conductor Talich. Within the first few years of the Republic, this council grew to include Novák, Ostrčil, Kovařovic, and Křička: Novák and Ostrčil were chosen as president and vice president, respectively, quite possibly with an eye to preserving the peace between the still-rampant ideological factions.[16] Similarly, at the Conservatory, a mere thirty-four days after Czech independence, an advisory committee was set up with regard to nationalization; meanwhile, Novák took over the administration (in place of the "utraquist" Kàan z Albestů), and was chosen as the first rector the following year. The main advisory board in this case included Janáček and Foerster—the former as a recognition of the composer's new popularity in Prague, the latter as a possible appeasement to the Nejedlý circle. The lack of German-Bohemian names on the roster is more than noteworthy, for the law that nationalized the Conservatory was simultaneously responsible for its de-Germanification, establishing a separate institution, the Deutsche Akademie für Musik und darstellende Kunst, under the directorship of Alexander Zemlinsky and privately operated with financial assistance from the state. Within the first year of the new Republic, the Společnost Národního divadla also capitulated to public demand, and was given over to the control of the Province of Bohemia: while Kovařovic and Schmoranz retained their positions of authority, a new artistic advisory board was incorporated, with Novák and Foerster as the two musical contributors.[17] While it is difficult to determine the influence of any of these figures in their newly appointed administrative or advisory positions (with the exception of the Conservatory, whose leadership had always been at least partly musical), the sheer presence of artists from multiple perspectives in the divided ideological climate of Czech music making is significant. For the cultural life of the early First Republic, the road to the democratization of art first necessitated the creation of an oligarchy of artists, grouped under the facade of cooperation—although, as we shall see, this spirit in no way carried over to other facets of musical interaction, which deteriorated into new and even more complex versions of previous ideological factions.

The demand for cultural change voiced before the end of the war by Helfert and Nebuška was continued in a similar tone after independence by various critics, including Nejedlý. The important difference, however, was that the new society had already come into being, and what was once merely critical posturing now took on the appearance of legislating cultural Czechness. In the first postindependence issue of *Smetana-Hudební list*, Nejedlý could not pass up the opportunity to expound his beliefs about the direction of Czech music in the new Republic, revealing a degree of nationalist fervor that carried over from wartime and the 1917 Smetana Exhibition. Under the exclamatory title "Freedom!" the critic rejoiced that the long-awaited day had arrived when Smetana's predictions could be realized: "Did anyone worry about the future of the nation when they perceived the joyful tones of *The Bartered Bride, Libuše*'s uplifting prophecy, or the triumphal, victorious march of *Blaník?* . . . Wasn't Czech independence already prepared in *Má vlast?* . . . We cannot therefore enter the new era with more dignity than to march under Smetana's leadership."[18] For the moment, Nejedlý's rhetoric was surprisingly inclusional, in that he optimistically envisioned, like Helfert, the free and willing participation of all "Czech" artists according to a plan of moral and socially responsible cultural achievement. Nevertheless, even in this celebratory mood, Nejedlý excluded those who did not fit into this plan: under the guise of attacking utraquism, Germanness, or noble status (equated with musical dilettantism), the critic could easily eject certain undesirable individuals from his concept of the Czech nation. In late 1918, Nejedlý's use of these terms to define "Czechness" negatively not only went unquestioned, but was openly accepted as true by a growing number of supporters. On the positive side, the critic restated his tried and tested views on the social responsibility of the artist toward the nation, "so that our culture retains its *lidový* (i.e., folk-like) character, which is the best sign of its internal health and strength."[19] In the new international artistic community, this internally healthy, *lidový* quality would garner more respect for Czech culture. In the absence of a "foreign" regime whose cultural ideology obstructed his own, Nejedlý would have the chance to test his (and Hostinský's) theories about the promulgation of art in a democratic society. Nejedlý and like-minded ideologues would have many struggles in the years ahead, trying to reconcile his assumptions of an "internally healthy" society, created in the image of Smetana and springing up alongside Czech political freedom, with the growing multiplicity of cultural directions. One thing particularly galling for Nejedlý was that his vaguely defined component of modernism, integral to his vision of Czechness, was not as easily accepted. When European modernism arrived for Czech culture in 1918, the new stimulus challenged the joyous idealism of the Prague critics, who had taken Nejedlý's construct of Czech modernism at face value. The resulting tension—between their eagerness toward the new cosmopolitanism and the inevitable disappointment guaranteed by traditionalist aesthetics—would define the new era for the first several years.

Listy Hudební matice and the Issue of Modernism

The discourse on the "direction" of Czech music is one that occupied critics and composers alike in the early years of the Republic, almost to the point of obsession. It is through these debates, concerned in part with international as well as domestic music making, that we can observe attempts by the musical community in Prague to redefine itself amid the onslaught of new stimuli. Although the factionalization of the critical spectrum and the details of the debate grew ever more complicated, it is possible to see a clear trend in Czech music criticism, from the optimism of 1919, through the rhetoric of "crisis" after 1921, to the conscious rejection of foreign influences around 1924.

Perhaps the clearest indicator of the postwar attitude toward international modernism in Prague was the stance that the critics of *Hudební revue* took toward French music and culture. Indeed, its second postwar volume inaugurated this trend with Václav Štěpán's article on the French pianist Blanche Selva, whom he virtually recruited over the next two years to help forge a link between French and Czech musical cultures.[20] Introduced to Czech piano music through the work of Suk, Novák, and Štěpán himself, she came to Prague in 1919 with a Conservatory-biased view of the larger musical community: the sudden and largely superficial nature of the cultural encounter gave rise to much rhetoric about the intrinsic interrelatedness of the musical spirit of the two countries.[21] The incident with Selva paralleled other, similar attempts to "reunite" the French and Czechs (as if some sort of "brotherhood" had previously existed), including performances of Roussel's music by the Czech Philharmonic, and, in the literary world, a fascination with Cocteau and Apollinaire. It comes as no surprise that anti-German slogans were not far behind in such an atmosphere: the orientation toward France was a conscious avoidance of all things German that would continue throughout the years of the First Republic. Štěpán himself promoted his liaison to Selva as a tremendous opportunity to promulgate Czech music abroad, despite the project's obviously limited scope. Nevertheless, the Štěpán-Selva vignette demonstrates the optimistic outlook among many Czech cultural figures to "open the windows wide" (*okna dokořán*) to new influences, particularly those of Western Europe. The latent nationalism embedded in the supposed kinship with French culture would, in subsequent years, be revealed more obviously as the Czech critical body continued its contact with the rest of Europe, although not always with positive results.

Concurrently with the above phenomenon, Nejedlý continued to develop his own vision of the future of Czech music, now shaped by the challenges of the new era. In "Into the Tenth Year," from the January 1920 issue of *Smetana-Hudební list*, the author made a clear separation between Czech culture of the war years and that of the present regime, in terms of ethics, aesthetics, and ideology.[22] In the new era, "we want to go after our goal in an uncompromising, direct manner: to help art to a true victory, without patronage, against all those who pursue any sort of inartistic agenda."[23] Beside the divisions along temporal and artistic lines, the critic emphasized an economic one: he warned against the demoralizing effect of money on art, which could thrive only in a situation where the "clean artist" could create "clean art."[24] Similar themes were carried over into Nejedlý's opening essay for the following year, "On a New Path," which dismissed the past decades' political intrigues in favor of a new society, where younger composers could feel the winds of change while still acknowledging their roots in the moral laws of art.[25] Nejedlý's increasingly anticapitalist rhetoric reflected his newfound interest in the Czechoslovak communist party (KSČ) which attained legal status in 1921. To underscore his protosocialist stance, Nejedlý declared that "the *individual*, be it in this or another of the arts, must be far more *modest*. . . . Today we must demand from them more modesty, more sacrifice to the whole."[26] The idea of collectivism in art had surfaced already in the debate over the reformation of cultural institutions prompted by Helfert and others even before the end of the war, and was largely an outcome of discussions within the Nejedlý circle formulated over a longer period. In the larger social context, this denial of subjectivity for the common good was ultimately the legacy of the Cultural Revival, now brought into the modern democratic era.

While Nejedlý's position easily synchronized with his earlier repudiation of the "subjectivism" of the music of Novák, Suk, and others, the specificity of the artist's task ("sacrifice") was new. This ideology surfaced in tandem with similar artistic trends abroad, particularly the German Neue Sachlichkeit and Busoni's Junge Klassizität, both of which entailed a decreased emphasis on the individual artist as creator, objectivity of expression, and accessibility to wider, democratic audiences.[27] The conspicuous absence of specific composers' names in Nejedlý's criticism, including those of his young protégés (such as Jirák), implies a philosophy of complete anonymity in an artistic collective. It was at the apparent prompting of these protégés that Nejedlý published "To the Young" the following November, in which he further elaborated on the ideal of artistic modesty and sacrifice, now in the context of the perceived aesthetic crisis that had beset the musical world.[28] The crisis for Nejedlý was as much a product of the previous generation's individualism as it was of the subsequent postwar break with the past, an event that occurred before any future direction had been decided. Art in the modern era was no longer happy and healthy, two factors that the critic demanded of truly modern music: a budding advocate of what would come to be known as socialist realism, Nejedlý declared that a healthy artistic modesty was both *lidský* (human) and *lidový* (of the people), and that a combination of these elements separated modernists from reactionaries, even within generations.

In several articles written around this time, Nejedlý began to formulate his concepts of "temporal" and "atemporal" modernism. Temporal modernism was that which was merely current and/or fashionable, whereas the immanently or atemporally modern carried traces of the modernist (i.e., progressive) aesthetic of past generations, and therefore lay closer to the essence of modernism in its embrace of tradition. To this end, in "To the Young" he divided composers into those "young by age" and those whose youth was a source of energy and moral truth. Although the truly modern artist needed to be aware of the changes in his society, his music could not afford to bow to fashion, which was dependent upon the vagaries of bourgeois taste. Such terms were derived ultimately from Hostinský, for whom the work must exhibit *důslednost*, not *náladovost* (see discussion in chapter 2). As he described in a contemporary article, Nejedlý perceived the epitome of temporal modernism in the Spolek pro moderní hudbu (Society for Modern Music), founded in 1921 on Novák's incentive to provide a performance venue for the latest trends in international modernism, such as atonality and the early neoclassicist work of Les Six.[29] Nejedlý's opposition to the new music group was likely founded on his decade-long quarrel with Novák and a certain jealousy that such a "reactionary" figure (now director of the Conservatory, no less!) could hold any power over modern music in Prague. Nevertheless, his remarks reflect the growing tension that the city's musical community felt over the flood of outside influences after 1918. Facetiously labeling Novák's group "The Society for Modish Music," Nejedlý at once criticized its temporal modernism as well as those composers who had denied their youth to follow such an ill-advised route: implicit in all of this was the critic's dismay over a perceived rejection of Smetana, whose supposed atemporal modernism and youth were sufficient for the continuation of moral traditions in the new era. Ironically, Nejedlý's criticism of the group was not unfounded (if not for the reasons he stressed): the Spolek, while purportedly a venue for the exploration of new music from abroad and the promulgation of homegrown talent, was in reality an excuse for the increasing conservatism of Novák and his followers to gain a stranglehold over composers in Prague in the 1920s.[30] Before long, the tensions between the old and new musical worlds produced a crisis of both composition and audience reaction, which was felt not just in Prague but across Europe throughout the interwar period.

Nejedlý attempted to deal with this issue in the article "Today's Crisis in Music," which appeared serially throughout 1922.[31] The article probed the social and artistic reasons for the widespread decline in audience interest in new music, a phenomenon that the critic assessed quite perceptively as an aesthetic separation between art and society. Although much of this argument was based on a differentiation between high and low art, dismissing the latter as a manifestation of the economic corruption of society, Nejedlý also made the useful observation that the artists of the early 1920s had lost the ability to create what their specific society needed.[32] This situation produced what he referred to as a "baroque" decadence in modern music, a natural period of decline in the organicist conception of artistic movements; hence the concentration on technical details in most modernist music, which he felt alienated the public.[33] While "decadence" referenced Nejedlý's earlier descriptions of prewar musical society and its attendant shortcomings, the article also sought to link the concept to that of *odbornickost*, meaning the dry, negative academicism he perceived as pervasive among adherents of the Novák school. Nevertheless, such factional distinctions did not play out so cleanly in the music criticism of the early 1920s: with regard to his work at the National Theater and his opera *Legenda z Erinu*, Nejedlý's own protégé Ostrčil suffered the accusations of both decadence and *odbornickost*.

In October 1921 a new journal appeared in the Prague music community, one that would change the image of music criticism during the First Republic. Replacing the UB organ *Hudební revue*, which had faithfully represented one side of the critical spectrum since 1908, *Listy Hudební matice* (Music Publishing-House Pages) was the journalistic branch of the newly formed Hudební matice Umělecké besedy (Music Publishing House of the Artists' Union, or UB). In the new spirit of democracy, *Listy Hudební matice* espoused a policy of open submissions, thereby attempting to leave factional interests aside. Its new editor, the thirty-four-year-old composer Boleslav Vomáčka, had been one of Novák's first students, and having seen the various disputes at close range, knew well to steer clear of direct confrontation with *Smetana-Hudební list*. Thus, when combined with Nejedlý's gradual withdrawal from the sphere of music criticism, the arrival of *Listy Hudební matice* produced a relative lull in the struggle over the domination of Prague's musical community. From a wider perspective, however, its unde-cided, nonconfrontational, and on the whole, passive approach to modernism came to characterize the members of Vomáčka's generation, who had com-pleted their studies before the war but were unable to begin their careers until the 1920s.[34] As a result, many of the most active members of the Prague musical community throughout the early 1920s never truly escaped a deep-seated con-servatism and fear of the world outside the Czech Lands.

All of this is not to say that Vomáčka himself was a man without ideas, as his first lead article, "On Musical Modernism," demonstrates. Alongside an unex-pected abandonment of the old social values, including the musical figureheads Novák and Suk, he adopted a critical stance toward international modernism.[35] In an aesthetic about-face that would prove fateful for the Czech compositional community in future generations, Vomáčka rejected the spirit of total openness toward all things foreign that had characterized the last two years of *Hudební revue*. In his new critical stance (ironically, although not coincidentally, like that of Nejedlý), he was skeptical of the novel musical techniques suddenly pouring in from abroad, with the rationale that such experiments lacked a certain ethi-cal and ideological refinement. In contrast to the cosmopolitan world, "Our masters, who with true Slavonic passion took up the pursuit of the world prob-lem of the technical modernists, stand morally infinitely higher than the origi-nators of this [contemporary] movement. They went into battle with the full conviction of the victory of modernist ideals and mere technique was never their goal."[36] Vomáčka's omission of names of these "technical modernists" is signifi-cant here, because it seems to conflate some sort of imagined Schoenbergian avant-garde with Czechs of earlier generations ("our masters," a common short-hand designation for Smetana, Dvořák, and Fibich). The true artist in this vision would reject the artificiality of modernism and turn inward, attaining perspec-tive on real human feelings and thus also "the tempo of life."[37] To cap off this mandate of quasi-isolationist modernism, Vomáčka, amid allusions to Beethoven and Smetana, declared that society was awaiting such an artist, "who will bring a work that will be an expression of the new era and the signpost for new paths"; this passage continues a thread of messianism already appearing elsewhere in the discourse, most notably in Helfert and Nejedlý.[38] Hence, despite many voices to the contrary in Czech society of the early Republic, conservative nationalism was still a dominant force over cosmopolitanism, even among those at the UB whose Czechness had been, and would continue to be, openly questioned.

Just who "our masters" were in 1921 was open to debate, and the subsequent issues of *Listy Hudební matice* did little to clarify the situation. Throughout the journal's first two years, several articles appeared that attempted to promote potential leaders among the younger generation in Prague's music community, most specifically Ladislav Vycpálek and Jaroslav Křička.[39] Both men, like Vomáčka, were part of the "dispossessed" wartime generation, and spent most of their careers in the shadow of Novák and his controversies; no longer fresh faces by the 1920s, they had little hope of attaining a leadership position in Czech musical life. While the articles' authors did not describe the composers in such messianic terms as Vomáčka's peroration suggested, much of their rhetoric would return throughout the period to indicate the positive qualities of a specifically Czech modernism. Václav Štěpán, for instance, lauded Vycpálek's rigorous contrapuntal textures and dexterous treatment of motives, while Vomáčka emphasized his "synthesis of human, social, and religious values": both concepts were founded on something perceived to be the inner core of the music and were thus musically justified (an assessment that echoes Hostinský's *důslednost*). Jan Löwenbach noted the immediacy of Křička's expression, praising his "sense for supple melodic line and sonically and formally effective thematic work."[40] Both composers were described in terms of manliness (*mužnost*), and although their oeuvres were significantly different, the implication of potential leadership was similar; neither composer, however, rose to the challenge.

The second and third years of *Listy Hudební matice* provided a forum for the continued debate over the future of Czech modernism, through Emil Axman's reports on the Spolek pro moderní hudbu, as well as through the significant contribution of Vomáčka's regularly appearing column, "Otázky dne" (Questions of the Day). The writings of both men demonstrate the tensions the Prague music community experienced in their relationship with the modernism of Western Europe, in that Axman's Spolek purported to be a venue for such music, and Vomáčka frequently surveyed the latest literature by figures such as Paul Bekker, all the while filtering these phenomena through personal or cultural biases. Although Axman reinforced his group's connections to important foreign artists, "with this reciprocation of performance, however, the Spolek does not seek to proclaim artistic cosmopolitanism. An artist does not become worldly by staggering through modern trends, but by working in an independent manner through what the world gives him."[41] Similarly, Vomáčka looked askance at Bekker's glorification of the physiological in music; on the other hand, the *psychological*, according to Vomáčka, prioritized ideas over mere effects, and thus was both inexhaustible and, via Smetana, quintessentially Czech.[42] Using the same argument, however, Vomáčka sought to include European modernists such as Křenek and Mahler under a rubric of Czechness (by virtue of their familial ties to Bohemia) and thereby to reconcile the readership of *Listy Hudební matice* to the foreignness of the novel compositional techniques. In a further installment of "Otázky dne," Vomáčka welcomed news of Ernst Křenek's first symphony, which he had not yet heard, but which "interests us, in that a Czech[!] is creating a path in German music that is the subject of serious discussion in the German musical world," that "path" being neoclassicism.[43] Accepted into the fold of his "homeland" by sole virtue of the distinctively Czech "ř" in his surname, Křenek's rejection would be just as swift once Prague audiences came to know the un-Smetanian nature of his music. By April 1923, Vomáčka had discarded all pretense of open-mindedness toward new international developments and called for Czech musicians to stand up, prepared to fight for "artistic-moral values."[44] At this point, however, the editors opened the discussion to other members of the musical community, including Doležil and Jirák from the opposing critical faction.

Doležil's sizable essay, "On the Future of Our Music," dwelt on a theme previously expounded by his mentor, Nejedlý: the individual artist and his potential self-abandonment to the collective, one of the "cardinal questions of today's art."[45] After some vague ruminations about the necessity that the artist reflect the "concreteness" of real life in the content of his work, Doležil weighed the artist's subjective view of the world against the objective goals of his creation. His conclusion, arrived at by comparing the achievements of Smetana and Foerster (which he labeled as collectivist and individualist, respectively), was that both viewpoints were necessary to synthesize a firmly grounded "new art." This concept of new art, like that of many of Doležil's contemporaries in Prague, was ideally the stimulus for a moral renaissance in the modern age, and did not necessarily mean the use of new musical techniques. Indeed, the author made clear his viewpoints on artistic primitivism, which he connected to artificiality, reactionary aesthetics, and a lack of clarity and moral worth.[46] Doležil summarized the core of his argument as follows: "In the end this connects with our moral requirements in art, in that we always believe those artists more if they express themselves through the fixed, concrete experience of their ideas and feelings, rather than forcing themselves into abstract schemas and contentless, bloodless mysticism."[47] That the proponents of moral modernism were in fact Czech, Doležil implied throughout the article; as such, his prose did much to reconcile the long-belligerent critical factions through a mutual sense of withdrawal from the influence of Western European culture.

Nowhere was such a withdrawal stated more directly than in Axman's article, "Leave Aside Foreign Tongues, Speak Your Own!" which appeared almost a full year later in February 1924, just three months before the ISCM festival.[48] For Axman, the main factor that separated Czech music making from international modernism was *feeling*—and in this instance, the separation was not only aesthetic but also racial:

We Slavs and Czechs, a soft and sensitive people, are already so used to considering feeling as the only source of musical expression, that we cannot really understand it when the West suddenly announces to us that this rich, never-ending source of musical beauty is a residue, a pigtail, for which there is no place in the music of today, and that music flowing from feelings and conversing through feeling is an anachronism.[49]

Such a pronouncement, coming at this stage in the debate on the future of Czech modernism, was a backlash of reactionism, virtually granting leave to justify antimodernist aesthetics on the basis of an imagined racial difference. This formulation, based directly on Herderian romantic nationalism and its designation of the Slavs as rich in tradition, also blatantly disallowed the possibility of multiple or simultaneous modernisms. Axman went on to pit the "intellectual chaos" of the West against the *důslednost* of Czech tradition, from which emanated the guiding lights of Janáček, Novák, Suk, and Ostrčil, who had created a new Czech culture.[50] Czechness for Axman was not necessarily antimodern, however, but a combination of humanness and modernity, such that the Czech artist would ideally lead his people from tradition to modernism without having to stoop to the amoral level of the music of Western Europe.[51]

Axman's main opponent appeared in the form of Karel Boleslav Jirák, a young composer who had also studied under Nejedlý. Jirák, writing in the January 1924 issue of *Nová svoboda* (New Freedom), rejected Axman's formulation of "soft and sensitive" Czechness, citing Hába and Křenek (again) as examples of Czechs who wrote "unemotional music."[52] For Jirák it was more a question of the presence or lack of "ideas" in music rather than feelings, a position that placed him firmly in the Nejedlian ideological camp, although he made no attempt to define what "musical ideas" were. Whereas Doležil demanded a solidification of the composer's relationship to lived experience, and Axman's formulation was directed toward making art intelligible to the public, Jirák felt that music should be created for the future, with little regard for the vagaries of public taste (i.e., Hostinský's *náladovost*).[53] To this end, he stressed that Smetana was appreciated only after his death, thereby linking his argument of "music for the future" to the same undercurrent of nationalism and traditionalism.

As the foregoing discussion shows, there was considerable confusion among the first generation of interwar ideologues in Prague's music community regarding the place of the Czech composer within international modernism. After the initial euphoria of independence and openness toward the West, many critics and composers began to shrink away from the perceived threat of foreign influences, which, they felt, lacked a certain moral fiber immanent in contemporary Czech compositions. Although the ideological camps were still present, with regard to these issues they were no longer as cleanly divided, in that several of the individual critical positions overlapped, particularly in the case of Doležil and Jirák. More likely, the commonality of ideology was symptomatic of the feeling of displacement experienced by the wartime generation, many of whom became spokespeople for the musical community in the early years of the Republic. The consensus was not without controversy even within the sphere of Czech composition, however, as was shown by the vehemence of subsequent debates and their effect on collective musical identity.

The "Suk Affair" and *Zrání,* 1918–19

On October 30, 1918, a mere two days after independence, the Czech Philharmonic gave its first concert in the new Republic, ushering in a new era with the premiere of an orchestral composition. The work was Josef Suk's tone poem *Zrání* (Ripening), a title that refers to the maturation of the individual through human experience, taken from the symbolist poem of the same name by Antonín Sova on which it is partially based. *Zrání* occupies an interesting position in the history of composition in Prague, in that not only was it received as a metaphor for the struggle for Czech national independence, but it also provoked a controversy of alarming proportions. The composition itself is a single-movement work of nearly forty minutes in length, using enormous orchestral forces, and in the final measures, a women's choir singing vocalise; it forms both a major component of Suk's autobiographical cycle of orchestral works and a landmark piece of Czech modernism. In the tone poem's novel and highly complex form (discussed in detail in chapter 6), Suk created a system of dramatic prefiguration and reminiscence that evoked the self-reflection of a maturing being, be it individual or collective. This form also mirrored the Czech historical consciousness of the time, which viewed the present in the context of past achievements that, in themselves, carried the seeds of the modern era. In the rampantly nationalistic atmosphere of the early days of the Republic, even Suk's introverted and autobiographical subjectivism could stand for the victory of the nation. Indeed, the suggestive power of the work was so strong that it forced the entire community to take sides over its composer's contribution to the Czech collective, prompting months of intense scrutiny that paralleled the purge of Czech cultural life after the war.

Most commentators, both at the premiere of *Zrání* and in the years since, connected Suk's work to a nationalist context, be it implicit or explicit. In his emotional "Open Letter to J. Suk," published in the November 1918 issue of *Hudební revue*, Václav Štěpán referred to *Zrání* as "a gift of enthusiasm, of artistic elevation, of joy from the heights that you reached; [a gift] that belongs to us all, to your brothers in the nation, through you."[54] Štěpán's implied meaning is that the goals of Suk's tone poem and the Czech nation were one and the same: maturation, attained through struggle, but also guided by fate. For Štěpán these two events culminated simultaneously:

> Today it appears to be the greatest mark of fate that the first performance of your work occurred two days after we finally became free. Like a celebration of our national victory, full of pure, internal dignity, your poem of victory resounded, achieved through work, moral strength, and love. And the words "By this sign you shall be victorious" engraved your music into the minds of us all: this is the path that each person must travel, so that he can attain his own goal, which stands behind all the sufferings of life; this is the path that the nation also has to travel, so that it can fulfill its mission.[55]

In Štěpán's vision of personal, artistic, and national maturation, the listener would realize the victory of the Czech people through the musical "victory" (described by conductor Václav Talich) in the closing moments of *Zrání*, and vice versa, merging art and life to become an indistinguishable whole.[56] The tone poem provoked reminiscences of the struggle for nationhood; both narratives, moreover, were enacted from the standpoint of the goal, rather than the struggle itself. As a portion of a larger, autobiographical cycle, *Zrání*'s "national" narrative became mapped onto the "personal" narrative of Suk the composer, merging the individual and the collective: the resulting maturation ("which belongs to us all . . . through you") would be felt at once vicariously and directly, as an audience member or a citizen.

Written somewhat later, Boleslav Vomáčka's assessment of *Zrání* in the context of Suk's compositional career introduced a theme that, as we have already seen, would be echoed in music criticism throughout the early years of the Republic. After a description of the work as an intertextual synthesis of the composer's entire living oeuvre, Vomáčka claimed: "*The high moral ground* on which Suk stands here gives true consecration to the work."[57] Only after some general statements about Suk's faithfulness to love, true art, and humanity, did Vomáčka connect moral superiority to the nation: "His works are similarly imbued with a national spirit, although they lack patriotic titles. Their national trait lies deeply within them."[58] The interiority of Suk's expression of Czechness is seen here in a positive light, a nuance we have encountered, interestingly, in Nejedlý's analysis of Smetana and others. Yet this very introversion is also intimately connected to the "subjective" realm of Suk's autobiographical cycle, the expression of an individual's private experiences enacted, rather paradoxically, in a public forum. Indeed, the "national" element—that *Zrání* might be taken to represent not only the artist or perhaps each listener as an individual but also an imagined collective with shared, internal characteristics—adds a problematic layer to an already complex equation. It was within this convoluted discourse of nation and artistic representation that Nejedlý began what was to become a veritable witch-hunt of national traitors among Czech cultural figures in postwar life.

In his review of *Zrání* that appeared in the November 1918 issue of *Smetana-Hudební list*, Nejedlý wrote the words that would provoke a backlash of controversy from both sides of Prague's critical divide, in many ways continuing elements of the polemic that had existed since the 1870s. The ensuing events would also inaugurate a disturbing period of purgation within Czech cultural life in the first years of the Republic, thereby devaluing the new sense of openness brought about by democracy and freedom. After a lengthy introduction in which Nejedlý acknowledged Suk's laudable attention to *důslednost* in pursuing the cycle he started with *Asrael* and *Pohádka léta* (A Summer's Tale), the critic suddenly changed course, asserting that the same problems found in these earlier works also persisted in *Zrání*:

> As I pointed out already with respect to the first two works, however, these themes [i.e., the programmatic subjects] do not penetrate into Suk's *musical* representation so deeply that they are directly translated into musical expression, but remain simply unused at the bottom of Suk's soul (whence his musical ideas are not gathered); such is the case also with *Zrání*.[59]

In one sentence, Nejedlý attempted to negate the myth of autobiography that surrounded Suk's orchestral cycle: not only were the works musically disconnected from their supposed source ("the bottom of Suk's soul"), but the composer was seemingly incapable of rendering his innermost feelings as musical ideas. With these comments, Nejedlý also attempted to sever Suk's achievement from the collective Czech identity. To do so, however, was to strip away a powerful reflection of the national legacy, and, as we shall see, resulted in a backlash against the critic himself. Nejedlý insisted that the idea of the human maturation process had to be imagined separately from the music itself, since nothing in the music gave the listener this idea. Similarly, the form of Suk's tone poem was "disunified and ineloquent," successful neither as a cyclical four-movement nor as a single-movement structure, since the dearth of "musical ideas" prevented the necessary organic freedom of flow.[60] The core of the work was missing for Nejedlý: the "musical idea" that necessitated the development of the remainder of the composition.

Such a reaction was evidently based on personal bias and a refusal to examine the work in any detail, since, as subsequent analysis will show, the entirety of musical material in *Zrání* is based on a Grundgestalt of motives given within the first twelve measures of the piece. With a similar attitude, Nejedlý also dismissed the extramusical connections of Suk's tone poem, because "I consider it pointless to analyze a work in terms of the ideological aspect when the idea exists only outside the work and in no part within the music itself."[61] As such, the critic could not even begin to consider *Zrání* an expression of "national ripening," as had Štěpán and Vomáčka. In a comparison with Suk's overtly nationalistic *Praga* and *Meditation on the Theme of St. Václav's Chorale*, both of which appeared on the program with *Zrání*'s premiere, Nejedlý opined: "it was quite instructive to hear these two works right next to *Zrání*, for they clearly showed that, if a similarly shallow expression is at least somewhat bearable in works with a private subject, in which we ascribe an insufficiency of depth just to a single personality, . . . such music is absolutely inadmissible when it comes to a national expression, in which I have to imagine the entire nation as the subject of the work."[62] Furthermore, Nejedlý asserted that to perform Suk's music on an occasion of such national importance was shameful to the point of immorality. The article concluded with the words:

> With regard to such national music there is, moreover, a need for a person quite other than one who, in the moment of our greatest national suffering, received the Order of Austria from the Austrian government, together with clerics and German traitors of the Czech cause. For such a person there is no place in *this* environment, even if he were to adorn himself now ever so much with the tricolor.[63]

When pressed in an open letter from Karel Hoffmann, Suk's colleague from the Czech Quartet, to justify his allegations, Nejedlý responded in the left-of-center journal *České slovo* that the Czech Quartet had willingly participated in pro-Austrian patriotic activities during the war, including a concert in Berlin in January 1918. Nejedlý asserted that although the concert was billed as a "good-will" action, its intent was purely nationalistic on the grounds that it was given to benefit ethnic Germans in Belgium; worse still was the fact that this "vater-ländische Betätigung" took place immediately after the Czech writers' rejection of Austrian military policy that same month, an act seen as a crucial step toward Czech self-determination. The critic concluded, "this perhaps will suffice for proof that we have every right to doubt whether the gentlemen of the *Czech Quartet* are that kind of *Czech artist* as we imagine belonging to such a category. My ideal of a Czech national artist is, at least, quite different."[64] In subsequent attacks, Nejedlý gave "proof" of Suk's immorality by citing the Czech Quartet's performance of Haydn's *Kaiserquartett* during the war, with its quotation of the Austrian national hymn.

Suk's supporters, particularly the critics at *Hudební revue*, were quick to retaliate. In an unsigned article ironically entitled "Josef Suk—National Traitor," one author quoted the final, accusatory statement from Nejedlý's *Zrání* review, with the words "we do not have enough sharp words to condemn this expression of national denunciation."[65] It is important to note that the majority of the Czech artistic community viewed any disrespect toward Suk and *Zrání* as an injury to the nation, and while Nejedlý and his circle exhibited growing sympathy for the communist movement, most of the cultural establishment remained social or national democrat in orientation. Citing many other unquestionably honorable Czech cultural figures who had been unable to refuse a distinction from the Austrian government, the author went on to repudiate Nejedlý himself on the grounds that, as an employee of the state-funded university, he relied on Austrian money for "his office, his bread, his existence, his reputation."[66] The general tone of the article is one of revulsion that such a tactic of cultural policing should be carried out in the public sphere, precisely when tyranny had been overthrown with independence only a month prior.

By the end of the year, Suk's supporters sought an honorary hearing to defend him against Nejedlý's claims of treason. The organization involved, called Maffie, was a tribunal of Czech artists, scientists, and public figures with no overall political or governmental affiliation. Suk's case was brought to their attention, and both parties were invited to submit claims, at which point the matter would be duly researched and considered.[67] On January 25, 1919, Maffie issued a statement that reviewed Nejedlý's charges against Suk, siding for the defendant. Their research revealed that while Suk certainly knew about his award, it was primarily given for a quarter-century of artistic performance, rather than for "a certain inclination toward Austrian activism"; that many other important Czech artists had also been decorated by the Austrian government, including Jaroslav Kvapil, one of the members of Maffie itself; and that Nejedlý's claims about a benefit concert in Berlin had no basis in fact.[68] As a counterclaim to the latter, Maffie's response cited a concert in Holland in late 1917, in which the

Czech Quartet was prevented from taking part, for fear that they might spread classified secrets to Masaryk's deputy-in-exile, Eduard Beneš. By this proclamation, not only were Josef Suk and the members of the Czech Quartet absolved of the charge of treason, but the implied heroism of foiled resistance activities also put them in a positive light.

Nejedlý reacted to the above proceedings in several different ways. In the January issue of *Smetana-Hudební list* he attacked the anonymous author from *Hudební revue*, openly challenging the national morals of the journal and its parent organization, the UB, with the implication of pro-Austrian collaboration.[69] Shortly thereafter, on February 2, Nejedlý published the article "E per si muove" [sic], which criticized Maffie's findings as having "missed the core of the matter, for it did not look at all into the question of *artistic and public morality*," focusing instead on issues of form.[70] When Suk's activity was contrasted with the legacy of Smetana, "it forces the question, what is true Czech art and what is not, and who is a *true Czech artist* and who is not!"[71] In the final analysis, the critic denied the efficacy of the Maffie proclamation, since "no tribunal has the right to judge *moral ideas* and *artistic* ideals."[72] In this manner, Nejedlý attempted to hide behind "ideology" as an undefined moral high ground, untouchable by Suk's defense, which concentrated only on mundane details. Nevertheless, Nejedlý would use his concept of "moral ideas and artistic ideals" as a yardstick by which to measure the wartime behavior of his compatriots. The implication is that only Nejedlý himself was capable of judging Czechness and artistry, as the final statement makes indubitably clear: "My standpoint is certainly *ideologically higher*, and this must always be victorious, if not now, then with even more certainty before *the judgment of history*."[73]

In the judgment of his contemporaries, however, Nejedlý was anything but victorious. From this point onward, the debate focused on the principles of national expression in art and its moral untouchability; Suk and his music, meanwhile, retained merely a symbolic, albeit emotionally charged presence. The "Suk Affair" turned quickly into the "Nejedlý Affair," a virtual backlash of public opinion against the critic, unleashed primarily by a feuilleton written by the heavyweight journalist Jan Herben in *Národní listy*, February 8 and 9, 1919. Herben sought to expose the instability of Nejedlý's moral basis: "I do not believe that a man can be raised to some sort of higher morality when he violates the prerequisites of the most primitive civil morality, which commands: *do not slander, do not bear false witness*."[74] Behind Nejedlý's "Jesuitism" was a set of "false cards"; Herben concluded with the following statements:

> Patriotism and morality are for him but a sacrilegious sham. Whoever has eyes to see, sees this: Zdeněk Nejedlý is a historian who is also a musician. He is a musician who is also a historian. Of this type of people there are few. The thought has gotten stuck in the head of Prof. Nejedlý that he can be the judge of Czech music, that he can prescribe the direction of Czech music. But Czech music is not listening to him.

Composers are wayward servants, and Janáček, Suk, Novák, and the others compose like free birds. . . . Prof. Nejedlý imagines his leadership as that of a bear-tamer, although the bears do not dance according to his baton. . . . For ten years this bear-tamer has maltreated Suk, and Suk grows from work to work, his own person, different from how the bear-tamer prescribed; when Nejedlý could not strike down *Zrání*, he struck the man.[75]

Herben's feuilleton attempted to shed Nejedlý of his disguise (designated by Šourek as that of a "false moralist"), thereby revealing the underlying reason for Nejedlý's attack on Suk—a will to power that Nejedlý felt to hold by right over Czech music making. While Nejedlý had tried to exercise this will on multiple occasions in the past, he had clearly overstepped with the "Suk Affair," in that his attack on *Zrání* seemed, by extension, to falsify the maturation of the Czech nation, and to tarnish the reputation of the artist who had depicted this in music.

Within a week of Herben's retaliation there appeared yet another anti-Nejedlý protest, much like the one published in 1912 with the signatures of thirty-one of Prague's most important musical figures.[76] The protest of February 16, 1919, printed in the right-wing dailies *Národní listy* and *Venkov* (The Countryside) with the title "To the Czech Public," bore an impressive fifty-six signatures, a total buoyed by the number of nonmusical personalities that lent their names to Suk's cause. Initially wanting to voice dissent with an affirmation of "the belief in honest patriotism and absolute trust in distinguished Czech artists," the group had held back, awaiting the outcome of Maffie's inquiry.[77] A solid decision in favor of Suk reinforced the signatories' ardor: "Maffie illuminated the groundlessness, suspicion, and treachery that heavily affected the personal and national honor of artists who are dear to the entire Czech world." Referring to the words of the anonymous author of "Josef Suk—National Traitor," the protest continued:

> We also will raise our voices against the same new "patriotic police." . . . With this we fulfill our duty to integrity and truth, and we warn the Czech press not to lend themselves to statements that suspect the honor of individuals and their patriotic purity and place a blemish on national morality.[78]

Although the text of the protest added relatively few new issues to the discourse around the "Suk Affair," it did attempt to strengthen the argument against Nejedlý: the critic himself, with his calls for purging Czech culture of immoral and unnational elements, had committed an offense against "national morality." For the group of protesters, it would be more detrimental to deprive the nation of leading cultural figures than to leave unquestioned their alleged pro-Austrian sympathy and have them continue to represent the Czech nation, both domestically and abroad. This brief declaration was perhaps also the most reactionary statement in the entire "Suk Affair," in that it asked the other representatives of the Czech press to ignore or exclude the opinions of Nejedlý and his followers. As such, the protesters not only turned Nejedlý's moral yard-stick back on him, but they also employed his exclusionary tactics with a virtual call for the postwar publishing industry to boycott him entirely.

The protest's text also had an impact through the personalities it was meant to represent. Musicians making a reappearance among the list of signatories included Karel Hoffmeister, Emanuel Chvála, Karel Kovařovic, Jaroslav Křička, and Václav Talich: new faces included Antonín Šilhan, Václav Štěpán, and Ladislav Vycpálek, while notably absent were Vítězslav Novák (having presumably learned his lesson!) and the members of the Czech Quartet, including Josef Suk himself. Perhaps more significant in the eyes of the general public would have been the participation of visual artists (Hugo Boettinger, František Kysela, Max Švabinský) and literary figures (K. M. Čapek-Chod, Karel Čapek, Petr Křička, and most importantly, Antonín Sova), bringing the "Suk/Nejedlý Affair" well beyond the boundaries of the musical community and into the general consciousness of contemporary Prague. As such, it befitted the origin of the controversy—in one artist's reflection of the collective—that all of Czech society should take an interest in its outcome.

While Nejedlý could not match the fifty-six protesters in quantity of supporters, he could outdo them in quantity of words: the article "My Case: Toward an Understanding of the Pathology of Czech Society in the Republic," originally published in *Smetana-Hudební list*, was reissued by Melantrich in 1919 as a forty-nine-page document. Taking its name from Herben's feuilleton "The Nejedlý Case," Nejedlý's subtitle reveals that the new regime had already become for him a source of disenchantment and cynicism, especially when compared to the unguarded optimism of "Freedom!" or his earliest political essays for the socialist press. From the outset Nejedlý blamed *Národní listy* for confusing its readers by focusing the debate on him, when it should have concentrated on the reality of an "ideological, emotional, and moral disruption in the first stages of the Republic."[79] Much like his rebuttal to the 1912 protest, in "My Case" Nejedlý listed his opponents and dealt with them individually, although with a greater dose of social theory.

Nejedlý started by rejecting the authoritarian implications of Maffie's verdict because it attempted to negate journalistic freedom: the trial was therefore not convincing to him with respect to the original moral issues of the case, which could be determined only by other free-thinking critics or artists. Since Kvapil and Machar, the only artistic members of Maffie, represented "typical artistic liberalism and eclecticism" instead of any sort of *důslednost*, the verdict was biased and unreliable. After a more or less slanderous attack on Herben's character and intellectual worth, during which the journalist was accused of having opened the floodgates to public misconceptions and potentially dangerous threats, Nejedlý turned his attention to the protest of February 16.[80] He rejected the protesters' attempt to ostracize him as an agent of cultural policing, since such ostracism was in itself an act of cultural policing. The multiplicity of signatories also implied an unquestioned tribute to authority and a dangerous lack of social responsibility, since the rhetorical effect of one critic's opinion had to be shared in this case by "an armada of names, so that it would seem to be the opinion of all our people."[81]

Behind each of his opponents in the "Suk Affair" Nejedlý perceived what he termed a *gray terror*, "a peculiar, invisible *power* that directs everything," an apparatus of which Maffie, Herben, and the fifty-six protesters were but the instruments.[82] The invisibility of this power made it alien to social responsibility, thus causing the "pathology of Czech society in the Republic" referred to in Nejedlý's subtitle: in other words, a tendency toward an absolutist social structure that was allegedly inherent in the Czech character. For Nejedlý, this type of society was the perfect breeding ground for opportunism, as evidenced by the general amnesty of Czech cultural figures called for by the Maffie proclamation and others, regardless of their wartime activity.[83] Suk, in his apparent attempts to capitalize on the celebratory atmosphere of the postwar period (i.e., with *Zrání*'s nationalist statement of maturation) after questionable behavior during the war, represented for Nejedlý the contemporary spirit of opportunism, and the call for Suk's amnesty encapsulated the entire unseen apparatus of "gray terror." The very idea of an amnesty was at once a rejection of Nejedlý's ideal of cultural purification (i.e., as mandated by supposedly free-thinking critics such as himself) and of the social responsibility of artists toward society: this latter issue was of necessity an individual responsibility, which the mass nature of an amnesty negated. Yet the concept of social responsibility had led to an impasse, with each side attempting to exclude the other from a larger definition of Czechness on the basis of morally reprehensible behavior. The near obsession with morality in art would continue to define the Czech musical community throughout the early 1920s.

By the beginning of the summer of 1919, the "Suk Affair" had tapered off, although it had long since left behind the musical reason for its commencement: *Zrání* and its reception as a work representing the maturation of the Czech nation. The discourse quickly entered the realm of cultural politics, and Nejedlý in particular had his first opportunity to observe a working example of artistic responsibility within a free society. More important for the majority of participants was the question of the purging and policing of culture: while for Nejedlý it was a crucial stage in social reform, for many others (including those who already enjoyed considerable cultural power) such a move would deprive Czech society of its cultural leaders and therefore its spiritual basis as well. On all sides, the "Suk Affair" represented the first hint that the new Republic would not fulfill all its promises of limitless intellectual liberty and humanistic equality. Over the next few years, there would be further cause to doubt the direction of postwar Czech culture, particularly at the most visible of Prague's musical institutions, the National Theater.

Years of Upheaval at the National Theater:
Kovařovic and Ostrčil, 1918–20

The metamorphosis of the National Theater that took place in the first two years of the new regime mirrored many of the tensions that appeared in other branches of the Czech musical community. The conflict between modernism and tradition had a long-lasting impact on the atmosphere in the theater, but equally potent were the issues of nation and institutional reform. All of these issues effected great changes in the outward structure of the venue in a relatively short space of time. By the time of Kovařovic's death in December 1920 and the inauguration of his replacement, Ostrčil, as opera director, the entire aesthetic program of the theater had changed, reflecting the new and cosmopolitan atmosphere of the democratic era. Nevertheless, artistic changes did not necessarily mirror administrative ones, and the institution was ill-prepared for the sudden burden of social responsibility it faced.

Starting with the tremendously popular Smetana Exhibition in 1917, to which it had contributed a series of celebratory concerts, the National Theater had grown steadily in the eyes of its Czech audience, to the point where it regained the status it enjoyed during the late nineteenth-century Cultural Revival.[84] This public enthusiasm, however, stood in stark contrast to the internal turmoil that shook the theater in the early years of the Republic. On June 30, 1918, the Young Czech-affiliated Společnost Národního divadla signed its fourth consecutive six-year contract as administrators of the theater: Kovařovic and the arch-conservative general director Gustav Schmoranz were thus guaranteed to hold their positions of power well into the new regime. The longer this administration existed within the changing cultural climate, however, the greater the tension that threatened to split the administration internally, including a schism between the long-time allies Schmoranz and Kovařovic. According to František Pala, historian of the National Theater and Nejedlý disciple, Kovařovic began to reach a belated maturation as opera director in the last two years of his life, finally organizing and performing a repertoire that fulfilled his duty as a Czech cultural leader, and demanding administrative reform.[85] For the Nejedlý circle, this reform meant performing operas by Smetana and his "lineage," including those by suitable contemporary artists. Nevertheless, the conductor continued his problematic relationship with the younger generation of Czech composers, favoring Němeček while excluding Jirák and Zich, and postponing Jaroslav Jeremiáš indefinitely. Practical concerns also exacerbated the situation. With political freedom came the seemingly limitless use of the National Theater, producing an overwhelming surge of activity, which now included daily opera performances plus matinees and spoken dramas. In the risky economic situation of the early interwar period, this maximum performance load created dire circumstances for the majority of musicians; space was at a premium with the conflicting demands of dramatic and operatic divisions, and pressure began to mount for the annexation of a second stage.[86] Economic factors, too, would cause friction between the increasingly modernist artistic direction at the National Theater and its administration, which demanded bel canto and operetta to appease its conservative subscribers. Over the next two years, multiple suggestions were made to alleviate the situation, some of which involved a merge with the Vinohrady Theater and/or a takeover of the Deutsches Landestheater in Prague's Old Town. The increase in workload also forced Kovařovic to begin a long-awaited search for a dramaturge, a person who would in effect take over half the directorial and planning duties that Kovařovic had shouldered since the beginning of his tenure in 1900.

The repertoire of Kovařovic's final two seasons shows a marked turn toward Czech composers, including greater attention to the operas of Fibich, Kovařovic himself, and especially Foerster.[87] Performances of Foerster, whose latest opera *Nepřemožení* (The Invincible Ones, December 19, 1918) was the first premiere of the new Republic, were at once a celebration of contemporary Czech opera and of the composer's return to Prague after a twenty-five-year absence. Amid this overt nationalistic display, the Austro-German repertoire of the National Theater virtually disappeared from the first two post-1918 seasons, with the exception of Gluck, Mozart, and Beethoven, each of whom was felt to have a special connection to Prague. Performances of Wagner, on the other hand, were rejected as an insult within the prevailing anti-German atmosphere: the first interwar production of *Tannhäuser* on January 17, 1919, met with disastrous results.[88] As Pala related, Jaroslav Hilbert, a prominent journalist, dramatic poet, and Kovařovic's own brother-in-law, launched an attack on the opera director for his lack of judgment in programming a work full of "the Germanic musical spirit."[89] In his feuilleton of January 21, Hilbert chastised Kovařovic for his tactless ignorance of the Czech political situation, in which German art and culture had little place. Despite the Czech nationalist basis of his viewpoint, Hilbert's text referred more to France and to international, rather than domestic, diplomacy:

> Simple tact tells us what we have to do. . . . If we celebrate France one day through her composers and her hymn in an honest call of praise and three days later we change our clothes to the German spirit and again applaud, we give the impression of comedians whose expressions have no worth and whose acts are not led by logic. Today we are not just hedonists, we are citizens of an as yet unformed state, which arose from Czech blood, but also from the blood and sacrifices of its allies.[90]

For Hilbert, too, Czech cultural activity had to be based on *důslednost* ("whose acts are . . . led by logic") rather than *náladovost* ("hedonists . . . whose expressions have no worth"). The situation grows more complicated when we consider that the Wagnerian basis for much of Czech romantic music, from Smetana and Dvořák to Ostrčil, Novák, and Suk (by means of Richard Strauss), was usually ignored in overly simplified juxtapositions of German and Czech culture.[91] Such radically anti-Wagnerian sentiments, however, would prove to be merely a manifestation of the current political rejection of Austro-German hegemony, since *Der fliegende Holländer* met with resounding success at the National Theater under Ostrčil just two years later. It seems that once total separation had occurred politically and culturally (with the takeover of the Deutsches Landestheater in November 1920), the Czechs could perform Wagner with a "clear conscience."

Among the other events that threatened the cohesion of the National Theater within the first year of independence was the premiere of Jaroslav Jeremiáš's opera *Starý král* (The Old King) on April 13, 1919. Jeremiáš, the young student who had demonstrated against (his former teacher) Novák's *Karlštejn* less than two years before, had submitted his opera to Kovařovic in early 1913. The conductor put *Starý král* on hold indefinitely, requesting revisions and time to gather more orchestral forces, a difficult task in wartime. By the final days of the war, Jeremiáš, living in destitution, had become fatally ill. Kovařovic, apparently having realized his error in overlooking the young composer until it was too late, was unable to arrange for the production of *Starý král* before Jeremiáš's death on January 16, 1919, and the situation became a public disgrace for both conductor and theater. The composer's younger brother, Otakar Jeremiáš, and the lawyer Jaroslav Mayer both agitated on behalf of *Starý král* as a duty for the National Theater to fulfill. The virulent Mayer in particular went as far as to make public declarations blaming Kovařovic for the death of Jeremiáš, and subsequently wrote an open letter to President Masaryk in late January, asking for a resolution to the matter.[92] The Nejedlý circle joined the fray, beginning with Helfert's open letter of February 23, in which he refuted Kovařovic's arguments that the theater orchestra was too depleted during the war to produce Jeremiáš's score.[93] Helfert's opposition to the theater administration led to a public meeting, attended by Mayer and several of Nejedlý's students including Helfert, Bartoš, and Jirák. For the most part, Jeremiáš's cause was used as an excuse to demand reform in the National Theater, as the resulting proclamation shows:

(1) Let the National Theater be given to the leadership of artists. It is necessary to demolish the system of the Družstvo, to introduce economic and artistic responsibility. (2) The state has the duty to support the theater, but it does not have the right to impinge on internal artistic relations. (3) The government does not have the right to impinge on the artistic leadership of whatever artistic corporation. (4) Let the interests of composers be protected by a proper organization, which would guard all interests of composers without regard for musical faction. We demand a free art in a free state.[94]

The so-called "Jeremiáš Affair" demonstrated how closely the issues of artistic responsibility, nationalistic demands for the purging of culture, and the practical urgency of institutional reform were linked. In a contemporary article, Nejedlý raised the issue that cultural organizations had a moral duty toward the youngest generation of composers: both Jeremiáš as a young modernist and the fate of his opera at the National Theater were representative of the woeful state of things.[95] Despite the public outcry, *Starý král* met with a mixed reception: both Šourek and Chvála, writing in conservative daily papers, appreciated the orchestration but rejected the symbolist libretto and the general style of the music, which Chvála described as "dramatically fruitless" in its "erotic lyricism."[96] These judgments, coming as they did from two fellow associates of the UB, meshed with Kovařovic's personal opinion of the work, thereby delineating the usual critical factions of Prague's music community. Upon pressure from the minister of culture to relate the theater's role in the affair, the conductor was eventually forced to admit that, as a result of the "perversely erotic character" of the work, there was no way he could have programmed the work during wartime.[97] Although in the short term, the controversy surrounding *Starý král* seems to have died out shortly after the opera's three performances in April 1919, the ensuing demands for reform and the public's involvement in internal theatrical politics seriously undermined the administration, ultimately causing its collapse within the year.

When Kovařovic began at long last to search for a dramaturge who would assist his organizational and directorial duties, he unwittingly ushered in a new era for the National Theater. Indeed, there was no way that the conductor could have known he was hiring the man who would replace him as opera director a year later: Otakar Ostrčil. From the outset, Ostrčil's commitment to institutional reform, musical and theatrical modernism, and especially to young Czech artists would revolutionize the image of the National Theater and provide the most tangible (and perhaps controversial) manifestation of Nejedlý's ideology. In the short term, however, the new dramaturge would have to be an authoritative name with suitable qualifications to reconcile the musical public with the theater.[98] Kovařovic's original choice, the Brno-based composer Jan Kunc, was unavailable, and so the vacancy was advertised in the Sunday papers on July 6, 1919.[99] Four applications were received by the end of the summer: while Jaromír Borecký, Karel Moor, and Ota Zítek were dismissed without much consideration, Kovařovic hesitated for several months over the possibility of Jaroslav Křička. Křička, whose experience as a conductor and composer outstripped all other candidates, had led Prague's historic Hlahol chorus for many years and was a loyal member of the UB, having signed both protests against Nejedlý. Like Vycpálek and Vomáčka, Křička belonged to a generation that began to reach maturity during the First World War, and as such was neither a new face nor a seasoned veteran of Prague's music sphere: his opera *Hipolyta*, produced by Kovařovic in 1917, was slated for publication and had attracted critical attention. Nevertheless, Kovařovic waited for a more definitive solution to present itself, which it did in the form of the "Vinohrady Theater Affair."

Ostrčil had worked as opera director at the suburban Vinohrady Theater since 1914, and had recently been dismissed as a result of a controversial administrative decision that liquidated the entire opera section in favor of spoken drama and operetta.[100] When Ostrčil, with five years of experience in opera direction, became a free agent in the fall of 1919, the job market changed drastically, and Kovařovic jumped at the chance to hire what now appeared to be the most promising candidate. Contact was made between the two conductors in November, and despite their historic factional differences, Kovařovic was able to offer Ostrčil the position within just a few minutes.[101] Pala went so far as to state that Kovařovic's decision was made in the conscious effort to appease the critical opposition he had faced so often in the past two decades of his tenure as opera director. Although Ostrčil had always acted somewhat independently from his supporters in the Nejedlý circle, his hiring indicates a certain rapprochement between the group and the National Theater; this unlikely turn of events owes much to the success of the Smetana Exhibition of 1917 and the Nejedlians' resultant increase in cultural power. An increasing number of individuals were echoing Nejedlý's call for social responsibility in the reform of cultural institutions, amounting to a rhetorical trend throughout the entire critical spectrum; in this particular case, such efforts merely amounted to hiring a younger conductor with modernist inclinations. As we shall see, however, this relatively calm shift of cultural power would eventually meet with critical disfavor from the opposing, conservative camp once the process of transition to Ostrčil's concept of the National Theater was complete in the early 1920s.

The new dramaturge's duties commenced immediately with preparations for the premiere of Janáček's opera *Výlety páně Broučkovy* (The Excursions of Mr. Brouček). Ostrčil also planned an extensive list of possible repertoire, representing a broad range of time periods and both Czech and foreign composers, which would serve as his guide to new productions and premieres for the next several years, including Zich's *Vina* and his own recently completed *Legenda z Erinu*. The first few months of Ostrčil's employment at the National Theater were comparatively uneventful, given the internal strife of the preceding season. This relative calm was disrupted, however, by political events that lay outside the realm of culture. On April 15, 1920, the National Assembly was dissolved in preparation for the first full elections under the new democratic regime. The landslide victory of the Social Democratic Party started the process of change throughout the many facets of Czech life that had remained undisturbed since Habsburg times. Nowhere was this change more instantaneous than at the National Theater: the National Democratic Party, which had continued to support the Young Czech-based Společnost Národního divadla after the war, had fallen from power, and their adherents now proceeded to do the same. On April 30, there appeared in Prague's daily papers an announcement that the Společnost, after twenty years of "progressive" and "economically significant" leadership, would relinquish the administration of the National Theater into the hands of the provincial Bohemian government, effective the next day.[102] While this event did not mean the completion of the nationalization process (which would only happen in 1930), it did spell the end of an administration whose goals for the theater had been based more on economic interests than artistic ones. Nevertheless, the archconservative Gustav Schmoranz retained his post under the new administration as general director, and, as such, continued his authority over Kovařovic, Ostrčil, and the rest of the opera division. The public ownership of the theater, however, would eventually produce a greater sense of social responsibility in the planning of productions throughout the years of the First Republic, a change that amounted to a greater appreciation for modernist operas by both Czech and international composers.

While May 1920 was the first month of the new theater administration, it was the last for Kovařovic as director: since the beginning of the year he had experienced health problems, and over the summer and autumn of 1920 he appeared only rarely at the theater, being confined mostly to a sanatorium. During this period, Ostrčil took over many of the administrative duties of the opera division with a fair amount of success, in terms of both his critical reception and the esteem of his fellow musicians. So impressive was his substitution for Kovařovic, in fact, that the latter raced back to Prague when rumors began regarding Ostrčil's alleged plans to usurp the position of opera director.[103] The ailing director's fears would be in vain for several reasons: not only was Ostrčil's position not fully assured with regard to either the operatic ensemble or the critics, but with Kovařovic's health failing rapidly, the administration had already begun to arrange for his permanent replacement. When Kovařovic died on December 6, 1920, the advisory council voted unanimously for Ostrčil to replace him as opera director, ushering in an era that would last for the next fifteen years, and see almost as much controversy as the previous twenty. That controversy would start prematurely, on the preceding November 16, with the sudden forceful takeover of the historic Deutsches Landestheater by a Czech mob. The event would be the most extreme in a series of anti-German incidents within the development of the Czech musical community of Prague.

"De-Germanification":
The Deutsches Landestheater and the Czech Philharmonic

Although with the start of the Czechoslovak Republic there had been minimal bloodshed and no revolution as in neighboring states, a series of incidents disrupted the musical life of Prague, with serious implications for cultural interaction in the city. While both Czechs and German-Bohemians had defined their musical identities in direct opposition to each other since the Cultural Revival, only now did they have a chance to put this negativity into practice—with disturbing results. In seeking to overturn the hegemonic force of the Austrian regime in the new democratic era, the Czechs imposed an even more active system of repression and exclusion on their German neighbors. The ejection of Germans from the Conservatory, Czech Philharmonic, and the Deutsches

Landestheater severed the most important ties between the two communities, but also paralleled the ongoing purge of potentially "traitorous" Czechs from their own cultural life. Furthermore, these events point to crucial issues of reforming musical institutions in the name of social responsibility, however exclusional and negative the outcomes might be.

The German-Bohemian musical community was a small but active one, which could trace its roots at least as far back as the era of Smetana, although in a less prominent fashion. With the exception of the theaters, where the language of performance was an inevitable roadblock, German- and Czech-speakers had initially shared most of the cultural institutions of Prague, and the history of "de-Germanification" depicts their gradual separation into linguistic camps. Alongside this process of separation, whose negative consequences were isolation and a willful ignorance (often hatred) of each other, was a positive circumstance, wherein the German-Bohemian community evolved into an independent entity, no longer in the shadow of Czech endeavors.

The first institution to separate was Prague University, an event that resulted in two parallel musicology departments in the city in 1883. While for the Czechs this concern did not consist of much more than the lectures of Hostinský and Stecker in musical aesthetics and theory, respectively, the German University had a full lecture series in music history under Guido Adler well before the turn of the century. This situation continued well into the First Republic under Heinrich Rietsch, who succeeded Adler in 1900 (after the latter had departed for Vienna) and who founded a musicology institute in 1909, the same year that Nejedlý became the first chair in Musicology at the Czech University.[104] There was negligible contact between the two departments, however, and neither seems to have been involved in each other's affairs, moving in mutually exclusive circles. Only with the efforts during the First Republic between Erich Steinhard and various individuals from the Czech community, under the aegis of the journal *Der Auftakt*, did the two scholarly groups attempt a tentative rapprochement. Another prominent personality of German musical life was Alexander Zemlinsky, whom Heinrich Teweles brought to the Neues Deutsches Theater in 1910 to add a modernist spark to that institution. Zemlinsky's work prior to Czechoslovak independence included a wide range of operatic and concert endeavors that included the music of Mahler, Strauss, Schoenberg, Berg, Schreker, and others, efforts that coalesced into the Verein für musikalische Privataufführungen in the early 1920s. Designed as a fixed link to musical life in Vienna and other German musical centers, the Verein also served to promote new music with a sense of openness that many Czech societies were reluctant to do. Zemlinsky's leadership was likely one of the major factors behind the choice of Prague as the site of the 1924 and 1925 ISCM festivals: indeed, his premieres of *Erwartung* and the *Drei Bruchstücke aus Wozzeck* were long considered a benchmark achievement for new music in Prague. Like Steinhard, Zemlinsky acted as a bridge to both the Czech and Austro-German musical communities, engendering fruitful interaction between individuals such as Schoenberg, Berg, Ostrčil, Talich, Novák, and Suk.

After independence in 1918, the Prague Conservatory was the first musical institution to split into linguistic camps, as a direct result of the Czech faculty's resentment toward the German presence as well as the aristocratic administration, headed by Jindřich Kàan z Albestů and Rudolf Freiherr von Procházka. They demonstrated these feelings in an ultimatum published in the daily papers on November 28, 1918, insisting on "a purge of the national character of the institution," and "the introduction of a democratic spirit in the administration," statements that resulted in the resignation of both Kàan z Albestů and Procházka. Four days later, however, there appeared in *Národní listy* the announcement of the opening of the new Deutsche Akademie für Musik und darstellende Kunst in Prag, under the directorship of Procházka.[105] The new institution, which involved instruction in instrumental and vocal performance, music history, theory, and composition, as well as drama and dance classes, pooled together such talents as Zemlinsky, the theorist Romeo Finke, his nephew the composer Fidelio Finke, and the finest German instrumentalists in the city. Despite its sudden thrust into existence, the Deutsche Akademie sustained its commitment to educating fine German musicians throughout the remainder of the First Republic, and, along with the Neues Deutsches Theater, became a bastion of German musical life in Prague.

As indicated above, the German theater underwent a tumultuous transition in the first years of the Republic. Since the 1880s there had been three main venues for opera in Prague: the original German Estates Theater, built in 1783 (known alternately as Deutsches Landestheater or Stavovské divadlo), the Neues Deutsches Theater, constructed in 1886 as its modern counterpart, and the Czech National Theater. Although the Deutsches Landestheater had never been administered by Czechs, nor had it been the site of any significant Czech premieres, it had long been the object of envy by a significant portion of the music-going public, such that after independence, the matter of its ownership became one of open debate. Couched in rhetoric regarding the necessity for the National Theater's expansion, the idea of taking over the Deutsches Landestheater grew to the proportions of a national duty—as though the Czechs, believing themselves to be the oldest ethnicity in the region, could by rights "reclaim" the oldest established theater. In the National Assembly on April 8, 1919, in the context of a motion given by the Social Democrats Uhlíř and Neumann regarding the nationalization of the National Theater, there was an urgent demand that "the German Provincial Theater be turned into a Czech theater for purposes of spoken drama."[106] Citing the misuse of the building for showing films and its negligible contribution to the state of German theater in Prague, the politicians proposed its use by the National Theater, at least on a temporary basis until a more modern building could be constructed.[107]

In the autumn of 1919 the administrations of the National and Vinohrady theaters discussed a possible amalgamation, to unite in solidarity against the growing "bolshevist movement" among the personnel.[108] By the following May, the question of the Estates Theater arose again at a meeting held just five days after the dissolution of the Společnost Národního divadla, and the issue of annexation became part of the larger project of restructuring the National Theater. A proposal that a permanent commission be established regarding the annexation of the Deutsches Landestheater to the National Theater never came to fruition.

A full year later, just days before the death of Kovařovic, more forceful actions would take precedence. On November 16, 1920, a mob of Czech-speaking Prague citizens broke into the Deutsches Landestheater with the intention of ensuring its transferal to Czech power. Around noon on that date, a demonstration began at the foot of the famous statue in Wenceslas Square, ostensibly directed against recent aggressive acts by German nationalists in the border towns of Teplice and Cheb.[109] Led by former members of the Czech Legion (who provided the occasion with an illusion of heroism), the mob entered the theater through a back door and took possession, announcing the fact to the public immediately with placards that read: "Estates Theater for Teplice and Cheb."[110] The German director Krammer was removed from his office by force and directed by the legionnaires to his vehicle. A decision was made to perform *The Bartered Bride* on the newly acquired stage that very evening, which, according to theater critic and playwright Otokar Fischer, was "by coincidence the very day when, fifty-eight years before, the last regular performance in our mother tongue had taken place there."[111] The theater was decorated in garlands and banners in the Czech colors, and despite the short notice, the performance was sold out. Prior to the overture, National Theater soloist Jiří Huml gave a short speech entitled "The Estates Theater Taken over According to the Will of the People."[112] Ostrčil, regretting the forceful nature of the annexation, delegated the role of conductor to Kovařovic's assistant Rudolf Zamrzla; over the coming years, in the face of pressure from the theatrical administration, Ostrčil would express his reluctance to involve himself with opera at the Estates Theater. Not only was the extension of the *opera* to the newly annexed building not in the rationale for any of the takeover plans voiced in the months previous (which concerned only spoken drama), but such an act of imperialism also went against the "idea of the National Theater" as a purified realm of "national" artistic expression. According to Pala, Ostrčil viewed the theater administration's support of the annexation as motivated by economic, not artistic concerns, an assumption confirmed when the Estates Theater began to be used mainly for light operatic productions by foreign composers in Czech translation.[113]

The day after the official annexation, on December 7, 1920, a formal interpellation was issued by the German-Bohemian politicians Mayr-Harting and Naegle to the senate, requesting the return of the theater, taken by "an unqualified aggressive act, committed upon German citizens of the city and the state."[114] In much the same way that many of the Czechs had seen the Estates Theater as a long-desired goal of historical significance, the Germans of Prague felt its loss acutely, as though a crucial portion of their cultural life had been amputated. Although already replaced as the director of the German theaters, Heinrich Teweles described the annexation as a great injustice, with the insinuation that the Czech usurpers went against the judgment of their own government in their continued occupation of the theater.[115] The editors of the new German-Bohemian music journal *Der Auftakt* mentioned the events in a last-minute addition, entitled "Prager Musikleben," to their first issue, which appeared in late November. After a lengthy discussion of the meritorious cooperation between the city's artistic institutions, the authors added the following:

> Between the printing of these lines and the appearance of the first number of *Der Auftakt* lie well-known political events. The Theater in the Fruitmarket has changed its proprietors. For German musical life this means a difficult loss. The German opera is experiencing a temporary abbreviation of the concerts of the German Kammermusikverein and of the German Singverein, which had found accommodation there, and which, because of the Parliament's move to the Rudolfinum, have become homeless. It is not yet foreseeable how the conditions will be cleared up. So we will hope that the energies of all concerned will be successful in creating a substitute for those forced out, so that Prague's musical life does not suffer permanent damage from the encroachment of politics on the peaceful realm of art.[116]

As laconic as the foregoing text is with regard to the takeover itself, one notices a distinct avoidance of any mention of the Czech community and their active involvement in the entire process. The final statement regarding the "encroachment of politics" uses the phrase as though referring to an impersonal entity, and, although the addendum makes clear the editors' dismay over having already printed the initial, laudatory text, in no way does the above passage seek to contradict the previous material directly. Nor does the "difficult loss" for German musical life seem to imply any impact on its opera production, under Zemlinsky at the Neues Deutsches Theater. Indeed, both the above commentary and the subsequent, favorable descriptions of "Tschechisches Musikleben" in *Der Auftakt* demonstrate the nonconfrontational stance that journal would take throughout its twenty-year history during the First Republic, an attitude personified by its conciliatory editor, Erich Steinhard.

Rather more marginal to the concerns of Prague's German-Bohemian community was the flurry of activity around the Czech Philharmonic in the first two years of the Republic. These events would, however, serve to define the Czechs' relationship with their own institutions with respect to the use of de-Germanification as a tool for fulfilling a responsibility toward society. Like the National Theater, the orchestra had been owned and administrated during the Habsburg era by a private company with conservative political interests (the České filharmonické družstvo), and conducted by a contentious figure, Vilém Zemánek. Zemánek, born to a German-speaking Jewish family in Prague, was involved with the Czech musical community for his entire career, including very close ties with the UB that resulted in his participation in the 1912 protest against Nejedlý. At the turn of the century the conductor had been the UB's choice for the Czech Philharmonic over L. V. Čelanský, and despite criticism about weak artistic merits, he continued his leadership through the war years. The latter period was especially difficult for the financially impoverished orchestra as a result of their abandonment by the České filharmonické družstvo in 1914, at which point Zemánek became both musical and financial director of the ensemble.[117] As we have seen, Zemánek was singled out by Helfert in his list of desired changes in Prague's cultural institutions, on the one hand because of his ethnicity, and on the other because the Nejedlý circle openly favored Čelanský for the conductorship. So staunch was Helfert's support of the latter that he helped stage a coup with the most prominent orchestra members against Zemánek in April 1918, committing what Oldřich Pukl referred to as the first act of nationalist purging, even before independence.[118] At this point, with six months left in the First World War, Zemánek voiced his reaction publicly by revoking his exemption from Austrian military service, a deed whose anti-Czech implications virtually ended his career in that cultural sphere.

The competition for the conductorship of the Czech Philharmonic after Zemánek produced candidates from each of the Czechs' rival musical factions. While Čelanský was at first the most obvious choice, considering his history with the orchestra and Helfert, the situation quickly turned sour when he failed to prepare the repertoire sufficiently or even in a professional manner.[119] According to reviews of the time, Čelanský was capable of performing only *Má vlast* and the *Slavonic Dances*, and was unable to respond to more complicated, stylistically varied, or especially modern material. By the final days of the war, two opposing camps supported either Čelanský or the UB's proposed candidate, Václav Talich. Talich had been a satellite figure within the Czech musical establishment, and he now seized the opportunity to gain a permanent footing in Prague—his vehicle being Suk's *Zrání* and the intense publicity generated by that work and its composer. Although as of February 1919, the initial solution was to employ both Čelanský and Talich as co-conductors, by the summer of that year Talich had clearly won favor with the cultural and political elite of the city, masterminding an economic plan for the orchestra that included subsidies from private banks.[120] Talich's era as sole conductor of the Czech Philharmonic, beginning in September 1919, was one of artistic achievement and relative economic stability, forming a direct parallel to Ostrčil's regime at the National Theater.

That the politics of orchestral music in Prague were still embroiled in a dense web of anti-German feeling is demonstrated by the series of conflagrations surrounding two other musicians, Oskar Nedbal and V. V. Šak. In this case, as with the preceding "Suk Affair," Czech musicians were at the center of the controversy, albeit now with greater implications for relations with German culture, both at home and abroad. Similar to Zemánek, the careers of both men were ruined by the ill feeling and disgrace associated with the events. Nedbal, formerly violist in the Czech Quartet and conductor of the Czech Philharmonic (1896–1906), had left Prague in 1906 to conduct the Tonkünstlerverein in Vienna until the end of the war. Upon his return to Prague at the end of 1918 (when he was also a likely successor to Zemánek), Nedbal was chastised for his long absence in the Imperial capital, as well as for having composed music to the patriotic poem "Austrie" by Dostál-Lutinov. The "Nedbal Affair," as it came to be known, was a short-lived series of anonymous attacks on the conductor in *Hudební revue* in December 1918 and the following March, stating, for example, that Nedbal "suffered long and hard from his Czechness when he discovered that he is really a subject of the Hungarian state, and that his father is a pure-blooded German."[121] Although it was Nedbal's activities, and not his parentage, that formed the official reason for his disfavor with the Czech establishment, the comment is strongly reminiscent of the rejection, only a few months before, of Zemánek, whom Helfert had called simply "the German."

The resulting publicity was enhanced by the entrance on the Czech scene of musician and impresario V. V. Šak, a young man from a wealthy Prague family who had initially been a prospective investor in Talich's plan to reorganize the postwar Czech Philharmonic.[122] When the latter began to approach banks as the sole investors over the summer of 1919, Šak immediately set about launching his own independent orchestra in competition with the Czech Philharmonic, with Nedbal as conductor. That anything should compete with a national institution that had survived so much financial hardship was considered shameful to the point of treason, in that it put monetary gain ahead of national pride. As soon as the offer to Nedbal became public knowledge, Novák, Ostrčil, and Talich each sent letters to Šak, condemning Nedbal for his alleged anti-Czech activity and insisting that he not be hired; by this point, however, Šak and Nedbal were firmly allied, in open opposition to Prague's musical establishment. This provocation prompted two significant responses: Nedbal threatened publicly to sue Novák, Ostrčil, and Talich; and Šak appealed to Maffie for a judgment that would settle the matter of Nedbal's Austrian sympathies.[123] While the tribunal's verdict *against* Nedbal did not settle the matter fully, the case provided a stark contrast to the "Suk Affair" of exactly a year before. Most significant in this regard is Nedbal's outright rejection by the UB, who had defended Suk so ardently in his time of need. Given the parallelism and proximity of the two cases, it is easy to read Nedbal's ostracism as the UB's attempt to offset the strong implications of favoritism they had faced with Suk. Nedbal, being more peripheral to the group than Suk, was thus an easy scapegoat, through which the UB could appear reasonably objective toward matters of national and ethical concern.[124]

Šak's entrance into the world of Czech musical politics aggravated the preexistent tensions between musicians and capitalist administrators that had already caused controversy in the National and Vinohrady Theaters. In fact, the so-called

"Šakova filharmonie" was formed largely by terminated members of the Vinohrady Theater orchestra, who simply changed administrations, along with Čelanský, recently discharged from the Czech Philharmonic. By early 1920, both Čelanský and Nedbal were signed on as co-conductors of the Šakova filharmonie, in a "salon des refusés" that openly defied the UB and its associates. Alongside the orchestra, Šak's company (entitled "Presto") inaugurated a concert agency, printing house, and the journal *Hudba*, which ran for two years with Foerster as editor, and which, despite its inclusion of serious analytical articles, served primarily as an advertisement and soapbox for Šak's endeavors.[125]

Prior to Nedbal's debut with the Šakova filharmonie, however, the group's founder began to feel the effects of the establishment's scorn: on April 5, 1920, Šak received a letter of condemnation from the Economic Club of Prague Municipalities for his plans to engage as guest conductors the Austro-Germans Leo Blech, José Eibenschütz, and Werner Wolf.[126] When the group accused Šak of willful national provocation in conducting business with German musicians, the entrepreneur turned around and declared, quite significantly, that the Czech musical atmosphere in Prague was small-minded in its refusal to admit its dependence on its own German minority. These remarks (perhaps calculated ones, given the politically charged atmosphere) won the acclamation of the main German-Bohemian newspaper *Prager Tagblatt*, as well as the Czech journals *České slovo* and *Tribuna*, both of which had already been sympathetic to the anti-establishmentarian tactics of Nejedlý. A war of words commenced between these three journals and the conservative-nationalist papers *Národní listy*, *Národní politika*, and the agrarians' *Venkov*, which branded Šak as an antipatriot.[127] *Prager Tagblatt*, whose connections to the Austro-German world were essential to its survival, succeeded in having its editorials on the "Šak Affair" reprinted in the journals of major German cities, making the controversy one of the most publicly known of Prague's musical "affairs," and winning Šak further acclaim throughout Central Europe. The Šakova filharmonie embarked on a tour of Germany in September 1920 with Nedbal as the sole conductor, undertaken in open defiance of Šak's opponents; nevertheless, such a venture ultimately ruined the public support Šak had hitherto enjoyed. Upon their return to Prague, the orchestra was unable to make up the financial losses incurred on the German tour, and despite the advertisements for an absolutely baffling second season of all nine symphonies of Beethoven, Bruckner, and Mahler, both the ensemble and its parent company "Presto" folded the next year. Čelanský and Nedbal, their protector defeated and with virtually every remaining door in Prague closed to them, left the city for work elsewhere; neither returned in a professional capacity for the remainder of their careers.

The "Šak Affair" demonstrates the direct impact of the Czech-German struggle on music making in Prague, especially when combined with the pitfalls of institutional reform, private ownership, and public opinion in the early years of the First Republic. In terms of both the alleged "national provocation" of hiring German conductors and the stigma already attached to Nedbal, Šak transgressed the accepted bounds of cultural interaction. The negative press, coming as it did even before the forced annexation of the Estates Theater, reveals the growing consciousness of the existence of the German-Bohemian musical community on the part of both Czechs and Germans. Prior to independence, there was little awareness among Czech journalists of the merits of German-Bohemian music making in Prague, since Czech music, from the time of Smetana, had been defined in opposition to music in Austria and Germany as a whole. Šak's rebuttals and the involvement of *Prager Tagblatt* are some of the first open acknowledgments of the minority community and its contributions to the larger cultural sphere. No longer Austrians, German-Bohemian musicians were for the first time beginning to shape a new identity for themselves, looking to individuals such as Alexander Zemlinsky, Fidelio Finke, and Erich Steinhard, at the Neues Deutsches Theater, Deutsche Akademie für Musik und darstellende Kunst, and *Der Auftakt*, respectively.[128] Indeed, this new identity would have an impact on the cultural interaction between Czechs and Germans in Prague throughout the First Republic. As we have seen with Zemánek, Nedbal, Procházka, and the Estates Theater administration, their rejection by the Czech community was based not on their foreignness per se, but was a reaction to their (perceived) German ethnicity within an independent Czech state. Although the above controversies were all highly negative and even disturbing, the mutual awareness of the two communities would grow to produce artistically vibrant—if not always unproblematic—musical endeavors.

Ostrčil at the National Theater: *Pelléas* and *Slib*

For a time long after the many smaller debates had subsided, the first few years of Ostrčil's directorship of opera at the National Theater would help to define Czech musical identity, especially as its early days overlapped with the peak of nationalist and modernist controversy in Prague. After Kovařovic's two decades of often stultifying power in the theater, Ostrčil's regime would span fifteen years and shape the musical attitudes and cultural interactions of the entire musical community, both Czech and German. In the wake of the takeover of the Estates Theater, the internal relations at the National Theater were scarcely better than before, despite hopes to the contrary. As head of the operatic ensemble, Ostrčil was suddenly left alone to face both the administration above him and the ranks of musicians below. What hitherto had been a welcome chance to encourage reform in the shadow of Kovařovic (even as he lay terminally ill throughout 1920) now became an onerous task, the completion of which Ostrčil would have to fight for, with varying degrees of necessity, throughout his entire tenure. Even within the first few years, the National Theater became a battleground for the contestation of issues of operatic aesthetics, modernism, and cultural interaction that once again divided the critics of Prague.

At first, however, the critics were the least of Ostrčil's problems, seeming largely benevolent to the leader-elect over the course of his first few productions as director. Significant in this regard is the letter of congratulation he received from the UB, a sign of allegiance and trust in his continuation of Kovařovic's legacy: the reference foreshadows the dissenting voices that Ostrčil faced when he began to deviate from their expectations.[129] Rather, the conductor's first opposition came from within the theater, mainly from the general artistic director Schmoranz and members of the orchestra who were unwilling to explore a more challenging repertoire by Czech and international modernist composers. The first six months of Ostrčil's tenure were crucial toward the development of his large-scale plan for the direction of opera at the theater, ideas that were hindered in their execution by a deep-seated conservatism left over from Kovařovic's regime.[130] After the death of his colleague, Schmoranz refused to see a future for the opera division any differently from the pattern he himself had laid out with Kovařovic: beginning with Ostrčil's earliest repertoire sketches for the first season, Schmoranz asserted his authority in an effort to weaken that of his new opera director. While the conductor's original plans for the upcoming season included two challenging modern operas, Debussy's *Pelléas et Mélisande* and Zich's *Vina*, Schmoranz insisted upon the production of *Slib* (The Promise), the opera that Kovařovic had left unfinished at his death, as a priority over the other two.

Pelléas et Mélisande would prove to be the first of many turning points in Ostrčil's fortunes as a high-profile cultural representative in the Czech music community. As we have seen, the process of de-Germanification also involved a conscious turn toward France as a bearer of modern European culture, whose perceived leadership in literature and music the Czechs felt themselves obliged to follow. With *Pelléas*, scheduled for its Czech premiere on November 1, 1921, Ostrčil endeavored to fulfill what many considered a long-awaited cultural need: to acquaint the Czech public with recent operas by contemporary European composers. To this end, he employed the young director Ferdinand Pujman, who quickly became known for his modernist operatic concept.[131] Others, however, disagreed with the new direction of the National Theater toward progressive art: both main tenors in the ensemble, Vladimír Wuršer and Hilbert Vávra, openly refused the role of Pelléas, to the point that the former was dropped from the company. Vávra finally agreed at the eleventh hour to study the part, eventually singing to the accompaniment of an orchestra that was on the brink of sabotaging the entire performance. These difficulties with personnel, unfortunately, came out in the quality of the performance itself, a point not lost on the body of music critics. Reviews in both *Čas* and *Lidové noviny* remarked on the artistically dismal state of affairs at the National Theater, which since the end of the war had shown a lack of direction: it was to be hoped, the critic in *Čas* conceded, that the production of *Pelléas* would be a turning point, allowing for more premieres instead of comfortable favorites.[132] Jan Löwenbach, on the other hand, felt that Ostrčil's authority was too weak to bring such a directional change about, an assumption that quickly gained ground among the more skeptical of the critical community.[133]

The premiere of *Pelléas et Mélisande* at the National Theater was significant in that it also represented the arrival of the first major piece of West European music in Prague after the war. As such, its reception, both within the theater and without, bore witness to the conflict in Czech society between the desire to forge cultural connections to the West and the desperate struggle not to surrender the system of artistic values in place prior to 1918. As Pala related, the newer, "progressive" attitude toward operatic production, involving modernist repertoire, direction, and set design, was all part of Ostrčil's "idea of the National Theater." This concept envisioned a theater making the transition from a spirit of insularity (as encapsulated in the proscenium motto, "The Nation unto Itself") to one of cooperation, with a responsibility toward Czech society to present works of high artistic quality, thereby fostering participation in the larger European cultural sphere. Such a future for the theater and for Czech music making in general would effectively fulfill the paradigms for art and society promulgated by Hostinský, Nejedlý, and their followers, among whom Ostrčil and his new lieutenant, Pujman, had undoubtedly placed themselves. In this context, the ranks of the opponents to Ostrčil and his plan for the future of opera at the theater were, by and large, made up of the faction that had stood against Nejedlý before the war and shortly thereafter in the "Suk Affair." As we shall see, however, the opposition to Ostrčil's modernism based its criticism in increasingly conservative artistic values in the new political era, since their demands stayed rigid despite the fast-moving cultural climate after 1918.

Ostrčil's difficulties with the conservative opposition within the theater and outside it came to a head with the proposed plans for a production of Kovařovic's fragmentary opera, *Slib*. Although Kovařovic worked on the opera continuously in his final years, only the prologue ever saw completion in vocal score. Ostrčil, who by the time of Kovařovic's death had overcome long-standing factional differences with the older conductor and had begun to view him as somewhat of a mentor, could nevertheless not condone the production of such a fragmentary, and in his opinion, artistically unsuitable work by his opera company. On October 30, 1921, Schmoranz suddenly intervened in Ostrčil's operatic program for the season, demanding the production of *Slib* and the comic opera *Cesta oknem* (Through the Window) for a first-anniversary memorial celebration of Kovařovic's death.[134] When Ostrčil openly resisted this encroachment upon his authority, Schmoranz conveyed the situation to the theater administration in what amounts to a virtual denunciation of his opera director.[135] In an act that demonstrated the thin line between art and politics, the administration decreed that the production of *Slib* should go forward.

As inconsequential as the performance of a twenty-five-minute segment in honor of a recently deceased conductor may seem, the circumstances reveal more than just an attachment to Kovařovič as a person or even as an artist. The criticism of the *Slib* premiere makes clear that there was a marked refusal to part with the pre-1918 past and its cultural values within a large portion of Czech musical society. Even before the performance, playwright Jaroslav Hilbert chastised Ostrčil for his apparent disrespect toward the aesthetic of his predecessor, for whom he was a doubtful replacement.[136] This rebuke seemed to open the floodgates in the critical community, providing the stimulus for a postmortem cult of Kovařovic that ran parallel to a surge of attacks against Ostrčil as a person of artistic authority. Through his perceived lack of respect for the past regime, Ostrčil was considered to be unworthy of his status: that this problematic issue had its basis in a new attitude toward repertoire, performance style, and even audience represented a parting of the ways between the conductor and the more conservative segment of Czech society, both musical and otherwise. As the years following *Slib*'s performance show, Ostrčil's main opponents in this struggle were Antonín Šilhan at the National Democratic paper *Národní listy*, and to a lesser extent, Otakar Šourek at the Agrarian paper *Venkov*. Šilhan, known for his sharp tongue, dwelt on the theme of the "promise" (i.e., "slib"):

> *The Promise*, the title of Kovařovic's unfinished opera, reminds me of another promise. It was the promise that [opera stage-director] Pollert gave at Kovařovic's graveside: "We promise that we will keep the opera of the National Theater at the height to which you raised it." Today, after one year, does this promise appear fulfilled in the operatic performances of the National Theater?[137]

Šilhan's rhetoric, steeped in a romantic nationalism in which Kovařovic figured as a descendant of the founders of the National Theater, was doubly powerful through the image of the hero's funeral. Indeed, the above passage is tied to a strong Czech tradition of artist burials and graveside memorials, whose symbolism was (and still is) echoed every year in the famous Slavín cemetery in Vyšehrad, and which constitutes a significant, spiritual component of Czech romantic nationalism.[138] It is no wonder, then, that Šilhan became the leader of the anti-Ostrčil faction when the new conductor's plan for the National Theater took a path different from Kovařovic's, precisely when the legacy of the latter was threatened. At this point, too, Šilhan had an abrupt change of attitude toward the directorship of Pujman, whose work (alongside Ostrčil's) he had appreciated in *Pelléas et Mélisande*. Ironically, many critics from all sides, including the hesitant Šourek and the Nejedlian Doležil, found *Slib* itself to be a disappointment, insufficient to retain a place in the National Theater repertoire—hence similar to arguments Ostrčil had given in his disagreement with Schmoranz. After a short run the work was dropped quietly from the repertoire.

These preliminary difficulties would set the tone for Ostrčil's decade and a half, fighting with critics as he introduced new operas or updated older ones. The most significant battles in the early 1920s would revolve around the production of Czech works, particularly *Vina*, the latest opera by aesthetics professor and ardent Nejedlian Otakar Zich, whose music seemed to represent for many the ideological encroachment of his faction (discussed in detail in chapter 6). The new, modernist productions of Smetana's eight operas, being the combined efforts of Ostrčil, Pujman, and the set-designer František Kysela in preparation for the Smetana Centennial, would prove to have an even greater impact on the critical sphere of Prague. With its sheer volume of groundbreaking productions, the year 1924 would be a turning point for the Czech community and its relationship both to its own sense of tradition and to the perceived threat of international modernism.

The Second ISCM Festival and the Smetana Year

In 1924, the concertgoers of Prague witnessed the culmination of two large-scale projects that had taken shape over the years preceding: the Festival of the International Society for Contemporary Music and the celebrations for the hundredth anniversary of Smetana's birth. These events also saw the beginnings of a cooperative effort from both the Czech and German musical communities in planning the ISCM festival. Chosen the year prior in Salzburg, Prague hosted the second annual orchestral showcase from May 25 to June 7, a phenomenon organized in large part by the Czechoslovak representatives Jirák, Štěpán, Löwenbach, and *Der Auftakt*'s editor Erich Steinhard. Although the Czechoslovak section was limited to only two orchestral selections, they were allowed to present two concurrent opera festivals in honor of Smetana's cente-nary, which included a full cycle of his operas as well as a cycle of those by his-torically important Czech composers. The reception of these compositions, both foreign and Czech, as well as the outcome of the event itself, did much to change ideas about Czech musical identity at this time, albeit not in a way that anyone could have expected. Long anticipated as the moment where Czech and European modernism would finally join in happy union, bearing the fruit of the cultural openness heralded in 1918, the international compositions at the festi-val proved to be somewhat of a disappointment to the insular Czechs. So, too, was the Czech contribution fraught with anxiety, attempting as it did to repre-sent the achievements of Czech culture to a world they found difficult to face.

For the most part, the celebratory operatic cycles had been planned well in advance of the festival, indeed almost from the beginning of Ostrčil's tenure at the National Theater. Each of the eight Smetana operas was given a daring, new production, most of which had been premiered in the preceding two seasons; the second cycle, which included Zich's *Vina*, Novák's *Lucerna*, and Janáček's *Káťa Kabanová*, also incorporated new or recent productions. As to the effect of these operatic cycles within the Prague context, the most striking aspect is the unusu-ally negative criticism that the majority of the modernist productions received, starting with the premiere of Smetana's *Tajemství* (The Secret) in May 1922. The most formidable resistance came with the new production of *The Bartered Bride* in May 1923, causing a furor that reached all the way to the level of parliamentary debate. Led by Šilhan, Ostrčil's perennial nemesis, the critics of the Czech conservative newspapers attacked the efforts of the conductor and his creative team of Kysela and Pujman, the latter of which had been reinstated as director after having been forcefully ejected after the premiere of Zich's *Vina* in 1922.[139]

In what was perhaps the pinnacle of his campaign against Ostrčil's modernist conception of the National Theater, Šilhan, in his review "The Three Discoverers of Smetana," ironically accused the trio of having presented *The Bartered Bride* as a tragedy, disrespectful of the legacy due a composer of such national importance. "It will be a sad celebration. I have the impression that the discoverers wanted not to celebrate Smetana in any way, but rather to distort the work and to disgust the nation such that it would be more receptive to the beauties of [Foerster's] *Nepřemožení*, *Vina*, and [Ostrčil's] *Legenda z Erinu*."[140] At this point the rarely vocal Ostrčil wrote an open letter to the liberal paper *Národní politika*, accusing Šilhan of being a mere provocateur. The debate raged throughout June 1923, the main issue being the roles of tradition and modernism in the theater. On June 14, eleven members of the prominent Dramatists' Union issued a protest against Šilhan and his "patented 'patriotism,' which so often masks artistic backwardness," thereby evoking Hostinský's distinction between the progressively national and the superficially patriotic.[141] The following day, the conservative playwright and political analyst Viktor Dyk defended Šilhan's right to open criticism, saying that anything less was a threat to culture; by the end of June, Foerster had entered the fray, defending Ostrčil's modernist concept in its adherence to an essentially Smetanian aesthetic of progressiveness, and tying his achievements to those of the Cultural Revival.

The debate continued throughout the summer and autumn of 1923, and on November 26, the agrarian politician František Hnídka spoke out in Parliament against the "joyless" interpretation by Ostrčil, Pujman, and Kysela, which he declared "anti-Smetana," the work of a "certain artistic clique"; Hnídka ended by expressing the hope that the audience would avoid the production entirely.[142] A response came two weeks later from Senator František Krejčí, who asked that any discussion regarding the direction of modern theater be left to the Ministry of Education and National Culture, or if not, to the artists themselves, lest aesthetic decisions be made by unqualified onlookers. His remarks were, indeed, a thinly veiled attack on the right wing's appropriation of cultural issues for their own political agenda, without having much interest or stake in the art works themselves. Krejčí's defense of Ostrčil's modernist outlook was a major victory for the conductor, encouraging a change in public attitude in the months prior to the international event the following May.

The 1924 orchestral festival of the ISCM was perhaps one of the most peaceful cultural events of its size to be held in Prague in the interwar period, considering the confluence of stylistic and ideological viewpoints gathered there and the attendant potential for controversy. Nevertheless, the event demonstrates the serious disappointment that Czech audiences (and musicians in particular) were feeling toward the European modernism they had sought for so long. Well-known as the occasion at which Zemlinsky premiered Schoenberg's *Erwartung*, the festival attendees also had the opportunity to see Ravel's *L'heure espagnole*, Ostrčil's *Symfonietta*, and Suk's *Zrání*, as well as lectures by Helfert, Nejedlý, and Jirák. With regard to the Smetana-related aspects of the festival, the lectures and related publications by Helfert and Zich weighted the proceedings toward the Nejedlý camp, in the same way that the Smetana Exhibition of 1917 had afforded the group an "official" status.

Perhaps even more significant with regard to the city's factionalization is the participation of the German-Bohemian community as a serious contributor to international modernism as well as Prague music making. The efforts of Zemlinsky and the German theater went a long way toward bridging the gap between Czechs and Germans, such that subsequent years brought even more collaborations, culminating in the rapprochement of both sides under the aegis of the avant-garde in the 1930s. Quite surprisingly, Bartoš wrote extensively in his article for *Smetana-Hudební list* about Zemlinsky's success with *Erwartung* and of the German-Bohemian involvement in general, singing the praises of the Verein für musikalische Privataufführungen and its organizational efforts.[143] The Verein, Zemlinsky's branch of Schoenberg's Viennese society, had been operational since 1922, serving as the German-Bohemian contingent of the Czechoslovak ISCM committee, and had organized its own concert of chamber music including the work of Schulhoff, Ullmann, and Finke. Bartoš went on to say that, although the interest in contemporary music among the Prague German public was stronger than among the Czechs, they "did not bring [to the festival] anything of their own that might smell like native soil and be as rooted in it as is Smetana's music and the music of our other great composers, which you will recognize from afar because of their tone of *warmth*."[144] It is interesting that Bartoš could write intelligently about *Erwartung*'s modernist music and staging and subsequently resort to blatant Herderian clichés: such was the confusion that the festival itself produced, however, between a desire for cosmopolitanism and a longing for isolation.

In the criticism of the 1924 ISCM Festival there was some tension between the *Listy Hudební matice* and *Smetana-Hudební list* factions over the artistic worth of international modernism and the attendant preservation of essential Czechness. Nevertheless, the general tone reveals a softening of the isolationist attitude encountered in the months prior, if only for the sake of presenting the best possible face to the outside world. As can be expected, the residual discomfort with Ostrčil's modernist operatic leadership was reflected by local critics, in conjunction with the fact that Novák's *Lucerna* was not performed at the National Theater as part of the main cycle, but was relegated to Brno instead. Šilhan and Šourek criticized the conductor for this oversight; Šourek also bemoaned the lack of Dvořák's music in the festival's program, especially since that composer had contributed to the modern artistic direction of Novák and Suk, whose music did appear.[145] Prior to the event, Jan Löwenbach, one of the principal organizers, penned an apologetic essay for *Listy Hudební matice*, in which he stated that doubts over the "ideological structure of the festival" could be laid to rest.[146] Fears that some sort of "grotesque" or "bizarre" style would be imposed on Czech music would prove to be false, since the stylistic attributes of the ISCM were quite diffuse and eclectic, and therefore impracticable as a unified and "exclusive expression of contemporary work."[147] Thus insulated, the Czech hosts could demonstrate to the foreign public (or as Löwenbach wrote, "convince them of") the value of Smetana as a guiding light for modernist music, a topic he made the primary focus of his post-festival review of non-Czech criticism.[148] Indeed, the majority of post-festival criticism dealt primarily with local contributions as opposed to foreign ones; hence the 1924 ISCM was judged a success, since the Czech community felt they had been able to prove their independence from the rest of Europe through the high moral standard of their artistic direction. By contrast, the thrilling variety of foreign compositions and their potential for cultural interaction were, by and large, ignored as inconsequential.

Very few individuals realized the irony of the situation or were able to look past local prejudices with any sort of objectivity. One critic in particular, Josef Stanislav, credited the ISCM festival as having "a far-reaching significance for the serious Czechoslovak artist and listener. For the first time an atmosphere of modern music is blowing over us in the true sense of the word, placed simultaneously opposite art of other streams, captivating us as though through a spy-glass."[149] Stanislav continued his comments, chastising the current tendency in Prague music criticism to use "comfortably convincing and attractive phrases about the decadence of foreign art and the elevation of our art above the art of all nations of the world, thus fostering a 'healthy' conservatism and petty-bourgeois indolence . . . within which Smetana's name appears like a *deus ex machina.*"[150] In this atmosphere of closed-minded self-congratulation, Stanislav's essay would scarcely have been comprehensible, particularly regarding the increasingly conservative stance of the generation that had come of age between the wars; hence, his insightful remarks were more indicative of a younger group that would come into its own much later in the decade.[151]

Stanislav's attitude of open-minded pragmatism would not have a lasting effect on the Czech musical community and its attitude toward cosmopolitan interaction. As the following year's ISCM festival, also held in Prague, would show, what had begun as a welcome opportunity to experience international modernism and display Czech achievements quickly wore thin, and the resulting disillusionment would shape not only the activities of Prague's musical community, but also its attitude toward its own merits and identity.

* * *

An examination of the first six years of the Czechoslovak Republic reveals a society fraught with the tensions of democratization on all levels, much like other new regimes throughout Europe. While in late 1918 many critical voices expressed extreme optimism regarding the elimination of the old, oppressive administrations in cultural institutions, thereby introducing a new era of openness, these dreams quickly vanished with the unsteady pace of change. Even when change arrived—the salient examples being the de-Germanification of the Conservatory and Estates Theater and the Ostrčil administration at the National Theater—the results did not come without problems. Particularly in the case of Ostrčil this change caused a new factionalization of critics, loosely based on the critical divisions of pre-1918. New factors also emerged in the form of a witch-hunt aimed at artists who had not done their patriotic duty during the war (in an effort to ensure the socially responsible basis of Czech culture), altering the careers of Suk and Nedbal irrevocably. These years saw the anxiety of modernism spread throughout the musical community, affecting not only the attitude toward new music in Western Europe, but also the reception at home of works such as Suk's *Zrání*, Zich's *Vina*, and Ostrčil's *Legenda z Erinu*.

Chapter Six

Infinite Melody, Ruthless Polyphony

Czech Modernism in the Early Republic

The first few years of the Czechoslovak Republic were somewhat paradoxical regarding music composed by members of its own community and the issues surrounding the production of this music. On the one hand, as we have seen in chapter 5, much of the critical debate focused on the role of these composers' tradition-based fin-de-siècle modernism amid an increasingly present European avant-garde. Much of what was performed by the Czech Philharmonic and National Theater, however, consisted of the larger works of older Czech composers, written during the years of the First World War, at a time when fewer concert opportunities and performance forces had been available. As such, while ideologues (mostly younger composers of the wartime generation who had yet to write anything substantial themselves) debated about how to adapt to future directions of musical style, audiences were made to catch up on the recent past. Notably, this music was often presented *as though it were* avant-garde modernism, and critics, particularly those representing the conservative middle class, reacted accordingly. The result was an artificial environment designed to alienate mainstream audiences even when it was not especially warranted, since much more radical experiments were happening in almost every country of Europe. The sole exception, of course, is Janáček, most of whose operas gained favor with the Prague community upon their premieres under Ostrčil at the National Theater in the 1920s.

Beyond Janáček's idiosyncratic style, Czech modernism, even when practiced by the younger Prague generation, continued down the path set by Novák, Suk, and Ostrčil around 1900. The main hallmarks of this style were densely contrapuntal textures and on-running motivic development, with varying degrees of indebtedness to Wagner, Strauss, and after approximately 1925, Janáček. One significant device introduced in compositions around the First World War is the use of a kernel of motivic gestures, which appears at the beginning of a large-scale piece and serves to generate the rest of the musical material through a tightly knit motivic web. This structural technique is similar to Schoenberg's contemporary Grundgestalt, and like its outcome, developing variation, is derived ultimately from Wagner and Liszt's organicist conceptions of form. When combined with pervasive counterpoint in an orchestral setting—as it was for most Czech modernists—the result could be considered either an inspired mastery of boundless expression (as with Suk's *Zrání*), an opaque, cerebral exercise (Ostrčil's *Legenda z Erinu*), or even "the end of music" itself (Zich's *Vina*). That a technique employed so often should provoke such an array of responses indicates not only a possible variance in quality from work to work, but also that the perceived ideological position of each composer was a factor for critics. Inspired or not, each of these works shared a common—perhaps futile—goal of representing a cultural community at odds with international modernism, at a time when modernism itself had already begun to alienate its audience.

Reminiscence, Ripening, and Redemption: Suk's *Zrání*

As discussed in the previous chapter, one of the first musical events of the Czechoslovak Republic also ushered in one of its first ideological crises, with implications of national allegiance that went far beyond aesthetic concerns. The premiere of Josef Suk's tone poem *Zrání* (Ripening), two days after independence on October 30, 1918, created an atmosphere of public reverence around the composer, the work, and its perceived levels of meaning. Critics and audiences widely accepted the "ripening" of the title to signify that of not only the composer as an individual but also the Czech nation, hearing the maturation of a people in the ongoing development of motives from a tightly knit Grundgestalt across forty-five minutes of dense orchestral music. Suk's complex form of multiple movements subsumed into a single span, containing motivic reminiscences and prefigurations, can also be said to reflect the Czech historical consciousness of the time, which recast 298 years of Habsburg rule, a century of Cultural Revival, and national independence in a retrospective light of inevitability.

Suk composed *Zrání* throughout the years of the First World War as a continuation of the orchestral cycle he had begun with *Asrael* and *Pohádka léta* over a decade previously. The cycle was one of the most discussed aspects of Suk's career, in that it seemed not only to embody the main trajectory of the composer's artistic endeavors but also supposedly to provide a window into its creator's psyche that approached the autobiographical. This reading, never denied by Suk, dates from as early as the premiere of *Asrael*, the performance of which had become as much a collective act of grieving for Antonín Dvořák as for Suk himself, the young widower in the public eye. Thus, the ripening of *Zrání* held significance for the concertgoers of Prague as a serial installment of an intensely personal drama, writ large as a public spectacle. The choice of Antonín Sova's poem of the same name for his subject placed Suk among the symbolists, a literary group highly regarded in the early years of the century; the poem itself, republished with the score alongside Václav Talich's "official" analysis, did much to encourage the continued subjectivist, narrative reading of Suk's tone poem.

For the Prague audience of 1918, the title alone would connect Suk's piece to Sova's poem, itself an amorphous work with multiple suggested meanings. First encountered by the composer in 1912 during the beginning stages of his work on the tone poem, Sova's *Zrání* merges a human being with his/her natural surroundings, likening his/her maturation to the cyclical process of a day. The form of the poem offers a complex narrative layering, which, as we shall see, creates a parallel to the similar use of form in Suk's music.

Antonín Sova, *Zrání* (Ripening)

Across the plain the clouds float over the black forest . . .
The corn ripens and sings today
an amazing, rhythmic song of praise . . .

With faded bark the pine stands
solitary on the plain.
And flocks of birds swarm in the silent twilight,
in which the blood of the sunset
has faded, lightly pinkened . . .

Harmonious it is, the sacred calm,
over the water, over the grove, under the heavens,
in the far village, where not a person is heard,
in the far-off horizon, where black forests
droop at the edge of heaven,
and there like a memory it bubbles up from the depths,
now shooting up with sparks, now at rest,
and with the last flame ignites
the distance ablaze, where the brightness of the sun
is lost like a fanfare
in disappearing time . . .

From the depths how twilight exhales
before the glowing of the stars and into silence,
you believe you can hear a breath,
a greater calm, through which twilit worlds breathe,
a tuft among tufts, a blossom among blossoms,
and you dream:
Oh storms who have passed, downpours,
and winds who have roared wildly at our windows,
you violent torrents who have swelled into rivers,
and you persistent rains who were long unremitting:

Oh where did you go, you nervous, tearful pangs,
despairing days, nights, you reckless, courageous players?
You uncertain charms of love in the first Springs,
when the uncertain gold of primroses infused us with the gift
of ever more burning desire, from which the heart bleeds,
when it crawls after the far-off goal and staggers,
oh where did you get to, April sun and snow, where?
Where the fickle favor of hearts? Where the deception of smiles?

You festive quests into the unknown,
during which the consuming passion for human greatness
pursued our steeds
until their hooves struck sparks all around
and the horizons seemed to catch on fire at the break of day
already at the imminent goal of redemption?

Oh, not in vain did you pass, long ago,
oh storms, over the cape of highest Hopes,
you dense clouds in which there were no stars.
You helped bear the cruel lightning flashes!
You were driven by hundreds of tempestuous dangers,
that roared and whistled with an abysmal speech
filled with unfettered pains,
weeping for happiness! . . .

With destruction have you also borne the fertile ferment—
and now, when time has passed:
What was strong has had to force its way to the light,
to grow up and take to grain,
and live fully in ripening . . .
Whatever ripened could not know loss;
and thus only an immeasurable calm . . .

And I listen and gaze into the brightness.
In the cosmos are arranged thousands of stars . . .
And I measure the depths into which time has passed.
In this calm there is redemption.

In ripeness, come, oh final ripening,
oh sweet night, after the day.[1]

Many aspects of Sova's *Zrání* inform an understanding of the compositional
choices that Suk made when writing his tone poem, in that, while the music does

not necessarily conform programmatically to specific events in the text, it does achieve similar dramatic effects that evoke the process of human maturation. The apparent formlessness of the poem extends not only to its physical layout— line groupings of unequal size, rhyme without metrical structure—but also to its multiplicity of narrative modes, which combine internal monologue in both the past and present, exclamations directed at various natural forces, and the occasional statement offered to an audience separate from the author himself. Like the nature-inspired subject matter, the poem's form is cyclical, with references to ripening grain at either end that bracket a central sequence of complex reminiscences. These moments of past experience are in no way organized chronologically, nor do they achieve any sort of temporal unity, aside from their distance from the present: the sequence provides a variety of differing moods or characters, evoking emotions such as wonderment, fear, desire, anticipation, regret, and redemption. In this respect, the opening three lines of Zrání attempt to encapsulate (however laconically) the rest of the poem, in that a sense of nature-inspired danger is overcome by a process of maturation, to be celebrated by "an amazing, rhythmic song of praise."

The music of Zrání contributes to this narrative tendency, although as several contemporary critics claimed, Suk's initial conception for the work arose *before* his encounter with Sova's poem, such that any connection between the two media served more as a fulfillment of musical expression than as the basis for it. Václav Štěpán asserted that Suk's Zrání was in no way an attempt to paint Sova's Zrání in tones (echoing Hostinský's similar disdain for naturalism), such that the various musical episodes of the tone poem were not meant to correspond directly to the verbal descriptions of storms, daybreak, quests, and so on. Nevertheless, I contend that two substantial aspects of Sova's work seem to have had an effect on Suk's formal strategy. First, both works are inaugurated by an embryonic presentation of motives (or in contemporary Schoenbergian terms, a Grundgestalt) from which almost every subsequent expressive statement grows throughout the remainder of the work. Second, in both cases, this remainder is enacted formally through a complex series of reminiscences, after which the audience regains the state of mature understanding intimated in the opening gesture. Furthermore, the effect of collective maturation is captured in Suk's work by the offstage women's chorus, who sing wordlessly amid the musical and dramatic resolution of the tone poem.

Suk's Zrání is a masterwork of developing variation. The use of a Grundgestalt and its complex, contrapuntal Fortspinnung served to connect the work not only to the New German School and its latest representatives in Richard Strauss's tone poems and the early oeuvre of Schoenberg, but also to the contemporary conception of Czech modernism as a contrapuntal and motivic embodiment of *důslednost*. Suk's tone poem has the potential for yielding any number of possible formal schemes, several of which were discussed in the critical reception: among the most plausible is that of four movements subsumed into one large sonata form. Within this framework, Suk's marked use of reminiscences (of themes internal to *Zrání* as well as of preexistent works) and blurred formal divisions heighten the listener's interest and suggest a possible narrative of personal or collective maturation.[2] As such, the musical form itself held an awesome emotional power for the Czech public.

The twelve-measure Grundgestalt provides the basis for almost all of *Zrání's* subsequent motivic work, in terms of melodic and rhythmic cells, contours, and intervallic tendencies (ex. 6.1). Each of these components develops somewhat independently of the rest to form new thematic material in strikingly divergent directions; the generally contrapuntal texture and bitonal harmony of these twelve measures also presage the remainder of the piece. The very opening of *Zrání*, an unaccompanied melody for three solo violins, produces one of the most important themes, which is immediately subject to a fugato-like treatment. The intervals of this melody—predominantly seconds and fourths, hovering around E—are responsible for the majority of melodic gestures throughout the Grundgestalt. A countersubject encompasses the chromatic expansion of a minor second to a major sixth, a repeated-note passage in eighth notes, a dotted neighbor figure, and a rising three-note figure. As Štěpán pointed out, within the embryonic state of the opening, no one motive stands above the rest, and only with their development into independent themes do these fragments attain retrospective significance.[3] "All the motives, over which the melodic motion shifts, emerge, and disappear again, without our suspecting that these indefinite, merging lines, pointing nowhere, hide within themselves the same groupings of tones as later thematic crossbeams and pillars."[4] Štěpán went on to theorize about the individuality of Suk's conception in *Zrání's* introductory phrases, which, instead of presenting thematic or motivic material as bold, recognizable statements ("expressively and formally neutralized"[5]), offer a glimpse of melodic fragments in mid-transformation. Suk thus engages the members of his audience in a participatory form of narration, in that they discover a new understanding of the opening music amid a virtual enactment of the maturation process.

In his 1919 analysis, Talich (who was also the conductor at the premiere) described sixteen different motives in *Zrání*, all of which are derived from the initial theme in m. 1 (ex. 6.2).[6] To many of these, Talich also ascribed programmatic meanings, conforming to the generally accepted narrative of overcoming the hardships of life through maturation. As the music immediately following the Grundgestalt shows, the intervallic relationships of motive I are easily rearranged without destroying its developmental continuity; Talich's motives III, X, and XVI also demonstrate this process. A retrograde of three consecutive notes, found in motive I, forms a descending figure that appears in motives V, IX, XVI, and by extension, motives VI, VIII, and a host of developmental material not named by Talich. The dotted neighbor-note figure develops into an independent motive (II), and forms parts of motives III, V, and XIII; its

Example 6.1. Suk, *Zrání*, Grundgestalt (1–13).

Talich's program   **Formal layout**

I — Song of knowledge — Movt. 1: Principal theme

II — Song in praise of ripening

III — The human "I" — } Principal theme group

IV — Longing

V — Voice of the Earth — } Transitional themes

VI — Breath of the Infinite — Secondary theme

VII — Determination — (Movt. 4: Fugal subject)

VIII — Hymn of knowledge

IX — Song of youth — } Developmental themes

Example 6.2. Suk, *Zrání*, Talich's motives, programmatic meanings, and formal layout.

Example 6.2. (*continued*).

characteristic rhythm pervades much of the remaining material, most notably the vocalizations of the offstage women's choir at the very end of the work. The repeated-note figure, developed already in the Grundgestalt, eventually forms two important independent themes (Talich's motives VI and X, respectively). Two of the most extreme variations of the Grundgestalt material include motive IV, whose chromatic leaps are related to motive I and its countersubject, and motive VII, whose basic contour represents a chromaticization of I, a retrograde of VI, and whose triplets betray a connection to IV. Both of the latter motives function as independent themes that take on significance as *Zrání*'s form unfolds.

The formal layout of Suk's tone poem reflects the porous relation between past and present in Sova's narrative (as indeed, in the Czech historical consciousness). Although *Zrání* contains references to four large movements with complex internal forms, the disintegration of formal segments, the prefiguration of new ones, and the use of reminiscence serve to complicate a straightforward reading of the music. The Grundgestalt, in its presentation of the theme from which most of the motivic material derives, also takes on the role of a principal theme group in the context of a sonata-form opening movement (see annotations in ex. 6.2 and figure 6.1). A phrase of similar length develops and reinforces the principle theme (13–24) and leads to a transition dominated by motive IV (24–50).[7] Subtle appearances of motive VI prefigure its use in the secondary theme group (50–64), while IV recedes into sporadic fragments. A short transition, foreshadowing motive IX and highlighting an isolated appearance of motive VII, leads to a Fortspinnung of the secondary theme that ends in fragmentation (70–87). In a dynamic climax of the music so far, the principal theme appears in the full orchestra, now extended by motive VIII (87–100); a short codetta of two parallel phrases ends the exposition at m. 111. The development of what hitherto has been considered a "first movement" breaks down into a lengthy transition to a "second movement," with material based mostly on motives VI (i.e., the secondary theme), VIII, and IX; the latter two motives, through inversion and retrograde, become virtually indistinguishable. As with many of Suk's formal units, the lines of delineation become blurred through the use of motivic repetition and fragmentation (e.g., 180–212). A tranquil, fifteen-measure transition, offering three parallel phrases based on the VIII/IX complex, prepares the listener for the Adagio section, or "movement 2."

Perhaps the most formally and tonally fixed segment of the entire tone poem, the Adagio presents four relatively clear phrases of alternating themes (what Talich indicated as motives X and XI), separated by a central transition (245–61). Already within the context of the slow-moving second theme, however, Suk interjects motive XIII, whose unrelated rhythm, contour, instrumentation, and tempo undermine the prevailing mood (242, 244–50), eventually obliterating the fourth thematic statement completely (27off.). Gradually the new *scherzando* material of XIII takes over, after a prolonged transition containing reminiscences of X, interjections of IV and VIII, and prefigurations of the "third movement/scherzo" itself, which begins at m. 344. The scherzo is dominated by a short dotted motive (XIV) that undulates over the range of a third: Štěpán and others revealed this motive to be a paraphrase of the seventh piece from Suk's own piano cycle *Životem a snem* (ex. 6.3).[8] Another quote appears within the prevailing *moto perpetuo* in the form of the four-note "death motive" from the incidental music to the 1901 play *Radúz a Mahulena* (XV); perhaps the most recognizable of Suk's self-quotations, the combination of tritone and major-second intervals represents a chromatic variation of those found in motive I.[9] Texturally, the scherzo has much in common with the preceding material in

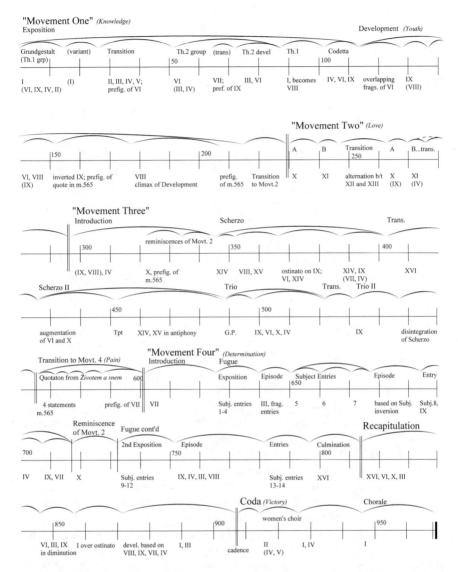

Figure 6.1. Suk, *Zrání*: schematic diagram of form with slurred subsections and motives (roman numerals refer to chart, Ex. 6.2).

Zrání, in that climaxes are attained and dissolved through repetition and fragmentation of motives: one such moment occurs with the arrival of a new motive, XVI, in the brass at m. 408. Formally, the scherzo is very diffuse, in no way bearing a resemblance to the repetitive form of its nineteenth-century origins; the dual appearance of motive XVI suggests a possible bisection of the movement at

Example 6.3. Suk, *Zrání*, quotation from *Životem a snem* (330–35)98.

Example 6.4. Suk, *Zrání*, fugal subject (624–27).

m. 425, but little other parallelism exists. After m. 487 the orchestration is greatly reduced, giving the effect of a trio that proceeds in four-measure phrases, in which woodwinds predominate; by m. 547 the complete disintegration of the scherzo is inevitable, when muted horns and timpani introduce a final statement of XV, given by the violas, *pizzicato*.

Formally, measures 565–600 represent a transition to the "final movement" of the tone poem; the majority of this music, however, is a substantial quote, again from the seventh piece of *Životem a snem*, now in greater detail and with the original rhythmic and metric designations. Delineated by four parallel phrases, the bass-register instruments present an undulating dotted figure whose climactic pitch climbs progressively higher, followed by repetitions of motive XIV. An orchestral crescendo brings a local climax after m. 586, and fragmentations of IV usher in the final movement, which begins with the faster tempo at m. 601. Motive VII is clearly the most salient material of the final movement, forming the subject of a fugue that begins at m. 624 (ex. 6.4); a relatively compact exposition of four entries lasts until m. 638, whereupon fragmentation of the subject inaugurates the first episode. Subsequent subject entries occur within a full-orchestral texture, alongside occasional inversions of the subject and brief appearances of other motives from earlier in the tone poem. The fugal/motivic interplay is temporarily interrupted by the extended reminiscence of motive X (i.e., the main theme from "movement 2") in the full orchestra, lasting fifteen measures. This reminiscence concludes the central portion of the fugue, after which commences the recapitulation of the four subject entries at m. 733. A climactic moment of fragmentation and inversion brings the climactic threefold appearance of motive XVI (801, 812, and 816) in the full brass, with which the fugue is forcefully concluded.

At this point in the form we encounter a precipitous recapitulation of motives from much earlier in the tone poem, including VI, X, III, and most prominently, motive I. The reappearance of material that had played such a key role (the main themes of the first two "movements") with such clarity and rapidity suggests that the music at mm. 820–907 represents a continuation of the opening sonata-allegro form. The principal theme (I) receives the most substantial treatment, in overlapping voices over an ostinato after m. 855, prolonged by developmental material (including the quotation from *Životem a snem*) that climbs to the highest climax in the work—the explosive cadence at m. 905, with six additional trumpets over the orchestra. The coda abruptly changes the mood, with a thinning of texture, a deceleration of tempo and the introduction of an offstage women's choir that sings vocalizations based on motive II (913ff.). Evoking the very opening of *Zrání* with the predomination of solo violin groups, the coda solidifies the feeling of finality with the reiteration of motive I. A chorale based on I concludes the work.

The above formal analysis represents only one of multiple possible readings provoked by the incredible scope and general amorphousness of Suk's single-movement tone poem. Reminiscence—and its counterpart, prefiguration—play a significant role in the drama that shapes *Zrání*, through not only the two prominent quotations but also the pervasive use of motives. Embedded within each section of the piece are marked statements of motivic material that appear "out of place," either because they have little to do with the immediately surrounding context of developing variation or because they have already received due treatment in earlier sections. While the largest reminiscence appears in the midst of the fugue at m. 716 (which acts as an interpolation of the second movement within the fourth), other transitional sections also demonstrate a more subtle technique of motivic disintegration, wherein new, antithetical material has already been introduced and is subjected to persistent interruptions by older material. The effect at mm. 270–344 (the transition between movements 2 and 3) is such that the interruptions to the Adagio (by means of motive XIII) gradually take over the texture, to the point where it is the reminiscences of the Adagio that appear as interruptions amid predominantly *scherzando* material (321, 334). The use of prefiguration, intimately connected to reminiscence, is equally effective throughout *Zrání*, in that Suk's ongoing thread of developing variation rarely admits motives without a clearly audible connection to the Grundgestalt. The quotation from *Životem a snem*, presented as a separate, transitional section to movement 4 at m. 565, has already been prefigured four times in earlier movements, and appears twice more in the recapitulation; although initially contextless, the music has become fully integrated into the work by the time we hear the quotation proper. Similarly, the fugal subject appears as early as m. 64 with virtually no connection to the surrounding material, prefiguring by far its reappearance in the introduction to movement 4 at m. 601.

In the context of the dramatic unfolding of *Zrání*'s form, Suk's use of reminiscence and prefiguration literally enacts the dissolution of past and present into each other, resulting in a suspension of the listener's formal perception. This process can easily be connected to the sense of cycle that Suk was attempting to achieve in his orchestral (and nonorchestral) compositions through the use of recycled quotations and autobiographical stimuli: the listener experiences more than just one composition in a single hearing. More significant for *Zrání* itself is the connection of these musical devices to the built-in reminiscences within Sova's poem, in which, we are told, Suk found the verbal fulfillment of his musical ideas. Each of the analysts of *Zrání* sought to interpret the structure of the work in terms of narrative, based on the events described in Sova's poem (despite Štěpán's caveat against this practice), and on the assumption of Suk's work as a link in the autobiographical cycle. The earliest of these publications, by Talich in 1919, eschewed traditional formal designations in favor of the following six-part scheme: Knowledge, Youth, Love, Pain, Determination, and Victory.[10] With respect to my formal analysis, these sections correspond to the exposition; the development of movement 1; movements 2 and 3; the transition to movement 4 (i.e., the quotation from *Životem a snem*); the fugue and recapitulation; and the coda, respectively. Clearly, Talich's formal sections gain their significance from the narrative outlined in Sova's poem, demonstrating the built-in cyclical formation (both Knowledge and Victory are in the present, postmaturation) as well as the affinity toward reminiscences (the entire central body of the work, including the fugue). Several motives also have specific designations in Talich's analysis, including "song in praise of ripening" (II), "the human I" (III), "longing" (IV), "Cupid's arrow" (transitional material prior to movement 2, or "love"), and "fate" (XVI). In this manner, Talich described the narrative of an individual (indistinguishable from the composer himself) who, in later years, looks back to the trials and tribulations of his youth, passing through amorous and tempestuous experiences before embarking on the inner struggle that brings maturity. As such, the musical reminiscences and prefigurations have a direct parallel to the extramusical ideas associated with the larger narrative scheme. Although Talich broadly cast all but the first- and last-hundred measures as a "reminiscence" in terms of the narrative, as we have seen, the various musical sections of the tone poem exhibit a more complex interrelationship between "past" and "present," interspersed with prefigurations of the future. While this latter designation was not used by Talich, one could suggest that, given the "narrative hook" implied by Sova's poem and reinforced by the cyclical tendency of the piece, the moments of prefiguration are in fact subtle reminders that the narrator him/herself has already achieved a mature state prior to the beginning of the narrative. By looking into the future within the context of the past we are reminded of the narrator in the present.

By 1918, of course, the Czechs were used to such exercises of historical consciousness. To a certain extent, any nationalistic composition that evokes a historical theme reenacts this same process of self-validation for the audience and their feelings of contemporary achievement. Parallel to *Zrání*—a landmark work marking Czech independence—is Smetana's *Libuše*, the inaugural opera composed for the National Theater in 1881, with its final half hour of musical and historical reminiscence. As the operatic drama draws to a close, Libuše assumes her role as clairvoyant in order to prophesy the next several hundred years of Czech history—which, for Smetana and the audience, are naturally already in the past. She accordingly "predicts" the glorious Přemyslid dynasty, the Hussite wars, the loss of independence in 1620, and the subsequent years of cultural darkness, closing with a strong implication that the Czech nation will rise again through the work of the Cultural Revival. That Smetana's oeuvre, the opera itself, and the theater for which it was written are all major landmarks of this final stage would not be lost on the audience, such that the words of the "historical" Libuše are fulfilled only by the operatic *Libuše*. The music for this scene (accompanied by textual descriptions sung by Libuše) is extraordinarily intertextual, with quotations of medieval hymns and Hussite chorales intermingled with motives from earlier in the opera itself. As with Suk, the musical and symbolic cyclicality are presaged in the opening and carried throughout, as though all the characters, as well as the modern audience, are already assured of the glorious maturation of the nation at independence.

Nevertheless, as the "Suk Affair" (outlined in chapter 5) attests, the unequivocal achievement of such a culturo-political project was a hard-fought battle in 1918. As a modernist compositional leader, Suk could hardly hope to capture the imagination of all factions of the Czech public for very long, and continued attempts to do so by other members of the Prague musical community—notably Ostrčil and Zich in the early years of the 1920s—would end in apathy or outright rejection. The harvest was over, but the crop was left to spoil.

From Sweet Cantilena to a Violent Scream:
Zich's *Vina*

Many of the issues surrounding the modernist representation of the Czech audience were magnified in the stream of controversies enacted between the upper-middle-class public and Ostrčil's regime at the National Theater over the course of the 1920s. As discussed in chapter 5, each new production in the first years of independence caused a furor from conservative critics, mostly centering on the modernist adaptations of Smetana and the incursions of foreign works. The premiere of Otakar Zich's opera *Vina* (Guilt) on March 14, 1922, therefore, introduced a polemic of a different stripe, in that the focus now shifted to a work by a current Czech composer. Set to Jaroslav Hilbert's play of the same name, Zich's work was considered by the majority of critics to indicate not only Ostrčil's direction for his opera company, for better or worse, but also his active influence among composers in Prague. Although the score of *Vina* is not, stylistically speaking, altogether different from the middle-of-the-road modernism of Zich's Czech contemporaries, its use of intensely discordant polyphonic textures to depict the fractures of bourgeois society sealed the opera's fate, both during the interwar republic and since that time.

The common stance of Zich and Ostrčil in contemporary cultural politics did not help the cause of *Vina*. The composer and conductor had shared a long association through the Nejedlý circle, and while still at the Vinohrady Theater in early 1915, Ostrčil guaranteed his support for the opera right after its completion. As the new dramaturge at the National Theater in 1919, Ostrčil brought *Vina* to the attention of Kovařovic (who had coldly dismissed it four years earlier) and, likely as a concession to rival critical factions, it was included in the roster for possible productions. When Ostrčil took the reins in 1920, that possibility became a reality, and the opera was produced eighteen months later, at what would prove a high-water mark in an anti-Nejedlý backlash among members of the press.

A true disciple of the operatic aesthetics of Nejedlý, Zich was attracted to Hilbert's 1896 play for its psychological element, which focuses on the unspoken tension in bourgeois family life, and on the guilt of one young woman, Mína, as she tries to hide her shameful past.

Characters:		
	Mrs. Maráková	alto
	Jiří Mařák, her son, a sculptor	baritone
	Mína Mařáková, her daughter	soprano
	Stanislav Hošek, Mína's fiancé	tenor
	Karel Uhlíř, a sugar merchant	bass

The action, in three acts, takes place in the living room of the Mařák household. Mína Mařáková, a twenty-three-year-old woman living with her widowed mother and older brother Jiří, is engaged to Stanislav Hošek, a friend of Jiří's. Tensions in the house are extreme, as Mrs. Mařáková has been unable to exhibit affection toward her two children for several years and openly resists their attempts to interact with her. When Jiří brings home a business associate, the sugar merchant Uhlíř, the past of both women returns with disastrous results: Uhlíř is the man to whom, seven years before, Mína gave her virginity, as a result of which she has lived a life of secret shame; he is also the son of Mrs. Mařáková's former lover, whose departure left her an empty shell. Uhlíř has arrived with the sole purpose of reclaiming Mína as his bride, and his persistence forces her, at the end of Act 2, to admit her "guilty" past to Hošek, who rejects Mína outright as shameless and unclean. With no other recourse, Mína reluctantly agrees to marry Uhlíř. When Hošek returns to grant forgiveness in Act 3, however, she herself cannot forgive his earlier treatment of her and rejects him in turn. Left alone, Mína's despondency overwhelms her, and she commits suicide by jumping from the window. Her body is discovered by Jiří and Mrs. Mařáková, whose tremendous guilt finally drives her to an outpouring of grief over the loss of the daughter she never knew.

Similar to Suk's *Zrání*, the audience's experience in *Vina* is one in which different layers of the past inform our understanding of the present as it plays out before us. Most striking among the characters in this regard is Mrs. Mařáková, who seems to be totally detached from present reality, and who can only express herself through an old-fashioned song, sung at the piano: in the original Hilbert, this character's desire to live life solely through reminiscence borders on the pathological. Zich, taking advantage of the musical possibilities inherent in this scenario, portrayed Mrs. Mařáková's obsession using a short, conventional arietta with a simple accompaniment.[11] The rest of *Vina*'s score, however, is a dense web of quasi-tonal counterpoint that offsets the conventionality of Mrs. Mařáková's reminiscences with the complexity of modern life: this thick texture also attempts to depict the constant psychological struggle that besets the rest of the characters in the opera. As such, Zich composed according to the aesthetic principles of "Czech" modernism espoused by Novák, Suk, and Ostrčil, where densely contrapuntal motivic work was held to represent both tradition and an atemporally modern Czech musical identity. With Mína's guilt as the focus, the climax of the psychological struggle in the plot coincides with an immense fugue, as the heroine attempts to write "a letter without words," unsuccessfully explaining her past to Stanislav.[12] In his analysis of the opera, the young musicologist Josef Hutter stressed the point that Zich's music augmented the "realism" of Hilbert's text through music, in that every psychological moment of the plot was magnified in the score, no note of which was superfluous to the narration.[13] Hutter went on to mention that Zich's "inimitable" modernism in *Vina* lay in the masterful gradation of psychological levels in the music of the opera, "from sweet cantilena of a songlike character . . . to a violent scream."[14]

One central task of analysis, given the extremes of positive and negative reactions in the contemporary press, must be to discover just how "modernist" Zich's music for *Vina* was, and how justified either the darts or laurels were in the various interpretations of its score. In many respects, *Vina* is a microcosm of the Czech modernism advocated in Prague, and can be taken as a yardstick for how successfully it could be applied to opera in 1922, as artists and the public entered the interwar era. Central to the debate are two key points: whether Zich could compose *at all* (and therefore whether his modernism was in fact authentic or fraudulent); and whether the application of his musical style to a fractured depiction of bourgeois society was well matched or aesthetically appropriate. To a certain extent, the second issue depends on the first, in that, if Zich's modernism simply masked a poor compositional ability, its dramatic statement about the psychology of bourgeois hypocrisy would be ineffective, or at best, accidental.

In musical terms, we are faced yet again with the disconnection between the vocal melody and the orchestral motivic web as a key marker of Czech modernism and its alienation of listeners (see discussion in chapter 4, pp. 76–77). How we get to this point, however, is somewhat unique to Zich's project in *Vina*. As stated in Hutter's hyperbole-charged analysis of the opera and its composer, Zich's intent was to provide a system of constantly shifting motives underneath a type of dramatic vocal declamation that firmly responded to the needs of Czech diction.[15] All aspects were to be first and foremost linear in construction, in order to give the listener the broadest possible psychological experience over

Example 6.5a. Zich, *Vina*, Act Two, staggered motivic entries (2: 42/2–4).

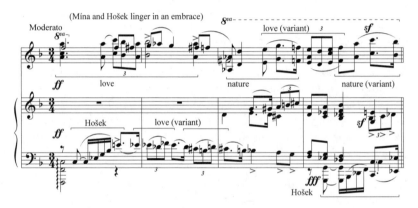

Example 6.5b. Zich, *Vina*, Act One, motivic combinations (1: 92/2–5).

the course of the opera. Motives appear with such intense frequency that they are often stacked in staggered entries in the style of a fugato (ex. 6.5a) or in combination with other motives (ex. 6.5b). Much further down the hierarchy of parameters was the use of traditional chords and harmonic progressions: these Zich derived, almost exclusively, from the coincidence of polyphonic voices. The resulting harmonies are, depending on the concatenation of musical events, either jarringly discordant or disappointingly mundane in the moment, and in the large scale, almost completely directionless. According to Hutter, such was Zich's plan.

These musical outcomes, naturally, relate to the drama of the opera, which relies on long-term psychological buildup in what is otherwise a mundane set-ting—a parlor in a bourgeois home in Prague. The first act fulfills its role in the

Example 6.5c. Zich, *Vina*, Act One, Mrs. Mařáková's motive (1: 1/1–5).

presentation of characters, motives, and emotional moods, but dramatically speaking does not offer any concrete events around which the music can be shaped: the atmosphere is introspective and outwardly lifeless in the sense of late Ibsen or Strindberg. Zich's music accordingly offers little differentiation from situation to situation amid the constant motivic Fortspinnung and loss of harmonic direction—a factor discussed at length in the criticism. Such a beginning, however, is perhaps a necessary evil, in order to depict the loveless and regretful family history among the characters and to prepare the audience for the enormity of the psychological impact of events in the second half of the opera.

Much of this impact depends, as elsewhere in opera, on a tension between internal and external emotional forces. Mrs. Mařáková, as the matriarch of the household, has imposed a repressive gloom on her children's emotional lives, and this effect is palpably renewed every time she enters the room: her motive, narrow in range and relatively conservative in its stepwise construction (ex. 6.5c) dominates the texture on each occasion. The first half of the opera can be charted by means of each of these entries, wherein she coldly interacts with Mína, Jiří, Stanislav, and Uhlíř in turn, provoking gradually increasing gradations of pent up anger in Mína. The central confrontational moment, as far as the music is concerned, arrives partway through Act 2, when Mrs. Mařáková finally expresses her buried emotions through a song from her past; Mína then enters and struggles to write a letter to Stanislav, accompanied in the orchestra by a five-voice fugue. Each scene is a soliloquy of sorts, wherein the women, provoked by present events beyond their control, are forced to come to terms with the past—Mrs. Mařáková with her lost love for Uhlíř's father, and Mína with her lost virginity to Uhlíř. Hilbert separated these parallel scenes by a single word, "Mamínko!" (Mom!), uttered by Mína just before her mother's wordless departure; Zich, on the other hand, provides music of startling contrast for each. Mrs. Mařáková's song is deliberately old-fashioned (and peculiarly "harmonic"), and yet appears as a seamless continuation of her own "conservative" motive (ex. 6.6a): her every word to this point in the opera

Example 6.6a. Zich, *Vina*, Act Two, Mrs. Maŕáková's "song" (2: 116/9–12).

Example 6.6b. Zich, *Vina*, Act Two, Mína's fugue (2: 121/9–18).

has thus contained a hidden reference to her past happiness, cruelly juxtaposed with the present. Her daughter's outpouring is much more aggressive, but wordless: the fugue speaks for her in a heightened version of the "ruthless polyphony" from elsewhere in the opera's first half, now dramatically attuned to the moment (ex. 6.6b). Although Zich constructs new material for the fugue's subject, there are intervallic and rhythmic connections to the motives for Stanislav, Uhlíř, love, defiance, confession, condemnation, and guilt.[16] The result, on Mína's side, is therefore just as cumulative as it had been for her mother, as though all motives but Mrs. Maŕáková's have been filtered through Mína's consciousness. Harmonically, the music of the fugue is even less constrained by vertical sonorities, thereby intensifying the "psychological" linearity of the earlier motivic web, which now buffets against the strictures of fugal form. The placement of these musically opposed scenes is no coincidence: it encapsulates the entire drama as a musical narration, taking the audience directly "from sweet cantilena to a violent scream," where formally structured music stands in for the direct declamation of each character and takes them beyond what they are able to express.

From this point onwards, through the initial split between Stanislav and Mína at the end of Act 2 up to the tragic final scene, the intensity of Zich's motivic web and nonmelodic declamatory vocal style is well matched to the dramatic moment. As the confrontations intensify, so too are the concrete events more plentiful, allowing Zich to shape the musical material more convincingly. Ironically, this musico-dramatic activity produces a second half and climax that feels much more traditionally melodramatic than the static, "psychological" first half. Thus, whereas the modernist, harmonically rootless linearity of the opening hinders the audience's perception of the drama, this very modernism becomes a necessary component of everything after the fugue. It would therefore seem that the interaction of parts in Zich's motivic web, although seeming outwardly haphazard and chaotic, seek to achieve a new, post-tonal, contrapuntal standard for music drama, perhaps a Czech parallel to *Erwartung* and *Bluebeard's Castle* in its distance from the average operagoer's experience. As with other modernisms, that of *Vina* was too easily confused with the lack of traditional compositional ability in its day, a judgment supported by assumptions regarding the Nejedlý faction in interwar Prague. Zich's *Vina* quickly became a pariah in the conservative press, a watchword for the dangers of modernism; as such, it fell victim to the critical factionalization of culture, rather than its own imperfections.

The production of *Vina*, conducted by Ostrčil and directed by Pujman, was reasonably successful with the public and stayed in the repertoire for three seasons, being periodically revived throughout the remainder of Ostrčil's tenure. The critical reception, however, was mixed to say the least, and demonstrates fully the growing fractures between modernists and traditionalists in the postwar Prague music community that were threatening Ostrčil's authority at the National Theater. Most laudatory in their analyses were Nejedlý, Bartoš, and Hutter, all three of whom belonged to the same musical faction as the composer, and who reinforced the notion that the crux of Czech modernism lay in elements of psychology and counterpoint. Basing his remarks in part on Zich's own influential study, *The Aesthetic Perception of Music* (Estetické vnímání hudby, published in 1910), Nejedlý claimed that *Vina* was a manifesto that sought to stretch the bounds of the audience's perception in opera.[17] Although he disagreed with the quality of Hilbert's original play, citing a lack of cathartic transfiguration in the tragedy, Nejedlý felt that these aspects were compensated for in Zich's operatic treatment, especially in the contrapuntal texture.[18] That such a work, wholly representative of the best of modern Czech music, should be performed and well received at the National Theater was indicative of a convalescent trend in the musical relations of Prague.[19] Bartoš, writing in the German-language *Prager*

Presse, celebrated the "polyphonic richness" and "spontaneity" of Zich's music, while Hutter, in his review for *Tribuna*, proclaimed Ostrčil and Zich the leaders of modern dramatic and instrumental counterpoint.[20]

In contrast to these positive remarks was a host of skeptical reviews, written from a variety of viewpoints. Vomáčka, although having little sympathy with members of the Nejedlý circle, agreed with them regarding instrumental characterizations of the individuals and dramatic situations in Zich's score, offering the (rather perceptive) observation that Ostrčil's *Poupě* had probably served as a model in this regard.[21] Nevertheless, Vomáčka went on to declare that Zich's work had limited effectiveness, in that its (and Hilbert's) theatrical realism was several years out of date. As a whole, *Vina* could do little more than express the "characterlessness and idealessness of bourgeois life, which arrives at tragic conflicts not from fateful necessity, but from an over-emotionality that originates in self-indulgence and apprehension before deliberating the consequences of actions and before the fixity of opinions in life."[22] Said another way, the effect of the whole for Vomáčka was more dependent on mood (*náladovost*) than on musical or moral consequences (*důslednost*), evoking Hostinský's aesthetic binarism for progressive art, now turned against *Vina*.

Interestingly, the Nejedlian Hubert Doležil echoed these criticisms in his review for *Československá republika*, emphasizing the dangerous relationship between realistic drama and musical naturalism, each of which could present operatic narrative only from a one-sided perspective. For Doležil, too many questions remained unresolved in *Vina*'s use of symbolism and transcendent thought, to the point that he doubted how appropriate it was to use Hilbert as a basis for opera at all. Zich's music produced a conflict, but only in that it seemed to be at cross-purposes with the drama. Similar to Doležil, Bartoš negated his favorable comments with the criticism that Zich's music "lacks a *catharsis* that would elevate us from the sphere of suffering and pain. His people believe little in the beauty of life, his music has little of a living basis—the ethical and living basis is missing in this music."[23]

Much more vehement in their rejection of *Vina* were Šourek and Šilhan, two conservative critics from within the ranks of the UB who had confronted members of the Nejedlý circle in the past. Now with the efforts of both Zich and Ostrčil before them, they did not mince words. Šourek's article in *Venkov*, despite Hilbert's own positive report on the operatic version of his own work, attempted to negate many of the specific claims made in the opera's favor. With the initial statement that "Zich is not an individual with a strong musical basis and inventiveness," Šourek proceeded to decry the "extremely modernistic character of his expression [and] his boldness in the construction of complex, harmonically ruthless polyphony," all of which was "only external garb."[24] The result of this "ruthless polyphony" was that the entire first half of the opera (up to the climactic fugue in the central scene of Act 2) was for Šourek a "monotonous, fragmented gray, without a particular inventive impulse and, most of all, without an intellectual, motivic expressiveness, from which only isolated lyric places rise like little islands of fresh, happy inspiration, able to capture the heart honestly." Zich's use of the orchestra, celebrated by Nejedlý and Vomáčka, was, for Šourek, unable to differentiate the characters in any meaningful, musical way.

In an article that would set a pattern for anti-Ostrčil attacks throughout the coming years, Antonín Šilhan's review of *Vina*, entitled "Finis musicae," was nothing less than a manifesto against modern music. It also reads as a statement of allegiance to the archconservative National Democratic paper (*Národní listy*) for which he wrote, and their repressive concept of traditional Czech culture:

> Modernism with Zich is merely false posturing. In essence, *Vina* is a product of primi-tivistic dilettantism, which covers up an inventive impotence, a lack of dramatic feeling, and a dramatic helplessness through harmonic monstrosities, collected cacophonies, and the coarsest naturalism. Parts of *Vina* are not song, but speech in a series of quite expressionless pitches. Only in a few agitated moments, here and there, did a tone flow from the throat of Mína that was like a flash of true feeling or emotion. Otherwise, everything that was sung on the stage would be just as well or as poorly suited to any sort of text whatsoever. If there are no fixed characteristics of the individuals in the vocal parts, neither are there in the orchestra.[25]

For Šilhan, every aspect of Zich's expressive vocabulary, from the harmonic language and horizontally based texture to the interrelationship of voices and orchestra, diverged from his expectations of how a modern opera should behave. Judging from his remarks about *Vina*'s vocal writing, Šilhan seems to have equated expression only with melodic lyricism; ignoring the opera's "modernist" psychological aspect, he dwelt solely on external features, unable to get past his personal prejudices toward modernism in music, the composer, and the aesthetic faction he represented. "True feeling or emotion," then, must be read in strict terms of nineteenth-century operatic convention, as though no other types were possible. The review went on to mock the staging and individual performers, the strong implication being that such a production was a reflection of Ostrčil's poor judgment as opera director. From the perspective of subsequent years, the combined effect of *Slib* and *Vina* produced a turning point in the critical atmosphere in Prague,[26] replacing a factional division based on differing views of modernism (i.e., the "lineages" of Smetana and Dvořák) with one in which Ostrčil and all things modern were an affront to a small but powerful bastion of conservative cultural figures.

The first consequence of the opposition to Ostrčil's production of *Vina* at the National Theater was the sudden removal of Pujman from his post as director in the opera department on April 1, 1922. The "Pujman Affair" resulted in a further increase in tension between the administration and Ostrčil, who had to revert back to his previous directorial staff for such crucial productions as Janáček's *Káťa Kabanová* (which premiered on November 30, 1922), Strauss's *Salome*, the first preparations for the jubilee Smetana cycle, and even his own

Legenda z Erinu. Throughout the 1922/23 season Ostrčil solicited National Theater intendant Ackermann for Pujman's reinstatement, an issue that joined a host of other similar controversies involving assistant conductors, soloists, the use of the Estates Theater, and lucrative versus aesthetically challenging productions. Although he had to wait until May 1923 to regain his favorite director, Ostrčil acquired an ally in František Kysela, a provocative young set designer, whose modernist work on *Hubička*, the second production of the new Smetana cycle, was initially well received, even in the pages of *Národní listy.*[27] Pujman's departure resulted in a slackening of the tension between Ostrčil and his critics, although the controversy would return, with far more serious implications, in the years ahead.

"A Dynamic of Elementary Strengths": Ostrčil's *Legenda z Erinu*

It was in this slight lull of theatrical politics that Ostrčil produced his long-awaited fifth opera, *Legenda z Erinu* (Legend of Erin), on March 12, 1923. Although it had received its premiere in Brno two years before, its exposure to the Prague circle of critics demonstrates Ostrčil's peculiar position in interwar Czech music as a representative of modernism and a role model for the younger generation, for better or worse. The opera itself was received alternately as an expression of pre-independent decadence, a manifesto of specifically Czech modernist techniques, and a socialist depiction of the heroic Czech collective. Oddly enough, the conservative faction of critics chose not to display their wrath toward Ostrčil as composer, as though to preserve some vestige of professional ethics toward Ostrčil as conductor of his own work.

Never prolific at the best of times, since the beginning of his tenure as opera director at the Vinohrady and National Theaters Ostrčil's creative production as a composer had become increasingly sporadic. Based on a text by the Czech decadent poet and playwright Julius Zeyer from 1885, *Legenda z Erinu* represents his only compositional effort from the Vinohrady period, completed in 1919 as he began his work as dramaturge at the National Theater. It is in many ways a problematic work, regarding both text and music, reflecting the growing crisis of operatic aesthetics in the Czech musical community throughout the mid-1920s in a way strikingly different from Zich's *Vina*: where the earlier opera provoked strong reactions as "the end of music," Ostrčil's barely warranted mention at all.

Part of the ambivalence toward the opera derives from contemporary attitudes regarding the author of its libretto. Zeyer (1841–1901) is largely considered to have been the leader of the Czech decadent movement, and was himself a great cosmopolitan figure in Czech literature, bringing in many different influences from abroad.[28] Appreciative of parallel literary trends in England and especially France, Zeyer created works that challenged the limits of his language in a superbly polished, poetic style of prose. Much of his creative work is set in other parts of Europe or Asia, and quite often, in distant historical periods (his story "Kunálovy oči," set in India and used by Ostrčil as the basis for his third opera, is typical), lending his work an aura of exoticism and mysticism.

Set in pre-Christian Ireland in the third century AD, *Legenda z Erinu* is itself full of legend: the characters in the drama are constantly telling tales, such that the action takes place as much in the "legendary past" as the "legendary present." Indeed, the entire first act revolves around instances of storytelling, which have a significant impact on the outcome of the drama. The long and complicated plot deals primarily with the supernatural healing powers of King Finn, his intended bride Grania, and her illicit love for the knight Dermat.

Characters:		
	Kormak, King of Erin	bass
	Grania, his daughter	soprano
	Finn, King of the Fenians	bass
	Ossian, his son	baritone
	Dermat O'Dyna, a knight	tenor
	Midak, son of King Kolga	baritone
	Dara, a druid	bass

In the opening scene, King Kormak relates an epic legend of his ally King Finn. The latter, as a young man, discovered a woman grieving for her lover, a hero recently killed in battle; when Finn retrieved the hero's ring, the woman changed herself into a white bird, bestowing healing powers upon the young man. Although he has never used it, Finn now has the power to restore health to the sick and dying who drink from his hand. Kormak is interrupted in his storytelling by the approach of Midak, who eventually identifies himself as the son of King Kolga, who had fought against Kormak and Finn and had died in battle many years before. Midak, raised by Finn, has come to seek advice from Kormak, convinced that his father was murdered. The two are interrupted in turn by the young knights Ossian and Dermat, who have come to seek the hand of Kormak's daughter, Grania, in marriage on Finn's behalf. As a token of good wishes Finn has sent a silver talisman to Grania, which Midak instantly recognizes as having belonged to his father. He swears revenge on Finn, his father's murderer. Grania, however, is lost to the world, and wanders around Kormak's castle in a trancelike state; she seems oblivious to Finn's gift and everyone in the room, including Dermat, who falls irrevocably in love with her.

In Act 2, Finn arrives at Kormak's court for his wedding, presenting the talisman to the semiconscious Grania. When she subsequently awakes, however, she wants no part of the proceedings. She uses a sleeping potion on all the wedding guests except Midak, Dermat, and Ossian, who are summoned to her presence. When Finn and Kormak are safely asleep, Grania and Dermat declare their love for each other, and arrange to flee; Midak offers his castle as a hideaway in an act of vengeance against Finn. When Finn awakes after the lovers' departure, he swears revenge on Dermat.

(*continued*)

Act 3 takes place at Midak's castle, where Dermat and Grania enjoy a blissful scene together, albeit marred by thoughts of guilt and premonitions of danger. When Midak arrives with the news that Finn has followed him, their fears are justified; assuring them of their safety, Midak insists on greeting Finn alone. Midak questions Finn about the details of Kolga's death. Dermat rushes onstage to defend Finn against the wrongful vengeance of Midak: in a dramatic coup de théâtre, Dermat reveals that it was his own father who murdered Kolga, not Finn, who had received the talisman from the same. Through this act of redemption, Finn and Dermat are seemingly reconciled, while Midak agrees to settle the debt of honor over Kolga's death.

Act 4 also commences with a scene between Dermat and Grania, who anticipate the arrival of Midak, Finn, and Ossian at their castle. Again full of premonition, Grania worries about Dermat's goodwill, having come from the castle without a sword. After she leaves to retrieve it for him, Midak appears, announcing his decision about the debt of honor: that he and Dermat will be reconciled if Grania will become his wife. When Dermat refuses, Midak stabs him, just moments before the arrival of Finn and Ossian. Finn, about to use his legendary healing powers to restore Dermat to health, stops cold when the dying man utters the name of his love, Grania; Finn, still angered over their elopement, lets Dermat die. Grania comes upon the bloody scene and gives a heartbreaking farewell over Dermat's body. With the words: "I brought your sword, too late for you, but not for me," she stabs herself and dies over her lover's corpse, to the horror of the rivals, Finn and Midak. The opera closes with a chilling psychological moment, in which both Midak and Ossian depart from Finn, wishing him farewell in the hope that he can live with himself after his betrayal of both Dermat and Grania, the only innocent characters in the drama. The legend of Finn has come full circle, in that the blessing he received from the white bird has become a curse.

Ostrčil used his own reduction of Zeyer's text as a libretto, taking a substantial portion of Zeyer's words and preserving their lyrical beauty and subtle rhythm in the long speeches that make up the various "legends" throughout the work. The use of such a decadent, subjectivist drama as a basis for modernist opera in the democratic era was highly problematic for Czech critics, who sought objective expressions of nationalism as a reflection of the Czech collective and its achievements. As with *Vina*, *Legenda z Erinu* presented a complex, introspective drama, set to a score whose density proved inaccessible to a large portion of the audience.

Ostrčil's music for *Legenda z Erinu* also reveals the strong tendency toward the contrapuntal textures favored by his contemporaries, with a harmonic language that occasionally employs functional chords and tonal references in a mostly polytonal context. These two elements work together, such that it is difficult to determine whether the harmony arises from contrapuntal necessity or it is the polytonality that complicates the voice leading: all in all it is much more harmonically "convincing," both in detail and long-range progression, than Zich. The melodic material of *Legenda z Erinu* relies to a certain extent on motives, although not exclusively so; indeed, Hutter made a distinction between conventional leitmotivic practice and that found in this opera.[29] While many of the motives serve a musico-dramatic function, Ostrčil developed much of the material in an ongoing variation process reminiscent of prewar Schoenberg. In light of the pervading bitonality and contrapuntal textures in *Legenda z Erinu*, Ostrčil's use of developing variation increased substantially over that of *Poupě*, whose score had extended passages of purely accompanimental music. As with many other operas of its generation, *Legenda z Erinu*'s motivic and melodic basis is found almost exclusively in the orchestral part, the voices having little interaction with what lies beneath. Not unlike the Suk and Zich works in the present chapter, Ostrčil attempted here to present a new voice for Czech modernism using musical techniques that still paid a strong allegiance to German modernism from the fin-de-siècle period. It thus became difficult to assert that such a score embodied either the achievements of Czech tradition or the new spirit of the democratic era. Nevertheless, Ostrčil created a work of awesome musical and dramatic insight, however apathetically it may have been received in its day.

Ostrčil's achievement in *Legenda z Erinu* is the specific way in which the intensely complex components of music and drama coalesce. Hutter argued that the twenty-four-page-long opening scene, the legend of Finn's youth as told by Kormak, behaves as an overture for the rest of the opera. Similarly, Nejedlý implied that Kormak's scene acts as a Grundgestalt, bearing the seeds of the themes for all four acts.[30] Not only is the full range of moods of the opera expressed in the opening few pages of Ostrčil's score, but several of the characters' specific motives appear in direct relation to the legend itself, even if those characters have not yet sung in the opera (see the chart of motives in ex. 6.7).

As the music of *Legenda z Erinu* progresses, a subsidiary drama is enacted in the orchestra between two opposing forces, which I will characterize as *tranquillo* and *pesante*. In this regard, long, legato phrases and thundering climaxes dissolve into each other with extraordinary rapidity, a tendency often greatly aided by the buildup and disappearance of contrapuntal voices. The passage marked *Tranquillo, largamente*, with its undulating triplets and luxurious melodic contour, will eventually form the basis of motives denoting Grania and Dermat, as well as the general mood of most scenes of which they are a part. The legend itself is characterized by an oscillating three-note motive, recurring throughout this initial scene, but also helping to shape many of the subsequent motives (motive I). On the other side of the spectrum, Kormak's narration of the Finn legend produces his "heroic" motive, a rhythmically charged passage dominated by three-note groupings marked *risoluto* (motive II). Midak's vengeance motive appears

Example 6.7. Ostrčil, *Legenda z Erinu*, motives.

Example 6.7. (*continued*).

marked *pesante* (motive III). In contrast to these aggressive motives is Finn's "gift" motive, a wide-ranging, largely legato passage that describes his ability to heal all those who drink from his hand (motive IV). Thus, even within the characterization of Finn (who is arguably the opera's dominant personality) we see the enactment of the *pesante-tranquillo* dichotomy, to which his conflicted role in the opera attests.

The remaining scenes of the first act are explorations of the musical motives first introduced in Kormak's legend. The scene between Midak and Kormak relies heavily on the motives for vengeance and Finn's heroism (III and II, respectively). Grania's trancelike entrance (with her own motive, V) in the midst of the scene changes the atmosphere completely, reintroducing the *tranquillo* music. A few measures later, when Ossian presents the golden talisman to mark her engagement to Finn, the suspicious Midak sings to the accompaniment of motive III (66).[31] The proximity of these occurrences and their mutual derivation from motive I (the "legend" motive) demonstrate the density of Ostrčil's musico-dramatic thought, which only increases as the drama progresses.

The second act commences with what is perhaps the composer's most austere contrapuntal passage: it is a four-voice fugue, 125 measures in length, based primarily on Finn's motive (II), with a middle section in which Grania's motive appears in augmentation, *espressivo*, above (74). Despite this rigorous prelude, reminiscent of the climactic psychological moment in *Vina*, the subsequent scene of Grania and Finn's engagement, wherein the latter sings an extended passage of *tranquillo* music, is surprisingly lyrical: it is the only such moment his character enjoys in the opera. Grania's awakening leads to further effusions of lyricism that reach a peak with the description of Dermat, whose motive appears in stretto (motive VI). This fluid texture gives way to several successive ostinati in the following "conspiracy" scene, alternating with soaring *legato* lines as Dermat and Grania profess their love for each other. Within the final passionate outburst from the lovers, a rhythmic motto appears for the first time that I will designate as the *sarabande*, which continues after their departure until the awakening of Finn and Kormak from their drugged slumber. The sarabande is related to both the initial legend motive (I) and to Grania (V), giving its every appearance a sense of urgency and fatefulness in terms of the dramatic outcome that the music narrates. The musical chaos spills into the final scene between Midak and Finn, at which point three thunderous statements of the vengeance motive (III) resound as the act closes, foreshadowing the plans for revenge of both Midak and Finn (119).

Act 3 opens with the most prolonged segment of undisrupted lyricism in the opera: it is a love scene between Grania and Dermat, in hiding at Midak's castle. The central portion of this scene is Dermat's description of the first time he beheld his beloved, in a texture governed by *legato*, *pianissimo* ostinati that culminate in a stretto of his own motive (VI) over tremolo chords (126): the effect is not unlike many such moments in *Pelléas et Mélisande*. The tremolos continue, however, through Grania's growing premonitions of impending disaster, alongside almost obsessive reiterations of the sarabande rhythm, which takes on a sense of almost violent urgency when coupled with the vengeance motive (III), marked *energico* upon Midak's entrance. Over the course of the remainder of the act, a palpable psychological change takes place, in which the music portrays a shift from the perceived guilt of Finn to that of Dermat's father: motive VI is gradually combined with III. As the act draws to a close, Ostrčil creates a theatrical effect by the insistent reiteration of the seminal three-note motto: the basic

[Finn? I am dying]

Example 6.8. Ostrčil, *Legenda z Erinu*, Finn's gift motive in Dermat's death scene (197/14–17).

material that governs the main motives of the opera (I, II, III, V, and VI) thus pushes the music toward a resolution in the fourth act.

Although the final act is the shortest of the four, it carries the responsibility of resolving the complicated narrative of the opera in a dramatically convincing manner. Act 4 also makes the most concessions to operatic convention than any of the preceding acts, largely as a result of the prevailing sense of melodrama in Zeyer's text at this point. The opening scene between Grania and Dermat forms a parallel with the preceding act, although Grania's premonitions (indicated by an "inquieto" motive) now far outweigh Dermat's calmness. Yet again, the sarabande motive overtakes the remaining happiness in their scene, underscoring Grania's worries about Dermat's lack of weapons. The "inquieto" music continues after Midak's entrance, now coupled with vengeance (III): the texture thickens with multiple reiterations of the latter, alongside fragments of Grania's motive (V) as Midak requests his retribution payment of her hand in marriage. When Dermat refuses, his stabbing brings the first moment of musical repose in the act so far, albeit in the context of extreme dramatic tension; it is followed by the entrance of Ossian and Finn to the latter's motive (II), marked *energico*. The lyricism of the early third act returns only with the dying Dermat's request for assistance from Finn's healing hand, and the orchestra is flooded with Finn's "gift" motive (IV) for the first time since Kormak's legend (ex. 6.8, 197). In a brilliant moment of motivic interplay, Ostrčil combined Finn's two motives (II and IV), alternating in registers amid snatches of Dermat's and Grania's motives. When Dermat utters his fateful cry, "Ó Granio!" the gift motive suddenly fragments into a frenzy of activity throughout the full orchestral range (200–201). Grania's subsequent lament over Dermat's body is perhaps the most touching scene in the entire opera, combining her own and Dermat's motives with the sarabande rhythm. The musical and dramatic pathos surrounding her subsequent suicide is parallel to that of Liù in Puccini's *Turandot*, which was being

Example 6.9. Ostrčil, *Legenda z Erinu*, Finn's two motives at the end of the opera (212/5–8).

composed around this time. In the final moments of *Legenda z Erinu*, as Midak and Ossian abandon the stage, the two motives of the grieving Finn gradually drift further apart in range, representing his inner psychological struggle between heroism and benevolence, the tragic outcome of which can be seen in the deaths of the young lovers (ex. 6.9, 212). Thus the dramatic potential of the initial legend of Finn plays out in Ostrčil's music throughout the greater legend of Grania and Dermat. Based on musical techniques of Grundgestalt and "psychological" motivic work inherited from German fin-de-siècle modernism, Ostrčil created a unique and challenging work, where the past and present merge musically and dramatically.

As with Zich's *Vina*, the reception of Ostrčil's *Legenda z Erinu* was mixed, forcing the critics of Prague to wrestle yet again with the issues presented by a modernist Czech opera, this time with an introspective and outdated, decadent libretto. As director of the opera at the National Theater, Ostrčil's reception would have a significant *political* difference to that of Zich, who was easily written off as an outsider from the University. In fact, Ostrčil's case is all the more complicated, in that the composer was already acknowledged as the main creative representative of Nejedlý's ideological faction, even though *Legenda z Erinu* by no means fulfilled their aesthetic paradigm of national, modern, socially responsible opera. Of all the critical reactions, only Hutter offered an unflinchingly positive analysis of *Legenda z Erinu* as a dramatic work by a leader of Czech musical modernism. All of the others, including significantly Nejedlý, found a sticking-point, either in the choice of Zeyer's play for a libretto or in the musical expression itself.

Nejedlý's review of the Brno premiere on June 16, 1921, was inconsistent in its praise of the opera, referring to the work as a "model example" of a modern music drama, while openly questioning its dramatic basis in Zeyer's play.[32] Nejedlý's unstated concern seems to have been Zeyer's status as the founder of Czech decadence, a movement anathema to the critic's aesthetic creed. As he would later state in his 1936 biography of the composer, "*Legenda z Erinu* [i.e., Ostrčil's opera, not Zeyer's play] is a work that stands quite consciously *opposed to everything decadent* that was pulling music apart at that time, and thus continues quite organically in Ostrčil's revivalist efforts."[33] Ignoring his protégé's predilection for Zeyer's fluid lyricism, Nejedlý championed the story's basis in heroic legend, a stance that hearkens back to the operas of the Cultural Revival, while also reflecting the critic's new affiliation with the communist party and an early form of socialist realist thought. To this end, he also asserted that Ostrčil was by no means a formalist in his musical expression, thereby attempting to repel the increasingly frequent charges of academic ("profesorský") stodginess hurled at the composer. Proof for Nejedlý of Ostrčil's nonformalist modernism was *Legenda z Erinu*'s ideological component, which was founded in the "stateliness, tragicness, and *heroicness* of the dramatic action."[34] These characteristics had their musical counterpart in the "concrete" thematic and formal layout of the opera, which, despite its awesome complexity, betrayed an "inner regularity and firmness."[35] These tenets were consistent with the idea that Czech modernism was based in complex contrapuntal and motivic work. In these respects Ostrčil was, for Nejedlý, distinct from most of his fellow (i.e., European) modernists, whose work had fallen into a state of "weakness, softness . . . like all baroque art."[36] As such, Nejedlý constructed a binarism wherein Czech modernism, represented by Ostrčil, was "firm," whereas that of the outside world was "soft," a paradigm that paralleled the moralist discussion happening contemporaneously in *Listy Hudební matice*. Indeed, the critic went so far as to say that the crisis of modern music, discussed so rampantly in the contemporary music press, had nothing to do with Ostrčil's opera, which was proof that a truly (non-"baroque") modern music was possible. Nevertheless, Nejedlý rather hesitantly included *Legenda z Erinu* alongside Ostrčil's premiere works, citing it as an example of the composer's prewar aesthetic, a victorious solution to the question of *l'art pour l'artismus*, but not completely connected to the present state of modernism.

Nejedlý's description of the composer as having struggled ("like a soldier") with problematic aesthetic issues such as *l'art pour l'artismus* skirts his hesitancy to accept the work wholeheartedly. Uncharacteristically, Nejedlý muddled through his dramatic analysis, claiming rather tautologically that Ostrčil's modernist musical style had rendered *Legenda z Erinu* a success, for only a work with a firm artistic basis and cultural significance could be considered truly modern. It is interesting to note that the oblique reference to the social necessity of art (i.e., the mysterious "cultural significance"), one of Nejedlý's clichés, is the only such mention in his writing on *Legenda z Erinu*, for clearly this is an opera that does not strive to represent the Czech collective. In Nejedlý's prose there is nevertheless a clear demarcation between the type of modernism he felt to be socially irresponsible— art created for its own sake and not in the service of the collective—and Ostrčil's oeuvre, which, through its "internal regularity and firmness," could be said to follow in the mold of Smetana. Such a designation served to place Ostrčil wholly on his own within European modernism, as the only up-to-date member of the Smetana lineage, which represented for Nejedlý the pinnacle of his paradigm. Since, however, this particular opera fit into the critic's aesthetic paradigm only with great difficulty, he chose to concentrate on the opera's theme of heroism instead, and its musical counterpart, the prevailing contrapuntal texture; both of these phenomena were thus the keys to the question of *l'art pour l'artismus*.

Although he agreed in many technical aspects with Nejedlý's review, Josef Hutter had one major point of divergence with his former teacher: he refused to admit that *Legenda z Erinu* was an example of *l'art pour l'artismus* in music.[37] In a quintessentially Nejedlian line of argument, Hutter claimed that such a classification was impossible, given the opera's ideological content and its realization in Ostrčil's music. Hutter's analysis of the opera reads like a manifesto, as though no other composer or work could claim precedence in the vanguard of music: "The work is even more significant, in that it represents not just a chance discovery and culmination of new paths, but the program of a new musical stage, in which Ostrčil is not only a leading composer, but *the direct embodiment of the idea of this musical culture*, not just Czech, but throughout the world."[38] Like Nejedlý, Hutter positioned Ostrčil on his own in the field of European modernism: he described the composer as having been misconstrued by both the conservatives and radicals. While the conservatives (whose demand for charm and optimism had resulted, interestingly, in *decadence*) might reject the modernist technical aspects of *Legenda z Erinu*'s music, the radicals would consider anything written before the war as having no soul, merely a technical display of *l'art pour l'artismus*. Although Hutter considered the conservative opponents to have espoused outdated subjectivist aesthetics, whose individualist expressions had been pulled apart by the "industrialization" of music, he also considered the new idea that the artist *must represent the collective* to be somewhat romanticized and hard to believe.[39] That this latter statement refers to Nejedlý's specifically socialist viewpoint (as well as the general mindset inherited from the Cultural Revival) is painfully obvious, although he is not mentioned by name. Ostrčil, meanwhile, was an example of "another dynamic, a dynamic of elementary strengths," specific to Czech modernism.[40] The hallmark of this style was for Hutter the "infinite melody" that Ostrčil's new style of polyphony produced, an instrumental melody that had little to do with harmonic convention, and that was at once musically and dramatically rationalized. Hutter considered the psychological effect of an essentially monothematic opera, whose developing variation and motivic expansion underscores the development of the drama in all its complexity, to be intrinsically Czech: "Not found elsewhere, with Ostrčil [this type of melodic writing] making itself known all the time. Thus through his person a Czech melody, even if not in a national sense; hence a Czech national genesis: 'made in Czechoslovakia.' "[41] As such, the derivation of the motives in *Legenda z Erinu* was neither Wagnerian nor Brahmsian, and was connected to Zeyer's prose only in the most external elements: rather, it expressed the human, psychological moments that the myth projected. With his nationalist viewpoint, Hutter attempted to sever Ostrčil's compositional techniques from their obvious provenance in German opera and place them in an independent Czechoslovak camp, the identity of which was increasingly difficult to define in the interwar era.

Most of Prague's other music critics were predominantly negative in their reception of *Legenda z Erinu*, including those from within the Nejedlý circle. Doležil supported Ostrčil's expressive techniques and the artistic potential of the work in his review for *Československá republika*, but disagreed with the ideological basis of the opera, in that its creative goals were not coextensive with the needs of Czech society. Bartoš was more direct: "Ostrčil's *Legenda z Erinu* will be counted among his typical works at whose birth the composer's uncommonly firm will and disciplined intellect did a lot more work than his heart."[42] From the other side of the critical spectrum, Šourek at first attacked the choice of Zeyer, whose "atmosphere is foreign to us, strongly recalling the Germanic myth of the Nibelungs, [and] its basic idea is icy cold"; Ostrčil's music was "similarly ruthless toward the performing musicians and the listener."[43] Nevertheless, by the Prague premiere in 1923, Šourek's attitude had improved to the point where the opera was described as a pinnacle of Ostrčil's art, both as a composer and conductor. It is not insignificant that Šilhan, writing in *Národní listy* on March 14, reported only the basic facts of the production with no critical remarks whatsoever, perhaps making a political statement through a total lack of aesthetic engagement with the opera.

The wide divergence of critical opinions, from the overly analytical Hutter to the uninterested Šilhan, indicates how problematic the state of modern Czech opera was for Prague's musical community. Among Ostrčil's supporters there was a marked attempt to carve out a niche for the composer within modernism, mostly by means of his predilection for quasi-tonal counterpoint and its function within the drama. The main stumbling block toward the acceptance of *Legenda z Erinu* as a flagship of modern Czech opera seems to have been its connection to Zeyer, although the sheer weight of the musical material certainly had a negative effect on Bartoš and Šourek. Perhaps the most striking aspect of *Legenda z Erinu*'s reception is its lack of revivals at the National Theater, throughout the Ostrčil administration and since that time: it would be Šourek's criticism about the rigors of listening rather than Hutter's nationalist model that would win out in the end. In comparison to Zich, whose more problematic music provoked attacks and counterattacks until the music was forced from the repertoire, *Legenda z Erinu* seems to have been thankfully forgotten by all, including some of the composer's most ardent supporters. Nevertheless, Ostrčil as a composer and conductor at the National Theater continued to have a tremendous impact on opera composers in the Czech music community throughout the late 1920s and early 1930s.

* * *

Ostrčil's problem, like Zich's, reflected a larger issue of integrating modernism, even in its Czech guise, into the musical life of Prague. As we have already seen, the social and political changes of the new era wreaked havoc in an artistic group long accustomed to isolation and one-sided battles against Vienna. In the new independent Republic, many forces and influences came into play, both from within the Czech community and without. Just as the new conditions brought change to the reception of opera, so did it affect the attitudes toward European musical modernism in general and the Czech role in it. The Germanic fin-de-siècle technique of using motivic webs as bearers of psychology in opera were no longer current elsewhere in Europe in the 1920s, but for the Czechs they were touted as extremely modern and definitive contributions to the history of musical style. This stylistic disparity is partly a result of the backlog of large compositions from before 1918, since some of these works had been conceptualized almost a decade before their performance; nevertheless, the criticism set up an artificial atmosphere of "avant-gardism" that alienated the public unnecessarily. In all three cases discussed in this chapter, the convoluted critical discourse prevented the works from being judged on their own musical terms. Regarding Suk's *Zrání*, the "national ripening" of the program and the political implications of Suk as a performer overshadowed the work itself. In the case of Ostrčil, *Legenda z Erinu* was made to measure up against his other pieces from decades before in a desperate attempt to save face. As for Zich, in what was potentially the most unrestrained modernist approach among any in the Czech community to date, the political machinations of Nejedlý and his opponents and the general resistance toward new ideas prevented his *Vina* from receiving any serious evaluation as a viable artistic contribution at all. Only sustained exposure to international influences could provoke a change in the community—influences that arrived, for better or worse, with the two festivals of the International Society for Contemporary Music and the Prague premiere of *Wozzeck*.

Chapter Seven

"A Crisis of Modern Music or Audience?"

Changing Attitudes to Cultural and Stylistic Pluralism (1925–30)

The late 1920s were years of transition for the musical community of Prague, as the last vestiges of the prewar rivalries receded substantially in favor of new alliances. This period also witnessed the rise of a new generation of younger composers and critics, many of whose values and aesthetic views bore only a faint resemblance to those of their forebears. During what were perhaps the most peaceful and prosperous years of the First Republic, the issue of "national music" lost much of the urgency it had carried in earlier years; only now and then did it stand as a marker by which to judge the latest modernist imports from Western Europe. Indeed, the attitude in the Prague compositional community at this time toward modernism was influenced by music from abroad as never before. Not so among the public: this new open-mindedness became a source of tension between artists and audiences, similar to crises in other European cities. Although the initial period of "nation building" had passed for First Republic society, the issue of the social responsibility of art, particularly regarding modern or even popular music, retained its focus as a priority for the younger generation. Again, the divergent views of musicians and their audiences reveals much about the cultural milieu of Prague in these years: while critics debated the social necessity for modern music, both domestic and foreign, attendance at performances dwindled to an all-time low.

For most audience members, both the Czech and the international compositions at Prague's 1925 International Society for Contemporary Music (ISCM) festival provoked widespread apathy toward foreign influences, reflecting somewhat the disappointment in European modernism at the previous year's event.

Despite the paucity of public support, a new desire slowly emerged in the majority of Czech musicians to be connected to the avant-garde of Western Europe. The prohibition of *Wozzeck* at the National Theater in November 1926 caused the greatest upheaval in the musical community in the entire First Republic era, and critics took the situation as a call to arms. Although a few right-wing individuals charged Ostrčil's regime with musical bolshevism,[1] almost all of Prague's composers and critics banded together in a show of support for the beleaguered conductor, as though performing the most current works of European modernism were a matter of cultural necessity, social responsibility, and even national pride.

Reactions to the "*Wozzeck* Affair" (as it became known) also cast into relief the new directions for Czech modernism in the late 1920s. Two operas from this time, analyzed in chapter 8, reflect the flexibility and multiplicity of styles now acceptable among Czech composers. Zich's one-act opera *Preciézky* (*Les Précieuses ridicules*, 1926) demonstrated an affinity with the aesthetics of Busoni's *Junge Klassizität* and the opera *Arlecchino*, thereby creating a new Czech subgenre termed "Nová Buffa." Meanwhile, Otakar Jeremiáš's theatrically modernist but musically moderate *Bratři Karamazovi* (The Brothers Karamazov, 1928) was received as the most promising example of dramatic music by a member of the next generation. Indeed, much of the musical community viewed these works as the long-awaited signposts for the future of Czech music, the perfect blend of tradition and cosmopolitanism necessary for contemporary society.

The late 1920s also witnessed the rise of popular music and culture, both inside and outside the ranks of Prague composers; this phenomenon can be seen as an extension of the new attitude toward cosmopolitanism in the Czech Lands and throughout Europe. The combined effects of a rising urban working class and a tremendously powerful nouveau riche changed the face of European culture, shifting the musical focus away from the exclusive monopoly of traditional concert venues and blurring the lines between genres. The overwhelming international popularity of Jaromír Weinberger's opera *Švanda dudák* (Švanda the Bagpiper, 1927) prompted a debate over the merits of light music in a concert sphere. Of greater significance locally, the young composer Emil František Burian arrived on the scene with a provocative blend of pro-Western populism and left-wing politics, gathering many supporters for the causes of dadaism, neoclassicism, modern ballet, and jazz, all of which he sought to assimilate into the compositional vocabulary of Czech music. While the movement of interwar Czech jazz and its effects on compositional aesthetics appears amid the larger discussion of populism in chapter 9, its importance in helping to shape the outlook of the younger generation of musicians in the late 1920s cannot be underestimated. Burian and his peers, while not as focused on the concept of Czech national music as the generation of their teachers, were conscious of the responsibility they bore in revitalizing their musical community through a new, cosmopolitan adherence to contemporary trends in Western Europe.

The Discourse on Modernism and Nation in the Late 1920s

By the middle of the decade, the word "crisis" seemed to be on the lips of every critic in Prague, be it with regard to audience attendance, foreign influences, the future of musical institutions, or the moral content of music by their own local composers. The anxiety that Czech critics felt at this time, while reflecting the words of their counterparts in other countries, had much to do with the expectation of great things from interacting with the European modernist community and their ensuing disappointment at the outcome. While artists and thinkers located the cause of the crisis in a variety of sources, including the laziness of the audience, the amorality of Western Europe, and the stubborn attitude of the critics themselves, few if any individuals offered concrete solutions to the problem of reconnecting with the audience.

Vladimír Helfert sought to create a definitive response to these issues in two articles that appeared at either end of the debate: "What We Need" from 1924 and "A Crisis of Modern Music or Audience?" from 1926.[2] In the earlier article he diverged from the post-Wagnerian ideology of his mentor Nejedlý, which he claimed was no longer sufficient amid the incoming tide of new values, styles, technologies, and social functions of art; such an adjustment was necessary, in Helfert's opinion, to resolve the question of Czech cultural individuality in relation to foreign music. Helfert sought an idealized middle ground that would serve as a dual warning against both the shortsighted rejection of European modernism *and* the uncritical mimicry of all foreign influences. Describing contemporary Czech society as existing in a state of intellectual crisis where slogans were propagated one-sidedly, Helfert held out hope for the moral regeneration of music, carried out by individuals who prioritized "musical thought" above all else. The young critic hoped that these individual composers would combine "new values" with their own personal creative method to attain a "new certainty," which would extend beyond the Czech environment into a new relationship with foreign works.

Two years later, in "A Crisis of Modern Music or Audience?" Helfert offered a sociopolitical reading of audience changes in the interwar era and concluded that economic factors had resulted in the lack of an ideal audience "that would create the necessary resonance for musical production." Where there was interest, he reasoned, there was no money, and those who had money lived in the absence of cultural tradition.[3] The workers, meanwhile, suffered from an insufficiency of cultural links to high art, and the students (who normally would act as mediators between the artist and other portions of the audience) showed a greater inclination toward the "fashionable tendency" of physical education than toward art. Such a statement reflects the class-based reading of culture common to proponents of the Czech communist party, which sought to work within the existing pro-Western democratic framework, rather than revolutionize society according to a Soviet or Spartacist model. In a nutshell, Helfert felt that music had lost the social, political, and national function it had enjoyed in the time of *Libuše* and *Jenůfa*, when both operas could be taken as a "manifestation of national thought."[4] Although he conceded that many contemporary compositional trends served only to negate the artistic movements of the past or each other, the critic did not lay the blame at the door of modernist music itself, asserting that the current state was not one of crisis but of transition. When musical works would begin to show a greater sense of definition and artistic purpose, he optimistically hoped, the audience would follow with a natural appreciation for the sense of certainty they evoked. It was up to the institutions of Czech musical life to rebuild the connections between artists and audiences, creating this certainty on both sides through socially responsible programming. With these articles, idealistic as they are, we witness in Helfert the maturation of one of the greatest thinkers of the interwar Czech cultural community, marked by an effort to distance himself from Nejedlý's short-sighted attitudes and the oppressive atmosphere of musical life in Prague.[5]

Another young, independently minded individual to stake a claim in the debate was the composer Bohuslav Martinů, who by this point had already moved to Paris to study with Albert Roussel, and whose first mature ballet, *Istar*, had been performed by Ostrčil at the National Theater (1924). In 1925 and 1926, Martinů sent opinion pieces to *Listy Hudební matice*, which, along with his idiosyncratic orchestral work *Half-time*, became a source of controversy in the Czech musical community. Martinů's viewpoint (coming, like Helfert's, from outside the Prague environment) served to introduce many issues that those entrenched in Czech musical life found too difficult to raise: his attacks on the state of music criticism, while certainly personally charged, are characteristic of his general acceptance of alternate modes of thought. He claimed, accurately, that the aesthetic one-sidedness of Czech critics (from both factions) forced them to throw out almost anything that did not fit their framework, creating an unhealthy, chaotic situation.[6] Their reliance on "old German aesthetics" took the joy out of music for Martinů, and their preference for the alleged "psychological" compositional layer seemed to prioritize "metaphysics to the detriment of pure music."[7] His observation that an inability to classify new influences had led Czech critics to "shrug their shoulders" and label compositions as merely "fashionable" resonates with the titles or theses of several articles at this time, most obviously with Mirko Očadlík's "Dnešní modnost a modernost" (Today's Fashion and Modernism).[8] From one perspective, Martinů was objecting to the Nejedlian binarism of the atemporally modern (i.e., music created in Smetana's image, now obviously stale) versus the ephemeral modernisms from abroad, a designation that implied mere experimentation and a lack of attention toward artistic and moral consequences. Alternately, his argument could apply just as easily to the older, more "traditionally conservative" generation of critics at the Artists' Union (UB) (e.g., Šilhan). In opposition to this attitude, Martinů proposed that each listener come to his/her own understanding of what modern music was, based on a historical understanding of style.[9] Such an enlightened viewpoint would (theoretically) overturn many misconceptions about current modernist trends, such as the ideas that "rhythmic dynamism," when employed in a composition, must force all other elements to the background; that primitivism is so widespread that it is in danger of being elevated to the level of a compositional principle; and that virtually anything resembling counterpoint can or should be considered progressive. The first two comments seem to reference Stravinsky's personal style (and somewhat ironically, that of Martinů himself); the final comment, meanwhile, would have struck a stinging blow to Prague's musicians, since artists of all persuasions had believed contrapuntal complexity to be an integral part of modernism since the turn of the century. All three points make a strong plea for stylistic multiplicity in an age of cosmopolitanism. He further attacked the Czech critics' inconsistent notion of tradition, in that for any given piece of new music, a composer could be applauded by one half of the critics as a successor to a perceived tradition, while being decried as a traitor to the same tradition by the other half. For Martinů, tradition was not a stable concept, even in history: the idea of "Czechness" in music was malleable, and his prediction of its continued transformation, while justified, also accounts for the cool reception his works received in interwar Prague.[10]

Martinů's attack on the musical community of Prague was an attempt to reconcile the divergent streams of modern music with the needs of contemporary society. This argument also addressed the necessity to "cleanse" musical style of its wartime expressionism, reducing its postromantic complexity to something simpler—and therefore more meaningful—for society in the late 1920s. While demands for the purgation of musical life had occurred immediately after the war (especially during the "Suk" and "Nedbal" affairs), seven years later this rhetoric had turned toward the ideal of a "pure music," a slogan that echoed not only on all sides of the critical spectrum in Prague but throughout contemporary Europe as well. As we shall see with the 1925 ISCM and Zich's *Preciézky*, the neoclassical implications of "pure music" met with difficulty in the predominantly post-Wagnerian Prague environment, where, as Martinů suggested, critics hailed compositions as modern based solely on their complexity, use of counterpoint, and an adherence to a Smetanian tradition. Although certainly not every Czech critic of the late 1920s took up the crusade of "pure music," with its associations of stylistic and ideological simplicity, such rhetoric left its mark on attitudes toward new music, its role in contemporary Czech society, and its relation to modernist trends in Europe.

More moderate than Martinů in his approach, Boleslav Vomáčka focused on the anxiety that Czech musicians felt toward both European modernism and their own domestic audiences in two substantial articles for *Listy Hudební matice* in 1925. Written in the context of the two ISCM festivals, Vomáčka's essay "The State of Contemporary Czech Music in the Stream of World Music" compared foreign compositional practice unfavorably with that of local composers, using "moral order," meaning, and poetic content as yardsticks.[11] Interestingly, his argument hinged on the assumption that the category of "pure music" derived solely from the ISCM, an institution to which the Czech community was not beholden. Thus, a certain degree of latent nationalist sentiment appeared in the essay (much like his "Otázky dne" contributions from earlier in the decade), with references to the inherent "Slavonic character" of his peers' compositions. Drawing on Zich's categorization of compositional types,[12] Vomáčka contrasted the trend toward "pure music" in the ISCM with a "poeto-musical" type, which he designated as being more historically and culturally important, and whose members included the Florentine Camerata, Gluck, Wagner, and the entire Czech community, past and present. Amid the universal push toward "pure music," he conceded that Czech music must seem "impure" in its predilection for romanticism and programmaticism, but with the confidence that "truth is deeper than slogans," he predicted that the value of the ISCM's "pure music" would remain only as a corrective against decadence. Although strange bedfellows, Vomáčka's ideology mirrored Nejedlý's paradigm, wherein the morally superior Czech compositional school was considered modern in a way that transcended time via a living tradition that was bound to outlast the trends of the day. It was precisely the type of aesthetic judgment against which Martinů was struggling.

Just two months later, Vomáčka's attitude toward his own audience painted a different picture of the perceived crisis of Czech modernism: while most modernist composers had posed as vain innovators, whose sole ambition was *épater les bourgeois*, Czech modernists were performing a social duty by exercising the brains of their audiences.[13] Any crisis in modern music, therefore, was a result of stupid audiences with no taste. The subscribers who resisted Talich, treated Ostrčil as dangerous, and drove the Spolek pro moderní hudbu (Society for Modern Music) to near bankruptcy were simply mentally lazy, and their reaction against (largely foreign) modernist music was unjustified. The combined effect of Vomáčka's articles was a depiction of Czech modernism stranded between the radicalism of the European avant-garde and the conservatism of the Prague audience, of whom "not 200, in words, two hundred . . . would have interest in what is new in the music of the present day!"[14] Vomáčka's judgment of his own cultural climate casts a strange light on his anxiety toward foreign influences, the moral "purity" of which was apparently not as great as that found in Czech practice; speaking for Czech interests in the face of the ISCM and for modernist interests amid the uncultured Prague bourgeoisie, Vomáčka's voice seems to represent no one but the musicians for whom he was writing. As such, his articles offered no concrete solution out of the perceived crisis of modern music, which for the author was coextensive with a crisis of Czechness in the modern era.

Coming as it did after much of the foregoing discussion, Helfert's "A Crisis of Modern Music or Audience?" touched on what was perhaps the most crucial issue of the day: the social necessity of certainty in art. All other issues, such as the ideological and stylistic simplification of music, the debate over post-Wagnerian "progress" versus neoclassicist "return," and local morality versus foreign influence, were attempts to resolve this main social question, on which hinged the very existence of the Czech musical community. Latent within this debate is the issue of national cultural interests, since, as Vomáčka stated, it was important not only to keep abreast of the developments of "representative works," but also to reflect the spirit of their present cultural milieu, so that Czech music could emerge to provide a secure direction for modernism.[15] In 1925, the second appearance of the ISCM festival in Prague would serve to redefine the terms of the debate by providing all involved with a greater exposure to modernist composers from the rest of Europe, for better or worse.

"A Festival Again?": The 1925 ISCM

While the seemingly fortuitous occasion of Prague's second consecutive ISCM festival boded well for Czech composition and its future in a European context, the reality was somewhat different. The result of an unexpected decision made by the executive committee of the ISCM, the organization's third annual orchestral festival was held again in Prague, just one year after the successful 1924 event. Despite the negative criticism penned by many of the Czech journalists at the time regarding the extreme degree of experimentation of the foreign entries, the 1924 festival had been, in general, the source of tremendous anticipation and wonderment throughout Prague's music community. Although one outcome of the event was the expression of disappointment and self-righteous isolationism from many voices in the Czech press, the sheer brilliance and magnitude of the festival (including the simultaneous Smetana and Czech opera festivals) outweighed the perceived failure of any individual work. No such anticipation, however, preceded the 1925 festival, which did not coincide with any nationalistic anniversaries; the Czech participation had also been scaled down by request of the ISCM directors. Deflated in their efforts to show off yet again to the international avant-garde, the body of Czech critics responded in kind: most of the reviews, with some notable exceptions, dismissed the festival as a whole and in its parts as a mistake, unworthy of the cultural status it claimed. This view, it must be said, was perhaps not unwarranted, since the 1925 concert schedule (three concerts, to which the Czechoslovak section added a vocal/choral concert, a concert of quarter-tone compositions, and a performance of Janáček's *Cunning Little Vixen*) did not happen to include many renowned composers among the international contingent. The exceptions were Vaughan-Williams's *Pastoral Symphony*, whose conservatism was rejected out of hand, Bartók's *Dance-Suite*, Berg's *Drei Bruchstücke aus Wozzeck*, and Stravinsky's *Symphonies of Wind Instruments* (which was struck from the program at the last moment). Milhaud and Křenek were not yet well known to Prague audiences, and the bill was rounded out by figures such as

Malipiero, Réti, Toch, and Kósy. Disappointing also were the official Czech contributions to the festival, namely Novák's 1906 tone poem *Toman a lesní panna* (Toman and the Wood Nymph) and Rudolf Karel's tone poem *Démon*, neither of whose styles were deemed to be representative of contemporary Czech compositional practice. Another contentious submission was Martinů's symphonic work *Half-time*, which the majority of Prague critics refused to admit was the product of a Czech composer, since it had been written in Paris in the perceived absence of traditional Czech aesthetics. Presaged by Martinů's contentious articles from Paris, the Czech community's rejection of their own prodigal son was an extension of their anxiety toward cosmopolitanism, European modernism, and the effects of these on the identity of Czech music. By contrast, Ladislav Vycpálek's thickly contrapuntal *Kantáta o posledních věcech člověka* (Cantata of the Last Things of Man), performed at the appended choral concert, received the most unqualified praise of the festival, including from Steinhard at *Der Auftakt*, who compared it favorably with the German-Bohemian contribution, Fidelio Finke's *Abschied*, a tone poem with vocal soloists to a text by Werfel.[16]

Surprisingly, the most positive of the Czech critics was Boleslav Vomáčka, who wrote contributions to *Listy Hudební matice* in a favorable tone both prior to and after the festival. Beginning his prefestival editorial with the nationalistic statement, "Our nation has a developed sense for internationalism," Vomáčka described the current situation as a continuation of a historical trend, wherein Czech musicians had always carefully evaluated the international influences on which they depended.[17] Although he admitted that familiarity with European modernism had bred a general contempt for it of late, modern Czech musicians could enter into this milieu with confidence, since their music had "already acquired sharp enough outlines," and could be easily defended against negative influences.[18] Vomáčka's self-assured tone continued into the postfestival review, where he applauded the chance for Czech musicians to propagate their music on their own soil.[19] Despite the shortcomings of most contributions to the festival, he deemed the experience useful for members of the Prague community, in that all participants "could create their own relationship to the motley picture of contemporary music according to their inclination and temperament."[20] Vomáčka provided such a picture for his readers: dividing the group into neoromanticists (i.e., post-Wagnerians), neoclassicists, and modernists, he judged few as having the "seal of mature art," including Novák and Karel, whose work had appeared outmoded in the context of the ISCM.[21]

Many of these opinions were echoed in the more aggressive reviews of Josef Bartoš, written for *Smetana-Hudební list*. Bartoš took a much more critical approach to all facets of the festival, including both the Czech and international contributions, the German community of Prague, and the ISCM administration. While he admitted that the 1924 ISCM had been a cultural necessity for Czech musicians in providing a welcome antidote to their pre-1918 isolation, the second festival had no such urgency for Bartoš, who described various works as "misrepresentative" (Novák), "pseudomodern" (Martinů), "gray on gray" (the entire second concert), having "no creative significance" (Hába), and generally "undeserving of fame."[22] The only works of value for Bartoš were Vycpálek's cantata and Berg's *Drei Bruchstücke aus Wozzeck*, the latter performed by Zemlinsky as a double bill with Dukas's *Ariane et Barbe-bleue*; Vycpálek, for Bartoš, was perfectly representative of Czech modernism of the atemporal (as opposed to fashionable) variety with its logical, monumental structure and its unaffected polyphony. His summation is indicative of the tension in the relationship between Czech and international modernism at this time: "For us Czechs, the spontaneous success of Vycpálek's *Kantáta* in front of foreigners is the best proof that, in the end, only artistic expression that is free of all makeup, pomade, and powder will be generally considered modern music, an expression that is truly human, non-l'art-pour-l'art-artistic [nelartpourlartartistní], and supported by a profoundly ethical life."[23] This reactionary attitude was at odds with Bartoš's review of the *Wozzeck* excerpts, in which he praised both Berg and Zemlinsky and blamed only the crisis situation of the German theater audience for the lack of a full production of the opera at the ISCM festival.[24] Bartoš's most telling statements were in the fault he found with the festival administration, which promoted an idealized "international music." That such a concept was artificial and valueless was demonstrated by the fact that the only truly successful compositions at the festival were those rooted in racial and domestic (i.e., national) soil.[25] In the absence of a full discussion of any compositions, including Berg's (which seems to have been the only foreign piece the critic was willing to accept on artistic terms), Bartoš's review amounted to a heavily self-righteous, reactionary attitude, wherein all outsiders were dismissed as unworthy, and curiously, unmodern.

Even more extreme in this regard were the two reviews penned by the critic and composer Jaroslav Tomášek, written for Helfert's Brno music journal *Hudební rozhledy*.[26] Tomášek echoed the prevailing skepticism of the Prague critics with the further distaste for anything demonstrably modern at the ISCM, on the grounds of the "Austro-Jewish" tendency displayed by the organization.[27] In this regard he mentioned Schoenberg by name (despite his absence from the 1925 program), later lumping him and Stravinsky together with the claim that their power in the international music community was stronger than the value of their own works.[28] Tomášek preached against the dangers of internationalism, wherein the "insufficiency of synthesis," the reaction against romanticism, and the cold objectivism of neoclassicism were demonstrative of diseased, decadent times: such an idea, of course, contradicted the mandate of neoclassicism, which arose in the effort to cleanse European culture of its decadent, diseased romanticism. The music of Czech composers (a category from which Martinů and Hába were excluded) was for Tomášek unable to compete in such an environment; nevertheless, their contributions, including the "well-chosen" Novák and Karel, were the highlights of the festival, in that they negated outside influences.

While Tomášek's anti-Semitic and highly chauvinist prose is not indicative of the full spectrum of Czech critics in 1925, many of his pro-isolationist sentiments were shared, albeit to a more moderate degree, throughout the community. Modernism, even in the hands of Czech composers such as Hába and Martinů, was still the object of distrust, and was virtually inseparable from cosmopolitanism as a threat against the more conservative efforts of the postwar Czech generation. Perhaps Jan Löwenbach assessed the situation best in his editorial "A Festival Again?" where he weighed the positive aspect of propagating Czech culture against the potential loss of national individuality. International modernism, he reasoned, would likely fail to recognize the distinctiveness of a small nation.[29] This insightful remark shows a certain attention to the perceived needs not only of Czech musicians but also of the entire national culture, not specifically Czech. Between the anxiety of isolation and the fear of outside influences, the musicians of Prague faced an uphill battle in contributing to European modernism. Indeed, even the negative criticism of the 1925 festival showed a marked improvement over the previous year's, in that Czech critics approached the music with a greater discernment between competing strains of modernism, assessing each differently. As we shall see, the hesitation of Prague's composers and audiences to accept the latest modernist trends from the rest of Europe was by no means a permanent situation, and the groundwork had also been laid for the positive reception of major foreign repertoire within the Prague critical community. The coming year would reveal a sizable shift in the attitudes and aesthetics of these musicians, not only toward each other but also toward modern European culture, and the social necessity of *change* as well. This sense of change would be captured most strongly in the "*Wozzeck* Affair" of 1926, which shaped the discourse more than anything else in its decade and became a defining moment for the younger generation.

The "*Wozzeck* Affair"

The scandal surrounding the premiere of *Wozzeck* in Prague on Thursday, November 11, 1926, represents perhaps the single most important event at the National Theater during the First Republic. The opera and its reception served to stir up a stagnating and apathetic musical community, provoking many to support international modernism from quite a militant stance. The scandal forced each member of the community to reconcile the Czech ideology of national self-sufficiency with the perceived social necessity of musical progressiveness. That the main opposition to the opera came largely from outside the ranks of Czech musicians served to solidify the latter, almost completely eradicating the factional divisions that had impeded their cooperation in the past. Much as the "Dvořák Affair" had for the previous generation, the "*Wozzeck* Affair" also provided the impetus for the younger generation to voice their opinions alongside their older contemporaries for the first time, a factor that would intensify efforts to create a Czech avant-garde, however belatedly.

Wozzeck was chosen as part of an effort to keep the National Theater and Czech concertgoers up to date with the latest operatic works from abroad, despite the disappointment and pessimism expressed so recently at the ISCM festivals. Inspired by Zemlinsky's performance of the *Drei Bruchstücke* at the 1925 festival, Ostrčil began his plans for a full production of Berg's opera almost immediately, working closely with both the composer and Zemlinsky. The production itself, with all its attendant difficulties of rehearsal and performance, represents one of the most important interactions between Czechs and Germans at this time: nevertheless, the credit for the production went entirely to the Czechs, in whose language it was sung (as *Vojcek*, translated by Jiří Maŕánek). Although the first performance was received positively in the theater, the controversy had already begun days before, as a result of a publication, *Alban Bergs Wozzeck und die Musikkritik*, issued by Universal-Edition to promote the work. Containing both positive and negative reviews by German critics from the Berlin premiere, the brochure reached their Prague counterparts in time to establish a significant bias either for or against the work. Most damaging in this regard was its effect on Antonín Šilhan, the formidable opponent of Ostrčil from the National Democratic daily *Národní listy*. In his article "In Foreign Service," Šilhan accused Ostrčil and the National Theater of falling prey to musical bolshevism in their decision to mount *Wozzeck*: this rhetoric echoed similar controversies surrounding the cultural administration of Leo Kestenberg in the neighboring Weimar Republic.[30] Two factors led Šilhan to this conclusion (in addition to his assumption that all modernist music was dangerously leftist): first, the rumor that Nejedlý, a known Marxist ideologue and friend of Ostrčil's, had influenced the conductor in his choice to perform the work; and second, the foreknowledge that the opera's third production had already been scheduled for Leningrad. That a center of bolshevism should accept a work alongside the National Theater was proof enough of conspiracy at the latter institution.

Never say never! When two excerpts of *Wozzek* [sic] were given on the occasion of the first festival of modern music at the German Theater, I mourned the person who would be forced to listen to the whole opera. I did not suspect that I myself would be one of those unfortunates and that I would meet with Mr. Alban Berg on the main Czech stage. . . . Why was *Wozzek* performed in the National Theater at all? . . . Suddenly it was clear to me. I got a hold of a list of the premieres at the St. Petersburg Opera, previously the Czarist, now the Bolshevist. And look! Amidst the new works there is nothing Slavic, but there parades—*Wozzek*. Ah so, "Leningrad!" And therefore also Prague! What a spiritual alliance! And already I saw the hands of the Bolshevist exponent in Czech cultural life [i.e., Zdeněk Nejedlý], who distributes prizes in the music section of the Academy of Sciences and who today also directs the opera of the National Theater, where Mr. Ostrčil is the mere executor of his will. Only now do I understand.[31]

Interestingly, the socialist implications of the opera's plot seem to have made little impression on Šilhan and the other detractors, possibly out of a lack of familiarity with the actual score and/or libretto. Other problems associated with the *Wozzeck* premiere included the insinuation that Conservatory students (who had been given free tickets to the performance) had served as a claque to support modernist music,[32] and that a conservative member of the Prague municipal council had died of a heart attack during the intermission in his box as a result of the music. In their reviews after the performance, both Šilhan and Emanuel Žák, the music critic from the right-wing clerical paper *Čech*, implied a direct connection between supposed "Jewish" and communist elements in Berg's music and the official's death. Žák went on to describe Berg as a "Berlin Jew" under the influence of none other than *Stravinsky*: clearly, the opposition was more concerned with anti-Semitic and anticommunist propaganda than with the music itself, which barely received mention.[33]

The majority of the music community, on the other hand, received *Wozzeck* with interest, if not with unequivocal welcome. Even those whose attitude toward the music was somewhat reserved admitted its enormous cultural importance for the community, and recognized its potential in shaping the future direction of national culture. As could be expected, Nejedlý openly criticized the stance of Šilhan and Žák, the first of whom was apparently conjuring up Bolsheviks everywhere in the theater and the Academy of Sciences, and the second of whom was incorrect with regard to Berg's supposed Jewishness.[34] The latter claim Nejedlý countered with an assurance that the composer was not only "the son of an unfalsified Viennese Christian Social," but had composed certain scenes that could only have been written by a Christian.[35] In an attempt at irony, Nejedlý pointed out that since the readers of *Čech* preferred *Les Huguenots* and *Carmen* (both by "French Jews") to *Wozzeck*, the newspaper itself was more Jewish than Berg's opera.[36] This small exchange between two critics, in the midst of a larger brewing storm, demonstrates how closely issues of nationalism and race lay below the surface of the debate: that Nejedlý could refute one anti-Semitic argument with another (albeit an indirect one) reveals the latent distrust for all those outside an imagined "ethnically Czech" category. Knowing the enormous political weight that the likes of Šilhan and Žák could wield, Berg's supporters feared a public demonstration at the second performance on Saturday, November 13. When this performance, too, went smoothly, the critics assumed that *Wozzeck* was on its way to public acceptance, and as such did not attend the third performance on the following Tuesday.

The events of November 16 would never have been recorded in such vivid detail had it not been for the young critic Mirko Očadlík, who attended the performance in order to study the music with the score.[37] Očadlík, who had started writing for *Listy Hudební matice*, *Národní osvobození*, and other papers just that year, established his career virtually overnight as a result of his role in the controversy. Since Tuesday nights were the traditional performances for subscribers, the vast majority of whom were wealthy, conservative, upper-middle-class businesspeople, the theater was filled with opponents to musical modernism; on this occasion there was also allegedly a large contingent of hired thugs. According to Očadlík, at precisely measure 736 in the second act, a sharp whistling emanated from the first balcony, accompanied by similar disruptions from the boxes and orchestra seating. Those who disagreed with the demonstration began to applaud, despite the threat of repercussions from the police who were stationed throughout the theater. Ostrčil was forced to stop the musicians, wait for the protest to subside, and, when it continued for more than half an hour, cancel the performance.[38]

In the days following, the members of the Provincial Council took the drastic measure of banning *Wozzeck* entirely from the National Theater, on the grounds that the potential violence might be more than the police could handle. Indeed, Berg's opera holds the distinction of being the only work ever to have been banned mid-run at the theater.[39] The theater's intendant Josef Nerad, while possibly not sympathetic to *Wozzeck*'s music per se, took issue with the infringement on his authority by nonartists, and resigned over the ban. Meanwhile, Očadlík hastened to inform his colleagues of the events, and along with Jirák and Vomáčka organized a public meeting of musicians affiliated with the UB in support of Ostrčil. Other cultural organizations, such as the Workers' Academy (Dělnická akademie), the Association of Dramatists, Hudební klub, the Mánes group of visual artists, and such recently formed groups as Přítomnost (The Present, a society for contemporary music), Devětsil (a group of avant-garde playwrights), and the Osvobozené divadlo (Liberated Theater) united to produce a statement of defiance against the authorities that banned *Wozzeck*.[40] The statement denounced the "terror against artistic work" that irresponsible forces had unleashed, thereby providing a dangerous precedent for other works of any genre. Significant in this and other related protest documents is the participation of younger musicians such as Emil František Burian, Iša Krejčí, Jaroslav Ježek, and Očadlík himself. The "*Wozzeck* Affair" provided their first opportunity to make a serious statement in the artistic community, and it is more than coincidental that the issue in question should involve a major work of European modernism: as we shall see, such a stance would characterize their generation more than any previous group. Many of the organizations listed above also sent letters of support to Ostrčil, or in support of him to his superiors; similarly, the UB music section officially requested that Šilhan's honorary membership be revoked, steps that were quite revolutionary in a group that had represented the musical establishment for so long. This latter point was disputed by the playwright Viktor Dyk, a sometime conservative politician and UB president, who ultimately denounced the entire music section in what amounted to an obvious political move. Curiously, Vítězslav Novák, who by now was regarded as the leader of the conservative musical establishment, signed the anti-Šilhan statement against the wishes of his superiors, although with the expressed reservation that his support was not for the music of Alban Berg, but rather for the separation of administrative and artistic concerns.[41]

While many of the Czech critics seem to have supported *Wozzeck* almost arbitrarily as a symbol of modernism, artistic freedom, or social/national duty, several found in the opera specific musical and dramatic elements that they considered as potential "signposts" for the future of music. Očadlík's extensive review, entitled "Operatic Innovation," foregrounded the stylistic, formal, and ideological unity he felt to be *Wozzeck*'s most significant contribution to opera, comparable only to *Tristan und Isolde* in its time.[42] The prevailing contrapuntal texture, the independence of melodic voices, their chromaticism to the point of atonality, the integration of forms from the realm of absolute music within a solid dramatic structure—these ingredients of expressionism demonstrated for Očadlík a "type of concentrated purism" that would cleanse the genre of its impressionistic influences, which were too much dependent on mood.[43] Like almost all Czech critics, Očadlík emphasized the direct relationship between contrapuntal texture and dramatic weight, a trend he felt to be shared by Zich's *Vina* (a significant example in its own right, given the ideological struggle surrounding its premiere three years before). *Wozzeck* was also a milestone in the struggle against "dramatic psychologism," whose proponents (including "verismo" composers, Strauss, Schreker, and the Czechs Karel and Zamrzla) were not led by logic and whose music had lost its unity through a false dependence on one single aspect of operatic creation.[44] Because of Berg's sense of unity, he could successfully incorporate expressionist orchestral techniques (glissandi, fluttertongue, col legno), which might otherwise be discredited as "the most horrendous naturalisms," but which had been used in a functional way that displayed their expressive value. With these stylistic comparisons the young critic seems to have envisioned a dual legacy of post-Wagnerian opera, one leading to the "logic" of Berg and Zich, the other, incorrectly, to the "psychology" of Strauss and Schreker. This duality maps easily onto Hostinský's *důslednost/náladovost* binarism, which the young critic would have gleaned through his teacher Nejedlý. Finally, the sociological statement of *Wozzeck* was not lost on Očadlík, since he felt it to be, like all other elements, of dramatic necessity to Berg's total creation. The critic did not seek to analyze the opera in terms of its class implications, however, leaving that particular field clear for his mentor.

Nejedlý applauded the efforts of Berg to find the human element in modern music, an endeavor that took him beyond the mere "decadence" of Schoenberg's music. In an immanent analysis that bears resemblances to the style of Adorno, Nejedlý felt that *Wozzeck* represented a new moral level of music drama, in both text and music, which reflected the ugliness of contemporary society. In Büchner's drama the categories of good and evil were blurred at each social level, revealing a complexity that Berg matched in his music. The opera's atonal musical language was therefore for Nejedlý not just an anarchy of notes, as he perceived to be the case with Schoenberg, but rather a meaningful social statement in the complex of melodic interrelationships. Nevertheless, Nejedlý did not consider the music to be extremely modern, at least no more so than that necessitated by the intellectual development of the modern era. The segments of Czech society that refused to accept the social truth of *Wozzeck* Nejedlý deemed indolent, predisposed to dislike anything new, and unable to use their brains at the opera. Rather idealistically, Nejedlý conjectured that "simple people" would understand the plight of the opera's hero and therefore appreciate Berg's work as a whole, or if not, go politely home. The critic read the *"Wozzeck* Affair" itself as existing outside the realm of art, perpetrated by reactionaries and their gang of hired fascist thugs in an act of false bravery. Charitably, he allowed that both sides had acted out of patriotism, since those who rejected *Wozzeck* did so with a sense of conservative, anti-German chauvinism, while those who supported Berg believed that progressive culture was a matter of national pride, even if its representatives were foreign. Nejedlý, like most other Czech commentators, cast Ostrčil as the hero in his drama of the controversy, since only a truly progressive artist could save art from the forces of capitalist society.

From the younger generation, Alois Hába also proposed a class reading of the opera and its reception.[45] He saw *Wozzeck* from a larger viewpoint of human development, wherein the opera mirrored the sociopolitical process of equality, not only through the dramatic situation but also in Berg's implementation of a nonhierarchized musical language. Almost baiting the majority of the theater-going public, Hába (himself an avant-garde composer and educator) declared that *Wozzeck* would satisfy only those with a higher dramatic sense, while those who might regret the lack of "passive triadic harmonies" were welcome to listen for them, played simultaneously, in the atonal cluster chords of Berg's score.

As the single Conservatory instructor who taught avant-garde styles of composition, Hába's reverence for the Second Viennese School was well known; the viewpoint of the youngest, neoclassicist-influenced circle of Prague composers, however, was much more problematic. Iša Krejčí, a composer who also reviewed music for the publishing-house journal *Rozpravy Aventina*, refused to consider *Wozzeck* as representative of modernism, since only Stravinsky and Milhaud were the true models for the younger generation.[46] According to Krejčí, these two composers had gained favor through their attempt at collective expression by means of immediate, "physiological" music, as opposed to the Second Viennese School, which was too self-absorbed to be accessible. Nevertheless, Krejčí (like Nejedlý) allowed that Berg had at least surpassed Schoenberg in the constructiveness of his forms and the extraordinary intensity of his opera as a drama. Similarly, the allegiance toward the neoclassical branch of European modernism evidenced in the writings of Burian, Ježek, and others did not stand in the way of their support of Berg and Ostrčil in the *"Wozzeck* Affair."

Many of the past "affairs" of the Prague music community had served to ostracize one of its more peripheral members, such as Zemánek, Nedbal, Šak, Nejedlý, or to some extent even Ostrčil and Zich, in that each "victim" had somehow transgressed against the reigning conservative ideology of the musical establishment at the UB. In the process of each, the latter institution was further buttressed against attack by means of a preserved moral superiority over foreign, ideological, or modernist musical threats. In the "*Wozzeck* Affair," however, the main enemy was in fact the upper-middle-class public, whose tastes had surpassed those of the UB in its own conservatism; the ostracized individual in this case was not the outsider (either Ostrčil or Berg), but rather the most conservative member of the UB itself, Šilhan. The rally of support behind Ostrčil cast him as the hero in a struggle between art and economics: Berg, when his name appeared in the debate at all, was never depicted as an outsider in the pro-*Wozzeck* criticism, and his non-Czech status barely entered the equation. Much more strongly situated in the rhetoric is the unquestionable necessity for Berg's music to become part of progressive Czech culture, for the good not only of social education but also of the Czechs' perceived relationship with "Western" Europe.[47] Determined to avoid embarrassment precisely at the moment when they felt they had gained the attention of the international modernist elite, the Czech musical community proclaimed a moral need to embrace a work whose own moral content might have been hotly debated under other circumstances. Indeed, given the undecided reception of much of the music at the ISCM festivals just months before, it is interesting to speculate as to how *Wozzeck* would have fared in critical opinion in the absence of public scandal.

Nevertheless, the change in attitude in Prague toward the avant-garde modernism of Western Europe was more than just arbitrary; rather, it was the result of the slowly changing aesthetic view of the generation that came of age during the First World War. Having oscillated between extreme nationalism in the wake of the Smetana Cult, the initial thirst for French culture after 1918, and isolationist conservatism when finally exposed to international modernism, with the passage of time this generation had not only tempered its reaction, but also gained ascendancy in the power structure of the musical establishment. As such, the moderately pro-Western outlook of Vomáčka, Jirák, and others had become the norm, amid which the radical antimodernism of Šilhan did not belong. While *Wozzeck*, in terms of the opera's specific style, may not have been the longed-for signpost pointing toward the future of Czech modernism, its positive reception—and the change in attitude it represented—served as a milestone in the attainment of Helfert's "certainty," at least within the confines of the musical community. Despite the gathering and reconciliation of artistic forces, however, the economic factor won the struggle: for two years following the disastrous premiere of *Wozzeck*, the National Theater administration denied Ostrčil the chance to present any work that could be perceived as inflammatory—or simply put, too representative of international modernism.

The Aftermath of *Wozzeck*: *Dědův odkaz*, *Švanda dudák*, and Antimodernism

For the remainder of the 1926/27 season at the National Theater, the administration struggled to retain the loyalties of its subscribers by means of appeasing them with either popular repertoire or premieres of operas by conservative composers. Although this situation implies a widespread backlash of antimodernism in Prague musical society, its composers and critics still maintained the ground they had won with the "*Wozzeck* Affair," continuing on the trajectory that would eventually lead them to the foundation of a true Czech avant-garde. Two years would pass, however, before any fruits of the cosmopolitanism earned through controversy would appear in the form of modernist Czech operas at the National Theater. In the meantime, operas by Novák, Weinberger, and Janáček provoked dissatisfaction among members of the community with the lack of progress in Czech culture and uncovered latent anxieties about the traditionalist roots of Czech identity as derived from the Cultural Revival.

Immediately after the *Wozzeck* fiasco, the administration forced Ostrčil to produce Novák's latest opera, *Dědův odkaz* (The Grandfather's Legacy), on December 22, 1926, much earlier than he had planned, resulting in an imperfect performance that insulted the composer and critics loyal to him. Šilhan and Šourek in particular bemoaned the fact that an opera by one of the most respected Czech composers came second to a problematic foreign work, and Novák resented its proximity to Christmas, when few patrons would be interested in the theater.[48] According to Lébl, while Novák had been at the forefront of the Czech modernist movement before the First World War and had retained his authority in the early years of the First Republic with an active interest in democratizing the cultural institutions of Prague, as society (and audiences) began to change he became quickly disillusioned with such a participatory stance.[49] His musical response, after the relatively challenging opera *Lucerna* from 1922, was to revert to a more conservative, academic style reminiscent of his earlier period; the material is dominated by a fascination with Moravian and Slovak folk song, indicative of conservative nationalism in general. The outcome, his fourth opera *Dědův odkaz*, is a work constructed of eight static scenes, linked by extensive symphonic interludes in the manner of the greatly successful cantata *Bouře* (The Storm) from 1910, when Novák was at the height of his popularity. The opera describes the life of an artist, constantly yearning for the perfect love he experienced once, briefly, in the past. The music borrows heavily from Novák's own tone poem *Of the Eternal Longing* from 1905, and in general stays at least a quarter-century behind styles current in the rest of Europe, being most closely allied with the *Märchenopern* of Humperdinck and d'Albert. Alongside this aesthetic, quite a lot of Novák's material comes from Slovak folk music, the preponderance of which was so great that *Dědův odkaz* was nominated for a prize of 20,000 crowns given by an American Slovak society for the first "Slovak opera."[50] It is nationalist in the straightforward, patriotic manner of the earliest UB generation.

As can be expected, such a retrospective opera did not win the favor of a critical community that had rallied behind a pinnacle of international modernism just weeks before. Indeed, even the more generous of Novák's colleagues were at best restrained in their praise of the work. *Dědův odkaz* provided Nejedlý with an opportunity to renew his venomous attacks on his archrival, creating a social reading of both the opera and its reception: as opposed to the truly national efforts of the Cultural Revivalists of the late nineteenth century, Novák's work portrayed only the smallness of contemporary bourgeois society.[51] The only portion of the nation the opera could be said to represent was therefore the moneyed classes who supported such works at the National Theater. This negative social factor, along with what Nejedlý described as the technical and inventive insufficiency of the work, he deemed damaging to the honor of art as a bearer of culture, particularly in that *Dědův odkaz* could be used as a model for younger composers and thus to deceive them from the true path of modernism.

Critics from the younger generation judged Novák all the more harshly. Očadlík reiterated many of Nejedlý's comments about *Dědův odkaz*, particularly with regard to the perceived dearth of invention: lacking synthesis or even concept as an opera, he viewed the work as "immature," "eclectic," and "inartistic," indicative of the extent to which Novák had fallen behind the modernist movement.[52] He also differentiated between modern attempts at continuing the Wagnerian principle of leitmotivs in the construction of new forms (as Berg and Stravinsky had) and the symphonic character of Novák's opera, which ran counter to the dramatic necessity of the genre and had more in common with techniques of the Italian verismo school.[53] The pugilistic Bedřich Bělohlávek, a newcomer to the critical sphere who laid out his entire view of Czech music history in the serial article "On Contemporary Czech Music," portrayed Novák as a composer who abused his official status in order to create "a series of compositions of lesser value," among which *Dědův odkaz* was merely "formally decorative" and superficial, never reaching any dramatic depth.[54] While not as ruthless as his younger contemporaries, the established critic Vomáčka (himself a former student of Novák) also found fault with his teacher's work, stating that despite its attempts at national feeling, the folk-play-cum-libretto was completely out of date and the opera's overwhelmingly lyrical passages were detrimental to the dramatic flow.[55] Vomáčka was simply exasperated with how distant Novák was from the "atmosphere of contemporary feeling," despite attempts to simplify his tone as a concession toward popularizing opera. The reception of *Dědův odkaz* reveals more than just the rejection of a substandard opera: Novák's growing status as a conservative composer was seen as representative of the musical establishment amid a critical environment increasingly hostile toward the power of the upper classes in the theater. Had it not been produced immediately in the wake of the "*Wozzeck* Affair," Novák's opera might have fared better, but the overall dismissive tone in the press indicates that such a "nationalist," isolationist aesthetic, coupled with an antimodernist score, was unacceptable by the late 1920s.

Four months after *Dědův odkaz*, the National Theater produced what would be the most successful production of the entire First Republic period, both at home and abroad: *Švanda dudák* (Švanda the Bagpiper), by the Czech-Jewish composer

Jaromír Weinberger. Its success was due in large part to the backing of Max Brod, who personally arranged its publication with Universal-Edition using his German translation, after which point it became popular internationally.[56] The opera, based on the well-known work by Revivalist playwright Josef Kajetan Tyl and conceived as a modern-day contribution to the folk-opera genre of Smetana's *Bartered Bride* and Dvořák's *Devil and Kate*, was dedicated to all three "national" artists in an act of humble allegiance to Czech tradition. *Švanda's* critical reception in Prague was unfortunately predicated as much on its overwhelming popularity as on its composer's perceived threat as a Jew within Czech culture. The anti-Semitism evident in this criticism appears only rarely in the history of Czech music, since historically very few Jewish composers from Bohemia had considered themselves Czech and not German prior to this point.[57] Weinberger's compositional style was certainly multivalent and populist; it was described by postwar musicologists Josef Bek and Oldřich Pukl as a mixture of romanticism, impressionism, Jewish and Christian sacred music, Czech and foreign folk styles, and popular music, perhaps more suited to the operetta genre, but not without its craftsman-like qualities.[58] As might be expected, such eclecticism was not well received by the consequence-driven critics of Prague, who trounced *Švanda* as a shameful fraud.

Many critics met the programming choice of Weinberger's work with utter disbelief, describing the opera, as Josef Hutter did, as a chain of kitschy, sentimental, grotesque, folk-like, and "national" scenes, comparing the total effect to the newly emergent revue genre.[59] Claiming that the dedications to Tyl, Smetana, and Dvořák were damaging to true national feeling, Hutter felt that Weinberger had "stolen" from other composers' scores (including that of *Libuše*), and as such, his ostentatious nationalism could be nothing but a conscious and cynical mockery of Czech tradition. Although admittedly brilliant and artful in its effects, the lack of invention that Hutter perceived stemmed from a threefold system of borrowing, on the levels of overall dramatic concept, organizational ideas, and the actual notes themselves.[60] Connecting *Švanda dudák's* style with the powerful forces of bourgeois musical tastes, Hutter declared that all critics would likely reject the work upon first hearing, with the notable exception of Šilhan.

As usual, Nejedlý was even more direct in his social reading of Weinberger's opera, which he felt was such a "galimatias" of quotes, it could not be considered the work of one composer.[61] The critic delineated the borrowings as follows: all occasions of majestic pomp were taken from *Libuše*, the merry scenes from *The Bartered Bride*, the dances from Dvořák's oeuvre, the character of the Devil from Janáček, and the moments of universality from the folksong repertoire on the one hand, and from Puccini on the other (the latter because of his popularity). Nejedlý bemoaned the fate of Czech national art that it was capable of producing such drivel as *Švanda dudák*, alongside which even *Dědův odkaz* seemed like a masterpiece. More specifically, he read in both the creation and reception of

Weinberger's work the demoralization of modern Czech society, claiming that the audience, with fascists in the lead, had flocked to the theater prepared to give the opera a tumultuous reception, much in the same way that they had come prepared to castigate *Wozzeck*. In a final salvo against the bourgeois subscribers, Nejedlý found it ironic that a Jew had composed what he predicted could become a fascist anthem (i.e., the opera's final celebratory chorus, "Na tom našem dvoře, všecko to krákoře"), to words by the same poet who had written the Czech republican national anthem ("Kde domov můj?" with words by Tyl and music by František Škroup).

The harsh reception of Weinberger's *Švanda dudák* bears witness to the anxiety from which the Czech musical community was suffering at the crossroads of modernism, populism, tradition, and international recognition. While for many it was a question of the correct representation of Smetanian tradition, folk customs, or false patriotism (including Novák, who judged it the work of an epigon),[62] *Švanda dudák* also exposed a certain embarrassment that such a work should attain worldwide renown before most of the Czechs' more "serious" composers. Bek and Pukl state succinctly what lay between the lines of many reviews at this time: that Weinberger's music, accepted abroad, would provide a fraudulent image of Czech music for the Western listener.[63] Even more significant with regard to international embarrassment (already encountered with the "*Wozzeck* Affair," when the eyes of the European avant-garde were trained on Prague) is the sense of discomfort that emerged through *Švanda dudák* with regard to the tradition itself. It seems as though folk operas, acceptable in the innocent nineteenth-century realm of the Cultural Revival, could never be "authentic" in the modern era, especially one that imitated *The Bartered Bride* so self-consciously.

As noted above, the issue of religious exclusion rarely came to the surface in the criticism of the time. Nevertheless, many of the artistic factors cited by the critics above (particularly the references to plagiarism, kitsch, grotesquerie, and ostentation) were long connected to anti-Semitic rhetoric in music, as was the charge of populism in general.[64] Weinberger himself had already been involved in an altercation with the young opera director Ota Zítek over the latter's supposed plagiarism in an article on Scriabin, an accusation that quickly developed into racist name-calling, public threats, and culminated in a court case.[65] Seven years later, a degree of latent animosity may have lain behind the vehemence with which *Švanda dudák* was rejected by the rest of the Czech musical community.

In spite of any anti-Semitic references the rejection of Weinberger may have had, most of the critical commentary seems to be aimed toward a growing consciousness of the place of Czech music in contemporary European culture. Ever since the ISCM festivals, the "*Wozzeck* Affair," and the lukewarm reception of *Dědův odkaz*, the musicians of Prague had gradually begun to place more priority on their own fledgling modernist school. Similarly, the reaction to *Švanda dudák*'s populism demonstrated a confusion between the wish for a greater audience appreciation for Czech music and a distaste for exaggeration and excess. Nevertheless, even a work both modern and popular could face difficulty in the troubled cultural environment of Prague in the late 1920s, as the hesitant reception of Janáček's *Věc Makropulos* would reveal.

As František Pala stated, the 1927/28 operatic season at the National Theater was chosen to be deliberately conservative in order to avoid the shadow of negativity that *Wozzeck* had created for the entire previous season.[66] Indeed, the only significant new production was *Věc Makropulos* (The Makropoulos Case, March 1, 1928), Janáček's penultimate opera, which had premiered in Brno in December 1926. The continued positive reception of the composer in Prague—ever since the belated premiere of *Jenůfa* in 1916—promised great things for the new work, based on a text by a favorite Czech playwright, Karel Čapek. After the romantically conceived *Káťa Kabanová* from 1922 and the nature-bound, childlike *Cunning Little Vixen* from 1925, both critics and audiences were ill prepared for the metaphysical realm of Čapek, set to some of Janáček's most provocative music. In the words of Jirák, *Věc Makropulos* was an "opera without music," whose orchestral accompaniment, with its boisterous accentuation, rendered the text unintelligible.[67] The conservative Borecký felt that Janáček was more suited to the primitive, natural world of *The Cunning Little Vixen*, rather than the "ideologically burdened" atmosphere of Čapek; many other critics agreed, receiving the opera without enthusiasm.[68] Even the usually open-minded and supportive Steinhard used words like "unpoetic," "manic," and "markedly undramatic" to describe *Věc Makropulos*, stating generally that the opera was a product of the current trend toward objectivism in musical genres.[69]

The reserved criticism matched the audience's reaction to Janáček's new opera: although *Věc Makropulos* went on to achieve international success and years later entered the permanent repertoire of the National Theater, its initial run lasted only five performances. The cosmopolitan implications of the opera's urban environment were unsettling to the Prague community, who had grown used to viewing Janáček as an interesting and somewhat untamed phenomenon from the Moravian countryside. Given the history of how foreign influences were received in Prague, especially those openly bearing the stamp of cosmopolitanism, it is not surprising that such an antiromantic, urban work by a Czech composer of international fame should be snubbed. Its urbanness no longer representative of the imagined Czech nation, and its score no longer demonstrably adherent to the tradition of post-Wagnerian operas (linked to the Czech identity through Smetana), *Věc Makropulos* and its composer confronted some of the most problematic issues facing Prague society and its cultural sphere in the late 1920s. The international popularity of Janáček and Weinberger forced critics and musicians to reconsider the inviolability of Czech traditions as descended from Smetana and the Cultural Revival, and therefore to reconfigure Czech musical identity toward the modern age. This renegotiation of culture affected no social group more than the younger generation of artists and musicians coming of age in the late 1920s.

The Younger Generation and Its Influences

New attitudes toward modernism, cosmopolitanism, and culture in general, appearing so gradually in the early postwar generation of Vomáčka and Helfert, became the dominant characteristic of the following generation of Prague musicians. Indeed, the similar aesthetic views of young composers and critics of the late 1920s and 1930s served to form a much more cohesive artistic group than any other in the twentieth century, such that Prague experienced a true avant-garde for the first time. Perhaps the most crucial factor in common was their acceptance of change on multiple levels in artistic life. These changes included an openness to foreign influences, almost without question; a passion for the popular as well as the avant-garde; a new sense of collaboration with the other arts, especially the theater; a keener social awareness with a tendency toward left-wing politics; and the acceptance of technology as a modern reality to be used and enjoyed. Odd as it may seem, they were the first generation of Prague musicians to declare their willingness to create music that was unabashedly new and unfettered by the constraints of the Smetana tradition. Such factors characterized a group whose most salient members were Alois Hába, Bohuslav Martinů, Erwin Schulhoff, Emil František Burian, Jaroslav Ježek, Iša Krejčí, and Mirko Očadlík.[70]

Technological changes, primarily radio and recordings, facilitated the influx of foreign and popular cultural products, which in turn created a sense of urgency surrounding the Central Europeans' contact with the outside world. The first Czechoslovak radio station opened just outside of Prague in May 1923, just a few months after similar endeavors in Britain; after a decade there were an estimated 600,000 radio sets in operation, owned by 16.5 percent of the country's population.[71] While the attitude toward these new machines was generally optimistic, many artists met the technology of radio with reservations or even consternation. In the Czechoslovak Republic, as elsewhere, performing musicians worried that recorded sound (or "mechanical music" as it was often termed) would spell the end of their livelihoods, and *Hudební věstník* (Musical Bulletin), a periodical dedicated to the rights of the struggling artist, duly condemned radio as a modern evil. The editor-in-chief, Julius Janeček, described in detail the negative competition that radio would bring to the live concert industry, predicting a "liquidation" of the theater audience, and consequently, widespread unemployment among musicians.[72] On the aesthetic side, critics debated the artistic merits of radio, and the larger issue of the mechanization of art. While never quite as philosophically based as the writings of Adorno and Benjamin on the subject, newcomers such as Gracian Černušák and Karel Vetterl weighed the educational value and popularization factor of the new technology. Černušák, somewhat pessimistic about the much-touted potential to educate vast segments of society about concert music via radio, claimed that the new audience, disunified in their relation to music in general, had largely given in to the lure of popular music by 1927.[73] Vetterl, on the other hand, rebutted both Černušák and Janeček, saying that through the creation of a "radio culture," composers would be free to create new genres, presenting music in its purest form; radio's natural orientation toward the modern era would necessarily assist cultural development, while the new competitive environment would weed out dilettantism among performers.[74] Drawing on the extensive writings of Heinrich Besseler on the social necessity of *Gebrauchsmusik*, Vetterl successfully tied his advocacy of radio to the Czech discourse on the promulgation of art in society, which had cycled through the music community continuously since the days of Hostinský.[75]

Talking films had much the same effect as radio on the musicians of Prague, in both negative and positive aspects. While Janeček and others at *Hudební věstník* bemoaned the effect of soundtracks in films on the unemployment rate of movie-house musicians, the editors of *Tempo-Listy Hudební matice* took an optimistic stance toward the new techology and its potential for artistic creation, as demonstrated by their reprint of Milhaud's article from the liberal German paper *Querschnitt* and a similar essay by the Czech Jan Branberger.[76] The latter acknowledged the worry that talking films would signal the end of movie-house orchestras, but identified the possibility of popular education through a new genre of music-based films, where the score made an artistic statement and was integral to the drama.[77] Perhaps most important for the young generation of composers, radio, gramophone, and talking films all made a profound impact through the foreign and popular music they introduced.

Popular music had existed in the Czech lands in various forms inherited from the early nineteenth century, particularly in terms of popularized songs and dances in folk-style, Singspiel couplets, and a strong tradition of brass-band ensembles.[78] Just prior to the First World War, Prague saw the establishment of a number of cabaret venues such as Montmartre and Alhambra, and performers such as Karel Hašler and the comedic ensemble Červená sedma (Červený's Seven, 1907–22), whose work can be viewed as a synthesis of satire, operetta, folk-like songs, and the earliest imports from Tin Pan Alley.[79] In this respect, Prague cabaret was similar to contemporaneous endeavors in the German-speaking world. As with the musical establishment, major changes occurred with regard to Czech popular music after 1918: as Gendron, Kater, Cook, and others have shown, jazz entered the European listening experience with the arrival of African-American troops in France and Germany at the culmination of the war.[80] While the first bands to tour the Continent, such as those of Will Marion Cook and James Reese Europe, did not include Prague in their itineraries, their activities and those of other ensembles in Paris and London strongly influenced the Czech musical sphere. Without the new technology of radio and the widespread circulation of recordings, however, the portion of Prague concertgoers in the 1920s that thirsted for jazz would have had to subsist on the infrequent visits of touring bands that ventured past the German-speaking lands. In the first few months of independence, the influence in Prague was still somewhat indirect, consisting mainly of a rejuvenation of preexistent traditional genres, now with more fashionable rhythms; Josef Kotek notes that until 1920, no one in the Czech musical community knew how to play the saxophone.[81] Nevertheless, by the mid-1920s, thanks to increased dissemination via technology, several Czech bands had formed whose intent was to replicate the new sounds from America, or at least to form a parallel to other, more upbeat European dance bands inspired by Tin Pan Alley. The new composer-performers Jara Beneš and R. A. Dvorský capitalized on the rage for the one-step, two-step, shimmy, and in 1920, the foxtrot, with names such as *The Consumptive Ostrich, Republican Foxtrot, Wyomingian,* and *Sing-Sing.*[82] Dvorský became somewhat of an entertainment industry all to himself, composing, performing, publishing sheet music, and taking under his wing dozens of young Czech jazz performers who would enjoy fruitful careers in dance bands, all the way into the postwar era. Nevertheless, several further developments would be necessary before Czech musicians would perform anything approximating jazz itself.

The sense of intercultural contact embodied by the Czech relationship to jazz between the wars is strange and problematic. Like that of other European societies, whose experience with the new music and dance came via Paris and London, the Czech discourse around jazz tended to conflate the images of those two cities, their imagined inhabitants, and lifestyles, with those of Africa, urban America, and even the Wild West.[83] This mixture of associations not only traces the path of the music from Africa and America to Europe, telescoping this long history into a single moment, but also encompasses the issues of exoticism, primitivism, and depersonalization connected with jazz. The apparent absence of history in America and Africa enchanted the European mind, which saw this new development as an exciting way to dispense with romanticism and its problems: the perceived sexuality of the dance also fit perfectly with the trend of anti-intellectualism in the new era. By the early 1920s, Paris had been firmly established as the main European port of call for American culture, a factor that resonated with the contemporary fascination with Parisian literature and music among the young intellectuals of Prague.[84] It is also important to note that for the Czechs, the espousal of jazz, both popularly and in the context of art music, was a conscious effort to escape from the cultural hegemony of the Austro-German world; while most German cities also experienced a similar jazz craze, Czech audiences viewed the phenomenon as having arrived "express" from Paris.

The dawn of jazz in Europe coincided with the dance craze as popular entertainment for the lower classes; as the history of Prague's younger generation of composers attests, dance affected artistic thinking as well, in that ballet, pantomime, and even popular dances began appearing in the oeuvres of several young artists, including Hába, Schulhoff, Martinů, and Burian. When the latter two composers had ballets successfully performed at the National Theater in the late 1920s, dance as a musical genre became the object of scholarly discussion, linked closely with French culture and Stravinsky (whose *Petrushka* was finally performed in Prague on February 25, 1925), neoclassicism, populism, "physiological music," and perhaps most important, the de-intellectualization of art. This last category, intimately connected with the emancipation of the body that dance produced, reinforced the Eurocentric attitude toward American culture in general and of African-Americans in particular as being physically oriented. As such, the entry of jazz into the Czech musical sphere served as a point of confluence for the multifarious streams of antiromanticism craved by the modernist-oriented composers of the young generation. Each of these phenomena had as its core the purification of the mind through a less cerebral art, which in turn could be used as a tool to socialize the newly emergent lower classes to culture.

The first climactic moment of jazz in Prague was doubtlessly the occasion of Josephine Baker's 1928 performance, occurring in the midst of her tour through Central Europe. The reception of this event, the most significant one of its kind in the First Republic, demonstrates the ideological jumble surrounding the dancer and her music. Preceded by a series of reviews by Otakar Štorch-Marien, the editor of *Rozpravy Aventina*, Baker's mythical status reinforced the confusion between African, African-American, Euro-American, and Parisian symbols. Baker's dancing was described as a mixture of animalistic gestures from Africa and refinement from America, a renaissance of the naked female beauty, and inseparable from the image of the Parisian revue.[85] Similarly, Štorch-Marien's review of her Prague performance referred to her as "a creature who always does what she likes," who is not ruled by cultivated thoughts, and yet captures the audience through the movements of her body; the rhythm of the music the critic found to be simply "wild," containing no psychological element whatsoever.[86] For musicians, the accomplishments of the Savoy Orchestra that accompanied her, as well as those of the British Jack Hylton and His Boys that followed eight months later, made an equally lasting impression. Although the critic "P.P." at *Hudební věstník* deplored the audience's approval of such undeserving, foreign compositions (in keeping with that journal's negative attitude toward jazz), both Jaroslav Ježek and Silvestr Hippmann assessed the performances with greater refinement.[87] Denying the rumors of an early demise to jazz, Ježek declared that Hylton's performance revealed something inexhaustible in the emotive quality of the music: "a piece of frivolous and brilliant Paris, a piece of that laughing life of the dancing halls and bars of Western metropolises, is leaving the gray and strict city of Prague."[88]

Ježek's commentary, based in a generally cosmopolitan viewpoint, highlighted the sheer joy that he and his peers derived from their attempts to merge the popular with the modern, creating an avant-garde movement for the first time within the musical community of Prague. Under the aegis of several interrelated institutions friendly to the cause of modern music by young composers, such as Ostrčil's regime at the National Theater, Zemlinsky's at the Neues Deutsches Theater (until his departure in 1927), Steinhard's open-minded editorial policy at *Der Auftakt,* and Hába's masterclass in quarter-tone composition at the Conservatory, the new group of young composers traversed the traditional boundaries of ethnicity and religion in the city. Their achievements would have lasting results, shaping the community all the way to the collapse of democracy in 1938.[89] In the late 1920s, when this compositional generation was still in its infancy, the most highly visible figure was Emil František Burian, who quickly came to represent the new cultural attitude through his prolific publications and youthful performances.

Emil František Burian and the Birth of the Czech Avant-Garde

The son of a principal baritone at the National Theater and the nephew of the internationally renowned tenor Karel Burian, Emil František Burian began his career as a performing artist in his teenage years. He thereafter styled himself as a composer, lyric tenor, pianist in both classical and jazz idioms, drummer, choral conductor, writer on music, librettist, actor, director, aesthetician, and theorist of the theater. That all of these transformations took place before his twenty-fifth birthday is one of the most astounding feats of prodigious creativity in the history of music in Prague. While not all of Burian's early projects were successful, of lasting value, or much more than vain sloganeering, it is apparent upon examination of the hundreds of pages of his writings from the 1920s that the young artist sought to create a new aesthetic that encompassed all the arts and their relation to a modern, cosmopolitan society. Taking on such gigantic issues as the legacy of Wagner, the crisis of the theater, popular culture, and the stigmas of lyric sentimentality and naturalism, Burian's artistic plan in many ways spoke for his generation in the late 1920s, at a time when many others were not yet in a position to express themselves publicly.

In many ways, Burian's attitude toward modernism stood in direct opposition to that of the Czech musical community in which he was raised, particularly in his love of mundane sentimentality and naturalism, abhorred by both the Nejedlý circle and the conservative elite. In a context where the individual artist was meant to negate his/her subjectivity in favor of contributing to the collective achievement of the Cultural Revival, Burian's aesthetic celebrated the personal and the experiential, from the perspectives of both artist and audience. As such, his ideas fit only partially with those of the neoclassical movement, which typically embraced the mundane with a greater sense of anonymity; nevertheless, Burian espoused many of the neoclassicists' tenets in his writings at this time.[90]

With his operatic pedigree, Burian was naturally drawn to the theater from an early age, composing three operas, *Alladine a Palomid* (1923, based on Maeterlinck), *Před slunce východem* (Before Sunrise, 1924), and *Mastičkář* (The Quack, 1925, based on commedia dell'arte) as well as a ballet, *Fagot a flétna* (The Bassoon and the Flute, 1925), while still studying with Foerster at the Conservatory. With *Před slunce východem* and especially *Fagot a flétna*, both premiered under Ostrčil at the National Theater (1925 and 1929, respectively), the young composer began to implement a new and highly individualistic aesthetic of music theater that he had developed through contact with Prague's avant-garde literary circles. Contemporary with the rise of the new compositional generation, a potent artistic force had developed in the form of Devětsil, a group of Czech poets, playwrights, and authors founded by Karel Teige in 1920. Eventually combining the creative energies of poets Vítězslav Nezval and Jaroslav Seifert, playwrights Jiří Voskovec and Jan Werich, and directors Jindřich Honzl and Jiří Frejka, Devětsil's mandate was the conceptualization of a new, optimistic understanding of life and art, which they termed Poetism.[91] Subject to "a synthetic organization of reality, in order to be able to satisfy every poetic hunger that afflicts this century," Poetism "sought out in films, the circus, sport, tourism, and in life itself the expressive possibilities which were not to be found in mere pictures and poems," in order to express what may be termed a lyrical, naturalistic view of life.[92] Obsessed with images of the cosmopolitan, the urban, and drawing on inspiration from the Futurists and Dadaists, the Poetists rejected the dry academicism of Czech (and European) tradition in favor of the everyday, the improvisational, the sentimental, and the grotesque. In musical terms these tenets manifested themselves in a predilection for jazz, revues, music halls, popular dance, street song, and urban sounds such as car horns and tram noises.[93] Burian had the fortune to be intimately involved with Devětsil in the early stages of the formation of this aesthetic, and was treated as a creative equal and musical authority. As such, many of the Poetist ideals appear in works such as *Fagot a flétna*, which the composer styled more as a ballet-revue than a straightforward ballet, with multiple simultaneous performance tableaux, including a text by Nezval.[94]

Burian himself theorized his personal contribution to the Poetist project as *Polydynamika*, a general aesthetic of art, wherein opposing elements were not blended into a harmonious *Gesamtkunstwerk*, but were instead liberated to create tension through contrasts and irregularities.[95] In a conscious rejection of Wagner, whose aesthetic of dense polyphony and homogeneity, according to Burian, produced a sensation of sluggishness and fatigue in the public, *Polydynamika*, a "harmony of diversities," would "exploit the details of the perception of the different elements of art" and intensify the audience's aesthetic response to each.[96] These different elements, encompassing musical parameters such as rhythm (which he prized above all else), polytonality, timbre, and form (which he sought ultimately to demolish), and also theatrical elements such as declamation, melodrama, dance, lighting, and spatiality, would interact in an ongoing counterpoint that involved the public in the creation of the work.[97] In his personal manifesto of *Polydynamika*, published serially in his own short-lived journal, *Tam-Tam* (1925), Burian attacked many of the traditional aesthetic tenets of Czech music, including anything to do with post-Wagnerian compositional practice, musical institutions, and academicism. In an aggressively anti-establishment essay entitled "Masked Conservatism," he rejected the notion of Czech tradition that granted the epithet "modernist" only to certain authorized artists, while discrediting all those who fell beyond a prescribed boundary as damaging to national culture.[98] In contrast to this false sense of tradition, Burian felt that "Czechoslovak art" was by nature international, *without a domestic tradition*, and was therefore obligated to pursue a cosmopolitan stance; with the Poetist predilection for urbanness and the multiplicity of the *Polydynamika* technique, he was ready to introduce jazz, dance, and street song into the vocabulary of Czech musical modernism.

In 1928 Burian published what amounts to a continuation of his manifesto of *Polydynamika*, fleshed out in an applied form. The extensive monograph *Jazz* contains everything from iconoclastic calls for the destruction of romantic forms, institutions, and ideologies; basic definitions of jazz; a Eurocentric history of the genre; an unscientific ethnography of African and African-American dance; discussions of Josephine Baker, modern dances, Křenek's *Jonny spielt auf*, and other efforts by Burian and his contemporaries; to an instructional manual of the musical parameters of jazz; a guide to orchestration; a glossary of instruments and terms; and a complete bibliography and discography. In *Jazz* Burian tackled almost every aesthetic issue of his generation, particularly the desire to replace worn-out concert-hall values with the dynamic culture of the streets, where Josephine Baker could be considered an important creative artist and where *Jonny spielt auf* was a model for modern opera. The very manner in which he described jazz is anti-establishmentarian and reflective of the *Polydynamika* technique in its disunity:

> A serious "secession" gentleman walked along the muddy street. He slipped. He moved in a dance rhythm of madmen and trained animals. This gentleman walked in quite a serious manner. *Chaplin* dances over the abyss on his hand and his left side. *Chagal* [sic] started his sketches dancing. *Stravinsky* wrote *Le sacre du printemps* and Blacks played *ragtimes* [sic] and *jazz*. "And thus it has come about that serious modernistic music and musicians, most notably and avowedly in the work of the French modernists Auric, Satie and Darius Milhaud, have become the confessed debtors of American Negro jazz." Yes, you Black man, bewitched by the culture of the renaissance European. It also happened that we [like you] were bewitched by a barbaric religion.[99]

Beyond the typical ethnocentrisms of his rhetoric, it is easy to see that Burian viewed jazz as a liberating element in multiple facets of music, predominantly for its inherently polydynamic character; that jazz supposedly best captured the sounds of the street made the new music doubly important. Furthermore, the new instruments that jazz introduced, particularly the drum set (often referred to as simply "jazz" by the Czechs), the saxophone, and other more ephemeral inventions such as the violinophon, offered a welcome expansion of the orchestrational palette, itself a key component of *Polydynamika*. The monograph advocated using the principles of jazz as building blocks for new, improvisation-based genres, wherein multiple media could join to form artistic works according to the personal taste of the listener.[100] The diminished importance of the individual creator that Burian perceived in jazz improvisation was akin to his generation's call for the de-intellectualization of art, in that both phenomena sought to remove cultural power from the romanticist establishment and the subjectivist approach it advocated. Alongside the destruction of authorial subjectivism and the de-personalization it suggests, ran the trends of populism (i.e., music for the masses) and the mechanization of art; the latter, via new instruments, popular films, and in particular the de-intellectualized dancing body, led directly back to jazz. Although at times Burian was able to distinguish African, African-American, Euro-American, and European streams of "jazz" with some lucidity, his prose often assumes an interchangeability between cultural products that is symptomatic of the European imagination at this time. The concatenation of cultures and genres was, for Burian in 1928, encapsulated by Ernst Křenek in his jazz opera *Jonny spielt auf*, in which the young Czech composer found symbols of "jazz, film, radio, sport, and revue. Brevity, speed, an easy conclusion, adventure, *naturalism and sentiment.*"[101] Of these elements, the idea of revue-as-opera expressed through the mundane world of the sentimental was the most appealing, and Burian set out to create his own opera in its image. Before doing so, however, he needed to fulfill his other declared goal: a new polydynamic genre, based on improvisational techniques and the lyrical naturalism so beloved by the Poetists.

Through his connections to Devětsil, Burian developed a series of working relationships with some of the most important young theater directors of the First Republic, particularly Jindřich Honzl and Jiří Frejka, who established in 1925 the first incarnation of the Osvobozené divadlo, in which Burian participated. Prior to the split of this partnership in 1928 (at which point Burian joined Frejka at the Divadlo Dada and Voskovec, Werich, Honzl, and ultimately Ježek re-formed the Osvobozené divadlo), Honzl and Burian engaged in debates regarding the artistic uses of the word, both spoken and sung. A left-wing workers' chorus, the Dědrasbor led by Josef Zora, was already experimenting with extended performance techniques, but Burian wanted to create an ensemble that would fulfill his aesthetic of *Polydynamika*, juxtaposing spoken text, rhythm, vocal contour, and verbal meaning. The result was Voice-band, a group of eight to twelve performers, by stipulation trained in oratory but *not in music*, who, under Burian's direction over a period of two and a half years, delivered major works of modern and revivalist Czech poetry using choral recitation.[102] Making its debut in April 1927, Voice-band performed poetry by Mácha, Erben, Neruda, and several of the Devětsil poets in a nonmelodic, recitative-like chant, articulated in syncopated rhythms that were meant to evoke popular dances, often to the accompaniment of Burian at the piano or the drums. By Burian's own description, the ensemble did not use formal notation (which would have been meaningless to the non-musicians) but devised their own new system as a collective, which, to the composer's surprise, turned out much like medieval neumes.[103] Burian, faithful to

Polydynamika, provoked the interplay between the declaimed text and its meaning, often distorting words from their typical pronunciation within a formalized poetic context and creating new associations through the juxtaposition with syncopated rhythms, polyphonic phrasing, and an idiosyncratic vocal contour. Following the aesthetic of the Poetists, he eschewed traditional formalism for pure lyricism and naturalist depictions of the text (however distorted) in his final sound-product. Received enthusiastically by the younger generation of artists from all disciplines (including Steinhard's *Der Auftakt*, where Burian's adventures were followed with great interest), the group was invited by Hába to participate in the sole Czech offering at the 1928 ISCM festival in Siena, where they were the smash hit of the festival.[104] Hailed upon their return as much for their modern experimentalism as for their newfound cosmopolitanism, Voice-band toured Czechoslovakia successfully, often performing with the participation of the modern dance ensemble of Jarmila Kröschlová, thereby adding a further element to the polydynamic mix. When Burian departed to take up new employment as stage director at the Brno Provincial Theater under Ota Zítek in mid-1929, however, future plans for concerts under that organization did not materialize, and the activities of Voice-band were adjourned until its reuse in Burian's theatrical efforts in Prague after 1933.

1929 also marked a turning point in Burian's compositional career, witnessing both the end of his largest work to date, the jazz opera *Bubu z Montparnassu* (Bubu of Montparnasse), as well as its surprising rejection by the National Theater. Begun in 1927 amid work on *Jazz*, the opera was a synthesis of the Poetist ideal of the lyric sentimentality of the urban street and Burian's own passion for jazz and *Polydynamika*. The novel of the same name by Charles-Louis Philippe, published in 1901 and translated by J. Votrubová-Veselá in 1919, had been celebrated by Teige and Nezval as a masterfully artistic rendering of reality, describing the modern world in a series of poetic pictures via multifaceted perception.[105] Together with his friend Ctibor Blattný (also a music critic), Burian transformed Philippe's somewhat unoperatic plot into a series of scenes designed not to tell a straightforward narrative, but to provide dreamlike, self-contained vignettes of the lives of his characters that are completed only in the minds of the audience members.[106] The effect was a deliberate reference to the newly emergent genre of film, already used by Křenek and Weill in modern opera; such an aesthetic was also in line with the predilections of Burian and the Devětsil toward multimedia.

Set in Paris, the opera revolves around three troubled characters: Mořic (also known as Bubu), a pimp and thief who has occasional pangs of conscience; Berta, a prostitute of Mořic who longs for an end to her life of depravity; and Petr Hardy, an innocent engineering student freshly arrived from the country. The performance of the opera took place on multiple planes, one occupied throughout the drama by dancers depicting the Seine. Musically, Burian employed sentimental and mundane street songs that contrast not only with the miserable lives of Mořic and Berta, but also with the sweetly lyrical world of Petr Hardy, whose music contains references to waltzes and impressionism.[107] In terms of vocal characterization, the composer exaggerated the difference in social realms by notating glissandi and tremolos in the vocal parts of the prostitutes and gang members, matching their slang speech, against which Petr Hardy's operatic conventionality seems out of place. While the score uses jazz initially to evoke all aspects of the Parisian demimonde, including a disruptive foxtrot and a grotesque tango to describe thugs and drunks, respectively, as the drama progresses Burian resorted increasingly to the expressionist vocabulary of his modernist Czech colleagues, in part as an inheritance from Ostrčil at the National Theater.[108] All of these elements coalesce into a dramatic "harmony of diversity" in the climactic final scene, in which the stage is divided between Mořic's jail cell and Petr Hardy's garret; each character sings in his own style simultaneously with Berta, whose voice projects from offstage through a megaphone. The musical and dramatic disjunction leads to a crushing conclusion, wherein the liberated Mořic forcefully retrieves Berta from Petr's arms, dragging her to her death in the Seine. Unlike the tragic demises of heroines in verismo operas, the death of Burian's Berta is perceived through a Poetistic lens of the mundane, reducing the sense of tragedy to the level of desensitization that the modern world has incurred toward all things.[109]

Revolutionary in its time, *Bubu z Montparnassu* was not given the opportunity to attain the influential status it deserved. Despite the fact that the composer's nonconformist *Před slunce východem* and *Fagot a flétna* had already received premieres at the National Theater, *Bubu* was dropped from the 1929/30 opera season as a result of pressure from the administration, which disagreed with the "lascivious action" of the plot.[110] Coming as it did on the cusp of Burian's departure for Brno and a career in theater direction, the disappointment was enough to silence *Bubu z Montparnassu* for the composer's lifetime. He never returned to full-scale opera in his career, and the opera received its premiere a full seventy years after its completion, on March 20, 1999. The work brought to a close an extraordinarily creative period in the life of one of the most prolific Czech composers of the 1920s; its fate symbolizes the excitement of Burian's generation toward the new impulses of avant-garde modernism, populism, and cosmopolitanism, as well as the continued hesitancy of the musical establishment to accept these phenomena. In the 1930s the musicians of the younger generation would follow Burian's lead in seeking other venues for musical theater and opera, attempting to reconnect with an audience long abandoned by mainstream modernism.

* * *

The late 1920s were years of tremendous, if not completely effective, transition for the musical community of Prague. From the time of the two ISCM festivals the issues of modernism and cultural interaction were debated hotly in the musical press, with many parties taking self-righteously isolationist or hesitantly open-minded attitudes. Although many different strains of European modernism became available at this time to Czech composers, it was neoclassicism, staunchly advocated by Martinů in absentia, which gained the most acceptance by 1926; this aesthetic stance would be filtered by Zich into his opera *Preciézky* of the same year (see chapter 8). The indecisiveness of the critical community came to a shattering conclusion with the "*Wozzeck* Affair," which saw the majority of creative musicians in the city united against the tyranny of the bourgeois opera subscribers. Modernism and cosmopolitanism became standards of national and cultural pride alongside a growing fear of embarrassment in the eyes of the international avant-garde. Nevertheless, despite the antimodernist hiatus that followed the tumultuous scandal, when conservative or openly populist productions such as Novák's *Dědův odkaz* or Weinberger's *Švanda dudák* appeased audiences and alienated critics, ground was being prepared for a more moderate attempt at modernism in the theater. Jeremiáš's *Bratři Karamazovi*, analyzed in the following chapter, achieved success through its combination of dramatic, cathartic intensity and relatively outdated musical effects, paving the way for more daring productions in the coming decade.

Meanwhile, a new generation had begun to take shape in the wake of the "*Wozzeck* Affair," one that put into action the modernist vows undertaken by so many at that time. While a host of new personalities, including Hába, Schulhoff, Krejčí, and Ježek had begun to emerge in the late 1920s, it was Burian who best encapsulated the aesthetic choices of his generation, which included a commitment to interaction with other arts, a predilection for anti-intellectualism, the everyday, and popular culture mixed with avant-garde creative impulses, all in a more cosmopolitan environment. Although this generation was able to luxuriate in the relative innocence of this prosperous decade, the political events and economic troubles of the 1930s would transform them entirely, thereby changing irrevocably the face of the musical community of Prague.

Chapter Eight

"I Have Rent My Soul in Two"

Divergent Directions for Czech Opera in the Late 1920s

The long shadows of the "*Wozzeck* Affair" extended over many endeavors of the Prague compositional community and its increasingly tense relations with the public in the late 1920s. As discussed in chapter 7, for several years after the November 1926 fiasco at the National Theater, all administrative decisions—largely conservative in the extreme—were made with *Wozzeck* in mind as a high-water mark of public reaction against modernism, never to be repeated. The reception of new works after this point, however, reflected something less tangible than box-office receipts. Almost invariably, operas of the late 1920s were afforded a new monolithic, iconic status, as though standing for something much greater than the musical and theatrical experience provided by an evening's entertainment at the National Theater. While the late operas of Janáček immediately achieved places in the national operatic canon, others, such as *Švanda dudák* and *Bubu z Montparnassu*, were vilified or blocked entirely. In between these two relatively extreme ends of the continuum, less contentious works were also treated as sole representatives of various aesthetic directions, each with the potential to resolve the crisis provoked by *Wozzeck*.

In many respects this legacy is echoed in the artistic choices of composers finally forced to reconcile their modernist styles with the expectations of a powerful paying public, and to resolve this dilemma in concrete, musico-dramatic terms. Operas premiered in the early 1920s, as we have seen in chapter 6, had dealt in musical and dramatic abstractions. Before *Wozzeck*, composers could present their pre-1918 work without worrying unduly about its overly negative (or even positive) impact on the public: Ostrčil's *Legenda z Erinu* is the prime example of this expressive distance, reflecting the general problems inherent in a "Czech modernism" based on dense contrapuntal textures and heavy orchestration. In the early 1920s, these works—written for the "desk drawer" in the years before independence—could have little chance of attaining iconic status in a new society. Conversely, everything after *Wozzeck* was forced to become iconic, even beyond the measure of the composer's design. Every opera was taken as a representative compositional stance with respect to the events of November 1926, and its relation to the public was always direct and fully conscious, since on all sides, particularly administratively, the risks of rejection were higher.

One benefit of all this to the repertoire of the late 1920s was precisely this greater consciousness, both on the part of composers as to the effect of their modernist artistic choices, and among audience members (including critics), whose perception of these choices was all the more acute. Each work from this half-decade presents a different method of defusing this potentially volatile set of circumstances, while still attempting to preserve a strong artistic voice. For Otakar Zich, the shift of consciousness had taken place three years earlier, after the premiere of *Vina*—in many respects, his own personal *Wozzeck*—prompting a shift toward neoclassicism in his *Preciézky*. Otakar Jeremiáš's *Bratři Karamazovi*, on the other hand, sought to resolve the dramatic intensity of contemporary opera with a score that paid homage to early modernist works of the past, such as Strauss's *Elektra*. Both composers attempted to recapture audiences at the National Theater, albeit via startlingly divergent paths.

Zich's *Preciézky* and the "Nová Buffa"

Half a year before the "*Wozzeck* Affair," Zich's opera *Preciézky* (*Les Précieuses ridicules*) premiered under Ostrčil at the National Theater, on May 21, 1926. The first identifiably "neoclassical" opera written and performed in the Prague context, it was an event that lingered in the memory of critics for a long time, as essays from several months and even years afterward demonstrate. Significantly, in the years after *Wozzeck*, the critical rhetoric seemed to merge this burgeoning Czech neoclassicism with the desire to gain distance from Berg's work and all it represented. Furthermore, Zich's opera heralded a communal change in attitude within Czech contemporary composition, not only toward the author himself but also toward the freshly cosmopolitan (and in its own way, modernist) viewpoint *Preciézky* was taken to represent. In the heavily post-Wagnerian atmosphere of Prague in the 1920s, the inroads of any preromanticist aesthetic presented a significant change in thinking. While Zich's musical language was still quite conservative for the standards of 1926, the critics' acceptance of its simplified harmony, melody, and orchestration mirrored the Czechs' gradually increasing interest in West European movements such as neoclassicism and *Neue Sachlichkeit*.[1] Indeed, the Prague musical community appreciated Zich's efforts to such an extent that they dubbed *Preciézky* the model of a new operatic subgenre, the "Nová Buffa" (New Opera Buffa).

As we have seen in past chapters, Zich had long been an outsider within Prague's musical establishment as a result of a series of events from earlier in his career: his longtime residence outside of the capital, his early association with Nejedlý, his outspoken stance in the "Dvořák Affair," his appointment as professor of aesthetics at Prague University, and not least, the critical controversy surrounding his previous opera *Vina*. With *Preciézky*, however, Zich scored a victory among many of the critics, including several from what had previously been the opposing aesthetic camp, as well as almost the entire younger generation. Such a turn of events, foreshadowing the consensus that would arise amid the "*Wozzeck* Affair," signaled the demise of the great aesthetic divide that had prevented any cooperation among Prague's musical institutions for a quarter-century. The positive reception of Zich's opera also bore witness to the aesthetic shift toward the acceptance of outside influences, in that *Preciézky* was taken to represent a variety of new musical directions from Western Europe, all related in some way to neoclassicism or objectivism. Finally, several critics also read a parody of contemporary bourgeois (specifically, Czech) society in the opera, not only in its dramatic situations but also in Zich's music in particular—a potentially volatile mix, in light of the forthcoming controversy surrounding *Wozzeck* and the bourgeois subscribers just a few months later.

Preciézky's most obvious link to neoclassicism is, ironically, its text. For the libretto Zich used his own translation of Molière's comedy *Les Précieuses ridicules* from 1659, with only minor textual deletions. The origin of the libretto is significant in light of the reception of the work, since it virtually guaranteed a connection to some form of neoclassicism; musically, however, Zich's score presents many additional layers of conservatism and *Vina*-style modernism, making the connection far from unequivocal. Nevertheless, the fact that Stravinsky had recently reworked Pergolesi's music as *Pulcinella* was not lost on the critics, who perceived an aesthetic similarity between Stravinsky's efforts and Zich's. Among the various branches of neoclassicism possible by 1926, the music of *Preciézky* has the most in common with Busoni's aesthetic of *Junge Klassizität*, which in retrospect can be judged as an early stage of neoclassicism, without the outright rejection of romantic operatic convention. Indeed, of all the European operas contemporary to Zich's work, one of the most dramatically and musically similar is Busoni's *Arlecchino*, premiered seven years before the composition of *Preciézky*. Busoni advocated a middle ground between conservative and avant-garde compositional streams for his students at the Prussian Academy of the Arts in interwar Berlin.[2] His aesthetic stance valued an organic sense of growth from the past to the future, taking from Classical-era music the "timeless values or fundamental truths, which transcended the boundaries of historical style," rather than any specific forms.[3] The result would be a fresh, utopian, modern music, which would rejuvenate the present and indicate the direction for future composition through a sense of unity, melodicism (which also included a renewed interest in counterpoint), and the renunciation of subjectivity.[4]

The similarity to the ideology of the Nejedlý school here is striking: although the Czech critic described his vision of atemporal modernism in terms of a specific national culture, the dual rejection of soulless modernity and antiprogressive conservatism has much in common, at least externally, with Busoni's aims. Writing in 1919, Busoni stressed the need for the "shedding of 'sensualism' and the renunciation of subjectivity (a path of objectivity—the author's retreat in the face of his work—a purifying path, a difficult course, a trial through fire and water)."[5] Both Busoni's and Nejedlý's aesthetic programs expressed the need for an outright rejection of the branch of German romanticism that had prevailed in European music from the turn of the century until the First World War. Like many others at this time, they both declared the social necessity of a moral purification of music, to be accomplished by stripping it of the excesses of composers like Strauss. Nevertheless, for Nejedlý the question of social necessity meant a political stance much more radically leftist than that of Busoni, who despised socialism. Similarly, for Nejedlý (and indeed most other Czechs), this antisubjective approach did not lead to an aristocratic essentialization of Mozart as it had with Busoni, but translated rather into the artist's selfless representation of the collective Czech identity. As such, the objectivity of Czech tradition and that of *Junge Klassizität* reached a point of confluence in Zich's music from diametrically opposed starting points. Zich's apparent adoption of both Nejedlý's rhetoric and *Junge Klassizität*, however, brings about a number of discrepancies, between the anti-Wagnerian, antinationalist approach of Busoni and the imagined heritage from Smetana, which was widely accepted as both Wagnerian and essentially Czech.

Although Zich's music for *Preciézky* in many ways confirms the connection to neoclassicism suggested by the choice of Molière, the overall tonal and gestural language of the score presents just as many complications to this theory. In the late 1920s the music journals of Prague were filled with articles and comments about the "return to melody" and "return to form" that neoclassicism advocated, as well as with discussions as to the replacement of late-romantic compositional paradigms with models from earlier eras. With regard to the theater, the perceived crisis of audience reception was often credited to the lack of communication between artists and operagoers. Each new operatic production was seen to be an attempt at a resolution of many of these questions, and *Preciézky* seemed for many to be central to these debates. Critics found the model for the strong melodic character of Zich's music in such varied sources as Mozart, Rossini, Pergolesi, and Foerster (whose melodic inventiveness had never been disputed in the Czech musical community), and those for the orchestration in Stravinsky and Strauss, in the "retrospective" periods of both composers. Important to Zich's operatic conception was the comic nature of the work, such that *Preciézky* became a hallmark of a new theatrical form, the "Nová Buffa." This genre, intimately connected to Stravinsky's *Pulcinella* and other commedia dell'arte-type works, attempted to resolve the crisis of the theater through a rejection of the oppressive psychologism of post-Wagnerian opera. Critics felt that Zich accomplished this break with Wagnerian tradition through the partial incorporation of numbers in his opera, as well as through the "objective" musical characterization of the people and events on stage. "Nová Buffa" also implied a parody of older musical styles: in the case of Zich, however, this did not necessarily mean the parody of preromantic forms, as it had with most of the neoclassicists. While the references to closed forms and the occasional use of eighteenth-century melodic or harmonic gestures allied *Preciézky* with the accepted neoclassical aesthetic, the majority of Zich's references were to musical styles much more contemporary to the composer. In fact, given his acknowledged melodic allegiance to Foerster (and by extension, to Smetana), it becomes difficult to determine precisely where adherence to tradition ends and where parody begins.

The situation becomes more complicated when placed in the discourse of Czech modernism, which, if the Nejedlians are to be believed, was based in post-Wagnerian operatic psychologism (of which Foerster's *Eva* was the frequently cited example), the idea that almost anything contrapuntal was inherently progressive, and the total rejection of retrospection in musical style. Indeed, *Preciézky* encapsulates the dichotomy of this ideology, in that its composer apparently upheld the tradition of Smetana (particularly in terms of the comic genre, descended from *The Two Widows*) while also pursuing the "most modern" trends of composition, which in this case were specifically retrospective. According to Nejedlý's reading of Smetana, the aesthetic of musical progress and adherence to tradition were one and the same, through the atemporal modernism on which the composer had based his conception of a national Czech music. As a result, the parody in *Preciézky* seems (rather inadvertently) to mock its own tradition of melodicism, severe contrapuntal textures, and even the general lack of avant-garde in Czech music making.

The plot itself does much to help delineate the characteristics of "Nová Buffa."

Characters:	Gorgibus, a Parisian nobleman	bass
	Madelon, his daughter	soprano
	Kathos, his niece	mezzo-soprano
	Marotte, their chambermaid	alto
	La Grange, a young nobleman	baritone
	Mascarille, his lackey	tenor
	Du Croissy, a young nobleman	tenor
	Jodelet, his lackey	bass

Set in a single scene in a seventeenth-century drawing room, *Preciézky*'s dramatic action revolves around the frivolous Madelon and Kathos and their romantic delusions about courtship. At the beginning of the opera two young noblemen, La Grange and Du Croissy, have just been spurned by the ladies and vow to take

(*continued*)

their revenge. The puzzled Gorgibus pleads in vain with his charges, who refuse to be married off unceremoniously, preferring not to "read the novel from the end" and therefore miss the adventure of having noble admirers and prolonged liaisons. Suddenly, the arrival of a mysterious marquis is announced (who is actually Mascarille, La Grange's lackey in disguise), and after some flirtatious pleasantries, the enthralled girls sit through his performance of an improvised song. The merriment continues, as Madelon and Kathos lavish praise on Mascarille's appearance and wit, causing him to fall into a vanity-induced faint; at this point, the gathering is interrupted by the arrival of another visitor, Du Croissy's servant Jodelet in disguise as a viscount. Declining the request to improvise a song of his own, Jodelet reminisces with his friend about imagined military exploits; the scene reaches a climax when musicians are called to accompany the four revelers in a dance. Suddenly, La Grange and Du Croissy rush onto the stage, demanding that their mischievous servants return the clothes they had borrowed; at the noblemen's command, Mascarille and Jodelet are beaten and stripped in front of the astonished girls. Gorgibus also enters, chases away the musicians (who are demanding to be paid), and after the sad departure of the humbled Mascarille and Jodelet, delivers a moral to the sulking girls, who flee to their rooms. Left alone on the stage, Gorgibus condemns the cause of this folly, "the stupid, idle, destructive entertainments of lazy souls, novels, riddles, verses and rhymes, sonnets and charms: may the devil take you all!"

Several critics, such as Očadlík, Nejedlý, and Krejčí, pointed to Zich's partial use of closed numbers in *Preciézky*, embedded within a through-composed score, as proof of the composer's attempt to unify the tradition of post-Wagnerian opera with a newer, more progressive "objectivity." While for Nejedlý the inclusion of numbers signified the implementation of logic in the compositional process, for Očadlík they provided greater formal flexibility, enabling Zich to achieve dramatic and musical unity.[6] Although Zich's score does reveal several extended passages that could be construed as consciously developed closed forms, these passages neither appear consistently throughout the opera, nor are they completely independent musical entities. Indeed, most of the aria-type segments lie in the first third of the opera (up to page 51 in the vocal score, which Očadlík referred to as the first scene), as do both passages specifically labeled "recit." Even beyond the convention of strict formal labels, cadences, or obvious caesuras to demarcate closed numbers, a closer reading of the opening portion of *Preciézky* reveals a larger plan of alternating arias, recitatives, and ensembles, which I have provided in table 8.1a.

Each of the segments I have designated "aria" demonstrates some degree of formal cohesion, be it tonal (Kathos's "Vskutku, strýčku" begins and ends in B-flat major), motivic (Gorgibus's "Pomádu na rty!" is dominated by the melodic major-seventh, a motive associated with this character), or accompanimental (i.e.,

Table 8.1a. Zich's *Preciézky*, references to closed-number format in first section

Type	Title	Character(s) involved	Pages[1]
—	Overture	—	3–16
Recitative	"Pane La Grange"	La Grange, Du Croissy	17
Aria	"Viděl kdo"	La Grange	18–22
Recitative	"Mám lokaje"	La Grange, Du Croissy, Gorgibus, Marotte	22–25
Aria	"Pomádu na rty!"	Gorgibus	26–27
Undefined	"A jakou vážnost"	Madelon, Kathos, Gorgibus	28–32
Aria	"Milenec, chce-li býti"	Madelon	32–36
Recitative	"Jakou slátaninu"	Gorgibus	36
Aria	"Vskutku, strýčku"	Kathos	37–39
Undefined	"Myslím, že se zbláznily"	Gorgibus, Madelon, Kathos	40–44
Trio	"Dovolte nám"	Madelon, Gorgibus, Kathos	44–46
Arioso	"Můj Bože"	Kathos, then Madelon	47–48
Recitative	"Nějaký lokaj"	Marotte, Madelon, Kathos	48–51

[1]The numbers in the charts and parentheses throughout this analysis refer to pages in the piano-vocal score. Otakar Zich, *Preciézky: Komická zpěvohra o jednom jednání*, Piano-vocal score by Karel Šolc (Prague: Hudební nakladatelství Foersterovy společnosti, 1926).

orchestral melody, types of chords, or articulation, generally consistent in all the above examples). In the case of La Grange's "Viděl kdo," the passage coheres through the use of an extended quotation from the overture (indicated *Allegretto vivo*, 13–16, and *Allegretto scherzando*, 20–22). Conversely, those passages I have labeled "recitative" (including the two from the score, 22 and 48) lack any sort of formal unity, particularly in the accompaniment, which is typically sparse and unconcerned with gestural consistency. Between these two forms are significant passages that defy easy categorization in a number-opera paradigm; in these, Zich generally structured the accompanimental music more than the obvious recitative-like passages, whereas the vocal parts are neither devoted to one singer for long enough to imply an aria, nor do they coalesce into an ensemble, as is the case with the climactic "Dovolte nám." These "undefined" passages are important in that they combine the opera's most dramatic interaction with a musical expression more sophisticated than simple recitative: simply put, they follow the Wagnerian principle of through-composed music drama, and their presence in *Preciézky* is an example of what the critics perceived as the merging of two operatic styles.

These through-composed passages gain in significance through the balance of the opera, the music of which is increasingly dominated by this style, as demonstrated in table 8.1b. After the entrance of Mascarille (and thus in the main body of the drama) the references to closed numbers grow much more sparse; the effect is such that what had once been the occasional reference to Wagnerian

Table 8.1b. Zich's *Preciézky*, dissolution of numbers in the remainder of the opera

Type	Title	Character(s) involved	Pages
Undefined	"Hola, nosiči, hola!"	Mascarille, Marotte	52–57
Undefined	"Dámy, smělost"	Mascarille, Madelon, Kathos	58–66
Duet	"Jsme tak zpraveny"	Madelon, Kathos	66–70
Trio	"To je to"	Madelon, Kathos, Mascarille	70–75
Undefined	"Ale, počkejme"	Mascarille, Madelon, Kathos	75–77
Impromptu	"Ach, ach, kéž bych se"	Mascarille	77–78
Undefined	"Ach, je to překrásná"	Madelon, Kathos, Mascarille	78–90
Arietta	"Nikde nedovedou"	Mascarille	91–92
Undefined	"Krásu díla"	Madelon, Kathos, Mascarille	92–98
Undefined	"Vikomte de Jodelet"	Mascarille, Jodelet, Madelon, Kathos	99–111
Dance-song	"Champagne, Lorain,"	Mascarille then Madelon	111–13
Undefined	"Co říkáš těmto očím?"	Mascarille, Jodelet, Madelon, Kathos	114–19
Ball	—	Mascarille, Jodelet, Madelon, Kathos	120–25
Undefined	"Ach, vy darebáci"	La Grange, Du Croissy, Gorgibus, others	125–34
Duettino	"Hle, takový je svět"	Mascarille, Jodelet	134–35
Epilogue	"To se ví"	Gorgibus	136–39

through-composition in a predominantly number-opera paradigm has now been reversed, not least with regard to the vocal writing. Beyond the brief "Impromptu" of Mascarille and the Ball scene with onstage musicians (both self-conscious "performances" in the context of the drama, 78–79 and 120–24, respectively), there are few breaks in the flow of arioso-style singing throughout the last two-thirds of the opera. In keeping with many post-Wagnerian operas of the early twentieth century, Zich's orchestra has the lion's share of melodic and harmonic material, over which the voices declaim their text, often in nonchord tones. In this respect, it is not surprising that substantial portions of the overture (which is itself a suite of four linked dances) should reappear in the orchestral accompaniment of later scenes under somewhat unrelated vocal material. Whereas the final segment of the overture shows up in La Grange's "Viděl kdo," parts 2 and 3 (*Andantino* to *Lento*, 5–13) form the basis of the entire preliminary discussion between Mascarille and the girls, now on a much grander scale (58–77). Although this music is quite overtly melodic in nature, only on very few occasions do the vocal parts take on the original melody from the overture, opting instead to add new (often rather angular) melodies to the already richly contrapuntal texture. This procedure also gives rise to moments of ensemble singing, wherein multiple melodies appear in staggered entries, sometimes with the same or similar text (as with the duet "Jsme tak zpraveny," 66, or the trio "To je to," 70). Nevertheless, such moments are merely fleeting references to number-opera convention, and in no way represent closed forms.

As mentioned previously, Zich's transparent use of melody, harmony, and counterpoint in *Preciézky* was a salient feature appreciated by the critics as indicative of a new, neoclassical direction for Czech modernism. At the same time, both the musical material and its reception present a problematic picture of how "Czech modernism" was perceived in 1926, in that the opera's overall conservatism, coupled with the problematic sense of parody, inhibits a straightforward reading of Zich's intentions. As Foerster put it in his "Introductory Word to Zich's *Preciézky*," modern Czech composers had no need to *return* to melody or form (as the neoclassicist slogan demanded) when they had never abandoned these principles.[7] Although Foerster's remark implied a certain adherence to Nejedlý's axiom of atemporal modernism in Czech post-Smetana tradition, it also, rather ironically, pointed to the reluctance that prevailed in Prague to join the European avant-garde musical community (revealing them not to be modernists at all). Whereas neoclassicists such as Stravinsky and members of Les Six did in fact "return" to preromantic styles and gestures *after* having worked with more avant-garde methods, and even then incorporated these retrospective elements into a modernist framework, with Zich no such stylistic separation exists. While it is true that *Vina* had presented a more dissonant harmonic vocabulary based on the concatenation of expressionist gestures and a tight contrapuntal framework, there were also moments of extreme conservatism arrived at by similar means, and to a certain extent, the musical language of *Preciézky* merely echoes the latter result. To further complicate matters, the material that Zich used to create the sense of stylistic (and possibly, parodistic) retrospection in *Preciézky* is not actually preromantic, but rather *pre-avant-garde*, such that his melodic (and in many cases, harmonic) point of reference resembles the "mainstream" nineteenth-century operas that were still dominating the theaters of Europe, such as those by Gounod and Massenet. Indeed, the difference between parody and outright conservatism is achieved in *Preciézky* only by the comedic nature of the drama, in that the nineteenth-century musical parody does not match the time period of Molière's play, thereby evoking a general (if somewhat undefined) sense of irony. And yet, these musical references are not at so great a temporal remove from Zich's own practice as to be recognizably parodistic from his own viewpoint, as was obviously the case with *Pulcinella*. As the criticism shows, however, the issue of stylistic discrepancy and/or parody does not seem to have been a grave problem in 1926, as most of the Czech musical community seems to have taken Zich's "historicism" at face value.

In many respects, Zich's music for this opera resembles the self-consciously mundane Parisian world of Les Six, a factor that rather curiously coordinates with the similar setting of *Preciézky*, albeit of almost three centuries earlier. As such, it

Example 8.1. Zich, *Preciézky*, "Parisian" waltz (62/24–31).

is difficult to determine whether such musical references are in homage to Les Six as representatives of neoclassicism or a parody of them as Parisians. Specific examples of this sort of reference are the prevailing waltz-tempi with ties over the barline and sequential, circle-of-fifths progressions. Particularly in the initial scene between Mascarille, Madelon, and Kathos, where the orchestral music derives from the overture, we hear extended moments of this "Parisian" music amid discussion of the social life in that city: at p. 62, when Mascarille asks, "So, my ladies, what do you think of Paris?" a waltz begins that underscores the remainder of the conversation, typical for Zich in its chromaticism and occasionally unexpected chordal shifts (ex. 8.1). The repeating melody at p. 60, alternating between measures of $\frac{3}{8}$ and $\frac{4}{8}$ with *rubato*, appears as a distortion of this phenomenon, complete with an atypical sequential progression. As the girls begin to imagine a circle of fashionable Parisian poets, the waltz continues, now with a proper sequence of seventh chords descending by fifth, with two overlapping melodies, both tied over the bar line (ex. 8.2, 69); the moment seems almost a direct copy of Poulenc, whose music had recently become known in Prague. It is interesting that such overt French influence should pervade the music of a composer whose work had been upheld as the future of Czech modernism, especially by a critical community that had chastised others on similar charges of "Frenchness" (notably Kovařovic), or had rejected French modernism en masse at recent concerts. Indeed, it becomes difficult to distinguish between the use of pseudo-French music as a parody or as an excuse to write mundane, harmonically conservative music, especially since Zich reconciled these references with his own style by means of an ever-present contrapuntal texture.

Criticism of *Preciézky* added to the ongoing discourse on counterpoint as a marker of Czech modernism. Such claims had been made regarding a variety of major compositions since the turn of the century, including those by Novák, Suk, Vycpálek, Ostrčil, and most significantly, Zich's *Vina*. In the judgment of

[So we will find out at the right time: Mr. So-and-so wrote a poem about such and such...
So we will find out at the right time: Miss So-and-so wrote the words to this and this song...]

Example 8.2. Zich, *Preciézky*, "French" circle of fifths (69/1–8).

critics such as Nejedlý, Očadlík, and Hutter, Zich's predisposition toward free counterpoint in *Preciézky* gave unshakable proof of his modernist outlook, regardless of the resultant harmonies. In some cases (such as ex. 8.2), the multiple melodies produce conventional harmonic progressions, while in others, particularly in the music that accompanies the cantankerous Gorgibus, the result is quite discordant. An example of this latter phenomenon can be seen in Gorgibus's rage-aria "Pomádu na rty!" where that character's major-seventh motive pervades the four-voice texture, causing some rather incisive harmonies (ex. 8.3, 26). Even the sheer abundance of independent melodies in a less caustic context produces a directionless sense of progression, as heard in Gorgibus's

Example 8.3. Zich, *Preciézky*, Gorgibus's major sevenths (26/11–16).

Example 8.4. Zich, *Preciézky*, complex voice leading (29/4–6).

statements about his charges' upbringing (ex. 8.4, 29). As with the latter example, however, many of Zich's moments of dense, chromatic voice leading have an effect similar to those in Richard Strauss's music, to whose *Rosenkavalier* and *Ariadne auf Naxos* Zich's opera was favorably compared.[8] At times, Zich's contrapuntal work, like Strauss's, consists merely of harmonic textures disguised by moving inner parts. In any event, owing largely to the comic nature of *Preciézky* and the purported neoclassical simplicity of the score, the use of counterpoint in no way approaches the depth of either *Vina* or *Legenda z Erinu*, in whose tradition Zich had supposedly continued.

In general, Zich's music for *Preciézky* is well suited to its comic plot, and the composer succeeded in characterizing both individuals and dramatic situations through different types of music. The major-seventh motive of Gorgibus has already been mentioned in this regard, and Jodelet's scene is characterized by an almost perpetual series of dotted rhythms to denote his assumed military status. Beyond these examples, motives do not play a large role in *Preciézky*, since none of the other characters is associated with specific music, including the three main characters—Madelon, Kathos, and Mascarille—around whom the drama revolves. The young critics Očadlík and Krejčí termed Zich's method "characteristic music" (*příznačná hudba*), which they placed in opposition not only to Wagnerian leitmotifs (which are called "příznačné motivy" in Czech), but also to all the negative things they associated with late romanticism, such as subjectivism and psychologism in opera.[9] According to Foerster, a large part of Zich's characterization technique stemmed from the orchestration, which the composer used to stave off any sense of turgidity that the vocal score, riddled with overlapping voices, might imply.[10] Nevertheless, the incessant contrapuntal treatment of multiple melodies in $\frac{3}{4}$ or $\frac{3}{8}$ time, with the same degree of chromaticism and little or no obvious harmonic direction, tended to reduce the impact of any one dramatic moment, as the young composer and critic Jaroslav Vogel observed.[11]

Although the reception of Zich's *Preciézky* was generally positive, as Hutter pointed out, the Czech criticism was divided into two distinct groups with regard to their assessment of the opera. German critics, on the other hand, were apparently unified in their praise.[12] Hutter's observation, although it implies the traditional factional divide among Czech critics, does not reflect the changes the community was experiencing with regard to musical modernism and foreign influences. While Šilhan's venomous negativity could be expected, the typically unenthusiastic Vomáčka and Šourek, although not completely unequivocal in their praise, provided positive and insightful comments regarding the orchestration and dramatic characterization, respectively.[13] Meanwhile, younger critics such as Očadlík, Krejčí, Bedřich Bělohlávek, and František Bartoš joined traditional Zich supporters (i.e., the Nejedlý camp) in their laudatory assessment of *Preciézky*, forming a group that excluded only Vogel, who judged the work harshly, likely as a result of its proximity to his own *Mistr Jíra* from the same year.

Perhaps the element of *Preciézky* most problematic for the critics was the relationship to Molière's text, which, as Jaromír Borecký reported in *Národní politika*, evoked a fundamentally different aesthetic than Zich's music.[14] Jirák found the text to be the sole bearer of lyricism in the work, and Vogel went as far as to say that Molière carried the drama in its entirety with no help from the composer.[15] As mentioned previously, Zich's choice of Molière seems to have been one of the decisive factors in the opera's assessment as a work that reflected the current trend toward neoclassicism and objectivity. To question the text, then, was also to cast aspersions on *Preciézky*'s representation of these trends in the first place.

Almost every critic referred to the issue of neoclassicism in some respect, a phenomenon that shows not only the general familiarity with this musical style in Prague at the time, but also the importance of an aesthetic of such demonstrably foreign provenance. Nejedlý and Jirák attempted to straddle the gulf between "objective music" and "feeling," declaring that Zich had not explored this route out of a lack of consideration for his audience; Jirák, writing more than half a year later, believed that the main impulse of *Preciézky* was based strongly in traditional operatic psychologism. Most other critics, however, sought to overlook these aspects of Zich's work and concentrate on the perceived rejection of post-Wagnerian aesthetics. For Očadlík, Zich had created a work inspired by small forms (i.e., the "numbers" described above), but which had been combined in such a way as to produce a graduated, unified whole; Očadlík's concept of operatic unity involved the equal participation of periodicity, imitation, counterpoint, clear orchestration, and "characteristic music." The historicism of the small ensembles and Mascarille's Impromptu impressed him with their pantomimic elegance and dramatic movement, qualities that Jan Löwenbach also credited to the work in his German-language review for *Der Auftakt*.[16] Hutter seems to have come the closest to Busoni's aesthetic of *Junge Klassizität* in his observation that Zich's work presented a new stylistic standard that brought the past and future together organically; for Hutter the merging of closed numbers with music drama led the listener through the work as part of a psychological, collaborative process.[17] Among all the critics, it was the young Iša Krejčí who most desired a split with the psychological, through-composed operas of the post-Wagnerian era: he found in *Preciézky* two simultaneous streams, which he termed the modern and the "old style of Italian buffa."[18] In this scenario, the declamatory style of singing and dissonant polyphony clashed with light melodies and homophonic moments to give comic opera a contemporary flavor. In what he considered the main contribution to opera in his generation, Krejčí felt Zich had captured the emotional shift between two eras in the stylistic dichotomy of his music.[19]

For many critics, the idea of "Nová Buffa" as it appeared in *Preciézky* was associated with the influence of one or more composers from the past, not necessarily from the Czech Lands, and often from wildly divergent time periods. Although never a major point of controversy, the issue of the heritage of "Nová Buffa" is the most divisive in the reception of this opera, particularly regarding whether its roots lay in the comic operas of Smetana or elsewhere. Curiously, although Nejedlý had always supported Zich as a successor of Smetana's aesthetic legacy, he felt that *Preciézky* lay in opposition to the style of *The Two Widows* and *Poupě*, in that the characters are viewed objectively to the point of ridicule rather than sympathetically.[20] Jirák and Vogel concurred, the latter stating that the ending of Zich's opera, with the absolute lack of reconciliation it offers, was not comic in the Smetanian sense of the word.[21] On the other hand, not only did several prominent figures (such as Foerster, Očadlík, and Krejčí) include *Preciézky* among modern Czech comic operas descended from Smetana, but Hutter even pointed directly to the influence of *The Two Widows*. Nevertheless, the inheritance from Smetana was, possibly for the first time in Czech operatic history, not a factor in its general acceptance, since other composers, including Pergolesi, Rossini, Mozart, Verdi, Strauss, and Foerster, were credited as possible sources for the "Nová Buffa." Krejčí virtually embraced Zich's opera as "Rossiniovská," comparing it favorably with *The Barber of Seville* and its perceived prototype, *La Serva Padrona*, while still being quintessentially modern.[22] Očadlík relished the Mozartian elegance and clarity of Zich's music, for which he found a modern counterpart also in Strauss's *Der Rosenkavalier* and *Ariadne auf Naxos*. Both Hutter and Krejčí, on the other hand, rejected any connection with Mozart whatsoever, since the characters of *Preciézky* did not develop in the manner of Mozart's; for Krejčí in particular, this factor seems to have been a major virtue of Zich's work, indicative of its modern (read: Italianate) outlook. Vogel, meanwhile, was not impressed by the "Italian style" of the whole opera, particularly the overture and the attempts at archaic-sounding music (e.g., the descending-fifth sequences), which came across as "trite melodic turns."[23] Such a blanket rejection of even the moderate neoclassicism of Zich's music indicates an aesthetic predisposition on the part of the critic, who was likely trying to defend his own compositional territory (i.e., his opera *Mistr Jíra*) or that of Janáček, whose music he had begun to study in earnest and to whom he had unfavorably compared Zich.

The "archaic" elements of *Preciézky*, however, did not impede Nejedlý in his quest for a social reading of the opera, as both drama and music. Referring to the work as a folk opera transferred to the salon, Nejedlý defended Zich's choice of subject with the claim that his music showed a distinct bias toward the downtrodden people, namely, the lackeys who had been forced to parade in salon garb for the pleasure of the upper class. Conversely, the aristocrats for Nejedlý were the focus of the opera's parody, in that the comic music made the audience see these characters' internal emptiness. As such, Nejedlý viewed *Preciézky* as a "negative" comedy that made a significant social statement; its performance in modern dress, however, would have made the statement clearer, assuming that Zich in fact desired to parody the moneyed classes of his own day.

Zich's *Preciézky*, while certainly not an undisputable representative of neoclassicism in opera, reveals much about the hesitant acceptance, on the part of both composer and critics, of the latest products of European modernism in 1926. Zich succeeded in marking his score with enough neoclassical elements (such as the suite-like overture, the numerous references to closed numbers, and the use of circle-of-fifth progressions) for his audience to recognize his intent, but in such a way as not to abandon the innate conservatism of the Czech operatic context. Still further elements, particularly the mundane waltzes, may have deliberately referenced the Parisian epicenter of neoclassicism as a contemporary movement, while obliquely forging a link to the historicist element of Molière's text. Each of these elements, however, serves to problematize Zich's work as a contribution to neoclassicism as a subset of interwar modernism, particularly since the pervasive counterpoint and conservative harmonic language can be read from multiple perspectives. The critical evaluation of *Preciézky* as a quintessentially modern opera also revealed the mindset of listeners in Prague at this time: while gradually coming to accept outside influences as positive elements in domestic composition, their narrow frame of reference was indicative of their degree of exposure so far. This attitude would continue to change in the months following *Preciézky*, and at no time more dramatically than with the Prague premiere of *Wozzeck*, just a few months later; indeed, Jirák's review of Zich, cited above, was written in light of these subsequent events, and any further assessment of modernist opera in Prague would of necessity also include similar reassessments of its meaning in the Czech and international contexts. Despite a two-year ban on anything but the most conservative works at the National Theater after November 1926, Czech composers still sought to bridge the gap toward their alienated but powerful middle-class audience. With an impetus provided by a younger generation keen on exploring the international avant-garde, a temporary solution would arrive in the form of a new opera on a familiar story, by a fresh face in the Prague musical community.

Jeremiáš's *Bratři Karamazovi*: "A Step Forward, a Step Backward"

Ever since the two International Society for Contemporary Music (ISCM) festivals of 1924 and 1925, the critical community of Prague had gradually begun to realize the need for a more participatory relationship with the rest of European culture, however tentative their steps may have been.[24] As the power of the older generations gave way to the new values of the younger generation, however, the attitude toward modernism, both at home and abroad, would change dramatically, first of all with a moderately provocative opera by a Czech composer, Otakar Jeremiáš.

After two full seasons of "safe" operatic productions at the National Theater to appease the wrath of the conservative subscribers, the administration finally allowed Ostrčil to pursue a more modernist path in his programming, and to select a work from the circle of younger contemporary Czech composers. His choice, Otakar Jeremiáš's three-act *Bratři Karamazovi* (*The Brothers Karamazov*, based on the novel by Dostoevsky), was a calculated risk: the thirty-six-year-old composer's first opera was modern enough not to be discarded as reactionary (as Novák's *Dědův odkaz* had been), while not so avant-garde as to offend either Czech audiences or the more sensitive critics. Premiered on October 8, 1928, *Bratři*

Karamazovi provided an interesting solution to the problem of modernist opera in Prague, in that its psychological intensity equaled that of *Wozzeck*, while the expressive style of much of its score hearkened back to the era of (if not before) *Elektra*. Ironically, in the opera itself, much of the dramatic intensity of the text is mirrored in the modernist music, amid relatively little action on stage. Furthermore, throughout the score, two sound-worlds, the modernist and antimodernist, are juxtaposed to highlight the main character's conflict with his repressive society. In this very act of juxtaposition, Jeremiáš's opera presented a compromise that would nevertheless prove a firm foothold for modernist opera in Prague, even if it remained shy of the European musical avant-garde of the late 1920s.

Part of the opera's success may be a result of the composer's status as an outsider in Prague, one who largely kept out of the city's ever-present ideological debates. Jeremiáš was from a highly musical family from the South Bohemian city of České Budějovice, whose musical life they virtually led; unlike his elder brother Jaroslav, whose brief, turbulent career and untimely death in 1919 had caused waves in the Prague community,[25] Otakar was merely one of many younger artists whose careers had yet to yield anything noteworthy. Perhaps more than in most European cities at this time, Prague composers still needed to prove themselves at the National Theater with a full-length opera to establish their careers fully, since to do so was to claim a spot in the pantheon of official Czech composers. As the era of musical modernism progressed, however, and audiences grew ever more alienated from new music, this accomplishment became increasingly unattainable.

While *Bratři Karamazovi* is a work of extraordinary dramatic power, its music was almost universally acknowledged to lie somewhere behind the frontlines of the avant-garde, not least of all in the opinion of the composer himself. Jeremiáš's article "The Development of Contemporary Music," published in 1924/25 amid work on the opera, outlined his aesthetic credo, taking an uncompromising approach to composition in his own cultural sphere as well as in the rest of Europe.[26] Citing Foerster and Janáček as two "healthy" alternatives within the prewar trends of naturalism, subjectivism, and formalism, Jeremiáš upheld moral and spiritual conviction above mere technical novelty in his own day as well. Just as Foerster and Janáček had not attempted harmonic, contrapuntal, or orchestrational innovations in the previous generation, Jeremiáš also shunned these devices in favor of a closer relation to "every detail of life," stating that "sometimes a step forward in art means a step backward in technique."[27] This aesthetic conservatism would also preserve a clear image of what was ideologically positive and negative in art, using Smetana as a model (whom Jeremiáš had discovered during the rebirth of the Smetana Cult in 1917), along with the new collectivist expression brought about by the democratization of art. Although he credited Stravinsky with opening new aesthetic horizons, by and large Jeremiáš felt that European modernist trends, including all of postwar German music, had overlooked both life and artistic expression. Echoing many of the Czech critics from around the time of the ISCM festivals, he credited Czech music alone with having preserved a synthesis of tradition and morality in the creation of new art, an endeavor that would surely prove the way out of the present crisis.

Jeremiáš found a reflection of his desire to connect with real life in the novels of Dostoevsky, in whose depiction of human suffering he found a reflection of his own sympathy toward the morally downtrodden of the world.[28] The composer admitted to finding and reading *The Brothers Karamazov*[29] only after having decided to create his first opera around a Dostoevskian story. Impressed by the optimistic conclusion, Jeremiáš felt the overall drama of the work would provide a suitable alternative to the novelist's other works, in which the opening catastrophe was followed by internalized psychology instead of action.[30] Although he entrusted the libretto to his long-time friend Jaroslav Maria, after receiving the draft of the first act it was clear that the composer would have to take a more active role in the organization of the text. Jeremiáš's later admission reveals that not only did he rewrite Act One completely, but also oversaw the remaining two acts, created "on the basis of musical laws. . . . According to my requirements and musical ideas it was always changed and adapted to a musical form."[31] The libretto, acclaimed for the quality of its dramatization of the original Dostoevsky, follows the outline of events in the book, highlighting the major scenes and referring to peripheral plot lines in passing. In this respect, *Bratři Karamazovi* depends on the audience's foreknowledge of Dostoevsky's plot, since many minor events and characters do not appear at all, and the two major female characters, Grušenka and Katěrina Ivanovna, enter only after the murder of Fedor, in the second and third acts, respectively. The audience must therefore rely on passing references or previous reading to understand their importance to Míťa and Fedor in the opening scene, and must already be aware of the liaison between Katěrina and Ivan before the climactic moment of the courtroom scene.

Characters:	Fedor Karamazov, the father	buffo bass
	Dimitrij (Míťa) Karamazov, eldest son	heldentenor
	Ivan Karamazov, middle son	baritone
	Alexej (Aljoša) Karamazov, youngest son	lyric tenor
	Smerďakov, Fedor's illegitimate son	baritone
	Agrafena (Grušenka) Světlova	soprano
	Katěrina Ivanovna	alto
	Musjalovič, a Pole, Grušenka's former beau	bass
	Vrublevský, a Pole, friend of Musjalovič	bass
	Tryfon Borysič, innkeeper in Mokré	bass
	Dr. Herzenstube	tenor-baritone
	Feťukovič, defense lawyer	tenor
	Grigorij, Fedor's old servant	bass
	Kalganov, Maximov, Judge, State Prosecutor, Chorus	

(*continued*)

Bratři Karamazovi takes place in a moderate-size Russian town and revolves around the problematic interrelationships of Fedor Pavlovič Karamazov and his four sons, Dimitrij (Míťa), Ivan, Alexej (Aljoša), and Smerďakov. The last of these, born after Fedor raped a mentally ill woman in the town, has been raised as a servant in his father's house and suffers from epilepsy. Míťa, an officer, leads a dissolute life full of gambling and debauchery, while Ivan is a cynical intellectual, and Aljoša seeks to enter a monastery. The plot focuses on Míťa, who is engaged to Katěrina Ivanovna, a respectable young woman of the town; at the same time he is also infatuated with Grušenka, a woman of low repute, who is also the object of Fedor's affections. Míťa, mad with jealousy, has spent money borrowed from Katěrina in order to win Grušenka away from his father.

Act 1 takes place in and outside Fedor's house, and is divided into two elided scenes, the second taking place later the same evening. The opera opens with a heated discussion between Míťa and Smerďakov over Grušenka's potential appearance at the house later that night, followed by a gentler, emotional scene with Aljoša that introduces Míťa's problematic relationship to Katěrina and her money ("Dnes slyš mou zpověď'," 23–44). With an abrupt shift in mood, the subsequent dialogue between Ivan and Smerďakov darkly foreshadows the brutal murder of their father; they are interrupted by the drunken Fedor, who disgusts and horrifies his two younger sons with anecdotes about his lust for Grušenka and his rape of Smerďakov's mother. Míťa and the servant Grigorij rush onto the scene, which ends dramatically with Míťa's attack on Fedor and Smerďakov's seizure. An interlude introduces the second scene, set in Fedor's garden. Alone, Míťa rushes onto the stage and sings a tormented soliloquy ("Ah! Světlo v pokoji," 114–22), oscillating between periods of lucidity and blind rage over his father's alleged meeting with Grušenka and his gift of 3,000 rubles. Finally provoked beyond reason, he gives the secret knock and Fedor appears, calling for Grušenka; in the darkness Fedor is murdered, and Grigorij, rushing to his master's assistance, is struck by the panicked Míťa fleeing from the scene.

Act 2 takes place in the inn at the neighboring village of Mokré, and begins with Míťa's precipitous interruption of a tryst between Grušenka and her Polish beau, Musjalovič. After tense greetings and a round of cards, Míťa takes Musjalovič aside in order to offer money if he leaves Grušenka forever. Seeking an excuse to be rid of Musjalovič, Grušenka condemns the Poles and sides with Míťa, whereupon the scene breaks into a celebratory atmosphere with local singers and dancers. Míťa, leaving the festivities, wavers between the determination to kill himself and the desire to live a new life with Grušenka ("Mám-li se zastřelit," 190–97); the latter, however, interrupts him and the two sing a soaring duet. In the final moments of the act their idyll is interrupted by the arrival of the police who have come to arrest Míťa for the robbery and murder of his father.

Act 3 is divided unevenly between the lengthy courtroom scene and the epilogue in Míťa's jail cell. In the intervening months, Katěrina has finally become disillusioned with the unpredictable Míťa and has turned her affections toward his brother Ivan. After Míťa's arrest, Ivan learned that it was in fact Smerďakov who killed their father upon his own mild suggestion. Following a brief introduction

(*continued*)

by the Judge and an apologetic lament by the defendant, the witnesses give their testimony in the order: Grigorij, Tryfon Borysič, Musjalovič, Míťa himself ("Pánové, jsem jistě lepší," 246–62), Herzenstube, Aljoša, Katěrina Ivanovna, and Grušenka. None of the character witnesses is able to sway the evidence against Míťa except Ivan, whose descent into guilt-ridden madness is enacted right in the witness box: he is interrupted finally by Katěrina's revelation of a damning letter written in Míťa's hand that seems to prove his guilt. A short but tumultuous interlude leads to the final scene in the jail cell, where Míťa and Aljoša ponder the future. After an impassioned reconciliation between Katěrina and Míťa, Grušenka arrives and the couple sings with renewed hope about a life of freedom in exile, seeking a life of redemption with the blessing of Aljoša.

Jeremiáš's *Bratři Karamazovi* provides an interesting problem in the context of early twentieth-century opera, in that it contains a psychological and dramatic intensity matched only in the most extreme of modernist operas, such as *Elektra* and *Wozzeck*, to which Jeremiáš's work was often compared. Musically, however, it straddles the modernist sound-world and that of the nineteenth century, only occasionally reaching the tonal complexity of *Elektra* (already two decades old) and never crossing paths with any of the avant-garde techniques of the late 1920s. Nevertheless, for all its outdated Wagnerianisms (particularly in the Act 2 duet, "Míťo, vždyť jsem ho milovala," 199–214, and the epilogue, 345–67), Jeremiáš's music contributes greatly to the propulsion of the psychological drama and provides a climax that was only possible in a modern, post-*Elektra* world.

Formally, *Bratři Karamazovi* is structured around long, aria-like segments that give the impression of closed numbers. Míťa alone receives four "aria" passages (one for each scene except the epilogue, see synopsis) as well as the Act 2 duet; there are also extended solo sections for Smerďakov and Fedor in the opening scene, for Grušenka in Act 2 ("Ach já, hloupá, hloupá," 165–72), for Aljoša in the epilogue, and for almost everyone in the courtroom scene in the form of testimonies. Although many of these make use of the traditional conventions of operatic arias—soliloquy or narrative, unified accompaniment patterns, climactic pitches—it is difficult to find caesuras or formal boundaries in many instances, especially in the case of the witness testimonies, which are often interrupted by other courtroom personalities. As opposed to *Preciézky*, where the closed-aria structure was more pronounced, creating a sense of stasis, the solo segments of *Bratři Karamazovi* are musically fluid. Their sheer number, however, induces a relative lack of onstage action in the opera; the major activity, when it appears, serves to delineate the ends of scenes (i.e., Míťa's attack on his father, Fedor's murder, Míťa's arrest, and Katěrina's revelation of the letter). Within this somewhat restrictive formal skeleton, the intensity of much of the vocal and orchestral music provides an element of freedom, a binarism that, as we shall see, is directly parallel to the emotional experience of Míťa throughout the opera.

Míta (9/1-2, opening of the opera)

Smerďakov (10/1-2)

Grušenka (17/1-2)

Katěrina (23/4-5)

Fedor (68/7-10)

Lawyer (227/3-4)

Example 8.5. Jeremiáš, *Bratři Karamazovi*, motives.

Example 8.5. (*continued*).

Jeremiáš also employed a relatively loose web of motives that pervade the opera, contributing in part to its inherent Wagnerianism and, as a result of their ongoing transformation, to its psychological intensity. As with the drama, almost all the characters are connected musically to Míťa, whose psyche can be said to pervade the opera, even when he is not onstage (which occurs for only one passage, 44–97). Míťa's motive, constructed of three tonally unrelated triads (F minor, E-flat major, B minor) and a chromatically altered seventh, contributes to the interconnectedness of the motivic web via its component parts—the sense of harmonic parallelism, the initial triplet rhythm, and the descending bass line.[32] As example 8.5 demonstrates, the parallel triads of Míťa's motive give rise to the oscillating thirds of Smerďakov's, which is also in triplets (10). The motives associated with Grušenka (17), Katěrina (23), and Fedor (68) also demonstrate a similar parallel motion, albeit with dotted rhythms, as do two motives, for Míťa's lawyer (227) and for Smerďakov's seizures (95), to a further harmonic extreme. Míťa's triplets, meanwhile, reappear for Smerďakov, Grušenka, Fedor (whose motive is a three-quarter variation of Katěrina's), and significantly, the murder motive (17). Another, equally powerful motivic force in the opera is exerted by Smerďakov through the distinctive oscillating contour of his motive's inner voices, which, when combined with the parallel motion from Míťa's motive, produces a rather unsettling modal mixture. This feature reappears in association with Fedor, Katěrina, Musjalovič, a rarely seen motive associated with Ivan (46), and interestingly, the love motive (116), showing that, as the true villain, Smerďakov's presence infiltrates all aspects of the opera's musical plot. Amid the plethora of other motives derived directly or indirectly from Míťa's, examples of characters whose music is unrelated to the hero's are rare: it is perhaps significant that Ivan and Aljoša, so temperamentally different from their older brother, should have dissimilar motives (46 and 19, respectively). As further analysis of Míťa's dramatic and musical development throughout the opera will show, the motivic web is central to the overall psychological effect of *Bratři Karamazovi*, producing a modernist intensity that struggles against the restrictions of the antimodernist framework in which it is placed.

The musical and dramatic concentration on Míťa is so great that it characterizes the entire opera, such as can be said for both *Elektra* and *Wozzeck*. Much like the title characters in these two operas, Míťa is an antihero whose status as protagonist continually challenges the audience's allegiance. The outcome of the plot of *Bratři Karamazovi* revolves around Míťa's acceptance or rejection by his society. This binarism is echoed in a host of others: social morality versus Míťa's perceived immorality; the rationality of others versus his irrationality; and most obviously in the music, his oscillation between lucidity and mental collapse. As the opera progresses and Míťa is wrongly condemned for his father's murder, his natural defiance is turned toward the hypocrisy of the society that makes him suffer: the binarism of morality/immorality turns into Míťa's moral ascendancy versus the false morality around him, and Míťa himself turns from antihero into hero. The most crucial question at the climax and into the epilogue becomes one of continuing in this defiance or of succumbing to social forces, thereby losing his heroic status.

Jeremiáš contributed greatly to this system of binarisms through the stylistic duality of his music, which hovers constantly between modernism and a nineteenth-century sound-world, or what may be termed antimodernism. In the score of *Bratři Karamazovi*, the antimodernist music belongs to the optimistic, rational, and hypocritical world of social forces, while Míťa (and other misfits, notably Fedor and Ivan during his mad scene) receives music that is modernist, irrational, and, given its scant chance of harmonic resolution, pessimistic. In this paradigm, even love becomes a normalizing force for Míťa, rationalizing his musical world both in terms of brotherly love (toward Aljoša, perhaps the most conservative character musically) and sexual passion (in the scenes with or referring to Grušenka). Since the optimistic epilogue of *Bratři Karamazovi* is the main point of differentiation between the fate of Míťa and those of Elektra and Wozzeck, whose manias force their demise at the end of their respective scores, it is important to determine how Jeremiáš's hero arrives at his conclusion in musical terms. Indeed, the progression of the drama in *Bratři Karamazovi* depends exclusively on Míťa's trajectory through the labyrinth of emotions conveyed by the extremes of Jeremiáš's music, and we can chart his course by examining the four aria-passages his character receives.

The heartfelt conversation between Míťa and Aljoša in the opening scene not only provides the first opportunity to relate the history of Míťa's relations with Katěrina, Grušenka, his father, and the money, but also serves to contrast the almost dictatorial image of the protagonist created in his initial encounter with Smerďakov. The aria-passage "Dnes slyš mou zpověď" (table 8.2, 23–44) demonstrates that Míťa's fragile mental state, in becoming increasingly volatile, mirrors the disintegration of the musical form, especially when juxtaposed with the relative calm of Aljoša. The opening portion, in which Míťa relates his act of generosity that has saved Katěrina's father from financial ruin, comprises a five-part rondo, based on a repeating section of music firmly grounded in C minor and dominated by Katěrina's motive. The two contrasting sections, both in faster tempi with intrusions of Míťa's own discordant motive, represent not only the narrator's heightened emotional state but also his growing obsession with personal shame—a factor of increasing importance throughout the opera. At the close of the five-part form, marked again by Míťa's motive, Aljoša delivers a single line in his characteristically lyric, almost static mode of expression: from this point onward, as Míťa's narrative continues, his grip on rationality loosens. As he begins to relate his story of meeting Grušenka and her powerful effect on him, her motive appears, and the orchestral accompaniment is dominated by a series of three-note ostinati, paralleling his obsession. Again, Aljoša interjects comments at evenly spaced intervals (five in all), providing a backdrop of calm against which Míťa's mounting hysteria comes into relief, even when the furor

Table 8.2. Form of "Dnes slyš mou zpověd'," 23–44

#	Page	Incipit	Tempo, meter changes	Motives	Musical attributes	Dramatic situation
1 (A)	23	Dnes slyš mou zpověd'	Moderato mesto, 3/4	Kateřina	c-, structured accomp.	Beginning of narrative:
2 (B)	24	Nabídl jsem mu peníze	Più animato Allegro, 4/4	Míťa, Kateřina	Tremolo, chromatic	Offers her father money
3 (A)	25	Aljošo, slyš, ona přišla	(ritardando molto), 3/4	Kateřina	c- then triplets from B	Kateřina's arrival
4 (C)	26	Aljošo, nikdy nebyl jsem	Lento	Aljoša variant	Lyrical; bitonal	Míťa's feeling of power
5 (A)	27	Jak veliké ponížení	Grave, Largo elevato	Kateřina, Míťa, Aljoša	Aljoša sings at end	Kateřina's supplication
6	30	Jsem sžírán touhou	Allegretto appassionato, 4/4	Grušenka	Chromatic over pedals	Desire for Grušenka
7	32	Ji stvořil bůh	Largo, molto appassionato	Love variant, Aljoša	Very lyrical, Aljoša sings	Greatness of Míťa's love
8	33	Aljošo, slyš dále	Più mosso agitato, 3/4	Míťa, Aljoša	Unstructured episodes	Involvement of Fedor
9	36	Eh, co mi vše platno	Allegro irato	Míťa variant, Kateřina	Mostly tremolo, triplets	Míťa's plan to get money
10	39	[Neb] věz, že vše	Lento tragico	Murder, Míťa variant	Ostinato, tremolo	Míťa's plan for revenge
11	41	Vyčíhám ji	Più mosso, con ira	Murder, Aljoša	Triplet oscillation, Aljoša sings	Murderous thoughts
12	42	Eh, vždyť ještě nevím	Risoluto, meno mosso 4/4	None	Tremolo, chromatic rush	Threats before departing

begins to affect Aljoša (cf. 38 and 42, where Aljoša's music returns in faster tempi). A new ostinato begins (36), marked *Allegro irato* and based loosely on Míťa's motive, as he describes his necessary split with Kateřina. The mania continues toward a description of the unavoidable confrontation with his father over the money, and the murder motive appears as a third ostinato, at climactic moments in conjunction with the other ostinati and character motives. The culmination of the scene, when Míťa declares his desire to kill his father before running from the stage, is punctuated by a single emphatic statement of the murder motive amid a stream of oscillating triplets. Formally, the second half can be considered the mirror image of the first. Whereas initially Míťa's straightforward narrative was interrupted by his own outbursts in a rondo format, after Aljoša's first comment it is he who becomes the stabilizing factor amid his brother's aberrational ravings. In the end, neither the normalizing force of Aljoša's music nor the rondo form can restrain the antihero, as he flees the scene to the accompaniment of chromatically descending triplet runs, through which all musical or dramatic structure for the scene dissolves into chaos. As we shall see, the open-ended climax of the passage presages many such moments for Míťa throughout the opera, compelling him inexorably toward judgment in the courtroom.

Míťa's second solo passage, the soliloquy "Ah! Světlo v pokoji" (table 8.3, 114–22), shows important similarities to the earlier scene, except that the interjections of another character are altogether absent here. The music of the "aria" nevertheless oscillates between the rational and the insane, perhaps all the more effectively for its status as an internal monologue. The two conflicting states in this instance are those of an unquenchable thirst for vengeance against his father and an extreme, almost childlike tenderness toward Grušenka; in the final moments of the scene these coalesce into a shout for revenge against both traitors of his love. Opening with Míťa's precipitous entrance on the stage to the accompaniment of frenetic tremolos, the mood turns quickly to one of indulgent self-pity marked Meno mosso-Andante, lyrically describing his susceptibility to Grušenka's charms (her motive appears throughout the accompaniment, labeled scherzando, along with a prefiguration of the love theme, 115). A single statement of Míťa's motive leads to a fiery phrase of extreme chromaticism ("When I blame, I threaten, I want to punish," 115), followed just as quickly by a lyrical phrase that brings us to the "love" motive proper, during which he declares his intent to "forgive, kiss, and love to death. To love and forget" (116). As with the previous aria-passage, thoughts of Fedor and money drive Míťa to a fiery rage; a final lapse into gentleness is also marred by a nightmarish vision of Grušenka's conspiracy with his father, and Míťa's imagination distorts her motive accordingly. To the accompaniment of the murder motive he denounces Grušenka, almost yelling, "Cunning weasel! If you permitted this crime, then woe to you, woe to you both!" (120–21); a chromatic and occasionally bitonal rush of sixteenth notes, punctuated by Míťa's motive, describes his precipitous approach to the door, the secret knock, and after a short interlude with Fedor's appearance, the climactic moment of the murder. While this passage is less delineated formally than Míťa's first solo, the alternation between opposing expressive styles is significant for both the character development of the antihero and the composer's portrayal of it. The portions of conservative, tonally uncomplicated music portraying the love of Grušenka, while at first seemingly tender and innocent, become quickly charged with uncontrollable hatred, with

Table 8.3. Form of "Ah! Světlo v pokoji," 114–22

#	Page	Incipit	Tempo, meter	Motives	Musical attributes	Dramatic situation
1	114	Ah! Světlo v pokoji	Meno mosso, 2/4	None	Tremolo, recit-like	Míťa sees light in room
2	114	Ach Bože, jaký jsem	Andante	Grušenka, Love variant	Lyrical, long phrases	Self-pity over love of Grušenka
3	115	Když vyčítám	Più mosso	Míťa	Accented, declamatory	Thoughts about punishing Grušenka
4	116	. . . tu ona plná nevinnosti	Andante con moto	Grušenka, Love variant	Lyrical	Grušenka as innocent
5	116	. . . a pak jen odpouštět	Poco allegro, amoroso	Love theme proper	Stable harmony, lyrical	Forgiveness, hope for future
6	117	Hle, tam vyžilý stařec	Più vivo	Fedor	Chromatic ostinato	Remembers Fedor's involved
7	118	A čím ji získal	Allegro con fuoco	None	Chromatic parallel chords	Hate toward Fedor
8	119	A ona přišla	Più lento	Grušenka	Dolce, leggiero	Imagines tryst of Fedor and Grušenka
9	120	Lstná kolčavo!	Poco più mosso, 3/4	Murder	Chromatic ascent	Plans for revenge against Grušenka
10	120	. . . pak běda tobě	Largo	Fedor, Míťa	Oscillating chords	Yelling threats
11	121	Teď opatrně k dílu	Meno mosso	Fedor	Similar to 9	Decision to take action
12	122	—	Lento, Molto allegro, 4/4	None	Tremolo, unstructured	Knocks on window

the result that lucidity turns to delusion, especially in the final such passage (119). "Ah! Světlo v pokoji" therefore represents a progression from "Dnes slyš mou zpověď'" in Míťa's spiraling descent into mental collapse.

Past the turning point of his father's murder (which in Míťa's eyes is actually the murder of Grigorij), this manic oscillation continues, with the difference that his state of lucidity is directed now toward the promise of future happiness, prefiguring the epilogue both dramatically and musically. In Act 2, when Míťa contemplates suicide away from the festivities of the crowd ("Mám-li se zastřelit," table 8.4, 190–98), the offstage dance music forms a framework of regularity, amid which his mind struggles between hope and annihilation. This duality is paralleled in an interesting fashion by the text, where the phrases, alternating between desperation and calm, each end in a word associated with "life," on a pitch in the highest tessitura of the tenor voice. As the dance music disintegrates in the opening phrase, Míťa contemplates his previous thoughts of suicide, singing, "there was no reason to live," to a relatively disunified accompaniment and a disjunct vocal line (191). Immediately following, however, the orchestra brings forth the love motive over a sympathetic, syncopated accompaniment, marked *espressivo, amoroso*; Míťa reasons that since his rival Musjalovič has fled the scene, "now it would be necessary to live," sung jubilantly

Table 8.4. Form of "Mám-li se zastřelit," 190–97

#	Page	Incipit	Tempo, meter	Motives	Musical attributes	Dramatic situation
1	190	Mám-li se zastřelit	Più mosso, 4/4	Dance, Míťa variant	Intercutting episodes	Míťa weighs options of suicide
2	191	Ale ted' onen její bývalý	Andante, 3/4	Love variant	Long, lyrical phrases	Realizes rival is gone
3	192	Proklatě! žít nemožno	Allegro con fuoco, 4/4	Míťa variant, Smerďakov	Accented triplets	Remembers Grigorij's "death"
4	194	. . . vyhladím stopy	Elevato/ allegro, 3/4	Míťa, Love variant	Tenuto, lyrical	Hope for new life
5	195	Ale ne, ach ne	Grave tragico	Míťa, Smerďakov variant, Dance	Accented, polyrhythmic	Gives up hope, dance interrupts
6	196	A což hodina, ba minuta	Poco allegretto, 4/4	Dance, Love, Grušenka	Steady pulse, polyrhythm	Rash hedonistic impulse

amid a powerful orchestral crescendo (192). Suddenly, however, he recalls what he believes to be his murder of Grigorij, and in a highly erratic passage dominated by heavily chromaticized variations of Míťa's and Smerďakov's motives, he utters a desperate prayer to God, who has "made miracles for greater sinners." At the cusp of desolation and hope, the music accelerates toward the line, "If however the old man were still alive," changing from *Allegro con fuoco* to *Elevato* (194). At this point Míťa sings of his hope for a new life of redemption, over his own motive, now marked tenuto; the elation lasts for several measures (with the text, "and with her I will start a new life," 195) before plunging yet again into despair. As he declares his resolution of suicide, "everything is lost, all is at an end," the offstage dance music interrupts the mood, and in a gesture of wild abandon, Míťa just as quickly rushes back to the pleasures

Table 8.5. Form of "Pánové, jsem jistě lepší," 246–62

#	Page	Incipit	Tempo, meter	Motives	Musical attributes	Dramatic situation
1	246	Pánové, jsem jistě lepší	Lento sostenuto, 3/4	Love variant	Lyrical, syncopated tenuto	Initial statement of regret
2	249	Ale taky podle lhal!	Poco più mosso	None	Disrupted, recit-like	Accusation of Grigorij
3	249	Nemohl jsem dosud mluvit	Pochettino più mosso	Kateřina	Chromatic parallel chords	Beginning of narrative
4	250	Nuž, vězte	Grave tragico	Murder	Tremolo, chromatic ascent	Declaration of innocence
5	251	Šlechetná Kateřina	Allegro appassionato	Kateřina	Triplets, syncopation	Tale of Kateřina's money
6	254	Druhou polovinu zašil jsem	Tempo allegro, più agitato, 4/4	Kateřina	Ostinati, tremolo	Description of pouch
7	258	V onu osudnou noc	Allegro inquieto	Grušenka, Love	Intercutting episodes	Narrative of night of crime
8	259	Při pomyšlení	Allegretto ben ritmico	Dance, Love, Grušenka	Regular pulse, climax	Description of events at Mokré
9	261	Učinil jsem vám	Largo grave	Murder	Intense lyricism	Míťa challenges accusers

of Grušenka, "at least for one night": the music of the dance, constantly accelerating, is intermingled with the motives of Grušenka, love, and with parallel chords denoting Míťa himself. Although the optimism of the future appears for the first time in "Mám-li se zastřelit" (and indeed, continues to resonate with musical references to the *elevato* music of 194), in the context of the antihero's increasingly delusional mania this moment can only be understood as a glimmer of conscience, colored by his obsessive shame over the events of his reprehensible past.

The climax of the opera, particularly as regards Míťa's character development, occurs during his testimonial statement, defending himself against his father's murder; it is here that Míťa confronts his obsession with his own shame, purges it publicly, then turns to question the morals of his accusers. "Pánové, jsem jistě lepší" (table 8.5, 246–62), although it contains many internal divisions along the lines of tempo and accompanimental patterns, has a larger structure of three unequal parts. The opening, marked *Lento sostenuto*, is a lament over his present situation and the misfortune that befell Grigorij, sung in long, lyrical lines over a tenuto syncopated accompaniment similar to that in "Mám-li se zastřelit" (191); as proof of his sincerity, variations of the love motive appear in the high violins. Interrupted by the Judge, demanding an account of his connection to the 3,000 rubles, Míťa is forced to recount his dealings with Kateřina, her money, and the two times he spent it on Grušenka at Mokré. Such a pedestrian list of contents, however, by no means describes the cathartic effect of this narrative: opening with a low ostinato based on Kateřina's motive, Míťa quickly progresses to the source of his torment, crying out "horrible shame" over an augmented octave (a phrase that, curiously, also describes the love motive, ex. 8.6, 250). After categorically denying his participation in the robbery and murder of Fedor, the music propels him almost uncontrollably through a description of his passion for Grušenka, with no harmonic resolution in sight; accordingly, we progress from the murder motive in ostinato to a series of disjunct motivic references to both Grušenka and love. Twice during the narrative Míťa approaches the brink of insanity with his cries, "Who will prove to me that I spent the entire three thousand? Nobody!" (254) and "Shame, shame!" (258), demonstrating his continued oscillation between defiance and torturous guilt, both sung at the highest extreme of his range. The conclusion of the narrative describes the compulsive decision to follow Grušenka to Mokré and spend Kateřina's remaining money, culminating in a phrase that spans Míťa's entire range; at its conclusion, the orchestra erupts into a polytonal and polyrhythmic frenzy (ex. 8.7, 260–61). The narrative finished and the demons of shame purged, Míťa turns to his accusers with the astonishing statement: "I have made a terrible confession for you. I have rent my soul in two. And you still want to make a record of it! Aren't you ashamed? And you poke your fingers into the gaping wound. Woe!" (261–62). In one of the most harmonically extreme moments in the opera, Míťa is finally free to confront his accusers and the

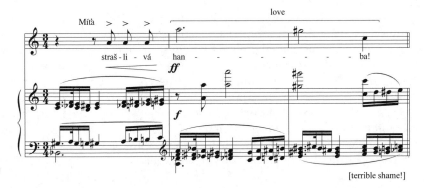

Example 8.6. Jeremiáš, *Bratři Karamazovi*, love theme on the word "shame" (250/5–7).

Example 8.7. Jeremiáš, *Bratři Karamazovi*, climactic catharsis of Míťa's testimony (260/8–10; 261/1–4).

hypocritical society that has forced him into this position, drawing strength from his catharsis moments earlier. At this moment, Míťa changes from antihero to hero, assuming a higher moral ground than those around him, winning victory over the emotional slavery that has plagued him the entire opera. Tellingly, his outburst is met with nothing but silence, as though no further questions or rebuttals are possible; the only portions of the remainder of the opera to approach the modernist intensity of "Pánové, jsem jistě lepší" are Ivan's mad scene and the revelation of Kateřina's letter, which serve to send the courtroom scene spiraling out of control, ultimately deciding Míťa's fate.

The epilogue to *Bratři Karamazovi* is set in Míťa's jail cell and depicts his reconciliation with Aljoša, Kateřina, and Grušenka; as mentioned previously, Jeremiáš chose to cast it in a broadly lyrical, conservative style (345–67). In many aspects it is the most problematic section of the work. Dominated vocally by the three visitors, Míťa has almost no opportunity to express himself, and despite the redemptive quality of such an optimistic ending, the resignation it implies lies wholly outside of his character, especially in the wake of his awe-inspiring "Pánové, jsem jistě lepší." To Jeremiáš's credit, this highly Wagnerian music, foreshadowed in the hopelessly blissful moments of "Ah! Světlo v pokoji," "Mám-li se zastřelit," and especially the love duet, has returned in the epilogue to receive its promised fulfillment—indeed, whole sections of the duet reappear, sung by the same characters. Perhaps the most striking aspect of this recapitulatory process occurs in the opera's final measures (ex. 8.8, 367), which reintroduces Míťa's motive, marked *elevato* in the manner of "Mám-li se zastřelit" (194). In this respect, the entire scene acts as a coda wherein the motivic web unravels, leaving only Míťa's motive to describe his apotheosis; moreover, the modernist harmonic disintegration of the rest of the opera finds ample resolution in its nineteenth-century lyricism. Míťa's apotheosis, from the same mold as that of *Jenůfa*,[33] not only undermines the issue of social hypocrisy raised by Dostoevsky.

Example 8.8. Jeremiáš, *Bratři Karamazovi*, Míťa's motive in the final measures (367/5–9).

As the criticism reveals, it also problematizes Jeremiáš's work in the context of modernist opera.

The indecision of Prague's critics as to whether *Bratři Karamazovi* represented a modernist masterwork or a reactionary bastion of tradition reflects the bipolar nature of the music itself. Much of the criticism was quite positive, especially from the Nejedlý circle, who still considered themselves outside the Prague musical establishment, and therefore sought to harness the composer's status as an "outsider" in Prague. In a series of articles, Josef Bartoš praised what he termed the "cathartic epilogue" whose basis in life reflected the composer's healthy optimism.[34] Describing Jeremiáš's music as lyrical and full of emotion yet unaffected, Bartoš distinguished the "concrete action" of *Bratři Karamazovi* from "pseudo-operatic dramaticness," such that the composer had elevated the drama above the merely symphonic (read: Novák's *Dědův odkaz*) to attain a modern sense of truth.[35] Bartoš's sense of modernism, clearly derived from Nejedlý's socialist, pro-Wagnerian stance, allowed for a strong adherence to tradition, but rejected any obvious dependence on foreign models, especially Italian verismo and naturalism; thankfully, no traces of these were to be found in Jeremiáš's work.[36] For Bartoš it boded well for the overall taste of the Prague audience that they had appreciated such a perfectly modern work.

Mirko Očadlík also gave a positive review of *Bratři Karamazovi*, but found fault with the Wagnerian tradition from which it was apparently derived, declaring the legacy of the Gesamtkunstwerk to be "an open wound, an unsolved problem" that outweighed its philosophical content.[37] Like Bartoš, Očadlík differentiated between the truly dramatic qualities of Jeremiáš's opera and what he termed the "histrionicism" of post-Wagnerian opera; indeed, the composer's main contribution to modern opera was the emancipation from histrionics, attaining a new "objective centralism," or internalized dramatic conflict. Realizing that *Bratři Karamazovi* was a far cry from the international avant-garde—whose music he had so recently praised in *Wozzeck*—Očadlík declared it unnecessary for every opera composer to search for innovation like Berg. Jeremiáš, in achieving a truly modern dramatic objectivity, had been revolutionary "in his own way." Recognizing the composer's debt to Ostrčil (particulary *Legenda z Erinu*) and Janáček (in terms of timbral detail), he nevertheless applauded the stylistic uniformity of the opera as well as the psychological development of Dostoevsky's characters through motivic variation. On the whole, Očadlík's assessment of *Bratři Karamazovi* adhered to Nejedlý's paradigm of an atemporally modernist, internally psychological work, despite the younger critic's dismissal of the obvious Wagnerian heritage of Jeremiáš's musico-dramatic concept.

Both Bartoš and Očadlík avoided a detailed social reading of *Bratři Karamazovi*, which their mentor Nejedlý provided in his article for the communist newspaper *Rudé právo*.[38] The critic took advantage of Jeremiáš's residence outside Prague to declare his oeuvre to be the work of a village dweller instead of an urbanite, through whose musical voice the proletarian rose up against his lords.[39] As such, the opera was modern in that it provided a "new view of the world," socially responsible in a way that the so-called "social" music of the bourgeois realm could never be. Although *Bratři Karamazovi* was unable to give a true portrayal of the life of the new working class (taking place as it does in the Czarist regime), Jeremiáš's musical portrayal of Dostoevsky was immeasurably closer to this ideal than anything that could be produced in bourgeois urban society. Even in the predominantly positive reception of the work, Nejedlý felt that most Prague the-atergoers had misread *Bratři Karamazovi*, captivated by its dramatic intensity rather than its inner human joy (which only the workers could feel). In contrast to Dostoevsky's "pessimistic" outlook, however, Jeremiáš had not written a lament over the evils of mankind, but rather a decisive blow against the society that mis-treats its downtrodden; as such, the opera was optimistic, expressing a new world rather than old Russia. In the portrayal of the characters as real humans, suffer-ing and exalting, Jeremiáš's work was comparable to *Wozzeck*; in fact, these two operas solved for Nejedlý the issue of the existence of modern opera, since side by side they showed the path of the genre for decades to come. Nejedlý's assess-ment of *Bratři Karamazovi* synchronized with those of Bartoš and Očadlík in that all three were based on the attempt to distinguish the work from the recent past of Czech opera, and from bourgeois art in general, which was ephemeral and therefore incapable of attaining atemporal modernism.

Not every critic was as unconditionally accepting of Jeremiáš's opera as the above three. Most others, particularly those outside the Czech-speaking com-munity, acknowledged the relative conservatism of the musical language, although this factor was by no means an impediment to its success. Perhaps the most openly critical was Karel Boleslav Jirák, whose short review of *Bratři Karamazovi* appeared in the very same issue as Bartoš's glowing appraisal.[40] Although he conceded that Jeremiáš's work was the greatest success at the National Theater since *Wozzeck*, Jirák felt that this esteem was a result of the com-poser's adherence to nineteenth-century operatic formulas, particularly the Wagnerianism and Straussianism of the older generation of Czech composers. While in general he felt that the libretto was the best possible dramatization of Dostoevsky's novel, it allowed for too many naturalistic or veristic effects, to the point where Míťa's arrest seemed "filmic." The apotheosis of the final scene, which he compared to those of *Faust, Tristan und Isolde*, and *Jenůfa*, weakened the dramatic effect of earlier scenes through conventional music. Jeremiáš's massive orchestral sound and occasionally "brutal" effects were, according to Jirák, Straussian, and the many other instances of foreign and Czech influences ham-pered the artistic quality of the opera through an insufficiency of individual style. Elsewhere describing *Bratři Karamazovi* as eclectic, reminiscent at times of *Rusalka, Hubička, Eva*, and *Vina*, Jirák lamented that such a compositional method in a conservative guise was no better than Weinberger's *Švanda dudák*. Being "alien and deaf to the modern attempts at new opera," Jeremiáš was forced to rely on such outdated mannerisms as $\frac{6}{4}$ chords and diminished sevenths at dramatic moments, the use of through-composed recitative to imitate speech, and the psychological working of Wagnerian leitmotivs, none of which was ideal in the modern conception of opera. In direct opposition to the reviews of Nejedlý, Očadlík, and Bartoš (and all but ignoring the social and dramatic importance of the work), Jirák's review described an opera that was too much like all that had come before.

Many of the more moderately critical reviews echoed the negative points of Jirák's article, albeit with a substantial admixture of praise, particularly for the overall dramatic atmosphere and Jeremiáš's musical characterization throughout such a large cast. Erich Steinhard, the leading German-Bohemian critic for *Der Auftakt*, allowed that one does not have to compose "problematic music" or find originality of expression in every opera, since a composer could attain musical potency even using a nineteenth-century language.[41] Vomáčka claimed that it was impossible to judge *Bratři Karamazovi* as having a specific musical originality; while not eclectic, Jeremiáš synthesized the great achievements of his time, including Smetana, Dvořák, and Strauss, into a new dynamic aesthetic.[42] Doležil, after a surprising attack on the overly "criminalistic" attributes of the libretto, which he deemed wholly unsuited to dramatization, credited the opera's "psychological modernism," attained without recourse to atonality or polytonality.[43] Interestingly, an unnamed critic from the Bremen journal *Weser Zeitung* drew a direct comparison between the music and drama of *Bratři Karamazovi* and that of *Elektra* and *Wozzeck*, with the reservation that the final scene evoked the Wagnerian paradigm of the unhappy hero redeemed by the comforting woman.[44] While an author from within the Prague circle, such as Erich Steinhard, may have submitted this review, it is tempting to consider that an outsider's point of view was the most objective in weighing the strengths and weaknesses of Jeremiáš's opera.

The various references to *Wozzeck*, *Elektra*, *Jenůfa*, Czech tradition, verismo, Wagner, anti-Wagner, modernism, and antimodernism throughout the reviews of *Bratři Karamazovi* demonstrate its problematic status in the atmosphere of 1928 Prague. The critics, for the most part, sensed that Jeremiáš's work was an important contribution to the discourse of modernist music in Prague, but questioned the composer's hesitancy to join the movement wholeheartedly. By 1928, the attitude toward modernism had changed so much that an opera written in continuation of the tradition of Ostrčil's *Legenda z Erinu* or Zich's *Vina* could not compete with the latest imports from abroad, including neoclassicism: even comparisons to Janáček, so much in vogue in the late 1920s, did not suffice in this regard. As we have seen, Jeremiáš's own opinion regarding modernism was somewhat reactionary, describing his work as "a step backward" from the trends of the international avant-garde. Nevertheless, his opera has a musical and dramatic intensity that is found only rarely in the genre.

As the above analysis has shown, Jeremiáš's music creates a binarism between modernism and antimodernism, reflected dramatically in the opposition between Míťa and his supporting cast, between insanity and morality, aggression and submission, and rather curiously, between the old life and the new. Whereas Míťa changes of his own accord from antihero to hero during his testimony in Act 3, thereby attaining moral superiority over his accusers, the final scene, designed as a cleansing apotheosis on the scale of *Jenůfa*, dissolves his aggression in the sound-world of the nineteenth century. As several critics noted (including Nejedlý, who disliked the overabundant lyricism of the music in this scene), such a reversion was dramatically and structurally at odds with the rest of the opera; Jeremiáš himself later described his need for an optimistic conclusion as a phase of his career to which he need not return.[45] Given the general hesitancy of Czech composers and audiences to accept the music of the European avant-garde in the late 1920s, the optimistic fate of Míťa in *Bratři Karamazovi* can be taken to represent Jeremiáš's reinterpretation of modernist opera, especially the brutally tragic conclusions of *Elektra* and *Wozzeck*. While Míťa approaches the state of criminal insanity of his counterparts, his successful return to conservative values forms an exact parallel to the Czech musical community, which explored European modernism and retreated to an aesthetic conservatism cloaked in moral authority. *Bratři Karamazovi*, while successfully received by the bourgeois theatergoers of Prague and performed the following year in Bern and Augsburg, did not directly influence the direction of modern Czech opera, or even stay in the repertoire of the National Theater, as many predicted it would. Nevertheless, its reception reflects an aesthetic shift in Prague, for both audiences and critics, in that not only were modernist works publicly appreciated for the first time in the city's history, but such a new work could be criticized for not being modern enough. After *Bratři Karamazovi*, there could never be a second "*Wozzeck* Affair."

* * *

Two operas of the late 1920s helped audiences and critics bridge the gap from the shocked conservatism of the early First Republic years to the easier acceptance of modern culture in the 1930s. This transformation was particularly important for members of the compositional community who, as the discussion in chapters 5 and 7 revealed, were often just as closed-minded as the bourgeois opera subscribers. Zich's *Preciézky* brought a certain freshness to the aesthetic palate of Prague, with its tentative exploration of neoclassicism, its tighter formal plan, and its lighter dramatic approach. Jeremiáš's *Bratři Karamazovi*, on the other hand, reinforced the Wagnerian legacy of modern Czech opera but flirted with a more extreme modernist style of expression, particularly as regards the correlation of music and internalized, psychological drama. Although both operas were arguably conservative within their respective trends, their positive reception by the Prague public of the 1920s led to a community where multiple possibilities of modernism and Czechness were acceptable, perhaps for the first time. It only remained for the younger generation of the 1930s to introduce into Czech culture further elements of populism and a more serious commitment to the avant-garde, however tempered by the new social and political conditions in the next decade.

Chapter Nine

Heaven on Earth

Socialism, Jazz, and a New Aesthetic Focus (1930–38)

In 1936, Jaroslav Ježek composed the music for a jazz revue entitled *Nebe na zemi* (Heaven on Earth) that was the smash hit of the Prague season. The title was an ironic statement on the political situation in the ailing First Republic as well as in the rest of Europe, particularly next door in the Third Reich. The political leanings of the revue's text were demonstrably socialist, although with a Western, prodemocratic focus and a growing sense of Czech nationalism. Ježek's score consisted of lively tangos, foxtrots, and other popular dances imported from America, as well as satirical, antifascist marches, all to the accompaniment of a jazz band based on that of Duke Ellington. The entire show, both musically and dramatically, was hailed as a significant contribution to Prague's avant-garde movement. That such a strange and wonderful amalgam of theatrical, musical, political, and social impulses should find place in a single work is indicative not only of the state of the Prague musical community in the 1930s, but also of the fundamental cosmopolitanism and awareness of its individual members as democracy was coming to a close.

The decade of the 1930s saw tremendous social, political, and economic changes throughout Europe, occasioned by the start of the Great Depression, the rise of Hitler in Germany and of offshoot fascisms in other states, the popularity of the socialist movement, and finally the total collapse of democracy and the start of the Second World War. While the first Czechoslovak Republic managed to retain its independent, democratic status longer than most states in Central and Eastern Europe, these international tensions were not without considerable effects locally as the decade progressed, particularly with the ascendancy of the communist party on the one hand, and after 1934, the unstoppable momentum of Henlein's fascist *Sudetendeutsche Partei*. These phenomena induced a rise in Czech nationalism in some quarters, such as had not been witnessed since the years before independence—much of it prodemocratic, but occasionally verging on fascist absolutism as well. The solidification of the working class as a powerful social and political force was also felt in Czech society, especially in connection with the new technological capabilities for mass communication.

For the members of the musical community of Prague (as for those throughout Europe), the economic effects of the Depression were especially harsh, not only in terms of the rise in unemployment among hundreds of their colleagues, but also in that audience attendance dropped substantially. The newly enfranchised working class sought its entertainment elsewhere—radio, dance halls, phonograph, and sound film—as they had already begun to do in the 1920s. Although Czech musicians were certainly employed in each of these new branches of the industry (if the product in question was domestically produced), the traditional cultural institutions of the city felt a palpable economic strain as popular culture became an institution in its own right.

Both the change in popular musical taste and the technological explosion of the 1930s had noticeable effects on the state of composition in Prague and on the aesthetic debates surrounding art music. Philosophically as well as practically, composers and critics discussed the quality of popular music production and its intersection, for better or worse, with their own artistic realm. Although in the early years of the decade the discourse tended to exclude issues of nationalism, it had everything to do with modernism and the social responsibility of art, in that musicians were torn between the moral duty they felt toward the audience and its cultural education on the one hand, and toward the purity of their craft on the other. As a result, the compositions of the era reveal a propensity for social themes as well as attempts at popularization, more than in any previous decade.

Despite these hardships and doubts, by the mid-1930s the Prague musical community was much more unified than it had been since the time of the early Artists' Union (UB). With respect to officially recognized institutions and clubs, the transition of power from the older generation to the younger began as early as 1928, when Štěpán and Axman relinquished their positions in the directorship of the Spolek pro moderní hudbu (Society for Modern Music) to Hába and Očadlík, thereby ending a long period of ambivalence and anxiety toward European modernism. Their takeover not only rejuvenated an organization whose conservatism had brought it to the point of stagnation, but also opened the floodgates to new musical developments, so long repressed by the group's older members (see discussion in chapter 5).[1] This point can also be considered an early milestone in the solidification of Prague's avant-garde, which was slowly transformed from a scattered group of individuals with differing agendas in the late 1920s into a network of linked organizations with a core of active members.[2] No longer having to prove themselves in an environment dominated by their elders, Czech musicians such as Hába and Ježek were free to make any associations they chose—that these were often with Germans or German-speaking Jews such as Schulhoff, Ullmann, and Reiner is also characteristic of the era. The

general attitude toward professionalism also ensured an end to the era of provocative manifestos (such as those by Burian in the previous decade); musicians could
now concentrate on the problems of the present and future of their art.

Another common trait, the general trend toward socialism and/or communism among the avant-garde, also served to link Prague's musicians with their
counterparts in other artistic and intellectual circles, both within and outside
the city. It is therefore evident that the sense of Czech musical identity during
the 1930s tended much more toward the collective than the individual, not only
reflecting the politics of the era but also fitting perfectly into the ideological
inheritance of the Cultural Revival. Although with this political bent there was a
certain interest in cultural policies and products from Soviet Russia, by and large
the Czech avant-garde communists were still predominantly Western in their
thinking, which is to say that they envisioned communism within a thoroughly
democratic context. All things considered, there was a strong urge to resolve
social issues through a modern art that was essentially Western in orientation.[3]

Just what version of musical modernism was supposed to accomplish this feat,
however, was open to question—an issue that itself became the main point of
contention in the Prague community. Already anxious about the overall ability
of European art music to have a social impact in its present disparate state,
Czech composers and critics of the 1930s espoused two main points of view.
Dalibor C. Vačkář, a young composer also active as a dramatist and journalist,
described the problem the most succinctly, albeit somewhat belatedly, in late
1935 for the avant-garde music journal *Rytmus*.[4] According to Vačkář, one group
of composers, whose inclination lay in the direction of neoclassicism, French
influences, or popular musics (such as the members of the Mánes Group),
wanted to use purely musical techniques to regain access to an audience they felt
had been alienated by late romanticism. A second group, among them the
inheritors of the socialist-minded Nejedlý school with the critic's son, Vít, at the
forefront, felt that music should in no way bend to popular taste, but should
seek to elevate the masses through the adoption of socialist themes and avant-
garde compositional techniques. Vačkář portrayed the intellectual standoff in
the following humorous manner:

> It's raining. Around a garden table sit composers from both camps, having a discussion.
> First: What shall we do so that we don't get wet? Second: Let's get umbrellas. Third: No,
> let's take off our clothes. Fourth: Let's run away and hide. Fifth: Is it absolutely import-
> ant that we don't get wet? Sixth: It makes me happy. Seventh: Let's make it stop rain-
> ing. Eighth: What, it's raining? I hadn't even noticed. And they kept on discussing this
> way, and everyone got soaked to the skin. They caught colds and died.
>
> **Moral**: When it's raining, let's act as though it's raining. But let's act![5]

Clearly, Vačkář's larger point was that neither faction was completely in the right
(of which I read the "odd-numbered" composers as socialists and the "even"
ones as neoclassicist/populists), as long as the deliberation itself prevented any

further activity. Within this framework, there are thinly veiled lampoons of those who were trying to solve problems beyond their grasp (the seventh composer), those oblivious to the seriousness of the situation (the fourth, sixth, and eighth), and those with radical, if impractical solutions (the third).[6] Nevertheless, part of Vačkář's statement seems to be the lack of clear delineation in the Prague musical community. That these two camps were not mutually exclusive or even adversarial is demonstrated by such works as Ježek's jazz revue *Osel a stín* (The Ass and the Shadow, 1933), with its serious, antifascist allegory, or the sheer numbers of composers of all stripes (including Jeremiáš and Křička) who wrote music for films. It is also important to note that providing the mass audience with its "own" music did not necessarily imply one specific compositional style, and the work of socialist-minded artists ranged from accessible mass songs to the most austere, abstract modernism. Similarly, not all of the work of the neoclassicists was as accessible as their purported mandate proclaimed. As a complement to the present discussion, in chapter 10 I analyze two operatic works that reveal the variety of reactions to these questions: Hába's *Matka* (The Mother, 1930), a quarter-tone opera with a socialist message; and Křička *Strašidlo v zámku* (A Ghost in the Castle, 1933), a comic Zeitoper with elements of jazz revue and operetta. These works were situated in an ongoing debate (ridiculed by Vačkář) that was largely generated by critics of the younger generation regarding the responsibility of modern music toward society and how a listenership should best be regained. It is this discussion that forms the focus of the present chapter.

Očadlík, *Klíč*, and the Musical Crisis in the Early 1930s

Early in the decade, the young Nejedlý student A. J. Patzaková (significantly one of the only women active in the discourse) described the gap between artists and audiences as one where "[the music] being produced today is in great discontinuity with what the people are living and thinking."[7] The article, "The Social Causes of Today's Musical Crisis," written for *Tempo* (the updated *Listy Hudební matice*) in 1931, represents one of the first attempts to delineate contemporary composers into the two aforementioned compositional factions. Although her division lay between socially responsible musicians and those espousing "academic historicism" (i.e., the neoclassicists), neither group, it seems, was capable of avoiding the isolation of high culture from "the new social realities of the new world."[8] For Patzaková, it was not that audiences did not crave inspiration and/or cultural leadership from the arts; in fact, in such a time of social anxiety, they were more in need than ever (a viewpoint that stood in opposition to Vomáčka's "stupid audiences"). It was all the more unfortunate, then, that artists should be in the midst of searching for a new direction and experimenting with new means of expression, precisely when they stood the greatest chance of distancing themselves from a public that needed them. Patzaková did not deny the proletarianizing trend in Czech society, what with the precipitous arrival of modern dances and new entertainment media; as such, the reaction of young composers was of paramount importance, since it could either guarantee the allegiance of the new society or alienate it permanently. In a related argument, she viewed the public's turn toward radio as being provoked not only by the rapid commercialization of culture but also by the collective need for anonymity and distance from an overblown artistic sphere. The resultant antagonism between the two sociocultural levels could nevertheless be bridged in one of two ways: first, culture via the radio could shape the "widest collectivization of artistic values" into a "new dilettantism," wherein the listener could achieve an unprecedented knowledge about music without any actual participation; alternatively, as Patzaková stressed in her conclusion, the older cultural institutions could adapt themselves to the new social reality.[9] The latter scenario would reaffirm music as a social endeavor of significance, oriented anew toward life, to be used as a means of social development. In short, the common public could participate in high-art culture and its institutions, instead of having the music simply waft over them via the radio. While Patzaková's attitude took into account the realities of the modern world regarding the prevailing taste toward popular culture and the radio, she still retained the belief that modern art music, if written with the proper "attitude toward life" and strategically circulated to a wide audience, could overtake popular music as a social priority. Although she never described the "proper" way of composing socially relevant music in concrete terms, it is noteworthy that much of Patzaková's rhetoric is almost identical to the previous generation of Nejedlians, when they called for operas written according to a Smetanian model. Such a position was obviously no longer relevant in a socially conscious discourse on music in the 1930s; nevertheless, an a priori compositional model still lurked behind Patzaková's argument, providing for the possibility of social change if ever a composer were to discover it, and an institution to promulgate it.

For all its abstraction and critical bias, Patzaková's article served to introduce to the Czech musical community the binarism that existed throughout the early 1930s, between those who wished to regain an audience through accessible music and those who believed the idea content of music should play a crucial role in social development. Central to the evolution of this debate in Prague was Mirko Očadlík, the young critic who, fresh from his education under Nejedlý, had come to the forefront of Prague music criticism through his efforts during the 1926 "*Wozzeck* Affair," and who, with Hába, took over the leadership of the Spolek pro moderní hudbu in 1928. Since that time, Očadlík had begun to formulate ideas regarding the best direction of modern Czech music, and importantly, its connections to tradition, individual leadership, collective identity, and social function. These efforts coalesced into the Spolek-based journal *Klíč* (The Key, 1930–34), for which he was the main editor and contributor. During the first half of the decade, this new journal became one of the most important musical voices in Prague, next to the UB's official organ, *Tempo*. Unlike *Tempo*, where contributors of all stripes could present ideas on equal, if somewhat tepid, terms, the writing in *Klíč* adopted a more radical tone, such that Očadlík could rightly declare that, by the start of its fourth year, "many have the opinion of this journal that it would be better if it had never been born."[10]

In his opening salvo in late 1930, Očadlík stated both his aesthetic creed and his goal for the journal: unlike many publications that dodged the central issues of the day, *Klíč* would be "a *key* to the resolution of problems and questions arising from the era and its needs."[11] Rejecting the romantic concept of music as a "mysterium of transubstantiation," the critic instead idealized "a pure art as a phenomenon that has shape, whose substance is an independent, formed thought that has volume, and whose expression is a new reality: technical, firm, logical, and convincing."[12] Accordingly, the goal of the journal was "to follow, research, and identify the growth of new art in all its components, to strike a path to new forms and new concepts, to remove sickly barriers slowing down the development of the new world. . . . There is no tradition or history except that which is enlightening and beneficial to new values."[13] For Očadlík, there was no question that new music would find its true place among the members of a society for whom culture would be more than just an abstract concept: they would be "convinced" by the logic that the "sickly barriers" of the past were a hindrance to achieving a unity between themselves and art, which would ultimately become "enlightening and beneficial." Although the rhetoric of the first *Klíč* editorial in part resembled that of the manifestos of the 1920s young avant-garde, with their wild abandonment of the past for its own sake, Očadlík's text was also guarded in its call for the new. His view of modernism was reasoned and goal oriented, a second Cultural Revival (or "Enlightenment") without literally returning to past musical expressions. Nevertheless, for all his disdain for the mysticism of the romantic past, what Očadlík envisioned was nothing less than a modern transubstantiation, wherein modern music and its public would unite into a new and satisfying whole.

Later in the first year of *Klíč*, Očadlík defined his project of solving the crisis of new music and society in more specific terms: the article "On the State of Criticism" began the task of "following, researching, and identifying" the reasons behind the separation of artists from society.[14] Rejecting financial concerns outright as the cause of social "disorientation," he claimed, much like his forebears in the Czech critical community, that a lack of artistic leadership had resulted in the alienation of the audience. Particularly important for Očadlík was the role of a critical leader, a position not filled "since the time when Zdeněk Nejedlý stopped his critical work" in 1927; among the others remaining, he noted a dearth of provocative viewpoints and a tendency toward over-intellectualism that amounted to little more than the misuse of poorly understood slogans.[15] The widespread application of uninformed opinions in the critical community, "without ideology or ideas, without thought, without originality, and without taste," was partially to blame for the social disorientation with regard to music, since such an inherent reactionism was unable to comprehend modernism.[16] Finally arriving at the crux of the issue—the possible resolutions for the current crisis—Očadlík called for a united front in both orientation and thought, away from insinuation and intrigue, in order to regain the lost audience. As with Patzaková's delineation of compositional attitudes, written around the same time, Očadlík described an incorrect as well as a correct path for criticism: those critics who sought to preserve the present state of affairs, particularly in the theaters, inevitably promoted the growth of splinter groups catering to public taste, while those who worked to mold new ateliers of artists were prepared to synthesize music with the new realities of life. Očadlík's utopian dream, despite the radical restructuring of society it advocated, was still based on images of the past, evoking *Meistersinger*-like guilds that would work for collective social development, including critics in the forefront.

Očadlík expanded his vision of the future of modern music and its role in society two years later in the lengthy article "The Essence of Modernism in Music."[17] In this study, he examined the dichotomy between tradition and modernism, which he took to mean the true understanding of the past and present, respectively. Each was imperative to the existence of the other, since tradition was not the past itself, but merely the modern view of it as a legacy; tradition was also the main limiting factor with regard to modernism, providing a systematic structure within which current experimentation could take shape. Očadlík concluded that, "the sense of new understanding is not just in the broadening of the contemporary horizon, but also in the deepening of a relation to the past," culminating in a "real synthesis," a "complete inclusion of the cosmos."[18] In this synthesis, the composer would sacrifice his/her own will to the collective, not only to solidify and unify the artistic presence in society, but also to regain that society's participation in culture, once and for all. Only in its somewhat frightening absolutism is Očadlík's view any different from that expressed by each generation of Czech critics since Hostinský (who had been his teacher's teacher). Interestingly, among all the different compositional factions and viewpoints he acknowledged, Očadlík declared Stravinsky to be the only contemporary composer who had achieved "real synthesis": "In Stravinsky we have felt that objectivizing, shared truth, depersonalizing and ascetically messianic, . . . the paean of collective life."[19] Among the young Czech composers, it was Hába and Krejčí, with their provocative use of new modes of expression and deep understanding of the present, that stood closest to Stravinsky's achievement, albeit still "in midjourney" by comparison.[20]

Očadlík's formulation was a problematic one, in that he confused the somewhat outdated desire for a musical Messiah, who would deliver Czech culture from its modernist crisis (a position expressed throughout the 1920s), with the protosocialist call for the collectivization of culture and the absolute erasure of the individual voice. The true leader would be the least individual, then, and typical of such post-Nejedlian constructions, the most worthy of the legacy from the Cultural Revival and ultimately Smetana (whom Očadlík evoked as a model of leadership and self-sacrifice).[21] His choice of Alois Hába and Iša Krejčí, too, was also problematic, since these composers were stylistically quite distant, and furthermore, were generally taken to represent the two ideological factions of the Czech avant-garde in the mid-1930s.

Alois Hába and the Quarter-tone School

The position of Alois Hába is unique, not only in the history of music in Prague but in the histories of Western art music and theory as well. Perhaps best known for his pioneer efforts in quarter-tone and sixth-tone composition, he was also instrumental in developing the athematic style, taking the twelve-tone system of the Second Viennese School (with whose adherents he was on good terms) in a new direction. Because of these theoretical advancements and the publication of his related treatises outside the Czech Lands, Hába became the most internationally recognized member of the Prague avant-garde, and after Janáček and Martinů, the most well-known Czech composer of the twentieth century. Not wholly unrelated to all of this, Hába was also one of the leaders of the Prague musical community in the 1930s, as much for the uniqueness of his compositional approach as for his organizational drive, without which his generation might never have coalesced into the unified force it became. Hába was also very much a leader for the faction of composers and critics within the avant-garde who espoused socialist themes for their uncompromising modernist compositions, to reach the audience via political education rather than pandering to current tastes for populism and neoclassicism. Nevertheless, Hába the person was never the messianic figure so long desired by Prague's critics: his leadership encouraged and cultivated a stylistic, and to some extent, ideological pluralism that had proved to be divisive at other times and in other places.

From a modest family from the Valašsko region in Eastern Moravia, Hába, like Janáček and Bartók, had a view of Western music strongly colored by his early experiences with local folk culture; much as his two antecedents had, he stood apart from the romantic tradition almost from the beginning of his compositional career. His early studies with Novák led to the fruitful exploration of new ways to apply Moravian musical traditions in art music (an endeavor long pursued by Novák himself), and his subsequent education under Schreker, Busoni, and less officially, Schoenberg, opened the road to free atonality and microtonality. Hába's application of the quarter-tone system as a method of rendering the folk music of Moravia in the most accurate (and modernist) fashion reveals the significant connection between avant-garde and national interests at this time. Although Hába was by no means the first to compose in quarter tones (Busoni had advocated such an exploration, as well as the Russian expatriate composer Ivan Višněgradskij), his systematic use of them led to larger forms than had ever been attempted. He also quickly developed an educational program at the Prague Conservatory, wherein quarter-tone and other microtonal systems were taught alongside Western harmony; Hába's notation, which incorporated several new accidentals to indicate intervals smaller than a semitone, were easily assimilated into the traditional system of notation. Requiring a fleet of new instruments to be specially manufactured for his music, including a quarter-tone piano, harmonium, clarinet, and trumpet, Hába found a patron in President Masaryk, who quite controversially chose to fund the instruments' construction.

Hába's return to Prague after almost a decade of study abroad (1914–23) met with widespread critical disdain, particularly from the Spolek pro moderní hudbu while under Axman's leadership, and from Bartoš in *Smetana-Hudební list*.[22] The one institution to afford him a foothold in the community was the Conservatory, with whom he was on good terms, likely via Novák. It was here that, from 1924 onward, he taught a course in quarter-tone music, largely at the instigation of the Ministry of Education and National Culture (MŠANO), despite the occasional opposition from administrators like Hoffmeister. Although the class attracted a good number of students from other composers' masterclasses, as well as from abroad, Hába's efforts were seriously threatened by the Conservatory's financial losses during the Depression. Only the change of rectorship to Josef Suk in 1933 saved the course from extinction, despite a MŠANO recommendation that it be discontinued.[23] From this secure vantage point, he was finally able to act as a leader for the younger generation of Prague composers and critics, coalescing into the highly influential artistic group Přítomnost (The Present) after 1933.[24]

Prior to this point, Hába's one venue for the promulgation of his (and his students') activities was the International Society for Contemporary Music (ISCM), of which the Spolek—after 1928 under his directorship—was the representative Czechoslovak section. While not in charge of organizing any events on Czech soil (after the lukewarm 1925 ISCM), it did contribute to other festivals, particularly in Siena in 1928, where Hába's quarter-tone concert was double-billed with Burian's Voice-band (see chapter 7). From the earliest days the circle of younger enthusiasts grouped around Hába included Miroslav Ponc and Karel Hába, the composer's brother; later students at the conservatory included Karel Reiner, Rudolf Kubín, Karel Ančerl (later a conductor of international fame), Schulhoff, Ježek, Ullmann, and several young composers from Yugoslavia.[25] Most of these composers did not continue with quarter-tone composition outside the classroom (with the exception of Ponc), and such was not their teacher's aim; rather Hába endeavored to introduce his new techniques within the context of an advanced discussion of West European harmony, including the theoretical approaches of Busoni, Schoenberg, Janáček, Novák, and others. Such was also the case with the later grouping of composers around Hába at

Přítomnost, where participants were not expected to conform to the leader's stylistic model, but rather to contribute to the overall pluralism of the group. As such, the new generation's attitude to musical contribution and collective identity, at least within the art world, was altogether different from that of their forebears, who had sought to exclude each other from definitions of modern Czechness. Given the repressively conservative atmosphere of the previous generation, it seems that only through this idea of pluralism could Prague musicians form a true avant-garde movement.

As we have seen, the Prague avant-garde as represented by the ascendancy of Hába and his followers was not without opposition among the city's conservative institutions and critics. Such was also the case with a number of individual composers reluctant to embrace techniques other than those of the accepted postromantic musical vocabulary. One encounter encapsulates the stylistic, cultural, and even political issues at stake between a figure such as Hába and his more conservative, perhaps even antimodernist, colleagues. Contemporary to the quarter-tone class's fight for existence in the early 1930s, a small polemic broke out between Hába and František Pícha, a former student of Jeremiáš, Foerster, Křička, Jirák, and Suk (!) who concentrated on arrangements of South Bohemian folk songs. It is interesting to note that the debate, although it culminated in a rally of voices for or against the avant-garde, actually began as a discussion of the effects of new technology and media on traditional compositional procedures. Pícha, in his pessimistic article "Sound Film" for the November 1931 issue of *Tempo*, expressed his doubts about the future of stage drama and opera as genres when more popular technology already existed on the screen. Since sound films could induce flights of imagination in the audience that an actor or singer on stage could not, "developmentally, the life of opera is concluded."[26] The physical and technical limitations of opera could never match the potential of film, the music for which, however, was (from the perspective of 1931) woefully inadequate. As a result, while one genre was destined to die out, the other was unable to make up for the resultant aesthetic gap: if the composer could not become the full director of all aspects of a musical film, the result would be a form of operetta on screen, at best.

Hába's response in *Klíč* pointed the debate toward his own issues. Although he began by "correcting" several of Pícha's misconceptions about the new technology (having assumed that the sound came from a phonograph, not the film itself), Hába asserted that opera did indeed have a future separate from film, although each might indeed be positively influenced by the other in the future.[27] Unlike sound films with music, whose structure was generated by images, he claimed that the main propelling force behind opera was music, which formed the basis of both its structure and its detail. For Hába, only in the twentieth century had artists begun to realize the true capabilities for operatic synthesis, a fact that Pícha as a nonopera composer had yet to understand. To this end, Hába recommended his own athematic compositional style as a possible remedy for the future direction of both modern opera and sound films with music. With athematicism Hába sought to negate the hierarchization of traditional musical form, particularly in terms of the role of melody: in practice, it was mostly associated with free atonality or twelve-tone composition. Operas would be enriched by the constant stream of melodic ideas that athematicism produced, a phenomenon necessary to a genre dependent on musical flow; coupled with "the mobile forces of social struggle" in the subject matter of modern operas (since folkloric and historical themes no longer had any import), athematicism would bring all components together in a unified artistic statement.[28] Films could also potentially benefit from Hába's athematic style if the director chose to match the pictorial mobility with a similar musical fluidity (for which he gave the example of Eisler's music to *Das Niemandsland*).[29]

From here the argument took a sharp turn toward criticism of the avant-garde under Hába's leadership: Pícha responded with an attack that encompassed atonality, athematicism, quarter tones, and a comparison between rival visions of modernism.[30] Proceeding from a strict delineation of tonality and atonality, Pícha asserted the necessity of a firm point of reference (or tonic), from which a thematic style of composition would "arise logically," thereby differentiating and hierarchizing musical ideas and creating a sense of "responsibility and obligation," presumably on the part of the composer toward the audience.[31] Atonality, on the other hand, along with the athematic style that "arises logically" from it, represented the destabilization of musical ideas and the "negation of all that is firm," through the strict equality of all elements and the total lack of melodic repetition.[32] According to Pícha, "it is impossible to realize the consequences of the athematic style," since "we think *thematically*," developing ideas internally through repetition, creating a hierarchy of thoughts in which all things are not equal.[33] Clear in Pícha's rhetoric is the connection to the Czech aesthetic tradition, specifically to Hostinský's concept of *důslednost*. He also assumed that in Hába's compositional system, "abstract reflexes won over musicality, and that he arrived at the athematic style speculatively," wholly apart from "living reality."[34] The lack of thematic and tonal hierarchization would also spell the total destruction of musical form, a step he considered unnecessary in the light of other modern Czech practices, such as Novák's monothematicism or Suk's polythematicism. Pícha's argument, especially when linked to the earlier discussion of new technology, demonstrated well the anxiety that gripped the older interwar Czech generation toward modernism. Once the sloganeering about the progressiveness of the new Republic had subsided in the 1920s, a large segment of the community was genuinely worried about the means "Czech music" would take to arrive at a truly modern state. Having finally arrived there, artists such as Pícha desperately fought for the aesthetic of the past, for which they would sacrifice modernism in any form.

Hába's response, published shortly afterwards in *Klíč*, attempted to clarify the basic tenets of his style by linking it to the European avant-garde: his work with quarter tones was simply an elaboration of Schoenberg's twelve tones, and athe-maticism had already been in practice in compositions based on regular chro-matic harmony (as evidenced by the growing usage of *Hauptstimme* markings).[35] The complete freedom from conventions of thematic transposition, diminution, augmentation, and so forth, would yield more expressive melodies, since the composer's consciousness would not be distracted by the intellectual exercise of compositional technique: "the only requirement of the athematic style is to write as much music as occurs to the composer."[36] These declarations were meant to place traditional techniques (as well as teaching methods based solely on tonal theory and classical form) in a negative light as a defense against attacks by a fel-low composer, his own age, who had resisted the trends of European modernism. Hába next brought the discussion around to another, extramusical agenda:

> This [athematic] style is the picture of a new society, over whose new order the entire world is struggling. It pertains to the fact that every person can develop their abilities in the planned collaboration of human society. Depending on the character of one's talent, [each individual] will acquire a more or less responsible function, but all will be needed equally. This ideal of society will become a reality! The athematic musical style is the sound, the musical prefiguration of a new, better society.[37]

The comparison between the equality of musical phenomena and that of social formations was not new with Hába: among others, Schoenberg used similar analogies in his *Theory of Harmony*.[38] The tangential character of the remark may seem somewhat out of place in a discussion of compositional technique, but it actually demonstrates the degree to which the young avant-garde of the 1930s still felt their creative efforts to be a responsibility toward society.

For Hába and many others, socialism was increasingly the answer to the prob-lems of modern culture in society, as evinced in the ever greater numbers of compositions written in the 1930s portraying socialist themes, and in the work of their colleagues in other disciplines, particularly the theater (see discussion below). Some of the generation's younger members, such as Vít Nejedlý and Burian,[39] were quite involved with communist activism on a musical level, through the Svaz dělnických divadelních ochotníků Československa (The Workers' Union of Theater Amateurs of Czechoslovakia, hereafter DDOČ), to which Hába also belonged. One key difference from their literary counterparts, however, was that the Czech musical avant-garde continued to approach the dis-course of political music along the lines of bourgeois cultural forms, as Hába's defense of the future of opera quite obviously reveals. Most of the musical avant-garde in Prague contributed at least a few compositions to the Communist party movement around the middle of the decade in the form of mass songs, but oth-erwise, the majority of the musical expressions of socialism or communism tended toward larger genres from the tradition of European bourgeois music making. Salient in this regard are Erwin Schulhoff's cantata setting of Marx and

Engels's *Communist Manifesto* (set in Czech as *Manifest*, 1932);[40] Burian's operatic "folk play with songs and dances," *Vojna* (The War, 1935); Vít Nejedlý's opera *Tkalci* (The Weavers, after Gerhard Hauptmann, 1938); and Hába's three operas, *Matka* (The Mother, quarter-tone, 1927–30), *Nová země* (The New Land, half-tone, 1935–36), and *Přijď království Tvé* (Thy Kingdom Come, sixth-tone, 1939–42). *Matka*, the only one of Hába's three to see performance, became a flagship representative of the socialist half of the Czech avant-garde movement (see analysis in chapter 10).

As the community continued to enjoy the benefits of peacetime in the early 1930s, the inherent pluralism of the avant-garde did not cause substantial internal difficulties, and new works were welcomed with interest and mutual encouragement. As the Vačkář quotation demonstrates, however, tensions had increased by the middle of the decade, particularly with the dire state of affairs in Central European politics: in the final years of democracy, aesthetic issues would once again grow into causes worth fighting for. The second faction, the neoclassicist/populists, although seemingly innocuous—even frivolous—in their earliest stages in the late 1920s,[41] also came to stand for something much larger than their transparent orchestrations and danceable rhythms would suggest.

Bagatelles, Burlesques, and Madrigals: Neoclassicism and the Mánes Group

In the 1932/33 season, despite the best efforts of Hába and Očadlík, the Spolek pro moderní hudbu reached a financial breaking point and was forced to close down its concert and promotional activities. While the society continued to exist until 1939, membership seems to have been merely nominal, and before long, other societies rushed to fill the gap, not only to provide a consistent outlet for new music in Prague, but also to rectify the stagnancy of the Spolek. For Hába, as mentioned above, this meant membership in (and soon after, leadership of) the new music society Přítomnost, a move solidified by the production of an all-microtonal concert in 1933.[42] For those not inclined toward postexpressionist modernism and socialist politics, other arrangements would have to be made.

Already on December 16, 1932, a singular event announced a new phenomenon in Prague musical life. At the Mánes Art Exhibition hall, perched over the Vltava River between the embankment south of the National Theater and Slovanský Island, visitors were treated to a recital of songs by young composers, all set to texts by the Poetist Vítězslav Nezval. The Mánes Group, established in 1887 as a forum for progressive painters and sculptors, had long maintained connections to other disciplines within the arts, and welcomed any opportunity to interact with young musicians and poets, particularly with the evolution of the 1930s avant-garde. As the pianist Václav Holzknecht put it, "The Mánes artists loved music, and when the musicians complained that they were now quite nicely out on the sidewalk, [the artists] congenially offered that they perform at their establishment. It was arranged in a café and came about in the great exhibition hall among the paintings and sculptures. It had a strange charm and created quite a unique atmosphere."[43] The first evening's programming was significant, in that it included works by E. F. Burian, Jaroslav Ježek, Pavel Bořkovec, and Iša Krejčí, with piano accompaniment provided by Holzknecht. With the exception of Burian, whose interests lay elsewhere, these musicians formed the core of the so-called "Mánes Group" (Hudební skupina Mánesa), together with František Bartoš, whose music first appeared the following November, and Bohuslav Martinů, who was considered a corresponding member and stylistic role model. Over the next five years, the group put on sixteen concerts in the Mánes hall, and a further two besides, with the last concert (at the French Institute) taking place just three weeks before the Nazi occupation of Prague. The programming always reflected the oeuvres of the group's main members and their particular stylistic allegiances: compositions by Les Six, Satie, Prokofiev, Shostakovich, Stravinsky, Hindemith, and the young neoclassicist Pierre-Octave Ferroud figured prominently in their concerts. Interestingly, Schoenberg was represented only by *Pierrot lunaire* and Berg in a memorial concert (alongside Ferroud) by the Piano Sonata and Seven Early Songs; all dodecaphonic works were avoided. Missing too are works by Hába and his circle, as well as by older Czech composers (with the exception of a single melodrama by Ostrčil, who had always been an inspirational figure for the young avant-garde), thereby creating the atmosphere of a *salon des refusés*, albeit somewhat artificially, for the young musicians.

The composers of the Mánes Group were all of similar ages, having met while studying at the Prague Conservatory in the late 1920s. It is significant that, of the four, three had graduated from the masterclasses of Suk and Foerster, who had the reputation of fostering new directions in compositional style, often vastly different from their own; Krejčí, the group's unofficial leader, had studied with Novák, but disagreed with his teacher's aesthetic leanings and growing despotism (as evidenced in the former Spolek). With Martinů as their spiritual guide in absentia, all four composers espoused some form of neoclassicism, either in the adoption of baroque and classical forms, the use of transparent instrumental textures, or in their pervasive "objectivity" and antiromantic expressive content. Besides their association with visual artists, all four were actively involved with the literary avant-garde: their Nezval evening operated as somewhat of a manifesto, with many other instances of collaboration with Biebl, Halas, Seifert, and Hoffmeister in their collective output.

The young artists' interdisciplinary activity was not confined to their choice of song texts. Following Burian's example, each had designs on avant-garde theatrical productions of various types, although as the following portion of this chapter will show, only Ježek achieved any appreciable success in this field during the 1930s. More consistently, the members of the Mánes Group turned to music journalism: starting in the late 1920s, Krejčí, Bartoš, and Ježek wrote substantial amounts of music criticism for a variety of publications issued by leading lights of the left-wing literary avant-garde. For the five-year run of the publishing-house journal *Rozpravy Aventina*, the three composers shared duties in writing short reviews, almost all of which included aesthetic discussions sympathetic to their modernist, cosmopolitan viewpoint. In the early 1930s, Krejčí and Bartoš transferred their efforts to Melantrich's *Listy pro umění a kritiku*, and by the end of the decade, to *Tempo*, which had gradually lost its UB-bias under new editorship. Thus, for almost as long a time as Očadlík, Krejčí (the group's most voluble member) was able to express his views in print, spelling out a program for what he conceived to be a specifically Czech neoclassicism based on clearly defined models from at home and abroad.

Krejčí's 1926 contribution to the "*Wozzeck* Affair" has already been discussed in chapter 7; his dismissal of Berg's modernism in favor of Stravinsky and Milhaud's music as the most "representative works of the West" would form a pattern for much of the rest of his criticism. In the very same issue of *Rozpravy Aventina* he also reviewed Martinů's first Piano Concerto, which happily provided an occasion for his initial sketch for a Czech neoclassical movement. After some moderate criticism of the work, Krejčí continued:

> Classicism, however, cannot be reconstructed to the letter; today it does not suffice merely to attempt [to regain] balance of expression and form on the one hand, and a classical, absolute musicality and vocality on the other. The spirit [of these things] should remain, but one must also create a music and form that is *new*. This is a subtle reminder directed toward the first Czech reconstructive attempt that, through its eruptive musicality and temperament, rightfully deserved the brilliant applause that it received during its premiere.[44]

Early in 1927, Krejčí refined his assessment of Martinů in a review of the ballet *Kdo je na světě nejmocnější?* (Who Is the Most Powerful in the World?), which had just been premiered at the National Theater. Martinů's list of credits now included such honors as being "the first to break the calm surface of the post-war Smetana tradition" and "the first Czech proponent of Stravinsky," who had reformed modernism in the dual direction of jazz and objective, unsentimental classicism.[45] As we have seen throughout the history of music journalism in Prague, it was increasingly rare for critics of any cultural faction to make negative implications about the legacy of Smetana and its positive effect on contemporary Czech composition. Elsewhere, Krejčí was even more uninhibited in his criticism of the older generation of Czech composers who had suppressed any exploration of cosmopolitan modernism. In a review of Burian's October 1927 concert, he wrote that the composer "brings us the echo of today's Europe, against which our current compositional community is hermetically sealed, unable to extricate itself from the Suk-Foerster influence."[46] Overall, he despaired that musical tastes in Prague were passé (*passeistický*) and overly dependent on the post-Wagnerian legacy, even within modernism; moreover, conservative critics had forced Czech musicians into a position of mediocrity, where "they will lose the little they have."[47]

What Krejčí missed in Prague was another world of musical expression, about which he was equally vehement: the triumvirate of Stravinsky, Milhaud, and Prokofiev was for him unparalleled in the history of music, in that it abandoned romantic subjectivism in favor of absolute forms and the physiological effects of rhythm. "It is the *conditio sine qua non.* All the rest will come to the good musician of its own accord."[48] Acknowledging the inheritance of Hostinský's romantic nationalist thought and its prioritization of collective identity, Krejčí nevertheless asserted that Stravinsky's was "the understanding of music in the sense of modern collectivism, which has nothing to do with the spiritual collectivism of the romantics; it is the demand for absolute form in art, linked with the demand for an absolute purposefulness of art."[49] Furthermore, "the social function of music and its collectivism consists solely and uniquely in its emotive content, which is subject to the immediate physiological agents of rhythm and sound. . . . Without this physiological effect, no sensory emotion is possible. [Music] has no social function if it is not also *immediately* sonically effective at the same time."[50] His view of the collective was thus not one of identity at all (and certainly not the spiritual "paean" that Očadlík envisioned in Stravinsky) but of visceral action and reaction.

Krejčí was incredibly exacting in his application of these principles to the works of his contemporaries. Vycpálek's use of counterpoint in his epic *Cantata of the Last Things of Man* was praised, but its lack of rhythmic interest and harmonic coloration fell short of Stravinsky's polyrhythmic polyphony.[51] Even Křenek's *Jonny spielt auf,* so adored by Burian and his younger contemporaries throughout Europe, came under heavy fire from Krejčí for its lack of single aesthetic purpose: it was simply a "miš-maš" of influences from operetta and the music for silent films, and the composer's dependence on expressionism showed him to be a romantic individualist of the worst kind.[52] Perhaps most significantly, Krejčí deplored the totally ineffective use of melody, harmony, and rhythm in the music of Soviet composers at a Spolek concert in 1927: "it is interesting how nothing of the whirlwind of contemporary revolutions in the Russian Lands has touched these musicians, . . . and how they leave unnoticed even the European conquests of Igor Stravinsky."[53] This realization seems to have marked a turning point for the young neoclassicist, dividing his initial predilection for socialist politics from his ultimate ideological formulation, given above, which prioritized purity of form and directness of impact as the most important social function, superseding politics. It was this decision that, by the 1930s, helped to divide his modernist faction from that of Hába and Vít Nejedlý.

How, then, was a modernist composer to achieve his goals, according to Krejčí? For one, he/she was to take compositional models from the preromantic (or even preclassical) period, since this era was aesthetically the closest to the daily experience of contemporary Europe, as he frequently claimed. As a result, most of the output of the Mánes Group consists of small forms, such as keyboard dance suites (reflecting both Baroque and modern jazz-inspired dances), sets of variations, short song cycles, sonatas for solo instrument and piano, string quartets, and small woodwind chamber groups of various combinations. Titles such as *Bagately, Burlesky,* and *Madrigaly* abound in the concert listings at the Mánes Exhibition Hall.[54] Krejčí's miniaturism extended even toward his titles, whether as diminutives (*Symfonietta, Concertino*) or via the adjective "little," as in the *Malá smutečná hudba* (A Little Funeral Music). This last composition, performed numerous times in the 1930s, helped to earn Krejčí the epithet of "Mozartian" through its connection to both *Eine kleine Nachtmusik* and *Maurerische Trauermusik*; the jovial expressive style of his music, its transparent orchestration, and crisp articulations also contributed in this regard.

Mozart and, in particular, Gluck seem to have been Krejčí's yardsticks for aesthetic value, especially when discussing the theatrical or operatic work of his colleagues. Tellingly, he compared his teacher Novák's celebrated cantata *Bouře* with Mozart's expressive style and Gluck's sense of drama as elements from the past that have had a lasting influence on the present—with the remark that it would have been better, had Novák followed their example.[55] Although he agreed in principle with Wagner's unification of the arts for the creation of music drama, "the realization of the neoromantics does not suit us today. To continue in this direction would mean to beat music theater to death. Today we do not require that music be subject to the words and that it psychologize the drama through its motives, but rather that it strengthen the immediate theatrical impression through its *absolute* musical beauty: through its rhythm and sound."[56] The concrete result was to be a play with songs and dances, set in closed numbers with stylized declamation: a Gluck for the modern era, as it were. As with the plethora of chamber music described above, the Mánes composers' predilection for incidental music may have had a pragmatic as well as an ideological function: not only were there ample opportunities to collaborate with the literary and theatrical avant-garde throughout the 1930s, but as we have seen in previous chapters, it was becoming increasingly difficult for young composers to introduce new work on the main operatic stages of Prague. With the exception of Bořkovec, each of the composers contributed music to a variety of plays for popular theaters in Prague, to authors ranging from Sophocles, Shakespeare, and Molière to Cocteau and the modern Czech novelist Vančura, all with an eye toward providing alternative venues for new music.

Alongside the Mánes composers' attempt to regain the audience came an openness toward popular culture and its music. As is typical for neoclassicism, both in its earlier, Burian-centered history in Prague and in major European centers like Paris and Berlin, jazz figured highly in both the chamber and incidental music categories of composition, since it lent itself to small forms on the one hand, and to popular theatrical spectacle on the other. Indeed, jazz was close to Krejčí's aesthetic formulation for neoclassicism, since it provided a visceral rhythmic element whose multilayered complexity could be easily transferred to modernist music. Although Krejčí himself did not compose jazz-inspired pieces, he greatly supported those who did—indeed, the most popular and successful of all Prague neoclassicists—Ježek and Schulhoff.

Popular Music and the Interwar Czech Musical Identity: Schulhoff and Ježek

The development of popular music in the Prague musical community, in both its concert-hall and music-hall incarnations, closely paralleled the larger social tensions between nationalism and cosmopolitanism, between ideas of the modern and the traditional, that were running through Czech (and indeed European) society at that time. As we have seen in chapter 7, jazz impacted the city's art musicians, in one form or another, all the way from the earliest days of independence, and by the late 1920s had become the single-most important musical influence from abroad. Through its strong connection to neoclassicism and its sheer popularity, the new music from America came to define Vačkář's "second group" of avant-garde Prague composers in the 1930s who appealed to the audience through accessible music, even if not every composition evoked jazz. In fact, their cosmopolitanism was not undifferentiated in its assimilation of popular elements, and the resulting stylistic variety revealed the breadth of associations this music had for musicians and audiences in interwar Prague.

The intersection of art musicians of the First Republic with jazz was a somewhat different story than the experience of the general public. As with the musical communities of other European centers after 1918, the younger generation was the one to be transfixed by the novelty of the cultural import from America, symbolizing as it did modernity, exoticism, frivolity, a sense of freedom, and the negation of the old. Jazz was also one of the strongest elements of the modern musical world that urged its participants into a cosmopolitan relationship with international culture, in a way totally unlike anything from the realm of art music. As we have seen with the foregoing discussion of Burian, the attitude of creative artists in Prague toward jazz involved its use as a tool within the context of European modernism, mostly assimilated into the vocabulary of Stravinskian neoclassicism and/or dadaism. The connections between neoclassicism and the European conception of jazz were manifold, particularly evident in the short dances and simple forms common to both, but also in the mutual sense of antiromanticism and asceticism. Most European jazz compositions, if not for solo piano, involved almost exclusively traditional orchestral instruments. With notable exceptions (particularly Ježek), few composers attempted to replicate the sound, instrumentation, structure, or even the improvisational technique of jazz, opting instead to incorporate syncopated rhythms, major/minor-third alternations, and riff-like instrumental solos—in essence, only the most external characteristics of the music. Martinů, whose experimentation with jazz took place almost entirely during his extended Parisian sojourn (1923–40), created convincing replications of modern dances (as in *La Revue de cuisine* and the Sextet for winds and piano) using instruments from the realm of art music almost exclusively. His use of jazz-inspired elements was closely tied to his admiration for the work of Les Six and Stravinsky. Martinů's characteristic folk-like style, in which angular rhythms are blended with a neoclassical clarity, also complicates the picture, in that certain rhythmic or melodic devices may stem from one of several possible sources of inspiration. As the problematic reception of the composer's *Half-time* at the 1925 Prague ISCM shows, both the work's jazz-like elements and its neoclassical influences were still difficult for the Czech critics to accept fully, despite the widespread fascination for both French culture and jazz at the time.[57]

At the same time as American popular music was making its first postwar forays into the Czech Lands, Erwin Schulhoff was touring Germany with several of his own virtuoso piano compositions based on popular dance types. Born in Prague to a prosperous German-Jewish family with a musical background,[58] throughout his career Schulhoff gradually transferred his allegiance to the Czech community, whose younger members were receptive to both his concert and popular music. Much of the populist side of Schulhoff's creative inspiration came as a result of his anti-establishmentarian tendencies, as well as his involvement with the Dada movement in Leipzig during his student years, 1919–22. Jazz-influenced works such as *Pittoresken, Ironien,* and the *Jazz-Suite für Kammerorchester,* composed during this period, may even have served as a populist counterpart to his ongoing predilection for Viennese expressionism, another byproduct of his studies.[59] Although it would take some time after Schulhoff's return to Prague in October 1923 before his jazz-dance pieces were fully accepted in the Prague musical community, the parallel to the slightly younger Burian, with their mutual connections to Dadaist circles, is striking. Much less were Schulhoff's efforts held to be acceptable by the German-Bohemians of the city, whose beleaguered position in the 1920s had induced a certain cultural openness (see chapter 5), but who were still unwilling to welcome a modernist jazz composer as one of their own. Despite his compositional and pianistic brilliance, he was refused a teaching position by the Deutsche Akademie für Musik und darstellende Kunst (presumably by the rector at that time, Zemlinsky, although this fact is not certain), leading him with increasingly greater certainty toward the Czech musical community, among which he was beginning to find valuable friends.[60] By the early 1930s, Schulhoff's name had appeared with much more frequency in the context of Czech cultural endeavors, including appearances as a pianist in Burian's Voice-band, Hába's quarter-tone masterclass (whose students' music Schulhoff propagated both at home and abroad), and Ježek's jazz orchestra at the Osvobozené divadlo, than among the

German-Bohemians.[61] To the latter's efforts he contributed articles on jazz and contemporary aesthetics to Steinhard's *Der Auftakt,* and after the departure of Zemlinsky from the Deutsche Akademie in 1927, forged a good relationship with his replacement, the German-Bohemian composer Fidelio F. Finke. Over the course of the interwar period, Schulhoff continued to use jazz as a means of expression, alternating with substantial forays into non-jazz-influenced neoclassicism and expressionism (as evinced by his numerous keyboard suites and the Schoenbergian opera *Flammen* of 1932, respectively). While his use of jazz was more extensive and thorough than that of Martinů or Burian, particularly in its application to the piano idiom, in the majority of his ensemble works Schulhoff, like his contemporaries, avoided replicating the instrumentation and idiomatic techniques of a jazz orchestra.

The 1930 jazz oratorio *H.M.S. Royal Oak* was the only one of Schulhoff's large-scale works that did not use European instrumentation as a means to distance the new composition from the jazz band as the original medium of inspiration.[62] The specific orchestra in the work is based on the model of Paul Whiteman, who by this point was no longer *en vogue*, even among Europeans: the instrumentation consisted of soprano, alto, and tenor saxophones (doubling on clarinets), two trombones, sousaphone, percussion, piano, celesta, banjo, and two accordions. Over the course of the thin dramatic action, which takes place during a mutiny on a cruiser where the captain has forbidden his sailors to play jazz, Schulhoff inserted a series of tangos, slowfoxes, waltzes, and sentimental songs that reflected back to the cabarets of a decade before. The "Hawaiian song" for tenor and orchestra, for instance, uses brasses and saxophones in a monotonous blend of repetitive gestures, over which the singer delivers a lyrical melody with self-consciously mundane German and English lyrics: from the dramatic context, however, it is not clear whether the overt sentimentality is meant ironically, as in *Bubu z Montparnassu* and *Mahagonny*, or to be taken on its own (Whitemanesque) terms. More intriguing is the "Rezitazione e fox-fugato," which describes the moment of mutiny both textually and musically. After an initial melodrama, beneath which the orchestra performs a series of erratic staccato chords (imitating the "shots" of a jazz band), Schulhoff presents a lengthy fugato that seems directly inspired by the famous contrapuntal passage in Milhaud's *La Création du Monde* from 1923. Unlike Milhaud, Schulhoff's "fox-fugato" uses no syncopation or blue notes in its subject, and the combined effect of all the fugal entries produces a terse, neoclassical effect rather than one of collective improvisation. Unfortunately for the composer, his attempt to wed somewhat old-fashioned jazz techniques with oratorio, a genre with a slim connection to drama or spectacle even historically, did not end in the success he had hoped for, and three productions (two of them for radio) became the extent of *Royal Oak*'s fate.[63] By the early 1930s, like many of his contemporaries including Martinů, Schulhoff virtually abandoned jazz as a stimulus, turning instead to a more aggressively socialist stance and large-scale symphonic genres, as seen with *Manifest* and the Third Symphony (which depicts the 1935 hunger riots in eastern Slovakia). In the final analysis, Schulhoff found, as did others such as Milhaud, that the hybrid between jazz and European concert music had a limited life span, dependent almost entirely on the fashion of the day and the open-mindedness of the concertgoing audience.

In contrast to Schulhoff, Burian, and Martinů, Jaroslav Ježek continued to use jazz to the end of his life, either as an element in the context of art-music compositions (such as the late works for piano, 1940–42), or more notably, as a replication of American jazz as heard on imported recordings and films, or the occasional live performance. Perhaps more than any other composer, Ježek's oeuvre consistently encapsulated the efforts of the Prague avant-garde to recapture their audience through more accessible artistic statements. As Holzknecht recounted, Ježek's fascination with jazz, whether in its American or subsequent European forms, started extraordinarily early in his career: at his Conservatory audition in 1925 he boldly chose to perform the "Boston" from Hindemith's *Suite 1922*, a composer and work not accepted by the establishment at that point.[64] Prior to his graduation in 1928, alongside a series of compositions in more traditional genres (which, like the 1927 Piano Concerto, contained references to jazz), Ježek had already turned to popular music in the form of contributions to numerous stage works. Starting in 1927, he composed incidental music for, among others, Cocteau's *Les Mariés de la Tour Eiffel* (performed as *Svatebčané na Eiffelce* at the Divadlo Dada with Burian in the cast), Goll's *Assurance contre le suicide* (*Pojištění proti sebevraždě*), and G. K. Chesterton's *The Man Who Was Thursday* (*Kamarád Čtvrtek*), to which he added both traditional preludes and interludes as well as modern dances. While many of the basic elements of the jazz idiom were in place at this time in his oeuvre, his expressive style in these early works had more in common with the prevailing European ideas of light dance music than with a replication of American jazz. Indeed, references to various forms of Czech pre-jazz popular music, such as marches, waltzes, and polkas, would always appear in contrast to his more concentrated jazz efforts. In this respect, the young composer's 1928 trip to Paris served to acquaint him with a multiplicity of new sounds and influences, learned directly from live bands and the latest recordings.

Ježek's limitations with regard to assimilating the sounds of jazz were similar to those of most enthusiasts in Prague, who could hear American bands only by undertaking a trip to West European cities, or less expensively, by listening to the recordings distributed throughout Europe at this time by American recording companies. Within this context, Ježek's music stands apart from that of his contemporaries in his reception of imported jazz and American culture, in that his study of recordings is well documented.[65] Indeed, over the next ten years, Ježek's assimilation of jazz elements into most of his compositions went beyond the majority of European efforts at this time, transcending the bounds of mere mimicry. Returning from Paris, he continued his work with avant-garde theater, composing incidental music for the comedian duo of Jiří Voskovec and Jan

Werich, both formerly of Devětsil. Their organization, called Osvobozené divadlo or Liberated Theater, began in the mid-1920s with shows to music by a variety of composers; after Ježek signed on in 1928, they became the single-most successful and popular theatrical attraction in Prague over a ten-year period, and are still considered an integral component of interwar Czech culture to this day. Voskovec and Werich presented witty political satires that lampooned the latest trends in European society, to the accompaniment of jazz-inspired songs and dances. In his music for the theater's jazz orchestra, one can witness Ježek's effort to put a subjective stamp on this music, creating a sense of agency that went against the depersonalizing trend that attracted so many neoclassists to popular music in the first place. The portrait of Czech life presented by the Osvobozené divadlo, while decidedly left-wing, was just as firmly Western and cosmopolitan in its outlook, largely as a result of Ježek's music. As the 1930s and the First Republic drew to a close, the theater's repertoire, both dramatically and musically, paralleled the resurgence of nationalism in Czech culture, often in direct opposition to the threat of fascism both within and outside their borders.

Ježek not only was an avid collector of American jazz recordings, he also internalized the gestures and nuances of jazz to such an extent that he was able to transfer that language as a whole to a multitude of new compositions. In cooperation with Voskovec and Werich, Ježek enlarged the theater's occasional musical ensemble into a permanent jazz orchestra, equipped to play more music than was customary for the average stage play. Invaluably, the composer had access to a real performing ensemble on a long-term basis, such that he could experiment with the jazz idiom over the progression of a whole decade.[66] Ježek, then, seems to fall into a distinct category of one who was trying to replicate the jazz idiom *as a whole* (with jazz musicians rather than classical ones), in its most current form from up-to-date recordings. This attitude also meant a continuous revision of his gestural and orchestrational language over the course of his decade at the Osvobozené divadlo, from his initial models of Paul Whiteman and Jack Hylton to an appreciation for Duke Ellington and Benny Goodman in the 1930s. The result was one of the closest examinations of American culture in Central Europe during the interwar period.

Between 1928 and 1938, Ježek supplied the music for twenty plays, each co-written by (and starring) Voskovec and Werich (see table 9.1). After the unanticipated popularity of Ježek's entr'actes for the first two, *Premiéra Skafandr* (which included the foxtrot "Tři strážníci," his first hit song) and *Líčení se odročuje*, the comedians decided to take a risk in creating a genre altogether new to Prague audiences. With the premiere of *Fata Morgana* in December 1929, the *jazzová revue* was born, in which music, dance, and film merged with a sharper level of political and cultural satire. Not only did Ježek's ensemble play more often during the dramatic action, but much of the dance music was performed on the stage itself, alongside the newly organized "Jenčíkovy Girls," a troupe of modern dancers named after the avant-garde choreographer, Joe Jenčík.[67] The success of

Table 9.1. Ježek's collaborations with Voskovec and Werich at the Osvobozené divadlo

	Title	Translation	Premiere	Performances
1	*Premiéra Skafandr*	The Diving Suit Premiere	October 12, 1928	61
2	*Líčení se odročuje*	Court is Adjourned	October 19, 1929	37
3	*Fata Morgana*	—	December 10, 1929	117
4	*Ostrov Dynamit*	Dynamite Island	March 11, 1930	101
5	*Sever proti jihu*	North Against South	September 1, 1930	158
6	*Don Juan & Comp.*	—	January 13, 1931	114
7	*Golem*	—	November 4, 1931	186
8	*Caesar*	—	March 8, 1932	191
9	*Robin zbojník*	Robin Hood	November 23, 1932	82
10	*Svět za mřížemi*	World Behind Bars	January 24, 1933	167
11	*Osel a stín*	The Ass and the Shadow	October 13, 1933	187
12	*Slaměný klobouk*	Straw Hat	February 27, 1934	83
13	*Kat a blázen*	Hangman and Madman	October 19, 1934	115
14	*Vždy s úsměvem*	Always with a Smile	January 1, 1935	108
15	*Panoptikum*	The Wax Museum	April 9, 1935	120
16	*Balada z hadrů*	Ballad from Rags	November 28, 1935	245
17	*Nebe na zemi*	Heaven on Earth	September 23, 1936	107
18	*Rub a líc*	Heads or Tails	December 18, 1936	189
19	*Těžká Barbora*	Heavy Barbara	November 5, 1937	179
20	*Pěst na oko aneb Caesarovo finale*	A Fist in the Eye, or Caesar's Finale	April 8, 1938	90
[21]	*Hlava proti Mihuli*	Hlava vs. Mihule	1938/39	0[1]
Films	*Pudr a benzín*	Greasepaint and Gasoline	1931[2]	
	Peníze nebo život	Your Money or Your Life	1932	
	Hej, rup!	Hip Hip Hooray	1934	
	Svět patří nám	The World Belongs to Us	1937	

[1] *Hlava proti Mihuli* was scheduled for performance when both comedians and composer were forced to flee to America in 1939: Ježek's music, already in rehearsal at the time, does not survive.
[2] The films of Voskovec and Werich used music by Ježek, mostly recycled from earlier plays, or vice versa.

the combination was absolute, with 117 performances and a degree of popularity to ensure ongoing public interest in their theatrical venture. Of the remaining seventeen jazz revues, only two productions stopped before a hundred performances, with the most successful, *Balada z hadrů*, reaching 245.

Ježek's contributions continued to revolve around set pieces, either preludes, interludes, or dances, as well as an increasing number of songs, usually performed by the main duo of Voskovec and Werich. These songs, while often in the style of one of the popular dances (such as blues, foxtrots, or the perennial favorite "Mercedes-tango" from *Sever proti jihu*), also included a large number of waltzes, comic cabaret songs, operatic parodies, and significantly, marches. This last category, mostly satirical in nature (such as the "March of the 100% Men" from *Golem*), grew to immense popularity in the late 1930s and during the Nazi occupation as a result of their antifascist lyrics, and represents not so much a stylistic retrenchment as a reflection of the growing nationalist feeling in Prague at the time. The predominance of so many songs meant that Ježek's music was necessarily subservient to the demands of the comedians' text. One of the most common places for Ježek's orchestra to demonstrate their prowess in jazz during the vocal numbers, however, was in the interludes between the verses, which generally occurred alongside shorter lyrics. In these, the listener would get a brief vignette of the jazz world, which in each case would appear as an instrumental variation upon the vocal melody immediately previous. It should be noted, however, that like most European jazz composers, Ježek almost always shied away from letting his instrumentalists improvise. Thus, even in the richly soloistic texture of the later songs and dances, audible in the many recordings cut for Ultraphon in the 1930s, the listener hears the illusion of improvisation, behind which lies a greater sense of compositional control.[68]

The significant body of purely instrumental numbers for the jazz orchestra of the Osvobozené divadlo, interspersed throughout the plays as preludes and dances for the chorus of Jenčíkovy Girls, was at the heart of Ježek's unfettered exploration of the jazz idiom. Without the constraints of a text or the necessity of balancing against a solo voice, the composer could more closely approximate the formal techniques of an American jazz band: namely, the introduction of a head, its subsequent elaboration by a series of soloists or sections of the combo, and the full return of the head to finish off the piece. Interestingly, Ježek gave English titles to most of these preludes and dances, such as "Spring on Broadway," "Rubbish Heap Blues," "City Lights," and "Echoes of the Music Hall," which conjured up scenes of urban America in a manner quite unrelated to the Czech satirical plays of which they were a part. In the absence of any specific link to the plots at hand, such instrumental numbers could easily have been written independently from their use in the theater, and as such may be taken to represent their composer's personal communion with American culture.[69]

Throughout Ježek's instrumental jazz repertoire, it is difficult to pinpoint the exact American sources of inspiration for the individual pieces, most of which represent a blend of assimilated gestures and techniques. A select few, however, stand apart, in that their American antecedents can be easily identified. The "Carioca" from *Kat a blázen* is directly modeled on the similar dance by that name from the 1933 movie *Flying Down to Rio* with music by Vincent Youmans. In the film, an American audience is treated to this Brazilian showpiece, wherein the dancing couples must keep their foreheads touching at all times; a surviving photograph from the Osvobozené divadlo shows that this choreographic detail was retained in its performance by the Jenčíkovy Girls.[70] A comparison between the two Cariocas reveals much more: not only did Ježek assimilate the specific musical traits of Youmans's Carioca to a startling degree of accuracy, but he also synthesized these elements to create a composition of much greater dramatic scope. While Youmans's Carioca is made up of a series of repeated musical units with no substantial ongoing variation, Ježek employed an intricate web of tonal and textural changes, with dramatic transitions between the sections. Ježek also changed the sound of the jazz orchestra in his Carioca from Youmans's model, which included flutes, clarinets, and a large string section. Conversely, Ježek's ensemble is dominated by trumpets and saxophones, which play off each other in a close-knit antiphony, a technique completely in line with arrangement techniques developed by Fletcher Henderson and others in the early 1930s. The surface similarities between the two Cariocas are many, not least of which is the pervading rumba rhythm, an element especially pronounced in Ježek's work. Evidently, Ježek sought to reinterpret this inherited musical vocabulary for his own creative ends: in his hands, the Carioca was transformed from a mildly flirtatious showpiece into a highly nuanced composition whose dramatic trajectory continues unabated throughout.

As an anonymous reviewer in *Rozpravy Aventina* described the music of the Osvobozené divadlo in 1930:

> Music is truly the element that makes this revue an international revue, since Ježek used American models in the creation of his orchestra and in the composing of pieces. He did not dwell on them, but took them only as a model, from which he could continue further into altogether new forms that can be defined as "Americo-Czech."[71]

The blending of stylistic elements from two widely divergent cultures in Ježek's music contributed to the larger artistic movement toward cosmopolitanism among the younger composers in Prague in the 1930s. While his music for jazz orchestra was one of the closest readings of American culture in the European context, he still included musical nuances that his audience perceived as markers of "Czechness," particularly in the antifascist march songs, but also in the hot and bluesy compositions. These nuances—particularly where the harmonic underpinning is mostly derived from a chromatic European vocabulary rather than a blues scale—only occasionally detract from their appreciation as full-fledged jazz band compositions. Ježek's lasting commitment to jazz reveals not only his personal love of the music, which extended beyond mere fashion, but also the attempt to make it part of modern Czech culture, indigenized instead of merely imported. In this, Ježek and the Osvobozené divadlo succeeded: the musical and theatrical portrait of interwar Czech cosmopolitanism they presented achieved a prodemocratic, nationalist significance. Ježek's role as purveyor of "Czech jazz" was further heightened to heroic status by the young composer's death in American exile during the Nazi occupation.

That this overtly populist oeuvre met with respect and even admiration among the other members of the Prague avant-garde musical circle is one of its most remarkable aspects, speaking to the lack of clear delineation between popular and art music in the early 1930s. Indeed, Ježek was always considered a full member of the art music community and an integral participant of the Mánes Group, where his "serious" compositions were routinely performed. As such, the music of Ježek, Schulhoff, and their colleagues added significantly to the ongoing debate between the role of modernist music as accessible entertainment and its potential to heal the ills of society. With the escalating political crisis in Central Europe, however, what had begun as a difference of opinion would develop into a full-blown polemic in the avant-garde music press—debated with a passion that betrayed the seriousness of the larger social situation—over the role of popular and art musics in modern Czech culture.

Rytmus, Popular Music, and the 1935 ISCM

The two factions of the Prague avant-garde having staked out their respective ideological territories, the debate regarding the direction of modern music remained at a standstill throughout much of the early 1930s. With the young compositional community more or less unified by a larger common goal, they were able to ignore dissenting, reactionary voices from outside their circle, such as Šilhan, who continued to provoke individuals (notably Očadlík) in the daily press. Očadlík's own publication, *Klíč*, folded in 1934 after only four years; its energetic and often hostile stance had not been appreciated by the older members of the establishment, and by and large, its content had failed to provide solid answers to the many questions it raised. Without an internal provocation to stimulate the debate further, it took outside political events to rouse the Prague musical community to take a stand against a perceived threat. The rise of German nationalism and the near disruption of the 1935 ISCM festival served to rekindle debates about the social role of Czech modernism, and subsequently, about the place of popular culture in the realm of art.

A year after the victory of National Socialism in Germany, 1934 saw the legalization of Konrad Henlein's *Sudetendeutsche Partei*, a fascist organization with direct ties to Hitler's government in Berlin. Henlein's machinations would prove to be sufficient justification for the takeover of the Czech border region at the Munich Conference four years later, thereby bringing the First Republic regime to an end. By the 1935 elections, many communities in these German-dominated areas, including the sizable spa town of Karlovy Vary (known internationally as Karlsbad), had elected SdP (Sudeten-German Party) representatives to the Czechoslovak parliament. Karlovy Vary had been selected by the 1934 ISCM jury as the site for the following year, beating out Brussels and Berlin, whose contingent had since boycotted the ISCM entirely, setting up its own parallel new-music society with a concurrent festival in Vichy.[72] Out of sheer political provocation, the German-Bohemian Karlovy Vary town council canceled its agreement with the 1935 ISCM a mere ten weeks before the festival was to take place. The musical organizers, Alois Hába, A. J. Patzaková, and Erich Steinhard, valiantly attempted to save the festival by shifting it to Prague, where an entirely new set of venues and performers would have to be contracted. Unable to get support in time for the original schedule, they were at the point of canceling entirely when Edward Dent, the ISCM president, agreed to a postponement from mid-summer to September. Financial support was pledged by MŠANO and the festival went forward successfully. Flush with victory and unified with a new sense of purpose, Hába's new music organization Přítomnost, which now represented the Czech portion of the ISCM's Czechoslovak section in place of the older Spolek, began to publish the influential journal *Rytmus* immediately prior to the 1935 ISCM. In many respects, *Rytmus* continued the work of *Klíč*, albeit with a less pugilistic stance than that taken by Očadlík in the earlier publication.

After the success of the ISCM, provocation continued to come from outside the community to stir opinions in Prague regarding the direction of new music, its interaction with popular music, and the public it was supposedly meant to address. The stimulus came from Frank Warschauer, a German-born film and theater critic who sought asylum in Prague after the start of the Third Reich. Within days of the festival's conclusion, Warschauer published the lengthy article "Music in a Deadlock (The Music Festival in Prague)" in the Czech-language cultural journal *Přítomnost* (not to be confused with Hába's group of the same name).[73] While the author congratulated the organizers for having succeeded in presenting the festival under such difficult political circumstances, the general tone of the article was one of reaction to modernism, warning composers not to feel too comfortable in the sheltered world of the ISCM, where the good reception of a work did not represent the prevailing attitude in society. Modern people were emotionally different from what modernist composers implied in their music, Warschauer claimed, and the public strongly desired to have their "living feelings" reflected in the music of their time. Typical of this distance was the fact that jazz, which had affected the course of art music only temporarily, had continued on, not as an integrated whole with art music, but as a distinct musical field with a closer connection to society. Warschauer concluded that it was the fault of modernist composers for not having bridged this gap when they had the opportunity to do so:

> Decidedly, however, we will only be able to speak about the success of modern music when it succeeds not just in filling a single concert hall, but when it penetrates among the multitudes of people again and becomes a component of their immediate consciousness and of their elementary musical expressions. In this sense, returning to the international festival, the creator of the *Lulu Suite* is an interesting musician. A modern composer in the sense that I just endeavored to explain, however, he absolutely is not. And similarly with so many other composers who brought us music that is certainly new, but absolutely not modern.[74]

One of the most interesting aspects of Warschauer's article was his claim that all of the modern music presented at the ISCM festival fell into one of two camps: either the composers wished to evoke light dance music, or they wanted to serve a political/revolutionary goal. While Warschauer's binarism is an extraordinary simplification, especially with regard to the wider representation from across Europe at the festival, it is strikingly close to Vačkář's formulation cited earlier. This binarism was one of the main points countered in the rebuttal of Hába's student Karel Reiner to Warschauer in the second issue of *Rytmus*. Claiming that the nonmusician had simply misunderstood many basic concepts (such as form, the athematic style, and dodecaphony), Reiner felt Warschauer's delineation of modernist camps had no basis in reality. While Reiner did well to expose the many weak points of his opponent's argument, his rebuttal failed to answer the key issues: rather he reinforced the distance between art and popular musics, claiming that "contemporary composers . . . turned away from jazz and similar trends and as such fight with all their strength for the purity of music."[75] Furthermore, he did his utmost to alienate any dissenting voices with his final statement, whose tone, at once socialist and nationalist, was increasingly characteristic of the avant-garde in the late 1930s:

> Czechoslovak musicians and the Czechoslovak public are not given to deception by such slogans and thus do not let themselves be brought to chaos by the destructiveness of irresponsible elements, who through their snobbery themselves have assisted the arguments of today's German regime against cultural bolshevism. They [i.e., the musicians and public] will find their path through constructive strengths and positive acts, preordained for them not only by a great and free tradition, but also by healthy thinking.[76]

As a close member of the Hába circle, Reiner's words demonstrate the importance they placed on political engagement as a crucial, defining component of art, particularly in a fragile democratic society: in retrospect, it also reveals how far these utopian dreams were from being accepted and realized amid that society, disillusioned as it was.

It is within this context, then, that Dalibor Vačkář proposed his delineation between two streams of socially conscious composers, the politically minded and the neoclassicist/populists, each of whom approached the issue of social function from opposing sides within modernism. Although the boundaries were certainly porous, Vačkář named Vít Nejedlý as the leader of the faction that upheld the social collective through tendentially oriented music, while Iša Krejčí represented those who felt that the immediacy of untendential, absolute music fulfilled a social function in and of itself. Nejedlý responded immediately in *Rytmus*, asserting that, while Vačkář had been correct in his basic delineation of the factions, he had missed the point that each viewpoint was descended from the ancient struggle between idealism and materialism.[77] For Nejedlý, the creation of art revolved around the relationship of the artist to the collective, working within the context of the class struggle toward the foundation of a new organization of society; whoever seeks to understand this reality must do so from within the struggle of life, rather than from the clouds (where he implied Vačkář, or perhaps Krejčí, was situated). Although it may seem natural that the son of Zdeněk Nejedlý should openly use Marxist terminology within the debate on musical modernism, so too is it indicative of the general level of engagement in the Prague avant-garde community.[78] For his part, Krejčí responded indirectly, with a further contribution to the debate the following year, regarding the interpenetration of popular and art musics, a discussion that continued simultaneously with Vačkář's.

Later that year, the debate on popular music took on a life of its own, reaching polemic proportions that had long been fueled by the success of jazz, Burian, and Ježek. "Does Light Music Exist?" asked Václav E. Babka in the title of his provocative essay for *Tempo* in December 1935.[79] Babka's viewpoint is one of outright snobbery toward populism in general, which he considered a threat to the world of art inflicted by technology and modern society; the fault lay squarely on the shoulders of society, not technology (in this case the radio) directly. Light music and its composers could not even bear the blame, since Babka neither considered it "music" nor its creators "composers." He proceeded in this condescending tone, concluding, "there really is no bad, light-weight, or simple music. There are just bad, light-weight, or simple listeners of that which is mistakenly called music."[80] It is unclear why a journal as professional as *Tempo* would consider running Babka's blatantly inflammatory text, if not simply to attract controversy and readership.

The responses to "Does Light Music Exist?" poured in to *Tempo* over the six months following its publication. The theorist František Sehnal replied with an even-tempered tone, reasoning that music could not be "light" from an aesthetic point of view: the differences between the two worlds lay in the binarism of abstraction versus what he termed "aesthetic primitivism."[81] The widespread popularity of dance, he claimed, was the result of a taste for physical movement among "people who think simply," for whom the appreciation of art music had likely been a struggle ending in failure. Thus, in Sehnal's eyes, the encroachment of popular music also represented a social, moral problem for the musical community itself: "Where are those who see the aesthetic and spiritual want of non-musicians? . . . Where is their conscience? It is very convenient to blame another for this lack."[82] The Brno composer Pavel Haas responded even more reasonably, saying that the distinction should not be made regarding the existence or propriety of popular music at all, but rather between good and bad production of it, since good-quality jazz had long been known to have made a significant contribution to the development of art music. Poor-quality popular music, however, was damaging in its destruction of public taste, "leading to laziness of thought and directly to stupid-mechanical perception," a phenomenon that was by no means a product of the twentieth century.[83] The editor of *Tempo*, Jaroslav Tomášek, continued this paternalistic attitude toward the listening public:

> Today it is clear that it is impossible to leave the broad social strata to their natural instincts in the things of intellectual culture without the danger that they will wander into the tortuous labyrinth of contemporary pseudo-culture. . . . [Nevertheless,] the developmental order of the world allows even uncultured errors the right to life. In this consists the dramatic tension of cultural development.[84]

The attitude that artists were responsible for the cultural salvation of the masses appeared, albeit somewhat indirectly, in the contributions of Jirák and Warschauer, who, being perhaps more in touch with the listening habits of the average resident of Prague, had fewer idealistic illusions in this regard. As the music director of Czechoslovak Radio, Jirák could introduce statistical percentages of listenership into the discussion, thereby revealing the full picture of what he termed "a poor state" that not even the radio could fix after "dozens of generations of neglect."[85] Agreeing with Sehnal, Jirák noted that the neglect of mass cultural education had produced "so many people who directly hate art music. *Here*, sirs, next to the general 'moral sickness,' is the root of the musical need."[86] Jirák's attitude was one of reconciliation with popular culture for the sake of social reconstruction; similarly, Warschauer, as a film critic, had less at stake in the preservation of a tradition of art music, and advocated an awareness of the means by which popular artists communicated with their audience. Warschauer insisted, like Haas, Tomášek, and Jirák before him, on a reclassification of the musical world, now under one single aesthetic category, such that all genres be judged by the same qualitative criteria, thereby eliminating what he termed a "double morality in music."[87] Siding with Jirák in the defense of radio against Babka's charge of social corruption, he saw in the recent increase in popular music production a reflection of a wider level of society that had found a political and social voice in the new technology. As such, it was undemocratic to ignore the tastes of what could be considered a new audience. Quite prophetically, Warschauer declared:

Whoever does not look for a way to the masses, but wants only to function in a small, limited circle, will gradually become quite an indifferent character and the world sooner or later will stop being concerned with him. The era has created the political and technical means that enable a musician to turn to everyone. If he does not act thus, he becomes an anachronism.[88]

Thus, the social responsibility of the modern artist, up to this point primarily understood in the context of the Cultural Revival, was turned back on the artists themselves, not as a responsibility to save society, but as a responsibility to themselves, not to be left behind; for an artist ignored by society could never hope to represent it in the cultural sphere.

Once Iša Krejčí responded to *Tempo* in early 1937, the musical representation of a greater cross-section of the listening public became the prime focus of the debate, marking its last stage during the First Republic. Entitled "Folk Song and Hit Song," Krejčí's essay contended that the sole mission of any type of music should be to give joy to the listener through sound and rhythm; it was a more populist version of his earlier aesthetic writings. The only differentiation between art and popular musics, by his reasoning, was that the latter was satisfied by this one criterion, whereas art music sought "to communicate to the perceptive listener the finest nuances of an internal emotional world."[89] The internal/external binarism in this rhetoric is strongly reminiscent of Hostinský's *důslednost* and *náladovost*, with the important exception that Krejčí sought to put the latter on an equal footing. The problem was that much of musical modernism had lost its all-important communicative basis and therefore the immediacy of its effect; thus, it was "silly to want modern music to approach life by artificially cramming a social or some other kind of idea or tendency into it."[90] While the epitome of social immediacy in music during the past century, the folk song, was no longer able to speak to the modern public, its modern counterpart, the hit song, had retained that ability, since "today's folk expression is typically an urban expression."[91] For Krejčí, the current market of dance music, despite having the appearance of an industrial workshop producing goods on demand, was at least able to guard music against "paper academicism," which led only to artistic reactionism. Thus, those composers who had successfully incorporated modern popular music into their compositional vocabulary, such as Stravinsky and Ježek, were truly modern artists in touch with the needs of society. Krejčí's particular defense of Ježek, whose work had long lain just below the surface of the entire debate, struck a chord of nationalism and political activism that had slowly become a significant factor in the identity formation of the younger generation:

Where today will you find so much primary inventiveness and so much immediate, physiological bewitching of the senses through refined and highly cultivated compositional technique as in Ježek's work? You say that the modern artist must not stand apart from the era and its political or social struggles and you are right. Who, however, has fought through their art for the progressive efforts of our society and against fascist reaction more than he? And in this way his art is modern, refined, completely individual, and *Czech*. . . . Say if there can be a more Czech music.[92]

Although neither Krejčí's justification for the espousal of modern popular music nor his nationalistic description of Ježek passed without rebuttal from other members of the Czech critical community, it is interesting that such a bald-faced chauvinist statement could even have arisen after a decade of cosmopolitanism and objectivity.[93] That Krejčí's expression of nationalism was a credo of both cosmopolitan and modernist aesthetics was symptomatic of the growing social and political tensions under which he was living. As the democratic era of the First Republic drew to a close, composers, critics, and their public would increasingly have to take a stand on political issues of which they were a part, but over which they ultimately had no control.

"A Little Bit to the Right": Nationalism, Socialism, and Antifascism in the Late 1930s

Political tensions, both within and outside the Czechoslovak state, forced the rise of Czech and German-Bohemian nationalism in the late 1930s to a degree not seen since the First World War and the early, patriotic years of the First Republic. This nationalism, however, was altogether different from that of previous generations, in that the phenomenon of fascism colored sentiments on both sides: for the majority of German-Bohemians (now self-identified as Sudeten Germans), fascism became a call for empowerment and unification with greater Germany, while for most Czechs, antifascism became an integral part of cultural identity. In the Czech musical community, this new resurgence of nationalism was still connected to the rhetoric of modernism and the social responsibility of art, albeit by the mid 1930s these issues had come to be seen through the lens of socialism and cosmopolitan avant-garde aesthetics. With the relatively unified ideological stance of the younger generation, the factional divide that had existed since the 1870s, after being prolonged an excruciatingly long time at the hands of Zdeněk Nejedlý, had seemingly moved far into the background. Curiously however, the explosion of political and cultural tensions in the late 1930s also brought about a recurrence of Nejedlianism, forming another parallel to the highly charged atmosphere of the pre-independence years, now cloaked in the new nationalism as the days of democracy came to a close.

Mention has already been made of the type of nationalism expressed in Ježek's jazz revues for the Osvobozené divadlo and their blend of antifascism and populism. The political statements in Voskovec and Werich's plays were directed quite specifically to the worsening international situation, and often had direct repercussions with regard to the reception of their work, along with Ježek's music. Having already lampooned the Mussolini regime in *Caesar* in 1932, the three creators of the jazz revue went on to provoke an international scandal with *Osel a stín* (The Ass and the Shadow) in 1933. The latter play, set in an ancient Greek state and modeled on Hitler's new fascist government, contained such caustic criticism that the German ambassador to Czechoslovakia demanded it be shut down (a request that Masaryk apparently ignored). The following year, *Kat a blázen* (Hangman and Madman) became the site of both Czech right-wing and left-wing demonstrations, forcing the temporary closure of the theater and its removal to a less than satisfactory location; *Nebe na zemi* (Heaven on Earth) saw the comedians' return in 1936, with a play that commented on the Sudeten-German victories in the Czechoslovak parliament that same year. One foxtrot in particular, "Politické nebe na zemi" (Political Heaven on Earth), described Czechoslovakia's chances for peace in Europe; after specific references to the political positions of England and France, the text continued with a parody of fascism and its leaders:

> Every person sees Heaven in his own way: / What one fights for, another is ashamed of. / One person sees in Heaven only work, peace, and calm: / Another, a means to hoax people. / "Strong like Goliath, I call you all to guard! / I am your Messiah. / You will give everything you have to me. / You will do what I order. / The world is ours, only ours. / Only I am willing to create Heaven on Earth. / With the rumble of thunder and even all kinds of horrors, / The day will come when I will lead you again to Verdun. / *Dann werden wir haben Himmel auf Erden!"*
>   . . . In this way, nobody would want to live in a German Heaven. / *Dreimal nein!* Perhaps Henlein . . . / Our Russian brother is a Slav, / But here again is the nuisance / That we want our Heaven to be / At least a little bit to the right. / Let's not beat around the bush for too long. / We want a small Heaven, but our own.[94]

The obvious references to Hitler, *Lebensraum,* and the Sudeten-German position were augmented by Ježek's music, which at this point turns from the nonchalant foxtrot into a military march; in the recording that dates from this era, Voskovec and Werich shriek the mock-quotation of Hitler with its German phrases in imitation of the Führer's infamous radio broadcasts. The final refrain (left out of the recording reissued under communism) attempts to define the Czech position with regard to socialism as well: while the Osvobozené divadlo was decidedly in the leftist camp of avant-garde theater, the reluctance to embrace a Soviet-style political and cultural policy is evident. Interestingly, the last line quotes a cliché expression that went hand in hand with the parochial, conservative nationalism popular in much of First Republic society: "malé, ale naše" (small but ours), which portrays the Czechs as diminutive but righteous Davids in the face of Hitler, the "Goliath" mentioned in the previous verse. The entire foxtrot, with its musical basis in the cosmopolitan aesthetic of the younger generation and its sense of political engagement and moral urgency, demonstrates the complexity of associations surrounding music and theater in the waning years of the First Republic.

    The confluence of Czech nationalism and antifascism appeared in many other works of the era, from a range of strikingly different stylistic worlds. One such work, the expressionist opera *Honzovo království* (Johnny's Kingdom) from 1935, represents the final large-scale work in the career of its composer, Otakar Ostrčil. The opera, based on an antitotalitarian allegory by Tolstoy, attempted to embody the new antifascist nationalism of the era, with negative representations of militarism and totalitarian government alongside a celebration of pacificism and popular uprisings. The composer, who died within a few months of its April premiere, soon came to be seen by Nejedlý and his (by now somewhat dissolved) circle as a martyr, offering up this last work after a career of fighting for the moral victory of modern music. *Honzovo království* received numerous analyses in print, and was soon considered one of the flagship works of its time, despite its stylistic proximity to older works such as *Legenda z Erinu* and *Bratři Karamazovi*, and only questionable lip service paid to neoclassicism; it was published by the newly created Otakar Ostrčil Society (Společnost Otakara Ostrčila), whose founding occurred simultaneously with the publication of Nejedlý's exhaustive biography of the composer.

Ostrčil's death on August 20 (occurring just weeks after that of Josef Suk on May 29) produced a relatively strong upheaval in the unity of the Prague music community. Not only did it occasion a series of nationalist retrospectives regarding his contributions at the National Theater, but it also brought about the problem of his succession as opera director. Although Jeremiáš had been groomed by Ostrčil as a potential replacement since the 1928 premiere of *Bratři Karamazovi* and had taken over some directorial duties after Ostrčil's illness in the spring of 1935, upon his mentor's death in August he found himself excluded from contention. MŠANO instead ruled in favor of Talich, the favorite of the musical establishment who had conducted the Czech Philharmonic for twelve years prior to leaving for the more prestigious and lucrative directorship of the Konzertföreningen in Stockholm in late 1930. His controversial "abdication" from the leading Czech orchestra was met with a brand of partisan criticism not seen since the "Suk Affair," especially from younger members of the Nejedlý circle such as Helfert and Očadlík, proving that the old rivalries were still, if somewhat irrelevantly, alive.[95] In the meantime, Novák had also stirred up controversy with an "affair" against Ostrčil early in 1931, in which he attacked the conductor for not paying sufficient attention to his four operas, particularly *Dědův odkaz*, which had been slighted in favor of *Wozzeck*. The ensuing debate witnessed the momentary return of the entire Nejedlý clique, restating the same issues that had lain dormant for an entire decade. Indeed, the key aspect of the so-called "Novák contra Ostrčil" affair was that it had absolutely nothing to do with contemporary music making in Prague, instead reducing the credibility of Novák even further in the eyes of the younger generation.

Thus, when Talich was chosen (with the strong assistance of the Conservatory, which promised him a full professorship) over Jeremiáš, the Nejedlý circle saw it as a direct provocation of their ideals of progressive, socially responsible modern art, in that Talich apparently represented the forces of reactionism. From 1936 to the end of the First Republic, critics such as Bartoš, Patzaková, and occasionally

Nejedlý himself campaigned against the artistic leadership at the National Theater, a cultural territory that they considered to be lost. Their venue was a new journal with an old name: *Smetana*, evoking not only the journal of the Nejedlý circle that had ceased operation in 1927, but also their somewhat outdated aesthetics. The partisan attitude of *Smetana* toward Talich provoked smaller controversies with other members of the Prague musical community, notably over a poor review of Axman's fifth symphony by H. W. Süsskind in *Rytmus*. This relatively minor event provoked harsh criticism on both sides with regard to each other's "tactics," to the point where the cultural position of Hába and the entire Přítomnost society was openly questioned. The controversy, otherwise irrelevant to the pressing issues of the contemporary social environment, highlights the differing senses of national representation and social engagement on both sides. While Nejedlý and his followers had always claimed to be representatives of Czechness and socialism, their commentary on the social responsibility of the modern artist, albeit infused with Marxist rhetoric, was strikingly passive in comparison to their actively socialist opponents at Přítomnost.

As indicated previously, the artistic decisions of Alois Hába, as musical and ideological leader of Přítomnost, in many ways determined the fate of the Czech musical avant-garde in the 1930s. This was particularly true after his laudable efforts to save the 1935 ISCM festival from disaster: as Vysloužil states, Hába's conviction in seeing the project to its conclusion demonstrated a duty toward not only organizational involvement, but also the preservation of social and democratic ideals in the face of impending danger.[96] As discussed in the analysis of the quarter-tone opera *Matka* (see chapter 10), the composer believed in the inseparable bond between modern art and society; his compositions from the mid- and late 1930s demonstrate this commitment to an increasing extent, owing in large part to his involvement with the DDOČ society. DDOČ organized agitprop-style meetings and cultural events and had several branches throughout Czechoslovakia; Hába, Schulhoff, Burian, and Vít Nejedlý all contributed mass songs to the movement. Several of the artists associated with DDOČ, including Hába and Schulhoff in 1933, also undertook diplomatic trips to the Soviet Union. Hába continued producing works that reflected the urgency of combining socialist subject matter with avant-garde art music, much like Schoenberg's compositions for workers' chorus from around the same time.[97] The quarter-tone cycle of ten men's choruses *Pracující den* (The Working Day, 1932) was meant to "show the path from the social oppression and the spiritual humiliation of the individual . . . toward the collective revolutionary act in the spirit of contemporary socialist humanism."[98] In many respects, the cycle presents a development of Hába's vision over that in *Matka*, particularly with regard to the portrayal of the proletarian woman in "Dělnická madona" The Worker's Madonna), which includes a lyrical, religious component. *Pracující den*, however, met the same fate as Hába's two other large-scale projects of the 1930s: the operas *Nová země* and *Přijd' království Tvé*, neither of which has ever been performed, both exhibit the treatment of radically socialist themes by means of avant-garde modernist compositional techniques. *Nová země*, which takes place in a fictitious Russian town of the same name during the collectivization period, was actually in preparation for production under Talich at the National Theater in 1936 when both the theater administration and MŠANO prevented the performance from going forward. According to a MŠANO report of November 26, 1936, the theater requested prohibitive measures because of an apparent danger from either protests against the opera in the theater, or demonstrations for the communist party at large.[99] The avant-garde community reacted to the disappearance of *Nová země* with shock and disappointment, as a contemporary article by Pala shows.[100]

Throughout the late 1930s, Schulhoff's path with regard to socialism and music shared many similarities with Hába's, with the exception that, in order to devote himself fully to the cause of the collective, he had to give up the most salient component of his career so far: jazz. Ironically, Schulhoff's first positive experience of politically engaged music making came as a result of working as a jazz pianist in the left-wing atmosphere of the Osvobozené divadlo theater orchestra; it was Voskovec and Werich, however, more than Ježek's music, which inspired him.[101] As mentioned previously, after *H.M.S. Royal Oak* and a few individual pieces around 1931, Schulhoff virtually abandoned jazz as a compositional element, turning toward a harmonically and rhythmically simplified musical language and a heavy-handed symphonic style. The new, anti-jazz style was based in neoclassicism (to which Schulhoff had been attracted in the past), with elements inspired by French Revolutionary songs, Soviet mass songs, Beethoven, and importantly, the early-classical Czech compositional school (particularly the Stamic family), whose work he had been employed to arrange for Jirák's radio orchestra.[102] Indeed, Schulhoff's involvement with the largely Czech DDOČ, contemporaneous with the rise of Sudeten-German nationalism (which excluded him as a Jew), served to align his interests with the Czech community, especially after 1933, when most of the German world became alien to him. Despite his increasing musical contributions to the socialist movement, notably after moving to Ostrava in 1935 where he assisted the DDOČ in the field, Schulhoff continued to rely upon jazz as a source of income, first as a popular piano duo with Oldřich Letfus, then in Ostrava as a performer of light entertainment music for the local radio station. As Letfus related in his postwar memoirs, these experiences were ideologically frustrating for the composer:

> For Schulhoff, this activity in the theater [i.e., Osvobozené divadlo] was only an occupation that ensured him a regular monthly wage: artistically it meant nothing to him. Schulhoff had by this point already refined his position with regard to jazz; he recognized that jazz did not signify a new epoch in the development of music.[103]

Thus, Schulhoff was constantly forced to compromise his artistic ideals for the purposes of what he considered bourgeois entertainment, by means of reaching into an earlier stage of his career he had hoped to conclude long before. It was Schulhoff's tragic fate that neither route held a future. In 1938 he fled Ostrava (which lay in the Sudetenland), and continued to work in Brno and Prague for the radio, surreptitiously, after the start of the Nazi protectorate. To save himself and his family he endeavored to gain Soviet citizenship, but waiting too long for the process, he was unable to leave Czechoslovakia before the dissolution of the Nazi–Soviet pact, making emigration to the East impossible. Schulhoff died in Wülzburg concentration camp from tuberculosis in 1942, amid composition of his Seventh and Eighth Symphonies, each of which contained socialist themes.

Schulhoff's negative attitude toward his own German heritage in the late 1930s was typical of other Jewish composers of his generation, notably Krása, who ultimately turned to Czech texts. Meanwhile, the changing fortunes of the non-Jewish German-Bohemian community were reflected in their attitude toward culture, particularly music, which for them had always lain in the shadow of the more active Czech musical community—a group that had forcibly excluded them in the first years of the Republic. After the accession of Konrad Henlein to power in 1934, their expressions of nationalism increased substantially, particularly in 1936 with the foundation of a new journal, the conservative and parochial *Musikblätter der Sudetendeutschen*, which served as an alternative to Erich Steinhard's cosmopolitan, liberal *Der Auftakt*.[104] Deliberately ignoring all German-Jewish musicians, past and present, *Musikblätter* had distinctly few local composers on which to concentrate, notably Fidelio Finke and Felix Petyrek, the second of whom had not lived in the Czech Lands since childhood. Although in its first issue the journal professed to be "unparteiisch," with an open-minded attitude toward a "musical exchange with the Czech people," its overriding parochialism soon came to the fore, particularly in the editors' relationship to Finke.[105] The director of the Deutsche Akademie für Musik since 1927, Finke pleased the German-Bohemian community greatly with the performance of his first opera, *Die Jakobsfahrt*, in 1936 at the Neues Deutsches Theater under Széll. The opera revolves around a group of German pilgrims en route to Santiago de Compostela, and contains medieval *Pilgerlieder* in the context of a Schoenbergian (perhaps even Ostrčilian) expressionism. The event produced a flurry of excitement in *Musikblätter*, with no less than four articles in as many issues; although Finke's musical debt to Schoenberg and even Debussy was acknowledged, critics foregrounded the Sudeten-German element in a work they felt would finally represent them on the operatic stage, thereby offering a strong sense of cultural legitimacy.

The honeymoon ended, however, when Finke was charged with communist sympathies after having taken part as the only German contingent in an "Exhibition of the Czechoslovak Avant-garde" at Burian's radical left-wing theater D37. In an article entitled "Der Fall Finke," the editors of *Musikblätter* strongly implied that the composer's musical roots did not lie in *Sudetendeutschtum*. Finke was forced to write an open letter to the journal, denying his interest in both the communist party and the exhibition itself, despite the submission of his work.[106] In a final show of patriotism toward the community, Finke wrote:

I clarify in all unequivocality: *I had and have never had any kind of connection to communism and I reject it with the deepest conviction. Similar is my relationship to Theater D37. My belonging and unchangeable loyalty to* Sudetendeutschtum, *however, will be indubitable to all who know me by my word and my work.*[107]

The urgency of the political situation demanded such a response, although its effect did not allow Finke to return to his momentary stardom: his name was never again mentioned in the journal during its remaining year of publication. From this point onward, *Musikblätter der Sudetendeutschen* became an increasing supporter of Nazism, with frequent articles referring to the racial purity of German music, supported by "inspirational" quotes by Henlein and Hitler.[108] Clearly, however, the journal's cultural position was not as stable as its editors assumed, and it was automatically discontinued at the start of the Protectorate.

Finke stayed on in Prague through the war and during the Third Czechoslovak Republic (1945–48) was deported, along with almost all the surviving German-Bohemian community, to what became East Germany. His petitions to Alois Hába in subsequent years for intercession and compassion, based on many years of cooperative intercultural efforts during the First Republic and the Protectorate, fell on deaf ears.[109] Undoubtedly, the nationalist divide that had progressively split the musical life of Prague into Czech and German camps after 1918 was incapable of being healed after such cataclysmic cultural and political events.

During a time when so many aspects of the democratic regime were coming to an end, various artistic statements emerged that attempted to codify the achievements of the past twenty years, as though with a consciousness of its impending conclusion. One of the most interesting documents to emerge from the Czech musical community in the late 1930s was Vladimír Helfert's book, *Česká moderní hudba* (Czech Modern Music, 1936).[110] An active and outspoken members of the Nejedlý circle in Prague before independence, Helfert had moved to Brno after the war to teach musicology at Purkyně University, where he gradually adopted a new vision of musical aesthetics and of the direction of modern Czech music, with a favorable attitude toward Janáček's music in particular. *Česká moderní hudba* presents an overview of Czech music history from the pre-Smetana generation to Helfert's contemporaries, thus forming a parallel to Nejedlý's pathbreaking work, the 1903 *Dějiny české hudby*, which had served to divide the musical community through its theory of compositional lineages. Helfert's work, on the other hand, revealed an effort to bury the partisan criticism that had long impeded the development of Czech culture. In this respect, his level-headed discussion of Smetana and Ostrčil, as well as his surprisingly generous assessment of such figures as Dvořák, Novák, Suk, and their students, presented as unbiased a narrative as was possible in the interwar period. Particularly striking is Helfert's frequent characterization of his composers' creativity as "heroic," a theme that runs throughout the study and that connects it to the new nationalist trend of the era. The only individuals to be given anything but the highest praise were Křička and Hába, the former for having sacrificed his artistic ideals in the name of superficial humor (see chapter 10), the latter because of his "mechanical" theoretical system, which for Helfert could never become the basis of musical inspiration.[111]

The most important section of the monograph, however, was the "Epilogue," which abandoned the narrative of music history and concentrated on the theme of ideology in music. In a nutshell, Helfert felt that Czech music had suffered from a lack of creative inspiration during the interwar period, thereby hampering the momentum of truly progressive art. Although the concept hearkens back to Hostinský's axiom of progressiveness in music, it also warns against the stifling of creativity through an overuse of ideology:

> The disastrous romantic opinion that the substance of compositional creativity lies in the expression of ideas and feelings, in the sense that the character of those ideas determines the worth of the work, endangers today not only the healthy development of our criticism and aesthetic opinions, but most of all, creative praxis as well. More than one young composer, despite presenting an open mind in his worldview and, through his convictions, going after the newest social ideals and being full of enthusiastic belief in the progress of the human spirit and human society, is nevertheless quite artistically removed from his own ideological consciousness. Why? Because he forgets that ideology itself does not suffice for a creative act. What is the worth of all ideology if such a composer does not have the ability to embody his ideals in an artistic work? And in this embodiment the decisive factor is not the worth of the ideas, but the worth of the *artistic means*. These, the character of the musical thoughts, their construction, and internal order, are the first and most incontrovertible condition that must be fulfilled if the ideas are to be applied to the creative function by which the composer was inspired. This alphabet of musical aesthetics should already be a certainty today.[112]

For Helfert, only musical creativity, with or without ideology, could enrich and deepen musical development. Proof of the insufficiency of ideology for this purpose alone was the current state of Soviet music, which had not benefited from what he considered the most progressive society in the world.[113] Indeed, he considered any unilateral discussion of the ideological direction of music to be "basically questionable, and for *free* work not only fruitless, but also dangerous,"[114] a statement that seems to link creative freedom with democracy. Simply put, the truly progressive artistic work carried its own social function through its moral strength. In attaining "a new greatness, new pathos, new monumentality, and a new heroism of ideas," music could regain its leading position in Czech culture.[115]

Česká moderní hudba attempted to put aside the factionalized and fractured system under which the Czech musical community had existed for generations, seeking to bring together differing views on artistic tradition, modernism, and the application of the composer's responsibility toward society. That these issues still held enormous currency after so many political, social, and cultural changes since the turn of the century speaks volumes, particularly because the author still viewed the resolution of aesthetic problems as taking place within a framework of Czech national identity. Although Helfert treated each of his subjects as individuals in his history, it was their contribution to collective Czechness and its moral future that took precedence throughout the text, albeit in a self-consciously nonideological way. For all its conciliatory efforts, however, *Česká moderní hudba* did meet with some opposition, not unexpectedly, from within the closed-minded Nejedlý camp;[116] nevertheless, it has come to be regarded as one of the most thorough musical texts of its kind from the First Republic era, despite the fact that its effectiveness was cut short by the end of democracy just two years after its publication. The new, long-term changes in aesthetic thought that Helfert's work might have introduced in the musical community of Prague were never to be realized.

* * *

In the 1930s, the Prague music community experienced more changes of ideology and compositional style in a shorter space of time than it had seen since the days of Smetana. Almost without exception, these changes were enacted by members of the younger generation, a group that finally welcomed influences from the international avant-garde with excitement and abandon. As Vačkář's humorous analogy expresses, the major difficulty faced by the young Czech avant-garde was whether to recapture the audience through socialist subject matter or accessible musical material. As time went on, both camps became more firmly entrenched in the ideology of their position, such that socialists could only compose in a rigid postexpressionist style, and the neoclassicist/populists refused tendential programs, lest they interfere with the public's experience of the pure musical form. After 1935, when the threat of international political extremism hit home with the sabotage of the Karlovy Vary ISCM, both sides began working with an energy that seems to mark an awareness of the limited time left to them as artists in a democratic, peacetime environment. Not only did the German-Bohemian community suddenly take on a new identity as a profascist Sudeten-German lobby group, viewing music through the lens of official Nazi culture, but the rhetoric of Czech critics also escalated with a brand of outspoken nationalism that did not sit well with their esoteric aesthetic goals. The music produced during this time also reflected the extremes of the time, inciting controversy over the ability of one stylistic path to represent the wider Czech collective. Indeed, traditional genres, more officially accepted by the establishment, had now to compete with the wildly successful jazz revues of Ježek discussed in the present chapter; in this, the operas of Hába and Křička, although from diametrically opposed perspectives on style and influence, faced similar challenges in what would prove to be an increasingly hostile environment.

Chapter Ten

"A Sad Optimism, the Happiness of the Resigned"

Extremes of Operatic Expression in the 1930s

The division of the young Czech avant-garde of the 1930s produced two camps, both aiming to resolve the question of how best to recapture an audience alienated by modernism.[1] Any opera composers of this generation would be daunted by the task of presenting their work before an audience that no longer considered opera a principal form of entertainment, or one that reflected their identity in the modern world. Each of the two compositional factions in Prague, however, faced a further uphill battle, in that neither of their aesthetic programs, in its purest form, was well suited to the traditional conventions of opera. For Hába and the postexpressionists, eager to use socialist themes to educate the audience, stage plays set to music were, in theory, an ideal way to capture the attention of large cross-sections of society, but their uncompromising, new musical vocabulary was not conducive to musico-dramatic narrative and pace without making significant concessions to tradition. Hába's quarter-tone opera *Matka* (The Mother) became the subject of discussion among Prague critics, but found an audience only in the more open-minded atmosphere of Munich in 1931. On the other side, Krejčí and the neoclassicists shied away from full-scale opera as a genre because this same issue of musico-dramatic narrative conflicted with their ideology that pure rhythm and sound should affect the listener directly through absolute forms, without the assistance of a program. The result was that composers of the Mánes Group devoted their energies to incidental music (including Ježek's jazz revues) instead of opera prior to the years of the Protectorate. Meanwhile, the populist side of the neoclassical movement was amply upheld by composers of light opera such as Weinberger (see chapter 8) and Jaroslav Křička, whose *Strašidlo v zámku* (A Ghost in the Castle) met with international success before coming to the National Theater in 1933, when critics questioned its merits as a modern contribution to music and/or theater at all. These two operas reveal the dilemma awaiting all modernist composers at mid-century, as potential audiences grew, and actual ones went elsewhere.

Hába's *Matka*: Modernism, Tradition, and Reference

Alois Hába's *Matka* was a pathbreaking work for its time, representing many "firsts" in the repertoire of European art music. Not only was it the composer's first attempt to write a vocal composition using the quarter-tone and athematic systems, but it was also the first such opera ever created, and the largest quarter-tone work written to that point. It was also the first work of any size by a member of the modernist Prague circle that truly and decisively broke with the musical vocabulary of romanticism, to the point where Hába's music is often considered to be outside the realm of "Czech music" even today. The opera, with its chamber orchestra of considerable size (twenty musicians), was the perfect showpiece for the ensemble of new instruments Hába had designed, such as the quarter-tone piano, harmonium, clarinets, and trumpets; it also demonstrated new techniques for the traditional instruments (double string quartet and contrabass, harps tuned a quarter tone apart, trombones, and timpani). Nevertheless, for all its revolutionary qualities, *Matka* was built upon a complex series of references to Czech and European operatic traditions, all enmeshed in a modernist musical exterior with a pronounced socialist message. Traces of operatic set pieces and vocal gestures abound in the first half of the work, but their absence from the second, "socialist" half implies a distinct separation of two aesthetic worlds for Hába. As one of the first socialist stage works written in the Prague musical community, Hába's opera provided a model for further endeavors in the hotbed of culturo-political activity that developed, as we have seen, later in the 1930s. In this respect, it also represented a milestone in a generation's efforts to realize the social responsibility of art in a concrete musical form.

By the time of the premiere of *Matka* on May 17, 1931, European audiences had come to know more than one overtly socialist opera. Aside from the stage collaborations of Brecht and Weill, one of the most noteworthy works of this type was Max Brand's *Der Maschinist Hopkins*, performed in Prague in October 1930 as *Strojník Hopkins*. A brief examination of its fate in Prague will set the stage for the reception of Hába's work. According to Vomáčka, although the opera met with "reasonable success" with the audience, among the critics the reaction was so mixed as to threaten a volatile polemic along the lines of earlier years.[2] That this did not happen is testament to the ascendancy of the younger generation to the institutions of Prague musical life; it also speaks to their disdain for belligerent figures such as Šilhan, who referred to the work as "the most disgusting German trash."[3] Like most of the critical voices, for or against Brand's opera, Šilhan compared the work to *Wozzeck*, in which he saw a parallel, not only in terms of the police presence in the theater, but also with regard to the communist threat he perceived in both works, "the inartistic and anti-Czech experiments of Mr. Ostrčil."[4] Others, such as the moderately conservative Šourek or the radical Očadlík, while negatively disposed toward *Strojník Hopkins* for various musical reasons, made the comparison to *Wozzeck* using much less pugilistic rhetoric: rather more disappointing was Brand's admixture of verismo or impressionist stylistic features with those of the Schoenberg school.[5] Of the critics from the daily papers, only Karel Hába, writing in *Československá republika*, spoke positively about the social tendencies of the opera, which "idealizes work—the world of machines, which receive and express the feelings and thoughts of the working masses."[6] Significantly, Alois Hába also took the sociopolitical aspects of Brand's opera seriously in his preview for the in-house publication *Národní divadlo*: the title character is described as "a man of the urban periphery, from which he arises, and which he does not betray."[7] Hába also cited the growing trend toward everyday situations and settings in opera, lauded the use of atonality and jazz songs in the score, and proclaimed it to be representative of the young generation's attempts at modern opera.[8]

The comments of both Hába brothers would have been made in the consciousness of their own operatic projects. By the time of *Strojník Hopkins*'s Prague premiere, *Matka* was already finished, and Karel Hába's first operatic attempt, the vaguely socialist, historical drama *Jánošík*, was halfway to completion.[9] It is important to note not only the great musical and theatrical disparity between these works but also the relative vagueness of their ideological stance toward socialism: indicative of the first years of the decade, their expressions of the workers' movement had not yet coalesced into firmer pronouncements such as Schulhoff's *Manifest* or Burian's work at D33.[10] In this respect, *Matka* represents a stage on the road to discovery of how best to combine socialist plot elements with modernist music; as we have seen time and again in the Prague community, such a project ultimately attempted to fulfill the social responsibility of art and lead Czech culture and society into a new era of synthesis.[11]

Set to the composer's own libretto written in his native Valašsko dialect, *Matka* mostly takes place in an unnamed village of the same region, over twenty-three years in an undefined era (most likely in the late nineteenth century, the time of Hába's own childhood).[12]

Characters:	Křen, farmer and itinerant musician	tenor
	Maruša, his second wife	soprano
	Křen's children from a previous marriage	S, S, MS, T
	Sister-in-law	alto
	Brother-in-law	bass
	Best man	tenor

<table>
<tr><td>(continued)</td><td></td><td></td></tr>
<tr><td></td><td>Lachrymose Old Women</td><td>S, S, A, A</td></tr>
<tr><td></td><td>Priest</td><td>tenor</td></tr>
<tr><td></td><td>Other neighbors and relations</td><td></td></tr>
</table>

The opera's plot revolves around Křen, whose first wife has died in childbirth, and who, throughout the course of the drama, must find a wife to help raise his six children. After a suitable mourning period Křen finds a willing helpmate in Maruša, and the wedding takes place in her neighboring village. From this point onward, the plot revolves around Maruša's struggle to be integrated into Křen's household, initially with the children of his first wife, then with Křen himself as his personality changes for the worse with the passing of time. The situation grows tense with the arrival of Maruša's own children by Křen, especially the youngest, Toneček, whom the others despise for his closeness to his mother. Unable to stand the penury and lack of future prospects on the farm, the older children leave to seek their fortune elsewhere, some as far away as America; the daughters marry and Maruša's own boys leave to get an education, with the exception of Toneček who stays on the farm. In the final scene, the elderly Křen and Maruša, now more kindly disposed toward each other, reflect on the hard struggle that has made up their lives, and the sacrifices the mother has made for her family.

With regard to the text alone, *Matka* has much in common with nineteenth-century folk opera, especially of the veristic type: like Janáček's *Jenůfa* and Foerster's *Eva*, it portrays the more unsavory aspects of Czech village life, where the woman is subjected to drudgery and often cruel disappointments. For the heroine Maruša, like her counterparts in Janáček and Foerster, sexuality and childbearing have elements of punishment as well as joy; as her husband Křen gets older, he becomes more sexually aggressive, to the point where his wife must defend herself physically. Taken as a whole, *Matka* reveals a sense of prevailing sadness, in the midst of which appear moments of joy, found mostly in local traditions such as weddings. Hába's social statement lies in the heroism of the title character, who receives neither a tragic death (as with Eva) nor an apotheosis (as with Jenůfa), but for whom mere survival into old age is a victory in itself. The implication is that, in representing the "everywoman," Maruša's victory is that of "the people." Hába's opera, however, in no way expresses this overtly: no single statement in the text refers to a larger, more philosophical view of the situation. While several critics have noted the connection to *Jenůfa* and *Eva*, they have been just as quick to point out the differences, many of which might have been taken as shortcomings by an audience in 1931. Altogether lacking the dramatic shape of romantic opera, Hába's open-ended work is of the lyric-epic type, akin to Brecht in its asceticism.[13] Indeed, rather like similar operas in Weimar Germany at this time, it is *Alltäglichkeit* taken to the extreme, the everyday so barren of poetry that it represents little outside of the harsh experiences it portrays. In this respect, it is a socialist opera of a type diametrically opposed to that of *Der Maschinist Hopkins*, which presented its hero struggling against forces stylized as machines. The sheer lack of dramatic stylization in *Matka* is more reminiscent of the social element in *Wozzeck*, by which Hába had been directly inspired.[14]

Musically as well as dramatically, *Matka's* ten scenes fall into three phases: the funeral of Křen's first wife, the period of mourning, the courtship of Maruša, and the wedding (scenes 1–4); the married life of Křen and Maruša, with their struggle to have a child together, the troubles of the growing family, and their increasing emotional separation (scenes 5–9); and the epilogue in old age (scene 10). Hába's music closely follows the dramatic mood of these phases, with a plethora of set pieces in the opening phase, including "phenomenal" songs and dances, and a distinct lack of them after the start of scene five.[15] These moments of formal clarity, especially in scenes one and four (the funeral and wedding scenes, respectively), represent some of the only musical references to the realm of traditional operatic convention. Otherwise, the quarter-tone musical material, athematic formal construction, and reduced orchestral forces offer *Matka* relatively little in the way of traditional dramatic shape.

Indeed, in the context of the Prague musical community of 1931, Hába's music was so new as to be almost wholly unrelated to its cultural context. The opera's vocal melodies and gestures have more in common with contemporary folk-song ethnography (in the manner of Janáček's speech melodies) than postromantic phrasing, although aspects of the "musical prose" of German modernist opera are also apparent, comparable to *Wozzeck* and *Erwartung*. Quarter tones are used to simulate the speech and singing styles of Moravian peasants, sometimes bisecting semitones as they ascend or descend in the melody, but more often replacing intervallic leaps from traditional chromatic harmony with ones slightly smaller or larger. In this respect, *Matka* represents a concatenation of the achievements of Janáček and the Second Viennese School, wherein the sounds of the local dialect are passed through a quarter-tone filter for greater accuracy of replication, but are also used to explore a revolutionary, interval-driven compositional technique.[16] Thus, any references, however hidden, to traditional operatic modes of expression, be they via the inclusion of set pieces or subtle references to them, imitative gestures in the orchestra, or even climactic phrases or pitches in the vocal line, would have become islands of stability for an audience unused to such an opera as a dramatic concept. Furthermore, as the following analysis will show, it is apparent from Hába's score that such references to operatic tradition lay somewhat outside the social message of the opera, since they are confined, with the exception of Maruša's lullabies and her more lyrical effusions in later scenes, to the ritualized events of the opening phase of the drama. The full impact of the struggle for existence in Valašsko life, moreover, comes only with the shedding of these formal niceties after the wedding scene: indeed, the lullabies that Maruša sings to Toneček are received harshly by the other characters, as though such expressions of tenderness did not belong in an environment of crushing darkness.

After an orchestral prelude, the first scene opens in a tense and somber mood as Křen and his sister-in-law (named only Švagrová, which translates directly) argue before the casket of the deceased first wife, Anča. Although much of this passage is an extended solo for Švagrová, its only marker of formal independence is the orchestral tutti at its conclusion on page 17, acting gesturally as a cadence; the vocal writing is neither lyrical nor dramatically declamatory, and prefigures much of the pessimistic dreariness from later in the opera.[17] After this point, the mood softens, and shortly thereafter Hába depicts the processional arrival of the neighbors to mourn Anča's passing; the use of $\frac{4}{4}$ time, *moderato*, with a regular succession of staccato eighths, slowly developed through rhythmic variation and orchestral crescendo, is an almost naturalistic portrayal of a ritual procession, as seen throughout the operatic repertoire.[18]

One of the only occurrences of simultaneous singing, the quartet of the Lachrymose Old Women—four villagers who perform a ritualistic song of mourning at the graveside—is the first set piece and the most cohesive passage in the opera (27–33).[19] Not unexpectedly, in the context of the stage action this scene is a moment of phenomenal music, performed with a distinct beginning and end: they are introduced by a neighbor ("Women, start then!") and concluded by Křen ("That's enough, women"). Constructed as a single solo line with three accompanimental voices (which mostly move chordally), it has its own formal shape, and is unified by a sustained accompaniment of lower strings and clarinets throughout. The melody of the top vocal line, when not joining the patter-style singing of the other three, has a tendency toward two-note groupings, the traditional symbol of lamentation or sighing in Western art music (28): this latter gestural type also sets the quartet apart from the majority of the vocal writing outside the set pieces, which is predominantly syllabic. The whole passage is divided musically into five unequal sections, separated by moments of rest (13, 10, 4, 8, and 11 measures in length, respectively) that produce a roughly symmetrical design, ABCBA. With the exception of the central segment—a single phrase of repeated notes—each of the other sections is constructed of smaller, arch-like melodic phrases, linked together by movement in the lower voices. Each of the four larger sections has a climactic pitch, on words that represent their respective textual content: "Oh you poor creature" (28), "poor orphans" (29), "Lord God" (31), and "laments and woe" (33). The last of these sections, which reflects back upon the performative act of the ritual itself ("You can't even hear our laments and woe, but perhaps your soul feels them in that other world"), has the most melismatic writing of the quartet, with the largest melodic intervals, particularly at the moment of climax (33). The opening scene concludes in a similar phenomenal vein with the arrival of the priest, who intones a series of prayers on a single pitch, and a funeral procession of considerable length (40–48). Each of these instances of phenomenal music provides a sense of dramatic structure for the opening scene that stands in relief against the amorphous quality found in later parts of the opera, particularly in its second, "domestic" phase.

Scene 4, as the climax of the opening phase of the drama, has the largest number of phenomenal moments: it is the wedding of Křen and Maruša, where the best man, groom, and bride all improvise songs for the guests. The whole is preceded by a dance in $\frac{5}{4}$ time, cast loosely in a five-part symmetrical form (again, ABCBA), with the chorus present in the outer sections: their exclamations of "Jucháj!" (Hooray) at Křen's suggestion for a dance (109–10) return amid the final accented chords in the orchestra (116–17), now with rhythmic clapping as well. All the other sections are distinguished by changes in orchestration, where different solo instruments take over the melodic line (violin and clarinet at 110, trumpet, clarinet, and piano at 112, violin and trumpet at 115) above an accompaniment of short, repeated rhythms. In his defense of the athematic style against Pícha's attacks (see chapter 9), Hába wrote that motives, such as those that serve to unify the funeral procession and the dance, do not lie outside the bounds allowed by thematic nonrepetition. Perhaps following Schoenberg's description of motives as short as a single melodic interval, Hába also allowed the use of such small building blocks in his otherwise free-form style. In the case of the wedding dance these motives serve as an accompaniment for ongoing "improvisatory" solos in the piano, violins, and clarinets that unravel after the conclusion of the five-part form (119–27); the whole instrumental sequence is wrapped up by a final cry of jubilation from the chorus. As we shall see, the chorus continues to create formal divisions between set pieces throughout the wedding scene.

The best man (or Družba) sings a relatively short song that has deliberate references to the folk style, identified by Vysloužil as a *kúlaná* from South Valašsko: the whole piece, twenty-four measures long, is divided into short two- or three-measure segments, wherein the singer, violins, and clarinets exchange rhythmic motives, providing a continuous sense of interest and festivity (130–32).[20] As the chorus enters for the final refrain and the slight orchestration builds to a fuller ensemble, the timbral distinctions between instrumental choirs gradually blend, after being sharply differentiated during the song proper (132–33). The chorus's laughter ("Chachachachacha") returns in a similar way during the transitional dialogue (136) and after the subsequent song by Maruša.

The bride's improvisation is the shortest of the three, a mere thirteen measures, but contains a surprising amount of internal repetition and variation. Hába's text itself repeats the lines in pairs, and the short melodic phrases, while never copied exactly in the repetition, produce a type of variation that stands out amid the prevailing athematic texture. While the character of Maruša's song is altogether different from the rest of the scene, it is linked with the preceding set pieces by way of the chorus's reaction, which changes the mood back to the jubilant dance for Křen's song. This final "improvisation" by the groom is perhaps the most overtly "folk-like" of the three, with its repeated melodic notes, partial refrain midway

Example 10.1. Hába, *Matka*, sc. 4, climax of Maruša's arietta (150/2–4).

through the stanza, and especially the persistent down-bow strokes in the string accompaniment. Nevertheless, Křen's vocal line has a thrilling climax reminiscent of romantic opera (145); moreover, the coda, which sums up the whole set of songs and dances with a combination of the Družba's refrain ("dyna dyna dyna") and the choral "Juchaj," evokes a decidedly operatic atmosphere, rather than the "modernist ethnography" Hába attempted in other places.

Continuing in this mode of traditional opera, the mood changes after the departure of Křen and the other guests when Maruša is left alone to contemplate the full import of her decision to marry. What transpires is in fact a fully independent arietta for the heroine (147–51), with an almost Puccinian climax, accompanied by the violins in octaves, including a high C on the word "Bóže" (God [help me to bear this worry], ex. 10.1, 150), sung pianissimo.[21] The moment of introspection concluded, Křen reappears, asking his wife the reason for her melancholy: her brief answer ("It's nothing, Francek, only all sorts of thoughts are passing through my head") indicates the lack of emotional unity in the couple: the lyricism ended, Křen stays forever outside of Maruša's psychological and musical world. This reality becomes apparent when the scene closes (in a cadential manner much more convincingly than any of the previous three, 152) and the realm of set pieces comes to an end. In the scenes depicting Maruša's married life, only in her moments of solitude, singing lullabies to her baby Toneček, does this lyrical, performative realm return.

The musical separation between Maruša's internal and external existences grows with each succeeding scene. The lyricism she expressed in scene four returns only fleetingly, absent from all of her statements to Křen and the older children: instead, she participates in the harsh patter-style of the others, confined to the direct imitation of speech through syllabic text setting, repeated notes, and mostly unmelodic gestures. After a long stretch of this type of angular, antiromantic music, during which Hába provides the listener with a strong feeling of the desultory and demoralizing nature of rural life, Maruša's brief lullaby (242–44) in scene seven comes as a moment of internalized lyricism, parallel to her arietta after the wedding. This sense of parallelism comes not only from the similarity of the musical gestures (most notably in the quiet climax, 243), but also from the reflective character of the text, which echoes Maruša's uncertainty at the wedding and reflects its outcome: "It's a difficult fate to be a mother and a wife . . . but you're the most important of all, Toneček." The intense lyricism of all voices (including multiple accompanimental parts), along with the sheer inner peace and joy she expresses in this moment of solitude, sets these fifteen measures apart from the rest of this phase of the opera.

If the solo segments at pages 147 and 242 form a parallel of inner joy, Maruša's extended aria in scene 8 (263–77) expresses a deep sadness parallel only to that of the quartet of Lachrymose Old Women in scene 1. As with the previous parallelism, the main distinction between the quartet and the aria is that the latter is not an example of phenomenal music, even though it too has elements of lullaby. Rather it is a cathartic outpouring of the character's psychological turmoil, perfectly in the tradition of romantic opera. Formally, however, it does not respond to the model of tension–climax–release associated with most arias: a multipart rondo (which by its very nature of constantly returning to an original state diffuses any sense of linear drama), it has much in common with similar long solos in *Bratři Karamazovi*, *Elektra*, and signficantly, *Erwartung*. In this regard, the progression of brief, interlinked musical and textual segments in Maruša's aria represents her changing psychological state, toward her children, her husband, and her life, thereby encapsulating the opera's emotional world in a sequence of vignettes. The main, recurrent portion of the rondo is a lullaby to her sleeping children; as she explains earlier in the scene, she must save these moments of tenderness for when her husband and the older children are not present, such that only we see her interior world, kept separate from the others. While apparent musical and textual references link these moments of repetition to create a larger form, the sense of return is largely psychological, since Hába's athematic style strongly prohibited the reuse of melodic material en masse in the manner of a traditional rondo.

As demonstrated in table 10.1, the lullaby (given in bold) always returns in the same tempo: it also employs a small tripartite textual structure, wherein the initial imperative ("Sleep!") is repeated after another short phrase ("my darling," etc.).[22] Musically this structure is consistently reflected in the opening three quarter notes, followed by some sort of syncopation, then a short descending figure (ex. 10.2, 263). In the intervening episodes, Maruša's thoughts dwell on tangential ideas pertaining to her children, particularly Toneček; the overall form of the aria is shaped by her attention, first to all the children, then Toneček alone, with a return to the group at the end. Despite a transparent overall structure, the aria does not build to a single, convincing dramatic climax with a resolution: indeed, Maruša receives two climaxes of vastly differing musical character and dramatic import, but neither at the conventional moment. The first of these, coming during the two parallel phrases on page 266 ("Perhaps you will understand sometime that it is motherly love. Perhaps you will not understand and will abandon my old knee"), displays an almost Puccinian brilliance for a moment of self-validation, and leads directly into a return to the lullaby. The second climax on page 271 is, surprisingly, a quieter one occurring on the word "Bóže" (God), just like Maruša's two moments of internal reflection so far—her aria after the wedding

Table 10.1. Hába, *Matka*: Form of Maruša's aria–lullaby, sc. 8

Page	Incipit[1]	Length	Textual content	Music content
263	**Toš spěte**	10 mm.	general wish for a healthy future for her children	Andante cantabile; quiet, sustained melodies in accomp.
264	Šak sem vás chtěla	10 mm.	describes suffering endured on their behalf	More rhythmic complexity, multiple string melodies
265	Ale nikdy jsem vás	8 mm.	describes occasional frustration with children	Thinner texture, upper strings and clarinets
266	Snáď nekdy pochopíte	4 + 6 mm.	perhaps they understand her maternal love	Two parallel phrases, builds to preliminary climax
267	**No spěte milánci**	4 mm.	return of lullaby	Tempo I, simpler texture
267	A co ten nájmenší	10 mm.	considers the youngest and his future	Quiet, sustained brass and clarinets, muted strings
268	**No spinkaj**	7 mm.	return of lullaby, directed at Toneček	Melody doubled at octave in violin
269	Nikdo ťa nechtěl	4 + 4 mm.	remarks on how no one wanted him but her	Two phrases with similar openings, poco animato
270	Aspoň v noci/Bože	4 + 7 mm.	she can only be motherly to him at night	Quiet climax in second half, doubled in violins
271	Chudery	7 mm.	comparison between Anča and herself	Disjunct, staccato accompaniment
273	**No spinkaj**	4 mm.	return of lullaby	Tempo I, melody tripled strings
274	A včil ešče zamísit	13 mm.	begins to prepare bread	Quasi allegretto, staccato and short phrases
275	Bóže, daj mi zdraví	10 mm.	short prayer for strength to continue for the children	Interlocking clarinet melodies
276	**Spinkajte, milánci**	3 mm.	brief return of lullaby	Melody in high register

[1]The incipits in this chart reflect the text found in the Filmkunst-Musikverlag score, and not the Supraphon libretto, which has substantial cuts in this scene.

Example 10.2. Hába, *Matka*, sc. 8, first refrain of Maruša's lullaby–aria (263/3–5).

Example 10.3. Hába, *Matka*: comparison of Maruša's different climactic pitches (150/2; 243/10; 271/4).

and the shorter lullaby in scene 7 (ex. 10.3 a–c). Not only does the hushed dynamic form a parallel to those on pages 150 and 243, but the melodic gestures show an obvious interrelationship as well. Nevertheless, a quiet central climax, followed by a considerable amount of further material before the final lullaby, does not help the aria to conform to the dramatic traditions of operatic performance. Rather it is wholly in keeping with Hába's vision of the second phase of the drama as the internalized social struggle of the everywoman. Although, in principle, such universality could be found in many operas that transcend their particularities of setting, *Matka*'s musical style forced it into a position of unconventionality—indeed, into a category all its own—for audiences in 1931.

Contemporary criticism at the time of the Munich premiere grappled with the issues of Hába's unconventionality in the face of tradition. Many from the Prague compositional community made the trip by train for the event, including Josef Suk, who had consistently supported the composer's pedagogical efforts. The young critics František Pala, František Bartoš, and the Munich-based Heinz Korffner were all positively disposed toward *Matka* as a quarter-tone composition, as a work in the athematic style, and a new dramatic statement for opera. For each, the social component figured highly in their assessment, especially when examined in conjunction with Hába's compositional techniques. Korffner could not decide whether the opera represented "a sad optimism, the happiness of the resigned, or . . . peace and reconciliation after aggression": the whole was, however, an example of "the psychological component without psychology," which is to say, without the overuse of the latter for an obvious dramatic purpose, as in the Wagnerian tradition.[23] His comment suggests that

Hába's characters, taken directly from actual life, made more of a statement than any sort of overly stylized representation that bowed to operatic convention, an issue that Bartoš also took up in his lengthy analysis for *Tempo*. According to Bartoš, in casting off the tradition of empty, romanticized folklore and using an uncompromising technique, Hába had found the true sense of social responsibility in his portrayal of the fates of living people. These he juxtaposed to his own realm of "pure music," which could never undertake such a task with its absence of ideological content.[24] Pala, meanwhile, relished the *Alltäglichkeit* of Hába's creation as a new type of dramatic work, where "everything is real," and the drama of "new people" was taken to a new level of "internal, conscious longing."[25] Korffner also sensed the novelty of *Matka* as a drama, which went along with the new quarter-tone sound: in it, dramatic relationships, particularly those in the second half, did not follow a linear direction, but rather arose through the juxtaposition of realities, as though the combination of different static planes produced a dynamic of its own, wherein the action was only symbolic of a higher artistic statement.

All three discussed Hába's music as something inevitable in music history; for Pala, the athematicism was "dictated by musical logic," which may or may not have been a reference to Schoenberg's defense of the twelve-tone system as necessitated by the logical progression of music history. Both Bartoš and Korffner described the use of athematic melody as a modern reassessment of the concept of "infinite melody," in a musical language (i.e., quarter tones) that was removed from the Wagnerian tradition. Quarter tones themselves were for Bartoš the "logical consequences" of Hába's analytical mind, producing a new system of "technical values."[26] Such a statement, albeit grounded in the rhetoric of Hostinský's *důslednost*, went against the grain of traditional Czech aesthetic thought in its application to an opera so wholly outside the bounds of Smetanian acceptability. Nevertheless, Hába's musical references to folk sources (notably the only such instance among all the quarter-tone composers) made the opera's score more region specific than the *Alltäglich* dramatic component may have wished: in this respect, according to Bartoš, he expressed himself as would a truly Czech composer.[27] In Bartoš's view, as well as that of other contemporary critics such as Očadlík, the achievement of Hába's quarter-tone system became a locus of nationalist pride in the midst of the generally cosmopolitan modernist movement. Whenever Hába and Schoenberg were compared in the Czech music literature of the time, it was to the detriment of the latter, whose twelve-tone system did not go far enough, either toward microtonality or athematicism. The rhetoric of such a statement would serve two purposes in the anxious climate of modernist music in Prague: not only would it defuse (if not belittle) the threat implied by Schoenberg's modernism and foreignness, but would also attempt to correct the assumptions that Hába's music had nothing to do with the Czech musical experience, and was therefore "not Czech."

All of this commentary seems to configure Hába's rather inaccessible musical language as a socially responsible gesture that took a step toward the cultural education of Czech society: such conjectures would have to remain strictly theoretical, as the opera did not receive a performance before a Czech audience until the so-called "Third Republic" in 1947. Certainly Hába's efforts at cultural education were in no way aligned to those of past generations, where Smetana's warm, folksy comedies and noble, historic tragedies served as untouchable models. As we have seen with *Poupě, Karlštejn, Preciézky,* and even *Bratři Karamazovi,* it was difficult for composers in Prague to extricate themselves from Smetana's legacy and, even if they had so desired, to make a statement of musical modernism within this framework that was accessible to the public. With regard to accessibility, *Matka* might have made more of an impact as a drama than through its music, since the action was derived in part from folk plays of the veristic type, albeit passed through a filter of Brechtian modernism. Even with the numerous references to operatic convention, folk music tradition, and scenes structured around moments of phenomenal music, the quarter tones and athematicism of *Matka's* score still ultimately fall short of the social statement its composer intended, simply because an audience (beyond that of artists and intellectuals) might not recognize the existence of a message at all. While Hába does admittedly succeed in portraying the stultifying atmosphere of the closed, parochial world of Valašsko, the large spans of undifferentiated musical material and directionless plot present the danger of stultifying the audience as well. Indeed, the main difficulty of *Matka* as a socialist opera is that the message, in both drama and music, lies solely in the implication that the absence of a straightforward narrative and of traditional modes of tonal expression expose the fractures of society. Furthermore, these absences also imply the absence of a subjective authorial voice, and as such, seek to represent the collective as an extension of those unfortunates presented on stage. Like many modernist attempts at cultural education, it presupposes a high level of cultural education in the audience to begin with, thus negating its own drive toward social responsibility. As Vačkář later suggested, however, the socialist-intellectualist approach to regaining the lost public was only one solution in the fragmented Prague musical community. The other faction endeavored to speak to the public through the music itself by making a more accessible artistic statement, a method that at its extreme was considered by many as a bow to cheap populism.

Křička's *Strašidlo v zámku:* Modernist Zeitoper, Populist Showpiece

By the early 1930s, the National Theater administration (now under state, as opposed to provincial, control) had begun to realize that financial danger was a very real possibility, and that its commitment to modernist music, largely via Ostrčil, did not yield the necessary revenue to rationalize their continued support. No single contemporary Czech opera, with the exception of Weinberger's 1927 *Švanda dudák*, had proved worthwhile financially, and several others, notably *Wozzeck* and *Strojník Hopkins*, had incurred substantial losses through expensive, unsuccessful productions. Hence, in October 1933, the National Theater took a risk, hoping to follow in the lucrative footsteps of Weinberger's opera, as well as Křenek's internationally successful *Jonny spielt auf.*

The opera they chose, the jazz-inspired *Strašidlo v zámku* by Conservatory professor Jaroslav Křička, had already proved to be a hit over the preceding four years in Brno, Wrocław, Leipzig, Vienna, and in Prague at the Neues Deutsches Theater.[28] Křička, as a member of the older generation that came of age during the First World War, was never associated with the Prague avant-garde, and as such, the use of jazz and popular culture in his opera lay outside the debate on the social function of modern Czech music. Indeed, Křička's compositional style had long existed at the conservative fringe of modern composers, even in Prague. His most forward-looking period—the years 1906–9, during which he aspired to a Novákian brand of impressionism—was spent in near total isolation as a music teacher in Ekaterinoslav, Ukraine. Upon his return to Prague, his affinities lay squarely with the older Conservatory set, where he was groomed as a replacement for the theorist Stecker; his work as conductor of the Hlahol Choral Society also supported the compositional output of the same circle. All through his career, Křička aspired to success on the operatic stage: *Strašidlo* was his second work to be accepted at the National Theater, the first being *Hipolyta* in 1917; he also wrote several children's operas, each displaying simplicity of style and directness of expression, yet without any sort of neoclassicist/modernist edge. Nevertheless, the populist and cosmopolitan implications of *Strašidlo*'s score helped to provoke a further polemic regarding the ability for such music to be called "modern art" at all.

Multiple sources, most of them conjectural, described Křička's decision to create a jazzy "light opera" as being based largely on the financial success of *Jonny spielt auf* and *Švanda dudák*.[29] Stylistically, *Strašidlo* bears direct connections to these works, both of which premiered in 1927, the year Křička began work on his opera; the prevailing stylistic references place it firmly in the larger generic category of Zeitoper, of which Křenek's *Jonny* is considered the flagship work. Zeitoper, as defined by Susan Cook, was a highly popular type of modernist opera in which the composer presented a stylized view of the modern world. The often comic or satirical plots would unfold to the accompaniment of a mixture of jazz and traditional operatic music, dancing, and new technology such as megaphones, loudspeakers, neon lights, machines of varous types, and importantly, film (for which reason they were often called *Filmopern*).[30] The setting was always modern, and mostly urban; plots tried to convey objectivity through various types of *Alltäglichkeit*, banality, sentimentality, and cliché, while still cloaking the action in an atmosphere of fantastic surrealism, rather like the telling of a modern legend. A showcase for cosmopolitan aesthetics, they often took an ironic stance toward this viewpoint for the purposes of making a political or social statement, as seen most prominently in the collaborations of Brecht and Weill, as well as in Burian's *Bubu z Montparnassu*. As the first Czech Zeitoper to be produced on the stage, Křička's work struggled with the duality of self-parody built into the genre, and it remains to be determined whether *Strašidlo* did in fact contain this modernist ironic distance, or whether it was merely a vehicle for its composer's success.

Based on Oscar Wilde's novella *The Canterville Ghost* from 1887, modernized, and reset in the fictional Bohemian castle of Satalice, Křička's *Strašidlo v zámku* lies somewhere between genres, as indeed most Zeitopern do, with their heavy stylistic borrowings from operetta, cabaret/revue, and operatic parody. The trouble that most of Křička's contemporaries had with *Strašidlo* was its lack of clarity in this regard: without the obvious irony of parody, the necessary banality of the sentimental, or the cultured surrealism of fantasy, these musical references could be read as naive, unselfconscious clichés. Particularly disturbing for the avant-garde Prague critics of 1933 would have been the lack of a Brechtian social message to accompany the populist music, since the art-music fascination with jazz purely as a cultural novelty had largely passed by the beginning of the Depression. Furthermore, the opera's juxtaposition of the modern elements of Zeitoper with devices self-consciously associated with traditional Czechness—namely, a sentimental folk song and a polka—were reminiscent of *Švanda*, a work the critics reviled. Given that Křička himself did not belong to the young avant-garde but to an older generation, *Strašidlo* quickly took on the specter of pandering to the taste of the conservative bourgeois subscribers, the cultural enemy of all sworn modernists since the "*Wozzeck* Affair." By the time it reached the stage of the Estates Theater in late 1933, having gained popularity in the Austro-German world, the work had also acquired a sense of Germanness its Czech public may not have appreciated.

Nevertheless, certain elements of *Strašidlo*, both musical and dramatic, have much in common with neoclassical reforms to the modern operatic genre. Cast in six large scenes of relatively equal length with four symphonic interludes, the music conforms loosely to a number-opera scheme, connected by moments of dramatic declamation and melodrama, such that the music is both highly episodic and continuous. A significant factor in the shaping of the large-scale musico-dramatic flow is the almost wholesale repetition of numbers with very little variation, especially to the accompaniment, which is pervasively homophonic. This aspect alone lends the opera a revue-like quality, wherein the audience has several chances to hear the main songs and dances prior to the final curtain. In keeping with the use of songs instead of arias, there are relatively few moments of extended lyrical melody in the vocal writing (Wagnerian or otherwise): the text is set mostly syllabically, in short, repetitive phrases, and patter-style ensembles appear as frequently as solo passages. Křička's harmonic language is always decidedly tonal, albeit peppered with clustered dissonances and momentary bitonal juxtapositions throughout: some of these arise from an outsider's (mistaken) perception of blues-based harmony, while others are simply theatrical grotesqueries. Interestingly, in no way is the use of dissonance related to the complex polyphony of other Czech modernists, since Křička's texture is comparatively thin, with very few moving voices; furthermore, its musical language is neither as concentrated as that of *Jonny*, with its basis in expressionism, nor as lighthearted as the jazz revues of Ježek, which have no pretensions to high art. *Strašidlo*—much like an earlier Czech attempt at neoclassical comic opera, *Preciézky*—sits in an ill-defined musical space, at once romantic in its overall format, antiromantic in its vocal style, and inconsistently modernist in its application of certain newer compositional techniques. Nevertheless, it can be argued that the resulting stylistic blend was designed to reflect the chaotic juxtapositions of the text, in which old and new, East and West collide for comedic effect.

In order to maximize the effect of cultural differences, Křička and his librettist made the necessary changes to Wilde's story in order to evoke a contemporary Czech environment, updating the action to the present and adding a new opening scene in Prague. The bustling real estate office we see in the first few minutes of the opera provides the only specifically "modern" or urban setting typical to Zeitopern, as the rest of the action takes place in a "historic" castle in the Bohemian countryside. The thin and uncomplicated plot unfolds as follows:

Characters:		
	Mr. Hollywood, American tycoon	bass
	Mrs. Hollywood, his wife	mezzo-soprano
	Elida, their daughter[31]	soprano
	Cedrik, their son	alto/mezzo-soprano
	Count Jiří of Satalice	tenor
	Theodor Proutek, Ex-minister	tenor
	Vendelín Taštička, realtor	bass-baritone
	The Chatelaine	alto
	Andulka, chambermaid	soprano
	Bob, a black servant	tenor
	The spirit of Count Kazimír of Satalice	baritone

Despairing of ever selling their main property, Satalice castle, in such difficult financial times, the real estate firm of Taštička & Co. advertises it to two potential buyers: the Czech Ex-minister Proutek and the American tycoon Mr. Hollywood. After the former is scared off by Taštička's mention of the 300-year-old ghost in the castle, Hollywood and his daughter Elida express delight at the novelty of residing in a haunted location, and agree to purchase it. The family travels by train to Satalice and receives a warm welcome by the young owner, Count Jiří, and his servants. During an evening of ping pong (mixed doubles, sung as a quartet) with her husband, daughter, and teenaged son Cedrik, Mrs. Hollywood discovers

(*continued*)

a red stain on the parquet floors. Servants explain to the family that this was the place where the Duke Kazimír of Satalice murdered his wife 300 years before, and that the stain will only disappear by breaking the castle's curse. The skeptical Cedrik decides that, with the help of the latest brand-name cleaning products from America, the stain will be removed; he sings and dances a black-bottom while the ensemble applies "Clerk's Universal Cleaner" to the floor.[32] As the scene draws to a close, Jiří and Elida begin to fall in love; they sing a lyrical duet, interspersed with an offstage polka and folk song, performed by local villagers. Overnight, Cedrik decides to set up a film camera, in order to discover the truth behind the alleged ghost. Meanwhile, unable to sleep, Elida descends and encounters Jiří, who has dressed up as a ghost in order to seduce her: the moment she discovers the truth, they are interrupted by Cedrik and by the servants, whose cries awaken the rest of the household. Disappointed by the apparent fraud, Mr. Hollywood declares the castle no longer enticing without the existence of a real ghost. Once everyone is finally asleep, the real Duke Kazimír appears; he is encountered by Hollywood, who makes an offer to bring him back to America as a museum exhibit. Later, the sleepless and now lovesick Elida also encounters Kazimír, who frightens her enough to make her call Jiří for help: the two are reconciled, and their kiss breaks the spell over the castle, whereupon the ghost gratefully disappears. In the morning, Ex-minister Proutek shows up prepared for a legal battle over the ownership of Satalice. He is met instead by a willing Hollywood, who leaves happily with his family and new son-in-law, Jiří.

While in the larger picture, the score to *Strašidlo* presents a mixture of elements inherited from jazz, cabaret, and operetta, certain specific musical tendencies arise with regard to individual characters and dramatic situations. The opening scene in the Prague real estate office is characterized by motoric rhythms and a rapid alternation between ensembles and short solo passages, emulating the frenetic pace of the urban business environment and setting the tone for the rest of the work; jazz references, mostly syncopations and hemiolas, occur in passing. This nervous energy carries over into the first interlude, which uses further motoric rhythms, an enhanced percussion section, and a sustained *accelerando* to depict the journey from Prague to Satalice via express train (50–54).[33] Taking a cue from Zeitopern such as *Royal Palace, Jonny*, and *Mahagonny*, Křička and the librettist Löwenbach insert a film sequence during the interlude, revealing images of the Bohemian countryside, complete with peasants working in the fields, as seen from the speeding train carriage. During the film, Křička presents the first musical moment of cultural difference on which the entire opera's premise is based: alongside the emulation of technology in the orchestra, the visual imagery of Czech tradition is brought into relief, and is gradually allowed to take over the music through the introduction of folk-like melodies.

Once the Americans arrive at Satalice, they themselves become the main locus of cultural juxtaposition in Křička's score. Although the entire Hollywood family is represented by music marked as "American," in the form of modern dances played by a jazz band embedded within the orchestra, it is Cedrik who is associated with the greatest number of such instances, as though his modern, skeptical attitude is the least "European" of the cast. This association with Cedrik also characterizes jazz reflexively, such that, as "Cedrik's music," it is set apart as "un-European," modern without a sense of history, and mundane without a taste for romance. Since Cedrik and his film are the dramatic catalysts at more than one point in the opera, jazz thus becomes somewhat of an agent in itself, intruding into everyday European life. As the main representative of jazz, Cedrik receives several numbers devoted to dances such as the black-bottom (which recurs throughout the score), the foxtrot, and at one moment, the black-bottom mixed with an offstage polka.

The first appearance of the black-bottom occurs during Cedrik's attempt to clean the bloodstained floor (enacting a parody of the dance's shuffling movements) with "Clerk's Universal Cleaner," and the song itself takes on the character of an advertisement for the same. After a brief introduction of "grotesque," neoclassicist-inspired cluster chords, the dance accompaniment produces a typical ragtime bass (with the alternation of bass notes and chords) and several instances of syncopation, all characteristic of the black-bottom (ex. 10.4, 83).[34] Above this, Cedrik sings a tune that is set apart from its accompaniment, merging only at moments of social or political commentary (Clerk's can apparently be used "for fabric, wood, the past," erasing everything without mercy: "I think that it should even be applied more in politics"[35]). Křička followed the black-bottom with a curious segment entitled *tempo di blues*, wherein the whole family and Jiří sing the praises of Clerk, to music much more reminiscent of operetta ensembles than of the blues. During the ensemble, Cedrik takes the opportunity to lampoon American values: "Clerk at work, / that is truly American, / for we purge puritanically / whatever disrupts our business."[36] Thus, these lighthearted moments manage to conflate Americanness with efficiency, level-headedness, sophistication, cutthroat capitalism, a classless society, and somewhat obliquely, with the glory of honest work. The music and the gestures of the dance, through popular stereotypes, both evoke their supposed African-American origin; conflated with the image of domestic servitude it strongly evokes the social inequality of contemporary America, although such an implication may not have been obvious to a European audience. In fact, an African-American domestic servant *does* appear in *Strašidlo*—Bob, whose flirtation with the Czech chambermaid Andulka parallels the Jonny–Yvonne relationship in Křenek's opera—but he is not always associated with jazz and almost never interacts with the rest of the cast.[37] Rather, the inclusion of Cedrik's black-bottom is aimed perfectly at the European perception of jazz as a light-entertainment medium, brought from America by the moneyed classes of Euro-American society. The dance reappears

[No matter where you find dirt, American "Clerk's" will clean it.
For fabric, wood, the past, it wipes everything clean without pity.
No matter where you find dirt, American "Clerk's" will clean it.
I think that it should even be applied more in politics.]

Example 10.4. Křička, *Strašidlo v zámku*, Black-bottom (83/1–16).

Example 10.5. Křička, *Strašidlo v zámku*, "Amoroso" music (100/12; 101/1–3).

twice more, both in connection to the disappearance of the ghost: first after Jiří's hoax is uncovered, then in the finale after his kiss to Elida has banished the ghost forever. Each time it contains a different commentary by Cedrik on the power of "modern methods" to dispel ancient superstitions, and thereby to link the cultures of America and Europe.

Diametrically opposed to the element of modern dance in *Strašidlo v zámku* is Elida and Jiří's duet, also recurrent throughout the opera as the embodiment of lyricism and old-fashioned romance. The duet (labeled *andante amoroso*) is probably one of the longest numbers in the opera, running through a series of interlinked sections in different keys and meters in each of its three incarnations; its prolonged melodies and arch-like phrasing mark it as the erotic focus of the work (ex. 10.5, 100–101). Its chromaticism, occurring at climactic modulations, is purely in a romantic vein, unlike the "grotesque" cluster chords in the rest of the opera, which can be traced to some sort of neoclassicist polytonality. Like the black-bottom/blues combination, the *amoroso* always contains an embedded piece of unrelated music, the first time an offstage polka (103), the second a "cavatina-duetto" of a slowfox character (134), and finally an offstage female chorus describing the disappearance of the ghost (210). In each case, the subsequent return of the *amoroso* music implies the end of an unwelcome distraction, intruding into the couple's private world in the midst of an extended courtship; the successive recurrence of this music gives a similar impression on a larger scale, as the opera gradually sheds its comedic, revue-like character. Nevertheless, as seductively operatic as these gestures appear out of context, their juxtaposition with the modern dances of Cedrik lends an aura of operetta to such expressions of lyricism, turning the apparently heartfelt into the sentimental and formulaic. Since there is no obvious hint of irony in the duet, either musically or dramatically, it seems not to be a parody of either traditional opera or operetta; so, too, the banality is not self-conscious enough to pass for that of the sentimental scenes typical to Zeitopern such as *Bubu*. Rather, the impression is that of naiveté, the positive world to the negative of the black-bottom with its disruptive energy. The cultured realm of true feeling, it is a European middle-class world, where norms and values are upheld unconditionally in lovers' duet thirds.

Křička juxtaposed the musical worlds of both the black-bottom and the *amoroso* directly with music that evokes a specifically Czech atmosphere, perhaps even more naively than the duet: a polka and a folk song, both performed offstage. These folk-like materials appear, unlike the jazz references, in moments of dramatic repose, such as scene endings; therefore, little musical tension comes across to the listener, despite the great stylistic disparity with the "onstage" music. Aside from their encroachment in the mechanistic film music described above, the first occasions for the polka and folk song to merge with the opera's vocal music occur in the context of Elida and Jiří's initial duet. These appearances, designed as a backdrop to Jiří's sentimental reminiscences, become a part of his attempts at courtship, such that Elida's perception of the neighboring village dance begins to blur with her own imagination of Jiří's past (ex. 10.6a, 103). The effect is strengthened with the folk song, sung by an unseen soloist (ex. 10.6b, 111), producing a meditative atmosphere that brings the couple closer together, symbolized by overlapping statements of the motto (113). At the end of the scene, when the solitary Elida repeats the folk song to herself, the dramatic stasis solidifies the sense of sentimentality in which Křička used the reference; the diatonic character of both the polka and folk-song melodies offsets the lush chromaticism of the duet proper.

The next inclusion of the polka in *Strašidlo*, combined with Cedrik's black-bottom (ex. 10.7, 158), has an entirely different dramatic function. As representatives of the Old and New Worlds, respectively, their simultaneous performance embodies either the clash of two cultures or their rapprochement, depending on the outcome of the opera. The scene is also an instance of the wholesale repetition of numbers in the manner of popular music theater; it was created during the 1930 revision with new verses for Cedrik and the chorus, and interspersed with a polka (with similar phrasing but a new melody) for the corps de ballet, complete with rhythmic foot stomping. When the black-bottom returns alongside the polka, it is perhaps the clearest moment of musical parody in the score, in that, through the sheer improbability of the juxtaposition itself, both elements are subject to ridicule and neither seems to be favored over the other.

The question of cultural clash or rapprochement reemerges at the very end of the opera. The ghost, representing the European past, has disappeared and the Americans are going home—with their new convert, Jiří—to go on with their lives as before. Cedrik reinforces this cultural separation with the reappearance of his black-bottom in the finale, now with the text: "The practical American spirit— / the romantic European spirit, / must apparently resist each other / —as you have observed."[38] Musically, however, this victorious mood is somewhat compromised by the continuous shifting of cultural references, now

Example 10.6a. Křička, *Strašidlo v zámku*, appearance of offstage polka (103/6–12).

Example 10.6b. Křička, *Strašidlo v zámku*, appearance of offstage folksong (111/7–14).

more extreme than elsewhere in the opera. For all Cedrik's objectivity, Elida intertwines a chromatic, lyrical melody amid the black-bottom, conveying conciliatory sentiments rather than alienating ones; her music elides with a reappearance of the operetta-inspired *tempo di blues* as the vocal ensemble builds. The *amoroso* music returns also, now in a march variant that seems to imply, through its newly desentimentalized state, the Americanization of European culture. The final moments of *Strašidlo v zámku* have some even more widely divergent implications: after the *amoroso*-march merges with the folk song in a victorious tutti reminiscent of the *Švanda* finale, the regular orchestra stops and an onstage brass band concludes the opera with totally unrelated music. The passage is meant to evoke the Satalice village band, playing unchallenging and mostly diatonic music with no trace of jazz influence whatsoever: the trio, which

[No matter where you find a phantom, American "Clerk's" will clean it;
without mercy it will rid everything of scary ghostliness.
Chorus: I say]

Example 10.7. Křička, *Strašidlo v zámku*, combination of black-bottom and polka
(158/1–8).

is repeated *ad libitum* as the villagers recede into the distance, includes a chorus
that sings about how it only takes a kiss to disperse worries.[39] It is a moment very
similar to the offstage interruptions from earlier in the work, particularly those
during the train-film sequence; as the final music in Křička's score, however, it
forces the listener to question which music is the norm among the many eclectic choices. While Cedrik's jazz is certainly the most dramatically influential in
the opera and has the greatest aura of modernity (if not of modernism per se),
it seems also to intrude on the prevailing operetta-based sound world of most of
the score, albeit not as obviously as the offstage folk-like material. In the final

moments, however, this dominance is reversed, in that Jiří and Elida's duet recedes in favor of a celebratory marching band, whose major-mode diatonicism is as unproblematic as it is decidedly antimodern.

With a few exceptions, the members of the critical community of Prague were surprisingly moderate in their reception of *Strašidlo v zámku*, especially given the tepid premiere at the Estates Theater, where many of the ensemble dance numbers passed without applause. Nor were the conservative critics overly laudatory toward what was in essence a normalization of jazz within the world of operetta. Šilhan, while admitting the presence of "musico-dramatic talent" in the moments of operatic parody, felt that the combination of such divergent elements resulted in many "secondhand ideas" producing a real "mishmash."[40] Jindřich Pihert from *Lidové listy* noted the successful production of a contemporary comic opera (which he disdainfully compared to Weill's *Dreigroschenoper* and *Mahagonny*), but viewed the synthesis of different musical styles as unsuccessful, leading to a situation where one was no longer able to differentiate between parody and truth.[41] These assessments echoed Robert Smetana's review of the 1929 Brno premiere, in which he bemoaned the reduction of serious Czech art to a series of musical caricatures, particularly when both composer and librettist could have offered a serious solution to the question of cultural polarity between America and Europe.[42]

As can be expected, two members of the younger generation, Patzaková and Očadlík, took a much harder line with Křička's opera, opening up avenues of criticism with greater aesthetic implications. Patzaková's review for *Národní osvobození* declared *Strašidlo* to be a moral failure, referring to the arbitrary combination of theatrical genres without any regard for the artistic whole, thrown together in an attempt at success on the international stage. For Patzaková, the work simply masqueraded under the slogan of "Nová Buffa" (recalling the slightly more "serious" *Preciézky* by Zich) or *Alltäglichkeit*. "The web of incongruous elements, the derivative, shallow and fruitless ideas, the mishmash of pseudo-folk sentimentality and fashionable dance cosmopolitanism, all of these earthbound, ephemeral, and transient fancies came out unabashedly. The more seriously the singers put on airs, and the more the theater tried to circumnavigate the jagged rocks of the light genre and adapt it to the higher requirements of the stage, the more obvious the vanity of such an artistic work becomes."[43] Clearly, Patzaková's negative opinion was formed by both the opera itself and the administrative decision to produce a popular and lucrative show after closing the door to more serious, modernist works.

Očadlík's mention of Křička, made only in passing amid his larger essay on modernism in music (see discussion above, p. 266), invokes an interesting paradigm that speaks to the larger issue of popular music and its role in art. "Instead of a new understanding, which often painfully shatters and undermines a pleasant reliability, we get a cult of mediocrity, if not of the substandard level of the *Švanda-Jonny-Strašidlo* type. *Sicut erat in principio et nunc et semper.*"[44]

Apart from the low opinion of the quality of Křička's music, the implications in Očadlík's comparison to *Švanda dudák* are clear: for all the embarrassment Weinberger had caused with his too-close reading of Czech tradition, *Strašidlo* erred doubly, in that it cloaked its fraudulent Czechness in modernism. For the critic, this modernism was, like Křenek's, only of the fashionable variety, and as such, not modern in a manner that reflected moral or artistic consequences (or *důslednost*). With the juxtaposition of all three operas, Očadlík declared the incompatibility of both the naive folk style and fashionable jazz dances with modern opera. While Křička's two precedents were both very popular and lucrative works on the European operatic stage, it should be noted that they achieved success for widely differing reasons: whereas *Švanda dudák* capitalized on the popularity of *The Bartered Bride*, *Jonny spielt auf* was the most spectacular Zeitoper of its time, a status that in no way tarnished its modernism. Indeed, it is curious that Očadlík should suddenly forget how influential Křenek's music had been on the Czech avant-garde of his generation, particularly Burian. Clearly, to some extent all three composers were "guilty" of the sin of intentional populism, which would serve to exclude them from the modernist camp: all three could now be excluded from the collective Czech identity also, as indeed Weinberger and Křenek already had been, for different reasons. Očadlík's statement points to a larger problem, which, as we have seen in chapter 9, came into open debate by the mid-1930s: the relevance of popular music as a whole and its artistic impact on concert music. In the solution to this question the members of the Prague avant-garde were slowly beginning to see a resolution to their crisis with society. As the decade came to a close, however, so did the democratic environment that had fueled these artistic experiments, successful or otherwise, and the vociferous debates that perpetually surrounded them.

* * *

The almost total lack of success that *Strašidlo* met with among Czech critics is symptomatic of the larger position of populism, modernism, and opera in 1930s Prague. Why did Ježek's jazz revues receive such accolades from the younger generation as "modern, refined, completely individual, and Czech," when an equal number of Americanisms in Křička relegated his work to merely "fashionable dance cosmopolitanism," "ephemeral and transient fancies?" This same community could also turn respectfully to Hába's compositional leadership, even though his music had little chance of gaining a widespread audience, and when he himself did not insist that his students write in a similar style. As described in chapter 9, much of the solution to this perplexing riddle lies in the political quagmire that was worsening year after year in Central Europe: although the work of Ježek and Hába is certainly not without its internal problems, the politics of these composers were never in doubt, and as such, the role of their music in any sort of culturo-political narrative was unequivocal. For *Strašidlo*, on the other hand, the simultaneous acceptance and rejection of Western values, for no obvious reason, did little to clarify the author's political stance at a time when such statements were becoming increasingly necessary.[45] In many ways, the pressure that earlier generations of Czech composers had felt—for every composition to be a contribution to collective identity—had transformed in the 1930s into a pressure to shape the political consciousness of the Czech public. Just as composers of Novák's heyday around the First World War had faced the charge of betraying the nation through subjective fancy, so now were younger artists threatened with the implication that apolitical music opened the door to fascism. So firmly did these idealists believe in the power of their art to preserve their fragile democracy that they forced each other to uphold the rhetoric of militancy, either through aesthetic pronouncements such as Krejčí's or Očadlík's, or in the prosocialist or pro-Western (i.e., populist) compositional factions. It is, of course, impossible to determine whether the modernist art of the 1930s could ever have regained the European society it so desperately wanted to save, had it been given the chance to run its course without political interruption. After the Second World War, that society had changed irrevocably, and the balance of popular and high-art cultures had shifted substantially. Perhaps the power of operas such as *Matka* and *Strašidlo* lies in the growing consciousness they reveal of a social order in its waning years. For this consciousness demonstrates the increasing need they felt of voicing, perhaps for the last time, the tremendous cultural expression of the interwar Czechoslovak Republic, before it was no longer possible.

Chapter Eleven

The Ideological Debates of Prague Within a European Context

In the words of Emil František Burian:

> **Tradition.** A hiding place. And it doesn't cost us a lot of sweat to find the usual philistinism and unconscious conservatism in it. It is one of those words that we can throw countless times and it will never come back to us, not even discredited. How many reviews, articles, and analyses abound in this overused definition:
>
> > If you are a futurist, you are not traditional.
> > If you are a dadaist, same thing.
> > If you are a poetist, still the same.
> > If you are a romantic = ?
> > Impressionist = ?
> > Decadent = ?
>
> If you are traditional, you are a romantic, impressionist, decadent (everything that does not mean tradition for the Czechoslovak Republic).
>
> If you are traditional, you are a **conservative**, an epigon, chewing the cud of everything tried, tested, and true, ad nauseam.
>
> Why are you a conservative (in the above sense)? Because it hasn't occurred to you to be anything else, because "you are not gifted from above, you cannot buy it at a pharmacy."
>
> Tradition, the comfortable "pharmacy," provides you with a peaceful life, disturbed by nothing. You dissolve with happiness that you, too, are finally a creative artist. It authorizes you, though (and this is the main thing), to be for once in your life a competent artist, provides you the advantage of a "licensed" poet or painter, leads you infallibly by impassible roads and gives you the crest of modernism. All the others, the so-called untraditional malefactors of national culture we cast off, discredit, denounce, in order to use them again, "when" forced by circumstances we understand them, for our own apish genius, for a new tradition, or conservatism, *vulgo* incapability.
> Long live tradition. Our poor tradition.[1]

In his idiosyncratic, anti-establishmentarian style, Burian voiced many of the larger concerns facing the Prague community over the course of the early twentieth century. Despite the multiple waves of Smetana-worship that passed through the ranks of its composers and critics on all sides of the ideological divide, there were also dissenting voices that pulled against the confines of such an overly restrictive tradition. Burian's astute perception of tradition, not as the noble preservation of national culture and identity, but as a "hiding place" for conservatism, indolence, and sheer inability seems to laugh in the face of everything the Cultural Revivalists held dear. That the bearers of an increasingly irrelevant lineage from past masters should have done so only out of a lack of ingenuity—or said another way, of any impulse toward modernism—speaks volumes about the role of new music in this society. As a young artist in a stagnating musical atmosphere, Burian would have keenly felt, on one hand, the compulsion to be "modern" at all costs out of a social responsibility toward the nation, and on the other, the collective resistance toward new influences from the rest of Europe and North America. Despite the first of these ideologies, taking up the challenge to bring modern art to local audiences in Prague meant most likely to be "cast off, discredited, denounced" as un-Czech. Increasingly after 1900 and particularly after 1918, the concept of modernism was cross-referenced to contemporary activities in the European musical scene. Even the term "modernism" itself, as it was used in the Czech press, was specifically charged with a sense of coming to terms with the European avant-garde, whether it be with an attitude of "catching up" to it, or surpassing it on a moral level. Thus, modernism itself was just as often rejected as a signpost for the future—either consciously, through the reaffirmation of tradition, or unconsciously, by positing a conservative "Czech modernism" as the morally correct alternative to the questionable activities of cultures abroad. It would be this conflicted attitude that would define music making in Prague across this whole era, just as much as the compositions its participants produced.

Modernisms, Influences, and the Czech Historical Consciousness

In many ways, the main question in the Czech critical discourse on music was whether outside influences could have a positive impact on Czech composition as a whole, and if so, which composers and styles would best "suit" an a priori image of Czech musical identity. These discussions, as we have seen throughout this history, revolved not so much around the individual composer's tastes, but rather around the imagined needs of Czech society, such that the whole phenomenon of intercultural influence acquired the trope of social responsibility. Fashions, whether or not figures such as Nejedlý would ever admit to it, played a large role in this part of the discourse; hence, for example, when Nejedlý and Ostrčil first embraced Strauss's modernism, later to reject him in favor of Mahler, their change of heart was influenced by similar shifts throughout the

European compositional elite. When critics turned this decision back against composers who continued to be influenced by Strauss (such as Novák and Jeremiáš), what started as an aesthetic judgment became the basis of a moral one, as though the perceived lack of modernity in an artist's choice of influences had a socially damaging effect. A stronger implication is that any such artist, by ignoring the alleged cultural needs of the Czech nation, brought on the specter of subjectivism, which is to say that no self-respecting disciple of the Cultural Revival could possibly stray from an imagined canon of Czech musical aesthetics as to make artistic decisions based on personal taste, for to do so would be self-ish to the point of national betrayal. Almost until the end of the interwar period, despite the advances made by the 1930s avant-garde, musical consequences were equated with moral ones, and foreign influence was often held to be just as arbitrary as the individual composer's mood.

Many of these influences have already been discussed in the context of a more detailed historical narrative. As described in chapter 1, the debates inherited by the generations of the twentieth century were sparked by pan-European nine-teenth-century polemics over the merits of program versus absolute music, par-ticularly surrounding Brahms and Wagner. Especially because Dvořák, in the final stage of his career, joined the Wagnerian cause, each of the belligerent fac-tions after 1900 was principally on the side of program music, even though their consciousness of this state of affairs grew ever more hazy. Their vehement argu-ments, therefore, can be partially explained by differences in interpretation of Wagner as a foreign authority on musical aesthetics: while the Nejedlians held that Smetana and his lineage were the only composers to blend Wagner's tech-nique with "Czechness," those at the Conservatory stood behind Dvořák, and eventually Novák and Suk, to a similar degree. As long as these imagined line-ages lasted, so were their respective Wagnerian inheritances progressively embedded into their compositional styles, until the differences in the music between factions became virtually unrecognizable.

The most striking aspect of foreign influences in the Habsburg era, however, came with the wave of early modernism of the 1890s in Western Europe, felt in the subsequent decade in Prague. While Mahler's music gained support among the Nejedlians (who, it seems, failed to understand his irony), and Debussian impressionism became an important expressive device for those associated with Novák, it was Strauss who made the greatest impact across the widest segment of Prague musical life. While the influences of all three revolutionized the orches-tration and harmonic language of contemporary Czech music, the perceived subjectivism of Strauss's music also left its followers and their compositions open to attack, particularly by the members of the Nejedlý circle. Impressionism was also felt to be akin to subjectivism and weakness, whereas the ironic distance in Mahler's musical expression (e.g., the inclusion of military, folk-like, and chil-dren's music, however distorted) was taken to stand for a collectivist aesthetic, and therefore closer to the legacy of the Cultural Revival. Thus, to mimic a foreign model perceived as weak was "un-Czech," while to embrace one spiritually aligned with Smetana was to do honor to tradition by embodying it in a modern form.

One of the only other prewar compositional movements to gain ground among Czech composers was that of early Schoenbergian expressionism, often described as constructivism in the context of the Czech orchestral style. Here the influence was somewhat indirect, having been adapted to a more conservative approach; certainly no Czech (or German-Bohemian) composer attempted anything as avant-garde as the Second Viennese School until the arrival of Hába and the quarter-tone composers. As a result, most commentators viewed such extreme modernism as a marker beyond which no musician in Prague could go without censure; Schoenberg himself received mention in the Czech music press only a handful of times before the war, despite the general knowledge of his activities. Nevertheless, a few individuals explored the world of proto-expressionism in however limited a capacity: Suk's second string quartet op. 15 (1916), Vomáčka's piano cycle *Hledání* (Seaching, 1914), and the oeuvres of Ostrčil, Vycpálek, and the short-lived Jaroslav Novotný all bear witness to the impact in Prague of *Verklärte Nacht* and the first two published string quartets by Schoenberg. By the time of the "*Wozzeck* Affair," Schoenberg was a household name, reappearing in Czech critical rhetoric—if only to be compared unfavorably with Berg, whose more accessible modernism was deemed necessary for Czech society. As with Wagner and Strauss, Schoenberg's influence could be accepted or rejected at will, depending on the changing needs of historical consciousness.

After four years of war, during which the subject of foreign influence was quite self-consciously avoided, Czech musicians entered the realm of democratic independence with just as self-conscious a desire to "catch up with Europe." It is a moment of almost quixotic aesthetic change in our historical narrative, when a group that had continuously defined itself as "modern" suddenly became both aware of its own parochialism and driven by this same innate modernism toward Western influences. As we have seen in chapter 5, in the first few years of the First Republic the overriding cultural tendency throughout most artistic circles in Prague was to embrace French culture in all its facets, encapsulated by the virtual adoration of Cocteau and Apollinaire, and musically by the fascination with Parisian revues and modern dances, Les Six, and Stravinsky (who by this time was accepted as a Parisian phenomenon). Nevertheless, such potential influences were just as quickly abandoned by the intrinsically conservative Spolek pro moderní hudbu, the leaders of which adopted a self-righteously traditionalist stance. Even Křenek, who had been hailed as an exiled son, now making a name for himself internationally, was swiftly disowned (along with his "physiological music") as "Czech" once his music actually became known to Prague audiences in the mid-1920s. As always, nomenclature was important for identity: the Spolek could easily serve as gatekeepers by identifying what was and was not "moderní," just as they could include or exclude certain composers under a rubric of Czechness, often through the very same logic.

The ultimate testing ground for these expectations of new music and its effect on Czech composition was the 1924 International Society for Contemporary Music (ISCM) festival, which was terribly disappointing for most artists in the home audience, whose worst fears with regard to European modernism were fulfilled. Primarily, it showed that what they had always considered to be modernist at home paled in comparison to the full-fledged avant-garde communities from across Europe. Conversely, the Czech contingent proved itself to be staunchly conservative and backward in the eyes of the international attendees, who were treated to a barrage of Smetana and outdated compositions by older modernists instead of anything more radical. By the 1925 ISCM, the mood was one of resigned isolationism, to the point of excluding even their "own" Martinů, whose music had strayed too far from the accepted canon of traditional aesthetics and compositional techniques to be considered "Czech." Behind all of this, however, still lay the desire of a great many musicians to be accepted on the international concert or operatic stage without compromising the artistic values with which they had been raised. In a much more explicit manner, as Burian's inflammatory text at the beginning of this chapter indicates, a fledgling avant-garde was beginning to carve out a new identity not based on any of the previous values, but rather one that was inherently and unapologetically cosmopolitan. Nevertheless, it would require a substantially different change in atmosphere before any reconciliation could be made with European modernism, without the nationalist baggage of the early postindependence years.

This reconciliation was brought about, extremely tentatively, by the interest in Zich's (at least nominally) neoclassical opera *Preciézky* in early 1926. Although Zich's music was more or less aligned with Busoni's *Junge Klassizität*, its basis was still on the conservative side of Czech expressionism (i.e., late romanticism), and was ultimately derived from Smetana. Nevertheless, the Czech critical community accepted *Preciézky* with its evident debt to non-Czech influences, thereby opening the door to other, more radical possibilities. That the "*Wozzeck* Affair" would transpire just months later is a testimony to this change of attitude, albeit somewhat surprising in its vehemence. The controversy was not so much about Berg or the Germanness of the music, but rather its modernism, the idea of which the vast majority of Czech musicians still cherished, albeit in a moderately conservative way. As such, the controversy said more about the Czechs' image of themselves as belonging to the European cultural sphere than about their acceptance of the music itself. Ironically, it had absolutely nothing to do with the German-Bohemian musical community, whose leader Zemlinsky had premiered the *Drei Bruchstücke*, prompting its complete performance in the first place. The "*Wozzeck* Affair" also lay on the cusp between generations, as Hába and Očadlík were to take over the Spolek pro moderní hudbu just one year later, signaling the rise of a new attitude toward modernism and cultural interaction.

Hába, as perhaps the most internationally recognized Czech composer of his generation besides Martinů, held an important position in the Prague musical community, in that he was able to direct the attention of "his" organizations—the Spolek and Přítomnost—toward an international outlook much more consistently than ever before. The fact that these organizations involved both Czech and German composers was integral to their cosmopolitan worldview—indeed, it can be said that Hába's leadership shifted the collective identity of Czech composers from the overwhelming burden of historical consciousness to a cosmopolitan consciousness, where one's place in modern Europe far outweighed one's legacy from the past. From the time of the 1928 Siena ISCM, which saw a concert of quarter-tone music as well as of Voice-band, the composers of Prague participated more actively in European festivals, culminating in the Herculean efforts surrounding the 1935 Prague ISCM, a testament to their cooperative spirit on an international level. No longer were the Czech representatives begrudging and miserly in their enthusiasm for European modernism, and the expectations of mutual acceptance had long since disappeared. Simply put, Hába's generation was the first in Prague actually to be modernist, in full appreciation of what the term signified.

As the most cosmopolitan Czech composer of his generation, Martinů's role as correspondent from Paris should also not be overlooked. Although after 1923 he ceased to interact with the Prague community on a daily basis, both his thought-provoking articles and his compositions proved to be divisive in Czech critical opinion. Indeed, Martinů was a constant reminder of the Czechs' sudden embrace of French culture in the early years of independence; for those who resorted to a comfortable, conservative isolation, he would have seemed an embarrassment. Nevertheless, his attitude toward cultural interaction had a positive effect on the community he left (particularly among the Mánes Group), even though his influence often took the form of polemics with the more conservative composers and critics.

Martinů's problematic position serves to highlight a larger issue in Czech musical identity: that of the success of their composers abroad, and both the petty professional jealousy and collective anxiety it seems to have produced. In certain situations, as in the case of Janáček after the Prague premiere of *Jenůfa* in 1916, individual international success helped to bring European modernism to the Czech community, and vice versa. Although Janáček had avoided the constant ideological battles of Prague musical circles in favor of the more peaceful environment in Brno, his operas produced a substantial following in the capital, followed by even greater successes in the Austro-German world, where his individualism was appreciated. All of these factors, however, also served to exclude him from many of the musical debates in Prague, including those surrounding nationalism, modernism, and the social responsibility of art. His music, at once individual, regional, and international, lay outside of the bounds created by Nejedlý, who had done much to exclude Janáček many years before. To a further extreme, Weinberger's international success, coupled with his Jewish heritage and his predilection for operetta, excluded him from Czech identity entirely, turning his doting replication of a Smetanian aesthetic in *Švanda dudák* into merely an embarrassing forgery. Interestingly, while the avant-garde movement of the 1930s did much to overturn the attitude toward the validity of music making in the rest of Europe, it still could not put aside the stigma of foreign success: Očadlík's comparison of Křička's popular *Strašidlo v zámku* to *Švanda* and *Jonny spielt auf* demonstrates that even the most open-minded modernists could feel threatened by the outside world.

International politics also played a substantial role in the identity of the Prague music community and the role of their art in society, both at home and abroad. The dawn of the communist party in Czechoslovakia in 1921 was somewhat a revelation to all facets of the arts in Prague, which had long exhibited a fascination with protosocialist politics, particularly with regard to the promulgation of art in society. The new politics, however, produced certain tensions within the archconservative administrations of cultural institutions such as the National Theater, and continued those divisions already existing in Czech music. Nejedlý's socialism, expressed most vociferously in the communist journals *Var* and *Rudé právo* in the 1920s, was often tangential to the main debates of the musical community, from which he gradually distanced himself after the messy "Suk Affair." Nevertheless, his blend of nineteenth-century romantic nationalism, calls for the social responsibility of the artist, and for the overhaul of the cultural establishment made their mark on the left-wing thinkers of the arts community in the interwar period, outdated though his position was. Nejedlý as an interwar communist had little to do with the violent, revolutionary atmosphere in Russia and Germany in the years immediately previous: only much later did he match his passive-aggressive political commentary with actual activism. In rather a different way, left-wing political ideology was also the territory of the younger interwar generation, each member having a slightly different attitude toward its bearing on their music. The earliest of these, Schulhoff and Burian, kept their oeuvres separate from their pseudo-revolutionary politics in the 1920s, opting instead to revolutionize music making through jazz and multimedia projects; they both would turn to more overt communism by the end of the First Republic, contributing musically to organized workers' events. Only in this latter phase did either express an affinity with Soviet politics and culture (perhaps triggered by Burian's publication, *On Modern Russian Music*, in 1926), coinciding in each case with the virtual abandonment of jazz. Hába, while not greatly influenced by jazz or popular culture, also held sympathies toward Soviet Russia through his choice of dramatic or textual themes in the 1930s (particularly in the case of *Nová země* and *Pracující den*), which melded the most rigorous brand of Czech modernism with the communist movement. The Czech avant-garde socialists still retained a degree of skepticism regarding the Soviet regime, however, in that their largely idealist thinking occurred in the context of a West European democratic system; this difference was somewhat exacerbated by the treatment of Shostakovich and others in the early Stalinist era, which profoundly shocked the Prague avant-garde community. Nowhere else is their pro-Western socialism more explicit than in the antifascist jazz revues of Ježek at the Osvobozené divadlo, which coalesced issues rampant in the music press since the "*Wozzeck* Affair" in an artistic statement of allegiance to both Western populism and Czech independence. The same protofascist political divisions expressed in 1926 by Šilhan and Žák over *Wozzeck* later caused the Osvobozené divadlo to be shut down after factional demonstrations in the auditorium in 1934. Much like modernism, socialism was often conveyed in the press as an influence from outside, construed as either necessary or destructive, depending on the faction, but almost never as a native Czech phenomenon.

The larger picture reveals an anxiety on the part of Czech musicians and ideologues toward global culture and their acceptance in it, simultaneously begrudging other nations for not having noticed them and dismissing those of their own who gained too much exposure; only occasionally did they express the desire to "catch up" with the rest of Europe. This condition, brought on by a combination of long isolation, a lack of collective self-worth, and an overabundance of self-righteous indolence and conservatism, is as much at fault for the fate of Czech music in the early twentieth century as the subsequent political circumstances of Nazi occupation and postwar communism. It is undeniable that the totalitarian regimes of the mid- to late twentieth century had an adverse effect on the dissemination of all forms of culture beyond the country's borders. Nevertheless, had the composers and critics of interwar Prague more actively encouraged a participatory relationship with the rest of European culture in their day, such historical excavations as this book, some three-quarters of a century after the fact, might not have been necessary.

The End of the "Affairs": The Prague Community after 1938

The crumbling of democracy that started with the Munich Accord of September 30, 1938, and ended with the fall of Czecho-Slovakia (i.e., the Second Republic) 166 days later on March 15, 1939, made most of the artistic questions of the past four decades irrelevant. The effects were almost instantaneous: the 1938/39 concert season at most institutions was largely truncated or filled with insignificant performances, and many publications ceased circulation overnight. Cultural debates that had focused on the distant horizon of past legacies and modernist directions suddenly narrowed to questions about the very survival of Czech culture and democracy in Europe. Such a schism, however, did not necessarily spell the end of musical life in what was now the *Reichsprotektorat Böhmen und Mähren.*

Nazi occupation, as elsewhere in Europe, actually spurred on local cultural events out of a feeling of patriotic resistance, as evinced in the annual Czech music festivals beginning in mid-1939, with literally hundreds of participating venues in both urban and rural communities.[2] While these became increasingly difficult after the arrival of Nazi governor Reinhard Heydrich in October 1941 and the progressive bans on operas with inflammatory subjects, it was not until August 1944 that Goebbels shut down Czech concert life completely.[3] The compositional community meanwhile came under intense scrutiny, with their organizational structures reconfigured so as to appear conciliatory toward the occupying regime. Certain individuals, such as Novák, Vycpálek, Burian, and Krejčí, carried on their artistic activities with equal or greater vehemence out of a sense of defiance, even if much of this work stayed in desk drawers until after the war. Nevertheless, despite an overall trend toward conservatism (out of either the capitulation to Nazi cultural agendas or a new wave of Smetanian patriotism), new music societies continued to give concerts in Prague, possibly because the concept of "Entartete Musik" was not applied as thoroughly in the Czech lands as in Germany.[4]

The years following 1938 dismembered the Prague musical community. The Jewish musicians Ullmann, Krása, Haas, Klein, Reiner, Ančerl, and many others were sent to Terezín in 1941, of which only the last two survived the war. All six contributed to the unbelievable flowering of musical life in that concentration camp, the details of which have been described at length elsewhere;[5] Ullmann, Krása, and Haas perished upon deportation to Auschwitz in November 1944, while the Conservatory graduate Klein survived until the death marches in January 1945. Schulhoff, as a Soviet citizen, was sent to Wülzburg in Bavaria, where he died after numerous bouts of torture. The music journalist Erich Steinhard was deported on October 26, 1941, to the Łódź ghetto, one of 25,000 arrivals at that time: it is the last record of his survival in the war. Non-Jews in Terezín included Burian and Helfert, interned for communist-related resistance activities; both were released, but Helfert died, his health broken, in May 1945. Rudolf Karel, the former Czech legionnaire, was imprisoned first in Prague's Pankrác prison, then in Terezín's "Little Fortress" for his work in the resistance; after famously composing an opera (*Tři vlasy děda Vševěda*) using only charcoal and scraps of toilet paper, he succumbed to injuries from torture in March 1945. Other figures in musical life, such as Martinů's pupil Vítězslava Kaprálová and the Brno conservatory student Milan Harašta, both young composers, died from illnesses acquired in adverse wartime conditions.

The community also suffered through emigration. Ježek, together with Voskovec and Werich, emigrated to New York during the Second Republic, but suffered poor health and died in 1942 (as did Zemlinsky, another exile formerly of Prague). The Nejedlý family fled to the Soviet Union in June 1939, enacting Zdeněk's ideology of total noncollaboration in Czech cultural life under the Protectorate; Vít, after working for a time as bandleader for the Czech patriots in the Red Army, died from battle-related injuries at the infamous Dukla Pass on New Year's Day 1945. After the war, the German-Bohemian population (including Finke) was ethnically cleansed from the Third Czechoslovak Republic (1945–48), deported to Bavaria and the southern portion of what became East Germany; other Czech musicians, such as Jirák and Löwenbach, emigrated shortly after the war, and many exiles like Martinů and Weinberger never returned. By the time of the communist revolution in February 1948, Czechoslovak society had attained an artificial homogeneity that bore little resemblance to the cosmopolitan life of the First Republic.

Isolated from the world, this new society shunned the liberal, bourgeois culture that had grown from their own Cultural Revival through the entire first half of the twentieth century. The leading musical figures of that bygone era who were still alive after the war were either too old to have much effect on cultural life (such as Novák and Foerster, who both died in the early years of communism), became unquestioning members of the communist party (such as Burian), or no longer tried to provoke Czech society with modernist ideals (as with Hába and his school). All others from the interwar contingent—Krejčí, Jeremiáš, Axman, Vycpálek, Vomáčka, Křička, Očadlík—lapsed into a conservative, unoffensive middle ground: the musical avant-garde, as it was known in the First Republic, virtually ceased to exist, along with any form of liberal cultural activity, for forty years of the postwar era. The new generation of composers after 1948 espoused the sterile models of officially sanctioned Socialist Realism, following a program put forward by the new minister of culture and education— none other than the unsinkable Zdeněk Nejedlý, who finally had the chance to implement his critical mandate, already propagated for half a century in print, as law. In so doing, he was able to enforce an educational system for music education, with all its revisionism and artificial homogeneity, the vestiges of which were felt all the way to the fall of the Iron Curtain.[6] Only now with the return of democracy and freedom since 1989 can we once again explore, on its own terms, the magnificent creative spirit of the Prague musical community in the early twentieth century.

Conclusion: The Prague Community in the International Sphere

In his 1939 essay, "Modern Czech Music in the World Forum," Helfert wrote the following:

> Indeed, his name has not yet made its way abroad in the way that it deserves, but this should not be a barrier simply preventing us from recognizing him as a significant phenomenon who kept step with modern European music and was able, in his own way, to express that contemporary longing for a new style, having already laid the main emphasis on the firm, technical aspect of musical creation.[7]

Although Helfert's sentence refers specifically to Ostrčil, it could, of course, be applied with good reason to any of the artists or thinkers discussed in this study.

Drawing on Helfert's thoughts, it follows to question the extent of the overall contribution of Prague's musical community to early twentieth-century modernism as a whole, as well as to our understanding of it. Although it is not likely that specific composers or stylistic features had a direct influence on composition in Western Europe (as they did in Yugoslavia, see p. 268), nor is it unfounded to posit that a Czech voice was audible amid the more prominent personalities of the European compositional elite. This presence, I believe, extended beyond the works of a few individuals of international fame—Janáček, Martinů, and Hába—to something less tangible: a larger sense of the interconnections of musical modernism with nationalism and the social responsibility of art. Indeed, the reactions of the Prague community, both critically and compositionally, to music in the rest of Europe puts that "mainstream" narrative into relief, since their response was always a mixture of positive and negative elements. That these reactions also involved active contributions in the international sphere (the ISCM festivals at home and abroad, performances of Czech music throughout Europe, and permanent connections to Paris, Vienna, and Berlin) speaks to the importance of their inclusion as a vital component within a larger history of European music in the early twentieth century. Furthermore, the many debates that raged throughout the Prague community ultimately reflected larger ones from the outside world through a highly nuanced and idiosyncratic prism of the local.

A reexamination of Prague's fin-de-siècle and interwar musical community has direct implications for the narrative of music history in other local environments, particularly in metropolises such as Berlin, Vienna, Paris, or even New York. Indeed, similar studies have already taken place with regard to the musical life of the Weimar Republic, where nationalism and antimodernism were daily realities alongside cosmopolitanism and modernism, and where the resultant mix proved shockingly volatile.[8] Such de-hierarchized narratives, by which I mean historical accounts where priority is given not just to the most "progressive" and prominent individuals, are imperative for the re-creation of nonteleological views of the past. This democratization of history is especially important for the study of culture in the early twentieth century, a time when the ideology of progressiveness or modernism was a benchmark to which almost all aspired—albeit often fallaciously, as is evident from the many ideological standpoints of the Prague community. The concept of modernism itself, as preached and practiced in the fin-de-siècle and interwar periods, existed as a construct against a background of antimodernism, its binary opposite, in a porous, dialogic relationship that traversed national and cultural boundaries. As more music of this era becomes accessible, through performances, recordings, and scholarship, it is increasingly clear that many shades of modernism and antimodernism existed beyond the early twentieth-century "mainstream," and that those individuals left out of the history virtually engulf the relatively few commonly studied. If a historian's endeavor is to recreate as closely as possible the situation "as it really was," then it is necessary even for our understanding of, say, Schoenberg and Stravinsky to explore daily life in the musical communities of Europe, so that we can begin to discover the basis of these composers' experiences. Each of the lesser-known figures from local cultural spheres also reacted, in his/her way, to modernist composers of international fame, producing a highly variegated and multifaceted image of the era. Within this context, other local discourses, such as those on nationalism or the alleged responsibility of art toward a specific society, could intersect with modernism in ways that were at once unique to their time and place and parallel to other cultural centers. As we have seen in the previous ten chapters, the musicians of Prague constantly shaped a communal identity, largely by means of contesting the individual's representation of his/her own community, but also by coming to terms with the continuous stream of contemporary music emerging from abroad. Thus, Prague, even at its most antimodernist and isolationist, can widen our understanding of the modern, cosmopolitan world.

In many respects, Prague can be as representative of music making in the early twentieth century as any capital in Europe, since every community had its conservative elements, particularly those where national interests were at stake. While conservative musical aesthetics were not always linked directly to nationalist sentiments, any attempt to locate a "national music" was usually done in reference to an imagined tradition, whether in the effort to preserve or to modify it for the present day. Thus, any local environment where nationalism played a disproportionately large role would have had an extraordinarily complex relationship to both musical modernism and foreign influence, since in these situations the modernist impulse would most likely come from abroad. In Prague, this resulted in an imagined Czech modernism that could never escape the legacy of the Cultural Revival, and an avant-garde whose individuals were often excluded from the category of "Czechness." The idea of "national traditions" was therefore one of the strongest obstacles to the exploration of modernist aesthetics in the early twentieth century, acting as a force either to ensure its application for the good of society or to prevent its existence entirely. In the most extreme cases, as in the Third Reich, when mixed with political power, these aesthetic attitudes had sinister implications for the continued freedom of musical and cultural endeavors. Even in the relatively moderate political climate of fin-de-siècle and interwar Prague, nationalism and social responsibility acted as constant limiting factors toward music, ultimately preventing the compositions of this era from achieving a broader impact beyond the borders of the Czech Lands.

While this book has not sought to present a complete picture of life and discourse in the musical community of Prague in the early twentieth century, it has attempted to provide a suitable overview of the ideological and aesthetic debates of some of its members. Indeed, many more studies of a more specific nature, regarding individual composers, compositions, and the ideas surrounding them, are yet to be explored. Nevertheless, it is hoped that the portaits presented here of critics such as Hostinský, Nejedlý, Očadlík, and Šilhan, and of composers such as Novák, Ostrčil, Zich, Hába, Jeremiáš, and Ježek, will provide ample opportunity for a reexamination of musical modernism and society in twentieth-century Europe. Although it is just one piece of the puzzle, it is quite possibly crucial to the retelling of history.

Appendix One

Personalia

The abbreviations throughout this appendix can be found in Notes to the Reader, p. xviii–xix.

Augusta, Václav. (1897–1939) Critic, editor of *D* (1919). Contributor to *HR*. Espoused extreme views on the de-Germanification of Czech culture, including Wagner.

Axman, Emil. (1887–1949) Composer, musicologist, and archivist. Studied with Nejedlý, Hostinský, Novák, and Ostrčil. Head of the National Museum, music department. Secretary of the Spolek pro moderní hudbu under Štěpán (1920–27). Compositional influences from Moravian folk music and WWI. Contributed to *S-HL*, *T-LHM*.

Bartoš, František. (1905–73) Composer and critic. Studied with Jirák, Křička, and Foerster. Member of the Mánes Group. Co-editor of *T-LHM* (1935–38, 1946–48). Late romantic and neoclassicist influences in chamber compositions, choruses, and incidental music (to plays by Vančura, Molière, Schiller, Gogol).

Bartoš, Josef. (1887–1952) Critic and musicologist. Studied with Stecker, Hostinský, and Nejedlý. Participant in almost every one of Nejedlý's "affairs." Translated Bergson, Carrière, and Croce into Czech. Articles and books on nineteenth- and twentieth-century Czech music including opera at the Prague Provisional Theater. Czech music critic of *PP* (1921–38), contributed to *ND* and *PL*, editor of *S-HL*.

Bělohlávek, Bedřich. (1902–91) Critic. Studied at the Conservatory and musicology at the University (dissertation on J. Jeremiáš). A radical, anti–establishmentarian voice in the context of 1930s criticism, with socialist leanings. Contributed to *NSv*, *RP*, *PL*, *ČH*, *Čin*. Librettist for Burian's *Před slunce východem*.

Bennewitz, Antonín. (1833–1926) Violinist, teacher, and administrator. Professor (1865–82) and director (1882–1901) of Prague Conservatory. Made violin school world famous. Taught Ševčík, Ondříček, Suk, and Nedbal. Appointed Dvořák, Ševčík (violin) and Hanuš Wihan (cello) to staff, but unable to hire Fibich.

Branberger, Jan. (1877–1952) Critic, secretary to the interwar Ministry of Education and National Culture (MŠANO). Editor of *HR-S*. Contributed to *HR*, *T-LHM*.

Burian, Emil František. (1904–59) Composer, stage director, and writer. Studied with Foerster. Director, dramatist, and actor for the Moderní Studio, Voskovec and Werich's Divadlo Na

Slupi, and Divadlo Dada. Co-founded Přítomnost society for contemporary music. Founded Voice-band (1927) and the left-wing newspaper *Levá Fronta*. Established his own theater, D 34 (1933). Contributed to *TT, VPR*. Interned in Terezín for resistance activities (1941). Latterly adopted the precepts of socialist realism. Operas: *Alladin a Palomid, Před slunce východem, Mastičkář, Bubu z Montparnassu, Maryša, Vojna*. Ballet: *Fagot a Flétna.*

Čapek, Bedřich. (1878–?) Critic. Studied musicology with Hostinský. Participated as a pianist in the Hudební klub. Contributed to *Lumír, D, HR, S-HL.*

Čelanský, Ludvík Vítězslav. (1870–1931) Conductor and composer. Studied composition at Prague Conservatory. Championed by the Nejedlý circle despite heavy criticism of his professional caliber. Unsuccessful tenures at the Vinohrady Theater (1907–13), Czech Philharmonic (1918–19), Šakova filharmonie (1919–21) before continuing his career in Kraków and Lwów. Opera: *Kamila.*

Doležil, Hubert. (1876–1945) Critic, musicologist. Studied with Nejedlý. Worked in Brno before independence and subsequently moved to Prague. Involved in the Hudební klub, "Dvořák" and "Novák Affairs." Contributed to *ČR, ČS, ND, S-HL, T-LHM.*

Dvořák, Antonín. (1841–1904) Composer, conductor. Studied with Antonín Liebmann, K. L. Pitsch. Principal violist in Provisional Theater Orchestra under Smetana. Taught Suk, Nedbal, Novák, and Karel. Spent 1892–95 in the United States. Operas: *Alfred, Král a uhlíř, Vanda, Šelma sedlák, Dimitrij, Tvrdé palice, Jakobín, Čert a Káča, Rusalka, Armida.*

Dyk, Viktor. (1877–1931) Journalist, playwright, and National Democratic politician. President of the Artists' Union in the early twentieth century. Contributed to *NL*. Texts set to music by Křička, Vomáčka, Jirák, O. Jeremiáš, Ostrčil, Petrželka, and Vačkář.

Fibich, Zdeněk. (1850–1900) Composer and teacher. Studied at Leipzig Conservatory with Moscheles and E. F. Richter, and privately with Jadassohn. Deputy conductor at the Provisional Theater in Prague (1875–78). Dramaturge at the National Theater and instructor at Prague Conservatory (1899–1900). Members of his extensive private composition studio included Kovařovic, Chvála, Ostrčil, and Nejedlý. Operas: *Bukovín, Blaník, Nevěsta messinská* (to a libretto by Hostinský), *Hippodamie, Bouře, Hedy, Šárka, Pád Arkuna.*

Finke, Fidelio Friedrich. (1891–1968) German-Bohemian composer, teacher. Studied with Novák at Prague Conservatory and with his uncle, Romeo Finke, at the Deutsche Akademie, where he subsequently directed composition master classes (1927–45). Co-editor of *A* for fifteen years. Contributed to *MdS*. After expulsion from postwar Czechoslovakia, director of the Dresden Akademie für Musik und Theater (1946–51) and professor of composition at the Liepzig Musikhochschule (1951–59). Operas: *Die versunkene Glocke, Die Jakobsfahrt*. Cantata: *Abschied* (1925 ISCM).

Foerster, Josef Bohuslav. (1859–1951) Composer, writer, teacher. Studied at the Prague Organ School, succeeding Dvořák as organist of Sv. Vojtěch (1882–88). After 1893 in Hamburg, where his wife was a principal soprano for Mahler; critic and professor of piano at Hamburg Conservatory. Professor of composition at the New Conservatory in Vienna (1903), music critic for *Die Zeit* (1910). In Prague, professor of composition at the Conservatory (1919–31), lecturer at the University (1920–36). President of the Czech Academy of Sciences and Art (1931–39). Conservative, lyrical compositional style, championed by Nejedlý. Taught Jirák, Bořkovec, K. Hába, and Burian. Contributed to *NL*. Operas: *Debora, Eva, Jessika, Nepřemožení, Srdce, Bloud.*

Haas, Pavel. (1899–1944) Composer. Studied at Brno Conservatory with Janáček. Interned in Terezín and died in Auschwitz. Contributed to *HRo, T-LHM*. Opera: *Šarlatán.*

Hába, Alois. (1893–1973) Composer, theorist, and teacher. Studied with Novák, Schreker, and Busoni. Established a masterclass of microtonal music at Prague Conservatory, attended by Ponc, Karel Hába, Osterc, Reiner, Ullmann, Schulhoff, Ježek, and Ančerl. Pioneered the construction of quarter-tone instruments. Director of the Spolek pro moderní hudbu and Přítomnost. Organizer of 1935 ISCM. Contributed to *A, ČR, K, ND, R, T-LHM*. Operas: *Matka, Nová země, Přijď království Tvé*.

Hába, Karel. (1898–1972) Composer, violinist, and teacher. Brother of Alois Hába. Studied with Novák, Hoffmann, and in his brother Alois's quarter-tone master class. Head of the music education department for Prague radio. Contributed to *ČR, ND, T-LHM*. Operas: *Jánošík, Smolíček*.

Helfert, Vladimír. (1886–1945) Critic, musicologist. Studied in Berlin with Kretzschmar and in Prague with Hostinský. Professor of musicology at Brno. A salient member of the Nejedlý circle and a key figure in the "Dvořák Affair." Premiered Janáček's *Šárka* in 1925 and organized the Janáček Archives in Brno. Published a Janáček biography. Trained the first generation of Brno musicologists. Interned by Gestapo for resistance activities, died shortly after liberation. Edited *HRo*. Contributed to *ČK, ČS, S-HL*.

Herben, Jan. (1857–1936) Writer and literary historian. Supporter of Masaryk during the battles of his early political career. Prominent during the "Suk Affair."

Hilar, K. H. (1885–1935) Theater director. Led the spoken drama sections of the Vinohrady Theater (1913–24, whose opera program he disbanded amid the "Vinohrady Theater Affair"), and the National Theater (1924–35).

Hilbert, Jaroslav. (1871–1936) Playwright and editor of *V*. Brother-in-law of Kovařovic, whom he criticized for the postwar production of *Tannhäuser*. Author of *Vina*, used by Zich as a basis for his opera of the same name.

Hippmann, Silvestr. (1893–1974) Critic and Artists' Union concert organizer. Contributed to *T-LHM* and *R*.

Hoffmann, Karel. (1872–1936) Violinist, member of Czech Quartet. Prominent during the "Suk Affair," in which he was also charged with pro-Austrian sympathies.

Hoffmeister, Karel. (1868–1952) Pianist, Conservatory professor, music essayist. Studied with Hostinský and Kàan. Edited *HR*, contributed to *D, HRo*, analyses of Suk and Novák.

Honzl, Jindřich. (1894–1953) Theater and film director, member of Devětsil. Later director of Voskovec and Werich's Osvobozené divadlo.

Hostinský, Otakar. (1847–1910) Aesthetician, critic. Studied with Smetana, of whom he was a great supporter; also an early proponent of the Artists' Union. Professor of aesthetics at Prague University. Lectured on music history at the Conservatory. Published essays on music aesthetics and history, co-edited (with L. Procházka) *Hudební listy* and *Dalibor*, the sites of vehement polemics with the Pivoda circle. Taught Nejedlý, Ostrčil, Bartoš, Helfert, and Zich. Opera sketch: *Elektra*.

Hutter, Josef. (1894–1959) Musicologist, critic. Studied with Nejedlý and Zich at Prague University. Contributed to *HRo, ND*, analyses of Zich and Ostrčil. Persecuted by Nejedlý after 1948.

Janáček, Leoš. (1854–1928) Composer, theorist, educator. Studied at the Czech Teacher's Institute, with Skuherský at the Prague Organ School, and at the Leipzig Conservatory. Founded Organ School in Brno. Founded *Hudební listy*. Formulated theory of "speech-melody." His opera *Jenůfa* was the subject of controversy with both Kovařovic and Nejedlý. Operas: *Šárka, Počátek románu, Její pastorkyňa (Jenůfa), Osud, Výlety pana Broučka, Káťa Kabanová, Příhody lišky Bystroušky, Věc Makropulos, Z mrtvého domu*.

Janeček, Julius. (1868–1936) Editor, critic. Edited *HVk* (1908–16, 1918–21, 1933–34). General secretary of the Czechoslovak Musicians' Union, 1909–34. Promulgated socialist politics in favor of the common performer.

Jenčík, Joe. (1893–1945) Choreographer. Worked at the National Theater, Vinohrady Theater (*The Bartered Bride*, 1923), Neues Deutsches Theater, and most significantly, the Osvobozené divadlo (1929–36), where his troupe, the "Jenčíkovy Girls," performed modern dances to Ježek's music.

Jeremiáš, Jaroslav. (1889–1919) Composer and pianist. Brother of Otakar Jeremiáš. Studied piano with A. Mikeš at Prague Conservatory, composition privately with Novák. Brief connections with Hudební klub, likely as a result of anti-Novák sentiment. Opera: *Starý král.* Oratorio: *Mistr Jan Hus.*

Jeremiáš, Otakar. (1892–1962) Composer and conductor. Brother of Jaroslav Jeremiáš. Studied composition with Novák. Conductor of Prague SO, briefly opera director of the National Theater as heir apparent to Ostrčil. One of the last interwar Prague composers to demonstrate an inheritance from Wagner. First chair of the Union of Czechoslovak Composers. Contributed to *ČH, HRo.* Operas: *Bratři Karamazovi, Enšpígl.*

Ježek, Jaroslav. (1906–42) Composer and conductor. Studied composition with Jirák and Suk. Composer and conductor at Osvobozené divadlo. Member of the Mánes Group, heavily influenced by jazz. Emigrated to United States (1939). Founder-conductor of the Czechoslovak Choral Group in New York. Contributed to *RA, VPR.* Ballet: *Nervy.* For Osvobozené divadlo repertoire, see table 9.1, p. 282.

Jirák, Karel Boleslav. (1891–1972) Composer, critic, and conductor. Studied with Novák and Foerster. Director of Czechoslovak Radio Orchestra and music department. Emigrated to United States in 1947; professor of theory and composition at Roosevelt College, Chicago. Contributed to *NO, T-LHM.* Opera: *Apolonius z Tyany (Žena a bůh).*

Kàan z Albestů, Jindřich. (1852–1926) Teacher, administrator, pianist, and composer. Studied at the Proksch Institute and with Blodek and at the Prague Organ School. Accompanied Dvořák on his first visit to England. Director of Prague Conservatory (1907–18). Instituted master classes in composition under Novák. Ousted from the Conservatory administration in 1918 because of his noble status.

Kalenský, Boleslav. (1867–1913) Critic and close friend of Novák. Editor of *D* (1911–13). Contributed to *HR-S, HR.* Involved in the "Knittl Affair" and "Dvořák Affair" as a staunch supporter of the Artists' Union, including his mentor Pivoda.

Karel, Rudolf. (1880–1945) Composer and teacher. Dvořák's last pupil. Established a symphony orchestra in the Czech Legion (1918). Professor of composition and orchestration at Prague Conservatory. Interned for resistance activities and died in Terezín. Operas: *Ilseino srdce, Smrt kmotřička, Tři zlaté vlasy děda vševěda.*

Knittl, Karel. (1853–1907) Teacher, critic, conductor, and composer. Studied at Prague Organ School. Taught at Pivoda's music institute, and taught harmony and instrumentation at Prague Conservatory; Conservatory director (1904–7). Wrote for *HL* and *D.* Sided with Pivoda against Smetana's *Two Widows.* His death prompted the "Knittl Affair."

Konopásek, Max. (1820–79) Critic and pedagogue. Associated with the Pivoda circle and contributor to *Hudební listy.* Proponent of pan-Slavism in music.

Kovařovic, Karel. (1862–1920) Composer and conductor. Studied clarinet, harp, and piano at the Prague Conservatory and composition privately with Fibich. Director of Pivoda's opera school. Opera director of the National Theater (1900–1920). Premiered operas by Ostrčil, Foerster, and Novák, and reorchestrated Janáček's *Jenůfa* for the Prague premiere. Battled with Nejedlý over the direction of Czech music. Operas: *Ženichové, Cesta oknem, Crespo, Armida, Noc Šimona a Judy, Psohlavci, Na starém bělidle, Slib.*

Krása, Hans. (1899–1944) German-Bohemian composer. Studied with Zemlinsky in Prague, at the Berlin Conservatory, and with Roussel in Paris. Influenced by Stravinsky and contemporary French composers. Interned in Terezín and transported to Auschwitz. Operas: *Verlobung im Traum, Brundibár.*

Krejčí, Iša. (1904–68) Composer, critic, and conductor. Studied composition with Jirák and Novák, conducting with Talich. Manager of the music department of Czechoslovak Radio. A champion of neoclassicism, he founded the Mánes Group with Ježek, Bořkovec, F. Bartoš, and Holzknecht. Contributed to *ČH, K, LUK, ND, R, RA, T-LHM.* Operas: *Antigona, Pozdvížení v Efesu, Temno.*

Křička, Jaroslav. (1882–1969) Composer and teacher. Studied at Prague Conservatory and in Berlin. Associate of Novák. In Ekaterinoslav for three years, friend of Glazunov and Taneyev. Contributed articles on Russian music to Czech journals. Choirmaster of Prague Hlahol chorus, premiered works by Novák and Janáček. Professor of composition and rector of Prague Conservatory. Czech representative for the Nazi-based new music organization Ständige Rat (1934–45). Operas: *Hypolita, Ogaři, Strašidlo v zámku* [*Bílý pán*], *Tlustý pradědeček,* and others, particularly for children.

Kysela, František. (1881–1941) Set designer and professor at the Decorative Arts school in Prague. After collaboration with Ostrčil at the Vinohrady Theater on *The Bartered Bride,* he created modernist designs for Czech operas at the National Theater throughout the 1920s and 30s, including the 1924 Smetana cycle, *Karlštejn,* and *Honzovo království.*

Löwenbach, Jan. (1880–1972) Critic, librettist, musical administrator, and writer. Expert on copyright law. Helped found the Klub československých skladatelů (composers' guild) and the Ochranné Sdružení Autorské (authors' copyright association). Cultural attaché to the Czechoslovak Consulate in New York during the war. Edited *HR* and contributed to *A, T-LHM.* Opera librettos: Martinů's *Voják a tanečnice* and Křička's *Strašidlo v zámku.*

Lošťák, Ludvík. (1862–1918) Writer, music student. While still studying at the Conservatory, authored a manifesto of modern music that garnered short-lived support in the Prague community.

Martinů, Bohuslav. (1890–1959) Composer. Largely self-taught, studied with Suk in Prague and Roussel in Paris. One of the foremost proponents of neoclassicism, idolized by the Mánes Group. Championed by Talich and Koussevitsky. Moved to United States in 1941. Contributed to *T-LHM, ND, LN.* Operas: *Voják a tanečnice, Les larmes du couteau, Tři přání, Den milosrdenství, Hry o Marii, Hlas lesa, Veselohra na mostě, Divadlo za bránou, Alexandre bis, Julietta, Čím člověk žije, Ženitba, Zaloba, Mirandolina, Ariadne, Řecké pašije.*

Masaryk, Tomáš Garrigue. (1850–1937) Author, historian, politician, first president of the Czechoslovak Republic, 1918–35.

Maýr, Jan Nepomuk. (1818–88) Conductor. First director of opera at the Provisional Theater, chosen as the Old Czech candidate over Smetana. After Smetana's accession in 1866, Maýr became involved in a campaign against him, latterly replacing him, 1874–81.

Nebuška, Otokar. (1875–1952) Critic at *NL* and *HR* with staunchly conservative views.

Nedbal, Oskar. (1874–1930) Composer, conductor, and violist in the Czech Quartet. Studied with Bennewitz and Dvořák at Prague Conservatory. Conducted the Czech Philharmonic (1901–6) and Šakova filharmonie. Director of opera at the Slovak National Theater. Opera: *Sedlák Jakub.* Operettas: *Cudná Barbora, Polská krev, Vinobraní, Die Schöne Saskia.* Ballets: *Z pohádky do pohádky, Pohádka o Honzovi.*

Nejedlý, Vít. (1912–45) Composer and communist agitator, son of Zdeněk Nejedlý. Studied with Jeremiáš. Ph.D. in musicology, 1936. Wrote music criticism for *Čin* and *Haló noviny,* contributed to *R.* Emigrated to USSR in 1939, where he worked in radio and composed film music and mass songs. Joined Red Army in 1943 and died at the Czechoslovak front. Opera: *Tkalci.*

Nejedlý, Zdeněk. (1878–1962) Critic, musicologist, communist politician, and writer. Studied under Fibich, Goll, and Hostinský. Reader in musicology and professor at Prague University. Championed Smetana, Fibich, Foerster, Ostrčil, and Zich, antagonized Dvořák, Janáček, Suk, and Novák. Organized the Hudební klub and was main contributor to *S-HL.* Edited *Var, Směr, ČK, Hudební sborník,* and wrote music criticism for *RP.* Contributed to *A, ND, NL.* After 1948 the first communist minister of culture and education.

Novák, Vítězslav. (1870–1949) Composer and Conservatory professor. Studied with Stecker, Knittl, and Dvořák. Taught Vycpálek, Vomáčka, Josef Bartoš, the Jeremiáš brothers, Alois Hába, Steinhard, and many others during the First Republic. Main organizer of the Podskalská filharmonie. Involved in the "Dvořák Affair" and a polemic against Ostrčil in 1930–31. Compositional style heavily influenced by impressionism and R. Strauss. Contributed to *HR.* Operas: *Zvíkovský rarášek, Karlštejn, Lucerna, Dědův odkaz.*

Novotný, Jaroslav. (1886–1918) Composer. Studied with Friml and Novák. Choirmaster of the Vinohrady Opera and the František Pivoda Singing Institute. Joined the Czech Legion in Russia during the First World War and died during revolutionary fighting.

Novotný, Václav Juda. (1849–1922) Writer on music and composer. Arranger of Smetana's operas. Studied with A. W. Ambros, Bennewitz, and Pivoda. Contributed to *D, HR.* Translated 100 opera librettos into Czech.

Očadlík, Mirko. (1904–64) Musicologist, critic, editor of *Klíč.* Studied in Vienna, received Ph.D. at Prague University with dissertation on Smetana's *Libuše.* Head of music broadcasting of Czechoslovak Radio. Edited *Radioamatér, Volné směry,* and *Rozhlasová práce.* Defended the musical avant-garde between the wars, working alongside Hába in the Spolek pro moderní hudbu (1927–34). A key figure in the "*Wozzeck* Affair." Contributed to *NO, S-HL, T-LHM.*

Ostrčil, Otakar. (1879–1935) Composer, conductor, and administrator. Studied at Prague University with Gebauer, Hostinský, Masaryk, and composition privately with Fibich. Opera director at the Vinohrady Theater (1914–19) and National Theater (1920–35). Under attack during his entire directorship by conservative critics, notably Šilhan. Co-founder and president of the Spolek pro moderní hudbu; champion of the works of his younger contemporaries. One of the main proponents of a Czech modernism based on dense counterpoint and motivic webs. Operas: *Jan Zhořelecký, Vlasty skon, Kunálovy oči, Poupě, Legenda z Erinu, Honzovo království.*

Pala, František. (1887–1964) Musicologist. Graduate of Prague University, where he studied with Nejedlý. Wrote daily reviews for *ČS,* contributions to *S-HL (II)* and studies of Foerster, Novák, Janáček, and Axman. His major work was a four-volume documentary account of opera at the National Theater under Ostrčil, heavily influenced by Nejedlý.

Patzaková, Anna (A. J.). (1895–1990) Musicologist, critic. Studied piano with Hoffmeister and musicology with Nejedlý. Active in the planning of the 1935 ISCM. Music critic for *NO* (1930–39), also contributed to *R, T-LHM, S-HL (II).* Co-founder of the Otakar Ostrčil Society in 1936. Promoted Czech music in England during the Second World War.

Petyrek, Felix. (1892–1951) German-Moravian composer and teacher. Studied in Vienna with Schreker and Adler. Taught piano at the Salzburg Mozarteum and the Berlin Hochschule für Musik, the Odeon in Athens, Stuttgart Musik-hochschule, and Leipzig Conservatory and University. Assimilated East European folk music.

Pícha, František. (1893–1964) Composer and teacher. Served in the First World War and the Czech Legion in Russia. Studied with Foerster, Křička, Jirák, and Suk. Professor of composition at Prague Conservatory. Arranged folk songs of South Bohemia, studied Moravian and Slovak folk song. Engaged in a brief polemic with Hába over the direction of new music.

Pivoda, František. (1824–98) Singing teacher and composer. Founded a private singing school where many prominent nineteenth-century Czech singers were taught. Propagated conservative and confused theories on Slavonic music; antagonized Smetana.

Procházka, Rudolf Freiherr von. (1864–1936) German-Bohemian Conservatory administrator. A student of Fibich, he sat on the board of directors for Prague Conservatory (1906–18) until his ejection after independence, whereupon he co-founded the Deutsche Akademie für Musik und darstellende Kunst.

Procházka, Ludevít. (1837–88) Music critic and Smetana supporter. A friend of Hostinský, he co-edited *Hudební listy* (1870–72) and *Dalibor* (1873–75).

Pujman, Ferdinand. (1889–1961) Opera producer and writer on music. Joined Nejedlý's circle, contributing to *S-HL* and reviews for *Samostatnost*. Scenic director at the National Theater (1920–22, 1924–44, 1947–56). Collaborated with Ostrčil, producing eighty-eight operas. Wrote the libretto for Hába's opera *Nová země*.

Reiner, Karel. (1910–79) Composer, pianist, and administrator. Studied musicology at Prague University and composition at the Conservatory under Suk and Hába. Pianist and composer in D34. Conducted 1947 Czech premiere of Hába's *Matka*. Contributed to *R*.

Rektorys, Artuš. (1877–1971) Editor of music journals and member of the Nejedlý circle. Edited *D* (1904–10), *S-HL*, *Hudební sborník*, and collections on Smetana, Fibich, Foerster, and Nejedlý.

Šak, Vladislav V. (1894–1977) Music entrepreneur. Student of Jirák, Foerster, and Ostrčil. After failing to overtake the Czech Philharmonic administration, founded the Šakova filharmonie, employing Nedbal and Čelanský. His company Presto founded the journal *Hudba*, edited by Foerster. Pro-German sympathies prompted the "Šak Affair."

Šalda, František Xaver. (1867–1937) Literary critic and author. A friend of Nejedlý, he contributed to *ČK* and *Var*. He had a strong effect on music criticism in the fin-de-siècle period, particularly on Nejedlý, Helfert, and Pujman.

Schmoranz, Gustav. (1858–1930) Architect and theater director. From the Young Czech takeover of the National Theater he became general director, leading the administration of Kvapil (drama) and Kovařovic (opera). Opposed radical change after 1918.

Schulhoff, Erwin. (1894–1942) Composer and pianist. Studied with Kàan at Prague Conservatory and in Vienna, Leipzig, and Cologne. Studied with Reger and Debussy. Associated with Grosz, Klee, Däubler, and the German dadaists. Returned to Prague to teach piano, instrumentation, and score reading at the Conservatory. First to play quarter-tone piano works of Hába. Pianist in Ježek's jazz orchestra for the Osvobozené divadlo. Influenced by jazz and communist ideals. Contributed to *A*, *ND*. Died in Wülzburg concentration camp. Opera: *Plameny*. Oratorio: *H.M.S. Royal Oak*.

Šilhan, Antonín. (1875–1952) Critic. Notoriously antimodernist music critic for *NL* (1910–41). Contributed also to *HR-S*, *HR*, a history of the Artists' Union, and a 1932 Novák anthology. Antagonized Ostrčil during his entire tenure at the National Theater and was largely responsible for the "*Wozzeck* Affair," 1926.

Smetana, Bedřich. (1824–84) Composer and conductor. Studied with Josef Proksch in Prague. Conductor in Sweden (1856–62), returning to Prague concert life as conductor of the Hlahol choral society and first president of the Artists' Union. Conductor of the Provisional Theater (1866–74). Supported by Hostinský and L. Procházka and antagonized by Pivoda and Rieger. Subsequently championed by the Nejedlý circle and the subject of a nationalist exhibition in 1917. Operas: *Braniboři v Čechách, Prodaná nevěsta, Dalibor, Libuše, Dvě vdovy, Hubička, Tajemství, Čertova stěna, Viola* (fragment).

Šourek, Otakar. (1883–1956) Musicologist and critic. Biographer of Dvořák. Music critic for *V*. Contributed articles on Suk, Novák, and Karel to *HR-S, HR, T-LHM*.

Sova, Antonín. (1864–1928) Symbolist poet. A friend of Novák's, he conceptually co-founded the movement of Czech impressionism. His poems were set by Suk (*Zrání*), Hoffmeister, Novák, Vycpálek, Foerster, Jirák, Petrželka, and Vomáčka.

Stanislav, Josef. (1897–1971) Composer, pianist, administrator, communist activist. Studied with Jeremiáš, Foerster, Novák, Hoffmeister, and Nejedlý. Employed in Svaz DDOČ, active in Přítomnost. Helped form the Czech composers union, and his political songs were widely disseminated. Contributed to *D, R*.

Stecker, Karel. (1861–1918) Theorist, composer, and teacher. Studied aesthetics at Prague University and the Organ School. Professor of composition, organ, theory, and history at the Conservatory. Wrote textbook on history of musical forms. Polemicized against Nejedlý in the "Knittl Affair." Contributed to *HR, HR-S*.

Steinhard, Erich. (1886–194?) German-Bohemian critic. Student of Novák and Knittl. Editor of *A* (1921–38) and head of German-Bohemian section of ISCM, active in all three Prague festivals. Latterly professor at Deutsche Akademie. Transported to Łódź, 1941.

Štěpán, Václav. (1889–1944) Pianist, critic, pedagogue, and composer. Studied musicology with Nejedlý and piano with Blanche Selva in Paris. Gave Novák premieres (*Pan, Exotikon*). Taught aesthetics and piano at the Conservatory. Championed works by Suk, Novák, Axman, Křička, Vomáčka, and Smetana. President of the Spolek pro moderní hudbu (1920–27). Contributed to *HR*.

Suk, Josef. (1874–1935) Composer and violinist. Studied at Prague Conservatory with Bennewitz, Knittl, Stecker, and Dvořák. Played second violin in the Czech quartet (1891–33). Married Dvořák's daughter Ottilie. Professor of composition at Prague Conservatory (1922–35). Taught Bořkovec, Ježek, Martinů, Reiner, and Vačkář. Compositional style influenced by impressionism and Strauss. The subject of controversy in the 1919 "Suk Affair." Melodramas: *Radúz a Mahulena, Pod jabloní*. Autobiographical symphonic cycle: *Asrael, Pohádka léta, Zrání, Epilog*.

Talich, Václav. (1883–1961) Conductor. Studied with Ševčík and Kàan. Conductor of the Czech Philharmonic (1918–30, 1946–48) and the National Theater (1935–44, 1947–48). Gave preference to the works of Dvořák, Suk, and Novák, despised by the Nejedlý circle. Brought Janáček's works into the standard repertoire. Taught Krejčí and Ančerl.

Theurer, Josef. (1862–1928) Critic and music educator. Involved with Nejedlý in the "Knittl Affair." Contributed to *D, S-HL*.

Tomášek, Jaroslav (1896–1970). Composer and critic. Studied musicology with Nejedlý and composition privately with Novák. Contributed to *HRo, R*. Editor of *T-LHM*.

Ullmann, Viktor. (1898–1944) German-Bohemian composer. Studied with Schoenberg in Vienna. Helped Zemlinsky reestablish German musical life in Prague as assistant conductor of Neues Deutsches Theater. Studied in Hába's quarter-tone masterclass. Contributed to *A*. Deported from Terezin to Auschwitz in 1944.

Urbánek, Mojmír. (1873–1919) Music publisher. Apprenticed with his father, František. Founded his own printing house in Prague (1900). Published music by Foerster, Novák, and Suk, and the journal *D*. Established the Mozarteum Concert Hall.

Vačkář, Dalibor Cyril. (1906–84) Composer and critic. Studied composition with Hoffmann and Suk at Prague Conservatory. Contributed to *R, T-LHM, HVk* under the pseudonym Dalibor C. Faltis. Composed light music for the theater, including Osvobozené divadlo.

Vetterl, Karel. (1898–1979) Musicologist and folklorist. Studied musicology with Helfert in Brno. Contributed studies on the social effects of radio to *A*, *T-LHM*, *HRo*, *Hudba a škola* and *Radiojournal*.

Vogel, Jaroslav. (1894–1970) Conductor, composer, and critic. Studied violin with Ševčík, composition with Novák, and in Paris with d'Indy. Conductor at Ostrava, the Plzeň opera, National Theater, Brno State Philharmonic. Noted for performances of Smetana, Janáček, and Novák. Contributed to *ČR*, *T-LHM*. Opera: *Mistr Jíra*.

Vomáčka, Boleslav. (1887–1965) Composer and critic. Studied composition with Novák. Edited and contributed major articles to *T-LHM* (1923–35) and wrote music criticism for *LN*. Also contributed to *A*, *HR*, *HRo*. Leader of an increasingly isolationist generation of Prague composers that came of age during the First World War. Operas: *Vodník, Boleslav I, Čekanky*.

Voskovec, Jiří. (1905–81) Playwright and comedian. One of the original members of Devětsil, branched off with Jan Werich to form the Osvobozené divadlo (1928–38). Co-author and performer in more than twenty plays and several films that lampooned the political situation of contemporary Europe to the accompaniment of Ježek's jazz orchestra and the Jenčíkovy Girls. Contributed to *VPR*. In 1939, fled with Werich and Ježek to New York, where he began an American film career.

Vrchlický, Jaroslav. (1853–1912) Poet and playwright. Author of several works set to music by Czech composers, including Novák (*Karlštejn*), Fibich (*Hippodamie*), Foerster, Kovařovic, Ostrčil, Zich, and Nedbal.

Vycpálek, Ladislav. (1882–1969) Composer and Artists' Union administrator. Studied composition with Novák, whom he staunchly supported during the controversy with Nejedlý. After the 1925 ISCM performance of his *Kantáta o posledních věcech člověka*, recognized as a leader of the densely contrapuntal Czech modernist style. Contributor to *HR*.

Warschauer, Frank. (1892–1940) German critic of film, theater, and radio, an important voice on cultural theory in the Weimar Republic. Exiled to Prague, 1933–38, where he continued his critical efforts, culminating in the 1937 monograph *Prag heute*. Contributed to *P*, *T-LHM*, instigating a short polemic with Reiner over the 1935 ISCM.

Weinberger, Jaromír. (1896–1967) Composer. Studied with Křička, Karel, and Novák in Prague, and with Reger in Leipzig. His opera *Švanda the Bagpiper* made him an international celebrity, even though it was unanimously reviled by Czech critics. Moved to United States to escape Nazi persecution. Operas: *Švanda dudák, Milovaný hlas, Lidé z Pokerflatu, Valdštejn*.

Werich, Jan. (1905–80) Playwright and comedian, partner of Jiří **Voskovec**.

Zamrzla, Rudolf. (1869–1930) Conductor and composer. Assistant to Kovařovic and Ostrčil at the National Theater (1901–30). Editor of *D* (1911–13) after the dismissal of Rektorys. Operas: *Svatební noc, Simson, Jidáš Iškariotský*.

Zemánek, Vilém. (1875–1922) German-Bohemian conductor of the Czech Philharmonic (1906–18). Personally took over administration of the orchestra after the dissolution of the Družstvo České filharmonie in 1914. Ousted from his position by a coup of musicians instigated by Helfert out of anti-German feeling.

Zemlinsky, Alexander. (1871–1942) Austrian composer and conductor. Studied composition in Vienna with J. N. Fuchs. Conducted at the Wiener Volksoper and co-founded the Vereinigung schaffender Tonkünstler. Opera conductor of Neues Deutsches Theater in Prague (1911–27), where he premiered Schoenberg's *Erwartung* and engaged Webern, Ullmann, and Jalowetz. Gave masterclasses in composition at the

Deutsche Akademie für Musik. Kapellmeister at the Kroll Opera under Klempererer in Berlin. Fled to Vienna, then to the United States.

Zeyer, Julius. (1841–1901) Decadent poet, novelist, and playwright. Considered by many to be the founder of the Czech decadent movement. Plays set to music include *Šárka* (Janáček), *Kunálovy oči*, *Legenda z Erinu* (Ostrčil), *Pod jabloní*, and *Radúz a Mahulena* (Suk).

Zich, Otakar. (1879–1934) Composer and aesthetician. Studied with Hostinský and Stecker. Member of the Nejedlý circle, contributing to the "Dvořák Affair." A main focus of controversy during Ostrčil's National Theater regime. The foremost figure in Czech aesthetic thought after Hostinský, particularly with regard to phenomenology. Compositionally an early proponent of neoclassicism in the Czech sphere. Contributed to *HRo, S-HL*. Operas: *Malířský nápad, Vina, Preciézky*.

Appendix Two

Premieres and New Productions at the National Theater, 1900–1938

WP—world premiere; PP—Prague (National Theater) premiere; NP—New production
‡Premiere conducted by Kovařovic; *Premiere conducted by Ostrčil

Year	Date	Composer	Title (*translation*)	Production
1900	1/9	Fibich	Pád Arkuna (*The Fall of Arkun*)	WP‡
1901	3/31	Dvořák	Rusalka	WP‡
	11/22	Kovařovic	Na starém bělidle (*At the Old Bleaching House*)	WP‡
1902	1/24	Nedbal	Pohádka o Honzovi (*Legend of Johnny*) [Ballet]	WP
	12/28	Suk	Pod jabloní (*Under the Apple Tree*) [Incidental Music]	WP
1903	2/13	Charpentier	Louisa	PP‡
	7/14	Moor	Vij	WP
1904	3/25	Dvořák	Armida	WP
	4/14	Kàan	Olim [Ballet]	WP
	12/14	Ostrčil	Vlasty skon (*Vlasta's Passing*)	WP‡
	12/28	Anger	V baletním sále (*In the Ballet Hall*) [Ballet]	WP
1905	4/16	Foerster	Jessika	WP‡
	10/22	Moor	Hjördis	WP
1906	1/6	Rozkošný	Černé jezero (*The Black Lake*)	WP
1907	4/29	Bendl	Švanda dudák (*Švanda the Bagpiper*)	WP posth.

Appendix Two (*continued*)

Year	Date	Composer	Title (*translation*)	Production
	6/7	Prokop	Sen lesa (*The Forest Dream*)	WP
1908	1/25	Nedbal	Z pohádky do pohádky (*From Tale to Tale*) [Ballet]	WP
	11/25	Ostrčil	Kunálovy oči (*Kunála's Eyes*)	WP‡
1909	10/29	Kovařovic/ Zamrzla	Na záletech (*Going Courting*) [Ballet]	WP
1910	3/11	Zich	Malířský nápad (*The Painter's Idea*)	WP
	3/11	Piskáček	Divá Bára (*Wild Barbara*)	WP
	4/25	Strauss	Elektra [in Czech translation by Kovařovic]	PP‡
1911	1/12	Ostrčil	Poupě (*The Bud*)	WP
	3/4	Strauss	Růžový kavalír (*Der Rosenkavalier*)	PP‡
	4/28	Picka	Malíř Rainer (*Rainer the Painter*)	WP
	9/1	Nedbal	Princezna Hyacinta (*Princess Hyacinthe*) [Ballet]	WP
1912	3/29	Weis	Útok na mlýn (*The Attack on the Mill*)	WP
	11/12	Strauss	Ohně zmar (*Feuersnot*)	PP‡
1913	10/24	Zamrzla	Svatební noc (*The Wedding Night*)	WP
1914	1/1	Wagner	Parsifal	PP‡
	6/27	Piskáček	Ughlu	WP
	11/28	Nedbal	Andersen [Ballet]	WP
1915	10/10	Novák	Zvíkovský rarášek (*The Zvíkov Imp*)	WP‡
1916	5/26	Janáček	Její pastorkyňa (*Jenůfa*)	PP‡
	11/18	Novák	Karlštejn	WP‡
1917	10/10	Křička	Hipolyta	WP‡
1918	3/9	Chvála	Záboj	WP‡
	12/19	Foerster	Nepřemožení (*The Invincible Ones*)	WP‡
1919	4/13	J. Jeremiáš	Starý král (*The Old King*)	WP posth.‡
1920	4/23	Janáček	Výlety páně Broučkovy (*The Excursions of Mr. Brouček*)	WP*
	6/6	Weis	Lešetínský kovář (*The Blacksmith of Lešetín*)	WP

Appendix Two *(continued)*

Year	Date	Composer	Title (*translation*)	Production
1921	3/5	Zamrzla	Simson	WP
	11/1	Debussy	Pelléas a Mélisanda	PP*
	12/9	Kovařovic	Cesta oknem (*Through the Window*)	NP
	12/9	Kovařovic	Slib (*The Promise*) [Fragment]	WP posth.
1922	3/14	Zich	Vina (*Guilt*)	WP*
	4/28	Němeček	Královnin omyl (*The Queen's Mistake*)	WP
	11/30	Janáček	Káťa Kabanová	PP*
1923	1/17	Strauss	Salome	PP*
	3/14	Ostrčil	Legenda z Erinu (*Legend of Erin*)	PP*
	5/13	Novák	Lucerna (*The Lantern*)	WP*
	5/27	Smetana	Prodaná nevěsta (*The Bartered Bride*)	NP*
	10/2	Smetana	Dvě vdovy (*The Two Widows*)	NP*
	11/15	Foerster	Srdce (*The Heart*)	WP*
1924	1/9	Smetana	Dalibor	NP*
	2/2	Smetana	Čertova stěna (*The Devil's Wall*)	NP*
	3/2	Smetana	Braniboři v Čechách (*The Brandenburgs in Bohemia*)	NP*
	5/11	Smetana	Viola [Fragment]	WP posth.*
	5/12	Smetana	Libuše	NP*
	9/11	Martinů	Istar [Ballet]	WP
	11/11	Karel	Ilseino srdce (*Ilsea's Heart*)	WP*
1925	2/24	Zelinka	Dceruška hostinského (*The Innkeeper's Daughter*)	WP*
	2/24	Stravinsky	Petruška [Ballet]	PP*
	5/18	Janáček	Příhody lišky Bystroušky (*The Cunning Little Vixen*)	PP*
	11/24	Burian	Před slunce východem (*Before Sunrise*)	WP*
1926	3/30	Vogel	Mistr Jíra (*Master George*)	WP
	5/21	Zich	Preciézky (*Les Précieuses ridicules*)	WP*
	5/21	Milhaud	Zmatek (*Salade*) [Ballet]	PP
	11/11	Berg	Vojcek (*Wozzeck*)	PP*

Appendix Two *(continued)*

Year	Date	Composer	Title *(translation)*	Production
	12/22	Novák	Dědův odkaz (*The Grandfather's Legacy*)	PP*
1927	2/17	Ravel	Dítě a kouzla (*L'enfant et les sortilèges*)	PP
	2/17	Martinů	Kdo je na světě nejmocnější? (*Who Is the Most Powerful in the World?* [Ballet])	PP
	4/27	Weinberger	Švanda dudák (*Švanda the Bagpiper*)	WP*
1928	3/1	Janáček	Věc Makropulos (*The Makropoulos Case*)	PP*
	10/8	O. Jeremiáš	Bratři Karamazovi (*The Brothers Karamazov*)	WP*
1929	2/2	Burian	Fagot a flétna (*The Bassoon and the Flute*) [Ballet]	WP*
	4/11	Zich	Vina	NP*
	—	Burian	Bubu z Montparnassu (*Bubu of Montparnasse*)	Canceled
1930	4/19	Zamrzla	Jidáš Iškariotský (*Judas Iscariot*)	WP posth.
	10/7	Brand	Strojník Hopkins (*Der Maschinist Hopkins*)	PP*
1931	2/21	Janáček	Z mrtvého domu (*From the House of the Dead*)	PP posth.
	3/8	Novák	Signorina Gioventù [Ballet]	WP*
	3/8	Novák	Nikotina [Ballet]	WP*
	5/17	A. Hába	Matka (*The Mother*) [performed in Munich]	WP
	9/19	Zelinka	Devátá louka (*The Ninth Field*)	WP*
1932	10/21	Szymanowski	Král Roger	PP*
1933	1/27	Němeček	Rajská zahrada (*The Garden of Paradise*)	WP*
	3/31	Karel	Smrt kmotřička (*Godmother Death*)	PP*
	9/19	Martinů	Špalíček [Ballet]	WP
	10/10	Křička	Strašidlo v zámku (*A Ghost in the Castle*)	PP

Appendix Two *(continued)*

Year	Date	Composer	Title (*translation*)	Production
1934	2/23	K. Hába	Jánošík	WP*
	10/3	Blodek	Zítek [Fragment]	WP posth.*
1935	1/16	Vojáček	Jasice	WP
	4/3	Ostrčil	Honzovo království (*Johnny's Kingdom*)	PP*
	4/17	O. Jeremiáš	Bratři Karamazovi	NP
	5/11	Szymanowski	Zbojníci (*Harnasie*) [Ballet]	WP
	5/11	Ponc	Osudy (*Adventures*) [Ballet]	WP
1936	2/7	Martinů	Hry o Marii (*Plays about Mary*)	PP
	—	A. Hába	Nová země (*The New Land*)	Canceled
1937	3/2	Jirák	Žena a bůh [Apolonius z Tyany] (*Woman and god*)	PP
	11/17	Hůla	Modrý květ (*The Blue Flower*)	WP
	12/17	Vomáčka	Vodník (*The Water-Sprite*)	WP
1938	3/16	Martinů	Julietta aneb Snář (*Julietta, or the Dream-book*)	WP

Notes

The abbreviations throughout these notes can be found in Notes to the Reader, p. xviii–xix.

Preface

1.   Stainslav, "Moderní hudba a Mezinárodní hudebrí festival v Praze 1924," 115–16.

Chapter One

1.   The five provinces were: Bohemia (Čechy), Moravia (Morava), Slovakia (Slovensko, independent since 1993), Silesia (Slezsko, most of which now lies in Southern Poland), and Sub-Carpathian Ruthenia (Podkarpatská Rus, now part of Ukraine). The regime that existed from 1918 to 1938 is known as the First Republic, while that of 1938–39 is the Second Republic or Czecho-Slovakia. In using the term "Czech Lands" I refer to Bohemia, Moravia, and Czech Silesia, a geographical entity corresponding to the present-day Czech Republic.

2.   For a complete personalia of the composers, critics, and other individuals mentioned in this book, please refer to appendix 1.

3.   Cohen, *Politics of Ethnic Survival*, 92–93. Cohen's figures are based on Austrian censuses of 1900 and 1910 across all suburbs of the city.

4.   For a discussion of the role of Jews in Bohemian society, see Kieval, *Making of Czech Jewry*. Even by the turn of the century, Austrian censuses showed that a large proportion of Jews had begun to make cultural allegiances with the Czechs. See Cohen, *Politics of Ethnic Survival*, 102.

5.   The Czech Cultural Revival (Obrození) was a nineteenth-century phenomenon enacted by a small number of intellectuals whose goal it was to bring the Czech language into widespread modern usage, and subsequently to create a literature, art, music, and scholarship based in it. See further discussion in chapter 2.

6.   Beckerman, "In Search of Czechness in Music."

7.   Ibid.

8. Taruskin, *Defining Russia Musically*.

9. Ibid., xiii.

10. Ibid., xiv.

11. Rather than imitate or quote actual folk song, many more compositions from the fin-de-siècle and interwar periods used folk poetry as a basis or inspiration, set in a contemporary high-art style. Cf. Novák's *Dvanáct ukolébavek na slova lidové kolébavky moravské pro ženský sbor* [Twelve Lullabies on the Words of a Moravian Folk Lullaby for Female Chorus], op. 61, composed 1932.

12. In this regard, too, composers from aristocratic families such as Jindřich Kàan z Albestů could not escape the charge of djlletantism.

13. Taruskin, *Defining Russia Musically*, 16–18.

14. Axman, "Nechte cizích, mluvte vlastní řečí!" 24.

Chapter Two

1. Two of the most frequently used survey texts, Grout and Paliska's *A History of Western Music* and Stolba's *The Development of Western Music: A History*, begin their meager discussions of Czech nationalist music with Smetana; although both mention the earlier existence of Tomášek, Voříšek, and so on, they do so in a section altogether removed from Smetana, such that the latter's appearance is completely decontextualized. Plantinga's *Romantic Music*, providing a more in-depth discussion generally, begins the history of music in Bohemia with Charles Burney's account, moving quickly to "Tomášek and Smetana." These two, however, are differentiated precisely on national terms, Tomášek developed as "essentially cosmopolitan," while Smetana receives the laurel: "a native composer who sought to create a distinctively national musical art" (Plantinga, *Romantic Music*, 348).

2. Slovakia, never part of the Czech Lands, was ruled by Hungarians after the fall of Greater Moravia in 894; it remained under Hungarian jurisdiction within the Austrian Empire all the way to 1918, and as such maintained a distinct cultural identity during the period under examination. The Slovak language, which uses the Roman alphabet, is the closest linguistic relative to Czech, and cultural ties, strengthened by emissaries from the Prague intelligentsia during the Cultural Revival, form a series of parallels between Prague, Brno, and Bratislava. Nevertheless, Slovakia's high-art cultural development lagged behind the Czechs', largely because of the dearth of artistic institutions before 1918.

3. Burney, *Present State of Music in Germany, the Netherlands, and United Provinces*.

4. Kenneth DeLong describes a "fanatical cult of Mozart that developed in Prague in the years after his death and which continued to exercise a dominating influence over musical life in the city well into the twentieth century" ("From Tomášek to Smetana"), 4.

5. Although various short-lived aristocratic theaters had been in operation since 1701, the first permanent public theater in Prague opened in 1783, built by Count Nostitz. It saw the premieres of *Don Giovanni* and *La clemenza di Tito* and exists to this day, known as the Estates Theater. For further discussion see Tyrrell, *Czech Opera*, 13–17.

6. This slim access to performance venues was the work of a single Czech director at the theater, one Jan Nepomuk Štěpánek (1783–1844). See discussion in Tyrrell, *Czech Opera*, 20–22.

7. Herder, "Slavian Nations"; Wilson, "Herder, Folklore, and Romantic Nationalism."

8. The main figures of the movement were the philologist Josef Dobrovský (1753–1829), the lexicographer Josef Jungmann (1773–1847), the poet Karel Hynek Mácha (1810–36), the historian František Palacký (1798–1876), and the journalist and poet Karel Havlíček-Borovský (1821–56), the last a personal friend of Smetana's.

9. See discussion in Cohen, *Politics of Ethnic Survival,* 86–139.

10. DeLong, "From Tomášek to Smetana," 5–10.

11. Despite a promising continuation with *Libušin sňatek* (1835) and his twenty years as main opera conductor at the Estates Theater, Škroup did little to encourage Czech-language opera; he composed seven German operas, and performed others by Heller and Kittl. See Tyrrell, *Czech Opera,* 67.

12. Weber, *Alexander Zemlinsky,* 25–37.

13. See discussion in Beckerman, "In Search of Czechness."

14. See discussion in Prinz, "Das kulturelle Leben."

15. For a brief overview of the activities of the music division of the UB, see Antonín Šilhan, "Hudební odbor Umělecké besedy," in Jelínek, ed., *Padesát let Umělecké besedy 1863–1913,* 79–138. Presidents of the music division included Smetana (1863, 1865, 1868–70), Pivoda (1866–67), Dvořák (1880), Fibich (1890–92), Novák (1914–17), Kovařovic (1918–20), Ostrčil (1921), Foerster (1922–23), Suk (1924–28), and Vycpálek (1929–39), although in most cases this distinction seems to have been honorary; the real power was yielded by conservative critics such as Šilhan.

16. The term "utraquist" referred originally to the segment of Czech society that followed the reforms to religious doctrine implemented by the followers of Jan Hus in the fourteenth century (specifically, the right to receive Eucharist of both kinds, "in utraque species"). They did not adhere to the subsequent Protestant Reformation, however; as such, their middle-ground stance was blamed for the disintegration of Czech political power in the early seventeenth century, which led in turn to the loss of independence in the Thirty Years' War. Later, the term came to signify an almost traitorous collaboration with Austrian authorities, especially at an institutional level.

17. It burned after six weeks of performances, and was rebuilt, also as a result of public fundraising, and reopened in 1883.

18. See biographical discussion in Jůzl, *Otakar Hostinský.*

19. Ibid., 36.

20. Ibid., 42.

21. Pivoda, *Pokrok,* February 22, 1870. Quoted in Jůzl, *Hostinský,* 42–43.

22. Smetana, *Národní listy,* March 3, 1870. Quoted in Jůzl, *Hostinský,* 43.

23. Hostinský, "Umění a národnost," reprinted in Hostinský, *O Umění,* 67–74.

24. Jůzl, *Hostinský,* 46. Jůzl produced monographs such as *Hostinský* mixed with a fair amount of official Marxist doctrine.

25. Hostinský, "Wagnerianismus a česká národní opera," reprinted in Hostinský, *O Umění,* 343–57.

26. Hostinský responded to Pivoda's 1872 article, "A Few Thoughts About Czech Opera," with "A Few More Thoughts About Czech Opera," and to Pivoda's 1873 "Where Are We? Where Do We Want to Go?" with "Where Are We? Where Do We Not Want to Go?" Cf. discussion in Eva Vítová, "70. léta—doba zrání Otakara Hostinského," introduction to Hostinský, *Z hudebních bojů,* 9–12.

27. Hostinský, "O hudbě programní," reprinted in *O umění,* 235–80.

28. Ibid., 237.

29. Alongside this smaller article, Hostinský published the extended German-language feuilleton *Das Musicalisch-Schöne und das Gesamtkunstwerk vom Standpuncte der formalen Aesthetik,* which provides a rebuttal to Hanslick on similar terms. See the English translation (excerpts) in Lippman, ed., *Musical Aesthetics.*

30. Nejedlý, *Dějiny české hudby,* 172.

31. "Česká opera," *Hudební listy* 5, no. 16 (April 16, 1874), 68; quoted in ibid., 171–72. For extensive discussion of the "Knittl Affair," see Stanislava Zachařová, "Nejedlého polemika o Karla Knittla," in Zachařová, ed., *Z bojů o českou hudební kulturu*, 29–115.

32. See discussion in Nejedlý, *Dějiny české hudby*, 173.

33. See discussion in Lébl, *Vítězslav Novák*, 34–47.

34. Zachařová, "Nejedlého polemika," 43–57.

35. Zdeněk Nejedlý, "Paměť veřejného mínění," quoted in Jůzl, 266.

36. Hostinský, *Umění a společnost* (Prague: J. Otto, 1907). Reprinted in Hostinský, *O umění*, 7–66.

37. Ibid., 17.

38. Ibid., 27.

39. Ibid., 46.

40. Lošťák, "Otevřený list mladé hudební generaci," quoted in *Dějiny české hudební kultury 1890–1938*, vol. 1 (Prague: Academia, 1972), 83.

Chapter Three

1. Jaroslav Jiránek, among others, makes this connection explicit: "the death of Zdeněk Fibich decided the direction of Zdeněk Nejedlý's lifework: he wrote his first artistic monograph (*Zdenko Fibich, zakladatel scénického melodramatu*, Prague 1901), and decided to go into musicology." Jaroslav Jiránek, "Zdeněk Nejedlý—zakladatel české hudební vědy," in Zachařová, *Z bojů o českou hudební kulturu*, 15.

2. See discussion of the nineteenth-century polemics in chapter 2.

3. Perhaps the most famous aspect of Nejedlý's career is his tenure as the first Minister of Culture and Education under the communist regime, 1948–62. Besides implementing a repressive, statewide socialist curriculum, the effects of which were felt all the way to the fall of communism in 1989, Nejedlý is credited with the propagation of Socialist Realism in all areas of the arts; he is also held to have participated in the "show trials" of the 1950s, wherein many members of the Czech intellectual elite were tried, incarcerated, or executed. While many socialist aspects can be found in Nejedlý's early writings, it is important not to dismiss his music criticism on the basis of events, however horrific, from half a century later. See chapter 11, n. 6.

4. Nejedlý, "Dvořákova *Rusalka*," 205.

5. Ibid.

6. Such an accusation of plagiarism would by no means be the last in Nejedlý's career as a music critic; in this respect, the impact of such a serious charge was diminished by repetition, not to mention the striking lack of corroborative musical examples in most of Nejedlý's criticism. For further discussion of Kovařovic, see below.

7. Even when quoting Smetana, Nejedlý neatly sidestepped the specific naming of Pivoda, Knittl, and others, including contemporary critics who may have written positive reviews of *Rusalka*.

8. As Judith Mabary has shown, the melodrama, for all its history in early romantic German opera, became revitalized as a "modern" Czech-language genre in the waning years of the nineteenth century, with Fibich's extensive *Hippodamie* trilogy in the forefront. Mabary, "Redefining Melodrama."

9. Josef Bohuslav Foerster, originally from Prague, spent a large part of his mature compositional career in Hamburg and Vienna (1893–1918), such that his direct "inheri-

tance" from Fibich and any tangible collaboration with Ostrčil were negligible, both of which contradict Nejedlý's construct of lineages.

10. Other composers participating in the Conservatory administration at this time were Karel Knittl, Karel Stecker, and Jindřich Kàan z Albestů, all of whom Nejedlý readily included in Dvořák's faction.

11. See Notley, "Brahms as Liberal."

12. Vladimír Lébl related how, for Novák, the time with Stecker and Knittl produced a lasting loyalty to both teachers, making him thoroughly prepared for the even more valuable training under Dvořák (Lébl, *Vítězslav Novák*, 26–27).

13. Zachařová, "Nejedlého polemika," 33. Zachařová's strong Nejedlian bias is evident throughout her writing on the "Knittl Affair."

14. Much like Hostinský, Knittl had refrained from public controversy since the 1890s, possibly because Pivoda's and Dvořák's deaths had made him almost the only living adversary from the 1870s.

15. Josef Theurer, "O posledních dílech B. Smetany," quoted in Zachařová, "Nejedlého polemika," 31. The lecture was later published serially in *Naše doba* 14 (1907).

16. Ibid. The emphases are Theurer's.

17. Zdeněk Nejedlý, "Poslední skladby Smetanovy," *Český pondělník* 1, no. 6 (December 10, 1906): 3. Quoted in Zachařová, "Nejedlého polemika," 32. The emphases are Nejedlý's.

18. See chapter 5.

19. Zachařová, "Nejedlého polemika," 34–35.

20. Branberger, "Karel Knittl †."

21. Ibid. Emphasis in the original.

22. See discussion in chapter 2, pp. 28–29.

23. In Pivoda's *Hudební listy*, all articles were presented with pseudonyms or extremely indecipherable truncations such as "-tt." Kalenský and Stecker quibbled with minutiae in the effort to deny Knittl's authorship or collaboration with Pivoda at all. The "-tt." author, they claimed, could have been either Rutte, Mottl, Wittlich, or even Jindřich Böhm (who used the pseudonym "diavoletto"), all of whom were known to be contributors to Pivoda's journal. Knittl, on the other hand, had used slightly different forms of the signature ("tt," "-tt-," "-tt.-," etc.) in later decades for different newspapers. Knittl's supporters never felt the need to confront the 1874 article's content, since for them it had no provable connection to Knittl in the first place. Cf. Zachařová, "Nejedlého polemika."

24. Kalenský produced a letter from Jindřich Böhm ("the still living originator of the *Two Widows* review under the symbol 'tt' in *Hudební listy, by ill luck Dr. Nejedlý's own uncle*"), a belligerent opponent of Smetana's Wagnerianism, who was still alive and had later married the aunt of Nejedlý's wife Marie. Indeed Nejedlý, who had almost no contact with his wife's aunt's husband, eventually received a communication from Böhm that the latter did not in fact pen the *Two Widows* article. Boleslav Kalenský, "Na obranu zesnulého ředitele konzervatoře Karla Knittla," *NL*, July 31, 1907; "Protismetanovství a knittlovština," *HR-S* 2, nos. 16–17 (October 1, 1907): 245. Quoted in Zachařová, "Nejedlého polemika," 72.

25. Zachařová, "Nejedlého polemika," 77.

26. Letter of Zdeněk Nejedlý to Artuš Rektorys dated August 16, 1907, quoted in ibid. Emphasis in the original. For a more detailed description of Czech political life at this time, see chapter 2.

28. Zachařová, "Kovařovic a Nejedlý," 91. Urbánek's *Dalibor* (1879–1913, 1919–27) was not the same journal as that by Procházka and Hostinský in 1873, which folded after only three years.

29. *Hudební revue*, the organ of the Umělecká beseda, started publication in 1908, with many of its members as contributing authors. It was largely a continuation of the short-lived *Hudební revue-Smetana*, which had published many of the pro-Conservatory articles during the "Knittl Affair."

30. Nejedlý used this emphasis in a number of critiques of the National Theater at this time. Cf. Zachařová, "Kovařovic," 98.

31. Both Nejedlý and Ostrčil had supported Kovařovic's reappointment as director in 1906 for this very reason. It is also likely that they held him in sympathy as a fellow student of Fibich's, albeit of a different generation. Cf. *Zdeněk Nejedlý—Otakar Ostricil Korespondence.*

32. Nejedlý at this point viewed the preceding decade as merely a period of difficult transition that had now ended. Zachařová, "Kovařovic," 93.

33. The entire letter of dismissal is quoted in ibid., 103–4.

34. Although there is no surviving evidence to prove Kovařovic's influence in this matter beyond doubt, Zachařová makes a strong case, in that subsequently, the journal *České slovo* received a request from the National Theater administration for the dismissal of Nejedlý's supporter Artuš Rektorys in 1913, which the editors ignored. The letter from theater director Gustav Schmoranz to *České slovo*, dated May 17, 1913, is included in ibid., 137–38.

35. Nejedlý, "Růžena Maturová."

36. Zachařová, "Kovařovic," 122. Šilhan, meanwhile, would serve as music critic at *Národní listy* until 1941 when the paper ceased publication; he used his power and influence to discredit Nejedlý and Ostrčil at every turn, particularly after the latter's ascent to the leadership of the National Theater opera. See discussion in chapters 5 and 7.

37. Nejedlý and his contingent temporarily moved en masse to the monthly publication *Pražská lidová revue*, which had very little circulation and, like *České slovo*, was not likely to be pressured by the Young Czechs, whom they opposed politically. See n. 34.

38. Nejedlý, "*Psohlavci* a jich smetanismus," 5–8.

39. Vladimír Helfert, "Hudební věda na naší univerzitě," *S-HL* 1, nos. 4–5 (December 16, 1910): 74. Quoted in Čornej, "Hudební klub v Praze," in Zachařová, ed., *Z bojů o českou hudební kulturu,* 119.

40. Ibid., 127. At the date of the inauguration of Hudební klub Nejedlý would have been thirty-two, Zich and Ostrčil thirty-one, and Helfert and Bartoš in their early twenties. Doležil, not in Prague full time at this point, was thirty-five.

41. Ibid., 119.

42. For a full list of the Hudební klub's activities, see Čornej, "Hudební klub," 158–63.

43. The examples were played in arrangement for piano duet. Ostrčil's participation in the Hudební klub, while limited to occasional musical performances, signals the renewal of his friendship with Nejedlý, from whom he had been estranged in 1906. See further discussion in chapter 4, p. 75.

44. Quoted in Čornej, "Hudební klub," 129.

45. Bartoš, "Antonín Dvořák," 5.

46. Ibid. Such explicitly Marxist references are rare prior to the First World War, even for a follower of Nejedlý.

47. See discussion in chapter 2, p. 25.

48. Bartoš, "Antonín Dvořák," 5. Emphasis in the original. The view that Dvořák's failing was in allowing himself to be molded by conservatives, both at home and abroad, is in consensus with a similar discussion in Nejedlý's *Dějiny české hudby* (see above, p. 41).

49. Ibid., 5–6. Emphasis in the original.

50. An assemblage of Nejedlý's recent university lectures, this publication was conceived as a sequel to *Zpěvohry Smetanovy* from 1909.

51. Nejedlý rationalized his choice to exclude Dvořák in terms of space, stating that a serious study of the latter's operas would necessitate a monograph unto itself (which the critic never wrote). Nejedlý, *Česká moderní zpěvohra po Smetanovi*, 3.

52. Ibid., 25. Although questions about the social function of art had been part of Hostinský's aesthetic platform, Nejedlý had refrained from fully adopting similar ideas until his initial exploration of left-wing politics with the approach of the First World War.

53. Löwenbach, "Smetana contra Dvořák."

54. As for Bartoš's article in particular, Löwenbach refused to accept the unquestioned comparison between Smetana and Dvořák, arguing that "their development and oeuvres directly force us to differentiate them and to interpret them separately, from within." As a direct contradiction of Bartoš's argument, Löwenbach denied that Smetana was at all even in his artistic development, whereas, even in his sketches, Dvořák's compositional technique showed a high degree of artistic conception. Ibid.

55. In the year previous, Vycpálek and Nejedlý had had a short, but vitriolic, exchange over the generally low level of musical analysis in Nejedlý's essay on *The Bartered Bride*. Vycpálek successfully demonstrated that several musical examples had chords incorrectly identified by Nejedlý.

56. Interestingly, Vycpálek's commentary did not touch upon Nejedlý's formulation of the social responsibility of progressive Czech music. Ladislav Vycpálek, "Česká moderní zpěvohra po Smetanovi."

57. Ibid.

58. The title of Helfert's article refers to a slogan apparently originating at a Dvořák festival in the German spa town of Pyrmont in 1911. Helfert described how the phrase was subsequently taken up by the conservative establishment at home; its use in his title is therefore ironic and derogatory toward the "weak, fumbling spirit of the majority of our artistic culture of today." Helfert, "Více Dvořáka!"

59. Vycpálek refuted this claim in several reviews throughout this period in *Hudební revue*.

60. "Protest 15.12.1912," *NL, V, PL, Čas*, December 15, 1912.

61. Nejedlý, "Boj o Dvořáka. II. Personalie," 104. The mention of Novák's "opinions on Dvořák's work" refers to his alleged negative assessment of some of his teacher's compositions, including the cantata *Svatební košile*, whose poem Novák eventually set as a completely new cantata.

62. Nejedlý, *Vítězslav Novák: Studie a kritiky*.

63. Cf. Lébl, *Novák*, 154, which contains a quote from Novák's memoirs on the subject.

64. Bartoš, "XI. koncert Filharmonie," 128.

65. See further discussion of Novák's compositional style in chapter 4.

66. Helfert, "Konce hudebního naturalismu."

67. Nejedlý, "Zvíkovský rarášek."

68. Ibid.

69. Nejedlý, "Leoše Janáčka *Její pastorkyňa*," 117.

70. Ibid., 118. See chapter 2 for a discussion of Pivoda's pan-Slavonic aesthetic of opera.

71. Nejedlý's posturing did not go unchallenged, and was countered by a lengthy article by Václav Štěpán in *Hudební revue* that overturned all of the critic's claims with specific examples from the opera. Štěpán, "*Její pastorkyňa*."

72. The central committee included the composer Adolf Piskáček, the singer Bohumil Benoni, the sculptor Jindřich Čapek, and the painter and set-designer František Kysela. Nejedlý provided the guide booklet of descriptions and historical studies for the exhibition.

73. Pihert, "Smetanova výstava," 359.

74. Helfert, "Smetanova výstava." Helfert uses the term "důslednost" to describe the objectivity of the exhibition. The term "věcnost," or objectivity, would later be used to translate the German musical trend of *Neue Sachlichkeit*.

75. Ibid., 114.

Chapter Four

1. Today this building houses the Státní opera.

2. *Dějiny české hudební kultury*, vol. 1, 84.

3. A comprehensive list of concert programs is given in Antonín Šilhan, "Dějiny Hudebního odboru Umělecké besedy," in Jelínek, ed., *Padesát let Umělecké besedy*, 79–138; xxxvii–xlvii. Šilhan does not give details of composition titles or performers for the "Young Vienna" concert, and it is unclear if 1911 represents the end of such activity.

4. An informal account of the Podskalská filharmonie, its membership and activities is given in Richard Veselý, "Hrstka vzpomínek," in Srba, ed., *Vítězslav Novák*, 345–75.

5. Members and regular guests of the Podskalská filharmonie included Josef Suk, Jaroslav Křička, Rudolf Karel, Antonín Šilhan, Boleslav Kalenský, Jan Branberger, Otakar Šourek, Václav Talich, Jan Löwenbach, Václav Štěpán, Ladislav Vycpálek, Boleslav Vomáčka, and the Jeremiáš brothers, all of whom appear elsewhere in the present narrative.

6. The most direct and audible influence of Mahler in Czech music occurs in the *Suita c-moll* by Ostrčil; the composer most credited with a Schoenbergian compositional approach is Jaroslav Novotný (1886–1918), whose career was tragically cut short by his death as a Russian prisoner of war, after serving in the Austrian army during the First World War.

7. Popular legend has it that Nejedlý's hatred of both Dvořák and Suk stemmed from his early romantic interest in Otilie Dvořáková, who jilted the young critic in favor of Suk; given the multitude of other ideological factors involved in Nejedlý's criticism, however, there is little reason to include the tale in a scholarly assessment of his reception of the two composers, and of the compositional lineages promulgated by him throughout his career.

8. Vítězslav Novák, *Paměti*, 175, quoted in Lébl, *Novák*, 89. Lébl's extensive article "Pražské ohlasy Debussyho tvorby," 195–233, demonstrates that Debussy's music was unknown in Prague before 1905. Interestingly, while many Czech composers were influenced by impressionism over the years, Debussy's style was not well received by critics in Prague until the years of the First Republic, after Debussy's death. Novák did, however, mention Grieg and Schumann as important influences in his earlier career. Cf. Novák's letter to Theurer, March 13, 1898, in Lébl, *Novák*, 54–55.

9. Dvořák's growing distaste for his student's latest work can be sensed in the tepid reception with which both the G-major Quartet op. 22 (1899) and the *Sonata eroica* met in the competition for the Czech Society of Chamber Music, on whose adjudicating panel Dvořák served. Submitted in 1901 under the subtitle "Independence!" the *Sonata eroica* received second place, since "none of the submitted works were recognized as qualified for the first prize." This relatively minor event demonstrates the generational and ideological gap that had developed between two artists who had formerly shared a similar viewpoint. Remarks of the Český spolek pro komorní hudbu are quoted in Lébl, *Novák*, 397.

10. Nejedlý, *Vítězslav Novák*. See also discussion in chapter 3, p. 59.

11. Throughout 1906, Novák worked seriously at sketches for an operatic setting of the legend of the Slovak folk hero, Jura Janošík: looked to with great anticipation by various

Slovak cultural figures, *Janošík* was to be the first "Slovak opera." Although *Janošík* was never completed, Novák did not give up on the genre, making substantial operatic studies along the way: the cantatas *Bouře* (The Storm, 1910) and *Svatební košile* (The Wedding Shirt, 1913) both attest to the composer's growing boldness in dramatic form and scope, each of which was discussed in greater detail in chapter 3. With regard to the concept of "Slovak opera," see the discussion of *Dědův odkaz* in chapter 8.

12. See discussion in Lébl, *Novák*, 95.

13. See discussion in chapter 3, p. 62.

14. According to Nejedlý, the older composer apparently doted on the boy like a paternal figure. Nejedlý, *Otakar Ostrčil*, 35.

15. This rather one-sided state of affairs is somewhat detrimental to the modern view of Ostrčil, since it is almost impossible to circumvent Nejedlý's oft-rehearsed characterization of his friend, especially in view of the fact that the composer himself rarely divulged his own artistic thoughts in print.

16. Nejedlý, *Otakar Ostrčil*, 36–38.

17. Ibid., 82.

18. Ibid., 78.

19. This view was fallacious on many levels, since Fibich's cosmopolitanism led him more frequently to non-Czech subjects, often from classical sources, and both men (particularly Ostrčil, who was raised in Prague) were middle-class urbanites their entire lives.

20. Nejedlý, *Otakar Ostrčil*, 84–89.

21. Ibid., 79.

22. Letter to Nejedlý from June, 1902, quoted in ibid., 80.

23. The influence of Strauss on *Kunálovy oči* may be explained by the fact that much of the opera was composed away from Nejedlý's domineering ideology (particularly in the final stages of work after 1906: see discussion later in the paragraph). Indeed, Lébl asserts that the opera is Ostrčil's most Straussian composition, and the score reveals little of the quasi-expressionist density of *Poupě* and the later works. See Lébl, "Pražské Mahlerovství," 129.

24. Nejedlý, *Otakar Ostrčil*, 127–29.

25. Vladimír Lébl credited *Poupě* for having introduced a new modernist flavor to Czech opera (Lébl, *Novák*, 166–68). The work was performed at the National Theater with relative regularity, with a new production every decade, up to 1960, after which point it disappeared from the repertoire. An unpublished recording of the opera (with minor cuts) from September 1956 with the Czechoslovak Radio Orchestra under the direction of Václav Jiráček exists in the archives of Czech Radio in Prague. The high professional quality of this recording easily demonstrates the worth of *Poupě* to achieve a wider listenership.

26. Nejedlý, *Česká moderní zpěvohra po Smetanovi*, 338.

27. Ibid., 329. Note that, at the time of Nejedlý's writing, *The Two Widows* had been premiered only thirty-seven years before.

28. Ibid., 329, 331. *The Two Widows*, although its dialogue passages are somewhat lengthy, still contains a full contingent of conventional operatic set pieces and ensembles, and includes an extraneous chorus of peasants and two peasant lovers, whose only role seems to be to round out the key ensembles in each act.

29. Ibid., 330–31. The emphases are Nejedlý's; the term "musical comedy" refers to *Poupě*'s origin as a stage play (and analogous to "music drama"), as opposed to a "comic opera"; it should not be taken to imply the more popular genre from later in the century.

30. Ibid., 331, 334.

31. Cf. Nejedlý's cursory descriptions of key moments in the opera; ibid., 334–35.

32. The numbers in parentheses throughout this analysis refer to pages in the piano-vocal score. Otakar Ostrčil, *Poupě, komická zpěvohra o jednom dějství na slova komedie F. X. Svobody*, piano-vocal score by the composer (Prague: Umělecká beseda, 1911).

33. Čapek, *O. Ostrčila "Poupě."*

34. Although the story is completely fictitious, it makes use of four historical personages: Karel IV (1316–78), his fourth wife Elisabeth von Pommern (1347–93), Arnošt z Pardubic (1297–1364), and Count Ješek von Wartenburg (1294–1362). Historical records show that these four individuals could never have met under these circumstances, since Karel and Eliška married on May 21, 1363, several months after Ješek's death on September 27, 1362. Despite this oversight, the action takes place in the first year of the imperial marriage (according to Vrchlický, in June 1363), when the king was forty-seven years old and the queen a girl of sixteen. Stories of Eliška's phenomenal strength abound, including reports of splitting swords, horseshoes, and metal breastplates with her hands; after Karel's death she entered an abbey in Hradec Králové, a factor that may have influenced her portrayal as a spiritually intuitive character. Although Alena, in Vrchlický's original, is supposedly Ješek's niece, she is most likely a fictional character.

35. Quoted in Lébl, *Novák*, 180.

36. The librettist Otakar Fischer created the character of the Italian duke by merging two characters from Vrchlický's original: the politically threatening Bavarian Duke Štěpán, who wishes to exert influence over Karel, and the Christian King Petr of Jerusalem and Cyprus, who undertakes a puritanical crusade to find women in the castle. Fischer's conflation of the two roles streamlines the narrative, resulting an interesting—if somewhat contradictory—psychological study.

37. The numbers in parentheses throughout this analysis refer to pages in the vocal score. Vítězslav Novák, *Karlštejn* (Vienna: Universal-Edition, 1916).

38. In response to her servant's surprise at the aggressiveness of her words, Eliška sings: "No, Alena, it is neither hatred, nor spite, nor envy: only the wistfulness of the young heart. Do you know what Karlštejn is? I know it from Karel himself: there his heart beats most fervently. I will penetrate into his most secret soul and in hiding I will start his heart dancing. As soon as I enter the castle, where he is lonely and alone, there with a merry voice will I call: stop listening to the forest and the silent cliffs! How I love you, my Karel, my lord and King!"

39. Poliakova, "Vítězslav Novák i ego opera *Karlštejn*," 136.

40. The entire essay is reprinted in Bedřich Bělohlávek, *Jaroslav Jeremiáš*, 166–68. Bělohlávek related how, after studying with Novák privately for a year in 1909, Jeremiáš formed a negative opinion of his teacher's compositional aesthetic, eventually coming under the influence of the Hudební klub before his untimely death in 1918 at the age of twenty-eight. The feuilleton, sent to several Prague journals, was rejected unanimously, and was never published in Jeremiáš's lifetime.

41. According to Jonathan Bolton, Nejedlý's criticism of Fischer reflects a long-lasting undercurrent of resentment that, as a Czech Jewish playwright, Fischer should have the right to represent Czech historical figures (or even cultural life at all) on a stage as important as the National Theater. Nejedlý's "incomprehensible symbols" can easily be read as an anti-Semitic stereotype. Personal communication.

42. See the related discussion in chapter 3, p. 60.

43. Nejedlý, "Vítězslava Nováka *Karlštejn*," 23. The implied relationship to French culture was a common jibe of Nejedlý's, particularly with regard to Kovařovic: the above comment was perhaps a subtle reference to the conductor's role in replacing *Libuše* with *Karlštejn*.

44. Ibid., 19.

45. Vycpálek, "Hudba. Vítězslav Novák: *Karlštejn*," 90–91.

46. Ibid., 91.
47. Ibid., 92.

Chapter Five

1. Among the more prominent uses of the term "pathology" was the subtitle of Nejedlý's feuilleton, *Můj případ: k pathologii české společnosti v republice* (My Case: Toward an Understanding of the Pathology of Czech Society in the Republic).
2. For a discussion of utraquism see chapter 2, n. 16.
3. Vladimír Helfert, *Naše hudba a český stát*, reissued in Helfert, *Vybrané studie I*, 33. Helfert's Marxist terminology reflects his teacher Nejedlý's turn toward left-wing politics.
4. Ibid., 34.
5. Although Nedbal was in fact Czech, Helfert used the opportunity to link the composer's predilection for operetta and ballet-pantomime to foreign tastes. Nedbal had been a student of Dvořák's, a factor that may also account for Helfert's dismissal of his music.
6. Helfert, *Naše hudba*, 37, 39. The three operas were Zich's *Vina*, Jeremiáš's *Starý král*, and Jirák's *Apollonius z Tyany*, all loosely connected to the Nejedlý circle, giving further cause for Helfert's disapproval of their rejection.
7. Ibid., 41. Emphasis added. It is difficult to say whether Helfert's remark referred to Zemánek's German university and musical training, or if it was meant as a veiled anti-Semitic statement, conflating the conductor's Jewish roots with the unwanted German domination of Czech cultural life. There are no other references to Zemánek's religion in contemporary literature.
8. Ibid., 43. Emphasis in the original.
9. Ibid., 45.
10. Ibid. Emphasis in the original.
11. Ibid., 46–49.
12. Nebuška, "Česká hudba," 378. For a discussion of the Umělecká beseda (UB), see chapters 2, p. 21, and 3, pp. 49–51.
13. Nebuška, "Česká hudba," 379.
14. Ibid., 384. Emphasis added.
15. Jaroslav Jiránek and Oldřich Pukl, "Hudební život v prvních letech republiky," Section 1, chapter 2 in *Dějiny české hudební kultury*, vol. 2: 1918–1945, 63.
16. Although the authors of the *Dějiny české hudební kultury* do not make this claim, František Pala made a similar statement with regard to Kovařovic's choice of Ostrčil as dramaturge at the National Theater at this time. See below, pp. 136–37.
17. According to Pala, neither composer had much influence on the administrative proceedings of the theater, preferring to remain as figureheads in this situation.
18. Nejedlý, "Svoboda!," 2.
19. Ibid., 3.
20. Štěpán, "Blanche Selva."
21. Selva, "Blanche Selva."
22. Redakce, "Do desátého ročníku." Although the article's author is listed only as "editor," Nejedlý's role in the magazine is well known, and the style of the prose is consistent with his other criticism.
23. Ibid.
24. Ibid.

25. Nejedlý, "Na Nové cesty [sic]," 1.

26. Ibid., 2. Emphasis in the original.

27. It would be some time before these concepts were *au courant* in Czech musical discourse: see discussion in chapter 7. I use the terms *Neue Sachlichkeit* and *Junge Klassizität* according to the definitions given in Levitz, *Teaching New Classicality*, 74–76; and Messing, *Neoclassicism in Music*, 68–70.

28. Nejedlý, "Mladým."

29. Nejedlý, "Spolek pro moderní hudbu." While Novák was the creator of the group and its spiritual leader, the president was officially Ostrčil, whose administrative duties were fulfilled by the acting president, Václav Štěpán, and especially the secretary, Emil Axman. With regard to Axman's regular reports to *T-LHM*, see further discussion below, p. 122.

30. Paralleling the critical developments of the early 1920s described throughout this chapter, the Spolek proceeded to reject the new music trends (Stravinsky, Schoenberg, Les Six) they initially sought to explore, and to maintain a monopoly over new music performance in favor of Novák and his disciples. Younger, more cosmopolitan composers whose allegiances lay elsewhere were effectively prevented from having their works presented under these official auspices. The demise of the group and its replacement by other new music societies is described in chapter 9.

31. Nejedlý, "Dnešní krise hudby."

32. Ibid., March 18, 1922, 35.

33. Although Nejedlý did not name any specific repertoire with regard to "baroque decadence," his usage seems to reflect his disdain for the "subjectivist" music of Richard Strauss, among others: given the absence of mention in the critic's writings regarding any neoclassical compositions at this time, it is likely that his use of the term "baroque" was only in a figurative sense. See discussion of Nejedlý's reaction to Ostrčil's *Legenda z Erinu*, below, p. 187.

34. Members of this generation included Rudolf Karel, Jaroslav Křička, Ladislav Vycpálek, Boleslav Vomáčka, Emil Axman, and Karel Boleslav Jirák.

35. Vomáčka, "O hudební moderně."

36. Ibid., 3.

37. Ibid.

38. Ibid.

39. Štěpán, "Vycpálkův sloh"; Vomáčka, "Ideová stránka"; Löwenbach, "Jaroslav Křička."

40. Löwenbach, "Jaroslav Křička," 13.

41. Axman, "Spolek pro moderní hudbu," October 15, 1922, 19.

42. Vomáčka, "Otázky dne," December 20, 1922, 65. The reference is to Paul Bekker's article "Künstlerische Körperschulung."

43. Vomáčka, "Otázky dne," February 20, 1923, 114. Vomáčka's discussion is in reference to Paul Bekker's article from *Musikblätter des Anbruch* 5 (January 1923). Křenek, born in Vienna to a family of Czech heritage, seems never to have acknowledged this national connection.

44. Vomáčka, "Otázky dne," April 20, 1923, 165.

45. Doležil, "O budoucnost naší hudby," 125.

46. Ibid., 130.

47. Ibid., 131.

48. Axman, "Nechte cizích."

49. Ibid., 165. The gendered terms in which Axman argues his point are similar to the dichotomy between "masculine" *Neue Sachlichkeit* and "feminine" expressionism at this time in Weimar Germany. Cf. Auner, " 'Soulless Machines.' "

50. Axman, "Nechte cizích," 166–67.

51. Ibid., 168–69.

52. Jirák, "K problému hudební moderny," 54–55.

53. Ibid., 55–56.

54. Štěpán, "Otevřený list J. Sukovi," *HR* 12, no. 2 (November 1918): 46.

55. Ibid.

56. Talich's analysis is given in chapter 6.

57. Vomáčka, "Josef Suk," *Cesta* 1, no. 52: 1447. Emphasis in the original.

58. Ibid.

59. See formal discussion in chapter 6. Nejedlý, "Josefa Suka *Zrání*," 9. Emphasis in the original.

60. Ibid.

61. Ibid.

62. Ibid., 10.

63. Ibid. Emphasis in the original. Nejedlý is referring to the notice in the *Wiener Zeitung* of May 28, 1918, which lists Josef Suk as a recipient of "das Kriegskreuz für Zivilverdienste · zweiter Klasse," alongside Hermann Bahr, Julius Bittner, Karel Hoffmann, Hugo von Hofmannsthal, Franz Lehár, Oskar Nedbal, Franz Schreker, and Vilém Zemánek. Reprinted in *Dějiny české hudební kultury 1890–1945*, vol. 2, plate 2. The tricolor in Nejedlý's remark refers to the new flag of the Czechoslovak Republic, red, white, and blue.

64. Emphasis added. Nejedlý, "České kvarteto," 31–32.

65. "Josef Suk—Vlastizrádcem," *HR* 12, no. 3 (December 1918): 128.

66. Ibid., 129. The author goes as far as to give the title "c.k. professor Nejedlý" (i.e., "císařský královský," the Czech equivalent of "kaiserlich und königlich"), evoking the designation of officials in the Austrian Imperial government.

67. Maffie began during the First World War as an anti-Austrian resistance movement, led by Dr. Přemysl Šámal. According to the list of signatories on the eventual judgment of Suk, Maffie's presiding body consisted of: Dr. Bohuslav Franta, politician in the National Democratic Party; Jan Josef Frič, astronomer; Dr. Antonín Hajn, newspaper publisher and politician; Jaroslav Kvapil, playwright and librettist of Dvořák's *Rusalka;* J.S. Machar, poet; Dr. Josef Scheiner, head of the Sokol organization; Dr. Přemysl Šámal; and Dr. Bedřich Štěpánek, minister of public hygiene.

68. "Pod čarou." Reprinted in *Dějiny české hudební kultury*, vol. 2, plate 3.

69. Nejedlý, "*Hudební revue* věnovala . . ."

70. Nejedlý, "E per si muove." Nejedlý's title misquotes Galileo's famous insistence ("Eppur se muove") that the Earth moves around the sun, despite all ecclesiastical claims to the contrary. The critic's invocation of the phrase in this instance implies a comparison between the Maffie and Galileo's disbelieving clerics, both of which bear a negative (albeit distant) association with Viennese counterreformational hegemony by extension. Cf. n. 75.

71. Ibid. Emphasis in the original.

72. Ibid. Emphasis in the original.

73. Ibid. Emphasis in the original.

74. Quoted in "Případ Nejedlého," 240. Emphasis in the original.

75. Ibid., 240–41. Herben's accusation of Nejedlý's "Jesuitism" is perhaps a backlash against the latter's anticlerical insinuations with the title "E per si muove." Cf. n. 70.

76. See discussion in chapter 3.

77. "České veřejnosti," *NL*, February 16, 1919. Reprinted in "Případ Nejedlého," 241.

78. Ibid.

79. Nejedlý, *Můj případ,* 4.

80. Nejedlý quoted a threatening note he allegedly received after the publication of Herben's feuilleton: "I just read the article by Dr. Herben in *Národní listy* and I hope that, perhaps next time, you will finally keep your moralizing principles to yourself. If, contrary to expectation, you ever continue [in this manner], I will answer you myself, not with words but with a physical act [athletickým činem]." Nejedlý refrained from publishing the author's name. Quoted in ibid., 21.

81. Ibid., 23.

82. Ibid., 36.

83. Ibid., 39. See also J. S. Machar's article "Amnestie," which appeared in the context of the "Suk Affair."

84. Pala, *Opera Národního divadla,* vol. 1, 1.

85. Ibid., 2–5.

86. Ibid., 56.

87. Pala described how, as a result of their patriotic subject matter by Jirásek and Němcová, respectively, Kovařovic's *Psohlavci* and *Na starém bělidle* attained a peak level of popularity with operagoers after independence. Ibid., 54.

88. The reaction to this production presaged the violent confrontation between Czechs and Germans at the Deutsches Landestheater less than two years later (described below).

89. Jaroslav Hilbert, "Ke sporu o vhodnosti . . . ," *V,* January 21, 1919. Quoted in Pala, *Opera Národního divadla,* vol. 1, 82–83.

90. Quoted in Pala, *Opera Národního divadla,* vol. 1, 83.

91. Nejedlý, surprisingly, is a big exception in this regard. In his co-option of Smetana's "lineage," Nejedlý stood behind Wagner as an important factor within his concept of "progressive art." Such a line of argument prevented his participation in this particular dispute: Czechness, which for him depended on progressiveness, could not be compromised by contemporary attitudes toward Germany.

92. The full letter is quoted in Pala, *Opera Národního divadla,* vol. 1, 116–19.

93. Jeremiáš had offered to reduce the score, but was ignored by Kovařovic. Vladimír Helfert, "Panu Karlu Kovařovicovi," *ČS,* February 23, 1919. Quoted in ibid., 119.

94. Quoted in ibid., 118–19.

95. Nejedlý, "Jar. Jeremiáše *Starý král.*"

96. Quoted in Pala, *Opera Národního divadla,* vol. 1, 123.

97. Quoted in ibid., 120.

98. Ibid., 136.

99. The text of the advertisement is given in ibid., 137.

100. The Vinohrady Theater was run by the Družstvo Národního divadla, which had previously directed the National Theater until 1900 and had moved to the nouveau riche Vinohrady suburb to set up its own theater in 1904 (see discussion in chapter 4). Although the Družstvo cited economic hardships incurred by the expensive and poorly attended operatic productions, the dismissal of the orchestra personnel was more likely a defense measure against possible unionization, which the administration and the director of spoken drama, K. H. Hilar, staunchly opposed. Although many of the musicians found employment in either the National Theater, the Czech Philharmonic, or the new Šakova filharmonie (see discussion below), the event caused a scandal in the music community; Nejedlý wrote a lengthy feuilleton, denouncing the capitalist tactics of the Vinohrady administration and Hilar. *Spor ve vinohradském divadle* reveals an early stage of Nejedlý's application of socialist politics to the criticism of culture.

101. According to theater archivist Václav Podrabský who witnessed the brief meeting, Kovařovic simply asked Ostrčil, "Would you accept the position of opera dramaturge at the National Theater?" When Ostrčil accepted, he was presented with the score of Janáček's most recent opera: "Would you like to study and perform it? Here you have it." Quoted in Pala, *Opera Národního divadla,* vol. 1, 179.

102. *NL,* May 1, 1920. Paraphrased in Pala, *Opera Národního divadla,* vol. 1, 219.

103. Pala, *Opera Národního divadla,* vol. 1, 240.

104. Burkhard Kippenberg, "Rietsch [Löwy], Heinrich," *New Grove Dictionary of Music and Musicians,* 6th ed., ed. Stanley Sadie (London and New York: Macmillan, 1980). One subsequent pillar of the German-Bohemian musicology community was the celebrated scholar of eighteenth-century music, Paul Nettl (1889–1972).

105. Reprinted in *HR* 13 (1919, no. 20): 87. Cf. Pukl, "K problematice českého hudebního života, 204–6.

106. Quoted in Pala, *Opera Národního divadla,* vol. 1, 97–98.

107. Ibid.

108. Ibid., 144. This remark preceded the dissolution of the Vinohrady opera section, which had been considering unionization. Cf. n. 100.

109. The German-Bohemian demonstrations were directed against the use of the Czech flag on schools and hotels, on November 10 and 13, respectively. Cf. Pala, *Opera Národního divadla,* vol. 1, 258–59.

110. Ibid., 260. Cf. the report of the events in *NP,* November 17, 1920.

111. Fischer, "Stavovské divadlo."

112. Pala, *Opera Národního divadla,* vol. 1, 262.

113. Ibid., 263. Elsewhere Pala related how even Mozart's *Die Entführung aus dem Serail* (performed in Czech as *Únos ze Serailu*) was deemed by Schmoranz as too heavy for the Estates Theater audience.

114. The passage is quoted in full in Pala, *Opera Národního divadla,* vol. 1, 264.

115. Teweles, *Theater und Publikum,* 229.

116. "Prager Musikleben," *A* 1, nos. 1–2 (November 1920): 14. The reference to the Fruitmarket is to the triangular space (now called *Ovocný trh*) that abuts the Estates Theater; the Rudolfinum, one of Prague's foremost concert halls, housed the National Assembly during the First Republic.

117. Pukl, "K problematice," 209.

118. Ibid., 210.

119. This situation forms a direct parallel to Čelanský's dismissal as opera director of the Vinohrady Theater in 1913, prior to Ostrčil's term there.

120. *Dějiny české hudební kultury,* vol. 2, 65.

121. "Očista," *HR* 12, no. 3 (December 1918): 130. The two claims made here are without basis in fact. The article is quoted incorrectly in Pukl, "K problematice," 199.

122. Pukl, "K problematice," 213–14.

123. Ibid., 199–201.

124. Appearing at the same time as insinuations about the low artistic merit of operetta at the Vinohrady and Estates Theaters, it is no surprise that Nedbal, predominantly an operetta composer, should be sidelined in favor of Suk, the composer of autobiographical symphonic poems. Also of interest is the near total absence of the Nejedlý circle in the "Nedbal Affair," with the exception of Ostrčil, who as we have seen, acted independently from the group as a performing musician. It was likely Nedbal's involvement with Šak that kept Nejedlý out of the fray, since in the continuing controversy the factions became increasingly amorphous.

125. Pukl, "K problematice," 216. Šak, through his "Barnum-esque" advertisements, promised to solve all the existing problems of musical society in Prague, namely, by providing a financially solvent orchestra that would offer opportunities and funding for young Czech composers, publishing, advertising abroad, and even a new concert hall. Understandably his boastfulness irritated the musical establishment, which was already skeptical of anyone who would hire both Čelanský and Nedbal.

126. Ibid., 217. The Czech title of the organization is Hospodářský klub pro města pražská.

127. Ibid., 217–18.

128. Ironically, many of these individuals, particularly Zemlinsky, Ullmann, and Schulhoff, have heretofore received more scholarly attention than those from the dominant Czech society, likely because of their connectedness to the Austro-German musical world.

129. The letter of congratulation, signed by playwright and conservative political commentator Viktor Dyk, is reprinted in Pala, *Opera Národního divadla*, vol. 2, 7.

130. Ibid., 39.

131. Ibid., 75. Pujman, according to the *Československý hudební slovník*, was the first to bring modernism to Czech operatic direction. See also Lébl, "Pražské ohlasy Debussyho tvorby." Debussy's opera had received its Prague premiere at the Neues Deutsches Theater on September 28, 1908, sung in German. The National Theater production of 1921 was sung in Czech.

132. V., "*Pelléas a Melisanda*," quoted in Pala, *Opera Národního divadla*, vol. 2, 77–78.

133. Löwenbach, "*Pelléas a Melisanda*," quoted in Pala, *Opera Národního divadla*, vol. 2, 78–79. Most of the other critics, including Antonín Šilhan and Otakar Šourek, were positive toward Ostrčil's production of the opera.

134. The event was to be a three-day Kovařovic festival, beginning with *Psohlavci* on December 7, and the comic opera *Na starém bělidle* (At the Old Bleaching House) on the following day. The prologue of *Slib* was completed and orchestrated by Rudolf Zamrzla in preparation for the premiere on December 9, on what would have been Kovařovic's fifty-ninth birthday. *Cesta oknem*, the composer's second comic opera from 1885, had been reorchestrated during the final months of his life for a possible new production at the National Theater. The texts of Schmoranz's and Ostrčil's memoranda are quoted in Pala, *Opera Národního divadla*, vol. 2, 41.

135. Schmoranz's memoranda to the administration, dated November 4 and 9, 1921, are quoted in Pala, *Opera Národního divadla*, vol. 2, 80–83.

136. Hilbert, "Vzpomínka na Kovařovice," quoted in Pala, *Opera Národního divadla*, vol. 2, 85.

137. Šilhan, "Kovařovicův *Slib*," quoted in Pala, *Opera Národního divadla*, vol. 2, 85–86.

138. Cf. Sayer, *The Coasts of Bohemia*, 25–28.

139. See discussion in chapter 6. Pala, *Opera Národního divadla*, vol. 2, 185–95.

140. Šilhan, "Tři objevitelé Smetany," quoted in Pala, *Opera Národního divadla*, vol. 2, 192.

141. Quoted in Pala, *Opera Národního divadla*, vol. 2, 194.

142. Ibid., 252.

143. Bartoš, "Mezinárodní hudební festival," 70–71. Bartoš's positive attitude is due in part to his connections to the German-Bohemian community, and mainly to his work as music critic for the daily newspaper *Prager Presse*. For further information regarding the Verein für musikalische Privataufführungen, see Horst Weber, *Alexander Zemlinsky*, 32–35, and Mahler, "Alexander Zemlinskys Prager Jahre."

144. Bartoš, "Mezinárodní hudební festival," 71. Emphasis in the original.
145. Pala, *Opera Národního divadla,* vol. 2, 314.
146. Löwenbach, "Mezinárodní festival."
147. Ibid., 270.
148. Löwenbach, "Pražský festival."
149. Stanislav, "Moderní hudba," quoted in Bek, "Mezinárodní styky české hudby 1918–1924," 417–18.
150. Ibid.
151. See discussion in chapters 7 and 9.

Chapter Six

1.   The translation is my own, based on the version printed in *Josef Suk: Zrání, op. 34, hudební báseň pro velký orkestr* (Prague: HMUB, 1919), 3–4. All ellipses printed in the poem occur in Sova's original.
2.   The compact, embryonic state of the motivic material in the Grundgestalt also approximates the imagery of Sova's poem, where the immature kernel ripens into mature corn.
3.   Václav Štěpán, "Sukův sloh a význam ve třech orchestrálních dílech: *Asrael, Pohádka léta, Zrání,*" in Květ, ed., *Josef Suk,* 262.
4.   Ibid., 264.
5.   Ibid.
6.   For the sake of convenience and consistency, I will use Talich's numbering of motives as they appear chronologically, despite his inclusion of motivic forms of widely differing importance. See Talich, "Rozbor V. Talicha," in *Josef Suk: Zrání, op. 34, hudební báseň pro velký orkestr* (Prague: HMUB, 1919), 7–14.
7.   The numbers in parentheses throughout this section refer to measures in the full score. Josef Suk, *Zrání: Symfonická báseň pro velký orchestr, op. 34* (Prague: Editio Supraphon, 1967).
8.   The motive in question, although somewhat different metrically and rhythmically, begins at m. 3 of the piano piece, which bears the expressive indication: "Forthright, later with the expression of overpowering force." The entire cycle (whose name is often translated as *Things Lived and Dreamed*) is one of the nonsymphonic pieces from Suk's output that is taken to represent an extension of the autobiographical cycle. The title itself evokes a similar sense of fluid consciousness as *Zrání,* both poem and tone poem.
9.   The "death motive" appears most significantly throughout *Asrael* in its representation of the Angel of Death; so pervasive was the cultural significance of Suk's motive that years later, in the concentration camp Terezín, the Bohemian-Jewish composer Viktor Ullmann used it for the same purpose in his opera *Der Kaiser von Atlantis.* In *Zrání* the final note appears down a tone from the original, which formed a series of two tritones.
10.   "Poznání, Mládí, Láska, Bolest, Odhodlání a Vítězství." Talich, "Rozbor V. Talicha," 8.
11.   This excerpt, the "Píseň paní Mařákové," is the only part of *Vina* to have been published (Prague: Em. Starý, 1922). All other passages in this analysis are taken from the fair-copy piano-vocal score housed in the music archive of the National Theater, MS. K177.
12.   Cf. the description in Pala, *Opera Národního divadla,* vol. 2, 103.
13.   Hutter, "Otakar Zich a jeho hudební drama *Vina,*" December 30, 1922, 135.

14. Ibid., 107. Note the resemblance of Hutter's reading of *Vina* to Nejedlý's appreciation of similar characteristics in Novák's *Bouře*.

15. Hutter, *Otakar Zich a jeho hudební drama "Vina,"* 25–39.

16. These motivic designations are given in ibid., 45–61.

17. Nejedlý, "Zichova *Vina.*"

18. Nejedlý's reaction to Hilbert was to be expected, given the playwright's editorship of the Agrarian newspaper *Venkov* and his previous attacks on Ostrčil.

19. Quoted in Pala, *Opera Národního divadla*, vol. 2, 104.

20. Quoted in "Ot. Zich: *Vina,*" 106–7.

21. Pala, *Opera Národního divadla*, vol. 2, 104–5. Pala did not recognize that "V.," the initial of the critic in *Čas*, indicated Vomáčka. A contemporary review of criticism edited by Vomáčka himself ("Ot. Zich: *Vina*") demonstrates this to be the case.

22. Quoted in "Ot. Zich: *Vina,*" 105.

23. Ibid., 106. Emphasis in the original.

24. Quoted in ibid., 105.

25. Antonín Šilhan, "Finis musicae," quoted in ibid., 106–7.

26. See discussion in chapter 5. Oddly, the criticism of historians under communism treated *Vina* as an unmentionable embarrassment in Czech opera history, despite the composer's allegiance to Nejedlý. As a result of the opera's subject matter and setting it was ultimately reconfigured as a product of the bourgeois society it sought to unmask.

27. The new production of *Hubička* premiered on February 9, 1923. Pala, *Opera Národního divadla*, vol. 2, 167.

28. Pynsent, *Julius Zeyer*, 5.

29. Hutter made the same dogmatic distinction in his analysis of *Vina*.

30. The term Grundgestalt was not used by Nejedlý, although he perfectly described its function.

31. The numbers throughout this analysis refer to pages in the piano-vocal score. Otakar Ostrčil, *Legenda z Erinu: Zpěvohra o 4 jednáních na slova Julia Zeyera* (Prague: Foersterova Společnost, 1920).

32. Nejedlý, "Ot. Ostrčila *Legenda z Erinu,*" 77.

33. Nejedlý, *Otakar Ostrčil*, 290. The term *obrodný* (revivalist) serves to connect Ostrčil to the Cultural Revival, and to operas such as Smetana's *Libuše* and *Dalibor* in particular. Emphasis added.

34. "Mohutnost, tragičnost, *heroičnost* dramatického děje." Nejedlý, "Ot. Ostrčila *Legenda*," 76. Emphasis in the original.

35. Ibid., 75.

36. Ibid., 76. Nejedlý's negative use of the term "baroque" implies both the larger stylistic judgment of superficial ornamentation and the critic's own dim view of a musical period that took place during the Czech "Dark Ages." He attempts to de-historicize the baroque and apply it to various branches of modernism. Cf. chapter 5, p. 120.

37. Hutter's divergence from Nejedlý's ideas would increase all the way to the end of his career. See chapter 9, n. 116.

38. Hutter, *Legenda z Erinu*, 30. Emphasis added.

39. Ibid., 4–8.

40. Ibid., 7.

41. Much of Hutter's prose is composed of aphoristic sentence fragments such as the above. The final phrase, "made in Czechoslovakia," is in English. Ibid., 11.

42. Bartoš, *Otakar Ostrčil*, 35. Quoted in Pala, *Opera Národního divadla*, vol. 2, 173.

43. Šourek, "Brněnská zpěvohra."

Chapter Seven

1. The phrase "musical (or more commonly, cultural) bolshevism" was in current parlance throughout the right-wing musical establishment of Weimar Germany, and was often used to express a fear that the communist movement would use the cultural sphere as a starting point for political domination. In Prague, this slogan had a slightly different connotation, especially since there was little threat of a communist revolution as there had been in the early days of German democracy; rather, it implied an intrusion from outside Czech society, either from the Soviet Union or in this case, Berlin. Cf. Nötzel, *Gegen den Kultur-bolschewismus.*

2. Helfert, "Čeho je potřeba"; and "Krise."

3. Helfert, "Krise," 74–75.

4. Ibid., 77.

5. The appearance of these and subsequent articles from the Brno-based journal *Hudební rozhledy* mirrors Helfert's relocation to Brno in 1919 to head the newly founded musicology department at what is now Masaryk University.

6. Martinů, "Ke kritice o současné hudbě," 185.

7. Ibid. Martinů's phrase is "metafysiky na úkor čisté hudby."

8. Očadlík, "Dnešní modnost a modernost."

9. Martinů, "O současné hudbě," 268–70.

10. The issue of Martinů's thorny relationship with Czech identity and the Prague critical sphere is dealt with extensively in Thomas D. Svatoš, "Martinů on Music and Culture." With regard to Martinů and the larger issue of Czech musical style, see Beckerman, "In Search of Czechness," 63–73.

11. Vomáčka, "Stav přítomné hudby české."

12. The work that Vomáčka cites is Otakar Zich, *Symfonické básně Smetanovy* (Prague: HMUB, 1924), for which publication he would likely have been on the editorial board. Zich met with increasing success as an author on aesthetics in the interwar period, especially in the realm of theater.

13. Vomáčka, "Krise moderní hudby."

14. Ibid., 83.

15. Vomáčka, "Mezinárodní hudební festival."

16. Although Steinhard credited Vycpálek with being the Czechs' "strongest talent," he placed the Cantata merely in a context of the "Volkstümlichen und Nationalen," such that "the vision of death with the resounding of the *Totentanz* is unparalleled in Slavic music." Finke, meanwhile, attempted Werfel's poem with "intensity," but failed to match the specific emotion of the text with the Mahlerian language he chose for its setting. Steinhard, "Vom Prager internationalen Musikfest," 217–18.

17. Vomáčka, "Mezinárodní hudební festival," 265.

18. Ibid., 267.

19. Vomáčka, "K festivalu," 339–40.

20. Ibid., 335.

21. Ibid., 335, 337. Vomáčka's phrase is "pečeť vyzrálého umění."

22. Bartoš, "Druhý mezinárodní festival."

23. Ibid., 51.

24. Ibid., 98. Vomáčka expressed similar views toward *Wozzeck* in the reviews discussed above.

25. Ibid., 99. Bartoš translated the phrase from Dent's German-language introduction as "internacionální hudba." These statements were echoed almost exactly in Václav Kálik's article, "O národnosti."

26. Tomášek, "Druhý orchestrální festival," and "Mezinárodní festival." The first portion is an editorial on the festival itself, while the second represents the review of the actual compositions.

27. Ibid., 161. Tomášek's word is "rakouskožidovský."

28. Ibid., 162.

29. Löwenbach, "Zase festival?" *T-LHM* 4, nos. 8–9 (May 15, 1925): 303–6.

30. Šilhan, "V cizích službách."

31. Ibid.

32. Iša Krejčí vehemently refuted this claim (and its implications for the Conservatory, which had procured the tickets) in the short article, "Skandály o *Vojcka* a Konservatoř."

33. "It would be lamentable if our main stage opposed every instance of progress that is expressed in the modern dramatic oeuvre. A new art has arisen that seeks to go further and higher. But it is not the task of the National Theater to go against its tradition and pursue every eccentricity in the field and to cultivate the operatic repertoire of the style of *Straviňský and his epigons*. There is no progress in the style of these modernists that would build on old foundations, but rather a revolution, which wants to destroy the old and create something quite different, new, to create new concepts of musical beauty, another musical aesthetic that is in opposition to the musical tradition of the ages. There is not just political, social, and economic "communism," there is also artistic communism. Musical anarchy" (Žák, "Albán Berg: *Vojcek*"). "Last Thursday at the National Theater an example of Bolshevik 'art' was given, a musically and textually perverse piece by the *Berlin Jew Berg*. The dragging out of such a piece onto our national stage was an example of unbounded impertinence and an arrogant provocation of music and of our art-loving nation" ("Skandál v Národním divadle," emphasis added).

34. Nejedlý, "Pan AŠ v *Národních listech*"; and "Blamáž našich klerikálů."

35. Nejedlý, "Blamáž." Nejedlý specifically mentioned the scene where Marie reads the Bible.

36. Nejedlý, "Blamáž." "*Čech* has apparently already been so musically *made Jewish* [požidovštěn], that it already likes only music of French Jews, and thus neither recognizes it when, among these Jewish *Huguenots* and *Carmens*, et al., there appears some straightforward Christian music—*Wozzeck*!" Emphasis in the original.

37. See Očadlík, "Skandál v Národním divadle"; and Lébl, "Případ *Vojcek*."

38. Lébl, "Případ *Vojcek*," 210–11.

39. Pala, *Opera Národního divadlo*, vol. 3, 235–55.

40. The full text of the protest and list of participating individuals and organizations is contained in "Za svobodu uměleckého projevu."

41. On this matter, Novák later expressed his dissatisfaction that his fourth opera, *Dědův odkaz*, was overshadowed by Ostrčil's production of *Wozzeck*. Šilhan also tried to portray Novák as a victim of the "*Wozzeck* Affair," such that these issues lingered in the reception history of Novák's opera as well. See the discussion below.

42. Očadlík, "Operní novatérství," 48.

43. Ibid., 50. Očadlík's phrase is "Proto se jeví expresionismus čistě hudebně jako druh koncentrujícího purismu, oproti rozptýlené náladovosti impresionistické." Note the actual use of the term *náladovost*.

44. The contemporary Czech attitude toward Italian opera of the verismo school (i.e., Puccini, Mascagni, Leoncavallo, and others) was one of righteous disdain, likely because of the bourgeois subscribers' constant demand for the style. Often equated with naturalism, Czech critics and composers felt that verismo dwelled too much on overt dramatic and

musical effects, providing a directness of expression that left little room for the idealization of art and life favored by Smetana and the Revivalists. As the criticism of *Wozzeck* and *Bratři Karamazovi* (see chapter 8) reveals, the use of the terms verismo and naturalism was often erroneous, implying either a lack or overabundance of psychological interrelationships in opera.

45. Hába's somewhat belligerent article was written and published prior to the premiere (oddly enough in the National Theater's in-house journal), but it is not known whether it stirred up any of the ensuing scandal. Hába, "K chystanému provedení opery *Vojcek*."

46. Krejčí, "Bergův *Vojcek*." See further discussion of Krejčí's aesthetic stance in chapter 9.

47. It is ironic that, while Vienna, the site of *Wozzeck*'s composition, lies further east than Prague, the entire German-speaking region has always been perceived by the Czechs as existing to the west, and as such has often represented a gateway to Western Europe, for better or worse. Whereas under the Habsburg regime this factor was perceived as a conservative barrier, in the interwar period many looked to the German Lands as a link to artistic progress.

48. Pala, *Opera Národního divadla*, vol. 3, 257.

49. Lébl, *Novák*, 195.

50. The prize was never awarded monetarily. Ibid., 427.

51. Nejedlý, "Vítězslava Nováka *Dědův odkaz*."

52. Očadlik, "*Dědův odkaz*."

53. Ibid., 55. The references to Stravinsky and verismo in this context are incorrectly applied.

54. Bělohlávek, "K případu Vítězslava Nováka," 599; "O současné české hudbě," February 16, 1928, 101.

55. Vomáčka, "Z hudebního života."

56. Entwistle, "The Turkey Takes Wing." By 1931, *Švanda dudák* had achieved more than 2,000 performances, including a run at the Metropolitan Opera in New York.

57. The notable exception from the turn of the century is Karel Weis, who composed operettas performed in both Czech and German; his importance as a folk-song collector in Southwestern Bohemia is often overlooked.

58. *Dějiny české hudební kultury*, vol. 2, 227. Bek and Pukl, in their descriptive terminology, reinforce many negative stereotypes of the eclectic, inartistic influence of Jewish musicians on European culture.

59. Hutter, "Divadla a koncerty," 134.

60. Hutter himself "borrowed" this threefold categorization of musical plagiarism from his teacher Zich. Cf. Zich, "Dvořákův význam umělecký."

61. Nejedlý, "Jaromír Weinberger." Nejedlý's term refers to the mixture of languages after the tower of Babel, an obvious reference to Weinberger's Jewish heritage.

62. Paraphrased in Pala, *Opera Národního divadla*, vol. 3, 282.

63. Pala, *Opera Národního divadla*, vol. 3, 283; *Dějiny české hudební kultury*, vol. 2, 227.

64. Knittel, " 'Ein hypermoderner Dirigent.' "

65. The entire business is reported in "Z mravů naší hudební společnosti," which reproduces an article from *PL*, January 1, 1920, entitled "Antisemitismus a muzika." Weinberger presented evidence in the journal *Kmen* that Zítek's article for *HR* contained uncited passages from the *Blaue Reiter* almanach, whereupon *HR* printed an unsigned article with the sentence: "[Weinberger makes his point] only so he can show the readers of *Kmen* how multifaceted and remarkable is the composer, pianist, theorist, writer, poet, essayist himself (*Gott, wie tallentvoll sind unsere Leut'!*) and what ignoramuses are all those who have ever made negative judgments about his compositions." Weinberger and Zítek both retaliated in print, and upon a chance meeting between the two men and Ladislav Vycpálek at the Representační dům in Prague, Zítek apparently said, "You dirty Jew,

during the pogrom we'll hang you from the lightpost first!" After the subsequent trial, both newspapers published a joint apology regarding the troubling affair.

66. Pala, *Opera Národního divadla*, vol. 4, 7.

67. Ibid., 62.

68. Ibid., 63.

69. Steinhard, "L. Janáček *Die Sache Makropulos*."

70. Because Martinů left Prague for Paris in 1923 and never again resided in the Czech Lands, I regard him only as a contributor from outside the group, although he shared many of the same ideals as his peers, and influenced them in the form of articles and operas performed at Czech theaters (particularly *Hry o Marii*, Brno, 1935, and *Julietta*, National Theater, 1938).

71. *Dějiny české hudební kultury*, vol. 2, 33.

72. Janeček, "Radio"; and "Radio a hudebníci."

73. Černušák, "Kulturní hodnoty hudebního rozhlasu."

74. Vetterl, "Hudba v rozhlase," May 1929; June–July 1929; and "O novou hudbu pro rozhlas."

75. Vetterl, "Rozhlasová hudba," October 24, 1929; November 20, 1929. Cf. Hinton, *The Idea of Gebrauchsmusik*.

76. Milhaud's article was originally published as "Apropos Tonfilm."

77. Branberger, "Zvukový film."

78. Kotek, *O české populární hudbě*, 117–202.

79. Kotek records the arrival of a few modern dances, particularly, the boston, cakewalk, maxixe, and in 1913, the tango; alongside these there were oddities such as the bear dance, apache dance, "Wackeltanz," and so on, which were little more than urbanized folk dances, or imagined exotic pantomimes. According to G. R. Opočenský, an observer at the *Montmartre* in 1913, Ema Revoluce and Jindra Venoušek danced the "Alexander-Twosteep" (sic., i.e., *Alexander's Ragtime Band* by Irving Berlin) to great acclaim: this occurrence is considered by Kotek to be the earliest "proof of the pre-jazz infiltration in Bohemia." Kotek, *Kronika české synkopy*, vol. 1: 1903–1938, 19–39. Cf. Kotek, *O české populární hudbě*, 175–87.

80. Gendron, "Fetishes and Motorcars"; Gioia, *History of Jazz*, 57–69; Kater, *Different Drummers*, 3–28; Cook, *Opera for a New Republic*, 41–55.

81. The prominent arranger and danceband leader R. A. Dvorský noted that in 1919 he still had to substitute the even more exotic "violinophon" for the saxophone for lack of players. František Alois Tichý was the first to incorporate a saxophone permanently in his instrumentation in autumn 1921. Kotek, *O české populární hudbě*, 197–99.

82. Ibid., 188–89. All titles are English in the original.

83. Gendron, "Fetishes and Motorcars," 143–45; Kotek, *O české populární hudbě*, 194. The cover page of one dance, the "Wentery Jazz," showed, among others, Indians with tomahawks, a Canadian Mountie, and a semiclad black slave amid the fashionable salon world of Paris.

84. In the first few years of Czech independence, the overriding cultural tendency throughout most artistic circles in Prague was to embrace French culture in all its facets, encapsulated by the virtual adoration of Cocteau and Apollinaire (the latter for his poem "Zone," which conflated Prague and Paris). See discussion in chapter 5, p. 117.

85. Štorch-Marien, "Kolem pařížských revuí."

86. Štorch-Marien, "Taneční umění."

87. P.P., "Savoy-Orkestr."

88. Ježek, "Jack Hylton and Hisboys" [sic.].

89. See continued discussion in chapter 9.

90. The West European composer closest to Burian's aesthetic might be Francis Poulenc, whose interest in mundane popular musics and banal lyricism is echoed in the writings of Burian, if not directly in his compositional style (see discussion below).

91. Valentová, "*Bubu z Montparnassu,*" 3.

92. Vítězslav Nezval, "Kapka inkoustu," *ReD* 1, no. 9 (1927/28), quoted in ibid.; Karel Teige, "The Poetist Manifesto."

93. Valentová, "*Bubu,*" 3.

94. Srba, "Les Pièces phoniques d'Emil František Burian," in *Colloquium Bohuslav Martinů,* 93.

95. Ibid., 90.

96. Burian, *Polydynamika,* quoted in ibid., 91.

97. Monmarte, "Honzl et Burian: Structuralisme et *Gesamtkunstwerk,*" 166–71.

98. Burian, "Maskovaný konservatismus," 24. See the quotation in chapter 11, p. 326.

99. Burian, *Jazz,* 18. Emphasis in the original. The secondary quotation is from Rogers, "Jazz at Home," 222.

100. Burian, *Jazz,* 14.

101. Ibid., 81. Emphasis in the original. Burian's embrace of lyric sentimentality somewhat contradicts his abandonment of authorial subjectivism identified above. The (rather sketchy) dividing line seems to be the centrality of the audience versus the artist, respectively: lyric sentimentality gives into the subjective whim *of the audience,* usually in order to make a social statement of a type not dissimilar to Brechtian epic opera.

102. Mikota, "E.F. Burian a jeho Voice-band." The name Voice-band (sometimes Voiceband) was always given in English, and was a deliberate reference to the popular term "jazzband." Although the group formally disbanded as an independent entity in the summer of 1929, Burian used similar techniques in his theater productions at *D35* in 1935, and a single concert was given in 1944.

103. Ibid., 95.

104. Ibid., 87–93. For the first time at this concert, the Voice-band repertoire included poetry by non-Czech authors, such as Apollinaire, Soupelt, Belloc, Heine, and Curci, in their original languages. Mikota provides a comprehensive summary of reviews from the occasion.

105. Valentová, *Bubu,* 4.

106. Ibid., 5–6.

107. Ibid., 9.

108. Ibid., 6–7. Notably, Křenek also employs expressionism as his base musical language in *Jonny spielt auf,* although the duality is reversed: since the opera begins in the "mainstream" European world, its initial expressionism is taken over by the populism represented by the title character.

109. The purposeless ending of *Bubu z Montparnassu* is not unlike that of Weill's *Royal Palace* (1925, one of the first Zeitopern), where the heroine Dejanira throws herself into the ocean through an inability to choose between suitors.

110. Pospíšil, *Opera Národního divadla,* vol. 5, 7–8. The earlier two Burian premieres had been prior to the "Wozzeck Affair," which likely accounts for *Bubu*'s rejection.

Chapter Eight

1. Indeed, Zich's work stands relatively close to many contemporaneous operas on a stylistic level, particularly Busoni's *Arlecchino,* Strauss's *Ariadne auf Naxos* and, in particular

(owing to the common textual origins), his incidental music to *Der Bürger als Edelmann*. As Susan Cook describes, the historicist quality of these early neoclassical operas was related to the Handel revival that took place in Germany in the early 1920s, although *Preciézky* does not necessarily reflect this link directly. The Parisian style of neoclassicism, among Czech composers most prominent in the work of the expatriate Martinů, did not gain a firm hold in Prague until the arrival of the younger generation in the 1930s; similarly, while "New Objectivity" was certainly discussed among the cultural elite in Prague, their acquaintance with it as a musical style was belated and likely did not predate Zich's opera. Cf. Cook, *Opera for a New Republic*, 3–26.

2. Levitz, *Teaching New Classicality*, 74. Levitz presents a thorough reading of Busoni's contribution to the early neoclassicist movement in the context of European modernism.

3. Ibid., 75.

4. Messing, *Neoclassicism in Music*, 68–70.

5. Busoni, "Junge Klassizität,"quoted in Levitz, *Teaching New Classicality*, 75–76.

6. Nejedlý, "Zichovy *Preciézky*"; Očadlík, "Otakara Zicha *Preciézky*," 17.

7. Foerster, "Úvodní slovo k Zichovým *Preciézkám*."

8. Očadlík, "Otakara Zicha *Preciézky*," 19.

9. Ibid.; Krejčí, "Zichovy *Preciezky*," 4.

10. Foerster, "Úvodní slovo," 2.

11. Vogel, "Z hudebního života," 346.

12. Hutter, "Zichovy *Preciézky*," 160.

13. Pala, *Opera Národního divadla*, vol. 3, 195–96.

14. Ibid., 196.

15. Jirák, "Otakar Zich," 109; Vogel, "Z hudebního života," 344.

16. Löwenbach, "Neue tschechische Opern," 135.

17. Hutter, "Zichovy *Preciézky*," 161.

18. Krejčí, "Zichovy *Preciezky*," 4.

19. Krejčí, "*Preciezky*," 2.

20. Nejedlý, "Zichovy *Preciézky*," June 26, 1926.

21. Vogel, "Z hudebního života," 345.

22. Krejčí, "Zichovy *Preciezky*," 4. "Zichovy 'Preciezky' jsou moderní buffou *rossiniovskou*." Emphasis in the original.

23. Vogel, "Z hudebního života," 345–46.

24. Regarding the ISCM festivals, see discussion in chapters 5 and 7.

25. See discussion in chapter 4 regarding Jaroslav Jeremiáš's role in the reception of Novák's *Karlštejn* and chapter 5 about the "Jeremiáš Affair."

26. Jeremiáš, "K vývoji současné hudby," October 10, 1924; February 15, 1925.

27. Ibid., 8. Jeremiáš's statement about the lack of innovation in Janáček is, of course, highly debatable.

28. Jeremiáš, "O vzniku opery *Bratři Karamazovi*." This short autobiographical article was published in connection with the revival of the opera at the National Theater under the composer's direction in 1935.

29. In the following discussion, the Czech title *Bratři Karamazovi* will be used to indicate the opera, while the English title will signify the book; out of consistency with the published score, I will use only the Czech spellings of the characters' names ("Míťa," "Grušenka," etc.), since the substitution of English transliterations would only result in confusion. Numbers in parentheses refer to pages in the vocal score, Otakar Jeremiáš, *Bratři Karamazovi* (Prague: HMUB, 1930).

30. Arguably, this phrase defines *The Brothers Karamazov* as well, since the father's murder is followed by a great deal of psychological, rather than physical, drama. Jeremiáš may have considered the debauchery and arrest at Mokré and the subsequent courtroom drama as "action," despite the relative paucity of activity onstage, particularly in Act 3 of the libretto.

31. Ibid., 5.

32. The motivic designations throughout this analysis are my own.

33. In this other, more famous Czech operatic apotheosis, the heroine and her somewhat violent admirer Laca are united under the banner of engagement, the dastardly Števa is socially punished, and even the murderous Kostelnička receives Jenůfa's forgiveness. It has often been criticized as the weakest act in Janáček's opera.

34. Bartoš, "Otakar Jeremiáš," October 24, 1928, 15, 5.

35. Bartoš, "Na okraj Ot. Jeremiášových *Bratří Karamazových*."

36. Bartoš, "Jeremiášovi *Bratři Karamazovi*." Similar rhetoric was used by the Nejedlý circle against Novák and Janáček; see discussion in chapters 3 and 4.

37. Očadlík, "Marginalia k *Bratrům Karamazovým*."

38. Nejedlý, "Jeremiášovi *Karamazovi*."

39. There is nothing in Jeremiáš's background to suggest a proletarian social class; he was raised in a family of music educators in České Budějovice, a small South-Bohemian city.

40. Jirák, "Z hudebního života."

41. Steinhard, "*Die Brüder Karamasoff* als Oper."

42. Paraphrased in Pala, *Opera Národního divadla*, vol. 4, 112.

43. Ibid., 113. Contrary to Doležil's claim, polytonality does appear at climactic moments throughout the opera.

44. Ibid., 112. *Weser Zeitung*, October 19, 1929.

45. Jeremiáš, "O vzniku opery *Bratři Karamazovi*," 5.

Chapter Nine

1. Under Hába and Očadlík's leadership the Spolek brought about a fresh interest in new music from abroad, including notable (albeit belated) productions of Stravinsky's *L'Histoire du Soldat* and *Svaděbka*. See also discussion below, p. 268.

2. For a more thorough discussion of this transfer of power and of specific organizations, see Vysloužil, *Alois Hába*, 132–33.

3. See discussion in Sayer, *The Coasts of Bohemia*, 195–220.

4. Faltis, "Sociální funkce umění? December 1935; January–February 1936. Faltis was the journalistic pseudonym of the composer Dalibor C. Vačkář.

5. Ibid., 54.

6. While it is difficult to determine whether Vačkář had specific composers in mind for the eight in the above quotation, the main neoclassicist/populists were considered to be Iša Krejčí, Pavel Bořkovec, Jaroslav Ježek, and František Bartoš (who formed the so-called "Mánes Group"), while the socialists included Alois Hába, Vít Nejedlý, Emil František Burian, and Erwin Schulhoff, among others.

7. Patzaková, "Sociální příčiny dnešní hudební krise," 81.

8. Ibid., 83.

9. Ibid., 85–86.

10. Redakce, "Na počátku ročníku."

11. Očadlík, "Svolejte naše hudebníky. . . ."

12. Ibid.

13. Ibid.

14. Očadlík, "O stavu kritickém," 1930–31.

15. Ibid., December 9, 1930, 101–2. After the collapse of the Hudební klub and *S-HL* in 1927, Nejedlý's music criticism had been confined to articles in the communist journal *Rudé právo*, which have been reprinted in *Kritiky II.*

16. Ibid., 103–4, 142. Očadlík mentioned Šilhan specifically, as well as "a group of younger so-called modernists."

17. Očadlík, "Podstata modernosti v hudbě."

18. Ibid., 79, 82.

19. Ibid., 83.

20. Ibid.

21. Očadlík reinforced this notion in his earlier editorial "Na konec ročníku," 291–92, where he urged the Czech musical community to be "rebellious and willful" like Hus, Havlíček, and Masaryk, thereby invoking three powerful figures from Czech history.

22. Vysloužil, *Alois Hába*, 133.

23. Also at Suk's suggestion, Hába's course became a full masterclass and Hába himself a full professor.

24. Actually, Přítomnost had existed since 1924, initially an amalgamation of the new-music societies Nezávislí, Několik, and Foerstrova společnost, it had a relatively conservative agenda until the early 1930s under the directorship of Karel Hanf, who welcomed first Karel Reiner then Hába to the group, effectively changing its artistic direction. See further discussion below, as well as Vysloužil, *Alois Hába*, 145.

25. Hába once wrote to Universal-Edition director Emil Hertzka that he would like to create "not only a Prague compositional school, but also a European one." Non-Czechs in Hába's classes included the Slovenes Dragutin Cvetko and Slavko Osterc and the Serb Ljubica Marič. See Vysloužil, "Hábova kompoziční škola," in *Alois Hába (1983–1973)*, ed. Vysloužil, 30–32.

26. Pícha, "Zvukový film," 89.

27. Hába, "Zvukový film a opera."

28. Ibid., 60.

29. Ibid., 59. The film, directed by Viktor Trivas, was first released in 1931. Hába's argument is similar to that of Schoenberg, who advocated a new direction for opera: "The theater crisis has been brought about in part by film, and opera finds itself in the same situation: neither can compete with the realism it offers. . . . In order to avoid the comparison with film, therefore, opera will probably turn away from realism or must otherwise find an appropriate path for itself." Arnold Schoenberg, "Is There an Opera Crisis?" 193.

30. Pícha, "Zvukový film, opera, netematický sloh," April 1932; May 1932. An editorial note mentions that the article, written some time earlier, was kept back from publication for reasons of space.

31. Ibid., 348.

32. Ibid.

33. Ibid., 348–49.

34. Ibid., 349–50.

35. Hába, "Budiž jasno o věcech základních." *Hauptstimme* markings would contribute to Hába's style in that they show the main melody in the absence of any distinct thematic material, particularly in the case of a multivoice composition. It is not by coincidence that

Schoenberg's music of the atonal period was recognized in Prague at this time for its artistic contribution, particularly since the flagship work of this style, *Erwartung*, had been successfully premiered there during the 1924 ISCM festival.

36. Ibid., 227.

37. Ibid., 226.

38. Schoenberg, *Theory of Harmony*, 151–52.

39. Starting in 1932, Burian (having returned to Prague from a three-year post at a theater in Brno) established and directed an independent theater that focused on avant-garde productions with overt socialist themes. Initially called D33, signifying "Divadlo" (Theater) and the number of the following year, the company changed name every season, so as to look progressively to the future. Burian introduced a substantial amount of music into his productions, although not as consistently as Ježek (see below); he is known to have sung light tenor roles, and Voice-band participated on more than one occasion. See Bořivoj Srba, "Les Pièces phoniques d'Emil František Burian."

40. The work was published and recorded during the communist period (i.e., after the composer's death) under the title *Komunistický manifest*.

41. For the beginnings of neoclassical opera in Prague, see the analysis of Zich's 1926 opera *Preciézky* in chapter 8.

42. *Dějiny české hudební kultury*, vol. 2, 170. The group's serial publication was *Rytmus*, discussed in detail below.

43. Holzknecht, *Jaroslav Ježek a Osvobozené divadlo*, 39–40. A complete listing of the concert programs and performers is given in the same volume, 415–17.

44. Krejčí, "Koncertní novinky," 71. Emphasis in the original.

45. Krejčí, "Boh. Martinu balet *Kdo je na světě nejmocnější.*"

46. Krejčí, "Večer skladeb E.F. Buriana," 32.

47. Krejčí, "O moderní hudbu," 119; "Moderní spolek," 101.

48. Krejčí, "Moderní spolek," 101.

49. Ibid.

50. Krejčí, "O sociální funkce hudby," 147. Emphasis in the original.

51. Krejčí, "Partitura Vycpálkovy *Kantáty*," 143; "Moderní spolek," 101.

52. Krejčí, "Německé divadlo," 11.

53. Krejčí, "Spolek pro moderní hudbu," 63. Somewhat bizarrely, Krejčí continued with a statement that, "Stravinsky is typically and deeply Russian like the entire current Russian revolution, is revolutionary like today's Russia, and is international like the ideas voiced by the current government of his homeland." Such a statement reveals Krejčí's intrinsic misunderstanding of his idol's political leanings, as well as a certain socialist idealism that proved virtually impossible to put into practice, as evinced by his subsequent output.

54. Ježek's *Bagately* were premiered on January 26, 1933; Bartoš's *Burlesky na slova V. Nezvala a M. Jacoba* on December 4, 1934; and Krejčí's *Madrigaly na slova K. H. Máchy* on May 9, 1938.

55. Krejčí, "Z hudebního života," 162.

56. Krejčí, "Opera?" Emphasis in the original. The author also paraphrases Gluck's statement about composing operas through absolute musical forms.

57. See discussion in chapter 7, p. 198. Cf. Svatoš, "Martinů on Music and Culture."

58. Schulhoff's great-uncle, Julius Schulhoff (1825–99), was a pianist and salon-music composer of European fame.

59. Bek, *Erwin Schulhoff*, 51–52.

60. Ibid., 62–64.

61. Schulhoff's *Songs on the texts of Petr Bezruč and anonymous folk poetry* were also performed at the Mánes Group concert of January 21, 1936, under the rubric of "New Czech Pieces" (*České novinky*).

62. See discussion in Bek, *Erwin Schulhoff*, 110–13, as well as documentary materials in Kotek, *Kronika české synkopy*, 83–89. Three excerpts of this oratorio were reconstructed and performed on the LP *Jazz a vážná hudba III: Ervín Schulhoff* (Panton, 1969).

63. *H.M.S. Royal Oak* was premiered on Frankfurt Radio in 1931, and was staged in Breslau (Wrocław) in 1932; its only Czech-language performance, with translations by Karel Balling, was given on Czechoslovak Radio on February 12, 1935.

64. Holzknecht, *Jaroslav Ježek a Osvobozené divadlo*, 243.

65. Ibid.

66. The jazz orchestra of the Osvobozené divadlo fluctuated in both size and stylistic attributes over the ten years of its existence. According to Josef Kotek, the ensemble's history can be divided into three periods: 1929–33, 1933–35, and 1936–38. The first, thirteen-member ensemble included three saxophones, two trumpets, trombone, sousaphone, two violins, viola, piano, banjo, and drums, and was based on the model of Paul Whiteman. The second, based on Duke Ellington's sound with sixteen musicians, included four saxophones, three trumpets, two trombones, sousaphone, three violins, piano, banjo, and drums. Finally, with the influence of recordings by Calloway, Henderson, Webb, Goodman, and others, Ježek added a third trombone in 1936; the violins were used sparingly, with a slight degree of improvisation, in the songs only, and were absent from the "hot orchestral compositions" altogether. See Kotek, "Jaroslav Ježek & orchestr Osvobozeného divadla 1930–1938," in Kotek, *O české populární hudbě*, 287–306.

67. For a discussion of each play and its musical component, see Holzknecht, *Jaroslav Ježek*, 105–43.

68. It should be noted, however, that at this time in America, many jazz recordings also exhibited a similar sense of compositional planning, not only in the Euro-American community (where improvisation was less likely), but also among African-American arrangers (e.g., Henderson) constructing a style that would become Swing. As a result, Ježek's project, although highly manipulated at times, can be seen to arrive at a similar orchestral Swing sound in the late 1930s, albeit by a different route.

69. According to a footnote in Holzknecht, the instrumental numbers were often rearranged or substituted from performance to performance. Cf. Holzknecht, *Jaroslav Ježek*, 413.

70. A reproduction is given in ibid., plate 123, opposite p. 305.

71. "*Fata Morgana*—Internacionální revuí."

72. The organization, called the Ständige Rat für die internationale Zusammenarbeit der Komponisten, was organized in June 1934 with Richard Strauss as its first leader. According to Splitt and Danuser, it was organized as a "musically conservative, politically opportunistic counter-institution" to the ISCM, which, through its strict control in choosing entries for its festivals, promulgated an antimodernist aesthetic. Representatives from eighteen countries were chosen according to the same principle; Jaroslav Křička served as the Czechoslovak representative for the entire duration of the Ständige Rat, a factor that has serious implications for his "musically conservative, politically opportunistic" opera, *Strašidlo v zámku*, analyzed in chapter 10. Hermann Danuser, *Neues Handbuch der Musikwissenschaft*, vol. 7 (Laaber: Laaber-Verlag, 1984), 123, quoted in Splitt, *Richard Strauss 1933–1935*, 176.

73. Warschauer, "Hudba na mrtvém bodě."

74. Ibid., 570. The Suite from Berg's *Lulu* had been performed at the 1935 ISCM.

75. Reiner, "Frank Warschauer na mrtvém bodě," 10.

76. Ibid., 12.

77. Nejedlý, "Ještě o tendenci."

78. For more discussion regarding this issue and Marxism, see Stanislav, "Věda, či pouhá osobní zkušenost?" Stanislav corrected some of the faulty concepts of Nejedlý, tending to be more generous toward Vačkář.

79. Babka, "Existuje lehká hudba?" Babka was a shadowy figure in the Prague musical community, appearing only in the context of the debate on popular music. It was likely a submission to *T-LHM* from a lay reader.

80. Ibid., 66.

81. Sehnal, "Hudba lehká a těžká."

82. Ibid., 78.

83. Haas, "Hudba lehká a vážná."

84. Tomášek, "V našem listě," 97–98.

85. Jirák, "Hudba lehká a vážná,"

86. Jirák, "Diskuse o vážné a lehké hudbě," 179. Emphasis in the original.

87. Warschauer, "Dvojí morálka v hudbě."

88. Ibid.

89. Krejčí, "Národní písen a šlágr," 104.

90. Ibid.

91. Ibid., 105.

92. Ibid. Emphasis in the original.

93. Among others, Dalibor Vačkář quibbled with the choice of Ježek as a representative of the nation, a composer whose music was based almost entirely on foreign models; his popularity, according to Vačkář, was a result of the fashionable status afforded the Osvobozené divadlo, the majority of whose antifascist expressions lay in the texts of Voskovec and Werich. Cf. Faltis, "Národní písen a šlágr a jiné."

94. In translating the text to this song, I have chosen to leave the original German phrases intact. The first two verses also contain substantial portions in English and French. Ježek, *Politické nebe na zemi.*

95. See Helfert, "Epištola o hudební kritice," and Očadlík, "Talichova abdikace."

96. Vysloužil, *Alois Hába,* 149, 257.

97. See discussion in Joseph Auner, "Schoenberg and His Public in 1930: The Six Pieces for Male Chorus, op. 35."

98. Vysloužil, *Alois Hába,* 270.

99. The report in question is quoted in Vysloužil, *Alois Hába,* 274.

100. Pala, "Co je s Hábovou operou?" Ironically, MŠANO's declaration comes almost exactly a decade after a statement rationalizing the ban on *Wozzeck* on similar grounds.

101. Bek, *Erwin Schulhoff,* 130. Schulhoff worked as a pianist under Ježek in the years 1933–35. Bek also mentions the composer's Spartakist sympathies in the early interwar period, as well as the powerful production of Weill's Schuloper *Der Jasager* of 1932 in Prague, in which Schulhoff's son Peter participated.

102. Ibid., 125, 127.

103. Quoted (in German translation) in Bek, *Erwin Schulhoff,* 130.

104. Steinhard had always presented an attitude of open-minded cooperation with the Czech musical community, offering them opportunities for publication of articles in German; his work also demonstrates a firm belief in the artistic efforts of the German-Bohemian community and their contributions to German culture at large.

105. Kinzel, "Wenn wir Sudetendeutsche darangehen."

106. "Der Fall Finke," *MdS* 1, no. 10 (August 15, 1937): 316–17.

107. Ibid., 317. Emphasis in the original.

108. Konrad Henlein, "Wir müssen . . ." *MdS* 1, no. 6 (April 15, 1937): 187; Adolf Hitler, "Die Kunst . . ." *MdS* 2, no. 7 (May 20, 1938): 230; Adolf Hitler, "Der Künstler . . ." *MdS* 2, no. 11 (September 15, 1938): 332.

109. Benetková, "Fidelio Friedrich Finke."

110. Helfert, "Česká moderní hudba," reprinted in *Vybrané studie I,* 163–312.

111. Ibid., 258, 302.

112. Ibid., 306–7. Emphasis in the original.

113. Ibid., 307. See Krejčí's similar criticism of Soviet composers performed by the Spolek pro moderní hudbu in 1927, p. 275 above.

114. Ibid., 308. Emphasis in the original.

115. Ibid., 311.

116. In fact, the Nejedlians viewed the epilogue of *Česká moderní hudba* as nothing less than the abandonment of (and therefore a direct attack on) their leader's ideological program. Given Helfert's embrace of Janáček from the earliest days of his Brno tenure, such a document was perhaps only a matter of time. The recently indoctrinated Nejedlian František Pala penned a long and scathing attack on the book in the new journal *Smetana-Hudební list,* quibbling with Helfert on all angles *except* the epilogue, but in language clearly inspired by it: Pala, "Studie o české hudební tvořivosti." Helfert responded in the feuilleton *Útok na Českou moderní hudbu* (Olomouc: Index, 1937, reprinted in Helfert, *Vybrané studie I.*), expressing his regret at the lack of mature critical discourse in the Czech context. Owing to the circumstances of history, Helfert, who died in 1945, avoided the wrath of his former teacher in the postwar communist regime. Not as lucky was his contemporary Josef Hutter, who had also gradually parted company with Nejedlý in the interwar period; his public approval of *Česká moderní hudba*'s anti-ideology outraged Nejedlý, creating a long-standing situation of professional antagonism that had disastrous results. See chapter 11, n. 6.

Chapter Ten

1. See discussion in chapter 9.

2. Vomáčka, "Z pražské opery."

3. Šilhan, "Operní premiéra s policejní asistencí."

4. Ibid.

5. Šourek, "Max Brand"; Očadlík, "*Strojník Hopkins.*"

6. K. Hába, "Max Brand."

7. "*Hopkins.*" Although no author is cited, the subsequent article, "Max Brand: *Strojník Hopkins*" is signed by Hába, whose frequent and often multiple appearances in the journal imply strongly that both articles are by him. "*Hopkins*" describes the plot of the opera more thoroughly, including its socialist implications and their considerable relevance for the dramatic outcome, in very respectful terms.

8. A. Hába, "Max Brand."

9. Premiered at the National Theater on February 23, 1934, *Jánošík* is a mildly modernist opera, combining Slovak folk song, nontonal gestures and Novákian impressionism; the subject matter revolves around the eighteenth-century Slovak robber-hero who is purported to have struggled for the freedom of his people.

10. See chapter 9, n. 39.

11. I use the term "synthesis" in reference to Očadlík's article "The Essence of Modernism in Music," discussed in chapter 9, p. 266.

12. While the locality is unidentified, one scene, that of the wedding, is set in the neighboring village of Lúčky, which may also be fictional. Valašsko lies in eastern Moravia, along what is now the eastern border of the Czech Republic. The dialect incorporates a variety of idioms and grammatical forms from Slovak, to which it is geographically adjacent; it is perhaps the most distant dialect from standardized Prague Czech.

13. Vysloužil, *Alois Hába*, 194–95. See also Korffner, "Před premierou Hábovy čtvrttónové opery," 146–47; and Sychra, "Hábova *Matka* jako hudební drama," 78. Sychra presented a binarism between the "drama-ballad" and the "new concept of village drama," of which the latter is represented in *Matka*.

14. According to Vysloužil, Hába constructed the libretto to *Matka* as a rural counterpart to the more urban *Wozzeck* so that the social statement would have a greater impact. See Jiří Vysloužil, "Hábova *Matka* jako sociální umění," in *Alois Hába (1893–1973)*, ed. Vysloužil, 26.

15. I use the term "phenomenal" after Carloyn Abbate, to signify the distinction between music consciously performed as music in the context of an opera, and "neumenal," that which is part of the composer's larger narrative, which the characters are unable to "hear." Cf. Abbate, "Mahler's Deafness": Opera and the Scene of Narration in *Todtenfeier*," chapter four in Abbate, *Unsung Voices*, 119–55. Vysloužil and Sychra also describe the dramatic shape of *Matka* in similar terms.

16. Hába's use of quarter-tone techniques, particularly with regard to vocal settings, eventually became linked to folk-song ethnography and the accurate representation of pitch. Vysloužil presents a cogent analysis of how Hába's method was consciously derived from Janáček's theories of melodic speech replication, which the younger composer greatly admired. See Vysloužil, *Alois Hába*, 203–7. Hába later became an expert on the microtonal music of the Arab world and contributed to conferences on the topic.

17. From this point onward, I will use simply a number in parentheses to represent a given page in the opera's full score. Alois Hába, *Matka/Die Mutter* (München: Filmkunst-Musikverlag, 1991). Reprint of autograph copy by F. Langmaier, 1947–48.

18. Cf. for example the procession of the villagers in *Così fan tutte* or the arrival of the guests in *Madama Butterfly*.

19. According to Vysloužil, the quartet represents the nenia, an ancient funeral singing ritual dating back to Roman times; Geoffrey Chew's description of the genre in *The New Grove Dictionary of Music and Musicians* matches Hába's musical setting and dramatic presentation, in that professional mourning women would sing to the accompaniment of funereal horns or lyres (here clarinets and strings). Cf. Vysloužil, *Alois Hába*, 216–18.

20. Vysloužil, *Alois Hába*, 210–12.

21. In my examples from this opera I have elected to use a standard quarter-tone font in place of Hába's own symbols found in the score (and explained in the inside cover of the Filmkunst-Musikverlag edition).

22. Significantly, the recurring refrain is also a feature of Marie's lullaby from *Wozzeck*, which may have been a model for those throughout *Matka*.

23. Korffner, "Před premierou Hábovy čtvrttónové opery," 146–47.

24. Bartoš, "Čtvrttonová opera," 320.

25. Pala, quoted in "O čem se píše: Čtvrttónová opera Aloise Háby," 350.

26. Bartoš, "Čtvrttonová opera," 317.

27. Ibid., 317, 322.

28. Křička's opera has a convoluted performance and publication history. Initially composed as *Bílý pán, aneb Těžko se dnes duchům straší* (The White Lord, or It's Hard to Be Frightened by Ghosts These Days), to a libretto by Křička's long time friend Jan Löwenbach(-Budín), it received its world premiere at the Brno National Theater on November 27, 1929. In preparation for this event, HMUB issued a printed libretto. In 1930 both the text and distribution of musical numbers were revised substantially with the help of Max Brod; the opera was given the new title *Strašidlo v zámku* and was translated by Paul Eisner into German as *Spuk im Schloss, oder Böse Zeiten für Gespenster*. Under this last title it appeared at German theaters in Wrocław (November 14, 1931), Prague (April 29, 1932), Leipzig (May 14, 1932), and Vienna (December 31, 1932); all of these productions presumably used the vocal score published by Universal-Edition in 1931, which has dual phrasings for both Czech and German in the notes, but only German text beneath. The Czech premiere of the new version, *Strašidlo v zámku*, occurred on October 10, 1933, in the smaller Estates Theater; a final performance, in Swedish translation as *Spöket pa slottet*, was broadcast by Stockholm Radio on June 3, 1937. One of the only available sources for the Czech text of the revised version (i.e., *Strašidlo v zámku*) is an unpublished bilingual piano-vocal score that lies in the archives of Universal-Edition; it likely served as proofs for the German-only published version, being twenty pages shorter and containing the composer's autograph corrections. A comparison between the 1929 Czech libretto and 1931 German vocal score reveals substantial changes, with certain scenes radically reorganized; many lines of original text were deleted and new lines (and entire scenes) were inserted in their place, sometimes with new musical accompaniments (such as those of exs. 10.5 and 10.6b), and other times with the music of earlier numbers repeated wholesale (ex. 10.7, whose text has no counterpart in the 1929 version). With the help of the unpublished bilingual proofs, however, one can reconstruct the 1933 Prague performance with relative ease.

29. Křička himself termed *Strašidlo v zámku* an "operka," a label that uses the Czech diminutive of opera, an indication of the work's levity rather than duration. See Křička, "Několik poznámek."

30. Cook, *Opera for a New Republic*, 27–39.

31. In the German vocal score, Elida and Jiří appear as Elinor and Georg, respectively, and Taštička is renamed Schnepper. All other characters retain their original names. Bob has been transformed into "Ein Cowboy aus Amerika": see discussion below, p. 319.

32. The black-bottom, while allegedly of African-American origin, was largely a theatrical dance popularized by *George White's Scandals of 1926*, and thereafter disseminated to White social dancing circles. Cf. Stanley Sadie, ed., *The New Grove Dictionary of Music and Musicians*, s.v. "Black-bottom." Significantly, Brand's *Der Maschinist Hopkins* also contains a black-bottom.

33. The title "Train Trip to Satalice" appears on a projection screen, in the manner of Brechtian music theater. The numbers in parentheses throughout this analysis refer to pages in the published piano-vocal score. Jaroslav Křička, *Spuk im Schloss, oder Böse Zeiten für Gespenster*, trans. Paul Eisner, ed. Max Brod (Vienna: Universal-Edition, 1931).

34. Křička's cluster chords are harmonically nonfunctional and are reminiscent of those interjected throughout Milhaud's *Saudades do Brasil*, for example.

35. The German translation is slightly less pointed: "Wo ein alter, wo ein neuer / Schmutzfleck auftaucht, putzt wie Feuer / Clerk, das viel-erprobte Mittel, / Kleider, Möbel, Adelstitel. / Wo ein alter, wo ein neuer / Schmutzfleck auftaucht, putzt wie Feuer / Clerk und putzt sogar in Ehre / die polit'sche Atmosphäre."

36. These lines appear only in the German version of Cedrik's part; in the unpublished bilingual edition, the Czech text merely repeats the black-bottom refrain throughout this ensemble. I have therefore used the German text (in which the word "Business" is given in English) as the basis of my translation.

37. Curiously, Bob is described in the German vocal score as "ein Cowboy aus Amerika," with various textual references to lassos throughout the libretto. Křička, however, very obviously codes him as African-American through a stereotypical banjo accompaniment (69) and attempts to replicate blues-based singing (note the whole-tone scales, 66–67, and glissandi, 219).

38. The German translation of this passage presents an altogether different picture: "Europa und Amerika, hurrah! Beide einig sieht man da."

39. The Czech text at this point of the unpublished vocal score (241–42) does not correspond to any passage in the finale of the 1929 Czech libretto; the entire closing scene was therefore added during the revision process.

40. Šilhan, "Jaroslav Křička: Strašidla [sic] v zámku." Šilhan's word, "všehochuť," which I translate as "mishmash," reappears in more than one review of Křička's opera.

41. Pihert, "Jaroslav Křička: Strašidlo v zámku."

42. Smetana, "Bílý pán na brněnském Národním divadle."

43. Patzaková, "Strašidlo v Stavovském divadle." Patzaková's word is also "všehochuť."

44. Očadlík, "Podstata modernosti v hudbě," 84.

45. Within a year, Křička's politics would be somewhat clearer, with his participation as the Czechoslovak delegate for the Reichsmusikkammer-sponsored new-music organization, Ständige Rat für die internationale Zusammenarbeit der Komponisten. While it is impossible to demonstrate that the composer had any leanings toward the ideology of Nazi Germany, his music for Strašidlo v zámku (and other works) is consistent with the anti-modernist aesthetic program of the Ständige Rat. See chapter 9, n. 72.

Chapter Eleven

1. Burian, "Maskovaný konservatismus," 23–24. The portion in quotation marks refers to a Czech proverb, which states "Whoever is not gifted from above cannot buy it [i.e., intelligence] at a pharmacy" [Komu není shůry dáno, v apatyce nekoupí]. Burian's paraphrase simply puts both verbs into the second person.

2. In chronological order, these were: Pražský hudební máj (1939), Český hudební máj (1940), the Dvořák centennial and Mozart sesquecentennial celebrations (1941), Jaro naší hudby (1942), Česká soudobá hudba, and Hudební máj (1943).

3. The operas that were banned had subject matter depicting Germanic oppression against the Czechs, or otherwise inflammatory political subjects: Braniboři v Čechách, Libuše, Psohlavci, and Dimitrij, among others. Other overtly patriotic operas such as The Bartered Bride and Dalibor were considered acceptable, as well as Smetana's tone poem cycle Má vlast. Beyond these individual cases, theaters were routinely closed or taken over during the years of the Protectorate. Cf. discussion in Dějiny české hudební kultury, vol. 2, 183–211.

4. Ibid., 194.

5. See, for example, Karas, Music in Terezin 1941–1945; Peduzzi, Pavel Haas; Slavický, Gideon Klein; and Klein, ed., Viktor Ullmann.

6. Nejedlý infamously took a leading role in the show trials of the early 1950s, making denunciatory speeches that resulted in a series of purges, arrests, and incarcerations of university professors. Although the official reasons for these actions listed high treason and espionage, it is clear that Nejedlý was continuing to settle old scores. Particularly heinous was his treatment of his former student, the musicologist Josef Hutter, who had sided with Helfert's *Česká moderní hudba* in 1936 and had been involved in the noncommunist wartime resistance: in 1950 Hutter was expelled from Charles University in Prague and sentenced progressively to thirty-nine years of imprisonment, of which he served six before being released on amnesty. Hutter died, broken, in 1959, three years before his teacher. Cf. chapter 6, n. 37 and chapter 9, n. 116.

7. Vladimír Helfert, "Moderní česká hudba na světovém foru," 190–92 in *Co daly naše země Evropě a lidstvu* (Prague: 1939), reprinted in Helfert, *O české hudbě,* 105–11.

8. See, for example, Thrun, *Neue Musik im deutschen Musikleben.*

Bibliography

The abbreviations throughout this bibliography can be found in Notes to the Reader, p. xviii–xix. Elsewhere in the bibliography, I have elected to convert all cryptic authorial abbreviations (such as "Lch." for Löwenbach and "ajp" for Patzaková) to full names, where known.

1. Scores and Libretti

Berg, Alban. *Wozzeck.* Oper in 3 Akten (15 Bildern). Autograph full score with text in Czech translation by Jiří Mařánek. HA-ND MS. H 200.

Büchner, Jiří [Georg]. *Wozzeck.* [Opera in three acts (fifteen scenes) by Alban Berg.] Czech translation by Jiří Mařánek, typescript on onionskin signed as "accepted for performance at the National and Provincial Theaters" by Otakar Ostrčil. HA-ND MS. H 200 L.

Burian, Emil František. *Bubu z Montparnassu.* [Lyric opera in three scenes after Ch.-L. Philippe, op. 51. Libretto by Ctibor Blatný and Emil František Burian.] Autograph piano-vocal score with typescript. Prague: Dilia, 1994.

Finke, Fidelio F. *Die Jakobsfahrt.* Oper in 3 Aufzügen nach dem Legendenspiel von Nietzenschmidt. Klavierauszug. Herausgegeben im Selbstverlag, [n.d.].

Hába, Alois. *Matka.* [Opera in ten scenes on a libretto by the composer.] Autograph full score. Munich: Filmkunst-Musikverlag, 1991.

Hilbert, Jaroslav. *Vina.* [Drama in three acts.] 5th ed. Prague: Buršík & Kohout, 1920. Copy of the play with textual deletions in ink and singers' vocal lines glued in. HA-ND MS. H 177 L.

Jeremiáš, Otokar [Otakar]. *Bratři Karamazovi.* [Opera in three acts and two scenes. Libretto by Jaroslav Maria and Otokar Jeremiáš after the novel by F. M. Dostoevsky.]

Piano-vocal score by the composer. German translation by Dr. Paul Eisner.] Prague: HMUB, 1930.

———. *Bratři Karamazovi.* [Opera in three acts and two scenes. Libretto by Jar. Maria and Ot. Jeremiáš after the novel by F. M. Dostoevsky.] Autograph full score with corrections by the composer. Vols. 1–3. HA-ND MS. H 720.

Ježek, Jaroslav. *Balety.* Prague: SNKLHU, 1952.

———. *Písničky 1928–1938. 35 písní Osvobozeného divadla na slova V + W.* Vol. 1. Prague: SNKLHU, 1955.

———. *Písničky 1928–1938. 27 písní Osvobozeného divadla na slova V + W.* Vol. 2. Prague: SNKLHU, 1955.

———. *Politické nebe na zemi.* Prague: Nakladatelství R. A. Dvorský, 1936.

———. *Tance.* Prague: SNKLHU, 1952.

Löwenbach-Budín, Jan. *Bílý pán, aneb Těžko se dnes duchům straší.* [Musical comedy in two acts with a prologue and epilogue. Text after a motive by Oscar Wilde.] Libretto to the first version of Křička's *Strašidlo v zámku.* Prague: HMUB, 1929.

Křička, Jaroslav. *Spuk im Schloss, oder Böse Zeiten für Gespenster.* Komische Oper in 6 Bildern (2 Teilen), op. 50. Text nach einem Motiv Oscar Wildes von Jan Löwenbach-Budín. Übersetzt von Paul Eisner, Bearbeitung von Max Brod. Piano-vocal score by the composer. Vienna: Universal-Edition, 1931.

———. *Spuk im Schloss, oder Böse Zeiten für Gespenster. Strašidlo v zámku.* Unpublished bilingual piano-vocal score with autograph corrections. Archive of Universal-Edition A.G. Wien, U.E. 1071.

Novák, Vítězslav. *Bouře.* [With the words of the sea-fantasy by Svatopluk Čech. Symphonic poem for orchestra, soloists, and chorus, op. 42.] Vienna: Universal-Edition, 1912.

———. *Dědův odkaz.* [Lyric opera in three acts (eight scenes) on motives from the poem of the same name by Adolf Heyduk, libretto by Antonín Klášterský, op. 57.] Prague: HMUB, 1926.

———. *Karlštejn.* Autograph full score. Vols. 1–3. HA-ND MS. H 35.

———. *Karlštejn.* [Opera in three acts after the comedy by Jaroslav Vrchlický, libretto by Otokar Fischer, op. 50. Piano-vocal score by Roman Veselý.] Vienna: Universal-Edition, 1916.

———. *Lucerna.* [Musical folktale in four acts after the play of the same name by Alois Jirásek, libretto by Hanuš Jelínek, op. 56. Piano vocal-score by Roman Veselý.] Prague: HMUB, 1923.

———. *Svatební košile.* [Ballad after K. J. Erben for solo voices, chorus, and orchestra, op. 48. Piano-vocal score by Roman Veselý.] Vienna: Universal-Edition, 1913.

———. *Zvíkovský rarášek.* [Comic opera in one act, op. 49. Libretto by Ladislav Stroupežnický. Piano-vocal score by the composer.] Vienna: Universal-Edition, 1915.

Ostrčil, Otakar. *Honzovo království.* [Musical play in seven scenes. Libretto (after L. Tolstoy) by Jiří Mařánek. Piano-vocal score by Karel Šolc.] Prague: Společnost Otakara Ostrčila, 1936.

———. *Legenda z Erinu.* [Opera in four acts on the words of Julius Zeyer.] Autograph full score with corrections by the composer. HA-ND MS. H 49.

———. *Legenda z Erinu.* [Opera in four acts on the words of Julius Zeyer.] Piano-vocal score. Prague: Foersterova Společnost, 1920.

———. *Poupě.* [Comic opera in one act on the words of the comedy by F. X. Svoboda.] Autograph full score. HA-ND MS. H 44.

———. *Poupě.* [Comic opera in one act on the words of the comedy by F. X. Svoboda. Piano-vocal score by the composer.] Prague: Umělecká beseda, 1911.

Suk, Josef. *Zrání.* [Symphonic poem for full orchestra, op. 34.] Prague: Editio Supraphon, 1967.

Weinberger, Jaromír. *Švanda dudák.* [Opera in two acts (five scenes).] Piano-vocal score. Vienna: Universal-Edition, 1928.

Zich, Otakar. *Píseň paní Mařákové z opery "Vina."* Voice and piano. Prague: Nakladatel Em. Starý, 1922.

———. *Preciézky.* [Comic opera in one act. Piano-vocal score by Karel Šolc.] Prague: Hudební nakladatelství Foersterovy společnosti, 1926.

———. *Vina.* [Opera in three acts. Drama by Jaroslav Hilbert.] Autograph full score. Vols. 1–3. HA-ND MS. H 177.

———. *Vina.* [Opera in three acts. Drama by Jaroslav Hilbert.] Autograph piano-vocal score. Vols. 1–3. HA-ND MS. H 177/1–3.

2. Articles and Books

Abbate, Carolyn. *Unsung Voices: Opera and Musical Narrative in the Nineteenth Century.* Princeton, NJ: Princeton University Press, 1991.

Aim, Vojtěch Bořivoj. "Otakar Jeremiáš: *Bratři Karamazovi.*" *Reforma,* October 10, 1928.

———. "Vítězslav Novák." *Reforma,* December 5, 1930.

Althusser, Louis. "Ideology and Ideological State Apparatuses (Notes Towards an Investigation)." In *Lenin and Philosophy, and Other Essays,* 127–86. Translated by Ben Brewster. London: New Left Books, 1971.

Ambros, Veronika. *Pavel Kohout und die Metamorphosen des sozialistischen Realismus.* New York: Peter Lang, 1993.

Anderson, Benedict. *Imagined Communities: Reflections on the Origin and Spread of Nationalism.* Rev'd. ed. London and New York: Verso, 1991.

Augusta, V. M. "Cesta moderní hudby." *D* 36 (1919): 46, 54–56.

———. "Česká hudební kritika." *HR* 12, no. 2 (November 1918): 68–69.

———. "Problém české hudby a případ Čelanského." *D* 36, nos. 12–13 (July 23, 1919): 91–93.

———. "Problém německé hudby a případ Wagnerův." *D* 36, no. 2 (February 15, 1919): 13–14; 36, no. 3 (March 3, 1919): 21–22.

———. "Stále totéž—a něco jiného." *D* 36 (1919): 61.

———. "Zápisník (Invektivy časového)." *D* 36, no. 1 (January 1919): 10.

Auner, Joseph. "Schoenberg and His Public in 1930: The Six Pieces for Male Chorus, op. 35." In *Schoenberg and His World,* ed. Walter Frisch, 85–125. Princeton, NJ: Princeton University Press, 1999.

———. " 'Soulless Machines' and Steppenwolves: Renegotiating Masculinity in Krenek's *Jonny spielt auf.*" *Princeton Journal of Women, Gender and Culture* 10, nos. 1–2 (1996): 58–72.

Axman, Emil. "K moderní hudbě." *S-HL* 10, nos. 7–8 (November 19, 1920): 96–97.

———. "Nechte cizích, mluvte vlastní řečí!" *T-LHM* 3, no. 5 (February 20, 1924): 165–70.

———. "O nové umění." *Hudba* 1, no. 1 (November 24, 1919): 8–9; 1, nos. 5–6 (January 12, 1920): 78–81; 1, no. 7 (January 31, 1920): 103–5.

———. "Reakce na postupu." *HRo* 2, no. 10 (June 20, 1926): 155–56.

———. "Spolek pro moderní hudbu." *T-LHM* 2, no. 1 (October 15, 1922): 19–20.

Axman, Emil. "Spolek pro moderní hudbu." *T-LHM* 3, no. 1 (October 15, 1923): 19–20.

———. "Spolek pro moderní hudbu." *T-LHM* 6, no. 1 (October 30, 1926): 18–20.

B. "Aus Zeitschriften. Stimmen aus dem tschechischen musikalischen Schrifttum. Das hohe Lied der Jazzmusik. Das Lied zur Arbeit." *MdS* 2, no. 6 (April 15, 1938): 217–18.

Babka, Václav E. "Boj o rozhlas." *P* 11, no. 2 (January 10, 1934): 20–21.

———. "Existuje lehká hudba?" *T-LHM* 15, no. 6 (December 17, 1935): 65–66.

———. "Intermezzo." *T-LHM* 15, no. 11 (March 19, 1936): 126.

Balthasar, Vladimír. "Ještě o nové pražské opeře a případu Stavovského divadla." *D* 38, nos. 8–9 (March 23, 1922): 59–62.

Bartoš, František. "XIII. Mezinárodní hudební festival v Praze." *T-LHM* 15, no. 1 (October 1, 1935): 4–6.

———. "Čtvrttonová opera Aloise Háby." *T-LHM* 10, nos. 9–10 (June 24, 1931): 317–24.

———. "Doslov k festivalu." *T-LHM* 15, no. 2 (October 15, 1935): 17–18.

———. "Otokar Jeremiáš: *Bratři Karamazovi*. Klavírní výtah." *RA* 5, no. 31 (May 1, 1930): 402.

———. "Zvukový film." *T-LHM* 11, no. 3 (November 1931): 110.

Bartoš, Josef. "XI. koncert Filharmonie." *S-HL* 3, no. 11 (1913): 128.

———. "Antonín Dvořák." *Hlídka Času*, October 18, 1911.

———. "Boleslav Kalenský: *Až do třetího pokolení*." *S-HL* 3, no. 8 (December 13, 1912): 83–86.

———. "*Die Brüder Karamazov* als Oper." *PP*, October 10, 1928.

———. "Druhý mezinárodní festival hudební v Praze." *S-HL* 15 (1925): 50–53, 97–101.

———. "Dvořákiana." *S-HL* 2, no. 20 (May 10, 1912): 294.

———. "Dvořákova hudba komorní." *S-HL* 2, nos. 5–6 (November 17, 1911): 69–72; 2, no. 13 (February 1, 1912): 177–80; 2, no. 15 (March 1, 1912): 206–10; 2, nos. 16–17 (March 22, 1912): 236–39; 2, nos. 18–19 (April 12, 1912): 267–69; 2, no. 20 (May 10, 1912): 281–82; 2, no. 21 (June 14, 1912): 300–301; 3, nos. 2–3 (October 18, 1912): 26–29; 3, nos. 4–5 (November 8, 1912): 44–48; 3, no. 12 (February 7, 1913): 138; 3, no. 14 (March 7, 1913): 165–68; 4, nos. 2–3 (October 10, 1913): 32–35; 4, no. 10 (January 16, 1914): 142–45; 4, no. 14 (March 27, 1914): 202–3; 4, no. 18 (May 22, 1914): 253–56.

———. "Dvořákův festival." *S-HL* 2, no. 14 (February 16, 1912): 203.

———. "Jeremiášovi *Bratři Karamazovi*." *T-LHM* 8, no. 2 (November 21, 1928): 55–57.

———. "Koncert Pensijního spolku Nár. Divadla: Dvořákovy *Svatební košile*." *S-HL* 3, nos. 6–7 (November 30, 1912): 70.

———. "Mezinárodní hudební festival v Praze 1924." *S-HL* 14, nos. 5–6 (November 30, 1924): 65–73.

———. "Mistr Vítězslav Novák." *S-HL* 3, no. 12 (February 7, 1913): 155–56.

———. "Na okraj Ot. Jeremiášových *Bratří Karamazových*." *ND* 6, no. 6 (October 6, 1928): 2–3.

———. *O proudech v soudobé hudbě*. Kdyně: Okresní sbor osvětový, 1924.

———. "Otakar Jeremiáš." *T-LHM* 8, no. 1 (October 24, 1928): 4–16.

———. "Otakar Jeremiáš." *ND* 6, no. 5 (September 29, 1928): 2–3.

———. "Otakar Jeremiáš et ses *Frères Karamazov*." *ND* 8 (1930): 15–16.

———. "Otakar Jeremiáš's Oper *Bratři Karamazovi* wurde . . ." *PP*, April 10, 1935.

———. *Otakar Ostrčil*. Prague: Česká akademie věd a umění, 1936.

———. "Prager Ostrčil-Premiere." *PP*, April 4, 1935.

———. "Případ Novákových *Svatebních košil*." *S-HL* 10, nos. 9–10 (December 30, 1920): 120–22.

———. "Smetanas *Dalibor* in ursprünglicher Gestalt." *PP*, January 11, 1924.

———. "Spolek pro moderní hudbu v Praze." *S-HL* 15, no. 2 (February 1925): 41–44.

———. "Zdeněk Nejedlý." *RA* 3, nos. 11–12 (1927–28): 127–28.

Bartoš, Josef, Hubert Doležil, Zdeněk Nejedlý, Mirko Očadlík, František Pala, A. J. Patzaková, and Artuš Rektorys. *Otakar Ostrčil či Vítězslav Novák: odpověď na brožuru Vítězslava Nováka "Vítězslav Novák contra Otakar Ostrčil."* Prague: Melantrich, 1931.

Bass, Eduard. *Jak se dělá kabaret?* Prague: Springer, 1917.

Beckerman, Michael. "In Search of Czechness in Music." *Nineteenth Century Music* 10 (Summer 1986): 63–73.

Bednář, Antonín. "K očistě konservatoře." *S-HL* 9, no. 2 (January 1919): 47.

Bek, Josef. *Erwin Schulhoff: Leben und Werk.* Translated by Rudolf Chadraba. Hamburg: von Bockel Verlag, 1994.

———. "Mezinárodní styky české hudby 1918–1924." *HVě* 4 (1967): 397–419.

———. "Mezinárodní styky české hudby 1924–1932." *HVě* 4 (1967): 628–48.

———. "Mezinárodní styky české hudby 1933–1938." *HVě* 5 (1968): 3–48.

Bek, Mikuláš. "Erwin Schulhoffs Oper *Flammen*—eine Entstehungsgeschichte." In *"Zum Einschlafen gibt's genügend Musiken": Die Referate des Erwin Schulhoff-Kolloquiums in Düsseldorf im März 1994,* ed. Tobias Widmaier, 99–104. Hamburg: von Bockel Verlag, 1996.

Bekker, Paul. "Künstlerische Körperschulung." *Frankfurter Zeitung,* October 20, 1922.

Bělohlávek, Bedřich. *Jaroslav Jeremiáš: život, doba, dílo.* Prague: L. Mazač, 1935.

———. "K případu Vítězslava Nováka." *NSv* 3, no. 46 (November 1926): 598–99.

———. "O současné české hudbě." *NSv* 5, no. 5 (February 2, 1928): 68–70; 5, no. 7 (February 16, 1928): 100–103; 5, no. 8 (February 27, 1928): 122–24; 5, no. 9 (March 1, 1928): 133–35; 5, no. 10 (March 8, 1928): 151–54; 5, no. 11 (March 15, 1928): 165–67; 5, no. 13 (March 29, 1928): 201–3; 5, no. 14 (April 5, 1928): 221–22; 5, no. 15 (April 12, 1928): 235–39; 5, no. 16 (April 19, 1928): 248–51.

———. "Oni a on, čili 'Případ Ostrčilův.'" *P* 10, no. 10 (March 8, 1933): 152–56.

———, ed. *Padesát let Zdeňka Nejedlého.* Prague: Dobrá edice, 1928.

———. *Povodeň hlouposti.* Prague: Dobrá edice, 1936.

Bendová, Anna. "Co čekají pokrokoví hudebníci od Talicha." *R* 1, nos. 2–3 (November 1935): 2–3.

Bendová, Anna, and Bedřich Bělohlávek. "O šéfa opery." *P* 12, no. 42 (October 23, 1935): 663–65.

Beneš, K. J. "Rozhlas a jeho posluchači." *P* 8, no. 46 (November 18, 1931): 732–34.

Benetková, Vlasta. "Alois Hába a Viktor Ullmann: doteky života a díla." *ZSVN* 22 (1993): 8–14.

———. "Festival mezinárodní společnosti pro soudobou hudbu v Praze 1935. Dokončení." *HVě* 33, no. 4 (1996): 337–55.

———. "Fidelio Friedrich Finke (1891–1968)." *HVě* 32, no. 3 (1995): 227–48.

———. "K historii československé sekce mezinárodní společnosti pro soudobou hudbu a jejích festivalů." *HVě* 33, no. 2 (1996): 139–58.

Berkovec, Jiří. *Josef Suk (1874–1935): život a dílo.* Prague: SNKLHU, 1956.

Bláha-Mikeš, Zdeněk. "Hudba u pražských Němců." *ČH* 35 (1931–32): 179–82.

———. "Politika a hudba." *ČH* 38 (1935–39): 66–69.

Blattný, Ctibor. "Černošské divadlo." *TT* 5 (December 1925): 6–8.

———. "Destrukce hudebních forem." *TT* 2 (July 1925): 4–5.

———. "Konstrukce hudebních forem." *TT* 3 (September–October 1925): 3–7.

"Boj o kulturní orientace." *ND* 2, no. 15 (December 5, 1924): 1.

Boleška, Josef. "Smetanismus—Kovařovicův a Nejedlého." *D* 33, no. 6 (November 25, 1910): 45–46.

Borecký, Jaromír. "*Bratři Karamazovi.*" *NP*, October 10, 1928.

———. "*Jánošík.*" *NP*, February 25, 1934.

Borecký, Jaromír. "Josef Suk: Relief." *D* 36, no. 1 (January 1919): 2–3.

———. "Otakar Ostrčil: *Honzovo království.*" *NP*, April 5, 1935.

———. "*Prodaná nevěsta* v novém nastudování." *NP*, May 29, 1923.

———. "*Švanda dudák.*" *NP*, April 29, 1927.

———. "Zpěvohra městského divadla Král. Vinohradů." In *Čtvrtstoletí Městského divadla na Král. Vinohradech, 1907–32*, 79–87. Prague: [n.p.], 1932.

Bouček, Dr. "Ostuda, a to několikerá." *NO*, November 18, 1926.

"Bouře v Národním divadle." *Večer*, November 16, 1926.

Branberger, Jan. "Karel Knittl †." *HR-S* 2, no. 7 (April 1, 1907): 83–85.

———. "Zvukový film." *T-LHM* 9, no. 2 (October 24, 1929): 80–81.

Brod, Max. "Shimmy und Foxtrott." *A* 2, no. 10 (October 1, 1922): 256–59.

Brodde, Otto. "Politische Musik." *MdS* 2, no. 6 (April 15, 1938): 162–68.

Bruegel, J. W. *Czechoslovakia Before Munich: The German Minority Problem and British Appeasement Policy.* Cambridge: Cambridge University Press, 1973.

Burian, Emil František. "Český synkopismus Voskovce & Wericha." *VPR* 1, no. 2 (1929): 2–4; 1, no. 3 (1930): 3–6.

———. "Danse africaine." *VPR* 1, no. 6 (April 15, 1930): 2–3.

———. "Estetika." *TT* 1 (May 1925): 1–3.

———. "Estetika v pokračováních." *TT* 2 (July 1925): 11–16.

———. *Jazz.* Prague: Aventina, 1928.

———. "Jazz." *TT* 6 (n.d.: ? January 1926): 7–8.

———. "Jsme opravdu v hudební krisi?" *P* 3, no. 20 (May 27, 1926): 313–14.

———. "Krise nebo diletantismus?" *TT* 1 (May 1925): 13–14.

———. "Maskovaný konservatismus." *TT* 5 (December 1925): 23–26.

———. "Můj jazz." *RA* 3, no. 14 (1927–28): 173.

———. "Muzika." *TT* 3 (September–October 1925): 21–23.

———. "Něco o jazzu." *HVk* 27, no. 7 (August 1, 1934): 2–3.

———. "O svébytnost recitačního umění." *LUK* 1 (1933): 527–33.

———. "Polydynamika." *TT* 3 (September–October 1925): 10–14; 4 (October–November 1925): 7–12.

———. "Slovo na jevišti." *LUK* 1 (1933): 198–202.

———. "Voice-Band." *A* 8, nos. 5–6 (May 20, 1928): 113–14.

Burian, Jarka M. "The Liberated Theatre of Voskovec and Werich." *Educational Theatre Journal* (May 1977): 153–77.

Burney, Charles. *The Present State of Music in Germany, the Netherlands, and United Provinces.* London: T. Becket and Co., 1773.

Busoni, Ferruccio. "Junge Klassizität." *Frankfurter Zeitung*, February 7, 1920.

Čapek, Bedřich. *O. Ostřila "Poupě": hudební rozbor.* Hudební knihovna časopisu *Smetana* no. 1. Prague: Knihtiskárna Nár. Soc. Melantrich, 1911.

———. "Otakar Zich a jeho opera *Malířský nápad.*" *HR* 2, no. 10 (December 1909): 513–18.

Čelanský, Ludvík Vítězslav. "Opera měst. Divadla na Král. Vinohradech." *HR* 1, no. 1 (January 1908): 30–31.

Černušák, Gracian. "Kulturní hodnoty hudebního rozhlasu." *HRo* 3, no. 7 (April 30, 1927): 112–14.

Černý, Miroslav. "Historismus a Nejedlého koncepce muzikologie." *HVě* 14, no. 1 (1977): 52–71.

———. "Zdeněk Nejedlýs Auffassung von Musikwissenschaft." *Beiträge zur Musikwissenschaft* 23, no. 1 (1981): 40–47.

České umění dramatické. Eds. František Götz and Josef Hutter. Prague: Nakl. Šolc a Šimáček, 1941.

"České veřejnosti." *NL*, February 16, 1919.

Československý hudební slovník osob a institucí. Eds. Gracian Černušák, Bohumír Štědroň and Zdenko Nováček. Prague: Státní hudební vydavatelství, 1963–65.

Chew, Geoffrey. "The Construction of Czech Music History, 1945–9." Forwarded to Czech and Slovak Music List, CSMSlist@artsci.wustl.edu, April 11, 1998.

Chlubna, Osvald. "Jak se komu líbí. O moderní melodii." *HRo* 3, nos. 4–5 (February 15, 1927): 56–57; 3, no. 8 (May 30, 1927): 132, 134.

Cohen, Gary B. *The Politics of Ethnic Survival: Germans in Prague, 1861–1914.* Princeton, NJ: Princeton University Press, 1981.

Cook, Susan C. *Opera for a New Republic: The Zeitopern of Krenek, Weill and Hindemith.* Ann Arbor, Mich.: UMI Research Press, 1988.

Čornej, Petr. "Hudební klub v Praze (1911–1927)." In *Z bojů o českou hudební kulturu,* ed. Stanislava Zachařová, 119–49. Prague: Academia, 1979.

Cvak, Ladislav, Jiří Voldán, and K. B. Jirák. "Národní píseň a šlágr." *T-LHM* 16, no. 14 (May 24, 1937): 186–88.

Čvančara, K. "Bouřlivá premiéra zhudebněného dramatu periferie." *Večer,* November 12, 1926.

———. "Symfonická báseň s jevištním doprovodem." *Večer,* December 23, 1926.

"Das neue sudetendeutsche Tonwerk. *Die Jakobsfahrt.* Aus einem Gespräch mit Fidelio Finke." *MdS* 1, no. 1 (November 15, 1936): 22–23.

David, Katherine. "Czech Feminists and Nationalism in the Late Habsburg Monarchy: 'The First in Austria.'" *Journal of Women's History* 3, no. 2 (Fall 1991): 26–45.

Dějiny české hudební kultury 1890–1945. Ed. Robert Smetana. Vols. 1–2. Prague: Academia, 1972.

DeLong, Kenneth. "From Tomášek to Smetana: Musical Life in Prague 1830–1860." Unpublished essay.

"Der Auftakt." *A* 1, nos. 1–2 (November 1920): 1.

Deutcher, Pavel. "O mechanické hudbě." *HVk* 22, no. 1 (January 1, 1929): 3–4; 22, no. 2 (January 16, 1929): 3; 22, no. 3 (February 1, 1929): 3.

"Die Uraufführung von Fidelio F. Finkes *Jakobsfahrt.*" *MdS* 1, no. 2 (December 15, 1936): 64.

"Divadelní krise pražská." *ND* 2, no. 31 (April 4, 1925): 1.

"Divadlo a národ." *ND* 6, no. 44 (June 14, 1929): 2.

"Dokumenty." *S-HL* 9, nos. 9–10 (June 1919): 103–7.

"Dokumenty. Liszt–Smetana–Dvořák." *S-HL* 2, no. 2 (October 20, 1911): 25–28.

Doležil, Hubert. "Claude Debussy: *Pelleas a Melisanda.*" *ČR,* November 3, 1921.

———. "Čtvrttónová soustava v hudbě." *ČR,* November 10. 1921.

———. "Doslov k úvahám o Novákově *Bouři.*" *S-HL* 2, no. 21 (June 14, 1912): 297–300.

———. "Dr. Zd. Nejedlý: *Česká moderní zpěvohra po Smetanovi.*" *S-HL* 2, nos. 8–9 (December 15, 1911): 115–19.

———. "Ervín Schulhoff." *S-HL* 10, no. 3 (March 29, 1920): 47.

———. "Jaroslav Křička." *T-LHM* 12, no. 1 (September 12, 1932): 1–5.

———. "L. V. Čelanský v České filharmonii." *ČR,* October 8, 1921.

———. "Nováková opera *Lucerna.*" *ČR,* May 15, 1923.

———. "O budoucnost naší hudby (Podnět k diskusi)." *T-LHM* 2, no. 6 (March 20, 1923): 125–32.

———. "Ostrčilova opera *Kunálovy oči.*" *ND* 16, no. 9 (February 22, 1939): 1–3.

Doležil, Hubert. "Ostrčilovo *Poupě*." *ND* 13, no. 3 (October 15, 1935): 2–4.

———. "Vít. Nováka *Bouře*." *S-HL* 2, no. 15 (March 1, 1912): 205–6; 2, nos. 16–17 (March 22, 1912): 225–28; 2, nos. 18–19 (April 12, 1912): 255–67.

Dorůžka, Lubomír, and Ivan Poledňák. *Československý Jazz: minulost a přítomnost.* Prague and Bratislava: Editio Supraphon, 1967.

Dostál, Jiří. *Jaroslav Křička.* Prague: HMUB, 1944.

———. *Vítězslav Novák a Umělecká beseda.* Prague: Melantrich, 1940.

Dostál, Josef. "Smysl modernosti." *T-LHM* 3, nos. 9–10 (July 15, 1924): 373–74.

"Důvěrou a hodnotou proti krisi." *ND* 10, no. 4 (October 15, 1932): 1.

"Echo z divadelního světa. Opera *Wozzeck*." *ND* 2, no. 10 (October 31, 1924): 8.

Entwistle, Erik. "The Turkey Takes Wing: Weinberger's *Schwanda* and the Aesthetic of Folk Opera." *Opera Quarterly* 12, no. 2 (1995–96): 35–46.

Faltis, Dalibor C. [Dalibor C. Vačkář]. "Hábovy čtvrttóny." *T-LHM* 15, no. 9 (January 1936): 101–2.

———. "Hábovy čtvrttóny (doslov)." *T-LHM* 15, no. 11 (March 19, 1936): 125–26.

———. "Národní píseň a šlágr a jiné." *T-LHM* 16, no. 10 (March 11, 1937): 128–31.

———. "O činnosti naší hudební kritiky." *P* 13, no. 51 (December 23, 1936): 805–9.

———. "Pokřik na kulturu (Rozhlas a posluchači)." *HVk* 29, no. 11 (December 1, 1936): 173–74.

———. "Sociální funkce umění? (O hudbě moderní)—Námět k diskusi." *R* 1, no. 4 (December 1935): 42–43; 1, nos. 5–6 (January–February 1936): 54–55.

"*Fata Morgana*—Internacionální revuí." *RA* 5, no. 17 (January 22, 1930): 203.

-fch-. "Pro moderní hudbu!" *HR* 13, no. 8 (May 1920): 317.

Felber, Erwin. "Schwer, ein Gespenst zu sein!" *A* 9, no. 12 (December 18, 1929): 309.

"Feuilleton. Pařížská sensace (Ze života černé Josefiny Baker)." *ND* 5, no. 15 (November 26, 1927): 4–5.

Finke, Fidelio Friedrich. "Der Fall Finke." *MdS* 1, no. 10 (August 15, 1937): 316–17.

Fischer, Otakar. "Stavovské divadlo." *Jeviště* 1, no. 47 (November 25, 1920): 530–33. Reprinted in František Pala, *Opera Národního divadla v období Otakara Ostrčila,* vol. 1, Prague: Divadelní ústav, 1962, 261.

———. "*Vojcek*." *NL*, November 27, 1920.

Fischer, Otokar [sic.], and Vítězslav Novák. "K premiéře *Karlštejna*." *HR* 10 (1916): 2–13.

Foerster, Josef Bohuslav. "Glossen zu *Pelleas und Melisande*." *PP*, January 29, 1922.

———. "Úvodní slovo k Zichovým '*Preciézkám.*'" *ND* 3, no. 37 (May 22, 1926): 2.

Foucault, Michel. *L'Archéologie du savoir.* Paris: Gallimard, 1969.

Frankl, Charles H. "Ripening." In Josef Suk, *Zrání, symfonická báseň pro velký orchestr,* vii. Prague and Bratislava: Editio Supraphon, 1967.

Fukač, Jiří. "'Novákova doba musí ještě přijít.' Vítězslav Novák: problémy stylu a recepce." *ZSVN* 15 (1989): 23–32.

———. "Recepce díla Vítězslava Nováka jako problém vědecký a praktický." *ZSVN* 14 (1989): 7–17.

———. "Vítězslav Novák v roce 1980: pokus o aktualizaci jasných i sporných otázek." *Opus Musicum* 12, no. 5 (1980): 130–34.

———. "Význam Vítězslava Nováka pro českou hudbu." *ZSVN* 17 (1990): 10–20.

Fuksa, František. "Vznik a vývoj městského divadla." In *Čtvrtstoletí Městského divadla na Král. Vinohradech, 1907–32,* 5–63. Prague: [n.p.], 1932.

-G-. "Umělecké výsledky pražského hudebního festivalu." *R* 1, no. 1 (October, 1935): 5–12.

Gellner, Ernest. *Nations and Nationalism.* Ithaca, NY: Cornell University Press, 1983.

Gendron, Bernard. "Fetishes and Motorcars: Negrophilia in French Modernism." *Cultural Studies* 4, no. 2 (1990): 141–55.

Gericke, H. P. "Die 'böhmische' Invasion in der deutschen Musik." *MdS* 1, no. 9 (July 15, 1937): 281–85.

G-i. "Ant. Dvořák, napsal J. Bartoš." *D* 34, no. 3 (November 11, 1911): 24–25.

Gioia, Ted. *The History of Jazz.* Oxford: Oxford University Press, 1997.

Grout, Donald J., and Claude V. Palisca. *A History of Western Music.* 6th ed. New York: Norton, 2000.

Haas, Pavel. "Hudba lehká a vážná." *T-LHM* 15, no. 8 (February 4, 1936): 90.

———. "O hudbě budoucnosti." *HRo* 3, nos. 4–5 (February 15, 1927): 58–59.

———. "O návratu." *T-LHM* 5, nos. 9–10 (July 25, 1926): 325–27.

Hába, Alois. "10 let kursů pro čtvrttónovou hudbu." *Výroční zprávy Státní konservatoře* 10 (1932–33): 57–58.

———. "Budiž jasno o věcech základních." *K* 2, no. 13 (1932): 224–28.

———. "Co jest revoluční umění hudební?" *T-LHM* 5, nos. 9–10 (July 25, 1926): 323–25.

———. "Ctvrttónová 'desetiletka' " [sic]. *ND* 9, no. 9 (November 3, 1931): 6.

———. "Diatonický, chromatický a bichromatický zvuk v hudbě evropské." *K* 1, no. 1 (1931): 2–5; 1, no. 2 (1931): 49–56.

———. "Hábovy čtvrttóny (Ke článku Dalibora C. Faltise)." *T-LHM* 15, no. 9 (February 20, 1936): 101–2.

———. "Hábovy čtvrttóny (Poznámky k doslovu D. C. Faltise)." *T-LHM* 15, no. 13 (April 30, 1936): 148–49. With an afterword by Jaroslav Tomášek.

———. "K chystanému provedení opery *Vojcek* od Albana Berga." *ND* 4, no. 8 (October 16, 1926): 5–6.

———. "K hudebnímu festivalu." *P* 12, no. 38 (September 25, 1935): 607.

———. "Max Brand: *Strojník Hopkins.*" *ND* 8, no. 5 (October 3, 1930): 2–3.

———. "Opera Albana Berga: *Vojcek.*" *ČR*, November 13, 1926.

———. "Organisace XIII. mezinárodního hudebního festivalu v Praze." *R* 1, nos. 2–3 (November 1935): 3–8.

———. "Premiéra opery Vítězslava Nováka *Dědův odkaz* v Národním divadle." *ČR*, December 24, 1926.

———. "*Švanda dudák.*" *ČR*, April 29, 1927.

———. "Vít. Novák: *Dědův odkaz.*" *ND* 9, no. 10 (November 10, 1931): 3–4.

———. "*Zvikovský rarášek* [sic]. *Karlštejn. Lucerna. Dědův odkaz.* Baletní pantomimy. *Slovácká suita.*" *ND* 8, no. 13 (November 28, 1930): 1–5.

———. "Zvukový film a opera." *K* 2, no. 4 (December 30, 1931): 57–63.

Hába, Karel. "K diskusi o romantismu." *T-LHM* 8, no. 6 (March 13, 1929): 220–22.

———. "Max Brand '*Strojník Hopkins.*' " *ČR*, October 9, 1930.

———. "Mladá generace a Otakar Ostrčil—skladatel." *ND* 6, no. 27 (February 23, 1929): 16–18.

———. "Několik slov o opeře *Janošík*" [sic]. *K* 2, no. 14 (1932): 306–8.

———. "Otakar Jeremiáš *Bratři Karamazovi.*" *ČR*, October 10, 1928.

Hannerz, Ulf. "Cosmopolitans and Locals in World Culture." *Theory, Culture and Society* 7 (1990): 237–51.

Hanuš, Otakar. "O českém kabaretu." In *Svátkův Divadelní almanach Republiky československé na rok 1922*, 94–98. České Budějovice: Svátek, 1922.

Hanuš, Stanislav. "Absolutnost a výrazovost." *T-LHM* 7, no. 1 (October 14, 1927): 42–43.

Hanuš, Stanislav, and Boleslav Vomáčka, eds. *Sborník na počest 60. narozenin Vítězslava Nováka.* Prague: HMUB, 1930.

Helfert, Vladimír. "Boj o Dvořáka. I. Polemika a demagogie." *S-HL* 3, no. 11 (January 21, 1913): 121–23.

———. "Čeho je potřeba." *HRo* 1, nos. 1–2 (October 10, 1924): 1–4.

———. "Epištola o hudební kritice." *Index* 3 (1931): 5–7.

———. "Konce hudebního naturalismu." *ČK* 2, no. 6 (December 19, 1913): 97–100.

———. "Krise moderní hudby či obecenstva?" *HRo* 2, no. 5 (January 23, 1926): 74–79.

———. "Novák i Ostrčil." *Index* 3 (1931): 65–66.

———. *O české hudbě.* Prague: SNKLHU, 1957.

———. "Otevřený list České filharmonii." *ČS*, December 1, 1918. Reprinted in *S-HL* 9, no. 2 (December 1918): 30–31.

———. "Panu Karlu Kovařovicovi." *ČS*, February 23, 1919.

———. "Smetanova výstava," *S-HL* 7, nos. 8–9 (June 21, 1917): 113–15.

———. "Více Dvořáka!" *ČK* 1, no. 4 (November 15, 1912): 114–18.

———. *Vybrané studie I.: O hudební tvořivosti.* Prague: Editio Supraphon, 1970.

Helfert, Vladimír, and Erich Steinhard. *Geschichte der Musik in der Tschechoslovakischen Republik.* Prague: Orbis-Verlag, 1936.

Herder, Johann Gottfried von. "Slavian Nations." In *Outline of a Philosophy of the History of Man,* bk. 16, chap. 4. London: L. Hansard, 1803.

Hilbert, Jaroslav. "Vzpomínka na Kovařovice." *V,* December 4, 1921.

Hinton, Stephen. *The Idea of Gebrauchsmusik: A Study of Musical Aesthetics in the Weimar Republic (1919–1933) with Particular Reference to the Works of Paul Hindemith.* New York and London: Garland Publishing, 1989.

Hippmann, Silvestr. "Moderna a obecenstvo." *T-LHM* 5, no. 5 (February 25, 1926): 171–75.

———. "Večer Jazz-revue Jacka Hyltona." *T-LHM* 8, nos. 4–5 (February 13, 1929): 158.

Hlavsová, Hana. *Otakara Jeremiáše Bratři Karamazovi (Tři pohledy na dílo).* Prague: Svaz čs. skladatelů, 1958.

"Hlídka." *Hudba* 1, no. 8 (February 16, 1920): 130–32. Includes "České veřejnosti!" and "Češi a Němci."

Hobsbawm, Eric. *Nations and Nationalism since 1780: Programme, Myth, Reality.* Cambridge and New York: Cambridge University Press, 1992.

Hoffmann, Karel, Jiří Herold, and Hanuš Wihan. "Prohlášení tří členů Českého kvartetta." *V,* December 24, 1912.

Hoffmeister, Adolf. "Devětsil." *RA* 1, no. 3 (November 1925): 33.

Hoffmeister, Karel. "*Bouře,* op. 42." *Hudební Rozpravy* 6 (1913): 1–9.

———. "Dvořákův festival." *HR* 5 (1911–12): 408–11.

———. "Vítězslava Nováka *Karlštejn.*" *HR* 10 (1917): 163–69.

Hofman, Vlastislav. "Výtvarné obdoby v hudbě." *HR* 12, no. 6 (March 1919): 221–25.

Holas, Miloš. "Hodinu u prof. Aloise Háby." *RA* 4, no. 9 (November 1928): 91.

Holzknecht, Václav, ed. *Dítě tu dávno není.* Prague: Editio Supraphon, 1976.

———. *Jaroslav Ježek.* "Seznam díla J. Ježka," 138–50. Prague: Horizont, 1982.

———. *Jaroslav Ježek & Osvobozené divadlo.* "Dílo Jaroslava Ježka," 407*ff.* Prague: SNKLHU, 1957.

"Hopkins." *ND* 8, no. 5 (October 3, 1930): 2.

Hostinský, Otakar. *Česká hudba 1864–1904.* Prague: Grosman a Svoboda, 1909.

———. *Das Musicalisch-Schöne und das Gesamtkunstwerk vom Standpuncte der formalen Aesthetik.* Leipzig: Breitkopf und Härtel, 1877.

———. *Herbarts Ästhetik.* Hamburg and Leipzig: Verlag von Leopold Voss, 1891.

———. *O hudbě.* Prague: Státní hudební vydavatelství, 1961.

Hostinský, Otakar. *O umění.* Prague: Československý spisovatel, 1956.

———. *Z hudebních bojů let sedmdesátých a osmdesátých.* Prague: Editio Supraphon, 1986.

Hostomská, Anna. *Opera: průvodce operní tvorbou.* With contributions by Lubomír Dorůžka, Emil Ludvík, and Jarmila Brozovská. Introduction by Mirko Očadlík. Prague: SNKLHU, 1955.

Hudba v českých dějinách od středověku do nové doby. Prague: Editio Supraphon, 1989.

Hutter, Josef. "Česká hudba na mezinárodním foru." *P* 1, no. 22 (June 12, 1924): 346–48.

———. "Divadla a koncerty. Národní divadlo v Praze. *Švanda dudák.*" *HRo* 3, no. 8 (May 30, 1927): 134–35.

———. "Divadla a koncerty. *Vojcek.*" *HRo* 3, no. 3 (December 15, 1926): 46–47.

———. "Hudba v Praze. *Před slunce východem.*" *HRo* 2, nos. 3–4 (December 24, 1925): 60–61.

———. "Jazz." *P* 2, no. 41 (October 22, 1925): 644–45.

———. *Legenda z Erinu: hudební drama na slova July Zeyera složil Ot. Ostrčil.* Rozpravy hudební sv. 29, ed. R. Zamrzla. Prague: Fr. A. Urbánek a synové, 1923.

———. "Moderní tance či moderní tanec?" *P* 2, no. 4 (February 5, 1925): 61–63.

———. "Nová česká zpěvohra." *ND* 2, no. 39 (May 30, 1925): 6.

———. "Opera v Praze. Vít. Novák: *Dědův odkaz.*" *HRo* 3, nos. 4–5 (February 15, 1927): 80–81.

———. *Otakar Zich a jeho hudební drama Vina.* Prague: Melantrich, 1922.

———. "Otakar Zich a jeho hudební drama *Vina.*" *S-HL* 12, no. 1 (January 25, 1922): 4–6; 12, no. 2 (February 25, 1922): 21–23; 12, no. 3 (March 18, 1922): 35–37; 12, nos. 9–10 (December 30, 1922): 135–36.

———. *Otakara Zicha Preciézky.* Prague: Foerstrova Společnost, 1926.

———. "Poslední vývojové období české opery." *ND* 1, no. 35 (February 25, 1924): 3–4.

———. "Postátnění Národního Divadla." *P* 5, no. 2 (January 19, 1928): 27–28.

———. "*Příhody lišky Bystroušky.*" *Tribuna*, May 20, 1925.

———. "Případ Václava Talicha." *P* 7, no. 51 (November 24, 1930): 804–6.

———. "*Věc Makropulos.*" *Tribuna*, March 3, 1928.

———. "Zichovy *Preciézky.*" *HRo* 2, no. 10 (June 20, 1926): 160–62.

"Idea a zábava." *ND* 9, no. 22 (February 13, 1932): 4–5.

"Individualism [sic] a kolektivismus v divadle." *ND* 9, no. 25 (March 19, 1932): 1.

J. F-a. "Koncerty. VIII. Koncert spolku pro moderní hudbu." *D* 38, no. 10 (April 13, 1922): 76.

Janda, Jindřich. "Mezinárodní hudební festival v Praze." *Hudba* 2, no. 1 (January–February 1925): 10–16.

Janeček, Julius. "Částečný úpadek jazzové hudby." *HVk* 26, no. 11 (December 1, 1933): 3.

———. "Je Praha česká nebo mezinárodní?" *HVk* 22, no. 17 (November 16, 1929): 5.

———. "Návrat k melodii." *HVk* 19, no. 5 (March 16, 1926): 2–3.

———. "Opera je luxus." *HVk* 20, no. 14 (October 1, 1927): 3–4.

———. "Radio." *HVk* 19, no. 17 (December 16, 1926): 2.

———. "Radio a hudebníci." *HVk* 20, no. 6 (March 16, 1927): 6.

———. "Salonní kapely a jazz." *HVk* 21, no. 1 (January 1, 1928): 4–5.

———. "Saxo- a jiné fony." *HVk* 19, no. 17 (December 16, 1926): 2.

Jelínek, Hanuš, ed. *Padesát let Umělecké besedy 1863–1913.* Prague: Umělecká beseda, 1913.

Jeníček, Rudolf. "Otakar Jeremiáš: *Bratři Karamazovi.*" *PL*, October 11, 1928.

———. "*Pelleas a Melisanda.*" *PL*, November 3, 1921.

———. "*Švanda dudák*, opera . . ." *PL*, April 29, 1929.

———. "Třetí premiéra Křičkovy komické opery." *PL*, October 12, 1933.

Jeremiáš, Otakar. "K vývoji současné hudby." *HRo* 1, nos. 1–2 (October 10, 1924): 7–8; 1, no. 7 (February 15, 1925): 111–14.

———. "Mravnost v umění." *ČH* 37 (1933–35): 229–33.

———. "O vzniku opery *Bratři Karamazovi.*" *ND* 12, no. 12 (April 27, 1935): 4–5.

———. "O. Jeremiáš o svých *Bratrech Karamazových.*" *ČS*, April 17, 1935.

Ježek, Jaroslav. *Dopisy z podzimu 1938.* Prague: V. Petr, 1948.

———. "*Harlekýn* Ferrichia Bussoniho" [sic]. *RA* 4, no. 1 (September 1928): 10.

———. "Hudba v Osvobozeném divadle." *VPR* 1, no. 1 (1929): 12.

———. "Jack Hylton and Hisboys" [sic]. *RA* 4, no. 15 (January 1929): 152.

———. "Pařížské dojmy z listopadu a prosince 1931." *K* 2, no. 6 (1932): 110–12.

———. "Skladatel Ježek o své hudbě k revui *Golem.*" *T-LHM* 11, no. 3 (November 1931): 117.

———. "Spolek pro moderní hudbu v Praze." *RA* 5, no. 10 (November 21, 1929): 119.

———. "V cyklu na oslavu padesátin Ostrčilových." *RA* 4, no. 30 (April 1929): 303.

Jirák, Karel Boleslav. "Alban Berg: *Vojcek.*" *NO*, November 13, 1926.

———. "Alban Berg: *Vojcek* (K zítřejší premiéře v Nár. divadle)." *NO*, November 10, 1926.

———, ed. *Das internationale Musikfest Prag 1924.* Prague: Průmyslová Tiskárna, 1924.

———. "Die Oper *Sache Makropulos* von Leoš Janáček." *A* 7, no. 2 (February 25, 1927): 48–50.

———. "Diskuse o vážné a lehké hudbě (závěr)." *T-LHM* 15, no. 16 (June 30, 1936): 179–80.

———. "E. F. Burian: *Před slunce východem.*" *NO*, November 26, 1925.

———. "Festival moderní hudby." *NSv* 1, no. 2 (January 1924): 42.

———. "Hudba lehká a vážná (K diskusi)." *T-LHM* 15, no. 10 (March 5, 1936): 114.

———. "Hudební kritika a rozhlas." *T-LHM* 16, no. 1 (October 7, 1936): 3.

———. "K problému hudební moderny." *NSv* 1, no. 3 (January 1924): 54–56.

———. "Mezinárodní hudební festival." *NSv* 1, no. 9 (February 1924): 151.

———. "Otakar Zich." *T-LHM* 6, no. 4 (January 25, 1927): 106–11.

———. "Pozdní výhonek českého wagnerismu." *NO*, October 10, 1928.

———. "Pražské němectví a česká hudba." *T-LHM* 3, no. 1 (October 15, 1923): 4–8.

———. "Romantismus—učitel a nepřítel." *T-LHM* 8, no. 3 (December 18, 1928): 83–86.

———. "Tristan bez Isoldy." *NO*, December 20, 1924.

———. "Úpadek kritiky?" *NO*, February 14, 1928.

———. "Více či méně hudby v rozhlase?" *T-LHM* 15, no. 2 (October 15, 1935): 14–15.

———. "Vítězslav Novák: *Dědův odkaz.*" *NO*, December 24, 1926.

———. "*Vojcek* na ruby." *NO*, April 29, 1927.

———. "Z hudebního života." *T-LHM* 8, no. 2 (November 21, 1928): 60–61.

Jiránek, Jaroslav. "Ostrčilův stylový přínos a jeho vnitřní polarita." *HVě* 5 (1968): 548–69.

———. "Zdeněk Nejedlý—zakladatel české hudební vědy." In *Z bojů o českou hudební kulturu,* ed. Stanislava Zachařová, 15–28. Prague: Academia, 1979

"Josef Suk—Vlastizrádcem," *HR* 12, no. 3 (December 1918): 128–29.

Jůzl, Miloš. *Otakar Hostinský.* Prague: Melantrich, 1980.

"K aféře Sukově." *HR* 12, no. 4 (January 1919): 171.

-K-. "Československá hudba v cizině." *T-LHM* 11, no. 4 (December 1931): 148.

"K novému životu, k nové práci!" *HR* 12, no. 2 (November 1918): 45.

K. "O českém muzikantství." *D* 35 (1912–13): 255–56.

"K případu *Vojcka.*" *PL*, November 18, 1926.

Kalenský, Boleslav. "Dvořákiana. I. Prof. dr. Zd. Nejedlý a Dvořák." *D* 34, no. 5 (November 25, 1911): 40.

Kalenský, Boleslav. "Dvořákiana. II. Dvořák v líčení Fibichově a Hostinského." *D* 34, no. 8 (December 16, 1911): 63–64.

———. "Dvořákiana. III. Až do třetího pokolení . . ." *D* (January 20, 1912): 90–91.

———. "Dvořákiana. IV. 'Nikdy dosti Dvořáka!'" *D* 34, nos. 42–43 (September 20, 1912): 306–7.

———. "Dvořákiana. V. Fr. X. Šalda—nový protidvořákovec. VI. 'Hudební klub' o Dvořákovi." *D* 35 (1912–13): 79–85.

———. "Ještě jiný případ vědecké kritiky." *D* 34, no. 26 (April 4, 1912): 194.

———. "K našim sporům a potřebám." *HR-S* 1, no. 15 (July 15, 1906): 193–98.

———. "Na obranu zesnulého ředitele konzervatoře Karla Knittla," *NL,* July 31, 1907.

———. "Protismetanovství a Knittl." *HR-S* 2, no. 14 (July 15, 1907): 196–202.

———. "Protismetanovství a Knittlovština." *HR-S* 2, nos. 16–17 (October 1, 1907): 238–44.

———. "Různé zprávy. Sešikování 'Protidvořákovců.'" *D* 34, no. 29 (April 25, 1912): 218.

———. "Zasláno. Ke sporům o 'knittlovštinu.'" *HR-S* 2, no. 11 (June 1, 1907): 157–58.

Kálik, Václav. "O národnosti." *T-LHM* 5, nos. 9–10 (July 25, 1926): 333–35.

Kallenberg, Siegfried. "Die erste Viertelton-Oper." *A* 11, no. 5 (May 25, 1931): 145–47.

Karas, Joza. *Music in Terezin 1941–1945.* New York Pendgragon, 1985.

"Karel Knittl †." *D* 29 (1906–7): 214–15.

Kareš, Miloš. "Názor libretistův o zpěvohře *Švanda dudák.*" *ND* 10, no. 12 (February 15, 1933): 2–3.

Kater, Michael. *Different Drummers: Jazz in the Culture of Nazi Germany.* New York and Oxford: Oxford University Press, 1992.

"Ke skandálu s Bergovým *Vojckem.*" *Čech,* November 18, 1926.

Kern, Stephen. *The Culture of Time and Space 1880–1918.* Cambridge, Mass.: Harvard University Press, 1983.

Kieval, Hillel J. *The Making of Czech Jewry: National Conflict and Jewish Society in Bohemia, 1870–1918.* New York and Oxford: Oxford University Press, 1988.

Kinzel, Hugo. "Unsere Sendung ist erfüllt, unser Ziel erreicht." *MdS* 2 (after September 15, 1938): 353–55.

———. "Wenn wir Sudetendeutsche darangeben . . ." *MdS* 1, no. 1 (November 15, 1936): 1–3.

Klein, Hans-Günter, ed. *Viktor Ullmann. Verdrängte Musik* 12. Hamburg: Bockel, 1996.

Klíma, Cynthia A. *A Tricultural Theatrical Tradition: The History of the German Theater in Prague, 1883–1938.* Ph.D. diss., University of Wisconsin-Madison, 1995.

Klíma, R. "Boj o Dvořáka. Trochu glos a polemiky." *D* 35 (1912–13): 123.

Knauer, Ernst. "Zur Frage des deutschen Rundfunks in der Tschechoslowakei." *MdS* 2, no. 11 (September 15, 1938): 330–32. [Followed by an inspirational quote by Adolf Hitler!]

Knittel, K. M. "'Ein hypermoderner Dirigent': Mahler and Antisemitism in *fin-de-siècle* Vienna." *Nineteenth Century Music* 18, no. 3 (1995): 257–76.

Kohn, Walter. "Je moderní hudba na mrtvém bodě?" *P* 12, no. 40 (October 9, 1935): 640.

Korffner, Heinz. "Před premierou Hábovy čtvrttónové opery v Mnichově." *K* 1, no. 5 (1931): 145–50.

Kotek, Josef. *Kronika české synkopy: půlstoletí českého jazzu a moderní populární hudby v obrazech a svědectví současníků.* Vol. 1: 1903–38. Prague: Editio Supraphon, 1975.

———. *O české populární hudbě a jejích posluchačích: od historie k současnosti.* Prague: Panton, 1990.

———. "Podíl jazzu v české umělecké avantgardě dvacátých let." *Estetika* 24, no. 1 (1987): 33–39.

Kovařovic, Josef. "Zdeněk Nejedlý a Karel Kovařovic." *HRy* 1971: 139–40.

Kovařovic, Karel. "Zasláno." *D* 35 (1912–13): 178.

Král, Václav. *Zdeněk Nejedlý a Gollova škola.* Prague: Univerzita Karlova, 1986.

Krásnohorská, Eliška. "Bohemia." In *The Woman Question in Europe: A Series of Original Essays,* ed. Theodore Stanton, 446–56. New York: G. P. Putnam's Sons, 1884.

Krejčí, Iša. "Bergův *Vojcek.*" *RA* 2, no. 6 (1926–27): 70–71

———. "Boh. Martinů balet." *RA* 2, no. 12 (1926–27): 143.

———. "*Dědův odkaz.*" *RA* 2, no. 8 (1926–27): 95.

———. "Dva typy tvůrčích duchů v hudbě." *HVk* 30, no. 8 (September 1, 1937): 139–40.

———. "Hudba a mladé divadlo." *LUK* 3 (1935): 307–8.

———. "Koncertní novinky." *RA* 2, no. 6 (1926): 71.

———. "Moderní spolek." *RA* 3, no. 8 (1928): 101.

———. "Národní píseň a šlágr." *T-LHM* 16, no. 8 (February 5, 1937): 104–5.

———. "Německé divadlo." *RA* 3, no. 1 (1927): 11.

———. "O moderní hudbě." *ČH* 30 (1927): 23–24.

———. "O moderní hudbu." *RA* 2, no. 10 (1926): 119.

———. "O sociální funkci hudby." *LUK* 2 (1934): 147.

———. "Opera?" *LUK* 2 (1934): 88.

———. "Otakaru Ostrčilovi . . ." *ND* 6, no. 27 (February 23, 1929): 18.

———. "Partitura Vycpálkovy *Kantáty o posledních věcech člověka.*" *RA* 2, no. 12 (1927): 143.

———. "*Preciezky*" [sic]. *ND* 3, no. 36 (May 15, 1926): 2.

———. "Richard Wagner a dnešek." *K* 3, no. 6 (1933): 136–38.

———. "Skandály o *Vojcka* a Konservatoř." *RA* 2, no. 6 (1926–27): 71.

———. "Spolek pro moderní hudbu." *RA* 3, no. 5 (1927): 63.

———. "Večer skladeb E. F. Buriana." *RA* 3, no. 3 (1927): 32.

———. "Z hudebního života. V. Novák: *Bouře.*" *RA* 3, no. 13 (1928): 162.

———. "Zichovy *Preciezky*" [sic]. *ND* 3, no. 35 (May 8, 1926): 4–5.

Křička, Jaroslav. "Několik poznámek k opeře *Strašidlo v zámku.*" *ND* 11, no. 3 (October 16, 1933): 1–2.

"Křičkova opera *Strašidlo v zámku* v zrcadle zahraniční kritiky." *ND* 11, no. 3 (October 16, 1933): 5–6.

"Krise obecenstva?" *ND* 9, no. 19 (January 23, 1932): 3–4.

Kvapil, Jaroslav. "Ke sporu o vhodnosti . . ." *V,* January 21, 1919.

Květ, J. M., ed. *Josef Suk: Život a dílo, Studie a vzpomínky.* Prague: HMUB, 1935.

Ladmanová, Milada. "Stylový přínos Přítomnosti, sdružení pro soudobou hudbu." *HVě* 5 (1968): 187–209.

Lébl, Vladimír. "Dramatická tvorba Otakara Ostrčila a její jevištní osudy." *Divadlo* 9 (1959): 294–302, 333–39.

———. "Pražské Mahlerovství let 1898–1918." *HVě* 12, no. 2 (1975): 99–135.

———. "Pražské ohlasy Debussyho tvorby v létech 1905–1921." *HVě* 6 (1969): 195–233.

———. "Případ *Vojcek.*" *HVě* 14, no. 3 (1977): 195–227.

———. *Vítězslav Novák: život a dílo.* Prague: Nakladatelství Československé akademie věd, 1964.

Levitz, Tamara. *Teaching New Classicality: Ferruccio Busoni's Masterclass in Composition.* Frankfurt: Peter Lang, 1996.

Lippman, Edward, ed. *Musical Aesthetics: A Historical Reader.* Vol. 2. New York: Pendragon Press, 1985.

Lošťák, Ludvík. "Otevřený list mladé hudební generaci v Čechách a na Moravě." *D* 18 (1896): 193–94.

Löwenbach, Jan. "Hudba před plátnem." *P* 12, no. 15 (April 17, 1935): 235–37.
———. "Jaroslav Křička." *T-LHM* 2, no. 1 (October 15, 1922): 8–18.
———. "K problému židovské hudby." *T-LHM* 5, no. 5 (February 25, 1926): 194–95.
———. "K začátku saisony. Nová hudba a denní kritika." *HR* 12, no. 1 (October 1918): 26–27.
———. "Mezinárodní festival a česká hudba." *T-LHM* 3, no. 8 (May 26, 1924): 269–71.
———. "Neue tschechische Opern." *A* 6, nos. 5–6 (May 1926): 134–35.
———. "Nezdravé zjevy našeho hudebního života." *HR* 13, no. 2 (November 1919): 58–61.
———. "Otakar Hostinský." *HR* 3, no. 2 (February 1910): 65–66.
———. "Ostrčilovo *Poupě*." *HR* 4, no. 1 (January 1911): 3–9.
———. "*Pelléas a Melisanda*." *LN*, November 3, 1921.
———. "Pražský festival v zrcadle cizí kritiky," *T-LHM* 3, nos. 9–10 (July 15, 1924): 333–57.
———. "Příklad Masarykův.—Čestné soudy." *HR* 12, no. 4 (January 1919): 148–49.
———. "Smetana contra Dvořák." *Hlídka Času*, December 6, 1911.
———. "Zase festival?" *T-LHM* 4, nos. 8–9 (May 15, 1925): 303–6.
Löwenbach, Josef. "*Die Schuld*. Oper von Ottokar Zich." *A* 2, no. 3 (March 18, 1922): 93–94.
-lth.- "Josef Hutter: Otakar Zich a jeho hudební drama *Vina*." *D* 38, nos. 8–9 (March 23, 1922): 67.
-M. "*PL* o Bergově *Vojcku*." *NL*, November 19, 1926.
Mabary, Judith. "Redefining Melodrama: The Czech Response to Music and Word." Ph.D. diss., Washington University, St. Louis, Missouri, 1999.
Machar, J. S. "Amnestie." *NL*, February 2, 1919.
Mahler, Arnošt. "Alexander Zemlinskys Prager Jahre," *HVě* 9 (1972): 239–46.
Mařánek, Jiří. "E. F. Burian." *TT* 5 (December 1925): 3–5.
———. "Rozhovor s Otakarem Ostrčilem." *RA* 4, no. 22 (February 1929): 215–16.
———. "Zrcadlo interviewu: Vítězslav Novák." *RA* 4, no. 33 (May 1929): 325–37.
Martinů, Bohuslav. "Ke kritice o současné hudbě." *T-LHM* 4, no. 6 (February 20, 1925): 184–87.
———. "O hudbě a tradici." *P* 2, no. 43 (November 5, 1925): 678–79.
———. "O současné hudbě." *P* 5, no. 17 (May 3, 1928): 266–67.
———. "O současné hudbě." *T-LHM* 4, nos. 8–9 (May 15, 1925): 268–73.
———. "O současné melodii." *T-LHM* 5, no. 5 (February 25, 1926): 163–66.
———. "Poučení z *Prodané nevěsty* v Paříži." *P* 5, no. 44 (November 8, 1928): 696–97.
———. "Přežila se opera?" *P* 12, no. 7 (February 20, 1935): 105–7.
———. "Případ *Half-timu*." *T-LHM* 4, no. 5 (January 20, 1925): 170–71.
Matoušek, Miloslav. *Zdeněk Nejedlý: pokus o ideový profil*. Prague: Rudolf Rejman, 1928.
Maszányi, Det Ectif [=Antonín Srba]. *"Nepokradeš!": hudebně anatomická studie o metempsychose a metamorphose motivů*. 2nd ed. Prague: Knihtiskárna V. Kotrby, 1913.
Messing, Scott. *Neoclassicism in Music: From the Genesis of the Concept through the Schoenberg/Stravinsky Polemic*. Ann Arbor, Mich.: UMI Research Press, 1988.
Mikoda, Bořivoj. *Dílo Otakara Jeremiáše*. Sborník Pedagogické fakulty v Plzni, Umění, vol. 4. Prague: Pedagogická fakulta v Plzni, 1965.
Mikota, Jan. "E. F. Burian a jeho Voice-band." In *Prolegomena scénografické encyklopedie* 14 (1972): 85–108.
Milhaud, Darius. "Apropos Tonfilm." *Querschnitt* 9, no. 8 (August 1929): 562.
Monmarte, Danièle. "Honzl et Burian: Structuralisme et *Gesamtkunstwerk*." In *L'Oeuvre d'art totale*, 157–77. Paris: CNRS Éditions, 1995.

"Náměstek pražského starosty dr. Vaněk mrtev." *Čech*, November 12, 1926.

"Národní divadlo: *Vojcek*." *PL*, November 13, 1926.

Nebuška, Otakar. "Česká hudba a česká samostatnost." *HR* 11, no. 10 (July 1918), 378–84.

———. "Divadla. Národní divadlo. *Kunálovy oči*." *HR* 1, no. 10 (December 1908): 483–85.

———. "Prof. Dr. Z. Nejedlý." *HR* 4 (1911): 229–31.

———. "Vinohradské divadlo a hudba." *HR* 13, no. 1 (October 1919): 14–16.

———. "Zd. Nejedlý a K. Kovařovic." *HR* 4 (1911): 116–17.

Nebuška, Otakar, Otakar Šourek, and Roman Veselý. "K otázce Smetanova *Karnevalu*." *HR* 4 (1911): 194–205.

Nejedlý, Vít. "Ještě o tendenci." *R* 1, no. 7 (March 1936): 77–81.

———. *Kritiky a stati o hudbě (1934–1944)*. Ed. Jaroslav Jiránek. Prague: Knižnice Hudebních rozhledů, 1956.

———. "Mladí lidé se dívají na svět." *Čin*, January 3, 1935.

Nejedlý, Zdeněk. "Affaira Dvořákovská vyvíjí se dále." *ČK* 1, no. 7 (January 3, 1913): 223–24.

———. "Antonín Dvořák mrtev." *Zvon* 4 (1904): 463–64.

———. "Antonín Dvořák: pohled na životní jeho dílo." *Osvěta* 34, no. 1 (1904): 517–25.

———. "B. Smetana a kulturní politika F. L. Riegra." *ČK* 2, no. 1 (October 3, 1913): 8–12; 2, no. 2 (October 17, 1913): 25–28; 2, no. 3 (November 17, 1913): 53–55; 2, no. 4 (November 21, 1913): 70–72; 2, no. 5 (December 5, 1913): 86–89; 2, nos. 7–8 (January 16, 1914): 115–17; 2, no. 9 (February 6, 1914): 140–43; 2, nos. 10–11 (February 27, 1914): 163–66; 2, no. 18 (June 5, 1914): 269–72; 2, no. 19 (July 10, 1914): 289–92.

———. *Bedřich Smetana*. Prague: Mánes, 1924.

———. "Bedřich Smetana." *Var* 3, no. 3 (March 15, 1924): 65–74.

———. "Blamáž našich klerikálů." *RP*, November 20, 1926.

———. "Boj o Dvořáka. II. Personalie." *S-HL* 3, nos. 9–10 (January 3, 1913): 100–110.

———. "Boj proti Ant. Dvořákovi." *ČK* 1, no. 6 (December 20, 1912): 186–88.

———. "Čechische Musikinstitutionen." *Čechische Revue* 1 (1906): 243–49; 350–55; 459–67; 752–60.

———. *Česká moderní zpěvohra po Smetanovi*. Prague: J. Otto, 1911.

———. "České kvarteto za války." *ČS*, December 15, 1918. Reprinted in *S-HL* 9, no. 2 (December 1918): 31–32.

———. *Dějiny české hudby*. Prague: Nakladatelství Hejda & Tuček, 1903.

———. "Divadla. Vít. Nováka *Karlštejn*." *S-HL* 7, no. 2 (December 14, 1916): 27–28.

———. "Divadlo. Zichova *Vina*." *S-HL* 12, nos. 4–5 (June 10, 1922): 60–64.

———. "Dnešní krise hudby." *S-HL* 12, no. 1 (January 25, 1922): 1–4; 12, no. 3 (March 18, 1922): 33–35; 12, no. 8 (November 10, 1922): 113–15.

———. "Dvořákova *Rusalka*." *Rozhledy* 11, no. 8 (May 25, 1901): 205.

———. "E per si muove." *ČS*, February 2, 1919. Reprinted in *S-HL* 9, no. 3 (February 1919): 61.

———. *Frederick Smetana*. London: Geoffrey Bles, 1924.

———. "Gustav Mahler." *Hudební sborník* 1, no. 1 (1913): 1–4 (úvod); 8–14.

———. *Historie mého smetanovství*. Prague: Státní hudební vydavatelství, 1962.

———. "*Hudební revue* věnovala . . ." *S-HL* 9, no. 2 (January 1919): 47.

———. "Individualismus." *Var* 3, no. 17 (November 15, 1923): 513–21.

———. "Jar. Jeremiáše *Starý král*," *S-HL* 9, nos. 7–8 (April 1919): 95–97.

———. "Jaromír Weinberger: *Švanda dudák*." *RP*, May 1, 1927.

———. "Jeremiášovi *Karamazovi*." *RP*, October 14, 1928.

Nejedlý, Zdeněk. "Ještě spor o Dvořáka." *S-HL* 3, no. 12 (February 7, 1913): 153–55.

———. "Josefa Suka *Zrání.*" *S-HL* 9, no. 1 (November 29, 1918): 9–10.

———. "K dějinám české hudby." *Osvěta* 34, no. 2 (1904): 638–45.

———. "Karel Kovařovic. Zemřel 6. prosince t. r." *S-HL* 10, nos. 9–10 (December 30, 1920): 116–19.

———. *Korespondence Zdeňka Nejedlého s historiky Gollovy školy.* Prague: Univerzita Karlova, 1989.

———. "Krise esthetiky." *ČK* 1, no. 1 (October 4, 1912): 19–23; 1, no. 2 (October 18, 1912): 42–47; 1, no. 3 (October 31, 1912): 76–78.

———. *Kritiky (Den 1907–1909).* Sebrané spisy Zdeňka Nejedlého, vol. 38. Prague: SNKLHU, 1954.

———. *Kritiky II (RP 1923–1935).* Sebrané spisy Zdeňka Nejedlého, vol. 39. Prague: SNKLHU, 1956.

———. "*Kunálovy oči.*" *ND* 6, no. 27 (February 23, 1929): 1–2.

———. "*Legenda z Erinu,* zpěvohra O. Ostrčila." *S-HL* 11 (1921): 86.

———. "Leoše Janáčka *Její pastorkyňa.*" *S-HL* 6, nos. 9–10 (August 4, 1916): 117–24.

———. "Letošní novinky Národního divadla v Praze. II. O. Ostrčila *Legenda z Erinu.*" *S-HL* 13, nos. 3–4 (June 21, 1923): 44–46.

———. "Lidově a pokrokově." *Var* 1, no. 1 (December 1, 1921): 1–13.

———. "Mladým." *S-HL* 11, nos. 7–8 (November 18, 1921): 101–6.

———. *Můj případ: k pathologii české společnosti v republice.* Hudební knihovna časopisu Smetana no. 29. Prague: Knihtiskárna Melantrich, 1919.

———. "Na Nové cesty" [sic]. *S-HL* 11, no. 1 (April 15, 1921): 1–2.

———. "Naturalismus naší opery." *ČK* 1, no. 21 (August 1, 1913): 671.

———. "O čtvrttónové hudbě." *S-HL* 13, no. 2 (April 19, 1923): 17–20.

———. *O divadle a jeho umělcích.* Prague: Panorama, 1978.

———. "O. Ostrčila *Vlasty skon.*" *ND* 6, no. 30 (March 15, 1929): 2.

———. *O umění a politice.* Prague: Melantrich, 1978.

———. "Ot. Ostrčila *Legena z Erinu.*" *S-HL* 11 (1921): 75–77.

———. "Otakar Jeremiáš." *S-HL (II)* 1 (December 2, 1936): 41–42.

———. *Otakar Ostřil: Vzrůst a uzrání.* Prague: Melantrich, 1935.

———. "Otakar Zich." *ND* 6, no. 33 (April 5, 1929): 2–3.

———. *Otakara Hostinského esthetika.* Prague: Nákladem Jana Laichtera, 1921.

———. "Pan Dr. V. Štěpán." *S-HL* 7, no. 1 (November 9, 1916): 14–15.

———. "Pan AŠ v *Národních listech.*" *RP,* November 14, 1926.

———. "Pokrokovost." *Var* 3, no. 12 (June 15, 1923): 353–65.

———. *Případ Vítězslava Nováka.* IV. leták Dobré Edice. Prague: Dobrá Edice, 1931.

———. "*Psohlavci* a jich smetanismus." *S-HL* 1, no. 1 (November 4, 1910): 5–8.

———. "Růžena Maturová." *NL,* February 7, 1910.

———. "Spolek pro moderní hudbu." *S-HL* 11, no. 1 (April 15, 1921): 5–8.

———. *Spor ve vinohradském divadle: k problému českého divadla.* Hudební knihovna časopisu Smetana no. 30. Prague: Knihtiskárna Melantrich, 1919.

———. "Svoboda!" *S-HL* 9, no. 1 (November 1918): 2–4.

———. "Tři retrospektivy. 2. Amnestie. 3. Nová pokroková strana." *Var* 1, no. 8 (March 15, 1922): 238–46.

———. "Úvodem." *Směr* 1 (1932): 1–7.

———. "Vítězslav Novák. K padesátým narozeninám." *S-HL* 10, nos. 9–10 (December 30, 1920): 112–14.

———. *Vítězslav Novák. Studie a kritiky.* Spisy menší Zdenka Nejedlého svazek II. Prague: Melantrich, 1921.

Nejedlý, Zdeněk. "Vítězslava Nováka *Dědův odkaz*," *RP*, December 25, 1926.

———. "Vítězslava Nováka *Karlštejn*." *S-HL* 7, no. 2 (December 14, 1916): 17–24; 7, no. 3 (January 4, 1917): 38–40.

———. "*Vojcek*." *Var* 4, nos. 16–17 (December 31, 1926): 441–61.

———. *Z české kultury*. Prague: Státní nakladatelství politické literatury, 1953.

———. "Z hudebního života dneška. Reakce i zde na postupu." *Var* 5, nos. 18–20 (1927): 452–63.

———. "Z pathologie naší hudební literatury." *ČK* 1, nos. 19 (July 4, 1913): 607–8.

———. *Z prvních dvou let republiky: politické stati*. Prague: Melantrich, 1921.

———. "Za Otakarem Ostrčilem." *ND* 13, no. 1 (September 5, 1935): 2–3.

———. *Zdeňko Fibich: zakladatel scénického melodramatu*. Prague: Hejda & Tuček, 1901.

———. "Zichova *Vina*." *S-HL* 12, nos. 4–5 (June 10, 1922): 60–64.

———. "Zichovy *Preciézky*." *ND* 3, no. 37 (May 22, 1926): 2–3.

———. "Zichovy *Preciézky*." *RP*, June 6, 1926.

———. *Zpěvohry Smetanovy*. Prague: J. Otto, 1908.

———. "Zvíkovský rarášek." *S-HL* 6, no. 1 (November 15, 1915): 1–5.

Nelson, Patricia. "Poznámky o negerských písních." Trans. F. K. *RA* 4, nos. 13–14 (1929): 134.

Němeček, Jan. *Opera Národního divadla v období Karla Kovařovice 1900–1920*. Vol. 1, 1900–1912. Prague: Divadelní ústav—Český hudební fond, 1968.

———. *Opera Národního divadla v období Karla Kovařovice 1900–1920*. Vol. 2, 1912–20. Prague: Divadelní ústav—Český hudební fond, 1969.

"Není nad důslednost." *HR* 6 (1912–13): 294.

"Není třeba vše . . ." *PL*, November 13, 1926.

"Nepokradeš!" *HR* 6 (1912–13): 549.

Netušil, Dluhoš. "Odněmčeme umění." *D* 36, no. 2 (February 15, 1919): 13.

Notley, Margaret. "Brahms as Liberal: Genre, Style, and Politics in Late Nineteenth-Century Vienna." *Nineteenth-Century Music* 17, no. 2 (Fall 1993): 107–23.

Nötzel, Karl. *Gegen den Kultur-bolschewismus*. Munich: P. Müller, 1930.

Novák, Mirko. "Vývoj a krise ideovosti." *T-LHM* 4, no. 10 (June 30, 1925): 329–35.

Novák, Vítězslav. "Doslov k *Bouři*." *HR* 6 (1912–13): 307–10.

———. *O sobě a o jiných*. Prague: Editio Supraphon, 1970.

———. "*Svatební košile*." *HR* 7 (1913–14): 61–67.

———. "Velectěná redakce!" *HR* 6 (1912–13): 294–95.

———. *Vítězslav Novák contra Otakar Ostrčil*. [Second edition with a foreword by the author.] Prague: Nakladatel A. Neubert, Knihkupec, 1931.

———. *Zdeněk Nejedlý v zrcadle své vědecké kritiky: s odpovědí na brožuru Otakar Ostrčil či Vítězslav Novák*. Prague: Nakladatel A. Neubert, Knihkupec, 1931.

Novotný, Antonín. "Móda." *S-HL (II)* 1 (December 2, 1936): 61–63.

"O čem se píše: Čtvrttónová opera Aloise Háby." *T-LHM* 9, nos. 9–10 (1930): 350.

O. L. M. "Divadlo. *Vina*." *D* 38, no. 10 (April 13, 1922): 75–76.

———. "Druhý Mezinárodní festival orchestrální hudby v Praze." *D* 41 (1924–25): 229–31.

"O novou buffu." *ND* 3, no. 36 (May 15, 1925): 2–3.

"O novou hudbu." *HR* 13, no. 8 (May 1920): 319–20.

Oberhel, Antonín. "Odstrčilovo *Poupě*" [sic]. *D* 36 (1919): 134.

Očadlík, Mirko. "50 let Otakara Ostrčila." *RA* 4, no. 22 (February 1929): 216–17.

———. "Alexander Zemlinsky se rozloučí . . ." *T-LHM* 6, nos. 9–10 (July 8, 1927): 323–24.

Očadlík, Mirko. "Čekáme na čin." *K* 2, no. 1 (1931): 1–2.

———. "*Čin* censuruje 'Pravdu o boji proti Talichovi.' " *LUK* 3 (1935): 533–34.

———. "Čtvrttónová škola." *K* 1, no. 9 (July 25, 1931): 308–11.

———. "*Dědův odkaz.*" *S-HL* 16, nos. 4–5 (July 1927): 54–56.

———. "Die Oper *Grossvaters Vermächtnis* von Vít. Novák." *A* 7, no. 2 (February 25, 1927): 50.

———. "Dnešní modnost a modernost." *Hudební Chvilka* 1, no. 5 (April 21, 1928): 1; 4.

———. "Ervin Schulhoff zápasí s ideami." *K* 2, no. 6 (1932): 113–17.

———. "Hábův *Jánošík.*" *ND* 11, no. 11 (February, 1934): 1–2.

———. "Jaký má být šéf opery Národního divadla." *P* 12, no. 38 (September 25, 1935): 602–3.

———. "K situaci." *K* 1, no. 5 (1931): 129–38.

———. "Marginalia k *Bratrům Karamazovým.*" *RA* 4, no. 5 (October 1928): 49–50.

———. "Mladí bez místa." *K* 2, no. 8 (1932): 177–80.

———. "Na konec ročníku." *K* 2, no. 14 (1932): 289–90.

———. "Na nových cestách. (O. Zich: *Preciezky* [sic]. D. Milhaud: *Zmatek.*) *NO*, May 23, 1926.

———. "Na prahu nové sezony." *K* 1, no. 1 (1930): 21–27.

———. "Národ sobě?" *K* 4, no. 2 (November 21, 1933): 20–24.

———. "Národní divadlo. Bergův *Vojcek.*" *T-LHM* 6, nos. 2–3 (December 15, 1926): 75–77.

———. "O směru." *K* 2, no. 13 (1932): 209–16.

———. "O stavu kritickém." *K* 1, no. 4 (December 9, 1930): 100–105; 1, no. 5 (1931): 141–45.

———. "Od negramotnosti k avantgardě." *LUK* 3 (1935): 308–11.

———. "Operní novatérství (K české premiéře Bergova *Vojcka*)." *T-LHM* 6, nos. 2–3 (December 15, 1926): 47–57.

———. "Osvobozené divadlo." *K* 1, no. 5 (1931): 177–78.

———. "Otakara Zicha *Preciezky.*" *S-HL* 16, no. 2 (September 1926): 17–20.

———. "Podstata modernosti v hudbě." *K* 4, nos. 5–6 (March 15, 1934): 68–85.

———. "Poměr starých k mladým." *K* 4, nos. 3–4 (January 16, 1934): 33–34.

———. "Poslední dílo Vítězslava Nováka." *K* 1, no. 6 (1931): 202–7.

———. "Postátněné Národní divadlo." *P* 8, no. 50 (December 16, 1931): 796–98.

———. "Posudky. Karel Hába: *Janošík* [sic]. Opera o 4 děj. Text A. Klášterského." *K* 4, nos. 5–6 (March 15, 1934): 90–93.

———. "Posudky. Z divadel. *Strojník Hopkins* na scéně." *K* 1, no. 3 (1930): 89.

———. "Poznámky. Novák i Ostrčil." *K* 1, no. 9 (July 25, 1931): 319–20.

———. "Skandál v Národním divadle." *NO*, November 17, 1926.

———. "*Strojník Hopkins.*" *K* 1, no. 3 (1930): 65–68.

———. "*Strojník Hopkins* na scéně." *K* 1 (1930): 89.

———. "Svolejte naše hudebníky . . ." *K* 1, no. 1 (1930–31): 1.

———. "Talich na obzoru." *K* 2, nos. 10–11 (1932): 153–55.

———. "Talichova abdikace." *K* 1, no. 4 (December 9, 1930): 117–23.

———. "Úvodem." *K* 1, no. 1 (1930): 1.

———. "Vítězslav Novák polemicisující." *K* 1, no. 8 (1931): 273–76.

———. "*Vojcek.*" *ND* 4, no. 11 (November 6, 1926): 2.

"Očista." *HR* 12, no. 3 (December 1918): 130.

Olšanský, Bohuslav. *Umělecké boje a české divadlo.* Edice Průboj svazek 1. Prague: Edice Průboj, 1931.

"Orientace Národního divadla." *ND* 2, no. 23 (February 6, 1925): 1.

Ostrčil, Otakar. "Hudebnímu referentu *N. L.* dr. Šilhanovi." *NP*, June 8, 1923.

————. "K provedení *Prodané nevěsty* na Národním divadle." *NP*, June 6, 1923.

————. "Otakar Ostrčil o své nové opeře." *ČS*, April 3, 1935.

"*Ostrov Dynamit* v kritikách." *VPR* 1, no. 6 (April 15, 1930): 24.

"Osvobozené divadlo!" *TT* 4 (October–November, 1925): 27.

"Ot. Zich: *Vina* (Revue kritik)." *T-LHM* 1, no. 7 (April 1922): 104–7.

P. P. "Savoy-orkestr." *HVk* 21, no. 8 (April 16, 1928): 3.

Paclt, Jaromír, ed. *Debussy, Szymanowski, Honegger, Stravinskij a současná česká hudba.* Prague: Státní Hudební Vydavatelství, 1962.

————. "Prag als Asylstadt, 1918–38." In *Musik in der Emigration, 1933–1945,* 153–74. Stuttgart: Metzler, 1994.

————. *Tři kapitoly o Zdeňku Nejedlém.* Prague: Knižnice Hudebních Rozhledů, 1937.

Pala, František. "Co je s Hábovou operou?" *S-HL (II)* 1 (1937): 88–89.

————. "Idea pokroku v české hudbě a leccos jiného." *S-HL (II)* 2 (1938): 79–81, 109–10.

————. *Opera Národního divadla v období Otakara Ostrčila.* Vols. 1–4. Prague: Divadelní ústav, 1962, 1964, 1965, 1970.

————. "Studie o české hudební tvořivosti." *S-HL (II)* 1 (1936–37): 71–72; 93–94; 100–101; 114–17.

Památce Otakara Ostrčila. Prague: [n.p.], 1936.

"Pan Zdeněk Nejedlý . . ." *D* 35 (1912–13): 168.

Pandula, Dušan. "Hábas Vierteltonoper." In *Tschechische Komponisten: Janáček, Martinů, Hába, Weinberger, Musik der Zeit: eine Schriftenreihe zur zeitgenössischen Musik,* ed. Heinrich Lindlar, Heft 8, 34–36. Bonn: Boosey and Hawkes, [n.d.]

Patzaková, Anna J. "Deset let od premiéry *Vojcka.*" *S-HL (II)* 1 (1936): 25–26.

————. "Ještě k 'Případu Emila Axmana v *Přítomnosti.*'" *S-HL (II)* 1 (1937): 135–36.

————. "Karel Hába: *Jánošík.*" *NO*, February 25, 1934.

————. "Mezi východem a západem." *LUK* 3 (1935): 550–53.

————. "O čem se píše. Diskuse o časových problémech." *T-LHM* 11, no. 4 (December 1931): 154–55; 11, no. 5 (January 1932): 191–92.

————. "O náš operní styl." *S-HL (II)* 1, no. 1 (October 8, 1936): 11–13.

————. "O našich poměrech." *S-HL (II)* 1, no. 1 (October 8, 1936): 3–5.

————. "O současné produkci." *S-HL (II)* 1 (May 13, 1937): 121–22.

————. *Otakar Ostrčil-Otakar Jeremiáš ve svých dopisech, v práci a zápasech o pokrokovou linii českého umění.* Prague: Společnost Otakara Ostrčila, 1959.

————. "Opera jako umělecký a politický výraz státu." *S-HL (II)* 1 (1937): 122–23.

————. "Pátá symfonie Emila Axmana." *S-HL (II)* 1 (November 25, 1936): 28–29.

————. "Případ Emila Axmana." *S-HL (II)* 1 (1937): 94–96.

————. "Rok po Ostrčilově smrti." *S-HL (II)* 1 (November 25, 1936): 37.

————. "Slavná premiéra (Ot. Ostrčil: *Honzovo království*)." *NO*, April 5, 1935.

————. "Slovo o kritice." *S-HL (II)* 1, no. 1 (October 8, 1936): 2–3.

————. "Sociální příčiny dnešní hudební krise." *T-LHM* 11, no. 3 (November 1931): 81–86.

————. "*Strašidlo* v Stavovském divadle." *NO*, October 12, 1933.

Payer, Otto. *Ottokar* [sic] *Ostrčil und die tschechische Opernbühne unserer Tage.* Prague: Mojmír Urbánek, 1912.

Peduzzi, Lubomír. *Pavel Haas: život a dílo skladatele.* Brno: Muzejní a Vlastivědná Společnost, 1993.

Peroutka, Ferdinand. *Jací jsme.* Published with *Demokratický manifest.* Prague: Středočeské Nakladatelství a Knihkupectví, 1991.

Pícha, František. "Radio." *T-LHM* 11, no. 5 (January 1932): 169–74.

———. "Zvukový film." *T-LHM* 11, no. 3 (November 1931): 86–89.

———. "Zvukový film, opera, netematický sloh." *T-LHM* 11, no. 8 (April 1932): 305–7; 11, no. 9 (May 1932): 347–51.

Pihert, Jindřich. "*Bratři Karamazovi.*" *LL*, October 10, 1928.

———. "Jaroslav Křička: *Strašidlo v zámku.*" *LL*, October 12, 1933.

———. "Smetanova výstava." *HR* 10, no. 9 (June 1917): 359.

———. "Z hudebního života. Praha. Národní divadlo. *Karlštejn.*" *HR* 10 (1916): 89–92.

Plantinga, Leon. *Romantic Music: A History of Musical Style in Nineteenth-century Europe.* New York: Norton, 1984.

Plavec, Josef. "*Honzovo království.*" *ND* 12, no. 11 (April, 1935): 1–2.

———. *Otakar Ostrčil: "Honzovo království."* Prague: [n.p.], 1934.

"Pod čarou: Josef Suk prof. Nejedlým obviněn z rakušáctví, Maffií očistěn." *V*, January 30, 1919.

Pohl, Emil R. "Fidelio F. Finke und seine *Jakobsfahrt.*" *MdS* 1, no. 4 (February 15, 1937): 103–8.

Poliakova, Liudmila. "Vítězslav Novák i ego opera *Karlštejn.*" *Sovietskaia Muzika* 10 (1970): 129–36.

Popelka, Iša. "Devětsil, Teige a Jazz." *Taneční Hudba a Jazz* (1968–69): 49–64.

Pospíšil, Vilém. *Opera Národního divadla v období Otakara Ostrčila.* Vols. 5–6. Prague: Divadelní ústav, 1983.

"Prager Musikleben." *A* 1, nos. 1–2 (November 1920): 13–14.

"Pražské divadelní aféry." *LN*, August 24, 1919.

"Přehled časopisů. Spor o Dvořáka." *HR* 6 (1912–13): 283–87.

Prinz, Friedrich. "Das kulturelle Leben." In *Handbuch der Geschichte der böhmischen Länder,* ed. Karl Bosl. Stuttgart: A. Hiersemann, 1967, 34–36.

"Případ Jaroslava Jeremiáše a veřejné otázky hudební." *HR* 12, no. 6 (February 1919): 260–61.

"Případ Nejedlého." *HR* 12, no. 6 (March 1919): 240–42.

"Pro moderní hudbu." *HR* 13, no. 8 (May 1920): 281–82.

Procházka, František. "Byl jsem na mluvícím a hudebním filmu." *HVk* 22, no. 12 (September 1, 1929): 2.

"Profesor Václav Talich pověřen správou opery Nár. divadla." *ND* 13, no. 4 (November 1, 1935): 6–7.

"Protest 15.12.1912." *NL, V, PL, Čas,* December 15, 1912.

"Protesty proti *Wojckovie.*" *Večer,* November 16, 1926.

Pujman, Ferdinand. "Glossy k novému provedení Smetanových oper v pražském Národním divadle." *ČR*, March 2, 1924.

———. "O pokroku v českém umění." *R* 4, no. 2 (November 1938): 9–10.

———. *Operní sloh Národního divadla.* Prague: [n.p.], 1933.

Pukl, Oldřich. "K problematice českého hudebního života po první světové válce (1918–1921)." *HVě* 2 (1965): 184–234.

Pynsent, Robert B. *Julius Zeyer: The Path to Decadence.* The Hague: Mouton, 1973.

———. *Questions of Identity: Czech and Slovak ideas of nationality and personality.* Budapest, London, and New York: CEU Press, 1994.

Rádl, Otto. "E. F. Burian čili divadlo aktuální." *P* 13, no. 16 (April 22, 1936): 248–49.

———. "Historie Osvobozeného divadla." *P* 12, no. 22 (June 5, 1935): 347–49; 12, no. 23 (June 12, 1935): 360–62.

———. "Konec revue." *P* 12, no. 20 (May 22, 1935): 313–16.

Redakce [Editor]. "Spor o Dvořáka." *HR* 6 (1912–13): 230–32.

Redakce. "Do desátého ročníku." *S-HL* 10, no. 1 (January 15, 1920): 1.

Redakce. "Na počátku ročníku." *K* 4, no. 1 (October 14, 1933): 1.

Redakce. "Zakladáme nový hudební časopis." *S-HL (II)* 1, no. 1 (October 8, 1936): 1–2.

Reiner, Karel. "E. F. Burian." *R* 3, no. 7 (February 1938): 74–75.

———. "Frank Warschauer na mrtvém bodě." *R* 1, nos. 2–3 (November, 1935): 4–12.

———. "Musikblätter der Sudetendeutschen." *R* 3, no. 2 (November 1937): 15.

———. "Otakar Ostrčil: *Honzovo království*." *R* 3, no. 3 (November–December 1937): 30.

Ritter, William. "*Bratři Karamazovi*." *ND* 7, no. 11 (November 8, 1929): 3–5.

———. "Jeremiášovi *Karamazovi* a cizina." *ND* 7, no. 4 (September 20, 1929): 4.

Rogers, J. A. "Jazz at Home." In *The New Negro: An Interpretation*, ed. Alain Locke, 216–24. New York: albert and Charles Boni, 1925.

Rok po premiéře Honzova království. Prague: Společnost Otakara Ostrčila, 1936.

Rutte, Miroslav. "Spor o Dvořáka. Kapitola o úpadku české polemiky." *Moderní Revue* 19, no. 26 (1912–13): 168–79.

Šak, Vladislav V. "Dokumenty. ['O orchestru Uměleckého klubu . . .']" *Hudba* 1, no. 1 (November 24, 1919): 18–19.

———. "Šakova aféra." *Hudba* 1, nos. 11–12 (April 30, 1920): 180–84; 1, nos. 13–14 (May 15, 1920): 197–204.

Šak, Vladislav V., et al. "Dva dopisy." *Hudba* 1, no. 10 (April 16, 1920): 159–63.

Šalda, F. X. "Affaira Dvořákovská." *ČK* 1, no. 6 (December 20, 1912): 191–92.

Sayer, Derek. *The Coasts of Bohemia: A Czech History*. Princeton, NJ: Princeton University Press, 1998.

Scherchen, Dr. Hermann. "Není více krise v hudbě." *K* 3, no. 5 (1933): 81–84.

Schnierer, Miloš. "Komposiční škola Vítězslava Nováka." *ZSVN* 6 (1985): 19–27; 7 (1986): 4–14; 8 (1987): 8–15.

Schoenberg, Arnold. "Is There an Opera Crisis?" Translated by Joseph Auner. In *A Schoenberg Reader: Documents of a Life*, 193. New Haven, Conn.: Yale University Press, 2003.

———. *Theory of Harmony*. Translated by Roy E. Carter. Boston and London: Faber and Faber, 1983.

Schulhoff, Erwin. "Arnold Schönberg (1874–1924)." *ND* 2, no. 5 (September 26, 1924): 6–7.

———. "Arnold Schönberg (Naroz. 1874)." *ND* 2, no. 10 (October 31, 1924): 5.

———. "Der mondäne Tanz." *A* 4, no. 3 (1924): 73–77.

———. "Eine Jazz-Affaire." *A* 5, no. 7 (July 1925): 220–22.

———. "Ervin Schulhoff k anketě o čs. hudbě." *R* 3, no. 12 (August 1938): 117.

———. "Nový operní sloh." *ND* 1, no. 35 (May 25, 1924): 7–8.

———. "Saxophon und Jazzband." *A* 5, nos. 5–6 (June 1925): 179–83.

"Sedmdesáté narozeniny Antonína Dvořáka." *S-HL* 2, no. 1 (October 6, 1911): 14–15.

Sehnal, František. "Hudba lehká a těžká." *T-LHM* 15, no. 7 (January 16, 1936): 77–78.

———. "Rytmus a civilisace." *T-LHM* 16, no. 10 (March 11, 1937): 127–28.

Seifert, Adolf. "Das Wirken rassischer Kräfte in der Musik des deutschen Volkes." *MdS* 1, no. 10 (August 15, 1937): 300–303.

Selva, Blanche. "Blanche Selva o Čechách a Francii." *HR* 13, no. 7 (April 1920): 247–49.

———. "Význam styků mezi francouzskou a českou hudbou." *HR* 13, no. 4 (January 1920): 133–37.

Semrádová, Mila. *Voice-band E. F. Buriana*. Prague: Ustřední dům lidové umělecké tvořivosti, 1971.

Šilhan, Antonín. "Claude Debussy: *Pelléas a Mélisanda.*" *NL,* November 3, 1921.

———. "Cyklus oper Vítězslava Nováka. *Zvíkovský rarášek.*" *NL,* December 3, 1930.

———. "Cyklus oper Vítězslava Nováka. *Dědův odkaz.*" *NL,* December 19, 1930.

———. "Finis musicæ." *NL,* March 15, 1922.

———. "Jaromír Weinberger: *Švanda dudák.*" *NL,* April 29, 1927.

———. "Jaroslav Křička: *Strašidla* [sic] *v zámku.*" *NL,* October 12, 1933.

———. "Kovařovicův *Slib.*" *NL,* December 11, 1921.

———. "Leoš Janáček: *Káťa Kabanová.*" *NL,* December 2, 1922.

———. "Leoš Janáček: *Výlety páně Broučkovy.*" *NL,* April 25, 1920.

———. "Mezinárodní hudební festival." *NL,* June 7, 1924.

———. "Nový *Fidelio.*" *NL,* December 23, 1921.

———. "Operní premiera a baletní reprisa." *NL,* February 26, 1925.

———. "Operní premiéra s policejní asistencí." *NL,* October 9, 1930.

———. "Ostrčilovo *Honzovo království.*" *NL,* April 5, 1935.

———. "Ot. Ostrčil: *Legenda z Erinu.*" *NL,* June 19, 1923.

———. "Otakar Zich: *Preciézky.*" *NL,* May 23, 1926.

———. "*Právo lidu.*" *NL,* November 14, 1926.

———. "Tři objevitelé Smetany." *NL,* May 29, 1923.

———. "Smetanův *Dalibor* v novém rouše." *NL,* January 11, 1924.

———. "V cizích službách." *NL,* November 13, 1926.

———. "Vítězslav Novák: *Dědův odkaz.*" *NL,* December 24, 1926.

Šíp, Ladislav. *Česká opera a její tvůrci: průvodce.* Prague: Supraphon, 1983.

"Skandál v Národním divadle." *Čech,* November 17, 1926.

Slavický, Milan. *Gideon Klein: A Fragment of Life and Work.* Trans. Dagmar Steinová. Prague: Helvetica-Tempora, 1995.

"Směs. Nový 'doklad' Knittlova 'antismetaniánství.'" *HR-S* 2, no. 20 (November 15, 1907): 300.

Smetana, Robert. "*Bílý pán* na brněnském Národním divadle." *RA* 5, no. 12 (December 12, 1929): 143.

———. "K premiéře Schulhoffových *Plamenů.*" *Index* 5 (1933): 22–24.

Šourek, Otakar. "Brněnská zpěvohra. Otakar Ostrčil: *Legenda z Erinu.*" *V,* June 19, 1921.

———. "Dr. Leoš Janáček: *Věc Makropulos.*" *V,* March 3, 1928.

———. "Falešný mravokárce usvědčen . . ." *HR* 12, no. 5 (February 1919): 190–94.

———. "Genese Dvořákova díla." *HR* 8 (1914–15): 18–23; 121–30; 162–76; 218–30; 249–57; 9 (1915–16): 121–27; 157–63; 198–204; 250–55; 318–22; 362–68.

———. "Jaromír Weinberger: *Švanda dudák.*" *V,* April 29, 1927.

———. "Jaroslav Křička—dramatik." *ND* 11, no. 3 (October 16, 1933): 4–5.

———. "Jaroslav Křička: *Strašidlo v zámku.*" *V,* October 12, 1933.

———. "Ještě 'Případ Nejedlého.'" *HR* 12, no. 7 (April 1919): 336–38.

———. "K dnešní premiéře Zichovy *Viny.*" *V,* March 14, 1922.

———. "K Dvořákovu festivalu." *HR* 5 (1911–12): 485–86.

———. "K *Vojcekově* aféře v Národním divadle." *V,* November 21, 1926.

———. "Leoš Janáček: *Káťa Kabanová.*" *V,* December 2, 1922.

———. "Max Brand: *Strojník Hopkins.*" *V,* October 9, 1930.

———. "Nahraďte fráze fakty." *T-LHM* 16, no. 3 (November 7, 1936): 32–33.

———. "Nová kniha o Dvořákovi." *HR* 9 (1915–16): 59–71.

———. "Novákův *Dědův odkaz* na Národním divadle." *V,* December 24, 1926.

———. "Novákův *Karlštejn.*" *ND* 13, no. 11 (March 20, 1936): 3–4. Reprinted in *ND* 16, no. 10 (March 1939): 2–5.

Šourek, Otakar. "Nově vypravená *Prodaná nevěsta.*" *V,* May 29, 1923.

———. "Nově vypravený *Dalibor.*" *V,* January 11, 1924.

———. "Operní a baletní premiéra. Otakar Zich: *Preciézky.*" *V,* May 23, 1926.

———. "Otakar Jeremiáš: *Bratři Karamazovi.*" *V,* December 10, 1928.

———. "Otakar Ostrčil: *Legenda z Erinu.*" *V,* June 19, 1921.

———. "Otakar Zich: *Vina.*" *V,* March 16, 1922.

———. "*Pelléas a Melisanda.*" *V,* November 3, 1921.

———. "Pohnutá operní premiera. Alban Berg: *Vojcek.*" *V,* November 13, 1926.

———. "Pražský hudební festival." *V,* June 1, 1924.

———. "Smetanovo *Tajemství.*" *V,* May 13, 1922.

———. "Ve věci Novákovy *Lucerny.*" *V,* May 18, 1923.

———. "Vítězslav Novák: *Lucerna.*" *V,* May 15, 1923.

Sova, Antonín. "Zrání." In *Josef Suk: Op. 34 Zrání, hudební báseň pro velký orkestr,* 3–4. Prague: HMUB, 1919.

Splitt, Gerhard. *Richard Strauss 1933–1935: Aesthetik und Musikpolitik zu Beginn der nationalsozialistischen Herrschaft.* Pfaffenweiler: Centaurus Verlagsgesellschaft, 1987.

Spilka, František. "Knittl a Dvořák." *HR-S* 2, no. 7 (April 1, 1907): 85–86.

Spurný, Lubomír. "Boj o Nováka?" *ZSVN* 17 (1990): 26–30.

Srba, Antonín. *Boj proti Dvořákovi.* Prague: Nákladem Lidového družstva tiskařského a vydavatelského, 1914.

———, ed. *Vítězslav Novák: studie a vzpomínky.* Prague: Osvětový klub, 1932.

Srba, Bořivoj. "Les Pièces phoniques d'Emil František Burian." In *Colloquium Bohuslav Martinů, his pupils, friends and contemporaries,* 88–97. Brno: Masarykova Univerzita, 1993.

Stanislav, Josef. "Ideologie a hudba." *R* 2, nos. 11–12 (May–June, 1937): 110–13.

———. "Moderní hudba a Mezinárodní hudební festival v Praze 1924." *D* 40 (1924): 115–16.

———. "Umělecká morálka a kritikové *Smetany.*" *R* 2, no. 7 (March, 1937): 69–72.

———. "Věda, či pouhá zkušenost? (K některým sporným otázkám hudební ideologie.)." *R* 1, no. 8 (March–April, 1936): 94–96.

———. "Zdeněk Nejedlý." *R* 3, no. 8 (March 1938): 79–81.

Štech, Václav. *Vinohradský případ: Román divadelní skutečnosti.* Prague: J. Otto, 1922.

Stecker, Karel. "Časopis *Smetana.*" *HR* 6 (1912–13): 356–57.

———. "K článku 'Smetanismus a Wagnerianismus.' " *HR* 4 (1911): 266–75.

———. "O stavu hudební vědy na české universitě." *HR* 6 (1912–13): 544–46.

———. "Za Karlem Knittlem." *S-HR* 2, no. 15 (September 15, 1907): 212–21.

———. "(Zasláno.) Ctěná redakce!" *S-HR* 2, no. 11 (June 1, 1907): 154–56.

———. "Zasláno. Čtenářstvu *Smetany!*" *S-HR* 2, no. 13 (July 1, 1907): 182–87.

Stecker, Karel, and Karel Hoffmeister. "Našim čtenářům!" *HR* 1, no. 1 (January 1908): 1–3.

Steinhard, Erich. "Alban Berg. Nach der *Wozzeck*-Uraufführung an der Berliner Staatsoper." *A* 6, no. 1 (January 1926): 10–12.

———. "Brand: *Maschinist Hopkins.*" *A* 10, no. 12 (December 12, 1930): 293–94.

———. "*Die Brüder Karamasoff* als Oper." *A* 8, no. 9 (September 20, 1928): 228–29.

———. "Die Domszene aus Dietzenschmidt Fidelio Finkes *Sankt Jakobsfahrt.*" *A* 15, nos. 7–8 (August 1, 1935): 132–34.

———. "*Die Jakobsfahrt* von Fidelio Finke." *A* 16, nos. 11–12 (December 1936): 191–93.

———. "J. Weinbergers *Schwanda der Dudelsackpfeifer* in Prag." *A* 9, no. 4 (April 20, 1928): 118–19.

Steinhard, Erich. "Jaroslav Křičkas *Spuk im Schloss.*" *A* 11, nos. 11–12 (December 1931): 283–84.

———. "Junge Musik in der Tschechoslowakei." *Die Musik* 17, no. 8 (May 1925): 561–77.

———. "Křeneks *Jonny spielt auf.*" *A* 7, nos. 7–8 (July 1, 1927): 185–86.

———. "L. Janáček *Die Sache Makropulos*: Erstaufführung Tschechisches Nationaltheater, Prag." *A* 8, no. 4 (April 25, 1928): 96–97.

———. "Modemusiker Erwin Schulhoff." *A* 9, no. 3 (March 20, 1929): 80–81.

———. "Sudetendeutschen Komponisten." *A* 8, no. 7 (June 20, 1928): 157–59.

———. "*Vojcek.*" *ND* 4, no. 11 (November 6, 1926): 2–3.

———. "Vom Prager Internationalen Musikfest." *A* 5, no. 5 (May 1925): 217–19.

———. "Wihtemans Jazzorchester in Paris" [sic]. *A* 6, no. 10 (October 1926): 221–22.

———. "Zug aus der Musikphysiognomie der Zeit." *A* 7, nos. 7–8 (July 1, 1927): 143–44.

Steinhard, Erich, et al., eds. *Von deutscher Kultur in der Tschechoslowakei.* Kassel and Wilhelmshöhe: Johannes Stauda, 1928.

Stolba, K. Marie. *The Development of Western Music: A History.* 3rd. ed. Boston: McGraw-Hill, 1998.

Štěpán, Václav. "Blanche Selva." *HR* 13, no. 1 (October 1919): 1–7.

———. "Estetický problém současné hudby." *T-LHM* 7, nos. 6–7 (April 4, 1928): 227–38.

———. "Francouzský vliv u nás.—Blanche Selva." *HR* 13, no. 4 (January 1920): 150–53.

———. "*Její pastorkyňa* (Odpověď na článek prof. Nejedlého)." *HR* 10 (1916): 28–40.

———. "Mirní konservativci a rozhodní pokrokovci." *HR* 7, no. 1 (October 1913): 1–8.

———. "Otevřený list J. Sukovi." *HR* 12, no. 2 (November 1918): 46. Reprinted in *Josef Suk: Zrání, op. 34 hudební báseň pro velký orkestr,* 5–6. Prague: HMUB, 1919.

———. "Pojednání." In *Josef Suk: Op. 34 Zrání, hudební báseň pro velký orkestr,* 15–22. Prague: HMUB, 1919.

———. "První pokus monografie o Novákovi." *HR* 8, no. 5 (May 1915): 180–84.

———. "Vítězslava Nováka *Zvíkovský rarášek.*" *HR* 8, no. 1 (January 1915): 2–10; 8, no. 2 (February 1915): 49–53; 8, no. 3 (March 1915): 92–96.

———. "Vycpálkův sloh." *T-LHM* 1, no. 5 (February 1922): 70–72.

———. "*Zvíkovský rarášek.*" *HR* 9, no. 1 (October 1916): 32–36.

Štorch-Marien, Otakar. "Chocolate Kiddies." *RA* 1, no. 3 (November 1925): 34.

———. "Kolem pařížských revuí." *RA* 2, no. 10 (1926–27): 114–16.

———. "Odpoledník *Národ.*" *RA* 2, no. 10 (1926–27): 119.

———. "Skandální rozhodnutí." *RA* 2, no. 6 (1926–27): 72.

———. "Taneční umění." *RA* 3, no. 17 (1927–28): 213.

Suchý, Viktor. "Případ Dvořákův." *Neruda,* December 21, 1912.

Suk, Josef. "Skladatel J. Suk proti prof. Nejedlého." *V,* December 28, 1912.

"Sukovo *Zrání.*" *HR* 12, no. 2 (November 1918): 84.

Svatoš, Thomas D. "Martinů on Music and Culture: a View from his Parisian Criticism and 1940s Notes." Ph.D. diss., University of California-Santa Barbara, 2001.

Svoboda, Jiří. "Před uzavřenou oponou (K Burianově opeře *Před slunce východem*)." *TT* 5 (December 1925): 5–6.

———. "Voice-band." *Hudba a Škola* 1, no. 6 (March 1929): 91.

Svobodová, Marie. *Hudební periodika v českých zemích 1796–1970 a na Slovensku 1871–1970.* Prague: Státní knihovna ČSR, 1979.

Sychra, Antonín. *Estetika Zdeňka Nejedlého.* Prague: Československý spisovatel, 1956.

———. "Hábova *Matka* jako hudební drama." *R* 11 (1947): 77–81.

Talich, Václav. "Rozbor V. Talicha s notovými příklady." In *Josef Suk: Zrání, op. 34, hudební báseň pro velký orkestr,* 7–14. Prague: HMUB, 1919.

Taruskin, Richard. *Defining Russia Musically: Historical and Hermeneutical Essays.* Princeton, NJ: Princeton University Press, 1997.

Teige, Karel. "The Poetist Manifesto." Translated by G. S. Evans. In "Dreams and Disillusion: Karel Teige and the Czech Avant-Garde." http://home.sprynet.com/~awhit/pmanifes.htm

Teweles, Heinrich. *Theater und Publikum.* Prague: Gesellschaft deutscher Bücherfreunde in Böhmen, 1927.

Thomson, S. Harrison. "Review Note: The Collected Works of Zdeněk Nejedly" [sic]. *Journal of Central European Affairs* 12, no. 2 (July 1952): 170–73.

Thrun, Martin. *Neue Musik im deutschen Musikleben bis 1933.* Bonn: Orpheus-Verlag, 1995.

Tomášek, Jaroslav. "Druhý orchestrální festival v Praze." *HRo* 1, no. 10 (June 12, 1925): 161–63.

———. "Mezinárodní festival hudební v Praze." *HRo* 1, no. 10 (June 12, 1925): 168–70.

———. "Třídění duchů. (K případu *Vojcka*)." *HRo* 3, no. 3 (December 15, 1926): 35–37.

———. "Úvodník [Lehká hudba]." *T-LHM* 15, no. 9 (February 20, 1936): 97–98.

———. "V našem listě rozvinula se debata . . ." *T-LHM* 15, no. 9 (February 1936): 97–98.

"Trapné otázky." *ČR*, November 18, 1926.

Tyrrell, John. *Czech Opera.* Cambridge: Cambridge University Press, 1988.

U. H., Dr. "Umschau. In der Austellung 'Entartete Musik' . . ." *MdS* 2, nos. 9–10 (July 15, 1938): 308.

Uggé, Emmanuel. "Hot-jazz na postupu." *HVk* 32, no. 3 (March 24, 1939): 51–52.

———. "Jazz." *HVk* 29, no. 8 (September 1, 1936): 125–26; 29, no. 9 (October 1, 1936): 138–39; 29, no. 10 (November 1, 1936): 153–55.

———. "Swing Music." *HVk* 31, no. 5 (May 1, 1938): 73–75.

"Úvodem." *S-HL* 1, no. 1 (November 11, 1910): 1.

V. "*Pelléas a Melisanda.*" *Čas*, November 3, 1921.

"V poslední době ohromný rozruch způsobily události v Národním divadle při provedení Bergerového *Woicka*" [sic]. *ČH* 29 (1926): 34.

Vachek, Emil. "Causa *Voycek.*" *NSv* 3, no. 47 (December 1926): 603–6.

Válek, Jiří. *Vznik a význam Ostřčilovy opery "Honzovo království."* Prague: Národní Hudební Vydavatelství/Orbis, 1952.

Valentová, Helena. "*Bubu z Montparnassu:* Lyrická opera E. F. Buriana." *Opus Musicum* 27, no. 1 (1995): 3–12.

vb. "Otakar Jeremiáš: *Bratři Karamazovi.*" *NL*, October 10, 1928.

Veidl, Theodor. "Das neue sudetendeutsche Tonwerk. Zur *Jakobsfahrt* von Fidelio Finke." *MdS* 1, no. 1 (November 15, 1936): 21–22.

Veselý, Richard. "K boji proti Dvořákovi." *HR* 8, no. 3 (March 1915): 96–103.

———. "Otakar Hostinský v dějinách české hudby." *HR* 3, no. 3 (March 1910): 121–26.

Vetterl, Karel. "Hudba v rozhlase." *Hudba a Škola* 1, no. 8 (May 1929): 116–18; 1, nos. 9–10 (June/July 1929): 134–36.

———. "O novou hudbu pro rozhlas." *T-LHM* 8, no. 10 (July 4, 1929): 327–330.

———. "Rozhlasová hudba." *T-LHM* 9, no. 2 (October 24, 1929): 53–57; 9, no. 3 (November 20, 1929): 94–98.

"Vlivy." *ND* 4, no. 38 (May 28, 1927): 2.

Vodička, Felix. "Kategorie kontinuity." *Plamen* 7 (1965): 47–53.

Vogel, Jaroslav. "Druhý pražský festival v zrcadle zahraniční kritiky." *T-LHM* 5, no. 1 (October 15, 1925): 11–14.

———. "E. F. Burian: *Před slunce východem.*" *ČR*, November 26, 1925.

———. "Otakar Zich: *Preciézky.*—Darius Milhaud: *Zmatek.*" *ČR*, May 23, 1926.

Vogel, Jaroslav. "Z hudebního života." *T-LHM* 5, nos. 9–10 (1926): 344–47.

———. "Židovství v moderní hudbě." *T-LHM* 5, no. 5 (February 25, 1926): 175–77.

"*Vojcek* a pan Bořivoj Vocásek." *PL*, November 20, 1926.

"*Vojcek*—Bergova 'opera' nebude již provozována." *Večer*, November 18, 1926.

Volek, Jaroslav. "Novák—'osová' osobnost české moderní hudby." In *Vítězslav Novák: Studie a vzpomínky k 100. narozeninám*, eds. Karel Padrta and Bohumír Štědroň, 21–42. České Budějovice: Jihočeské muzeum, 1972.

Vomáčka, Boleslav. "Alban Berg: *Vojcek*." *LN*, November 13, 1926.

———. "Čtvrtý mezinárodní hudební festival v Curychu." *T-LHM* 5, nos. 9–10 (July 25, 1926): 315–22.

———. "Ideová stránka díla Ladislava Vycpálka." *T-LHM* 1, no. 5 (February 1922): 73–75.

———. "Josef Suk." *Cesta* 1, no. 49 (1919): 1360–63; 1, no. 52: 1444–48.

———. "K festivalu." *T-LHM* 4, no. 10 (June 30, 1925): 335–40.

———. "Krise moderní hudby a hudebního obecenstva," *T-LHM* 5, no. 3 (December 18, 1925): 83–85.

———. "Max Brand: *Strojník Hopkins*." *LN*, October 9, 1930.

———. "Mezinárodní hudební festival v Praze." *T-LHM* 4, nos. 8–9 (May 15, 1925): 265–68.

———. "O hudební moderně." *T-LHM* 1/1 (October 1921): 2–3.

———. "Ohnisko nového života." *T-LHM* 3, no. 2 (November 25, 1923): 64–66.

———. "Otázky dne." *T-LHM* 2, no. 3 (December 20, 1922): 65.

———. "Otázky dne." *T-LHM* 2, no. 5 (February 20, 1923): 114.

———. "Otázky dne." *T-LHM* 2, no. 7 (April 20, 1923): 165.

———. "Otázky dne. K diskusi o moderní hudbě." *T-LHM* 3, nos. 9–10 (July 15, 1924): 379–81.

———. "Otakar Zich: *Preciézky*.—Darius Milhaud: *Zmatek*." *LN*, May 23, 1926.

———. "Stav přítomné hudby české v proudu hudby světové," *T-LHM* 5, no. 1 (October 15, 1925): 1–4.

———. "Z hudebního života." *T-LHM* 6, no. 4 (January 25, 1927): 118–19.

———. "Z pražské opery." *LN*, April 29, 1927.

Vrchlický, Jaroslav. *Noc na Karlštejně.* [Comedy in three acts.] In *Souborné vydání básnických spisů*, 13th ed. Prague: J. Otto, 1913.

Vučkovič, Vojislav. "Hudba jako propagační prostředek (Část kreda mladého moderního skladatele)." *K* 3, no. 8 (1933): 171–78.

———. "Idealismus a materialismus v hudbě." *R* 2, no. 4 (December 1936): 41–44; 2, nos. 5–6 (January–February 1937): 56–58; 3, no. 2 (November 1937): 14.

Vuillermoz, Emil. "Rag-time a jazz-band." *ND* 2, no. 24 (February 13, 1925): 5–6.

Vycpálek, Ladislav. "Česká moderní zpěvohra po Smetanovi." *HR* 5 (1911–12): 28–31.

———. "Hudba. Vítězslav Novák: *Karlštejn*." *Lumír* 45 (1916): 90–92.

———. "Jak se pan prof. Nejedlý učil harmonii." *HR* 4 (1911): 379–80.

———. "K Novákově instrumentaci." *HR* 6 (1912–13): 357.

———. "Opera a pokrokovost." *T-LHM* 11, no. 3 (November 1931): 99–100.

———. "Pan Nejedlý . . ." *HR* 6 (1912–13): 422–23.

———. "Prof. Zd. Nejedlý a *Prodaná nevěsta*." *HR* 4 (1911): 313–19.

———. "Symfonické koncerty České filharmonie." *HR* 6 (1912–13): 91–92.

———. "Symfonické koncerty České filharmonie." *HR* 6 (1912–13): 143–44.

———. "Symfonické koncerty České filharmonie." *HR* 6 (1912–13): 268–70.

———. "Zd. Nejedlý odpovídá . . ." *HR* 6 (1912–13): 258–60.

Vysloužil, Jiří. "Alois Hába in der Musikentwicklung des 20. Jahrhunderts." In *Gedanken zu Alois Hába*, ed. Horst-Peter Hesse and Wolfgang Thiess, 9–25. Salzburg: Verlag Müller-Speiser, 1996.

Vysloužil, Jiří. *Alois Hába: život a dílo*. Prague: Panton, 1974.

———, ed. *Alois Hába (1893–1973): Sborník k životu a dílu skladatele*. Vizovice: LÍPA, 1993.

Warschauer, Frank. "Co se děje s hudbou v této době." *P* 13, no. 6 (February 12, 1936): 93–95.

———. "Dvojí morálka v hudbě (k diskusi o lehké hudbě)." *T-LHM* 15, no. 13 (April 30, 1936): 150.

———. "Fantom opery." *P* 13, no. 43 (October 28, 1936): 680–84.

———. "Hudba na mrtvém bodě (K hudebnímu festivalu v Praze)." *P* 12, no. 36 (September 11, 1935): 567–70.

———. "Působil jazz na novou hudbu?" *P* 12, no. 45 (November 13, 1935): 718–20.

Weber, Horst. *Alexander Zemlinsky: Eine Studie*. Vienna: Verlag Elisabeth Lafite, 1977.

Weislová, Hana. "K historii mezinárodního festivalu v Praze 1935." *R* 1, no. 1 (October 1935): 4–11.

Wellek, René. "Twenty years of Czech literature, 1918–1938." In *Essays on Czech Literature*, 32–45. The Hague: Mouton, 1963.

Wilson, William A. "Herder, Folklore, and Romantic Nationalism." *Journal of Popular Culture* 6, no. 4 (1973): 818–35.

"Z hudebního života. O Bergovu operu *Vojcek*. Státní ceny." *S-HL* 16, no. 3 (November 1926): 47–48.

"Z mravů naší hudební společnosti." *S-HL* 9, no. 4 (March 1919): 87.

"Za svobodu uměleckého projevu." *T-LHM* 6, nos. 2–3 (December 15, 1926): 95.

Zachařová, Stanislava. "Kovařovic a Nejedlý." In *Zdeněk Nejedlý: doba, život, díla*, 89–170. Prague: Ústav pro českou a světovou literaturu ČSAV, 1975.

———. "Nejedlého polemika o Karla Knittla." In *Z bojů o českou hudební kulturu*, ed. Stanislava Zachařová, 29–104. Prague: Academia, 1979.

———, ed. *Z bojů o českou hudební kulturu*. Prague: Academia, 1979.

———, ed. *Zdeněk Nejedlý–Otakar Ostrčil Korespondence*. Prague: Academia, 1982.

Žák, Emanuel. "Albán Berg: *Vojcek*." *Čech*, November 13, 1926.

———. "Otakar Jeremiáš: *Bratři Karamazovi*." *Čech*, October 10, 1928.

———. "Vítězslav Novák: *Zvíkovský rarášek*." *Čech*, December 24, 1926.

Zelenka, František. "Návrhy inscenace Hábovy opery *Matka* pro Mnichov." *K* 1, no. 6 (1931): 200–202.

Zelenka, Miroslav. "Ethika v polemice." *D* 36 (1919): 72.

Zemanová, Zora. "K otázce moderní hudby." *T-LHM* 4, no. 6 (February 20, 1925): 181–84.

———. "Orchestr jazzu." *P* 5, no. 13 (April 6, 1928): 199–201.

Zich, Otakar. "Čtvrttónová hudba." *HRo* 2, no. 2 (November 14, 1925): 19–23; 2, no. 5 (January 23, 1926): 69–74; 2, no. 6 (February 15, 1926): 90–93; 2, no. 7 (March 15, 1926): 110–13; 2–8 (April 15, 1926): 121–23.

———. "Dvořákův význam umělecký." *Hudební sborník* 1, no. 3 (1913): 145–80.

———. *Estetické vnímání hudby*. Prague: Supraphon, 1981.

———. "K Novákově *Bouři*." *S-HL* 2, no. 20 (May 10, 1912): 282–85.

———. "Ke sporu o Dvořáka." *S-HL* 6 (1915–16): 29–36; 49–53.

———. "Otakar Ostrčil: *Kunálovy oči* (Rozbor opery)." *HR* 1, no. 10 (December 1908): 465–77.

———. "Smetanovská hesla." *P* 1, no. 1 (January 17, 1924): 10–11; 1, no. 2 (January 24, 1924): 25–27.

———. "*Vina*." *ND* 6, no. 32 (March 29, 1929): 8.

Zítek, Ota. "Česká hudba a válka." *HR* 11, no. 3 (December 1917): 89–92.

Z—k. "*Výlety páně Broučkovy.*" *LN,* April 24, 1920.

Zubatý, Václav. "Úkoly české hudby v českém státě." *HR* 12, no. 3 (December 1918): 98–100.

3. Discography

Burian, Emil František. *Bubu z Montparnassu.* Excerpt from the opera. Jiří Hruška, Katarina Vasar, Lubomír Havlák, Martin Bárta, Dagmar Vaňtáková, Orchestra and Chorus of the Prague State Opera, conducted by Bohumil Gregor. In *Éra Státní opery Praha 1992–2000.* ČRo archival recording SO 0017–2611.

———. *Dokumenty.* Contains "Náš tatíček," "Kmotr Matěj," and "Pohádka o koze," performed by Voice-band. Supraphon LP O 18 1529, 1974.

———. *Písničky a Songy.* Including *Coctaily* and *Milenci z kiosku.* E. F. Burian, Jindřich Jindrák, Helena Vondráčková, Pavel Sedláček, Voice-band, Ježkův orchestr Osvobozeného divadla conducted by Karel Ančerl, Orchestr Gramoklubu conducted by Jan Šíma, Milan Dvořák and his orchestra. Supraphon LP 1 13 1935 G, 1976.

Foerster, Josef Bohuslav. *Eva.* Complete opera recording. Eva Děpoltová, Leo Marian Vodička, Anna Barová, Jaroslav Souček, Libuše Márová, Karel Petr, Prague Radio Chorus, and Prague Radio Symphony Orchestra conducted by František Vajnar. Supraphon CD SU 3001–2612, 1996.

Hába, Alois. *Mother.* Complete opera recording. Vlasta Urbanová, Oldřich Spisar, the Prague National Theater Chorus and Orchestra, conducted by Jiří Jirouš. Supraphon CD 10–8258–2 612/10 8259–2 612, 1992.

———. *Nová země.* Excerpt from the opera. Jindřich Jindrák, Věra Krilová, Jaroslav Horáček, Ludmila Hanzalíková, Karel Berman, Antonín Votava, Orchestra and Chorus of Czechoslovak Radio, conducted by Václav Jiráček. ČRo archival recording HAB 20–2.

Jeremiáš, Otakar. *Bratři Karamazovi.* Complete opera recording. Ladislav Neshyba, Jiří Zahradníček, Ivo Žídek, René Tuček, Karel Berman, Helena Tattermuschová, Blanka Vítková, Orchestra and Chorus of the National Theater in Prague, conducted by Josef Chaloupka. ČRo archival recording JER 20–4.

———. *Bratři Karamazovi.* Excerpts from the opera. Jarmila Pechová, Drahomíra Tikalová, Václav Eremiáš, Antonín Zlesák, Vladimír Jedenáctík, Chorus and Orchestra of the National Theater in Prague conducted by Zdeněk Košler. Supraphon LP SUA 18593, 1964.

Ježek, Jaroslav. *Jaroslav Ježek a Orchestr Osvobozeného divadla, 1930–1938.* Original mono remastered recordings. Ježkův orchestr Osvobozeného divadla conducted by Jaroslav Ježek. Supraphon CD SU 5374–2, 2002.

———. *Osvobozené divadlo V+W.* Vols. 1–6. Jiří Voskovec, Jan Werich, Ježkův orchestr Osvobozeného divadla conducted by Jaroslav Ježek, Karel Ančerl, and others. Supraphon CDs 11 2550–2/2552–2 and SU 5028–2/5030–2, 1994–95.

———. *To bylo Osvobozené divadlo.* Vol. 2: 1934–38. Jiří Voskovec, Jan Werich, Ježkův orchestr Osvobozeného divadla conducted by Jaroslav Ježek. Supraphon LP 1018 7141/42 H, 1986.

Kovařovic, Karel. *Psohlavci.* Complete opera recording. Beno Blachut, Drahomíra Tikalová, Marta Krásová, Pavel Haderer, Ladislav Černý, Václav Bednář, Helena Tattermuschová, Zdeněk Otava, Ivana Mixová, Czechoslovak Radio Chorus and Prague Radio Symphonic Orchestra, conducted by František Dyk. Supraphon CD SU 3357–2 603, 1998.

Novák, Vítězslav. *Dĕdův odkaz.* Excerpts from the opera. Ivo Žídek, Jaroslava Vymazalová, Prague Radio Symphonic Orchestra, conducted by Jiří Pinkas. ČRo archival recording NO 22–3.

———. *Karlštejn,* op. 50. Complete opera recording. Václav Bednář, Zdenka Hrnčířová, Jaroslav Gleich, Eva Prchlíková-Liková, Karel Kalaš, Czechoslovak Radio Chorus and Prague Radio Symphonic Orchestra, conducted by Jaroslav Vogel. ČRo archival recording NO 21–1A.

———. *Lucerna.* Complete opera recording. Hanuš Jelínek, Eva Děpoltová, Jana Jonášová, Drahomíra Drobková, René Tuček, Václav Zítek, Karel Berman, Chorus and Symphonic Orchestra of Czechoslovak Radio, conducted by František Vajnar. Supraphon CD 1116 4671–1116 4673, 1986.

———. *Zvíkovský rarášek.* Complete opera recording. Karel Berman, Milada Šubrtová, Helena Tattermuschová, Beno Blachut, Miloslava Fidlerová, Ludmila Hanzalíková, Prague Radio Orchestra conducted by Josef Hrnčíř. Broadcast on Czech Radio, December 1, 2001.

Ostrčil, Otakar. *Honzovo království.* Complete opera recording. Soloists, Chorus and Orchestra of the Czechoslovak Radio Symphonic Orchestra, conducted by Václav Jiráček. Broadcast on Czech Radio, March 22, 2002.

———. *Kunálovy oči.* Excerpts from the opera. Alena Míková, Oldrich Spisar, Jadwiga Wysočanská, Jindřich Jindrák, Jaroslav Horáček, Chorus and Orchestra of the Smetana Theater in Prague, conducted by Josef Hrnčíř. ČRo archival recording OS 23–4.

———. *Poupě.* Complete opera recording. Karel Kalaš, Stanislava Součková, Antonín Zlesák, Václav Bednář, Czechoslovak Radio Symphonic Orchestra conducted by Václav Jiráček. ČRo archival recording OS 22–1.

———. *Vlasty skon.* Excerpts from the opera. Marie Steinerová, Jindra Pokorná, Antonín Jurečka, František Roesler, Jindřich Doubek, Jaroslav Jaroš, Chorus and Orchestra of the State Theater in Brno, conducted by František Jílek. ČRo archival recording Y 484–84.

Podvalová, Marie. *Operní recitál.* Contains excerpt of scene between Karel and Eliška from Act 3 of *Karlštejn.* Orchestra of the National Theater in Prague conducted by František Škvor. Supraphon LP O 12 0714, 1970.

Suk, Josef. *Zrání: Symfonická báseň, op. 34.* Women's Choir of the Prague Philharmonic Chorus and Czech Philharmonic conducted by Václav Neumann. Supraphon LP 1110 3640, 1985.

Weinberger, Jaromír. *Schwanda der Dudelsackpfeifer.* Complete opera recording, sung in German to a text by Max Brod. Hermann Prey, Lucia Popp, Siegfried Jerusalem, Gwendolyn Killebrew, Alexander Malta, Siegmund Nimsgern, Munich Radio Orchestra, and Bavarian Radio Chorus conducted by Heinz Wallberg. CBS LP 79344, 1981.

Zich, Otakar. *Preciézky.* Excerpts from the opera. Jarmila Pechová, Marie Ovčačíková, Jaroslav Horáček, Antonín Votava, Prague Radio Orchestra, conducted by Josef Hrnčíř. National Theater Orchestra conducted by Zdeněk Chalabala. ČRo archival recording ZIO 21–4-6.

Index

Eastman Studies in Music

This study presents a history and analysis of the Prague musical community from 1900 until the end of democracy in 1938. *Opera and Ideology in Prague* not only narrates the fascinating history of a local musical community but also reveals much about music and culture in Europe.

The fin-de-siècle period was dominated by the musicologist Zdeněk Nejedlý's polemics regarding the competing "legacies" of Smetana and Dvořák and the merits of modernism. After Czech independence in 1918, a new generation of musicians accepted modernist foreign influences only with extreme hesitation.

The 1926 Prague premiere of Berg's opera *Wozzeck* and the ascendancy of a young group of avant-garde composers changed the cultural climate entirely, providing new ground for the exploration of jazz, neoclassicism, quarter tones, and socialist music. As the Czechoslovak Republic drew to a close, a resurgence of nationalism appeared in the musical expressions of both Czechs and German-Bohemians.

The analyses of operas and tone poems by Novák, Ostrčil, Zich, Jeremiáš, Hába, Křička, and Suk provide a cross-section of musical life in early twentieth-century Prague, as well as a series of interpretations of Czech cultural identity. Populist endeavors such as jazz and neoclassicism represented some of the ways in which composers of the 1930s attempted to regain an audience alienated by modernism: in this respect, the trends in Prague mirrored those of the rest of Europe.

"At last we have a book that situates Prague properly at the forefront of the modernist music movement. Through a probing analysis of the heated press debates that accompanied the premieres of greater and lesser Czech operas, Brian Locke demonstrates that Prague, the amorphous capital of an amorphous nation, served as fertile ground for the cultivation of universal—not provincial—concepts of musical nationalism. The book greatly refines our understanding of the careers of Smetana, Dvořák, Janáček, and Martinů, while also documenting the astonishing impact of the music critic and politician Zdeněk Nejedlý on Czech culture."

—Simon Morrison (Princeton University),
author of *Russian Opera and the Symbolist Movement*

"This is truly a landmark book, filling a gap in our knowledge and understanding of early twentieth-century Czech music and culture, and, in the process, illuminating events in the rest of Europe and in America. The author relates this fascinating account with an engaging style that makes one eager to read on. The music (including a good number of in-depth analyses), the political intrigues, the main characters and events—all are presented with clarity and style based on solid research."

—Timothy Cheek (University of Michigan),
author of *Singing in Czech: A Guide to Czech Lyric Diction and Vocal Repertoire*